GOALLESS DRAWS

By the same author

THE ILLUSTRATED HISTORY OF FOOTBALL (2016)
THE ILLUSTRATED HISTORY OF FOOTBALL: HALL OF FAME (2017)

GOALLESS DRAWS

ILLUMINATING THE GENIUS OF MODERN FOOTBALL

DAVID
SQUIRES

First published by Guardian Faber in 2018
Guardian Faber is an imprint of Faber & Faber Ltd,
Bloomsbury House, 74–77 Great Russell Street,
London WC1B 3DA

Guardian is a registered trade mark of
Guardian News & Media Ltd,
Kings Place, 90 York Way, London N1 9GU

Typeset by Faber & Faber Ltd
Printed and bound by CPI Group (UK) Ltd, Croydon CR0 4YY

A CIP record for this book
is available from the British Library

ISBN 978–1–783–35162–6

FSC
www.fsc.org
MIX
Paper from
responsible sources
FSC® C020471

4 6 8 10 9 7 5 3

FOR ARTHUR

CONTENTS

INTRODUCTION

The first football cartoon I can remember drawing was in 1984, when I was nine years old. It was the day before the FA Cup final, a Friday school afternoon in May. I don't recall what the weather was doing, but let's say it was sunny, for atmosphere. Perhaps sensing an opportunity for a quiet end to the week, my teacher set the class a short assignment: we each had to create an imaginary football club, including team name, badge, kit and players. It was the first season I'd really got into football, but by this stage I was already so obsessed that my parents had begun to gently suggest I might occasionally like to read about, think about or talk about other subjects. This, then, was the perfect creative task for me.

The lad next to me called his team 'Liverpool' and included the Liverpool badge, the Liverpool kit and Liverpool players. Read the brief, mate. Others had been more imaginative, creating a select XI of pop stars or Care Bears or The Kids from 'Fame'. I tried for something more memorable.

It was around this time that my friends and I had become vaguely aware of the Second World War. We'd yet to be taught about it in school, but had cobbled together a few details from conversations with older kids and snippets of Sunday-afternoon war films. We were sketchy on the facts, but knew that Hitler was the baddie and would personally scrap it out with Winston Churchill in dogfights above the British skies, climbing into a Messerschmitt like Darth Vader piloting a TIE Fighter.

Combining these two burgeoning interests, I called my team The Berlin Burners and illustrated it with an action shot of Hitler goose-stepping a volley past a diving goalkeeper from distance. The badge included a choice of symbol more commonly seen in newspaper articles about vandalised cemeteries.

My teacher's cushy Friday afternoon lay in tatters, as she was now forced to deliver a serious lecture about the evils of the Third Reich. However, some of my classmates found it quite funny, perhaps because it was (a) silly, (b) naughty, (c) historically accurate. This wasn't the exact moment when I decided I wanted to draw cartoons for a living (after all, there'd be little time for it when I was captaining England to World Cup glory, while raising a family with the blonde woman from Heaven 17 who made me anxious when she was on *Top of the Pops*), but I definitely realised it was a nice feeling.

A less pleasant sensation resulted from one of my first paid jobs as a cartoonist, which was to create a caricature of the permanently angry midfielder Steve McMahon. A series of strange circumstances ended with me standing in a small office with the former Liverpool hard man as he gave me some very direct and robust feedback, which ended with a complaint that I had made him look like the TV magician Paul Daniels. Barely a day passes when I don't think back to that day, burned by the regret of not saying, 'So you liked it, but not a lot?' The incident did teach me a valuable lesson, though: don't go out.

Some years and several career changes later (none of which involved partnering Alan Shearer in the England attack – thanks a lot, Glenn Hoddle), making childish drawings about football somehow became a job. Since 2014 I've been producing them for my liberal luvvie snowflake comrades at the *Guardian*, and this book is a collection of some of my favourites.

Looking back through them has served as a reminder of quite how much insane stuff has happened in the last four years. Brexit, Trump, Leicester winning the Premier League, Hal Robson-Kanu eviscerating the Belgian defence – and that was just 2016. Some things have remained comfortably unchanged, though: FIFA is still abominably ridiculous, the most powerful clubs are still driven by an insatiable lust for more, and José Mourinho resolutely remains José Mourinho (although I think I'm getting closer to nailing his likeness, at least; I might even get there by the time he retires).

A lot happens in four years of football. Players and managers come and go (I remain hopeful that a club will take a punt on Harry Redknapp or Tim Sherwood again soon, as they are both fun to draw and have personalities that are ripe for cartoon material), empires crumble (I would consider sawing off a non-essential body part if it meant Arsène Wenger would return to Arsenal) and new stars and pantomime shitehawks rise to the fore.

So I hope that this book will help you to recall some of the events of the last few years and some of the characters who have come and gone, whether their contribution be big and significant (José, Pep, Hal Robson-Kanu, etc.) or brief and absurd (Sam Allardyce's reign as England manager, that bloke who shoved a dildo into the Sky Sports reporter's ear, and so on).

Naturally, my enthusiasm for football has dimmed since that – let's say sunny – afternoon in 1984. Frankly, it would be a bit strange if my bedroom walls were still decorated with the pictures of Mike Duxbury and Paul Rideout I'd torn out of magazines – you can just print them off now. But while the excesses of the modern game can be dispiriting, what has remained unchanged in the years that I've been producing these cartoons is the capacity of the game itself to thrill. When Gareth Bale scored with *that* overhead kick in the 2018 Champions League final, I was every bit as stunned and delighted as that eight-year-old boy whose disrespectful images of history's greatest monster ruined a primary-school teacher's plans to clear off to the pub early doors.

POPPYGATE

How many poppies are you wearing right now? If the lapels of your jacket are adorned with a dozen or fewer, then you might as well commit a faecal outrage in the Queen's hat and throw it at the Cenotaph, you traitor. If you aren't wearing *any* poppies – and I'm nauseated by the mere *notion* – then you are most likely in a terrorist training camp or are Channel Four newsreader Jon Snow, or both. Oh, you're reading this in June? Tell it to our war dead, *Johnny Jihad*.

There was a time – a darker time – when Remembrance Day would simply be recognised at football matches by a dignified silence to reflect upon the sacrifices made by people who were almost certainly fighting for our freedom to harass people into wearing poppies.

The practice of footballers being made to wear poppies on their shirts is a tradition that stretches as far back as our memories allow, to 2003. Leicester City were the first Premier League club to wear them, and after they'd won two consecutive games in their newly adorned kit, then-manager Micky Adams suggested they should become a permanent part of the strip. By 2009, nearly all the Premier League clubs were wearing them, thanks in part to an aggressive campaign of poppy-shaming from everyone's favourite vehicle of contrived moral outrage, the *Daily Mail*. Liverpool and Manchester United were the only clubs holding out, with United arguing that they sold poppies around Old Trafford, all their staff wore them and they did lots of work with armed forces charities throughout the year. Thankfully, by the following year this kind of treacherous talk had been quashed, the *Mail* doing what it does best – grinding everyone down into tired submission. Victory!

This sense of outrage reached a crescendo in 2016, when FIFA declared that England and Scotland could face a fine if they wore poppies during a World Cup qualifier due to be played on Armistice Day. Poppies, they argued, were political symbols, and therefore prohibited.

Plainly, this was nonsense. How could an object that had been hijacked by nationalist bullies, one that suddenly meant something to people only because of the crusades of opportunistic, military-fetishising right-wing tabloids, be considered a political symbol? To hammer home the point that poppies have nothing to do with politics, Prime Minister Theresa May criticised FIFA's decree in the House of Commons. There were populist points to be scored, and May snaffled them up like Gerd Müller or someone less German. Perhaps she should have called an early general election to hammer home this advantage?

Eventually, FIFA backed down, browbeaten and possibly bemused by the tsunami of indignation. Perhaps they realised that the fines wouldn't amount to much anyway, so shrugged and remembered their corporate values and mission statement: '*Ah well, sod it*' (it sounds better if you say it in a Swiss accent).

There are some notable poppy dissenters, of course. Tune in to any of the foreign leagues over remembrance weekend and you won't see any of them wearing poppies, not even in the countries that Britain carpet-bombed to freedom. Then there is James McClean, a man whose explanations for his decision not to wear a symbol that could be seen to commemorate the British armed forces that committed an atrocity in his home town are rightfully met with an annual chorus of boos and death threats.

With each passing year, the task of exaggerating the excesses of poppy season becomes more challenging. In 2017, I drew a cartoon featuring a person wearing a body suit covered in poppies. A few days later, someone wore this exact same outfit to a Leicester City match (Micky Adams?). The next few months were spent busily drawing images of Scarlett Johansson hand-delivering a Pulitzer Prize to my castle door, but it seems my powers of premonition were restricted merely to the sartorial choices of people in the East Midlands.

The cartoon that opens this section, featuring the Tommies in the trenches, was the first one I had published in the *Guardian*. It was a proud moment, enhanced by the delight of immediately being told, by a firing squad of several hundred tweets, that the cartoon contained a glaring typo. Instantly, I kissed goodbye to my sweetheart and raced down to the war office, determined to sign up for their most suicidal mission. Sadly, I was informed that the Great War had finished nearly a hundred years earlier, so there would be no need for me to march through a gore-littered bog towards a wall of machine-gun fire, armed only with a plastic fork sellotaped to a water pistol.

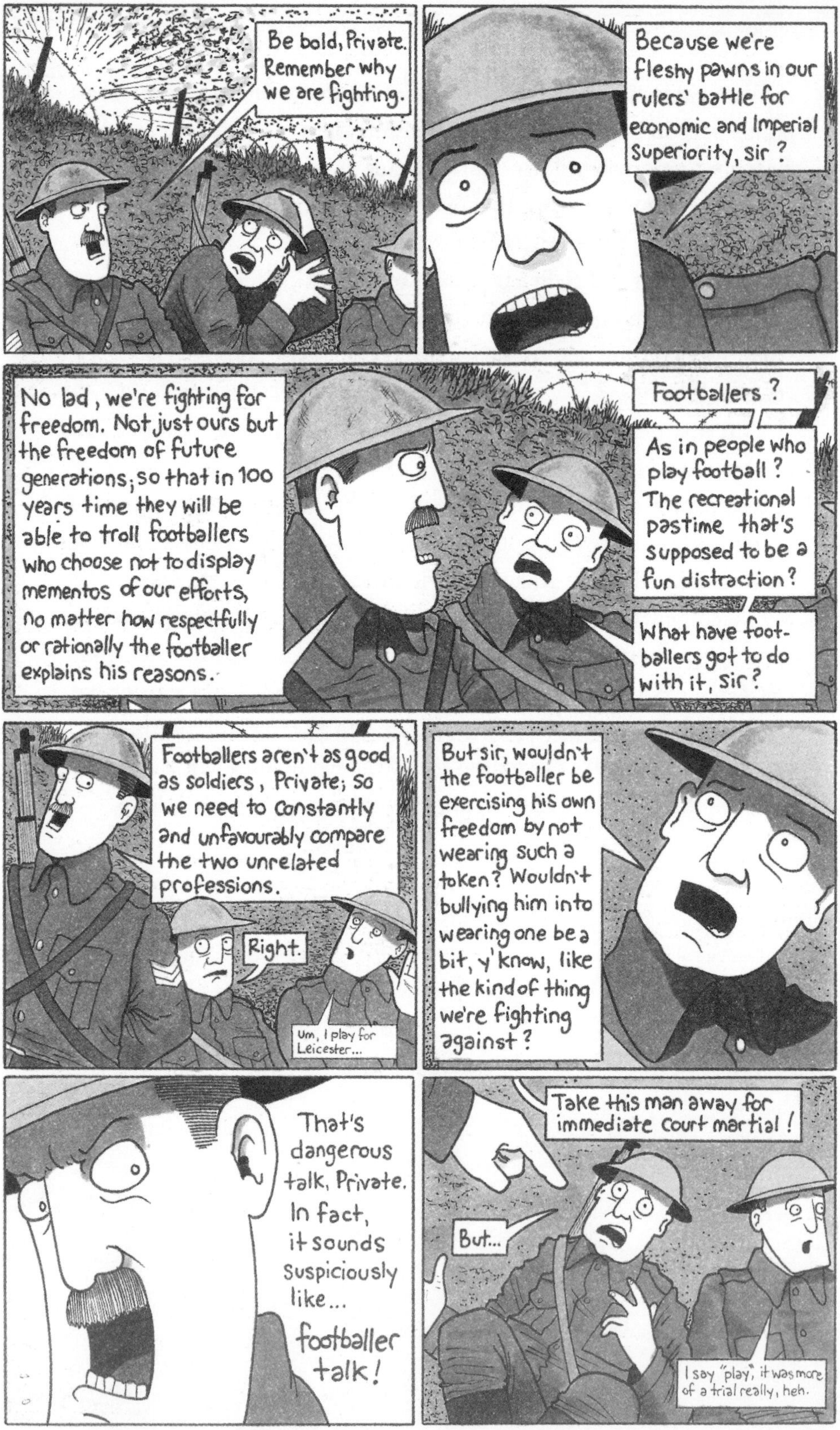
Be bold, Private. Remember why we are fighting.
Because we're fleshy pawns in our rulers' battle for economic and Imperial superiority, sir?
No lad, we're fighting for freedom. Not just ours but the freedom of future generations; so that in 100 years time they will be able to troll footballers who choose not to display mementos of our efforts, no matter how respectfully or rationally the footballer explains his reasons.
Footballers?
As in people who play football? The recreational pastime that's supposed to be a fun distraction?
What have footballers got to do with it, sir?
Footballers aren't as good as soldiers, Private; so we need to constantly and unfavourably compare the two unrelated professions.
Right.
Um, I play for Leicester...
But sir, wouldn't the footballer be exercising his own freedom by not wearing such a token? Wouldn't bullying him into wearing one be a bit, y'know, like the kind of thing we're fighting against?
That's dangerous talk, Private. In fact, it sounds suspiciously like... footballer talk!
Take this man away for immediate court martial!
But...
I say "play", it was more of a trial really, heh.

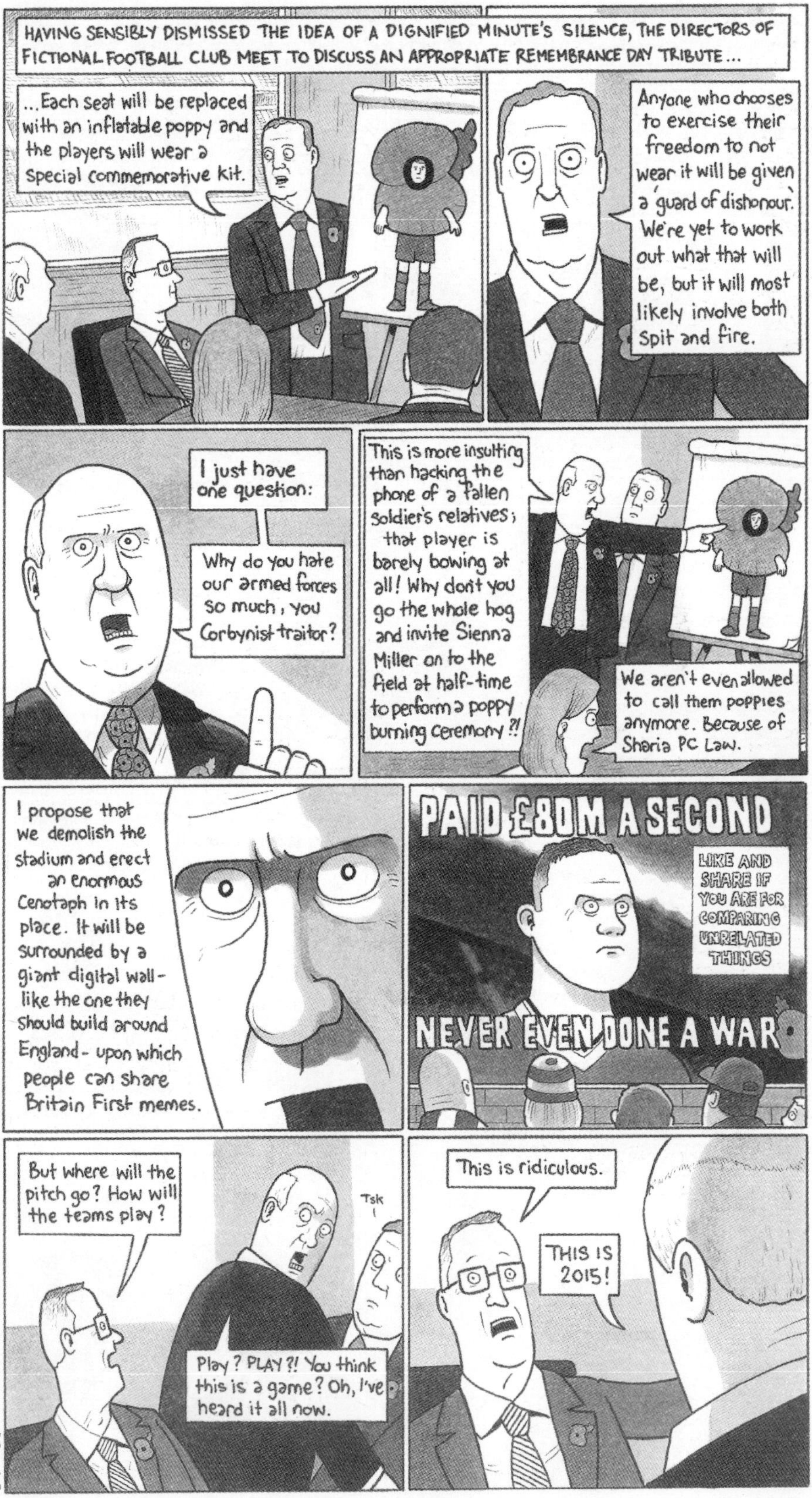
HAVING SENSIBLY DISMISSED THE IDEA OF A DIGNIFIED MINUTE'S SILENCE, THE DIRECTORS OF FICTIONAL FOOTBALL CLUB MEET TO DISCUSS AN APPROPRIATE REMEMBRANCE DAY TRIBUTE...
...Each seat will be replaced with an inflatable poppy and the players will wear a special commemorative kit.
Anyone who chooses to exercise their freedom to not wear it will be given a 'guard of dishonour'. We're yet to work out what that will be, but it will most likely involve both spit and fire.
I just have one question:
Why do you hate our armed forces so much, you Corbynist traitor?
This is more insulting than hacking the phone of a fallen soldier's relatives; that player is barely bowing at all! Why don't you go the whole hog and invite Sienna Miller on to the field at half-time to perform a poppy burning ceremony?!
We aren't even allowed to call them poppies anymore. Because of Sharia PC Law.
I propose that we demolish the stadium and erect an enormous Cenotaph in its place. It will be surrounded by a giant digital wall - like the one they should build around England - upon which people can share Britain First memes.
PAID £80M A SECOND
LIKE AND SHARE IF YOU ARE FOR COMPARING UNRELATED THINGS
NEVER EVEN DONE A WAR
But where will the pitch go? How will the teams play?
Tsk
Play? PLAY?! You think this is a game? Oh, I've heard it all now.
This is ridiculous.
THIS IS 2015!

THE POPPY FURY SEASON SEEMS TO COME ROUND EARLIER EACH YEAR; SOME PEOPLE HAD THEIR JAMES McCLEAN EFFIGIES UP IN **OCTOBER** THIS YEAR. WITH AN INTERNATIONAL BREAK COMING UP, THE BOARD OF **FICTIONAL FC** ARE FREE TO FOCUS ON THEIR OWN OUTRAGE. WE JOIN THEM IN THE KAY BURLEY SUITE...

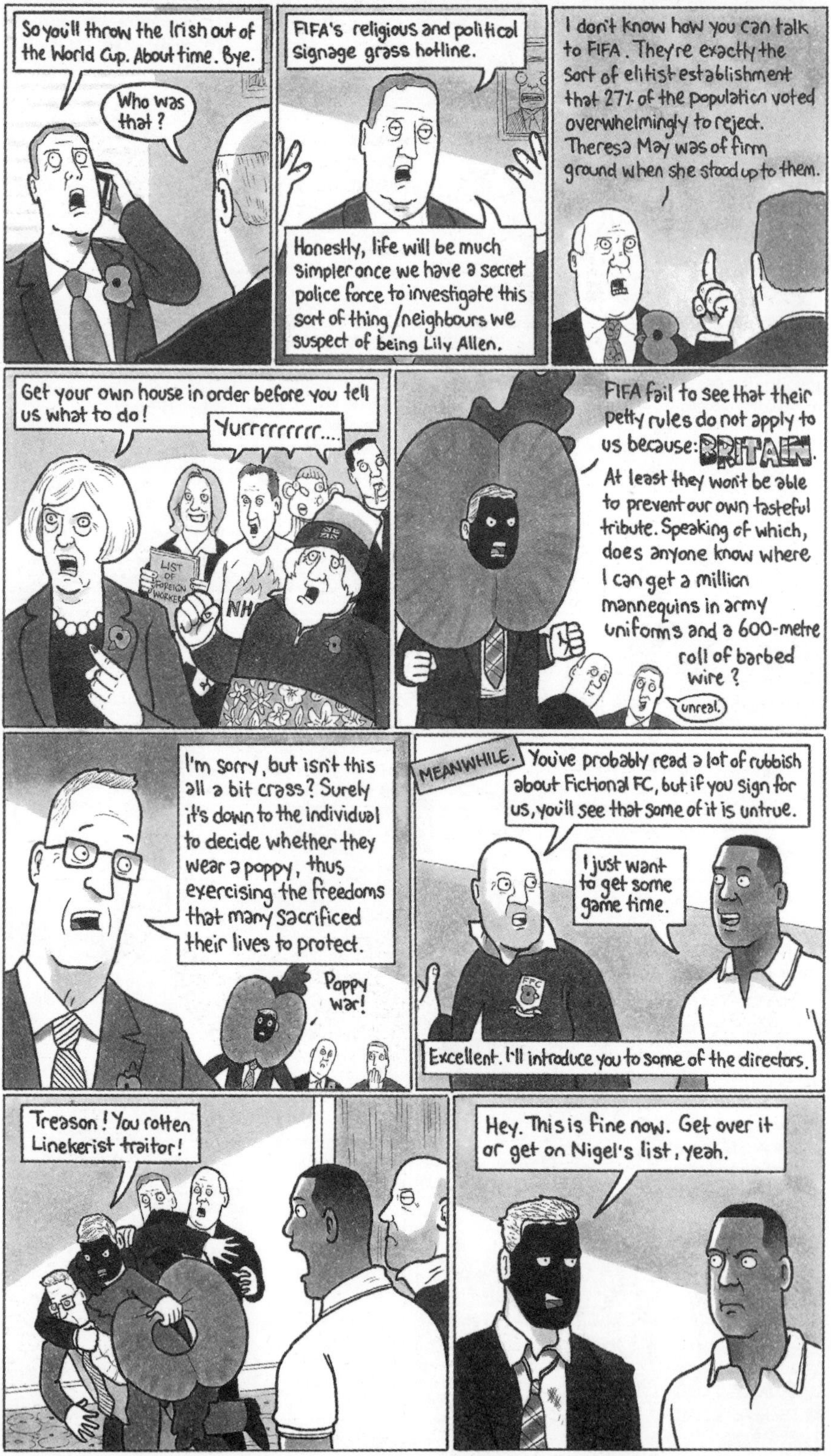

So you'll throw the Irish out of the World Cup. About time. Bye.
Who was that?
FIFA's religious and political signage grass hotline.
Honestly, life will be much simpler once we have a secret police force to investigate this sort of thing/neighbours we suspect of being Lily Allen.
I don't know how you can talk to FIFA. They're exactly the sort of elitist establishment that 27% of the population voted overwhelmingly to reject. Theresa May was of firm ground when she stood up to them.
Get your own house in order before you tell us what to do!
Yurrrrrrrrr....
FIFA fail to see that their petty rules do not apply to us because: BRITAIN. At least they won't be able to prevent our own tasteful tribute. Speaking of which, does anyone know where I can get a million mannequins in army uniforms and a 600-metre roll of barbed wire?
unreal.
I'm sorry, but isn't this all a bit crass? Surely it's down to the individual to decide whether they wear a poppy, thus exercising the freedoms that many sacrificed their lives to protect.
Poppy war!
MEANWHILE.
You've probably read a lot of rubbish about Fictional FC, but if you sign for us, you'll see that some of it is untrue.
I just want to get some game time.
FFC
Excellent. I'll introduce you to some of the directors.
Treason! You rotten Linekerist traitor!
Hey. This is fine now. Get over it or get on Nigel's list, yeah.

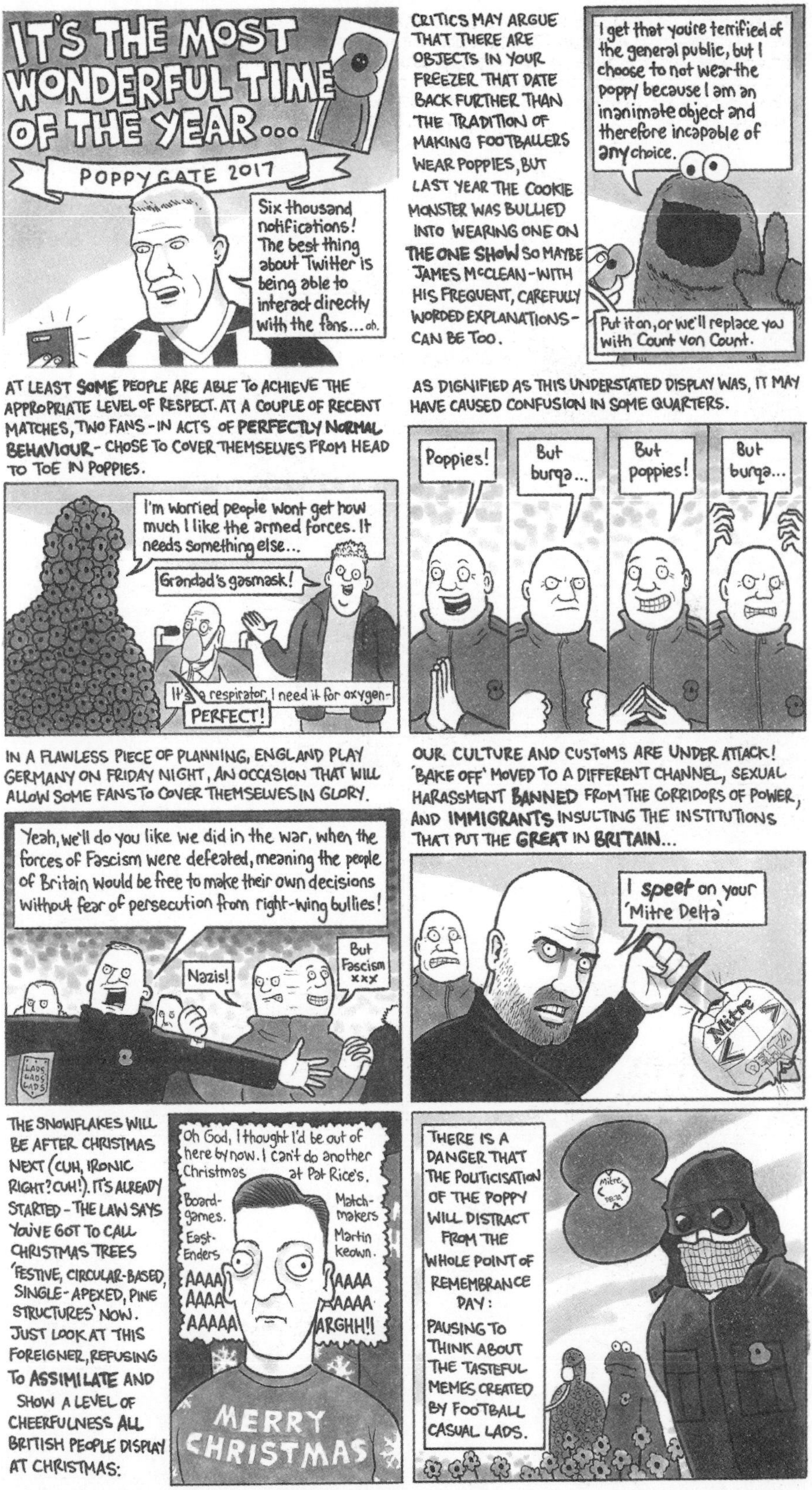
IT'S THE MOST WONDERFUL TIME OF THE YEAR...
POPPYGATE 2017
Six thousand notifications! The best thing about Twitter is being able to interact directly with the fans... oh.
CRITICS MAY ARGUE THAT THERE ARE OBJECTS IN YOUR FREEZER THAT DATE BACK FURTHER THAN THE TRADITION OF MAKING FOOTBALLERS WEAR POPPIES, BUT LAST YEAR THE COOKIE MONSTER WAS BULLIED INTO WEARING ONE ON THE ONE SHOW SO MAYBE JAMES McCLEAN - WITH HIS FREQUENT, CAREFULLY WORDED EXPLANATIONS - CAN BE TOO.
I get that you're terrified of the general public, but I choose to not wear the poppy because I am an inanimate object and therefore incapable of any choice.
Put it on, or we'll replace you with Count von Count.
AT LEAST SOME PEOPLE ARE ABLE TO ACHIEVE THE APPROPRIATE LEVEL OF RESPECT. AT A COUPLE OF RECENT MATCHES, TWO FANS - IN ACTS OF PERFECTLY NORMAL BEHAVIOUR - CHOSE TO COVER THEMSELVES FROM HEAD TO TOE IN POPPIES.
I'm worried people wont get how much I like the armed forces. It needs something else...
Grandad's gasmask!
It's a respirator, I need it for oxygen-
PERFECT!
AS DIGNIFIED AS THIS UNDERSTATED DISPLAY WAS, IT MAY HAVE CAUSED CONFUSION IN SOME QUARTERS.
Poppies!
But burqa...
But poppies!
But burqa...
IN A FLAWLESS PIECE OF PLANNING, ENGLAND PLAY GERMANY ON FRIDAY NIGHT, AN OCCASION THAT WILL ALLOW SOME FANS TO COVER THEMSELVES IN GLORY.
Yeah, we'll do you like we did in the war, when the forces of Fascism were defeated, meaning the people of Britain would be free to make their own decisions without fear of persecution from right-wing bullies!
Nazis!
But Fascism xxx
LADS LADS LADS
OUR CULTURE AND CUSTOMS ARE UNDER ATTACK! 'BAKE OFF' MOVED TO A DIFFERENT CHANNEL, SEXUAL HARASSMENT BANNED FROM THE CORRIDORS OF POWER, AND IMMIGRANTS INSULTING THE INSTITUTIONS THAT PUT THE GREAT IN BRITAIN...
I speet on your 'Mitre Delta'
Mitre
DELTA
THE SNOWFLAKES WILL BE AFTER CHRISTMAS NEXT (CUH, IRONIC RIGHT? CUH!). IT'S ALREADY STARTED - THE LAW SAYS YOU'VE GOT TO CALL CHRISTMAS TREES 'FESTIVE, CIRCULAR-BASED, SINGLE-APEXED, PINE STRUCTURES' NOW. JUST LOOK AT THIS FOREIGNER, REFUSING TO ASSIMILATE AND SHOW A LEVEL OF CHEERFULNESS ALL BRITISH PEOPLE DISPLAY AT CHRISTMAS:
Oh God, I thought I'd be out of here by now. I can't do another Christmas at Pat Rice's.
Board-games.
East-Enders
Match-makers
Martin Keown.
AAAA AAAA AAAAA
AAAA AAAA ARGHH!!
MERRY CHRISTMAS
THERE IS A DANGER THAT THE POLITICISATION OF THE POPPY WILL DISTRACT FROM THE WHOLE POINT OF REMEMBRANCE DAY: PAUSING TO THINK ABOUT THE TASTEFUL MEMES CREATED BY FOOTBALL CASUAL LADS.
Mitre
DELTA

THE GAME'S GONE:

Modern Football

When fans reach a certain age, it is common for them to complain about how football has changed. While you might despair about the prevalence of colourful boots or players wearing gloves in September, older generations may have shaken their heads at the sight of shorts with hems above the knee or footballs that were lighter than filing cabinets.

In many ways, Modern Football is better than Old Football. Our rose-tinted nostalgia for crumbling death-trap stadiums clouds the fact that modern grounds are structurally safer and more welcoming, and you're now less likely to get shanked in the liver with a screwdriver because you're wearing the wrong colour bobble hat. In the bad old days, some grounds didn't even offer fans the ability to pay an unreasonable subscription fee to observe, via a two-way mirror, the players trudging through the tunnel. How people coped without seeing their heroes roll their necks and pick their shorts out of their bums is a mystery. And just to add insult to injury, if you wanted to sample a range of artisan cheeses from the farmers' market on the concourse, you were out of luck (as you were if you were a woman wanting to go to the toilet).

But this brave new world isn't all rosy, of course. Attending the matches of certain Premier League clubs is now beyond the means of most people outside the top tax bracket. Prices have rocketed at a rate disproportionate to inflation or wage growth. Even in the lower leagues ticket prices are excessive, but at least there you can still sometimes sample the bygone delights of peeling paint and weeing against a wall. Little wonder then that people locked out of the game rail at the symbols of the modern era, like the half-and-half scarves of football tourists fulfilling a lifelong ambition of seeing their favourite team play and wanting a souvenir of the occasion, the shits.[1]

Arguably worse are people who eat healthy food in stadiums. There was public outrage in 2017, when an Arsenal fan was caught on camera dipping into a bag of carrot batons. Look at Lord Snooty with his vegetables! What's wrong with eating reconstituted offal compressed into a grey patty, microwaved to exactly the right temperature to encourage bacterial reproduction and jammed into a stale white roll, just like the rest of us? Bowel cancer's too good for you, is it, *Your Highness*?[2]

The most Modern Football thing I've seen was when my friend Richard, who lived next door to a baker, brought to a match six quiches in individual Tupperware containers for the LADS, LADS, LADS, LADS. For another game, he brought a whole roast chicken (which he tore apart with his hands, like an extra from *The Walking Dead*), a bag of mixed-leaf salad, six brioche milk buns, some fucking *aioli* and a packet of sliced Emmental, which admittedly was good for waving whenever there was a hefty challenge in front of our section.

Still, there are worse things to worry about than bourgeois condiments, many of them contributing to the feeling that football clubs are losing their connections with the communities they once represented. This has especially been the experience for fans of Newcastle United under the unpopular ownership of tracksuit-bottoms

---

1 OK, the half-and-half scarf thing is weird, especially the ones that have the names and pictures of opposing managers knitted into them. Does anyone actually buy the MARK HUGHES v. EDDIE HOWE scarves?

2 Incidentally, the worst burger I ever ate was at Chesterfield's old ground, Saltergate – which in itself sounds like a condition caused by a poor diet ('You heard about Dave? He's got Saltergate and all his limbs have swollen up like red balloons. I told him blue and green Pringles didn't constitute a balanced diet, but you know Dave').

magnate Mike Ashley. He forms the subject of the first cartoon of this collection on the theme of the modern game. The strip is based on a famous quote from Sir Bobby Robson, a man you could reasonably describe as the antithesis of Ashley, the anti-Mike. He wouldn't be hauled in front of a parliamentary hearing into Dickensian work practices at his rubbish-trainers empire, not Bobby.

> What is a club in any case? Not the buildings or the directors or the people who are paid to represent it. It's not the television contracts, get-out clauses, marketing departments or executive boxes. It's the noise, the passion, the feeling of belonging, the pride in your city. It's a small boy clambering up stadium steps for the very first time, gripping his father's hand, gawping at that hallowed stretch of turf beneath him and, without being able to do a thing about it, falling in love.[3]

Robson's position is at odds with many who occupy the boardrooms of English football, especially at the very highest level. No matter how rich and powerful, there always seems to exist an insatiable lust for more. The top executives of several Premier League clubs gathered for a secret meeting in early 2016, where topics covered may have included Liverpool's proposed ticket-pricing structure, which was causing them more pain than Jürgen Klopp's appendicitis.

However, even this group may be overshadowed by FIFA, who also came together in February 2016 to elect a new leader, one who would definitely stamp out corruption and end the self-serving culture of previous regimes. For some reason they stayed in the same Swiss hotel that was the scene of the dramatic arrest of several FIFA executives the previous year. Perhaps they wanted to relive

3 Bobby Robson, *Newcastle – My Kind of Toon* (2008).

the drama of seeing their associates bundled into the back of police cars, their heads cloaked by tablecloths, or maybe it just does a decent breakfast buffet.

As FIFA continued to eat itself, England's big five clubs met again to discuss the idea of restructuring the Champions League, apparently spooked by the idea of Leicester crashing their party – after all, nobody wants Jamie Vardy in their luxury yacht casino. Leading the discussion was Charlie Stillitano, a mysterious figure whose arguments for a closed-shop Champions League were at least based on a deep understanding of football culture, saying in a radio interview: 'What would Manchester United argue: did we create soccer or did Leicester create [it]? Who has had more of an integral role [in European football], Manchester United or Leicester? It's a wonderful story – but you could see it from United's point of view, too.'[4] Who could argue with logic like that?

Another bugbear of the modern game covered in this section is the always thorny issue of diving. If you discount all of the frequent and historic examples of English players throwing themselves to the ground, then it's clear to see why people were so outraged that that most English of players, Jamie Vardy, would be sent off for diving in a match against West Ham. *The very notion.* The debate occurred at a time when Britain was preparing to vote in the EU referendum, with politicians taking to the phones to try and convince people of their arguments. Well, one side did; the other just lied about it on the side of buses.

Perhaps the introduction of Video Assistant Referees will help to clear up arguments about diving with the same efficiency and clarity with which issues surrounding the outcome of the Brexit vote will be resolved. Time alone will tell . . .

---

4 'Charlie Stillitano's Champions League plans are an insult to Leicester City – and football', Sachin Nakrani, *Guardian*, 5 March 2016. theguardian.com/football/2016/mar/04/charlie-stillitano-champions-league-leicester

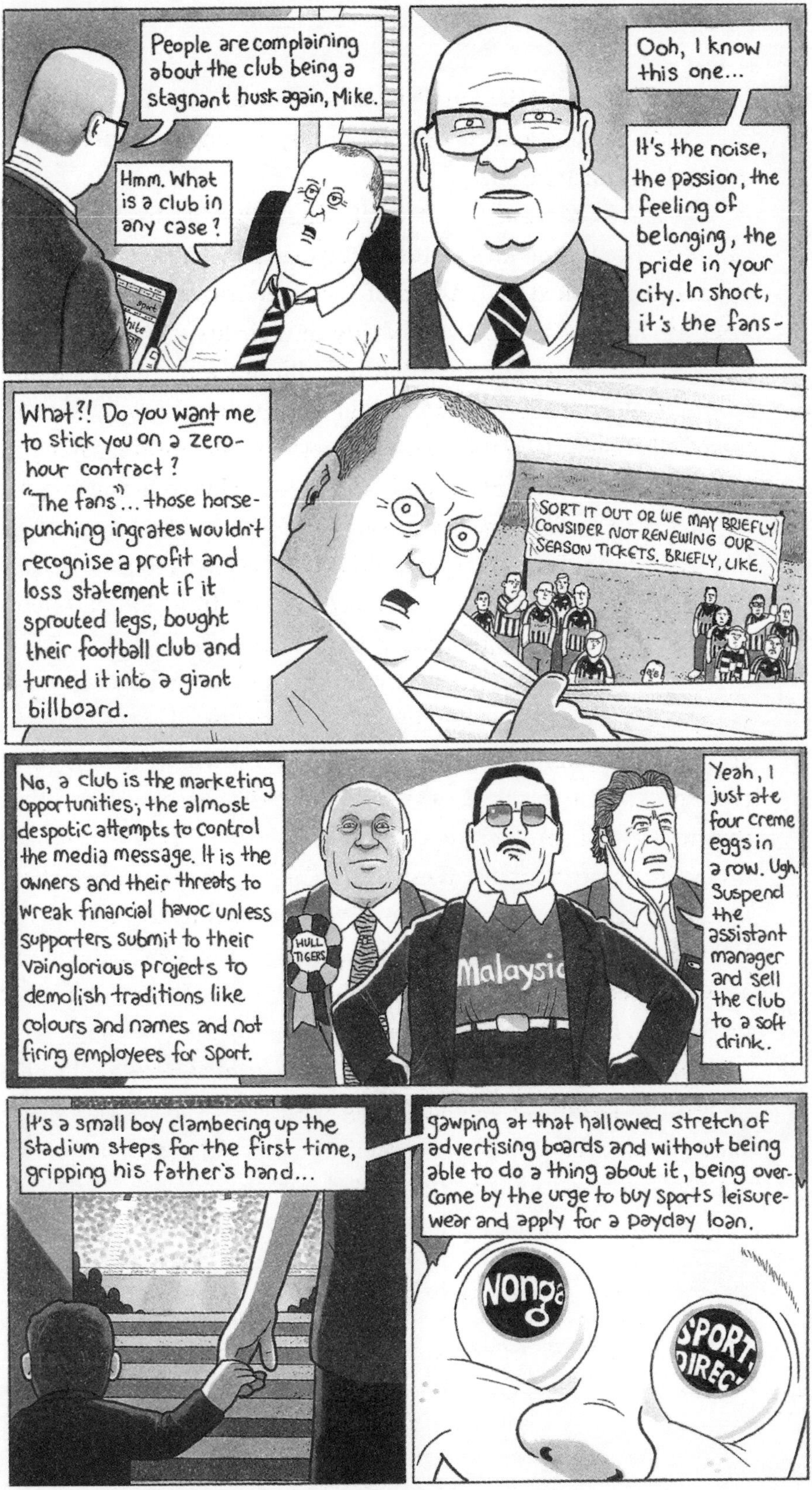
People are complaining about the club being a stagnant husk again, Mike.
Hmm. What is a club in any case?
Ooh, I know this one...
It's the noise, the passion, the feeling of belonging, the pride in your city. In short, it's the fans-
What?! Do you want me to stick you on a zero-hour contract?
"The fans"... those horse-punching ingrates wouldn't recognise a profit and loss statement if it sprouted legs, bought their football club and turned it into a giant billboard.
SORT IT OUT OR WE MAY BRIEFLY CONSIDER NOT RENEWING OUR SEASON TICKETS. BRIEFLY, LIKE.
No, a club is the marketing opportunities; the almost despotic attempts to control the media message. It is the owners and their threats to wreak financial havoc unless supporters submit to their vainglorious projects to demolish traditions like colours and names and not firing employees for sport.
HULL TIGERS
Yeah, I just ate four creme eggs in a row. Ugh. Suspend the assistant manager and sell the club to a soft drink.
It's a small boy clambering up the stadium steps for the first time, gripping his father's hand...
gawping at that hallowed stretch of advertising boards and without being able to do a thing about it, being over-come by the urge to buy sports leisure-wear and apply for a payday loan.

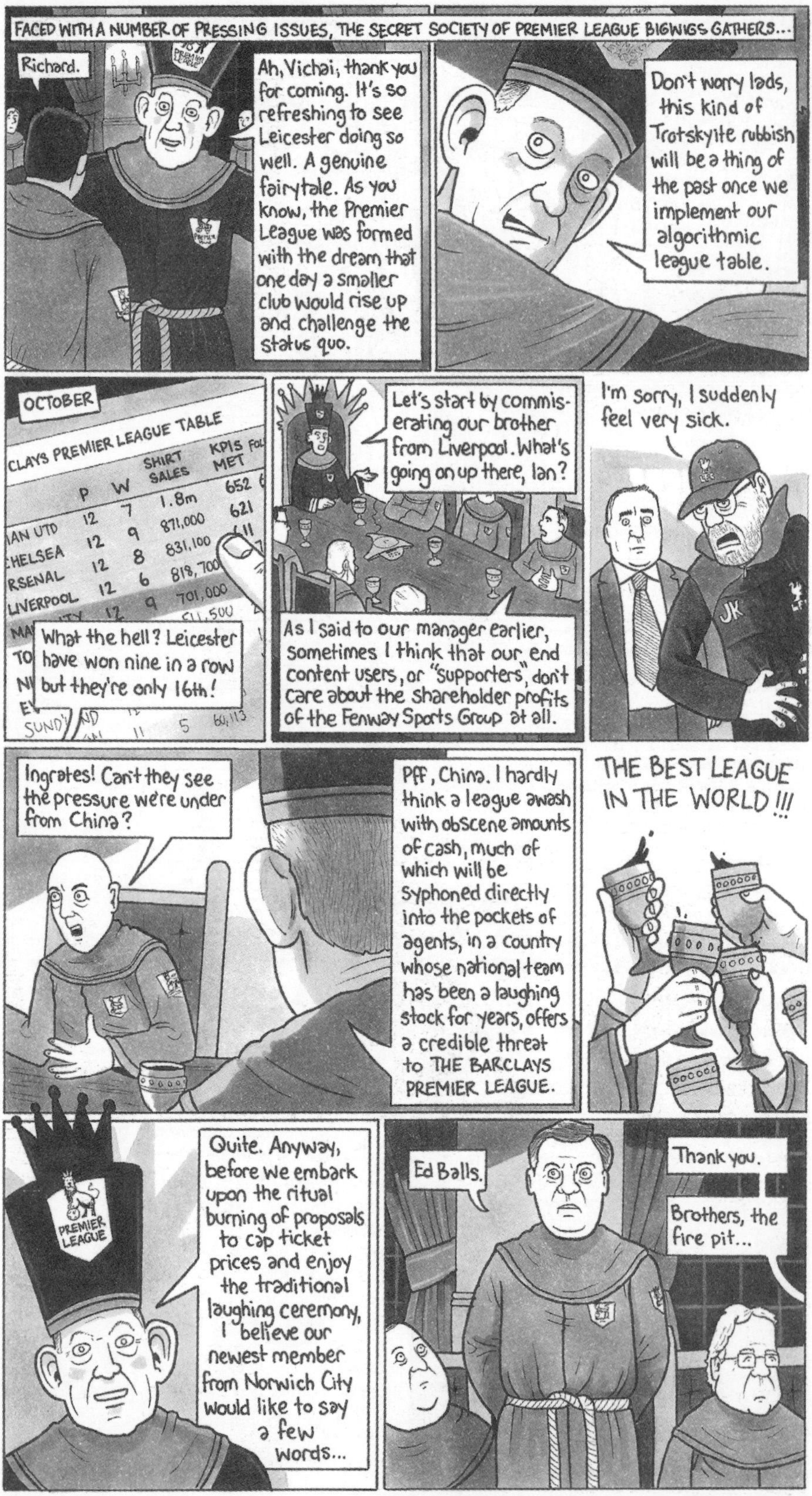
FACED WITH A NUMBER OF PRESSING ISSUES, THE SECRET SOCIETY OF PREMIER LEAGUE BIGWIGS GATHERS...
Richard.
Ah, Vichai; thank you for coming. It's so refreshing to see Leicester doing so well. A genuine fairytale. As you know, the Premier League was formed with the dream that one day a smaller club would rise up and challenge the status quo.
Don't worry lads, this kind of Trotskyite rubbish will be a thing of the past once we implement our algorithmic league table.
OCTOBER
CLAYS PREMIER LEAGUE TABLE
P W SHIRT SALES KPIS MET
AN UTD 12 7 1.8m 652
HELSEA 12 9 871,000 621
RSENAL 12 8 831,100
LIVERPOOL 12 6 818,700
What the hell? Leicester have won nine in a row but they're only 16th!
Let's start by commiserating our brother from Liverpool. What's going on up there, Ian?
As I said to our manager earlier, sometimes I think that our end content users, or "supporters", don't care about the shareholder profits of the Fenway Sports Group at all.
I'm sorry, I suddenly feel very sick.
JK
Ingrates! Can't they see the pressure we're under from China?
Pff, China. I hardly think a league awash with obscene amounts of cash, much of which will be syphoned directly into the pockets of agents, in a country whose national team has been a laughing stock for years, offers a credible threat to THE BARCLAYS PREMIER LEAGUE.
THE BEST LEAGUE IN THE WORLD!!!
PREMIER LEAGUE
Quite. Anyway, before we embark upon the ritual burning of proposals to cap ticket prices and enjoy the traditional laughing ceremony, I believe our newest member from Norwich City would like to say a few words...
Ed Balls.
Thank you.
Brothers, the fire pit...

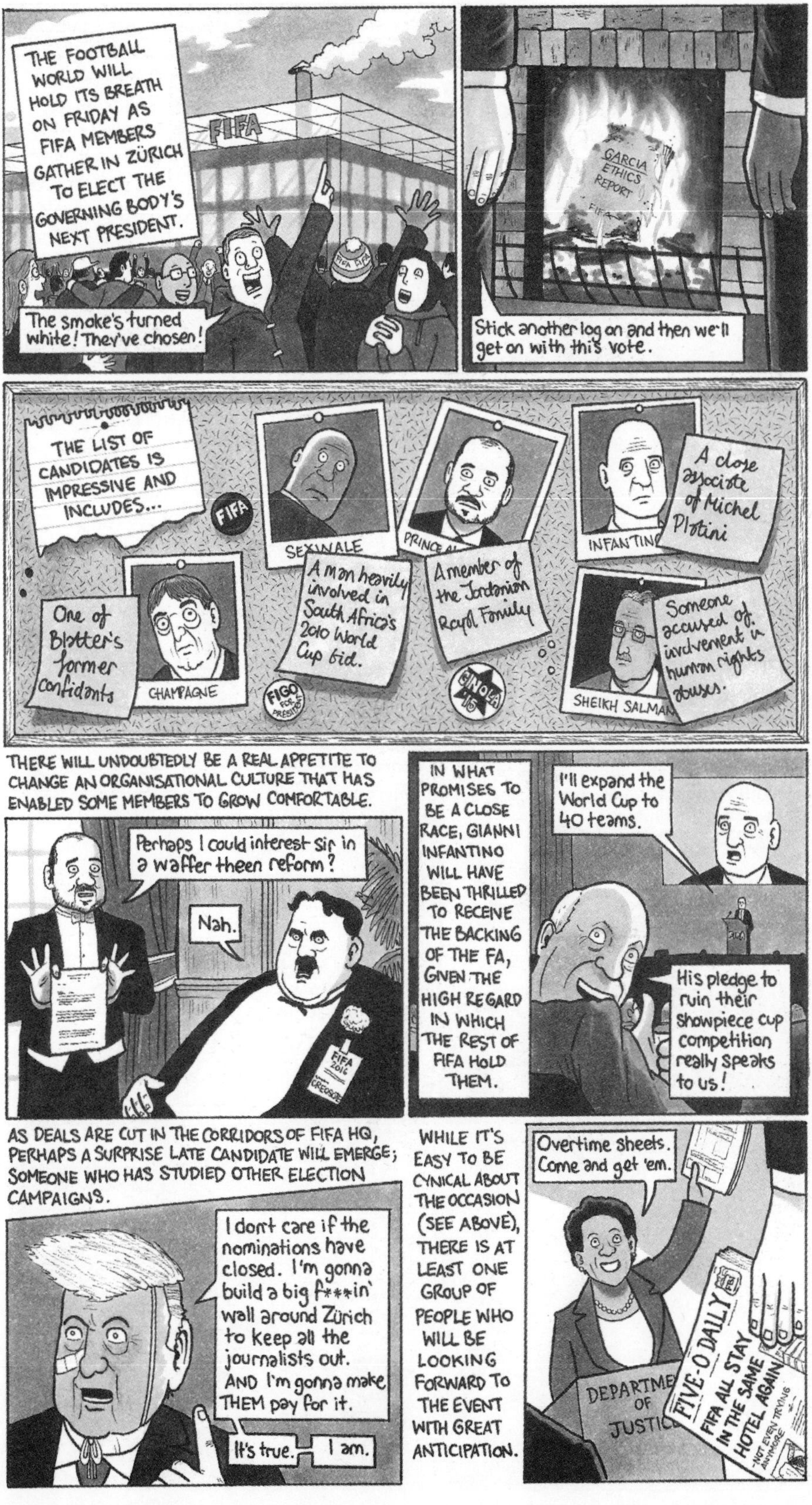
THE FOOTBALL WORLD WILL HOLD ITS BREATH ON FRIDAY AS FIFA MEMBERS GATHER IN ZÜRICH TO ELECT THE GOVERNING BODY'S NEXT PRESIDENT.
FIFA
The smoke's turned white! They've chosen!
GARCIA ETHICS REPORT
Stick another log on and then we'll get on with this vote.
THE LIST OF CANDIDATES IS IMPRESSIVE AND INCLUDES...
FIFA
SEXWALE
A man heavily involved in South Africa's 2010 World Cup bid.
A member of the Jordanian Royal Family
A close associate of Michel Platini
One of Blatter's former confidants
CHAMPAGNE
FIGO FOR PRESIDENT
Someone accused of involvement in human rights abuses.
THERE WILL UNDOUBTEDLY BE A REAL APPETITE TO CHANGE AN ORGANISATIONAL CULTURE THAT HAS ENABLED SOME MEMBERS TO GROW COMFORTABLE.
Perhaps I could interest sir in a waffer theen reform?
Nah.
FIFA 2016
IN WHAT PROMISES TO BE A CLOSE RACE, GIANNI INFANTINO WILL HAVE BEEN THRILLED TO RECEIVE THE BACKING OF THE FA, GIVEN THE HIGH REGARD IN WHICH THE REST OF FIFA HOLD THEM.
I'll expand the World Cup to 40 teams.
His pledge to ruin their showpiece cup competition really speaks to us!
AS DEALS ARE CUT IN THE CORRIDORS OF FIFA HQ, PERHAPS A SURPRISE LATE CANDIDATE WILL EMERGE; SOMEONE WHO HAS STUDIED OTHER ELECTION CAMPAIGNS.
I don't care if the nominations have closed. I'm gonna build a big f***in' wall around Zürich to keep all the journalists out. AND I'm gonna make THEM pay for it.
It's true.
I am.
WHILE IT'S EASY TO BE CYNICAL ABOUT THE OCCASION (SEE ABOVE), THERE IS AT LEAST ONE GROUP OF PEOPLE WHO WILL BE LOOKING FORWARD TO THE EVENT WITH GREAT ANTICIPATION.
Overtime sheets. Come and get 'em.
FIVE-O DAILY
FIFA ALL STAY IN THE SAME HOTEL AGAIN
"NOT EVEN TRYING ANYMORE"

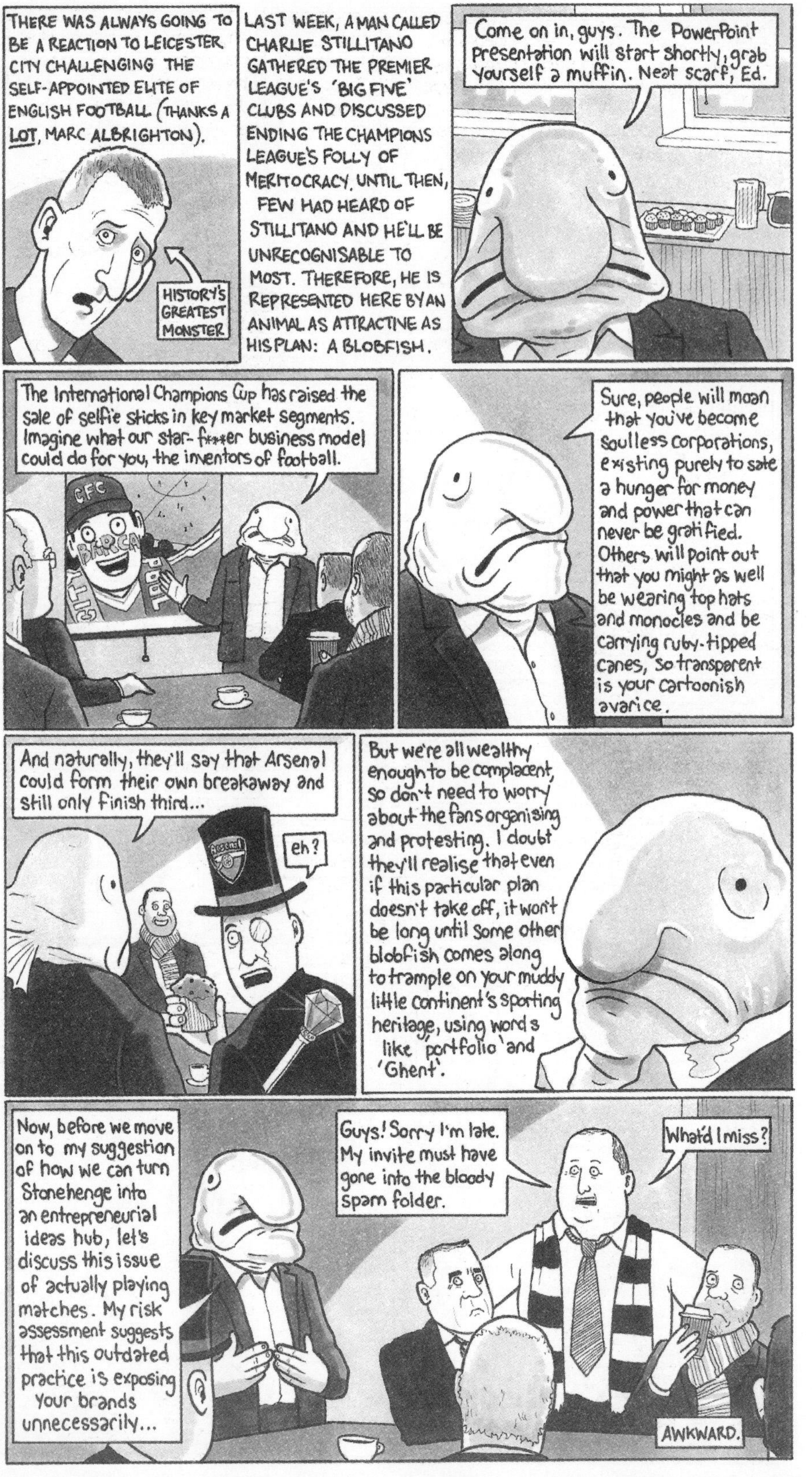
THERE WAS ALWAYS GOING TO BE A REACTION TO LEICESTER CITY CHALLENGING THE SELF-APPOINTED ELITE OF ENGLISH FOOTBALL (THANKS A LOT, MARC ALBRIGHTON).
HISTORY'S GREATEST MONSTER
LAST WEEK, A MAN CALLED CHARLIE STILLITANO GATHERED THE PREMIER LEAGUE'S 'BIG FIVE' CLUBS AND DISCUSSED ENDING THE CHAMPIONS LEAGUE'S FOLLY OF MERITOCRACY. UNTIL THEN, FEW HAD HEARD OF STILLITANO AND HE'LL BE UNRECOGNISABLE TO MOST. THEREFORE, HE IS REPRESENTED HERE BY AN ANIMAL AS ATTRACTIVE AS HIS PLAN: A BLOBFISH.
Come on in, guys. The PowerPoint presentation will start shortly, grab yourself a muffin. Neat scarf, Ed.
The International Champions Cup has raised the sale of selfie sticks in key market segments. Imagine what our star-f***er business model could do for you, the inventors of football.
CFC
BARCA
Sure, people will moan that you've become soulless corporations, existing purely to sate a hunger for money and power that can never be gratified. Others will point out that you might as well be wearing top hats and monocles and be carrying ruby-tipped canes, so transparent is your cartoonish avarice.
And naturally, they'll say that Arsenal could form their own breakaway and still only finish third...
eh?
Arsenal
But we're all wealthy enough to be complacent, so don't need to worry about the fans organising and protesting. I doubt they'll realise that even if this particular plan doesn't take off, it won't be long until some other blobfish comes along to trample on your muddy little continent's sporting heritage, using words like 'portfolio' and 'Ghent'.
Now, before we move on to my suggestion of how we can turn Stonehenge into an entrepreneurial ideas hub, let's discuss this issue of actually playing matches. My risk assessment suggests that this outdated practice is exposing your brands unnecessarily...
Guys! Sorry I'm late. My invite must have gone into the bloody spam folder.
What'd I miss?
AWKWARD.

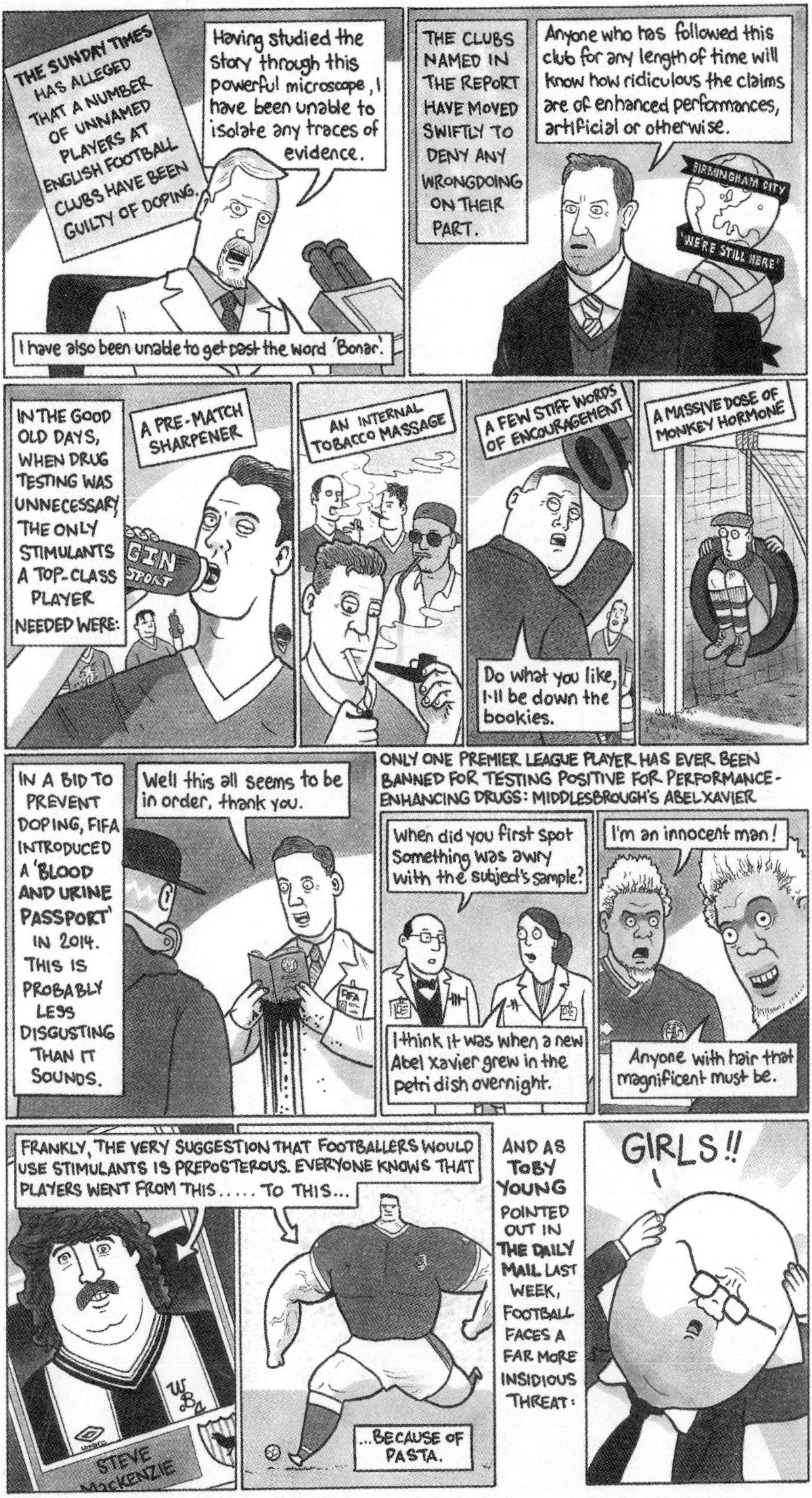
THE SUNDAY TIMES HAS ALLEGED THAT A NUMBER OF UNNAMED PLAYERS AT ENGLISH FOOTBALL CLUBS HAVE BEEN GUILTY OF DOPING.
Having studied the story through this powerful microscope, I have been unable to isolate any traces of evidence.
I have also been unable to get past the word 'Bonar'.
THE CLUBS NAMED IN THE REPORT HAVE MOVED SWIFTLY TO DENY ANY WRONGDOING ON THEIR PART.
Anyone who has followed this club for any length of time will know how ridiculous the claims are of enhanced performances, artificial or otherwise.
BIRMINGHAM CITY
'WE'RE STILL HERE'
IN THE GOOD OLD DAYS, WHEN DRUG TESTING WAS UNNECESSARY THE ONLY STIMULANTS A TOP-CLASS PLAYER NEEDED WERE:
A PRE-MATCH SHARPENER
GIN SPORT
AN INTERNAL TOBACCO MASSAGE
A FEW STIFF WORDS OF ENCOURAGEMENT
Do what you like, I'll be down the bookies.
A MASSIVE DOSE OF MONKEY HORMONE
IN A BID TO PREVENT DOPING, FIFA INTRODUCED A 'BLOOD AND URINE PASSPORT' IN 2014. THIS IS PROBABLY LESS DISGUSTING THAN IT SOUNDS.
Well this all seems to be in order, thank you.
FIFA
ONLY ONE PREMIER LEAGUE PLAYER HAS EVER BEEN BANNED FOR TESTING POSITIVE FOR PERFORMANCE-ENHANCING DRUGS: MIDDLESBROUGH'S ABEL XAVIER
When did you first spot something was awry with the subject's sample?
I think it was when a new Abel Xavier grew in the petri dish overnight.
I'm an innocent man!
Anyone with hair that magnificent must be.
FRANKLY, THE VERY SUGGESTION THAT FOOTBALLERS WOULD USE STIMULANTS IS PREPOSTEROUS. EVERYONE KNOWS THAT PLAYERS WENT FROM THIS..... TO THIS...
WBA
umbro
STEVE MacKENZIE
...BECAUSE OF PASTA.
AND AS TOBY YOUNG POINTED OUT IN THE DAILY MAIL LAST WEEK, FOOTBALL FACES A FAR MORE INSIDIOUS THREAT:
GIRLS!!

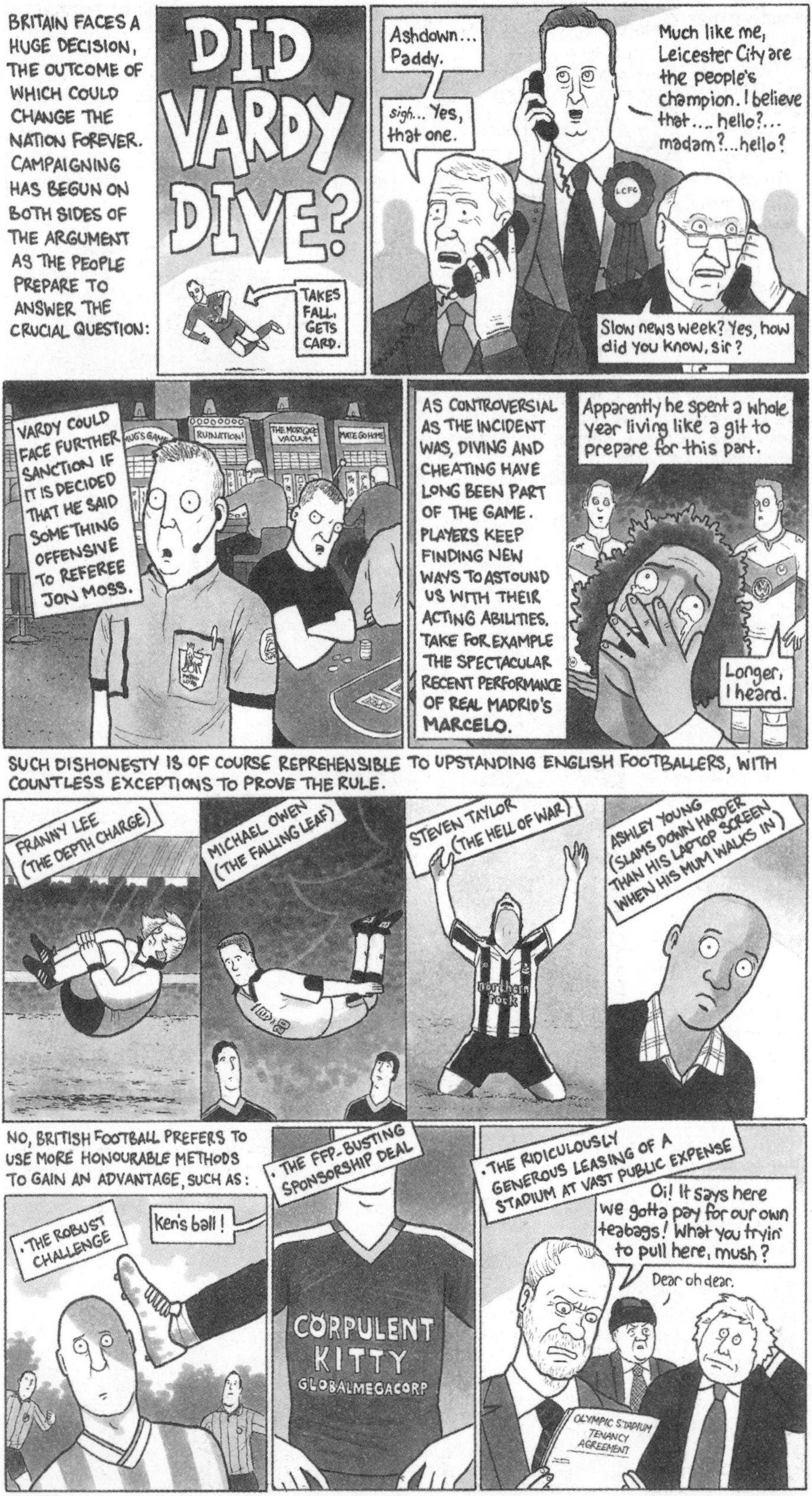
BRITAIN FACES A HUGE DECISION, THE OUTCOME OF WHICH COULD CHANGE THE NATION FOREVER. CAMPAIGNING HAS BEGUN ON BOTH SIDES OF THE ARGUMENT AS THE PEOPLE PREPARE TO ANSWER THE CRUCIAL QUESTION:
DID VARDY DIVE?
TAKES FALL, GETS CARD.
Ashdown... Paddy.
sigh... Yes, that one.
Much like me, Leicester City are the people's champion. I believe that.... hello?... madam?...hello?
LCFC
Slow news week? Yes, how did you know, sir?
VARDY COULD FACE FURTHER SANCTION IF IT IS DECIDED THAT HE SAID SOMETHING OFFENSIVE TO REFEREE JON MOSS.
RUINATION!
THE MORTGAGE VACUUM
MATE GO HOME
AS CONTROVERSIAL AS THE INCIDENT WAS, DIVING AND CHEATING HAVE LONG BEEN PART OF THE GAME. PLAYERS KEEP FINDING NEW WAYS TO ASTOUND US WITH THEIR ACTING ABILITIES. TAKE FOR EXAMPLE THE SPECTACULAR RECENT PERFORMANCE OF REAL MADRID'S MARCELO.
Apparently he spent a whole year living like a git to prepare for this part.
Longer, I heard.
SUCH DISHONESTY IS OF COURSE REPREHENSIBLE TO UPSTANDING ENGLISH FOOTBALLERS, WITH COUNTLESS EXCEPTIONS TO PROVE THE RULE.
FRANNY LEE (THE DEPTH CHARGE)
MICHAEL OWEN (THE FALLING LEAF)
STEVEN TAYLOR (THE HELL OF WAR)
northern rock
ASHLEY YOUNG (SLAMS DOWN HARDER THAN HIS LAPTOP SCREEN WHEN HIS MUM WALKS IN)
NO, BRITISH FOOTBALL PREFERS TO USE MORE HONOURABLE METHODS TO GAIN AN ADVANTAGE, SUCH AS:
• THE ROBUST CHALLENGE
Ken's ball!
• THE FFP-BUSTING SPONSORSHIP DEAL
CORPULENT KITTY
GLOBALMEGACORP
• THE RIDICULOUSLY GENEROUS LEASING OF A STADIUM AT VAST PUBLIC EXPENSE
Oi! It says here we gotta pay for our own teabags! What you tryin' to pull here, mush?
Dear oh dear.
OLYMPIC STADIUM TENANCY AGREEMENT

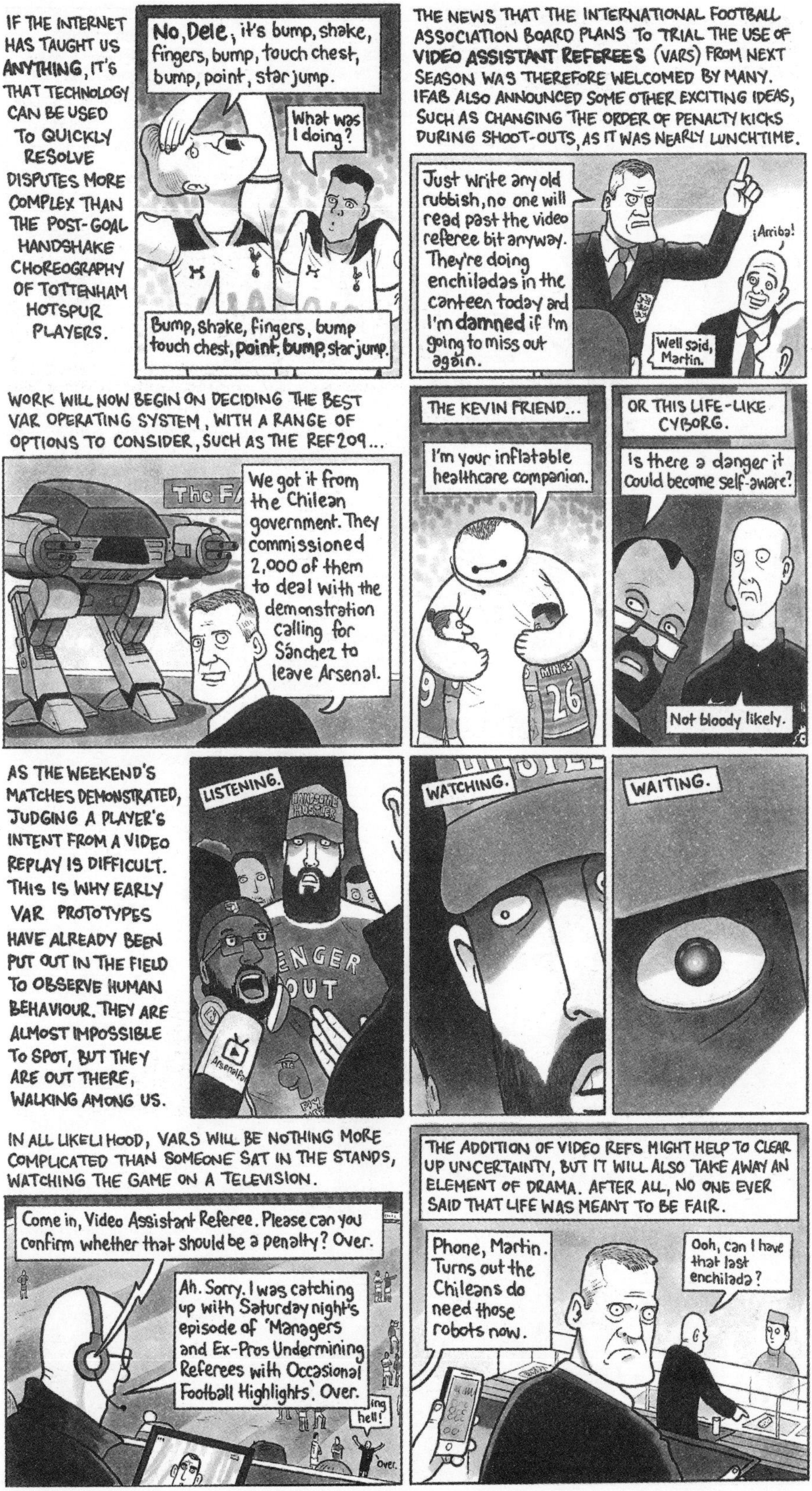
IF THE INTERNET HAS TAUGHT US ANYTHING, IT'S THAT TECHNOLOGY CAN BE USED TO QUICKLY RESOLVE DISPUTES MORE COMPLEX THAN THE POST-GOAL HANDSHAKE CHOREOGRAPHY OF TOTTENHAM HOTSPUR PLAYERS.
No, Dele, it's bump, shake, fingers, bump, touch chest, bump, point, star jump.
What was I doing?
Bump, shake, fingers, bump touch chest, point, bump, star jump.
THE NEWS THAT THE INTERNATIONAL FOOTBALL ASSOCIATION BOARD PLANS TO TRIAL THE USE OF VIDEO ASSISTANT REFEREES (VARS) FROM NEXT SEASON WAS THEREFORE WELCOMED BY MANY. IFAB ALSO ANNOUNCED SOME OTHER EXCITING IDEAS, SUCH AS CHANGING THE ORDER OF PENALTY KICKS DURING SHOOT-OUTS, AS IT WAS NEARLY LUNCHTIME.
Just write any old rubbish, no one will read past the video referee bit anyway. They're doing enchiladas in the canteen today and I'm damned if I'm going to miss out again.
¡Arriba!
Well said, Martin.
WORK WILL NOW BEGIN ON DECIDING THE BEST VAR OPERATING SYSTEM, WITH A RANGE OF OPTIONS TO CONSIDER, SUCH AS THE REF209...
The FA
We got it from the Chilean government. They commissioned 2,000 of them to deal with the demonstration calling for Sánchez to leave Arsenal.
THE KEVIN FRIEND...
I'm your inflatable healthcare companion.
26
OR THIS LIFE-LIKE CYBORG.
Is there a danger it could become self-aware?
Not bloody likely.
AS THE WEEKEND'S MATCHES DEMONSTRATED, JUDGING A PLAYER'S INTENT FROM A VIDEO REPLAY IS DIFFICULT. THIS IS WHY EARLY VAR PROTOTYPES HAVE ALREADY BEEN PUT OUT IN THE FIELD TO OBSERVE HUMAN BEHAVIOUR. THEY ARE ALMOST IMPOSSIBLE TO SPOT, BUT THEY ARE OUT THERE, WALKING AMONG US.
LISTENING.
HANDSOME HUSTLER
ENGER OUT
WATCHING.
WAITING.
IN ALL LIKELIHOOD, VARS WILL BE NOTHING MORE COMPLICATED THAN SOMEONE SAT IN THE STANDS, WATCHING THE GAME ON A TELEVISION.
Come in, Video Assistant Referee. Please can you confirm whether that should be a penalty? Over.
Ah. Sorry. I was catching up with Saturday night's episode of 'Managers and Ex-Pros Undermining Referees with Occasional Football Highlights'. Over.
ing hell!
Over.
THE ADDITION OF VIDEO REFS MIGHT HELP TO CLEAR UP UNCERTAINTY, BUT IT WILL ALSO TAKE AWAY AN ELEMENT OF DRAMA. AFTER ALL, NO ONE EVER SAID THAT LIFE WAS MEANT TO BE FAIR.
Phone, Martin. Turns out the Chileans do need those robots now.
Ooh, can I have that last enchilada?

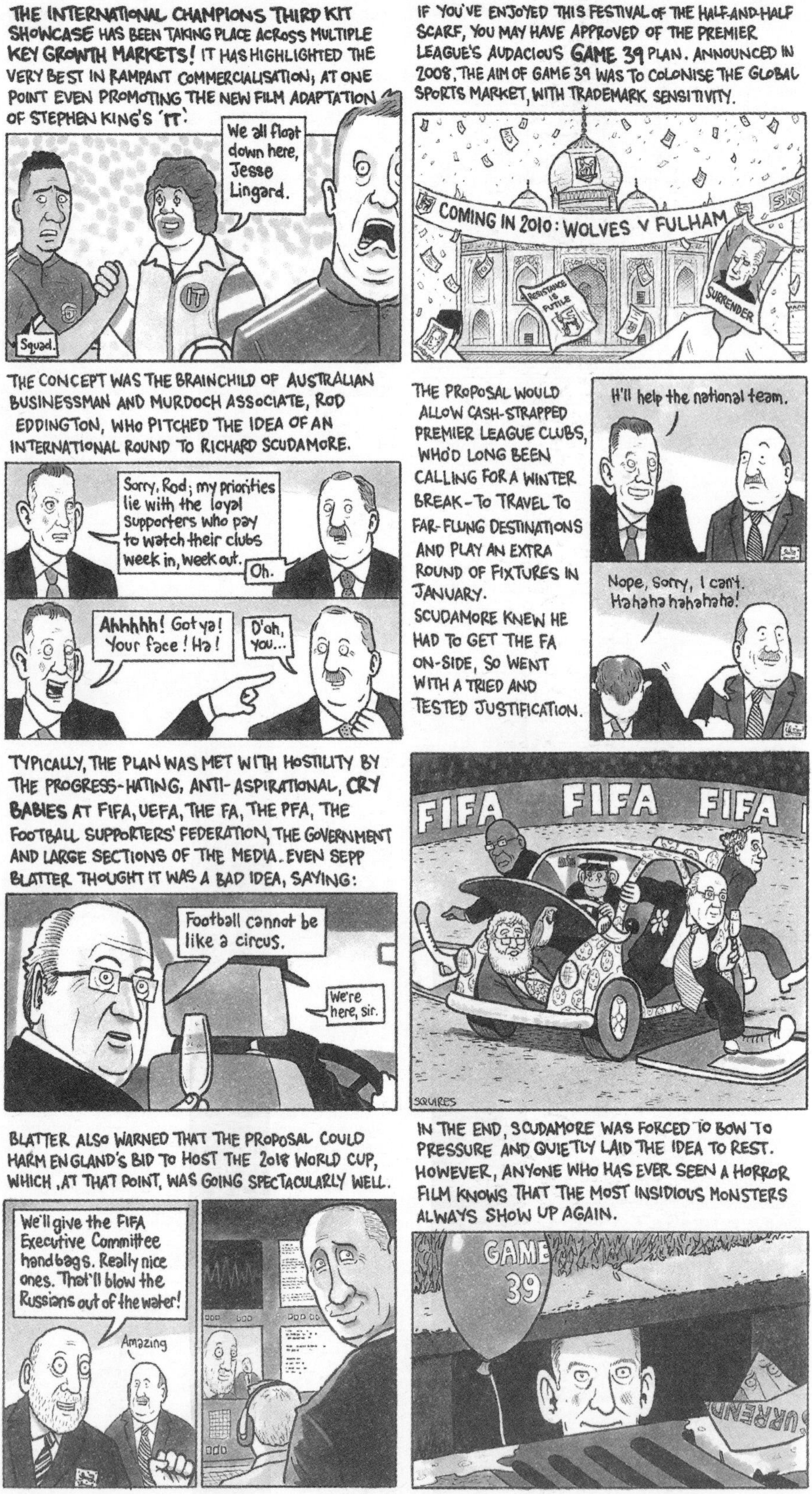

THE INTERNATIONAL CHAMPIONS THIRD KIT SHOWCASE HAS BEEN TAKING PLACE ACROSS MULTIPLE KEY GROWTH MARKETS! IT HAS HIGHLIGHTED THE VERY BEST IN RAMPANT COMMERCIALISATION; AT ONE POINT EVEN PROMOTING THE NEW FILM ADAPTATION OF STEPHEN KING'S 'IT'.
We all float down here, Jesse Lingard.
Squad.
IT
IF YOU'VE ENJOYED THIS FESTIVAL OF THE HALF-AND-HALF SCARF, YOU MAY HAVE APPROVED OF THE PREMIER LEAGUE'S AUDACIOUS GAME 39 PLAN. ANNOUNCED IN 2008, THE AIM OF GAME 39 WAS TO COLONISE THE GLOBAL SPORTS MARKET, WITH TRADEMARK SENSITIVITY.
COMING IN 2010: WOLVES V FULHAM
SKY
RESISTANCE IS FUTILE
SURRENDER
THE CONCEPT WAS THE BRAINCHILD OF AUSTRALIAN BUSINESSMAN AND MURDOCH ASSOCIATE, ROD EDDINGTON, WHO PITCHED THE IDEA OF AN INTERNATIONAL ROUND TO RICHARD SCUDAMORE.
Sorry, Rod; my priorities lie with the loyal supporters who pay to watch their clubs week in, week out.
Oh.
Ahhhhh! Got ya! Your face! Ha!
D'oh, you...
THE PROPOSAL WOULD ALLOW CASH-STRAPPED PREMIER LEAGUE CLUBS, WHO'D LONG BEEN CALLING FOR A WINTER BREAK - TO TRAVEL TO FAR-FLUNG DESTINATIONS AND PLAY AN EXTRA ROUND OF FIXTURES IN JANUARY.
SCUDAMORE KNEW HE HAD TO GET THE FA ON-SIDE, SO WENT WITH A TRIED AND TESTED JUSTIFICATION.
It'll help the national team.
Nope, sorry, I can't. Hahaha hahahaha!
TYPICALLY, THE PLAN WAS MET WITH HOSTILITY BY THE PROGRESS-HATING, ANTI-ASPIRATIONAL, CRY BABIES AT FIFA, UEFA, THE FA, THE PFA, THE FOOTBALL SUPPORTERS' FEDERATION, THE GOVERNMENT AND LARGE SECTIONS OF THE MEDIA. EVEN SEPP BLATTER THOUGHT IT WAS A BAD IDEA, SAYING:
Football cannot be like a circus.
We're here, sir.
FIFA FIFA FIFA
SQUIRES
BLATTER ALSO WARNED THAT THE PROPOSAL COULD HARM ENGLAND'S BID TO HOST THE 2018 WORLD CUP, WHICH, AT THAT POINT, WAS GOING SPECTACULARLY WELL.
We'll give the FIFA Executive Committee handbags. Really nice ones. That'll blow the Russians out of the water!
Amazing
IN THE END, SCUDAMORE WAS FORCED TO BOW TO PRESSURE AND QUIETLY LAID THE IDEA TO REST. HOWEVER, ANYONE WHO HAS EVER SEEN A HORROR FILM KNOWS THAT THE MOST INSIDIOUS MONSTERS ALWAYS SHOW UP AGAIN.
GAME 39

ANNOUNCE BERAHINO:

Football Transfers

Is there anything more exciting than your team buying a new player? Could it be that this young striker with hair like a First World War fighter pilot will be the final piece in the puzzle that unlocks your club's potential? If he plays as well as he strides towards the camera in the promotional gif on the club's Twitter feed, this could finally be the year that your heroes break into the third round of the Carabao Cup. Sure, his Wikipedia entry is as disturbing as a serial killer's (including lots of travelling around) and he did a bit of time for affray, but that is literally a victimless crime, and maybe – just maybe – it will be at *your* club where he achieves what he failed to do at eight other clubs across the lower leagues of Scotland and scores a goal.

Fans of 'selling clubs' (i.e. anyone other than Manchester United, Manchester City or Chelsea) also know the dread of discovering that your best player has decided that another club better matches his ambitions: owning a country estate in Cheshire and driving a car the size of a nightclub. I still wake in fright some nights, gripped by the memory of Swindon selling Jan Åge Fjørtoft (their solitary source of goals) to Middlesbrough on deadline day in 1995, a shrewd piece of business that saw the Robins relegated a few weeks later. It's still too soon for me to talk about Matt Ritchie's move to Bournemouth in 2013. I'm not sure I'll ever be able to.

Supporters of bigger clubs have different pressures and are required to have an encyclopaedic knowledge of every footballer in

Europe's top leagues. Oh, you don't know who Racing Santander's holding midfielder is? I thought you liked football? Novice.

The main focus of transfer business is, of course, deadline day. Like many other religious holidays, this often involves a whole load of money being wasted on tat, culminating in a huge anti-climax and weeks of bitter recrimination. Doing business in a mad panic, reliant on finding a functioning fax machine at 11.57 p.m., is clearly a better approach than considered planning and negotiation over the previous few months.

The 'transfer window' was only introduced in the 2002/3 season, and was a godsend for twenty-four-hour satellite news channels tasked with entertaining the patrons of Wetherspoons. A whole day of rumour, gossip and speculation: the golden nectar of content, sweet delicious content. Sparks would fly from the keyboards of the writers of the rolling news bar: 'BREAKING: LEROY FER SPOTTED AT ESTATE AGENT'S! . . . DONE DEAL: COSTEL PANTILIMON TO NOTTINGHAM FOREST (LOAN)! . . . GARETH BARRY IS ON THE M62, REPEAT, GARETH BARRY IS ON THE M62.'

Arguably, the most exciting transfer windows have been the ones in which clubs suddenly find themselves awash with cash, the plundering of minerals in faraway insignificant lands allowing them to sign Wayne Bridge. Roman Abramovich taking over at Chelsea led to such a wild spending spree, as did the arrival of Abu Dhabi's ruling family at Manchester City. City's immediate and understandable reaction was consistent with that of many lottery winners: they went nuts, buying all of the random gaudy stuff they'd denied themselves for years. If you won the exploited-labour lotto, tell me that you wouldn't buy yourself a Robinho too.

In the latter years of Arsène Wenger's reign at Arsenal, there was also a dramatic tension around deadline day. Gunners fans would wait expectantly, refreshing the live feed every few seconds, hoping that the manager had dipped into the transfer kitty to finally sign a functioning replacement for Patrick Vieira or Jens Lehmann. As day moves to night, the anxiety heightens: he's cutting it fine if he's going to secure the services of that lad from Racing Santander and get the obligatory photo of him giving the thumbs-up while undergoing a medical. Then, an update! Wenger spotted at the training ground! Could this be it? Nope, he's just retrieving a memory stick of Jupiler League highlights. After so many years of prudent austerity, can it be pure coincidence that in his final season in charge he broke the club's transfer record and signed Pierre-Emerick Aubameyang from Dortmund? Surely now they would let him stay? Surely now?

It wasn't always this way, of course. Transfers used to be conducted in car parks and smoky hotel bars. If a manager really wanted to sign a player, he would go round to his house, issue him with an aggressively worded ultimatum, ruffle his children's hair and demand to see him at training the following morning. The notion of hiring the services of an agent to help thrash out a fair deal was as outlandish as the idea of just changing jobs like in any other walk of life.

Football agents are broadly considered to be subhuman, the kind of vermin that help young people who lack confidence in negotiation and are inexperienced in workplace law and practice, preventing them from potentially being ripped off by unscrupulous employers. At the top end of the scale are the mega-agents, wealthy power-brokers who hold stables full of top international talent and have their slimy tentacles wrapped around some of the world's top clubs (and Wolves).

The first cartoon in this section is what prompted the *Guardian* to contact me with an offer to do some work for them. It depicts an event from the transfer deadline day in 2014, when Sky Sports News' roving reporter Alan Irvine was jabbed in the ear with a purple dildo during a live broadcast from the Everton training-ground car park. 'The Sports Reporter's Progress' – as the cartoon is titled

– shows the career path from enthusiastic young writer to rookie journalist through to poor sod stood outside a football stadium being humiliated by a herbert with a large marital aid. Is it weird that I owe my career to that herbert, to that love truncheon? I try not to think about it.

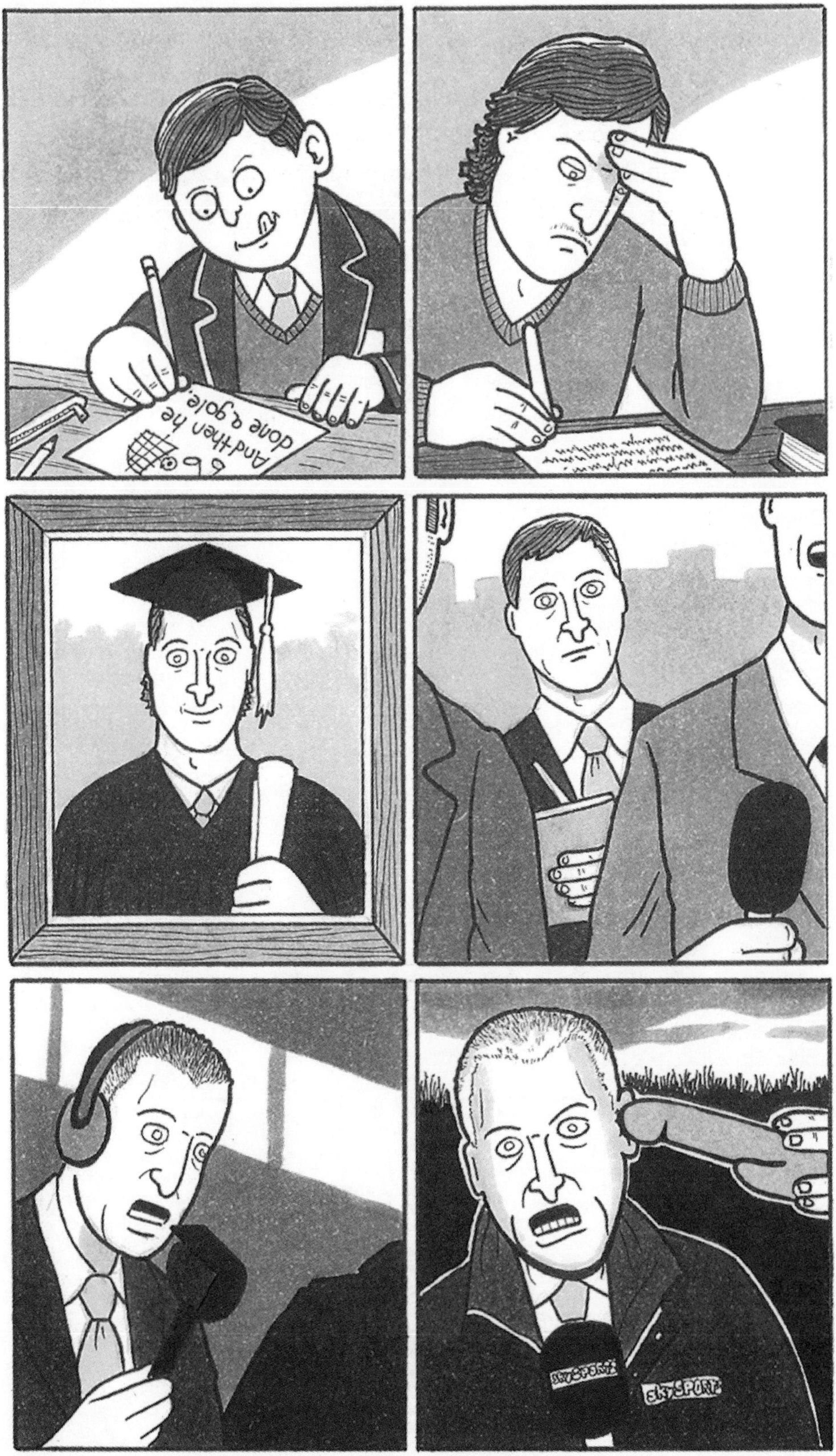
And then he
done a gole.

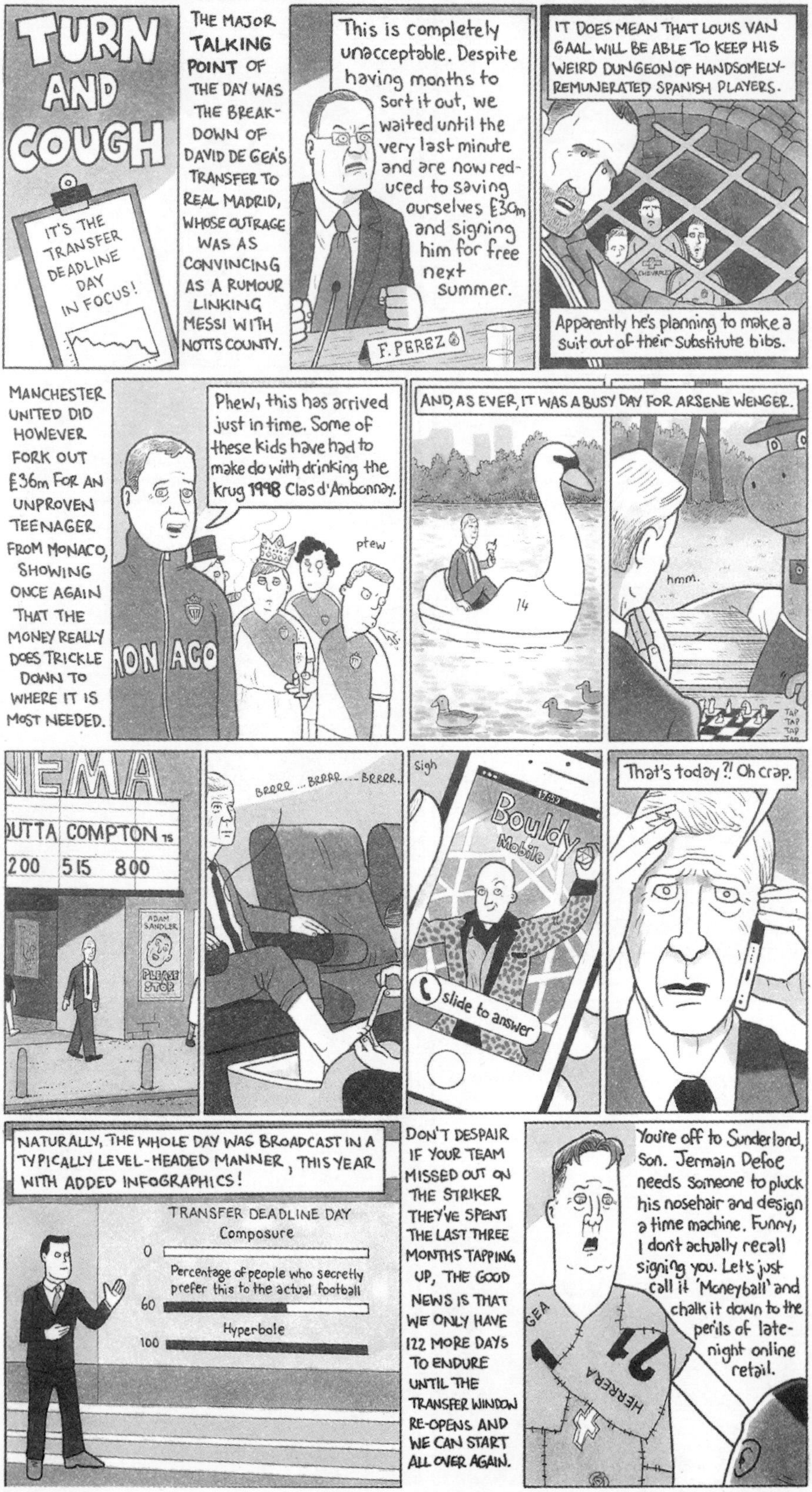
TURN AND COUGH
IT'S THE TRANSFER DEADLINE DAY IN FOCUS!
THE MAJOR TALKING POINT OF THE DAY WAS THE BREAK-DOWN OF DAVID DE GEA'S TRANSFER TO REAL MADRID, WHOSE OUTRAGE WAS AS CONVINCING AS A RUMOUR LINKING MESSI WITH NOTTS COUNTY.
This is completely unacceptable. Despite having months to sort it out, we waited until the very last minute and are now reduced to saving ourselves £30m and signing him for free next summer.
F. PEREZ
IT DOES MEAN THAT LOUIS VAN GAAL WILL BE ABLE TO KEEP HIS WEIRD DUNGEON OF HANDSOMELY-REMUNERATED SPANISH PLAYERS.
Apparently he's planning to make a suit out of their substitute bibs.
MANCHESTER UNITED DID HOWEVER FORK OUT £36m FOR AN UNPROVEN TEENAGER FROM MONACO, SHOWING ONCE AGAIN THAT THE MONEY REALLY DOES TRICKLE DOWN TO WHERE IT IS MOST NEEDED.
Phew, this has arrived just in time. Some of these kids have had to make do with drinking the Krug 1998 Clos d'Ambonnay.
ptew
MONACO
AND, AS EVER, IT WAS A BUSY DAY FOR ARSENE WENGER.
14
hmm.
TAP TAP TAP
COMPTON 15
200 515 800
ADAM SANDLER
PLEASE STOP
BRRRR ... BRRRR ... BRRRR
Sigh
Bouldy Mobile
slide to answer
That's today?! Oh crap.
NATURALLY, THE WHOLE DAY WAS BROADCAST IN A TYPICALLY LEVEL-HEADED MANNER, THIS YEAR WITH ADDED INFOGRAPHICS!
TRANSFER DEADLINE DAY
Composure
0
Percentage of people who secretly prefer this to the actual football
60
Hyperbole
100
DON'T DESPAIR IF YOUR TEAM MISSED OUT ON THE STRIKER THEY'VE SPENT THE LAST THREE MONTHS TAPPING UP, THE GOOD NEWS IS THAT WE ONLY HAVE 122 MORE DAYS TO ENDURE UNTIL THE TRANSFER WINDOW RE-OPENS AND WE CAN START ALL OVER AGAIN.
You're off to Sunderland, son. Jermain Defoe needs someone to pluck his nosehair and design a time machine. Funny, I don't actually recall signing you. Let's just call it 'Moneyball' and chalk it down to the perils of late-night online retail.
GEA
HERRERA
21

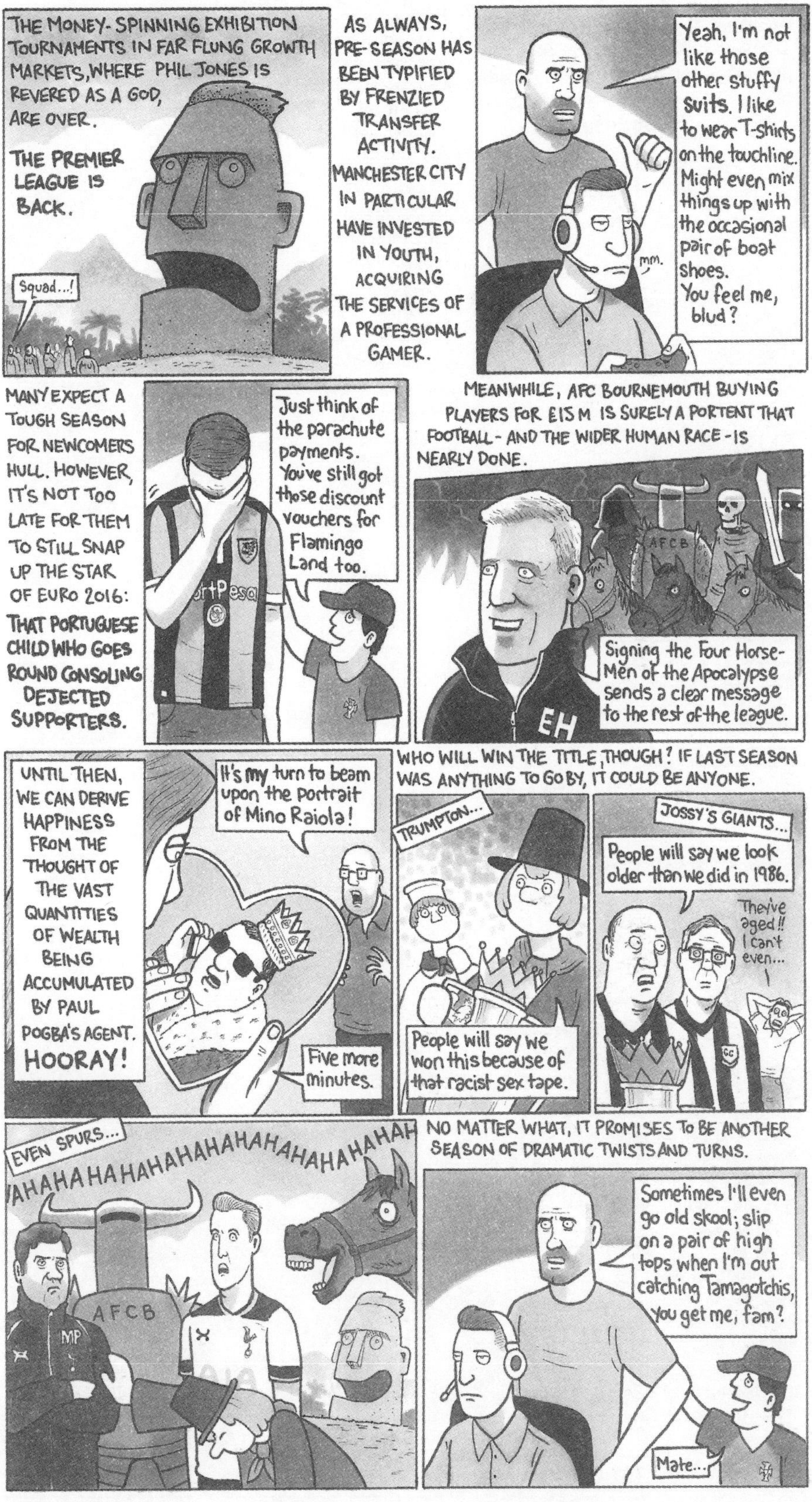
THE MONEY-SPINNING EXHIBITION TOURNAMENTS IN FAR FLUNG GROWTH MARKETS, WHERE PHIL JONES IS REVERED AS A GOD, ARE OVER.
THE PREMIER LEAGUE IS BACK.
Squad...!
AS ALWAYS, PRE-SEASON HAS BEEN TYPIFIED BY FRENZIED TRANSFER ACTIVITY. MANCHESTER CITY IN PARTICULAR HAVE INVESTED IN YOUTH, ACQUIRING THE SERVICES OF A PROFESSIONAL GAMER.
Yeah, I'm not like those other stuffy suits. I like to wear T-shirts on the touchline. Might even mix things up with the occasional pair of boat shoes. You feel me, blud?
mm.
MANY EXPECT A TOUGH SEASON FOR NEWCOMERS HULL. HOWEVER, IT'S NOT TOO LATE FOR THEM TO STILL SNAP UP THE STAR OF EURO 2016: THAT PORTUGUESE CHILD WHO GOES ROUND CONSOLING DEJECTED SUPPORTERS.
Just think of the parachute payments. You've still got those discount vouchers for Flamingo Land too.
MEANWHILE, AFC BOURNEMOUTH BUYING PLAYERS FOR £15M IS SURELY A PORTENT THAT FOOTBALL - AND THE WIDER HUMAN RACE - IS NEARLY DONE.
AFCB
Signing the Four Horse-Men of the Apocalypse sends a clear message to the rest of the league.
EH
UNTIL THEN, WE CAN DERIVE HAPPINESS FROM THE THOUGHT OF THE VAST QUANTITIES OF WEALTH BEING ACCUMULATED BY PAUL POGBA'S AGENT. HOORAY!
It's my turn to beam upon the portrait of Mino Raiola!
Five more minutes.
WHO WILL WIN THE TITLE, THOUGH? IF LAST SEASON WAS ANYTHING TO GO BY, IT COULD BE ANYONE.
TRUMPTON...
People will say we won this because of that racist sex tape.
JOSSY'S GIANTS...
People will say we look older than we did in 1986.
They've aged!! I can't even...
EVEN SPURS...
HAHAHAHAHAHAHAHAHAHAHAHAHAH
AFCB
MP
NO MATTER WHAT, IT PROMISES TO BE ANOTHER SEASON OF DRAMATIC TWISTS AND TURNS.
Sometimes I'll even go old skool; slip on a pair of high tops when I'm out catching Tamagotchis, you get me, fam?
Mate...

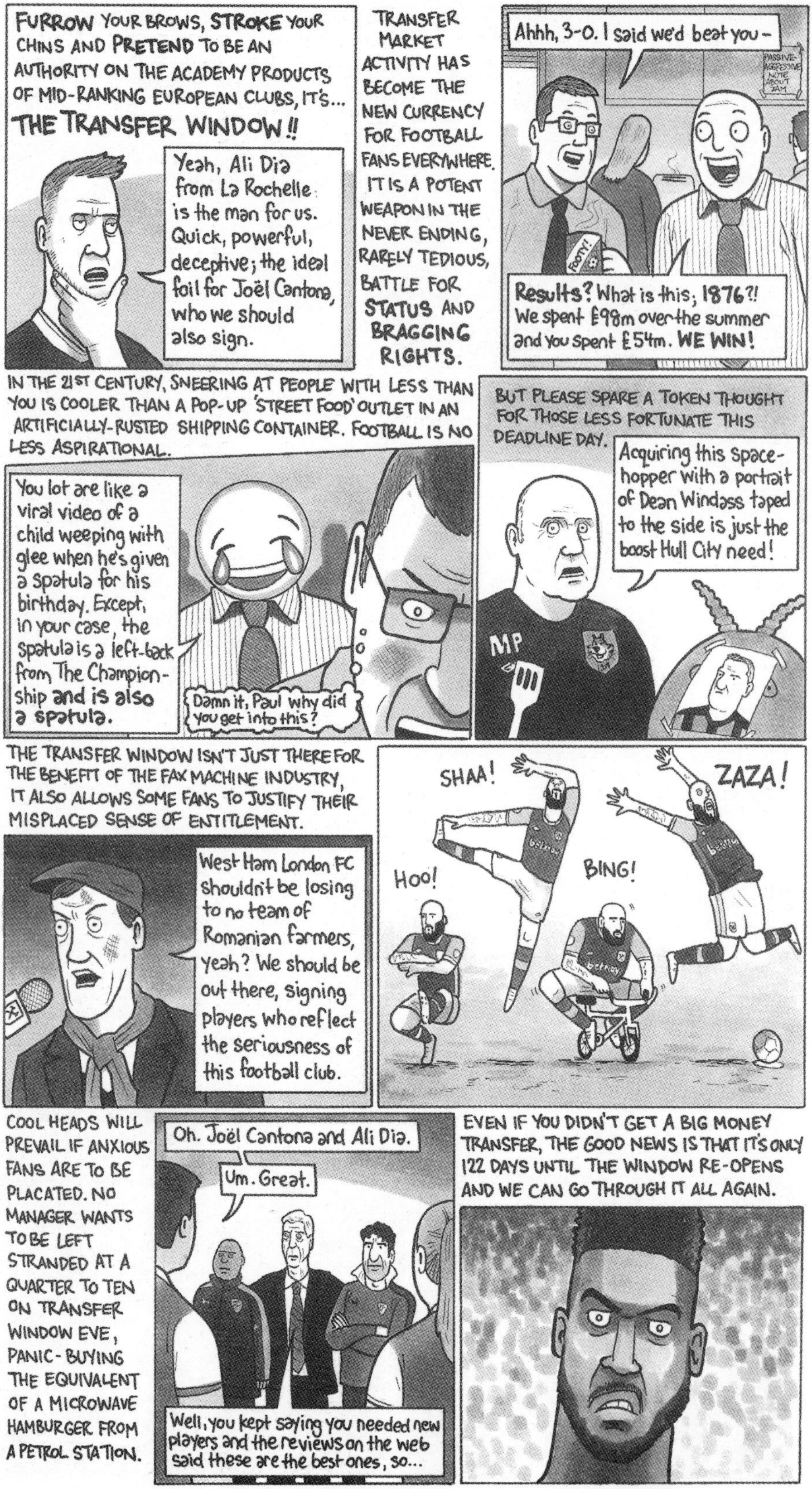

FURROW YOUR BROWS, STROKE YOUR CHINS AND PRETEND TO BE AN AUTHORITY ON THE ACADEMY PRODUCTS OF MID-RANKING EUROPEAN CLUBS, IT'S... THE TRANSFER WINDOW!!
Yeah, Ali Dia from La Rochelle is the man for us. Quick, powerful, deceptive; the ideal foil for Joël Cantona, who we should also sign.
TRANSFER MARKET ACTIVITY HAS BECOME THE NEW CURRENCY FOR FOOTBALL FANS EVERYWHERE. IT IS A POTENT WEAPON IN THE NEVER ENDING, RARELY TEDIOUS, BATTLE FOR STATUS AND BRAGGING RIGHTS.
Ahhh, 3-0. I said we'd beat you –
PASSIVE-AGGRESSIVE NOTE ABOUT JAM
FOOTY!
Results? What is this; 1876?! We spent £98m over the summer and you spent £54m. WE WIN!
IN THE 21ST CENTURY, SNEERING AT PEOPLE WITH LESS THAN YOU IS COOLER THAN A POP-UP 'STREET FOOD' OUTLET IN AN ARTIFICIALLY-RUSTED SHIPPING CONTAINER. FOOTBALL IS NO LESS ASPIRATIONAL.
You lot are like a viral video of a child weeping with glee when he's given a spatula for his birthday. Except, in your case, the spatula is a left-back from The Championship and is also a spatula.
Damn it, Paul why did you get into this?
BUT PLEASE SPARE A TOKEN THOUGHT FOR THOSE LESS FORTUNATE THIS DEADLINE DAY.
Acquiring this space-hopper with a portrait of Dean Windass taped to the side is just the boost Hull City need!
MP
THE TRANSFER WINDOW ISN'T JUST THERE FOR THE BENEFIT OF THE FAX MACHINE INDUSTRY, IT ALSO ALLOWS SOME FANS TO JUSTIFY THEIR MISPLACED SENSE OF ENTITLEMENT.
West Ham London FC shouldn't be losing to no team of Romanian farmers, yeah? We should be out there, signing players who reflect the seriousness of this football club.
SHAA!
ZAZA!
Hoo!
BING!
COOL HEADS WILL PREVAIL IF ANXIOUS FANS ARE TO BE PLACATED. NO MANAGER WANTS TO BE LEFT STRANDED AT A QUARTER TO TEN ON TRANSFER WINDOW EVE, PANIC-BUYING THE EQUIVALENT OF A MICROWAVE HAMBURGER FROM A PETROL STATION.
Oh. Joël Cantona and Ali Dia.
Um. Great.
Well, you kept saying you needed new players and the reviews on the web said these are the best ones, so...
EVEN IF YOU DIDN'T GET A BIG MONEY TRANSFER, THE GOOD NEWS IS THAT IT'S ONLY 122 DAYS UNTIL THE WINDOW RE-OPENS AND WE CAN GO THROUGH IT ALL AGAIN.

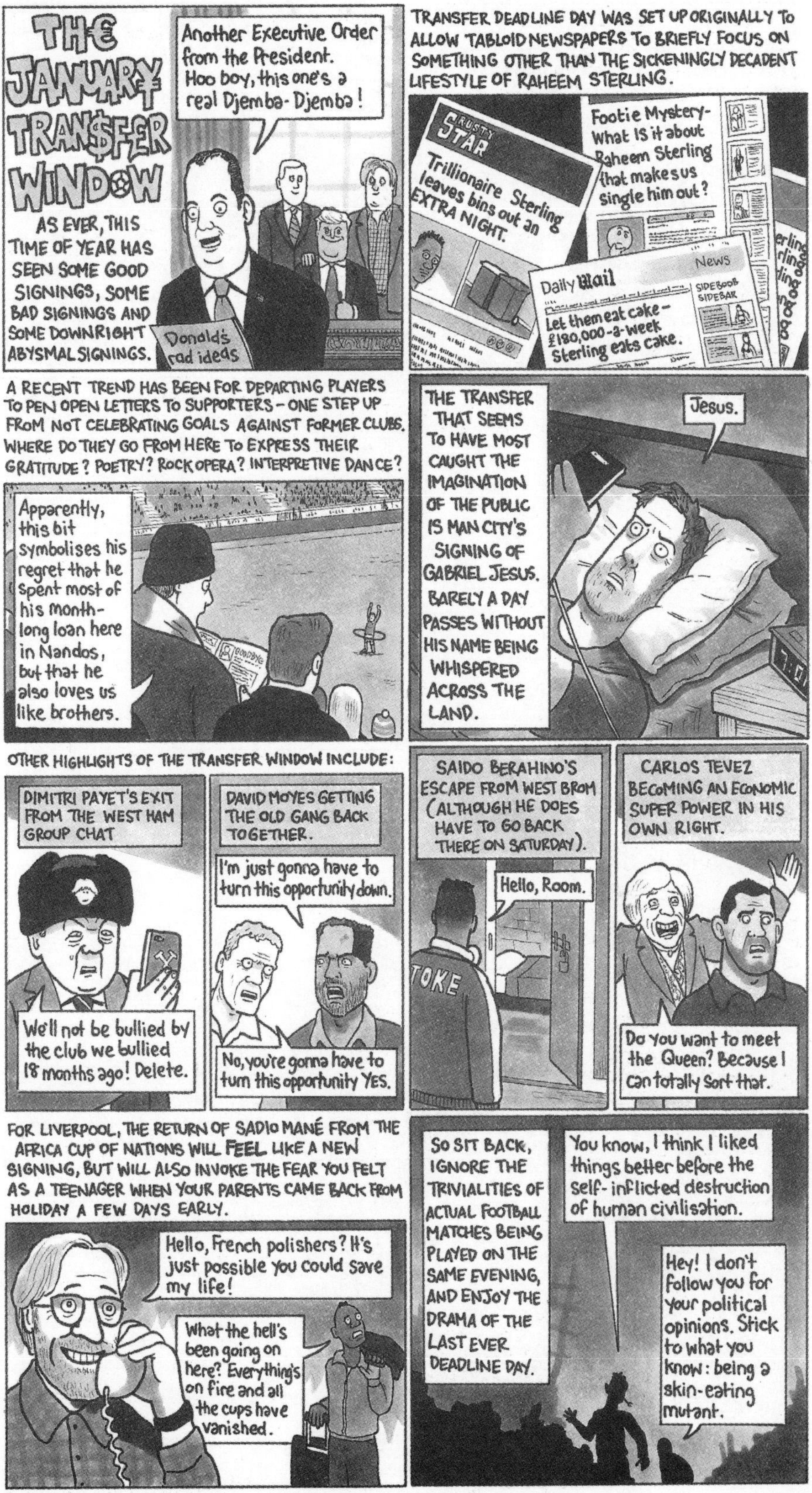
THE JANUARY TRAN$FER WINDOW
AS EVER, THIS TIME OF YEAR HAS SEEN SOME GOOD SIGNINGS, SOME BAD SIGNINGS AND SOME DOWNRIGHT ABYSMAL SIGNINGS.
Another Executive Order from the President. Hoo boy, this one's a real Djemba-Djemba!
Donald's rad ideas
TRANSFER DEADLINE DAY WAS SET UP ORIGINALLY TO ALLOW TABLOID NEWSPAPERS TO BRIEFLY FOCUS ON SOMETHING OTHER THAN THE SICKENINGLY DECADENT LIFESTYLE OF RAHEEM STERLING.
RUSTY STAR
Trillionaire Sterling leaves bins out an EXTRA NIGHT.
Footie Mystery- What IS it about Raheem Sterling that makes us single him out?
Daily Mail
News
SIDEBOOB SIDEBAR
Let them eat cake - £180,000-a-week Sterling eats cake.
A RECENT TREND HAS BEEN FOR DEPARTING PLAYERS TO PEN OPEN LETTERS TO SUPPORTERS - ONE STEP UP FROM NOT CELEBRATING GOALS AGAINST FORMER CLUBS. WHERE DO THEY GO FROM HERE TO EXPRESS THEIR GRATITUDE? POETRY? ROCK OPERA? INTERPRETIVE DANCE?
Apparently, this bit symbolises his regret that he spent most of his month-long loan here in Nandos, but that he also loves us like brothers.
GOODBYE
THE TRANSFER THAT SEEMS TO HAVE MOST CAUGHT THE IMAGINATION OF THE PUBLIC IS MAN CITY'S SIGNING OF GABRIEL JESUS. BARELY A DAY PASSES WITHOUT HIS NAME BEING WHISPERED ACROSS THE LAND.
Jesus.
OTHER HIGHLIGHTS OF THE TRANSFER WINDOW INCLUDE:
DIMITRI PAYET'S EXIT FROM THE WEST HAM GROUP CHAT
We'll not be bullied by the club we bullied 18 months ago! Delete.
DAVID MOYES GETTING THE OLD GANG BACK TOGETHER.
I'm just gonna have to turn this opportunity down.
No, you're gonna have to turn this opportunity YES.
SAIDO BERAHINO'S ESCAPE FROM WEST BROM (ALTHOUGH HE DOES HAVE TO GO BACK THERE ON SATURDAY).
Hello, Room.
TOKE
CARLOS TEVEZ BECOMING AN ECONOMIC SUPER POWER IN HIS OWN RIGHT.
Do you want to meet the Queen? Because I can totally sort that.
FOR LIVERPOOL, THE RETURN OF SADIO MANÉ FROM THE AFRICA CUP OF NATIONS WILL FEEL LIKE A NEW SIGNING, BUT WILL ALSO INVOKE THE FEAR YOU FELT AS A TEENAGER WHEN YOUR PARENTS CAME BACK FROM HOLIDAY A FEW DAYS EARLY.
Hello, French polishers? It's just possible you could save my life!
What the hell's been going on here? Everything's on fire and all the cups have vanished.
SO SIT BACK, IGNORE THE TRIVIALITIES OF ACTUAL FOOTBALL MATCHES BEING PLAYED ON THE SAME EVENING, AND ENJOY THE DRAMA OF THE LAST EVER DEADLINE DAY.
You know, I think I liked things better before the self-inflicted destruction of human civilisation.
Hey! I don't follow you for your political opinions. Stick to what you know: being a skin-eating mutant.

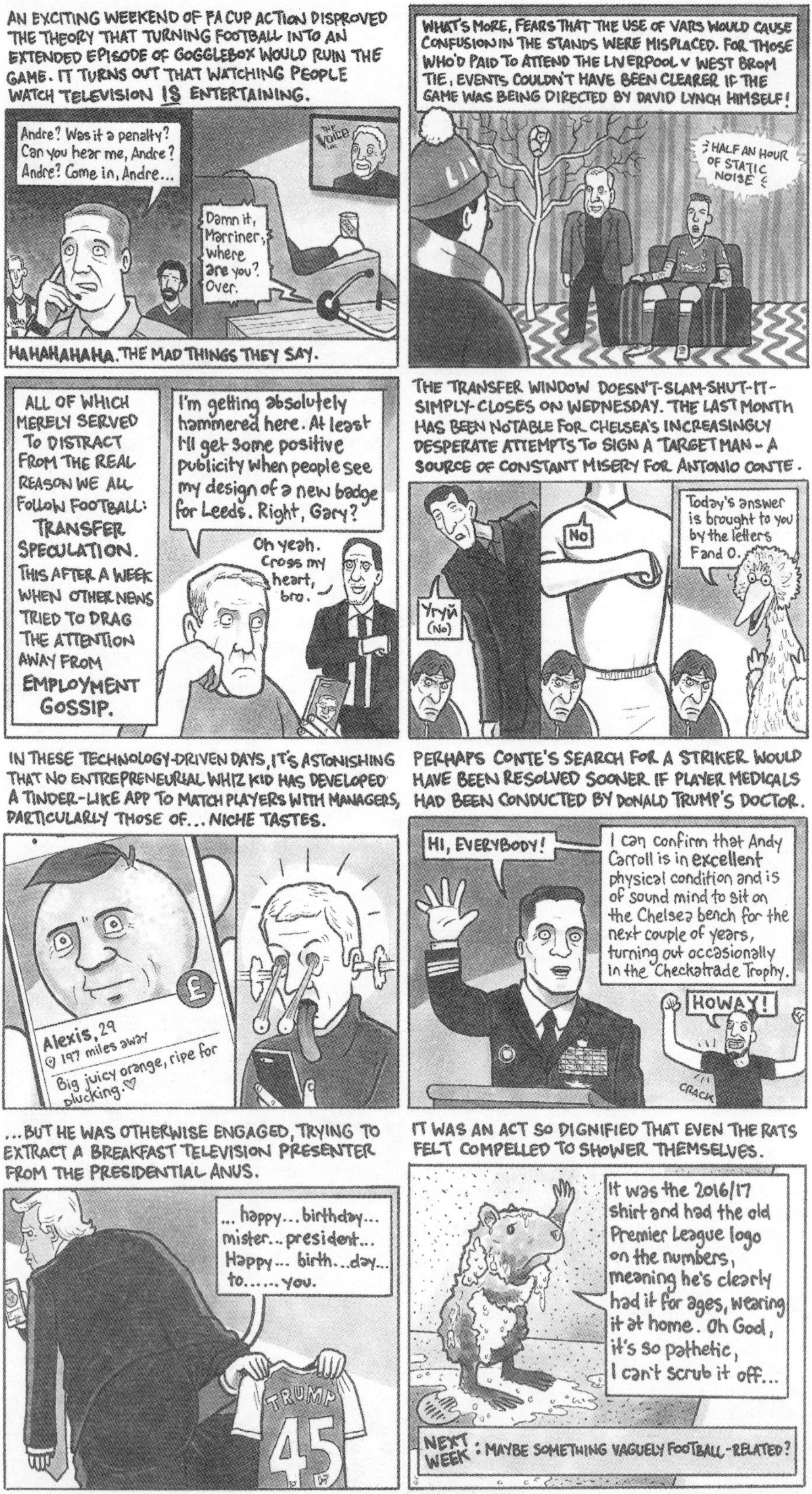
AN EXCITING WEEKEND OF FA CUP ACTION DISPROVED THE THEORY THAT TURNING FOOTBALL INTO AN EXTENDED EPISODE OF GOGGLEBOX WOULD RUIN THE GAME. IT TURNS OUT THAT WATCHING PEOPLE WATCH TELEVISION IS ENTERTAINING.
Andre? Was it a penalty? Can you hear me, Andre? Andre? Come in, Andre...
THE VOICE UK
Damn it, Marriner, where are you? Over.
HAHAHAHAHA. THE MAD THINGS THEY SAY.
WHAT'S MORE, FEARS THAT THE USE OF VARS WOULD CAUSE CONFUSION IN THE STANDS WERE MISPLACED. FOR THOSE WHO'D PAID TO ATTEND THE LIVERPOOL V WEST BROM TIE, EVENTS COULDN'T HAVE BEEN CLEARER IF THE GAME WAS BEING DIRECTED BY DAVID LYNCH HIMSELF!
HALF AN HOUR OF STATIC NOISE
ALL OF WHICH MERELY SERVED TO DISTRACT FROM THE REAL REASON WE ALL FOLLOW FOOTBALL: TRANSFER SPECULATION. THIS AFTER A WEEK WHEN OTHER NEWS TRIED TO DRAG THE ATTENTION AWAY FROM EMPLOYMENT GOSSIP.
I'm getting absolutely hammered here. At least I'll get some positive publicity when people see my design of a new badge for Leeds. Right, Gary?
Oh yeah. Cross my heart, bro.
THE TRANSFER WINDOW DOESN'T-SLAM-SHUT-IT-SIMPLY-CLOSES ON WEDNESDAY. THE LAST MONTH HAS BEEN NOTABLE FOR CHELSEA'S INCREASINGLY DESPERATE ATTEMPTS TO SIGN A TARGET MAN - A SOURCE OF CONSTANT MISERY FOR ANTONIO CONTE.
Угуй (No)
No
Today's answer is brought to you by the letters F and O.
IN THESE TECHNOLOGY-DRIVEN DAYS, IT'S ASTONISHING THAT NO ENTREPRENEURIAL WHIZ KID HAS DEVELOPED A TINDER-LIKE APP TO MATCH PLAYERS WITH MANAGERS, PARTICULARLY THOSE OF... NICHE TASTES.
£
Alexis, 29
197 miles away
Big juicy orange, ripe for plucking.♡
PERHAPS CONTE'S SEARCH FOR A STRIKER WOULD HAVE BEEN RESOLVED SOONER IF PLAYER MEDICALS HAD BEEN CONDUCTED BY DONALD TRUMP'S DOCTOR.
HI, EVERYBODY!
I can confirm that Andy Carroll is in excellent physical condition and is of sound mind to sit on the Chelsea bench for the next couple of years, turning out occasionally in the Checkatrade Trophy.
HOWAY!
CRACK
...BUT HE WAS OTHERWISE ENGAGED, TRYING TO EXTRACT A BREAKFAST TELEVISION PRESENTER FROM THE PRESIDENTIAL ANUS.
... happy... birthday... mister... president... Happy... birth...day... to...... you.
TRUMP 45
IT WAS AN ACT SO DIGNIFIED THAT EVEN THE RATS FELT COMPELLED TO SHOWER THEMSELVES.
It was the 2016/17 shirt and had the old Premier League logo on the numbers, meaning he's clearly had it for ages, wearing it at home. Oh God, it's so pathetic, I can't scrub it off...
NEXT WEEK: MAYBE SOMETHING VAGUELY FOOTBALL-RELATED?

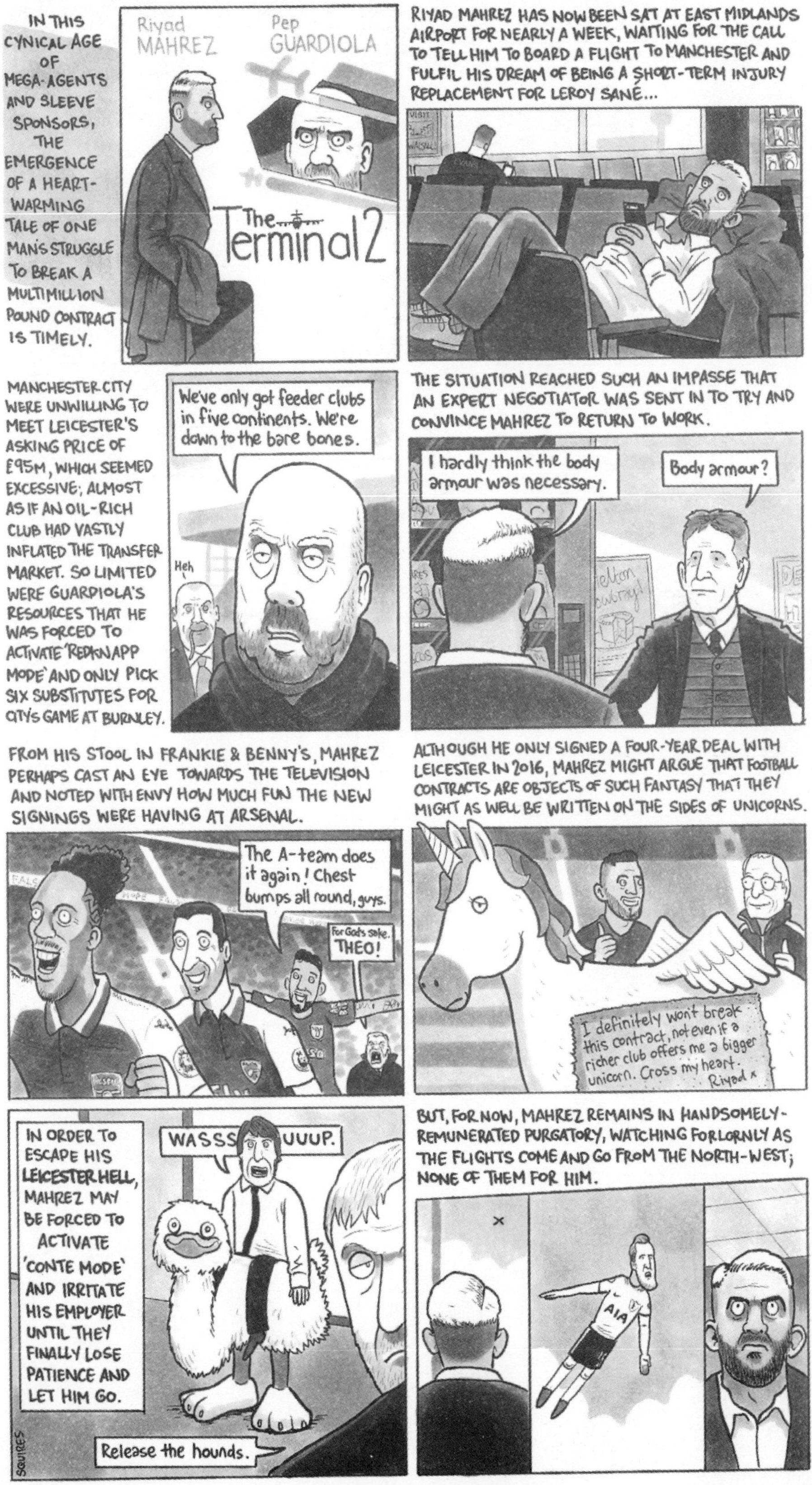
IN THIS CYNICAL AGE OF MEGA-AGENTS AND SLEEVE SPONSORS, THE EMERGENCE OF A HEART-WARMING TALE OF ONE MAN'S STRUGGLE TO BREAK A MULTIMILLION POUND CONTRACT IS TIMELY.
Riyad MAHREZ
Pep GUARDIOLA
The Terminal 2
RIYAD MAHREZ HAS NOW BEEN SAT AT EAST MIDLANDS AIRPORT FOR NEARLY A WEEK, WAITING FOR THE CALL TO TELL HIM TO BOARD A FLIGHT TO MANCHESTER AND FULFIL HIS DREAM OF BEING A SHORT-TERM INJURY REPLACEMENT FOR LEROY SANÉ...
MANCHESTER CITY WERE UNWILLING TO MEET LEICESTER'S ASKING PRICE OF £95M, WHICH SEEMED EXCESSIVE; ALMOST AS IF AN OIL-RICH CLUB HAD VASTLY INFLATED THE TRANSFER MARKET. SO LIMITED WERE GUARDIOLA'S RESOURCES THAT HE WAS FORCED TO ACTIVATE 'REDKNAPP MODE' AND ONLY PICK SIX SUBSTITUTES FOR CITY'S GAME AT BURNLEY.
We've only got feeder clubs in five continents. We're down to the bare bones.
Heh
THE SITUATION REACHED SUCH AN IMPASSE THAT AN EXPERT NEGOTIATOR WAS SENT IN TO TRY AND CONVINCE MAHREZ TO RETURN TO WORK.
I hardly think the body armour was necessary.
Body armour?
FROM HIS STOOL IN FRANKIE & BENNY'S, MAHREZ PERHAPS CAST AN EYE TOWARDS THE TELEVISION AND NOTED WITH ENVY HOW MUCH FUN THE NEW SIGNINGS WERE HAVING AT ARSENAL.
The A-team does it again! Chest bumps all round, guys.
For God's sake. THEO!
ALTHOUGH HE ONLY SIGNED A FOUR-YEAR DEAL WITH LEICESTER IN 2016, MAHREZ MIGHT ARGUE THAT FOOTBALL CONTRACTS ARE OBJECTS OF SUCH FANTASY THAT THEY MIGHT AS WELL BE WRITTEN ON THE SIDES OF UNICORNS.
I definitely won't break this contract, not even if a richer club offers me a bigger unicorn. Cross my heart. Riyad x
IN ORDER TO ESCAPE HIS LEICESTER HELL, MAHREZ MAY BE FORCED TO ACTIVATE 'CONTE MODE' AND IRRITATE HIS EMPLOYER UNTIL THEY FINALLY LOSE PATIENCE AND LET HIM GO.
WASSSUUUP.
Release the hounds.
SQUIRES
BUT, FOR NOW, MAHREZ REMAINS IN HANDSOMELY-REMUNERATED PURGATORY, WATCHING FORLORNLY AS THE FLIGHTS COME AND GO FROM THE NORTH-WEST; NONE OF THEM FOR HIM.
AIA

RIVALRIES

There was a time, in the hot-headed days of my youth, when I could explain on demand why I hated every club that wasn't Swindon Town.

Aldershot? I'll never forgive them for the Freight Rover Trophy Southern Area semi-final of 1987.

Newport County? They failed to show an adequate level of remorse when they relegated us to the fourth division in 1982.

Rochdale? Oh, where do I *start*?

Thankfully, as I matured into a man who makes a living from drawing pictures of footballers and colouring them in with felt-tip pens, I discarded those small-minded, provincial grudges. After all, we're all just people, football fans. Just because you were born in a different area or developed an affection for a football club that wasn't Swindon Town – as unlikely as that may seem – it doesn't mean we're so different. Obviously, this does not apply to the fans, players, officials, mascots, catering staff, ballboys and other employees of Oxford United, Bristol City, Bristol Rovers, Reading, MK Dons or Gillingham, who can all fuck off.

I've sometimes wondered how I would maintain my objectivity if any of those clubs were promoted to the Premier League. How would I remain emotionally detached if, say, the world were swept along by the fairy-tale story of Oxford United advancing to the latter stages of the Champions League? After much introspection, I've concluded that it wouldn't be a problem, as by that point I would have either moved to a remote village in the Amazon or dissolved into a puddle of pink effluent.

Regardless, it is a universal truth that there is a real anxiety associated with a loathed rival succeeding. As I write this, Liverpool and Real Madrid are about to play the 2018 Champions League final. I'm looking forward to the match, as it features two teams who regard defending as a suggestion rather than a requirement. Liverpool fans of my acquaintance are beside themselves with excitement and nerves. However, the flip side is the all-consuming dread felt by my friend Mike, a Manchester United fan. He's planning to avoid the match by going for a long cliff-top walk. If the result doesn't go the way he wants (anything less than a humiliatingly large win for Real Madrid being considered a disaster), he'll presumably throw himself from the ledge, his fall cushioned by a groaning mass of United and Everton fans.[5]

Rivalries sometimes present opportunities to look at the world in a different way, too. You may be surprised to learn that Swindon weren't always the well-run financial behemoth of today, with their vast wealth casting a shadow over at least six other League Two clubs. Unbelievably, there were times in the club's not-so-distant past when it seemed likely that they might even go out of business completely. The prospect of Swindon Town vanishing from the football map presented me with a quandary. I'd find it hard to pick another league team, considering how many of them I had seen inflict defeat on Swindon with scant regard for my emotional well-being. I therefore considered the idea of becoming a full-time 'anti-fan'.

As a London-based supporter I couldn't always afford a train or bus ticket back to the Wembley of the West to watch Swindon

---

5 SPOILER ALERT: He needn't have worried; in fact, I think he may even have had a hand in script development.

matches. Needing a Saturday football fix, I would sometimes study the fixtures and see if any of the teams devoid of redeeming features (see above list) were playing in the capital. I would then go and sit among the home support and become their most passionate fan for ninety minutes, occasionally drawing baffled looks from those positioned around me who were probably trying to remember why, for example, Brentford had such a vehement dislike for, say, Bristol Rovers (like *that* needs any explanation). The question was, could I do this every weekend?

No, of course not, it would be weird and – even for me – unhealthily negative.

Over the last decade, the emergence of social media has provided a further outlet for supporters of rival clubs to interact with one another in a respectful and adult fashion. The opportunities for sophisticated discourse in the online space are limitless. Some will choose to make spiteful references to a tragic event in a rival club's history; others will ridicule the historical economic hardship of an opponent's region, justified in their snooty contempt by the fact that they grew up in a town that had a Pizza Express. For the traditionalists, there is the old-fashioned approach of calling a stranger a bad nonce because they are wearing the football shirt of a team you don't like. Fans with an advanced knowledge of the Internet will sometimes furnish these exchanges with the cry-laughing emoji.

When combined, it all helps to make the world a better place, bringing strangers together through conversation. At no point over the last decade, when scrolling through my timeline, have I fantasised about all the smartphones in the world being bulldozed into a quarry which would then be filled in with radioactive waste. We're not so different, guys. Come on, let's have a cuddle (yeah, not you Newport County fans, it's still *way* too soon).

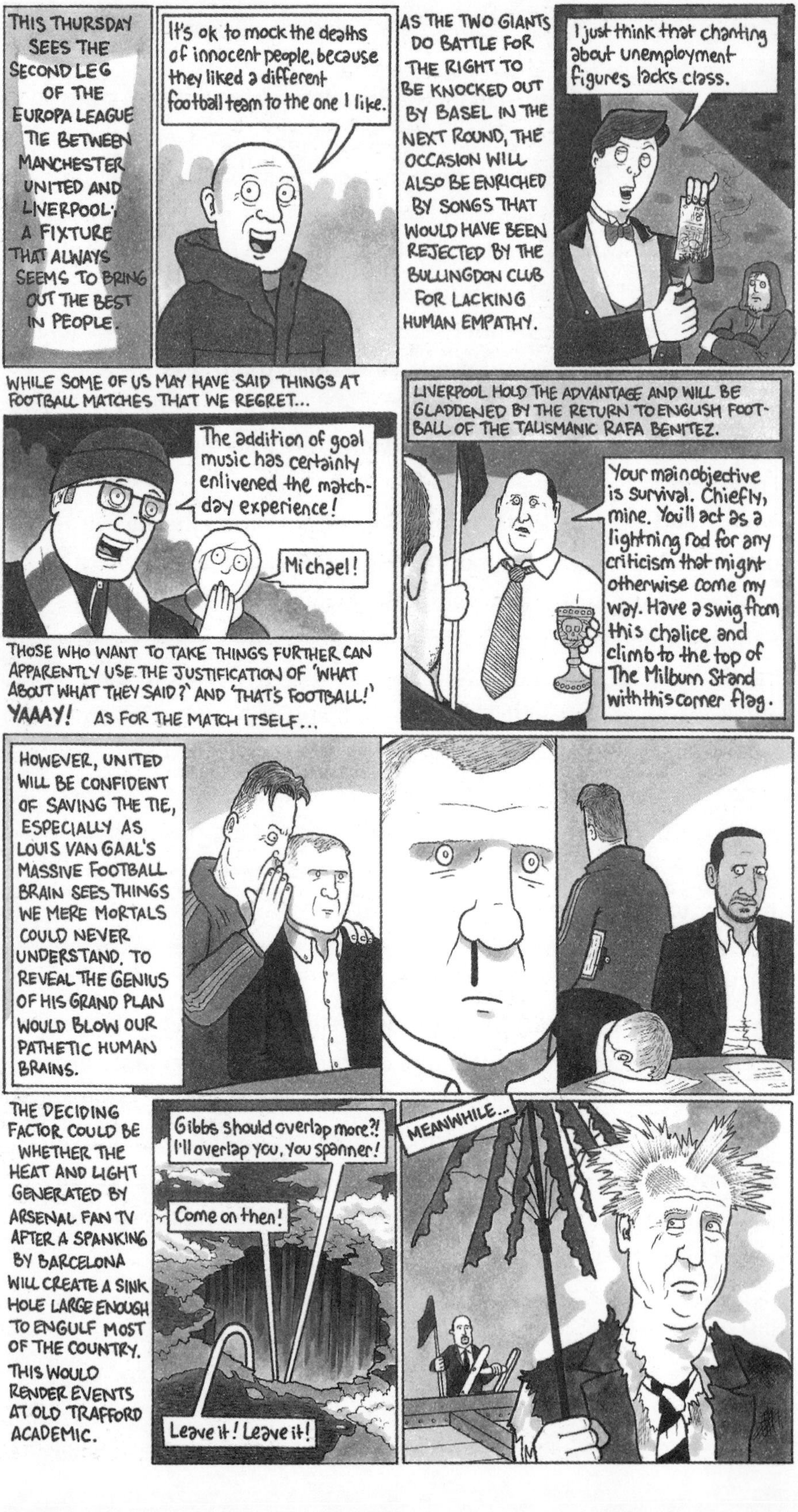
THIS THURSDAY SEES THE SECOND LEG OF THE EUROPA LEAGUE TIE BETWEEN MANCHESTER UNITED AND LIVERPOOL: A FIXTURE THAT ALWAYS SEEMS TO BRING OUT THE BEST IN PEOPLE.
It's ok to mock the deaths of innocent people, because they liked a different football team to the one I like.
AS THE TWO GIANTS DO BATTLE FOR THE RIGHT TO BE KNOCKED OUT BY BASEL IN THE NEXT ROUND, THE OCCASION WILL ALSO BE ENRICHED BY SONGS THAT WOULD HAVE BEEN REJECTED BY THE BULLINGDON CLUB FOR LACKING HUMAN EMPATHY.
I just think that chanting about unemployment figures lacks class.
WHILE SOME OF US MAY HAVE SAID THINGS AT FOOTBALL MATCHES THAT WE REGRET...
The addition of goal music has certainly enlivened the match-day experience!
Michael!
THOSE WHO WANT TO TAKE THINGS FURTHER CAN APPARENTLY USE THE JUSTIFICATION OF 'WHAT ABOUT WHAT THEY SAID?' AND 'THAT'S FOOTBALL!' YAAAY! AS FOR THE MATCH ITSELF...
LIVERPOOL HOLD THE ADVANTAGE AND WILL BE GLADDENED BY THE RETURN TO ENGLISH FOOTBALL OF THE TALISMANIC RAFA BENITEZ.
Your main objective is survival. Chiefly, mine. You'll act as a lightning rod for any criticism that might otherwise come my way. Have a swig from this chalice and climb to the top of The Milburn Stand with this corner flag.
HOWEVER, UNITED WILL BE CONFIDENT OF SAVING THE TIE, ESPECIALLY AS LOUIS VAN GAAL'S MASSIVE FOOTBALL BRAIN SEES THINGS WE MERE MORTALS COULD NEVER UNDERSTAND. TO REVEAL THE GENIUS OF HIS GRAND PLAN WOULD BLOW OUR PATHETIC HUMAN BRAINS.
THE DECIDING FACTOR COULD BE WHETHER THE HEAT AND LIGHT GENERATED BY ARSENAL FAN TV AFTER A SPANKING BY BARCELONA WILL CREATE A SINK HOLE LARGE ENOUGH TO ENGULF MOST OF THE COUNTRY. THIS WOULD RENDER EVENTS AT OLD TRAFFORD ACADEMIC.
Gibbs should overlap more?! I'll overlap you, you spanner!
Come on then!
Leave it! Leave it!
MEANWHILE...

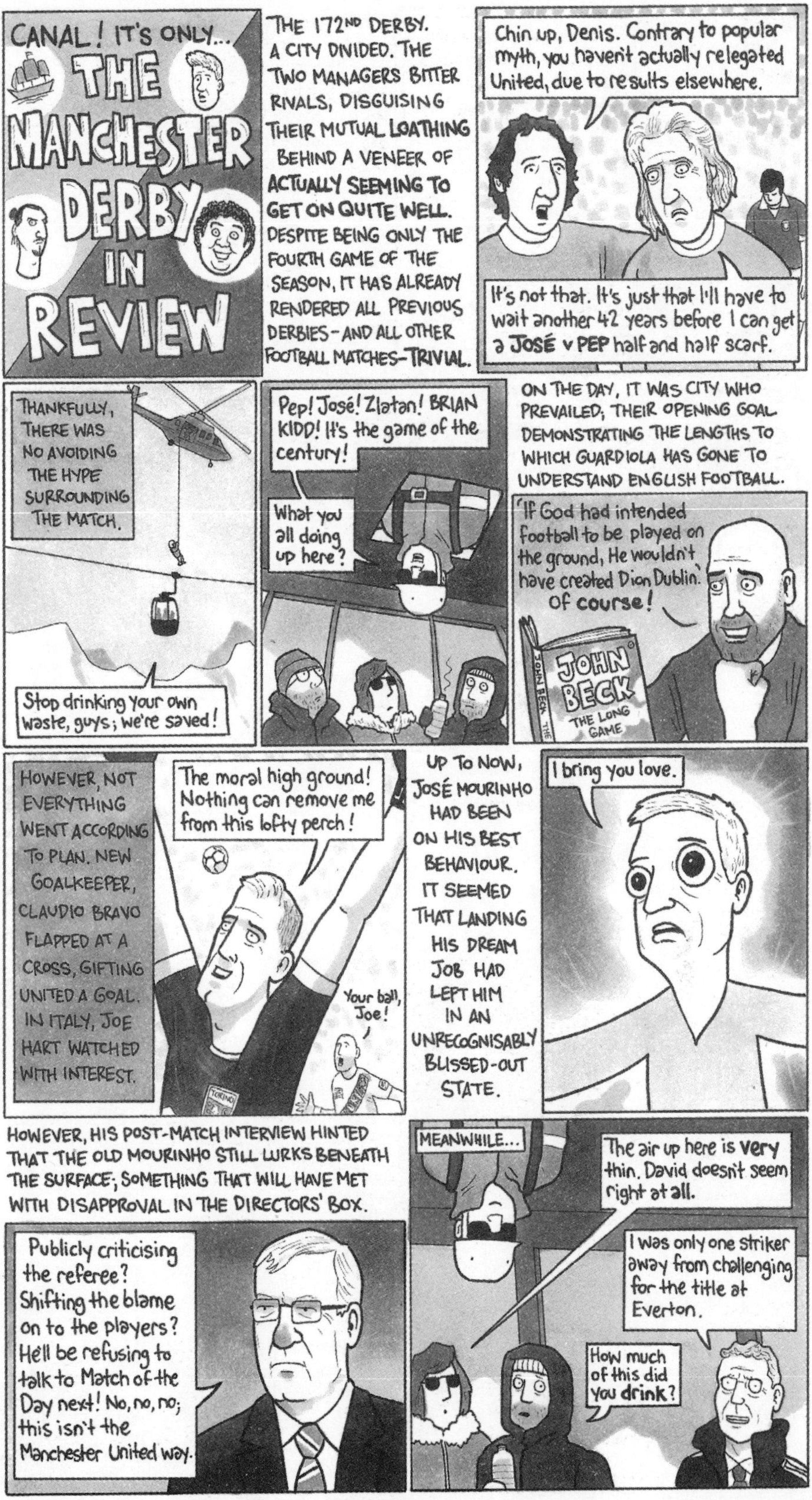
CANAL! IT'S ONLY...
THE MANCHESTER DERBY IN REVIEW
THE 172ND DERBY. A CITY DIVIDED. THE TWO MANAGERS BITTER RIVALS, DISGUISING THEIR MUTUAL LOATHING BEHIND A VENEER OF ACTUALLY SEEMING TO GET ON QUITE WELL. DESPITE BEING ONLY THE FOURTH GAME OF THE SEASON, IT HAS ALREADY RENDERED ALL PREVIOUS DERBIES – AND ALL OTHER FOOTBALL MATCHES – TRIVIAL.
Chin up, Denis. Contrary to popular myth, you haven't actually relegated United, due to results elsewhere.
It's not that. It's just that I'll have to wait another 42 years before I can get a JOSÉ v PEP half and half scarf.
THANKFULLY, THERE WAS NO AVOIDING THE HYPE SURROUNDING THE MATCH.
Stop drinking your own waste, guys; we're saved!
Pep! José! Zlatan! BRIAN KIDD! It's the game of the century!
What you all doing up here?
ON THE DAY, IT WAS CITY WHO PREVAILED; THEIR OPENING GOAL DEMONSTRATING THE LENGTHS TO WHICH GUARDIOLA HAS GONE TO UNDERSTAND ENGLISH FOOTBALL.
'If God had intended football to be played on the ground, He wouldn't have created Dion Dublin.'
Of course!
JOHN BECK THE LONG GAME
HOWEVER, NOT EVERYTHING WENT ACCORDING TO PLAN. NEW GOALKEEPER, CLAUDIO BRAVO FLAPPED AT A CROSS, GIFTING UNITED A GOAL. IN ITALY, JOE HART WATCHED WITH INTEREST.
The moral high ground! Nothing can remove me from this lofty perch!
Your ball, Joe!
UP TO NOW, JOSÉ MOURINHO HAD BEEN ON HIS BEST BEHAVIOUR. IT SEEMED THAT LANDING HIS DREAM JOB HAD LEFT HIM IN AN UNRECOGNISABLY BLISSED-OUT STATE.
I bring you love.
HOWEVER, HIS POST-MATCH INTERVIEW HINTED THAT THE OLD MOURINHO STILL LURKS BENEATH THE SURFACE; SOMETHING THAT WILL HAVE MET WITH DISAPPROVAL IN THE DIRECTORS' BOX.
Publicly criticising the referee? Shifting the blame on to the players? He'll be refusing to talk to Match of the Day next! No, no, no; this isn't the Manchester United way.
MEANWHILE...
The air up here is very thin. David doesn't seem right at all.
I was only one striker away from challenging for the title at Everton.
How much of this did you drink?

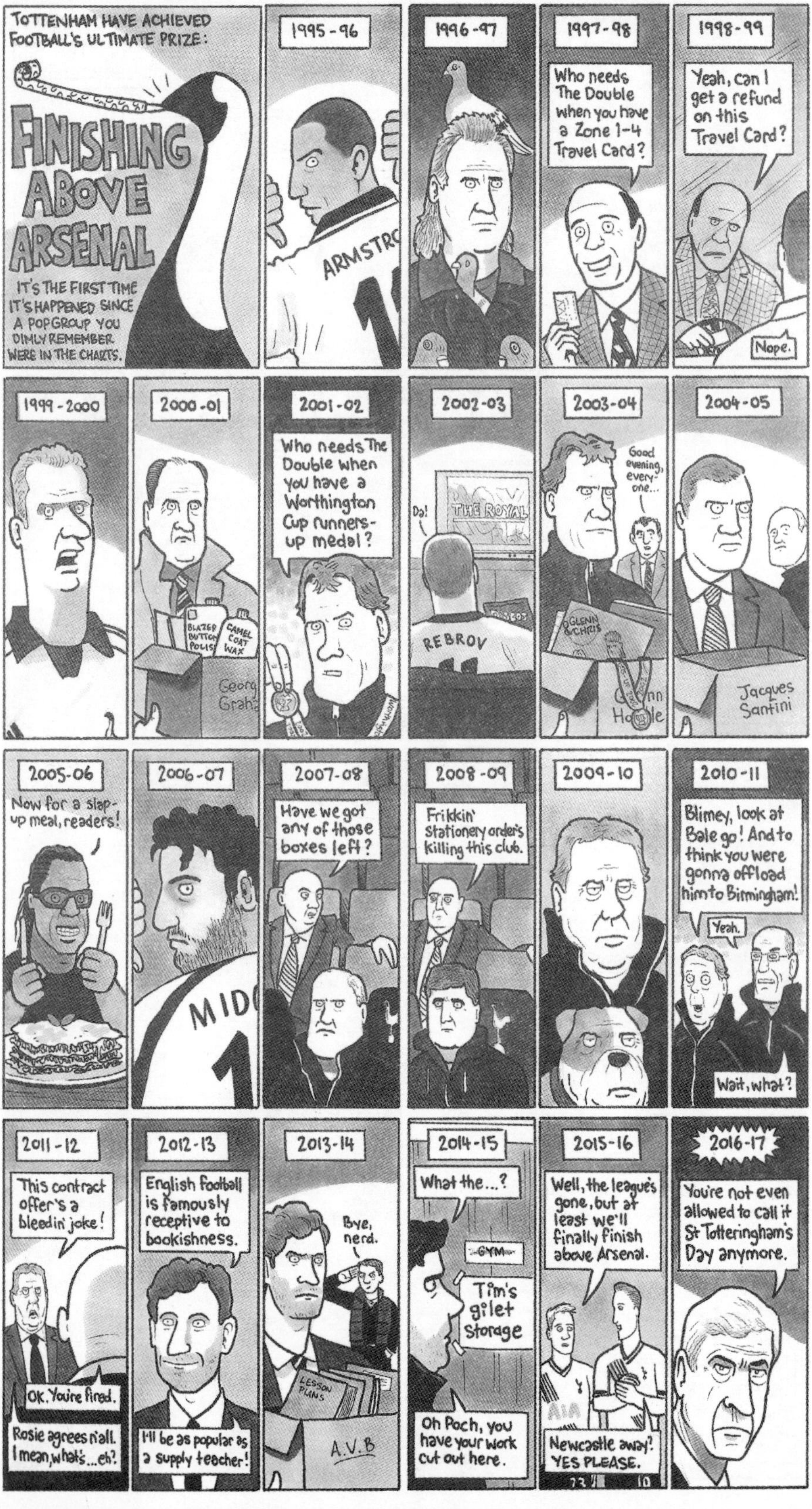

TOTTENHAM HAVE ACHIEVED FOOTBALL'S ULTIMATE PRIZE:
FINISHING ABOVE ARSENAL
IT'S THE FIRST TIME IT'S HAPPENED SINCE A POPGROUP YOU DIMLY REMEMBER WERE IN THE CHARTS.
1995-96
ARMSTRO
1996-97
1997-98
Who needs The Double when you have a Zone 1-4 Travel Card?
1998-99
Yeah, can I get a refund on this Travel Card?
Nope.
1999-2000
2000-01
BLAZER BUTTON POLIS
CAMEL COAT WAX
Georg Graha
2001-02
Who needs The Double when you have a Worthington Cup runners-up medal?
2002-03
Da!
THE ROYAL
REBROV
2003-04
Good evening, everyone...
GLENN & CHRIS
2004-05
Jacques Santini
2005-06
Now for a slap-up meal, readers!
2006-07
MID
2007-08
Have we got any of those boxes left?
2008-09
Frikkin' stationery order's killing this club.
2009-10
2010-11
Blimey, look at Bale go! And to think you were gonna offload him to Birmingham!
Yeah.
Wait, what?
2011-12
This contract offer's a bleedin' joke!
OK. You're fired.
Rosie agrees n'all. I mean, what's...eh?
2012-13
English football is famously receptive to bookishness.
I'll be as popular as a supply teacher!
2013-14
Bye, nerd.
LESSON PLANS
A.V.B
2014-15
What the...?
GYM
Tim's gilet storage
Oh Poch, you have your work cut out here.
2015-16
Well, the league's gone, but at least we'll finally finish above Arsenal.
Newcastle away? YES PLEASE.
2016-17
You're not even allowed to call it St Totteringham's Day anymore.

DERBIES!

– A TIME FOR GETTING TOGETHER WITH THOSE CLOSEST TO YOU AND BEING GRATEFUL THAT YOU'RE ONLY OBLIGED TO SEE EACH OTHER TWICE A YEAR. EVERTON CLAIMED A STUNNING 1-1 VICTORY IN **THE MERSEYSIDE DERBY** AS BIG SAM PUT INTO ACTION HIS TRUSTED 'SOUR RELATIVE AT CHRISTMAS' TACTICAL PLAN: SIT BACK, SOAK IT ALL UP, AND THEN HIT THEM WITH A PSYCHOLOGICAL HAYMAKER.

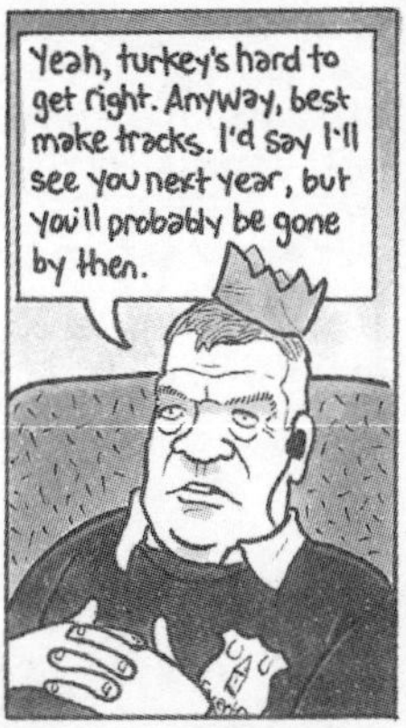
Yeah, turkey's hard to get right. Anyway, best make tracks. I'd say I'll see you next year, but you'll probably be gone by then.

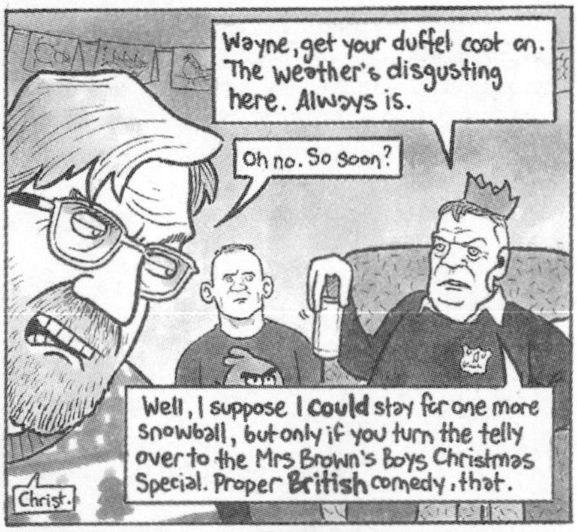
Wayne, get your duffel coat on. The weather's disgusting here. Always is.
Oh no. So soon?
Well, I suppose I **could** stay for one more snowball, but only if you turn the telly over to the Mrs Brown's Boys Christmas Special. Proper **British** comedy, that.
Christ.

JÜRGEN KLOPP WAS PARTICULARLY UPSET ABOUT THE PENALTY DECISION THAT GIFTED EVERTON THE ONE POINTS. HE BELIEVED THE INCIDENT TO BE AS HARMLESS AS ANY SNOW-BASED TALE ABOUT A YOUNG BOY AND A MAN WHO FREQUENTLY OFFERS THE DEFENSIVE RESISTANCE YOU'D EXPECT FROM SOMEONE MADE ENTIRELY OF WATER AND CARROTS.

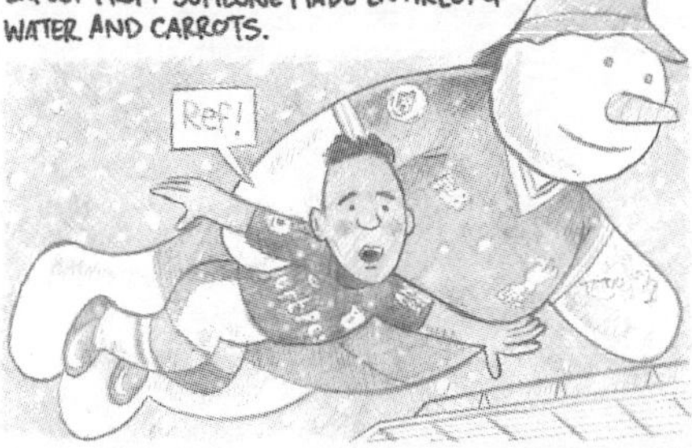
Ref!

WEST HAM RECORDED A SURPRISE WIN AGAINST CHELSEA IN THE **WE HATE TOTTENHAM AND WE HATE TOTTENHAM DERBY**, BUT THE SIGHT OF THE CHELSEA SUBSTITUTES TRYING TO KEEP WARM SEEMED TO BREAK SOMETHING IN THE MIND OF 'MATCH OF THE DAY' COMMENTATOR, JONATHAN PEARCE.

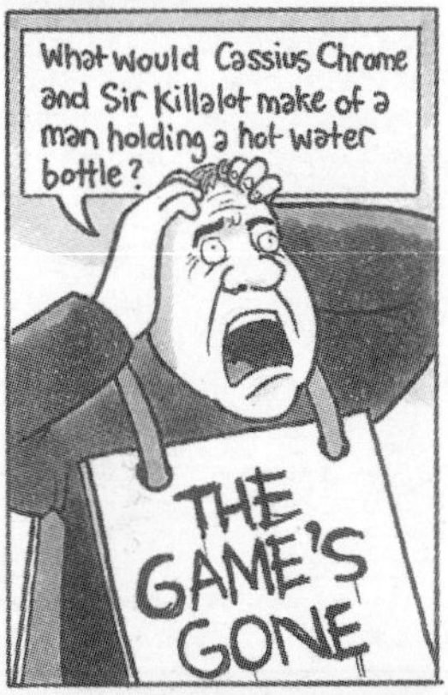
What would Cassius Chrome and Sir Killalot make of a man holding a hot water bottle?
THE GAME'S GONE

THE MANCHESTER DERBY WAS MARRED BY SCENES THAT **NOBODY** WANTS TO SEE (SHOW US, SHOW US, SHOW US, SHOW US). A MASS BRAWL IN THE PLAYERS' TUNNEL, APPARENTLY STARTED WHEN JOSÉ MOURINHO BECAME INCENSED BY THE ENTHUSIASM WITH WHICH THE MANCHESTER CITY PLAYERS WERE CELEBRATING THEIR 2-1 WIN. THEY WERE PLAYING **MUSIC!**

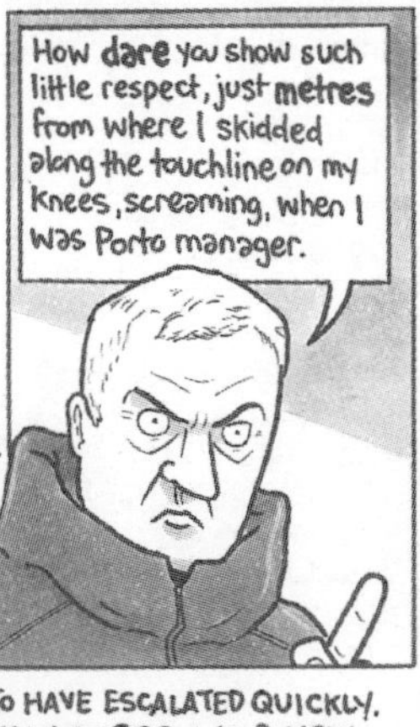
How **dare** you show such little respect, just **metres** from where I skidded along the touchline on my knees, screaming, when I was Porto manager.

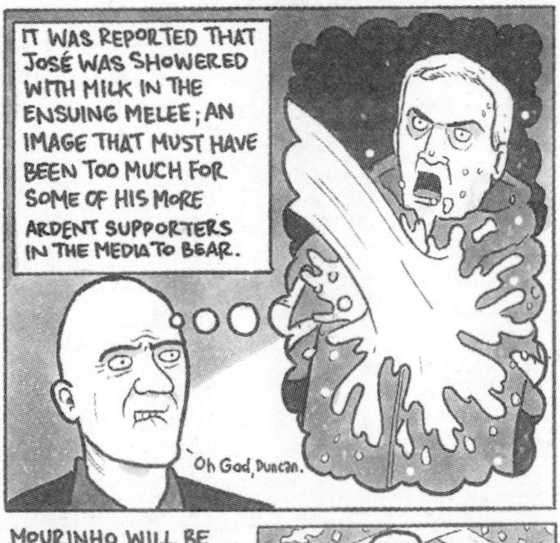
IT WAS REPORTED THAT JOSÉ WAS SHOWERED WITH MILK IN THE ENSUING MELEE; AN IMAGE THAT MUST HAVE BEEN TOO MUCH FOR SOME OF HIS MORE ARDENT SUPPORTERS IN THE MEDIA TO BEAR.
Oh God, Duncan.

THE SITUATION SEEMS TO HAVE ESCALATED QUICKLY. THERE WERE HORSES, A MAN ON FIRE AND ROMELU LUKAKU KILLED A GUY WITH A TRIDENT.

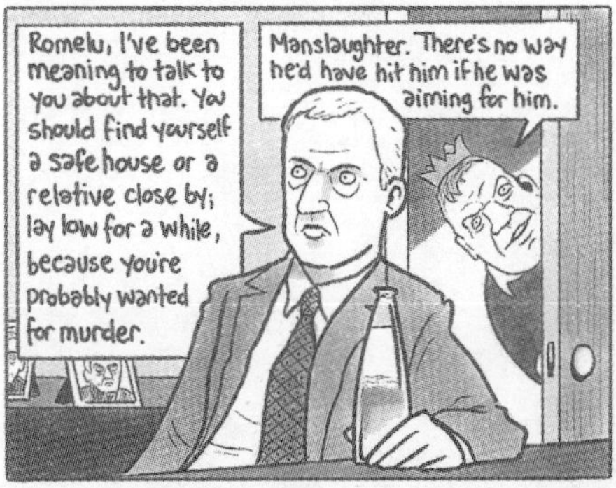
Romelu, I've been meaning to talk to you about that. You should find yourself a safe house or a relative close by; lay low for a while, because you're probably wanted for murder.
Manslaughter. There's no way he'd have hit him if he was aiming for him.

MOURINHO WILL BE **FURIOUS** THAT THE INCIDENT HAS DIVERTED ATTENTION FROM HIS TEAM'S POOR PERFORMANCE. WITH CITY NOW MATHEMATICALLY CERTAIN TO WIN THE LEAGUE, PEP GUARDIOLA CAN GO ON HOLIDAY WHILE THE REST OF US ENJOY SIX MONTHS OF ANALYSIS ABOUT **MILKGATE**. IT'S ODD, BECAUSE THERE'S NOTHING ABOUT PEP'S DEMEANOUR TO SUGGEST HE'S AN EVIL GENIUS.

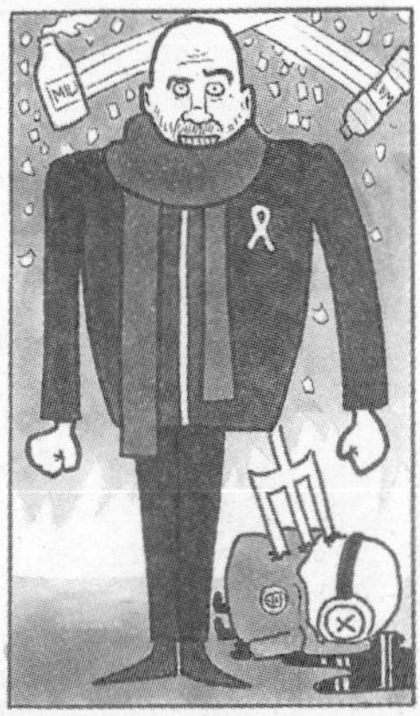

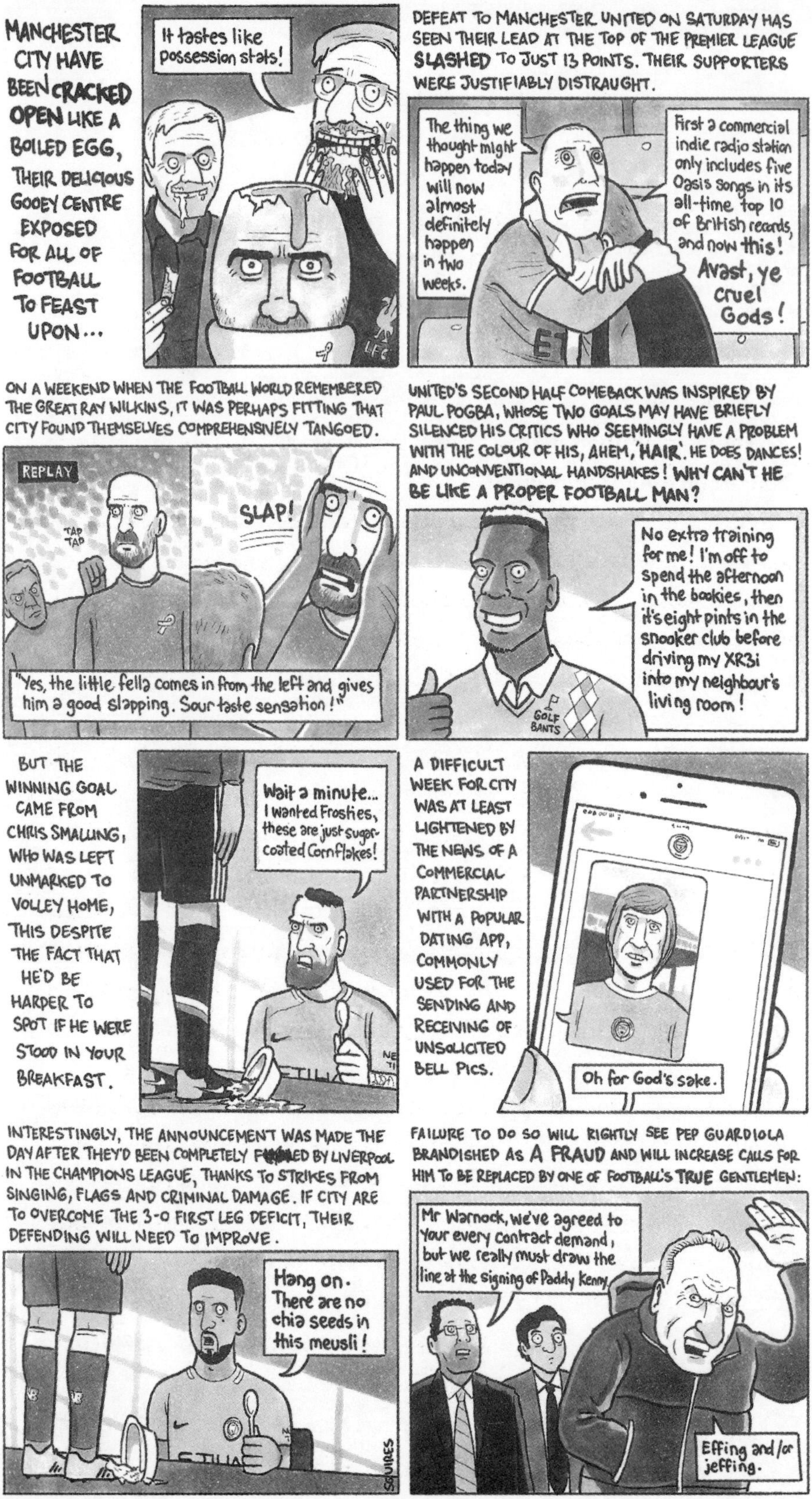
MANCHESTER CITY HAVE BEEN CRACKED OPEN LIKE A BOILED EGG, THEIR DELICIOUS GOOEY CENTRE EXPOSED FOR ALL OF FOOTBALL TO FEAST UPON...
It tastes like possession stats!
DEFEAT TO MANCHESTER UNITED ON SATURDAY HAS SEEN THEIR LEAD AT THE TOP OF THE PREMIER LEAGUE SLASHED TO JUST 13 POINTS. THEIR SUPPORTERS WERE JUSTIFIABLY DISTRAUGHT.
The thing we thought might happen today will now almost definitely happen in two weeks.
First a commercial indie radio station only includes five Oasis songs in its all-time top 10 of British records, and now this! Avast, ye cruel Gods!
ON A WEEKEND WHEN THE FOOTBALL WORLD REMEMBERED THE GREAT RAY WILKINS, IT WAS PERHAPS FITTING THAT CITY FOUND THEMSELVES COMPREHENSIVELY TANGOED.
REPLAY
TAP TAP
SLAP!
"Yes, the little fella comes in from the left and gives him a good slapping. Sour taste sensation!"
UNITED'S SECOND HALF COMEBACK WAS INSPIRED BY PAUL POGBA, WHOSE TWO GOALS MAY HAVE BRIEFLY SILENCED HIS CRITICS WHO SEEMINGLY HAVE A PROBLEM WITH THE COLOUR OF HIS, AHEM, 'HAIR'. HE DOES DANCES! AND UNCONVENTIONAL HANDSHAKES! WHY CAN'T HE BE LIKE A PROPER FOOTBALL MAN?
No extra training for me! I'm off to spend the afternoon in the bookies, then it's eight pints in the snooker club before driving my XR3i into my neighbour's living room!
GOLF BANTS
BUT THE WINNING GOAL CAME FROM CHRIS SMALLING, WHO WAS LEFT UNMARKED TO VOLLEY HOME, THIS DESPITE THE FACT THAT HE'D BE HARDER TO SPOT IF HE WERE STOOD IN YOUR BREAKFAST.
Wait a minute... I wanted Frosties, these are just sugar-coated Cornflakes!
A DIFFICULT WEEK FOR CITY WAS AT LEAST LIGHTENED BY THE NEWS OF A COMMERCIAL PARTNERSHIP WITH A POPULAR DATING APP, COMMONLY USED FOR THE SENDING AND RECEIVING OF UNSOLICITED BELL PICS.
Oh for God's sake.
INTERESTINGLY, THE ANNOUNCEMENT WAS MADE THE DAY AFTER THEY'D BEEN COMPLETELY F[redacted]ED BY LIVERPOOL IN THE CHAMPIONS LEAGUE, THANKS TO STRIKES FROM SINGING, FLAGS AND CRIMINAL DAMAGE. IF CITY ARE TO OVERCOME THE 3-0 FIRST LEG DEFICIT, THEIR DEFENDING WILL NEED TO IMPROVE.
Hang on. There are no chia seeds in this meusli!
SQUIRES
FAILURE TO DO SO WILL RIGHTLY SEE PEP GUARDIOLA BRANDISHED AS A FRAUD AND WILL INCREASE CALLS FOR HIM TO BE REPLACED BY ONE OF FOOTBALL'S TRUE GENTLEMEN:
Mr Warnock, we've agreed to your every contract demand, but we really must draw the line at the signing of Paddy Kenny.
Effing and/or jeffing.

JUST ABOUT MANAGING

Free monogrammed bench jackets aside, what possible incentive is there to be a football manager?

When you're not waiting about in hotel receptions, you're crawling along motorways in a bus that might as well be emblazoned with the slogan 'Do the universal masturbatory sign at me, fellow motorist'. It must be like a new circle of hell, where you're supervising an endless geography field trip. 'Sir, Jordan's blocked the chemical toilet!'

When you're not travelling, you're patrolling the training ground, turning your extremities to icicles as you observe your young charges fail to grasp the fundamentals of your football philosophy. Jesus, it's not hard. Did they not study the colour-coordinated ring binders you gave them with their USB sticks? Still, while you're out here watching them crash into each other, at least you're not in the dressing room listening to their grime playlists. You're not even sure what grime is, but you don't bloody like it. At least you could work out what UB40 were saying.

You have to spend an inordinate amount of time with footballers (depending on which club you're managing, you might see more of Andy Carroll than members of your own family), and if the recalcitrant adult babies don't perform, it's you who gets insulted in your local curry house. Unless you're Pep Guardiola, the fans will question your appointment. They guided Fleetwood Town to a trio of Champions League titles on Football Manager, so they're entitled to critique your track record. At best, you'll have a grace period of three matches. Rome wasn't built in a day, but you weren't on that job. If you had been, you'd have just hired your best mate to assist you, the same stooge who has followed you around from disaster to failure for the last fifteen years, like some dutiful tracksuited spaniel. Having failed to organise a defence to adequately repel the Visigoths' set pieces, you'd have been mutually consented the hell out of there and forced to flee for the hills, your compensation silver spilling from your toga.

Then there's the media: press conferences, post-match interviews, club website videos, questions, questions, questions. If you're lucky, you'll have some journalist friends who'll champion your cause every time some other poor sap gets the elbow and a lucrative vacancy arises.

You've spent your whole adult life in the closeted environment of football, but eventually, when there are no clubs left to hire you, the reaper's scythe falls and your managerial shelf life expires. Sure, you'll get the occasional scouting job and the odd charity gig – going through the motions, giving team talks to reality TV stars and the carpenter off a home renovation show – but you are now in the final stage of your career: punditry. You have been Curbishley-zoned.

The lucky few will be invited to sit next to Gary Lineker as a special guest for the duration of a major international football tournament. You've never really been able to carry off the open-shirt-and-light-jacket look, though, and the closest you've ever been to a World Cup was in 2002, when you were photographed in a local paper to help promote a bar that was staying open for the duration of the tournament. The floor was sticky and the bunting featured flags of teams that hadn't qualified, but you didn't say anything and you smiled for the photographer. The journalist who wrote the story works at Sky now; maybe you could add him on LinkedIn and see whether you can become one of those lads who talks about the football match they are watching on a monitor on a Saturday afternoon? Anything to replace the giddy excitement of a match day: the buzz of the crowd; the dressing-room dubstep; the improvised plumbing repairs to a chemical toilet filled with crisps. God, you miss it.

This next selection of cartoons is dedicated to those who live out most of their adult lives on this absurd merry-go-round. We start with Sunderland and the sacking of Gus Poyet, then it's on to Louis van Gaal's emotional summary of the 2014/15 season. Manchester United's football under van Gaal was dreary, but at least he provided good value elsewhere: flinging himself to the ground on the touchline, slapping Ryan Giggs, leading singalongs at end-of-season functions and oversharing with descriptions of how he felt during cup ties ('I had a twitchy ass'). He also had a unique nose – not in the sense that he was able to sniff out a bargain (hello, Morgan Schneiderlin), just that it looked like it was made of punched-in plasticine.

There is also a cartoon here about Aston Villa's relegation season, a curious outcome given that they started the season with master tactician Tim Sherwood in the dugout. By the autumn, Randy Lerner had replaced him with Rémi Garde, who stuck it out until the end of March. (Admit it, you'd forgotten about Rémi Garde's time at Aston Villa. It's OK, we've all pushed it down into our subconscious – most of all, Rémi.) By then, Villa were experiencing a relegation-induced mania of such severity that they were reportedly considering Andy Townsend for the position of Director of Football.

The final cartoon of the set focuses on Arsène Wenger's release from Arsenal after twenty-two years. How would he cope on the outside? The motor car had barely been invented when he took over from Bruce Rioch in 1996, but now the old coach would need to fend for himself without the regimented routine of the institution. Some birds aren't meant to be caged.

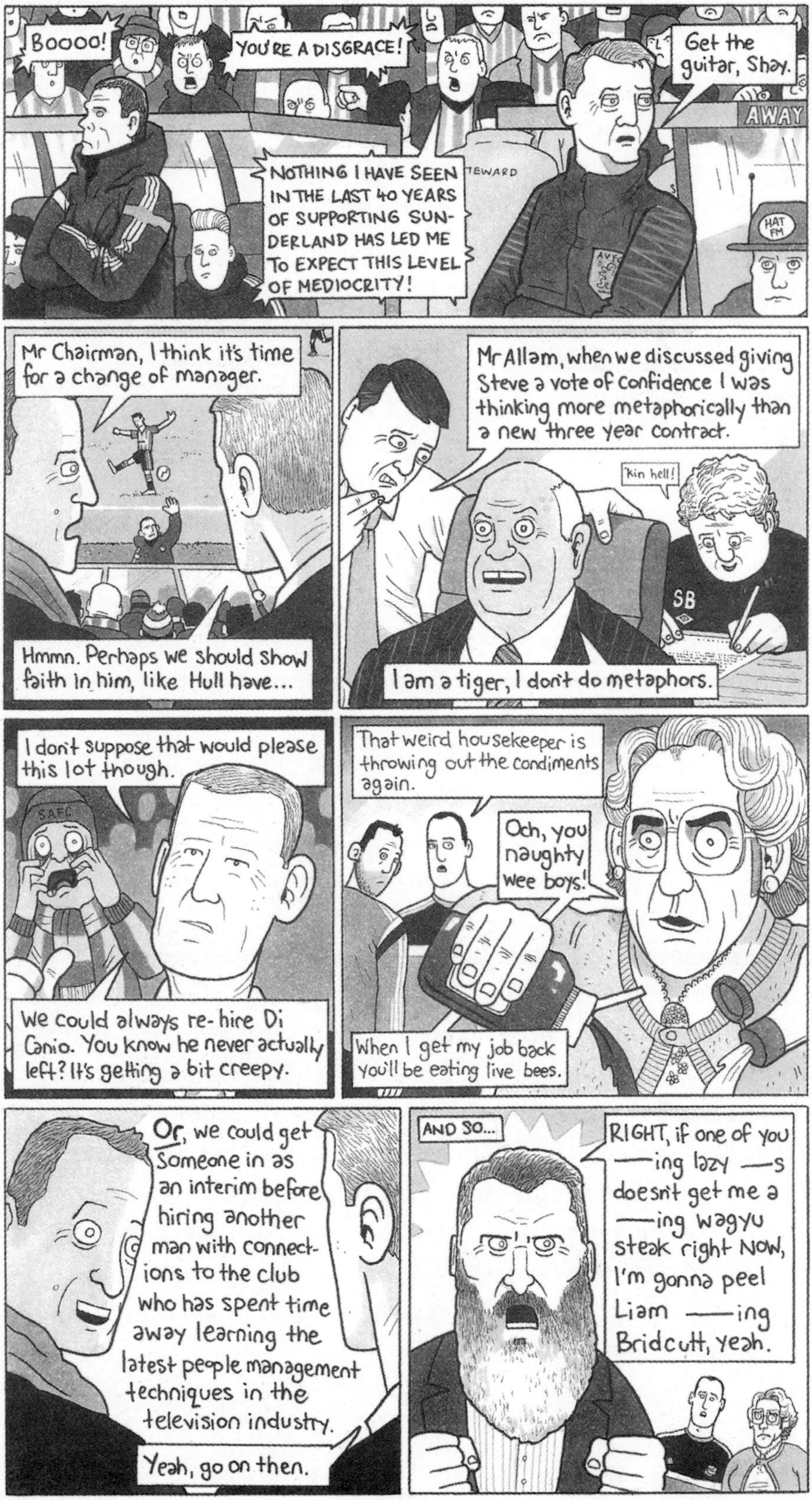
Boooo!
YOU'RE A DISGRACE!
NOTHING I HAVE SEEN IN THE LAST 40 YEARS OF SUPPORTING SUN-DERLAND HAS LED ME TO EXPECT THIS LEVEL OF MEDIOCRITY!
Get the guitar, Shay.
AWAY
HAT FM
Mr Chairman, I think it's time for a change of manager.
Hmmn. Perhaps we should show faith in him, like Hull have...
Mr Allam, when we discussed giving Steve a vote of confidence I was thinking more metaphorically than a new three year contract.
'Kin hell!
SB
I am a tiger, I don't do metaphors.
I don't suppose that would please this lot though.
SAFC
We could always re-hire Di Canio. You know he never actually left? It's getting a bit creepy.
That weird housekeeper is throwing out the condiments again.
Och, you naughty wee boys!
When I get my job back you'll be eating live bees.
Or, we could get Someone in as an interim before hiring another man with connect-ions to the club who has spent time away learning the latest people management techniques in the television industry.
Yeah, go on then.
AND SO...
RIGHT, if one of you ——ing lazy ——s doesn't get me a ——ing wagyu steak right NOW, I'm gonna peel Liam ——ing Bridcutt, yeah.

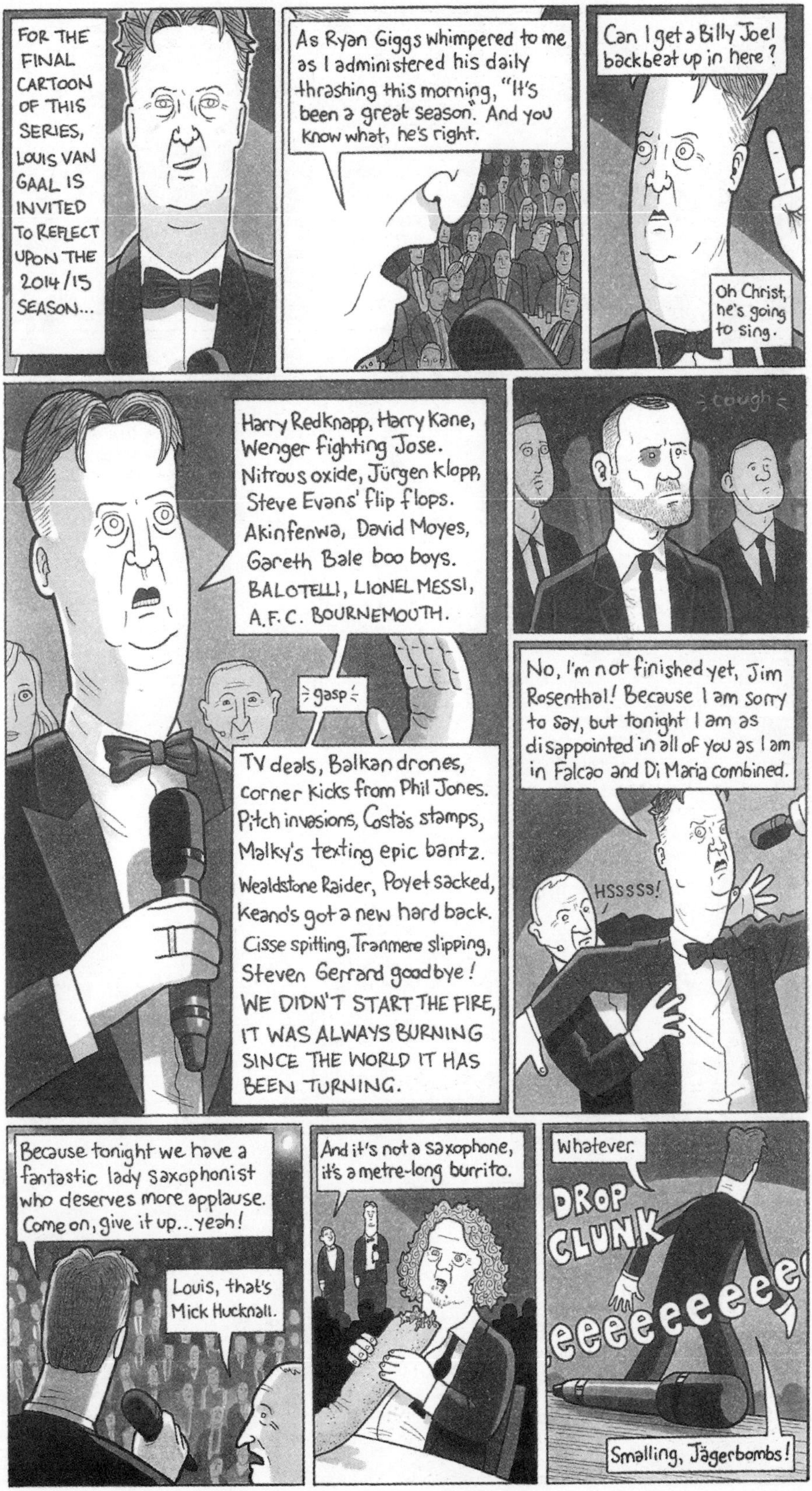

FOR THE FINAL CARTOON OF THIS SERIES, LOUIS VAN GAAL IS INVITED TO REFLECT UPON THE 2014/15 SEASON...
As Ryan Giggs whimpered to me as I administered his daily thrashing this morning, "It's been a great season". And you know what, he's right.
Can I get a Billy Joel backbeat up in here?
Oh Christ, he's going to sing.
Harry Redknapp, Harry Kane, Wenger fighting Jose. Nitrous oxide, Jürgen klopp, Steve Evans' flip flops. Akinfenwa, David Moyes, Gareth Bale boo boys. BALOTELLI, LIONEL MESSI, A.F.C. BOURNEMOUTH.
gasp
TV deals, Balkan drones, corner kicks from Phil Jones. Pitch invasions, Costa's stamps, Malky's texting epic bantz. Wealdstone Raider, Poyet sacked, Keano's got a new hard back. Cisse spitting, Tranmere slipping, Steven Gerrard goodbye! WE DIDN'T START THE FIRE, IT WAS ALWAYS BURNING SINCE THE WORLD IT HAS BEEN TURNING.
cough
No, I'm not finished yet, Jim Rosenthal! Because I am sorry to say, but tonight I am as disappointed in all of you as I am in Falcao and Di Maria combined.
HSSSSS!
Because tonight we have a fantastic lady saxophonist who deserves more applause. Come on, give it up... yeah!
Louis, that's Mick Hucknall.
And it's not a saxophone, it's a metre-long burrito.
Whatever.
DROP
CLUNK
eeeeeeeeee
Smalling, Jägerbombs!

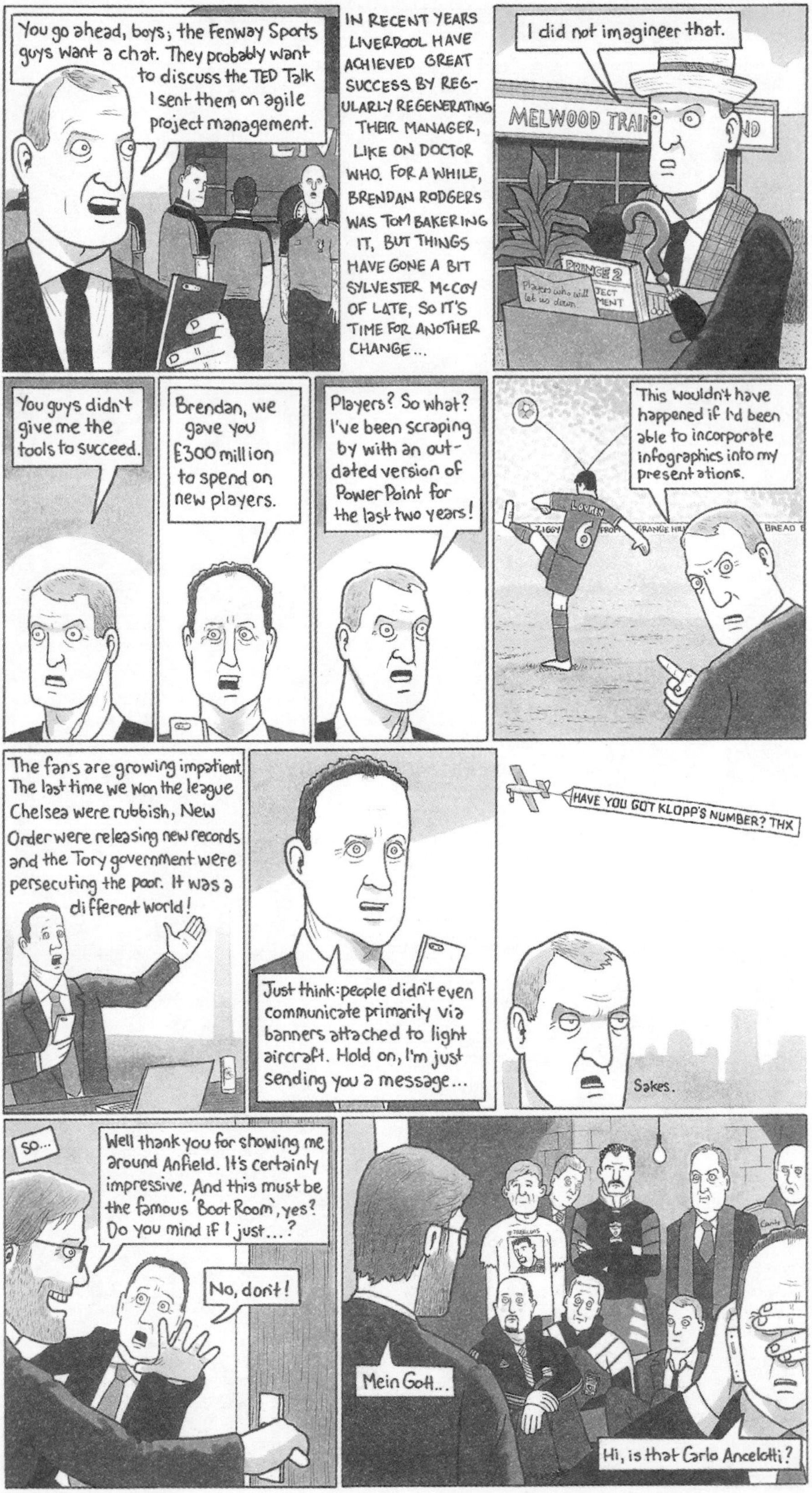

You go ahead, boys; the Fenway Sports guys want a chat. They probably want to discuss the TED Talk I sent them on agile project management.
IN RECENT YEARS LIVERPOOL HAVE ACHIEVED GREAT SUCCESS BY REGULARLY REGENERATING THEIR MANAGER, LIKE ON DOCTOR WHO. FOR A WHILE, BRENDAN RODGERS WAS TOM BAKERING IT, BUT THINGS HAVE GONE A BIT SYLVESTER McCOY OF LATE, SO IT'S TIME FOR ANOTHER CHANGE...
I did not imagineer that.
MELWOOD TRAI
PRINCE 2
Players who will let us down
You guys didn't give me the tools to succeed.
Brendan, we gave you £300 million to spend on new players.
Players? So what? I've been scraping by with an out-dated version of PowerPoint for the last two years!
This wouldn't have happened if I'd been able to incorporate infographics into my presentations.
LOVREN
6
The fans are growing impatient. The last time we won the league Chelsea were rubbish, New Order were releasing new records and the Tory government were persecuting the poor. It was a different world!
Just think: people didn't even communicate primarily via banners attached to light aircraft. Hold on, I'm just sending you a message...
HAVE YOU GOT KLOPP'S NUMBER? THX
Sakes.
So...
Well thank you for showing me around Anfield. It's certainly impressive. And this must be the famous 'Boot Room', yes? Do you mind if I just...?
No, don't!
Mein Gott...
Hi, is that Carlo Ancelotti?

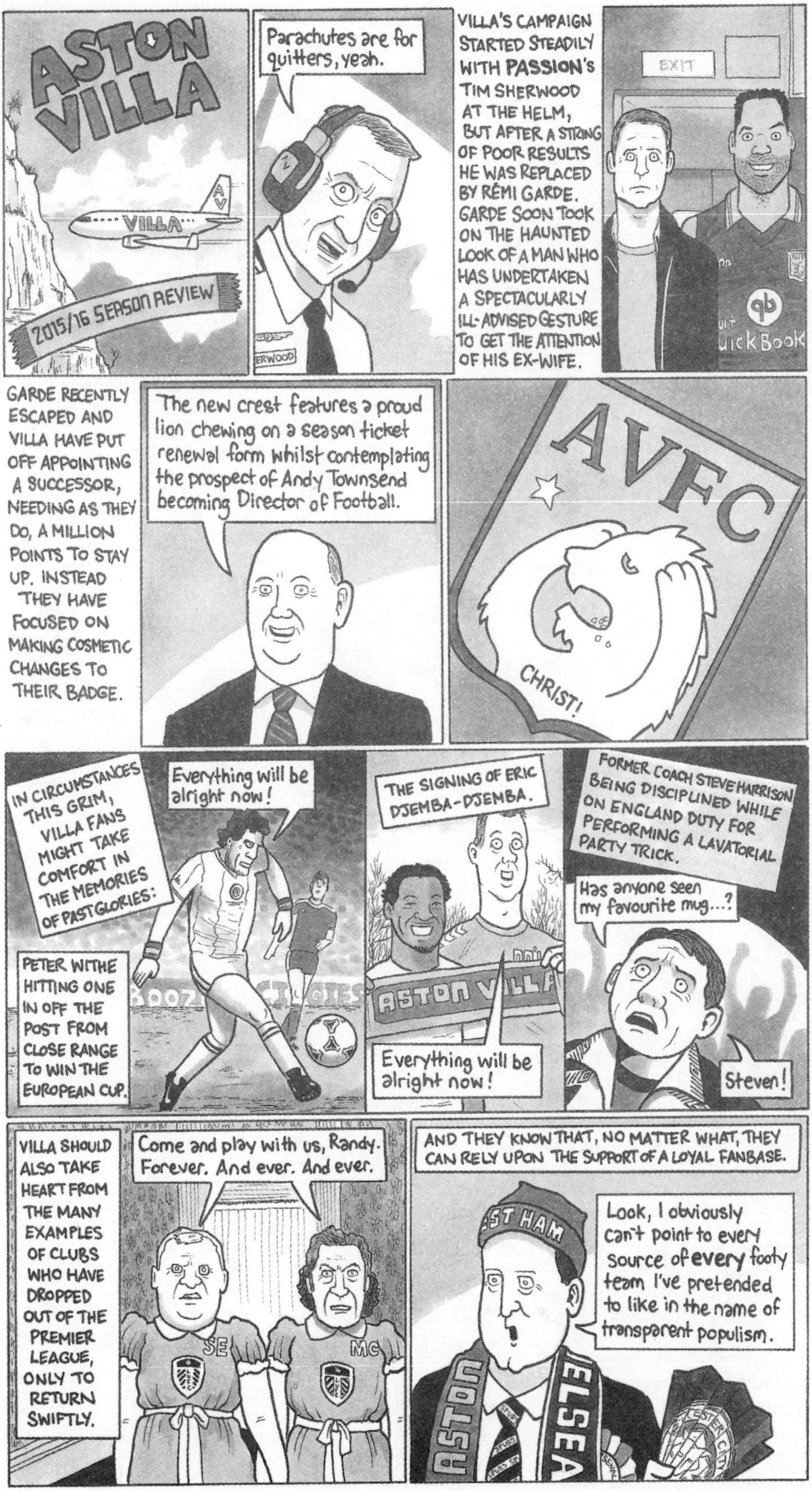

ASTON VILLA
AV
VILLA
2015/16 SEASON REVIEW
Parachutes are for quitters, yeah.
ERWOOD
VILLA'S CAMPAIGN STARTED STEADILY WITH PASSION'S TIM SHERWOOD AT THE HELM, BUT AFTER A STRING OF POOR RESULTS HE WAS REPLACED BY RÉMI GARDE. GARDE SOON TOOK ON THE HAUNTED LOOK OF A MAN WHO HAS UNDERTAKEN A SPECTACULARLY ILL-ADVISED GESTURE TO GET THE ATTENTION OF HIS EX-WIFE.
EXIT
uickBook
GARDE RECENTLY ESCAPED AND VILLA HAVE PUT OFF APPOINTING A SUCCESSOR, NEEDING AS THEY DO, A MILLION POINTS TO STAY UP. INSTEAD THEY HAVE FOCUSED ON MAKING COSMETIC CHANGES TO THEIR BADGE.
The new crest features a proud lion chewing on a season ticket renewal form whilst contemplating the prospect of Andy Townsend becoming Director of Football.
AVFC
CHRIST!
IN CIRCUMSTANCES THIS GRIM, VILLA FANS MIGHT TAKE COMFORT IN THE MEMORIES OF PAST GLORIES:
Everything will be alright now!
PETER WITHE HITTING ONE IN OFF THE POST FROM CLOSE RANGE TO WIN THE EUROPEAN CUP.
THE SIGNING OF ERIC DJEMBA-DJEMBA.
ASTON VILLA
Everything will be alright now!
FORMER COACH STEVE HARRISON BEING DISCIPLINED WHILE ON ENGLAND DUTY FOR PERFORMING A LAVATORIAL PARTY TRICK.
Has anyone seen my favourite mug...?
Steven!
VILLA SHOULD ALSO TAKE HEART FROM THE MANY EXAMPLES OF CLUBS WHO HAVE DROPPED OUT OF THE PREMIER LEAGUE, ONLY TO RETURN SWIFTLY.
Come and play with us, Randy. Forever. And ever. And ever.
SE
MC
AND THEY KNOW THAT, NO MATTER WHAT, THEY CAN RELY UPON THE SUPPORT OF A LOYAL FANBASE.
ST HAM
Look, I obviously can't point to every source of every footy team I've pretended to like in the name of transparent populism.
ASTON
ELSEA
SPURS

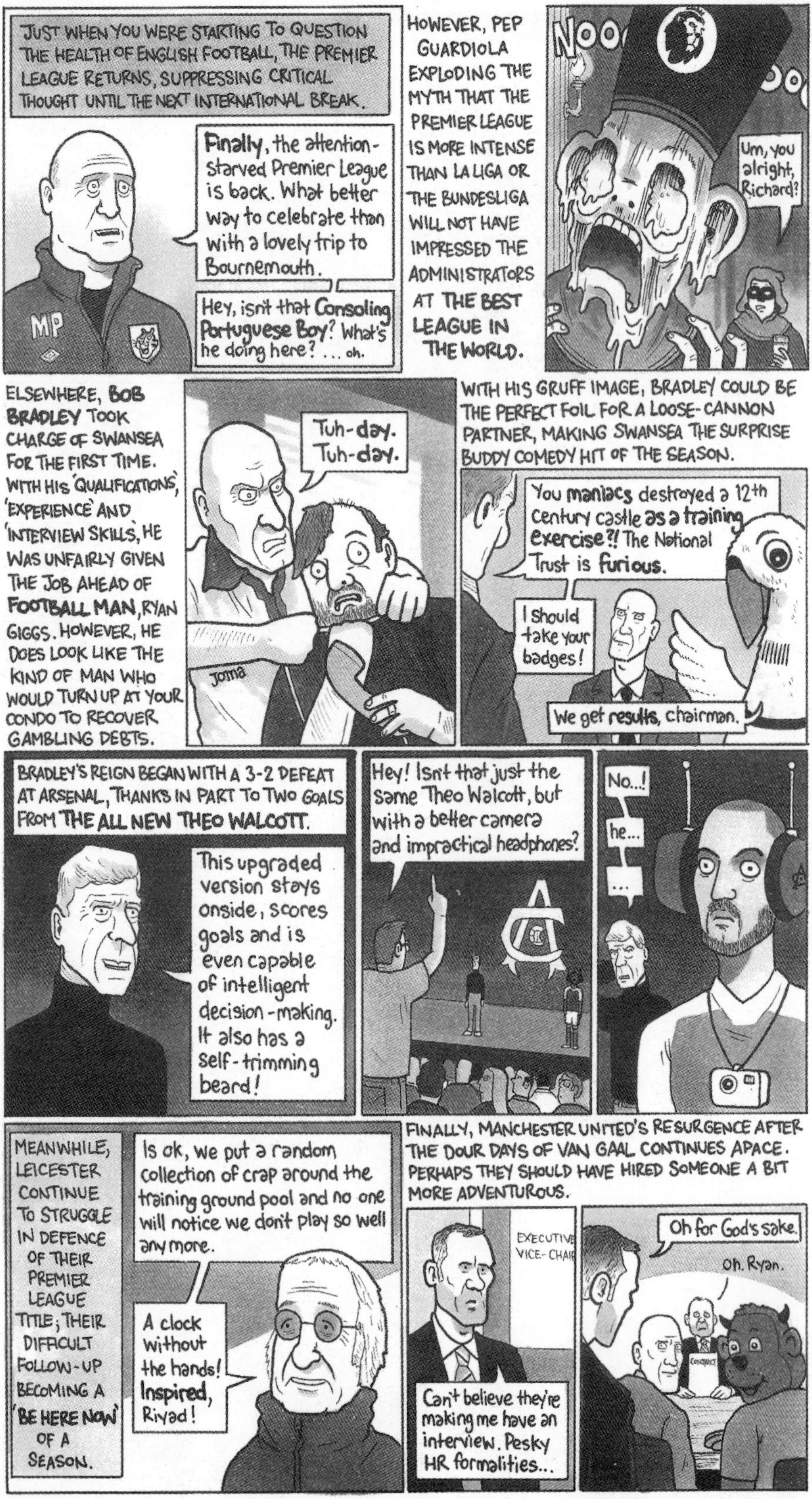
JUST WHEN YOU WERE STARTING TO QUESTION THE HEALTH OF ENGLISH FOOTBALL, THE PREMIER LEAGUE RETURNS, SUPPRESSING CRITICAL THOUGHT UNTIL THE NEXT INTERNATIONAL BREAK.
Finally, the attention-starved Premier League is back. What better way to celebrate than with a lovely trip to Bournemouth.
MP
Hey, isn't that Consoling Portuguese Boy? What's he doing here? ... oh.
HOWEVER, PEP GUARDIOLA EXPLODING THE MYTH THAT THE PREMIER LEAGUE IS MORE INTENSE THAN LA LIGA OR THE BUNDESLIGA WILL NOT HAVE IMPRESSED THE ADMINISTRATORS AT THE BEST LEAGUE IN THE WORLD.
Nooo
Um, you alright, Richard?
ELSEWHERE, BOB BRADLEY TOOK CHARGE OF SWANSEA FOR THE FIRST TIME. WITH HIS 'QUALIFICATIONS', 'EXPERIENCE' AND 'INTERVIEW SKILLS', HE WAS UNFAIRLY GIVEN THE JOB AHEAD OF FOOTBALL MAN, RYAN GIGGS. HOWEVER, HE DOES LOOK LIKE THE KIND OF MAN WHO WOULD TURN UP AT YOUR CONDO TO RECOVER GAMBLING DEBTS.
Tuh-day. Tuh-day.
Joma
WITH HIS GRUFF IMAGE, BRADLEY COULD BE THE PERFECT FOIL FOR A LOOSE-CANNON PARTNER, MAKING SWANSEA THE SURPRISE BUDDY COMEDY HIT OF THE SEASON.
You maniacs destroyed a 12th century castle as a training exercise?! The National Trust is furious.
I should take your badges!
We get results, chairman.
BRADLEY'S REIGN BEGAN WITH A 3-2 DEFEAT AT ARSENAL, THANKS IN PART TO TWO GOALS FROM THE ALL NEW THEO WALCOTT.
This upgraded version stays onside, scores goals and is even capable of intelligent decision-making. It also has a self-trimming beard!
Hey! Isn't that just the same Theo Walcott, but with a better camera and impractical headphones?
No...!
he...
...
MEANWHILE, LEICESTER CONTINUE TO STRUGGLE IN DEFENCE OF THEIR PREMIER LEAGUE TITLE; THEIR DIFFICULT FOLLOW-UP BECOMING A 'BE HERE NOW' OF A SEASON.
Is ok, we put a random collection of crap around the training ground pool and no one will notice we don't play so well any more.
A clock without the hands! Inspired, Riyad!
FINALLY, MANCHESTER UNITED'S RESURGENCE AFTER THE DOUR DAYS OF VAN GAAL CONTINUES APACE. PERHAPS THEY SHOULD HAVE HIRED SOMEONE A BIT MORE ADVENTUROUS.
EXECUTIVE VICE-CHAIR
Can't believe they're making me have an interview. Pesky HR formalities...
Oh for God's sake.
Oh. Ryan.

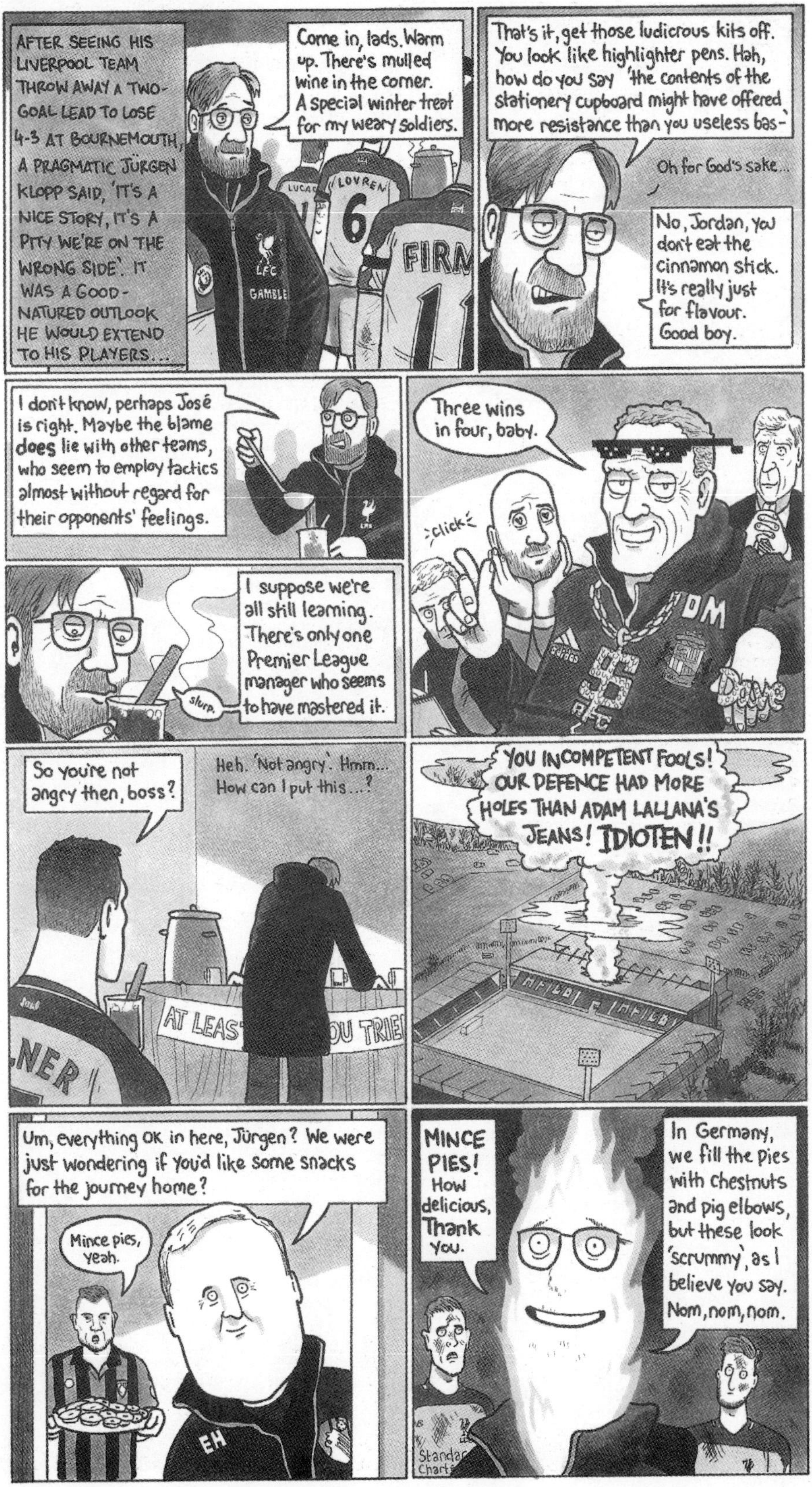
AFTER SEEING HIS LIVERPOOL TEAM THROW AWAY A TWO-GOAL LEAD TO LOSE 4-3 AT BOURNEMOUTH, A PRAGMATIC JÜRGEN KLOPP SAID, 'IT'S A NICE STORY, IT'S A PITY WE'RE ON THE WRONG SIDE'. IT WAS A GOOD-NATURED OUTLOOK HE WOULD EXTEND TO HIS PLAYERS...
Come in, lads. Warm up. There's mulled wine in the corner. A special winter treat for my weary soldiers.
LUCAS
LOVREN
6
FIRM
That's it, get those ludicrous kits off. You look like highlighter pens. Hah, how do you say 'the contents of the stationery cupboard might have offered more resistance than you useless bas-'
Oh for God's sake...
No, Jordan, you don't eat the cinnamon stick. It's really just for flavour. Good boy.
I don't know, perhaps José is right. Maybe the blame does lie with other teams, who seem to employ tactics almost without regard for their opponents' feelings.
Three wins in four, baby.
click
DM
I suppose we're all still learning. There's only one Premier League manager who seems to have mastered it.
slurp.
So you're not angry then, boss?
Heh. 'Not angry'. Hmm... How can I put this...?
AT LEAS
OU TRIE
NER
YOU INCOMPETENT FOOLS! OUR DEFENCE HAD MORE HOLES THAN ADAM LALLANA'S JEANS! IDIOTEN!!
Um, everything OK in here, Jürgen? We were just wondering if you'd like some snacks for the journey home?
Mince pies, yeah.
EH
MINCE PIES! How delicious, Thank you.
In Germany, we fill the pies with chestnuts and pig elbows, but these look 'scrummy', as I believe you say. Nom, nom, nom.

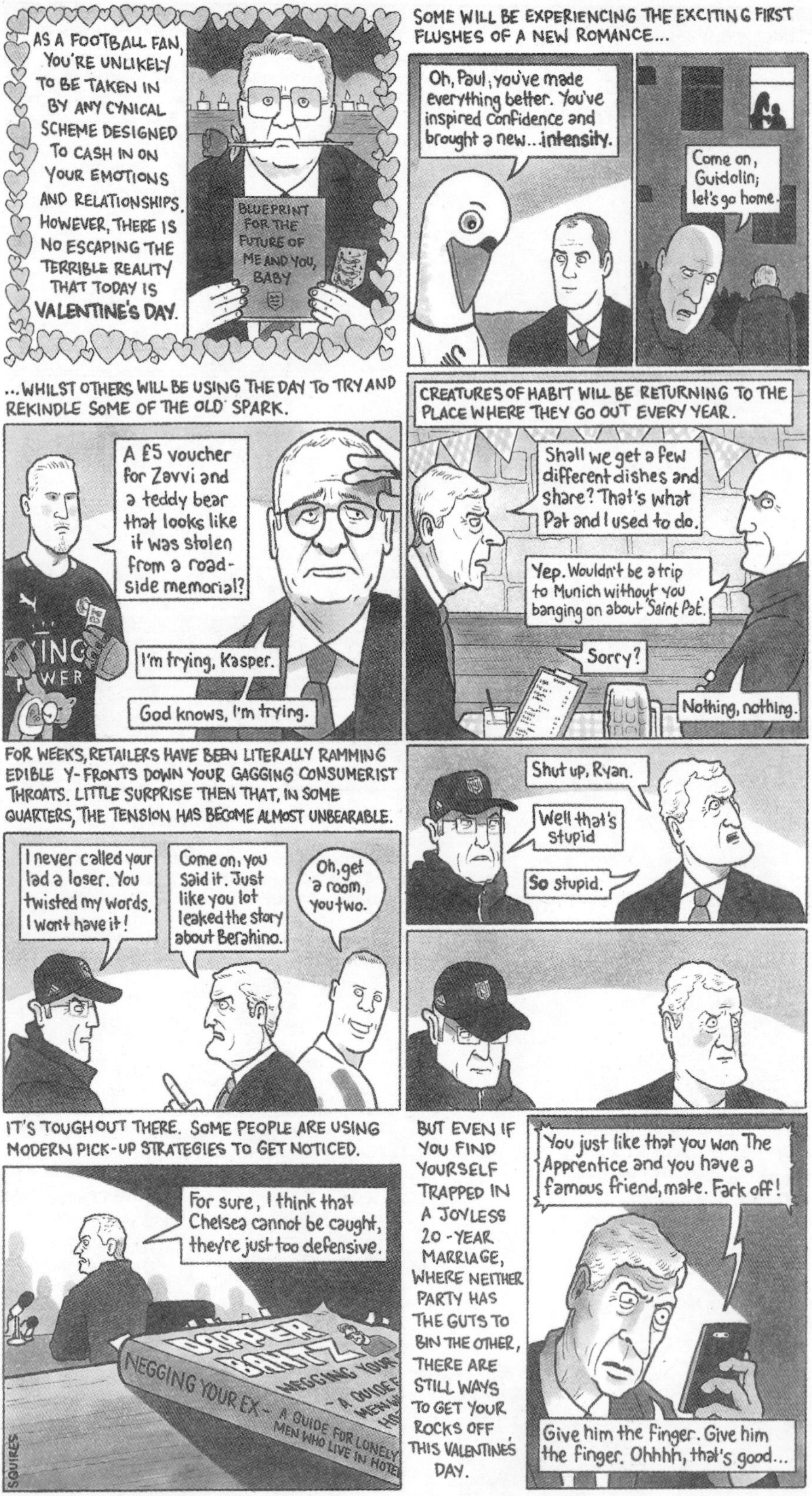
AS A FOOTBALL FAN, YOU'RE UNLIKELY TO BE TAKEN IN BY ANY CYNICAL SCHEME DESIGNED TO CASH IN ON YOUR EMOTIONS AND RELATIONSHIPS. HOWEVER, THERE IS NO ESCAPING THE TERRIBLE REALITY THAT TODAY IS VALENTINE'S DAY.
BLUEPRINT FOR THE FUTURE OF ME AND YOU, BABY
SOME WILL BE EXPERIENCING THE EXCITING FIRST FLUSHES OF A NEW ROMANCE...
Oh, Paul; you've made everything better. You've inspired confidence and brought a new... intensity.
Come on, Guidolin; let's go home.
...WHILST OTHERS WILL BE USING THE DAY TO TRY AND REKINDLE SOME OF THE OLD SPARK.
A £5 voucher for Zavvi and a teddy bear that looks like it was stolen from a road-side memorial?
I'm trying, Kasper.
God knows, I'm trying.
CREATURES OF HABIT WILL BE RETURNING TO THE PLACE WHERE THEY GO OUT EVERY YEAR.
Shall we get a few different dishes and share? That's what Pat and I used to do.
Yep. Wouldn't be a trip to Munich without you banging on about 'Saint Pat'.
Sorry?
Nothing, nothing.
FOR WEEKS, RETAILERS HAVE BEEN LITERALLY RAMMING EDIBLE Y-FRONTS DOWN YOUR GAGGING CONSUMERIST THROATS. LITTLE SURPRISE THEN THAT, IN SOME QUARTERS, THE TENSION HAS BECOME ALMOST UNBEARABLE.
I never called your lad a loser. You twisted my words. I won't have it!
Come on, you said it. Just like you lot leaked the story about Berahino.
Oh, get a room, you two.
Shut up, Ryan.
Well that's stupid
So stupid.
IT'S TOUGH OUT THERE. SOME PEOPLE ARE USING MODERN PICK-UP STRATEGIES TO GET NOTICED.
For sure, I think that Chelsea cannot be caught, they're just too defensive.
DAPPER BANTZ
NEGGING YOUR EX - A GUIDE FOR LONELY MEN WHO LIVE IN HOTE
BUT EVEN IF YOU FIND YOURSELF TRAPPED IN A JOYLESS 20-YEAR MARRIAGE, WHERE NEITHER PARTY HAS THE GUTS TO BIN THE OTHER, THERE ARE STILL WAYS TO GET YOUR ROCKS OFF THIS VALENTINE'S DAY.
You just like that you won The Apprentice and you have a famous friend, mate. Fark off!
Give him the finger. Give him the finger. Ohhhh, that's good...
SQUIRES

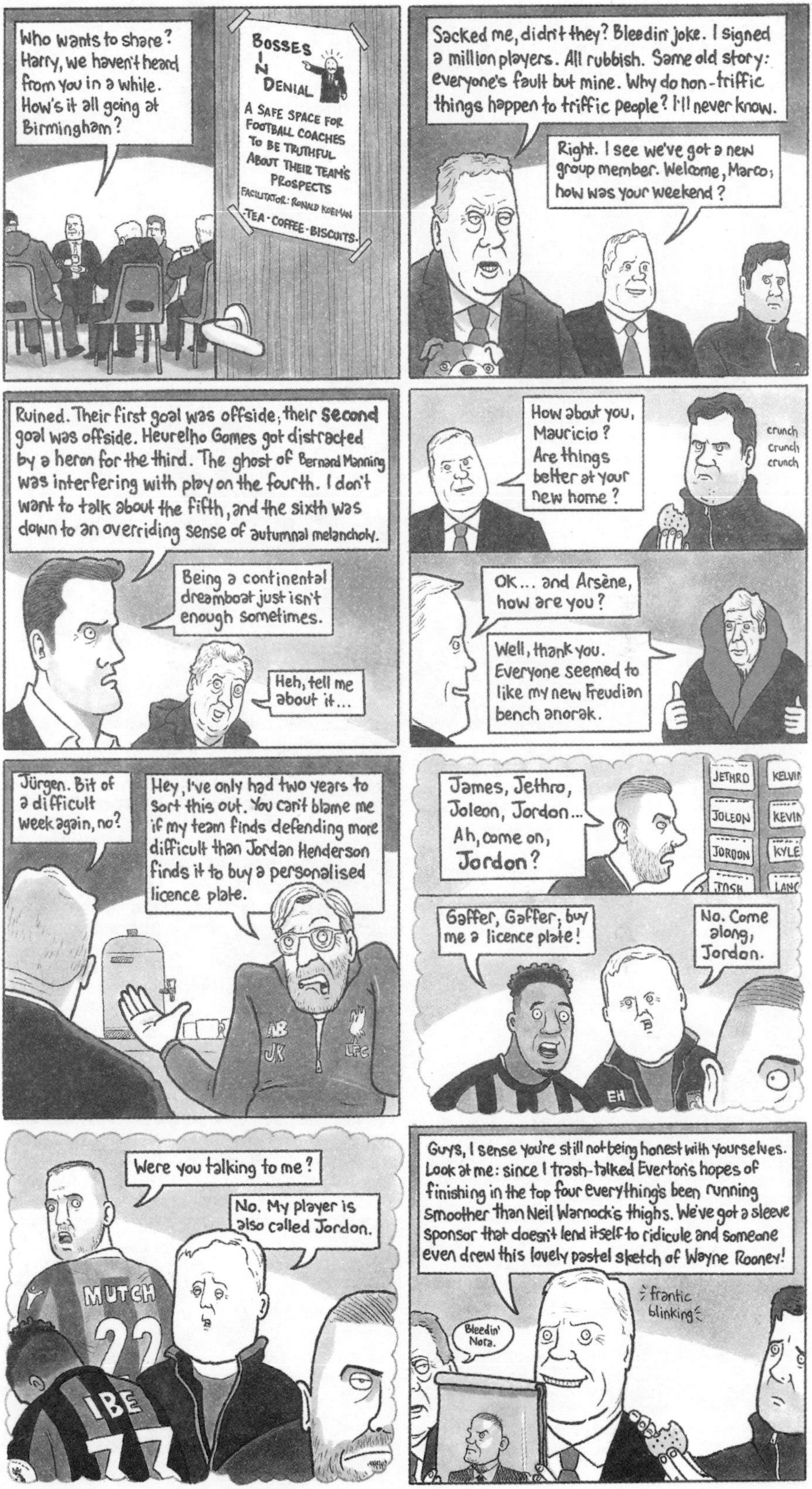
Who wants to share? Harry, we haven't heard from you in a while. How's it all going at Birmingham?
BOSSES IN DENIAL
A SAFE SPACE FOR FOOTBALL COACHES TO BE TRUTHFUL ABOUT THEIR TEAM'S PROSPECTS
FACILITATOR: RONALD KOEMAN
-TEA - COFFEE - BISCUITS-
Sacked me, didn't they? Bleedin' joke. I signed a million players. All rubbish. Same old story: everyone's fault but mine. Why do non-triffic things happen to triffic people? I'll never know.
Right. I see we've got a new group member. Welcome, Marco; how was your weekend?
Ruined. Their first goal was offside; their second goal was offside. Heurelho Gomes got distracted by a heron for the third. The ghost of Bernard Manning was interfering with play on the fourth. I don't want to talk about the fifth, and the sixth was down to an overriding sense of autumnal melancholy.
Being a continental dreamboat just isn't enough sometimes.
Heh, tell me about it...
How about you, Mauricio? Are things better at your new home?
crunch crunch crunch
OK... and Arsène, how are you?
Well, thank you. Everyone seemed to like my new Freudian bench anorak.
Jürgen. Bit of a difficult week again, no?
Hey, I've only had two years to sort this out. You can't blame me if my team finds defending more difficult than Jordan Henderson finds it to buy a personalised licence plate.
JK
LFC
James, Jethro, Joleon, Jordon... Ah, come on, Jordon?
JETHRO
JOLEON
JORDON
KYLE
Gaffer, Gaffer, buy me a licence plate!
No. Come along, Jordon.
EH
Were you talking to me?
No. My player is also called Jordon.
MUTCH
22
IBE
Guys, I sense you're still not being honest with yourselves. Look at me: since I trash-talked Everton's hopes of finishing in the top four everything's been running smoother than Neil Warnock's thighs. We've got a sleeve sponsor that doesn't lend itself to ridicule and someone even drew this lovely pastel sketch of Wayne Rooney!
Bleedin' Nora.
frantic blinking

THERE IS NO GREATER BARRIER TO EMPLOYMENT THAN BEING A WEALTHY, WHITE, MIDDLE-AGED, BRITISH MALE. DENIED OPPORTUNITY AT EVERY TURN, THIS VICTIMISED MAJORITY IS FORCED TO FLEE TO THE STUDIOS OF MIDDLE-EASTERN TV STATIONS. HOWEVER, IN AN INSPIRING PLOT TWIST, IT TRANSPIRES THAT THERE IS A PLACE WHERE EXTINCT REPUTATIONS ARE NO IMPEDIMENT TO EMPLOYMENT.

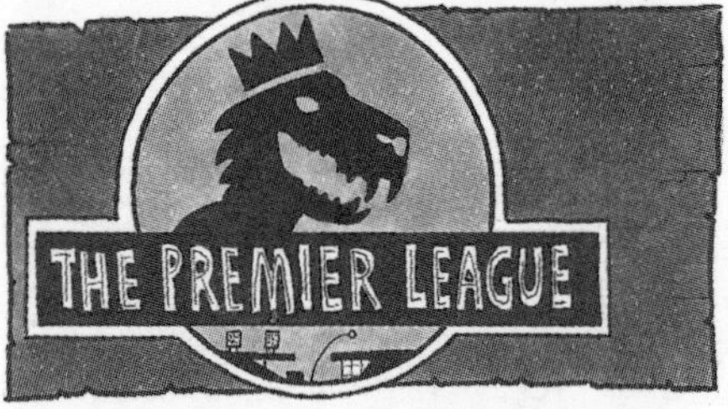
THE PREMIER LEAGUE

COULD IT BE THAT SAM ALLARDYCE WAS EXAGGERATING WHEN HE DESCRIBED THE PREMIER LEAGUE AS 'A FOREIGN LEAGUE IN ENGLAND'? (DOES A SUNDERLAND FAN CRAP IN THE STANDS?) THE RECENT RETURN TO TOP-FLIGHT MANAGEMENT FOR BIG SAM, ALAN PARDEW AND DAVID MOYES HAS BEEN CRITICISED, BUT TO LIKEN THEM TO DINOSAURS WOULD BE GROSSLY UNFAIR, **SO HERE GOES...**

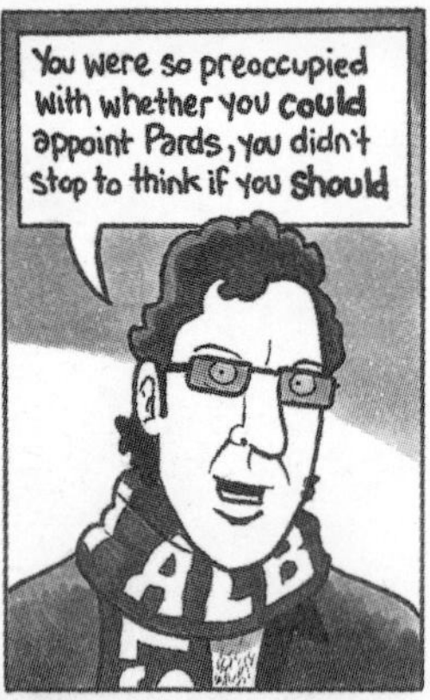
You were so preoccupied with whether you **could** appoint Pards, you didn't stop to think if you **should**

ALLARDYCE ACTUALLY HAS SOME PROGRESSIVE IDEAS. HIS CHEWING GUM IS JUICY FRUIT AND THAT EARPIECE HE WEARS PUMPS OUT AN OUTHERE BROTHERS SPOTIFY PLAYLIST. ALONGSIDE SAMMY LEE AND CRAIG SHAKESPEARE, HE WAS ABLE TO START HIS EVERTON REIGN BY OUT-WITTING HUDDERSFIELD'S DAVID WAGNER FOR AN ATYPICAL SCRAPPY WIN.

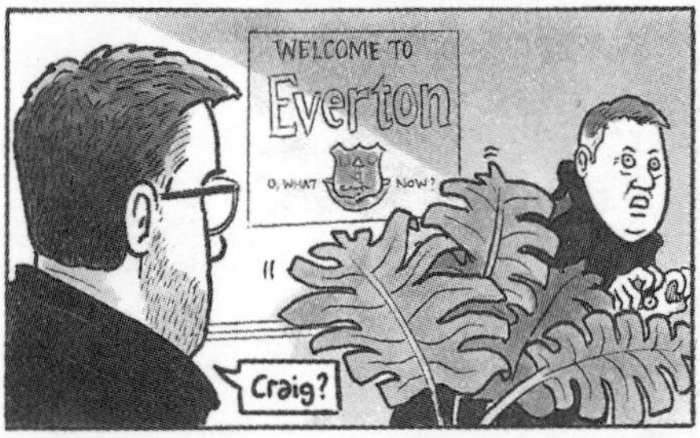
WELCOME TO
Everton
Craig?

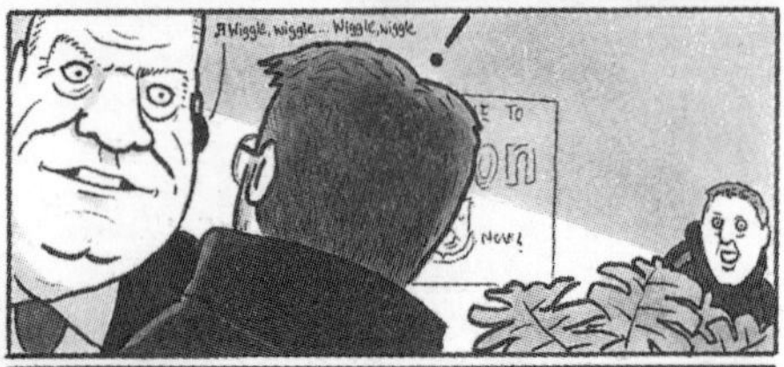
♫ Wiggle, wiggle... Wiggle, wiggle
!

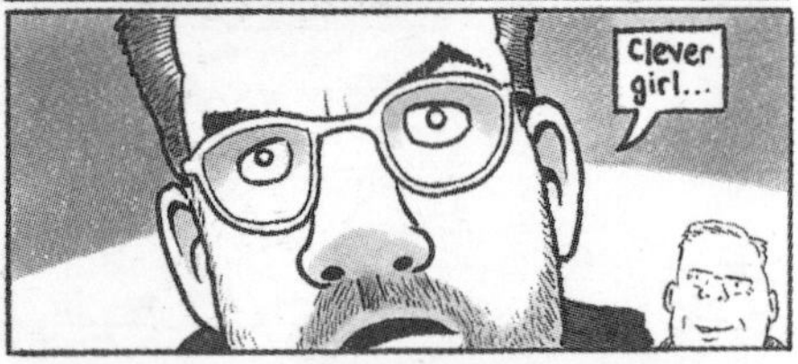
Clever girl...

IT WAS WHEN SHAKESPEARE WAS REPLACED BY CLAUDE PUEL AT LEICESTER THAT THE DEBATE ABOUT FOREIGN MANAGERS RESURFACED. DESPITE LEICESTER'S SUBSEQUENT UPTURN IN FORM, RIYAD MAHREZ'S NEW HAIRDO SHOWS THAT ANARCHY RULES. FOR GOD'S SAKE, NO ONE SHOW GARTH CR-

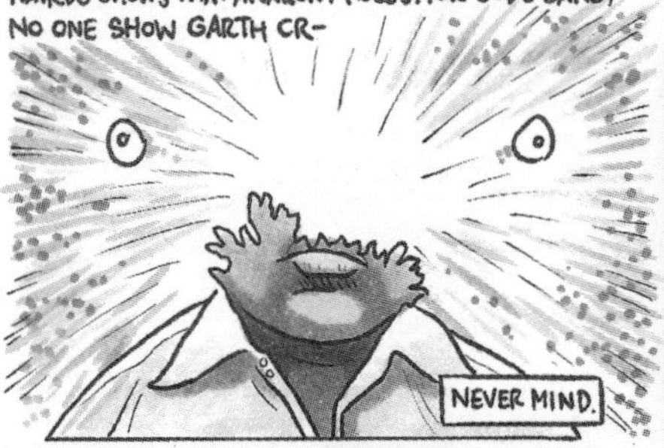
NEVER MIND.

THE FANS OF SOME CLUBS MIGHT FEEL LIKE THEY'RE AT THE BACK OF A MANAGERIAL CENTIPEDE, DIGESTING THE FOOTBALL OF A STRING OF TIRED JOURNEYMEN, BUT THEY ARE SPARED THE **TYRANNY** OF OVERSEAS COACHES, WITH THEIR FANCIFUL IDEAS ABOUT MAKING SPURS GOOD AND GIVING TEAM TALKS TO OPPOSITION PLAYERS.

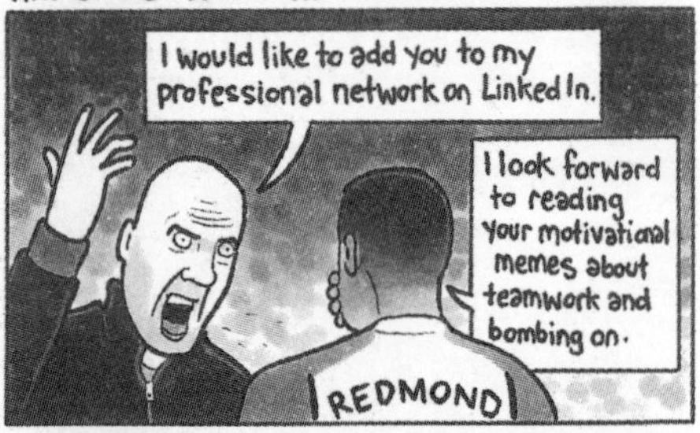
I would like to add you to my professional network on LinkedIn.
I look forward to reading your motivational memes about teamwork and bombing on.
REDMOND

ONE FORMER PREMIER LEAGUE MANAGER, ANDRÉ VILLAS-BOAS, HAS EVEN QUIT HIS JOB TO DRIVE IN THE DAKAR RALLY. ONE CAN ONLY HOPE THAT HE HAS THE FORESIGHT TO TAKE WITH HIM A CAMERA CREW AND TIM SHERWOOD AS CO-DRIVER. INSTANT TV GOLD.

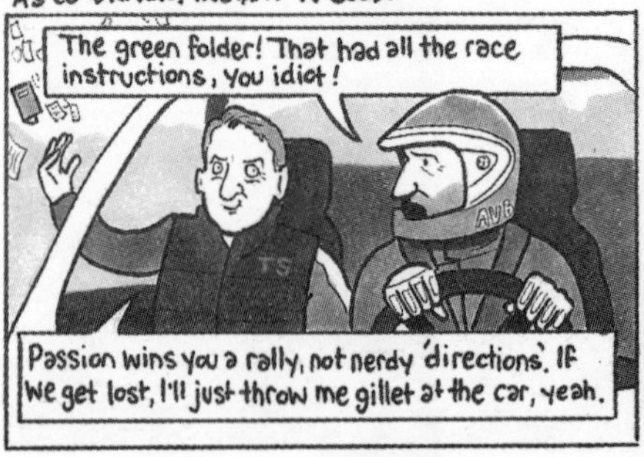
The green folder! That had all the race instructions, you idiot!
Passion wins you a rally, not nerdy 'directions'. If we get lost, I'll just throw me gillet at the car, yeah.

PERHAPS THE REVIVAL OF THE BRITISH MANAGER WILL PAVE THE WAY FOR THE RETURN OF THE SUPREME ALPHA RELIC; CRASHING THROUGH THE UNDERGROWTH TO A DUGOUT NEAR YOU, LIKE A BULLDOZER CLEARING THE WAY FOR SOME LUXURY APARTMENTS.

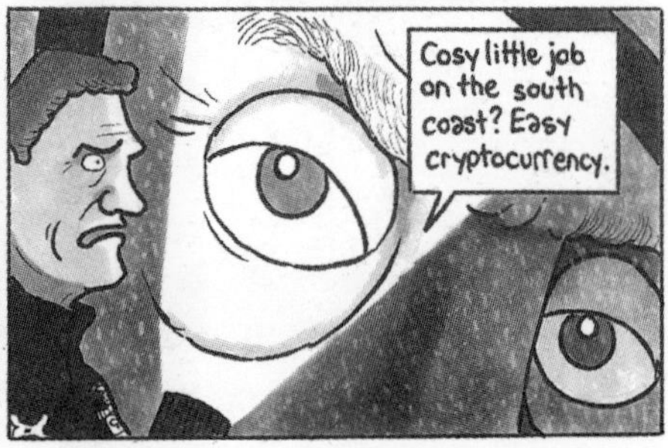
Cosy little job on the south coast? Easy cryptocurrency.

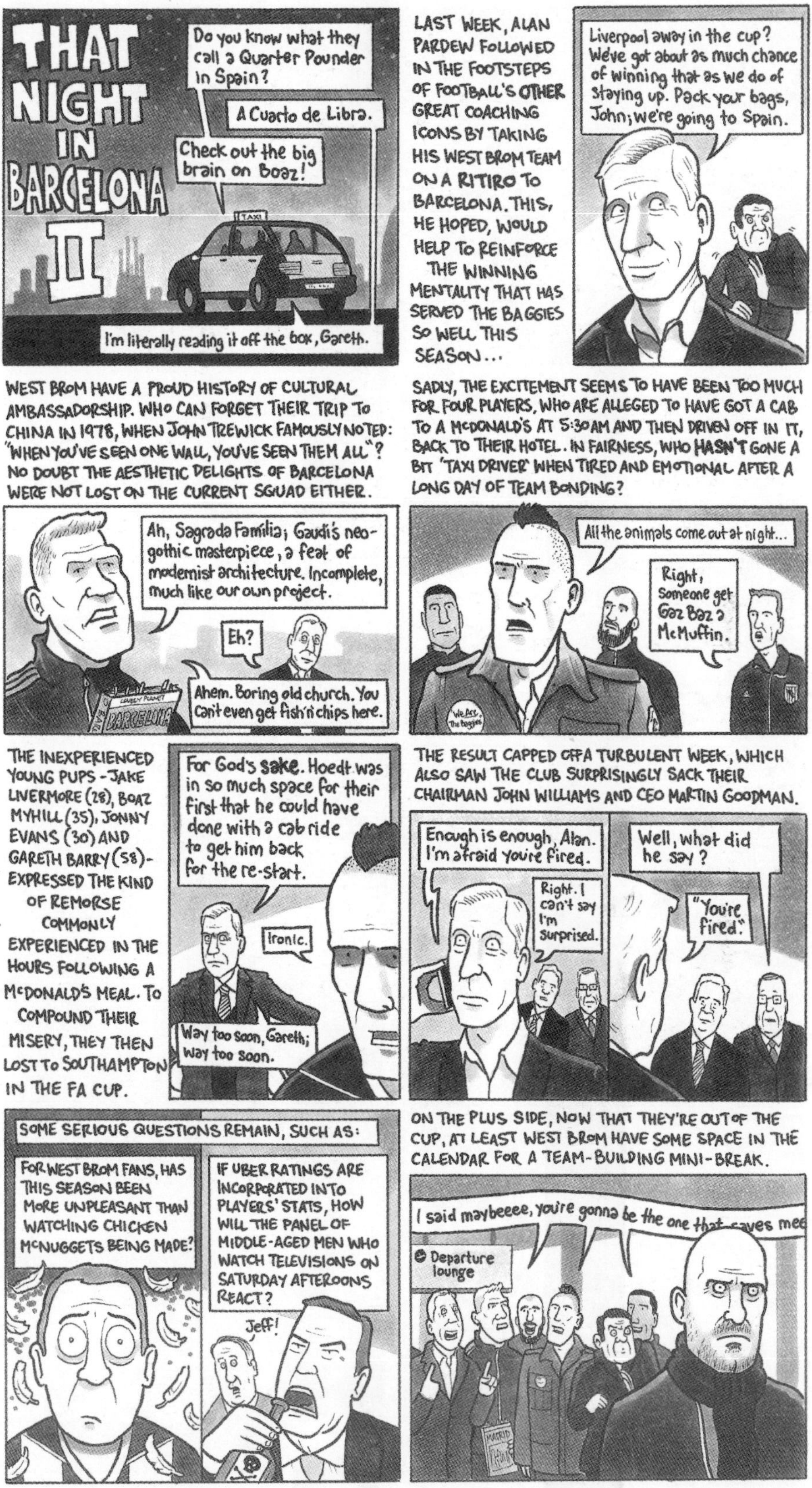

THAT NIGHT IN BARCELONA II
Do you know what they call a Quarter Pounder in Spain?
A Cuarto de Libra.
Check out the big brain on Boaz!
TAXI
I'm literally reading it off the box, Gareth.
LAST WEEK, ALAN PARDEW FOLLOWED IN THE FOOTSTEPS OF FOOTBALL'S OTHER GREAT COACHING ICONS BY TAKING HIS WEST BROM TEAM ON A RITIRO TO BARCELONA. THIS, HE HOPED, WOULD HELP TO REINFORCE THE WINNING MENTALITY THAT HAS SERVED THE BAGGIES SO WELL THIS SEASON...
Liverpool away in the cup? We've got about as much chance of winning that as we do of staying up. Pack your bags, John; we're going to Spain.
WEST BROM HAVE A PROUD HISTORY OF CULTURAL AMBASSADORSHIP. WHO CAN FORGET THEIR TRIP TO CHINA IN 1978, WHEN JOHN TREWICK FAMOUSLY NOTED: "WHEN YOU'VE SEEN ONE WALL, YOU'VE SEEN THEM ALL"? NO DOUBT THE AESTHETIC DELIGHTS OF BARCELONA WERE NOT LOST ON THE CURRENT SQUAD EITHER.
SADLY, THE EXCITEMENT SEEMS TO HAVE BEEN TOO MUCH FOR FOUR PLAYERS, WHO ARE ALLEGED TO HAVE GOT A CAB TO A McDONALD'S AT 5:30AM AND THEN DRIVEN OFF IN IT, BACK TO THEIR HOTEL. IN FAIRNESS, WHO HASN'T GONE A BIT 'TAXI DRIVER' WHEN TIRED AND EMOTIONAL AFTER A LONG DAY OF TEAM BONDING?
Ah, Sagrada Familia; Gaudi's neo-gothic masterpiece, a feat of modernist architecture. Incomplete, much like our own project.
Eh?
Ahem. Boring old church. You can't even get fish'n'chips here.
LONELY PLANET BARCELONA
All the animals come out at night...
Right, someone get Gaz Baz a McMuffin.
We Are The Baggies
THE INEXPERIENCED YOUNG PUPS - JAKE LIVERMORE (28), BOAZ MYHILL (35), JONNY EVANS (30) AND GARETH BARRY (58) - EXPRESSED THE KIND OF REMORSE COMMONLY EXPERIENCED IN THE HOURS FOLLOWING A McDONALD'S MEAL. TO COMPOUND THEIR MISERY, THEY THEN LOST TO SOUTHAMPTON IN THE FA CUP.
For God's sake. Hoedt was in so much space for their first that he could have done with a cab ride to get him back for the re-start.
Ironic.
Way too soon, Gareth; way too soon.
THE RESULT CAPPED OFF A TURBULENT WEEK, WHICH ALSO SAW THE CLUB SURPRISINGLY SACK THEIR CHAIRMAN JOHN WILLIAMS AND CEO MARTIN GOODMAN.
Enough is enough, Alan. I'm afraid you're fired.
Right. I can't say I'm surprised.
Well, what did he say?
"You're fired."
SOME SERIOUS QUESTIONS REMAIN, SUCH AS:
FOR WEST BROM FANS, HAS THIS SEASON BEEN MORE UNPLEASANT THAN WATCHING CHICKEN McNUGGETS BEING MADE?
IF UBER RATINGS ARE INCORPORATED INTO PLAYERS' STATS, HOW WILL THE PANEL OF MIDDLE-AGED MEN WHO WATCH TELEVISIONS ON SATURDAY AFTEROONS REACT?
Jeff!
ON THE PLUS SIDE, NOW THAT THEY'RE OUT OF THE CUP, AT LEAST WEST BROM HAVE SOME SPACE IN THE CALENDAR FOR A TEAM-BUILDING MINI-BREAK.
I said maybeeee, you're gonna be the one that saves mee
Departure lounge
MADRID

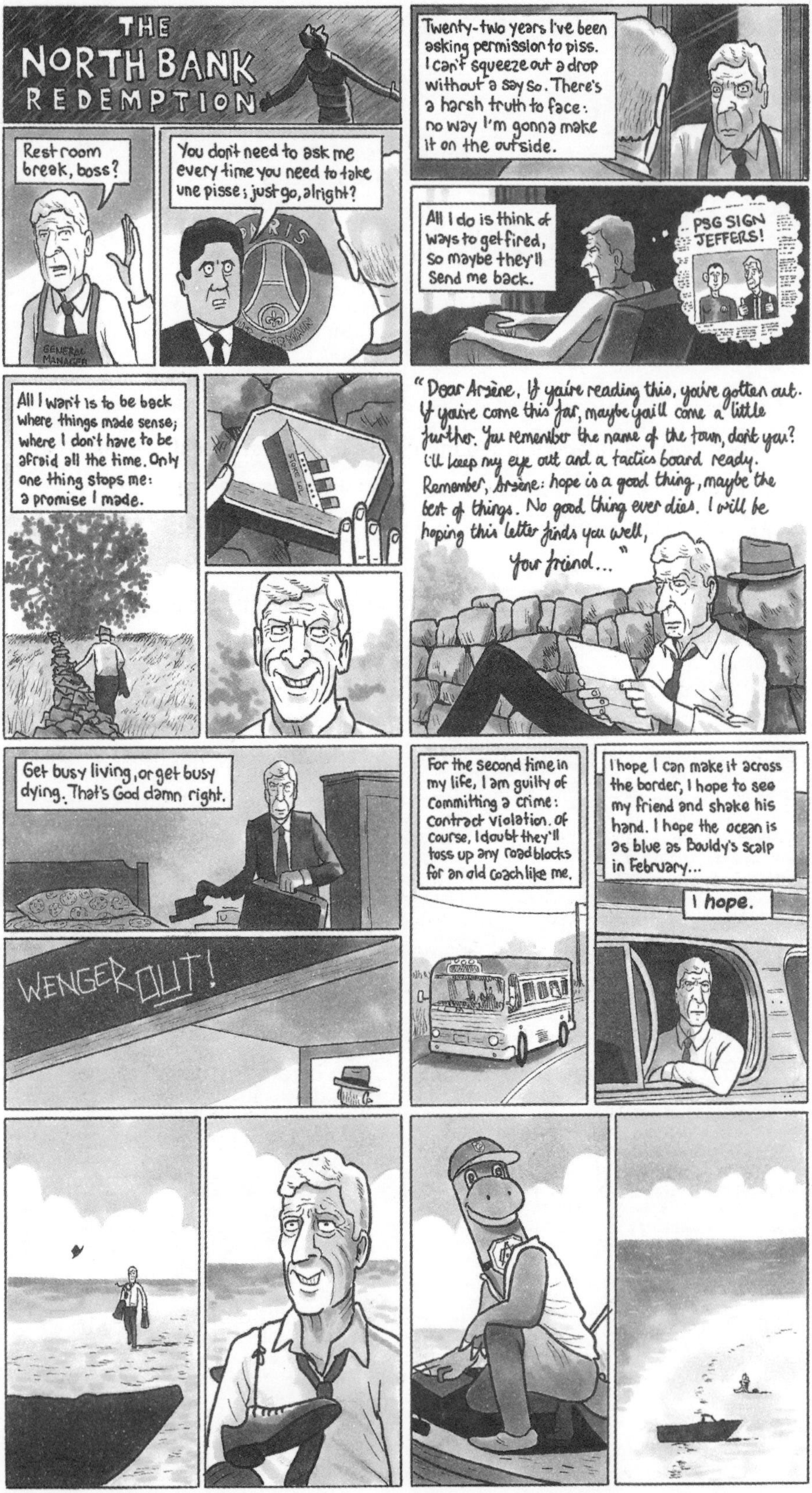
THE NORTH BANK REDEMPTION
Twenty-two years I've been asking permission to piss. I can't squeeze out a drop without a say so. There's a harsh truth to face: no way I'm gonna make it on the outside.
Rest room break, boss?
You don't need to ask me every time you need to take une pisse; just go, alright?
GENERAL MANAGER
All I do is think of ways to get fired, so maybe they'll send me back.
PSG SIGN JEFFERS!
All I want is to be back where things made sense; where I don't have to be afraid all the time. Only one thing stops me: a promise I made.
"Dear Arsène, If you're reading this, you've gotten out. If you've come this far, maybe you'll come a little further. You remember the name of the town, don't you? I'll keep my eye out and a tactics board ready. Remember, Arsène: hope is a good thing, maybe the best of things. No good thing ever dies. I will be hoping this letter finds you well,
Your friend..."
Get busy living, or get busy dying. That's God damn right.
For the second time in my life, I am guilty of committing a crime: contract violation. Of course, I doubt they'll toss up any road blocks for an old coach like me.
I hope I can make it across the border, I hope to see my friend and shake his hand. I hope the ocean is as blue as Bouldy's scalp in February...
I **hope**.
WENGER OUT!

MARC WILMOTS'S DISCO MIX:
Euro 2016

The 2016 European Championship was the greatest football tournament ever held, if you were Welsh, Icelandic or a highly strung, spray-tanned Portuguese man-baby with an ego the size of Crewe.

Undoubtedly, it was Ronaldo's tournament. His performances improved as the tournament progressed and he was responsible for dragging an unremarkable Portugal team to success, his subordinate teammates perhaps hoping that it would shut him up. He even had the added bonus of learning that his arch-nemesis, Lionel Messi (with whom he actually seems to get on quite well), had been found guilty of tax evasion.[6]

Time and again, Portugal's hero demonstrated a world-class dedication to petulance. He dismissed Iceland as having 'small mentalities' for celebrating their draw with Portugal; he threw a reporter's microphone into a pond; he had a hissy fit on the pitch during a draw with Hungary. Standing there screaming, legs rigidly akimbo, for a moment it looked like he might actually soil himself in frustration, tiny dehydrated pellets shooting angrily into the turf like machine-gun fire. However, come the end of the competition, it was impossible to begrudge him his moment, standing

---

6 Ronaldo's *Schadenfreude* would last little more than a year, however, as he too was charged with tax evasion in July 2017.

there with his hands on his hips, chest pumped out, huge trophy balanced on his head like a hat.

The championship was played in a festival atmosphere in France; when England were in town, the festival it specifically evoked was the Leeds Festival of 2002, when there was a huge riot and all the toilet cubicles got burned down. As ever, England fans brought colour to the occasion, their sunburnt shoulders, in every shade of cerise, heaving in the market squares as they sang songs about war victories that they contributed as much to as they did to the development of a cure for tuberculosis.

However, on this occasion there was an ugly end: the traditional 'throwing of the white garden furniture' and 'scuffles with baton-windmilling cops and local toughs' was completely ruined by a squadron of Russian hooligans who'd apparently received expert training. The age-old battle between amateur gentlemen and cynical professionals played out on the cobbled streets of Marseille. What chance does Darren from Stevenage stand against an ex-Special Forces trooper with a GoPro strapped to his head who treats the whole thing like a side-mission from Grand Theft Auto?

On the pitch, England's defeat to Iceland came a few days after the Brexit vote. Leave really did mean leave. It was ironic that, in Roy Hodgson, England were managed by a well-travelled man with a passion for European culture and a thirst for learning that saw him take the excellent decision to go on a boat cruise with his assistant Ray Lewington rather than scout Iceland.

Everyone else seemed to have fun, though. As always, Ireland's fans enjoyed themselves as if they were on a month-long summer holiday, travelling around France, drinking beer and watching football with their friends. No wonder Roy Keane looked indignant: this wasn't a bloody *barbecue*.

Croatia's supporters also had a laugh, briefly holding up their team's game against the Czech Republic with a barrage of flares and fireworks thrown onto the pitch in protest at corruption within the Croatian football association. One firework exploded just as it was about to be picked up by a steward who clearly hadn't been traumatised by bleak British public information films in the 1980s.

Another memorable feature of the match was Vedran Ćorluka picking up a head injury and then experimenting with various forms of protective headwear, from the understated (bandage) to the elaborate (water-polo cap decorated with the Croatian flag). Petr Čech, whose own scrum cap seemed bland in comparison, watched on impassively at this peacocking try-hard.

It was also an unforgettable championship for Wales, who enjoyed their best ever performance at a major tournament. It's possible there are still some Welsh fans in Lille, blinking into space, unable to believe that they have seen Hal Robson-Kanu execute a perfect Cruyff turn to send three Belgian defenders the wrong way, before slamming the ball into the net. In the rest of Britain, desperate attempts were made to clamber upon the bandwagon. Many people were already scouring ancestry websites for evidence to support an EU passport application, so it was a short diversion to unearth a distant aunt from Caersws. Wales eventually fell to Portugal in the semi-final – the only game that the Portuguese won in normal time throughout the entire tournament: they drew all three of their group matches, edged past Croatia with a last-minute goal in extra time and overcame Poland on penalties.

France seemed to have done the hard bit by beating Germany in the other semi-final, having been sent on their way thanks to a Griezmann penalty after a reckless Schweinsteiger handball. Once Dimitri Payet had hacked down Ronaldo in the eighth minute of the final, it seemed like a formality that the hosts would prevail. Ronnie sat sobbing on the Saint-Denis turf, a large moth sucking at his hot, salty tears. He was carried to the touchline on a stretcher and was substituted, the dream over.

But then, the resurrection – Cristiano rolled back the wall of drinks coolers and rose from the dugout like Jesus from the caves of

Jerusalem! Soon he was patrolling the touchline, barking instructions at his colleagues. Portugal coach Fernando Santos smiled on indulgently, aware that his own role was primarily ceremonial. As the game wore on into extra time and France's play became increasing laboured, it became obvious that Portugal would scab a winner, which is exactly what they did when substitute Eder let fly from twenty-five yards, his low strike skidding past Hugo Lloris.

For Eder, the goal was the glorious conclusion to an emotional narrative arc. He'd endured a tough start to life, raised in hardship and sent to an orphanage at the age of eight. From there, he battled to establish himself as a professional footballer, rising through the lower ranks of Portuguese football to the periphery of the national team. He'd been the subject of abuse after Portugal's poor showing at the 2014 World Cup. A scapegoat for their failure, he suffered a period of crippling self-doubt, but slowly rebuilt his confidence with the assistance of a psychologist. Yet now here he was, the scorer of the most important goal in his small nation's footballing history. On any other occasion, in any other team, *this* would have been the story of the tournament, but fuck all that because look over there, Ronaldo is standing in his pants, roaring at the night sky.

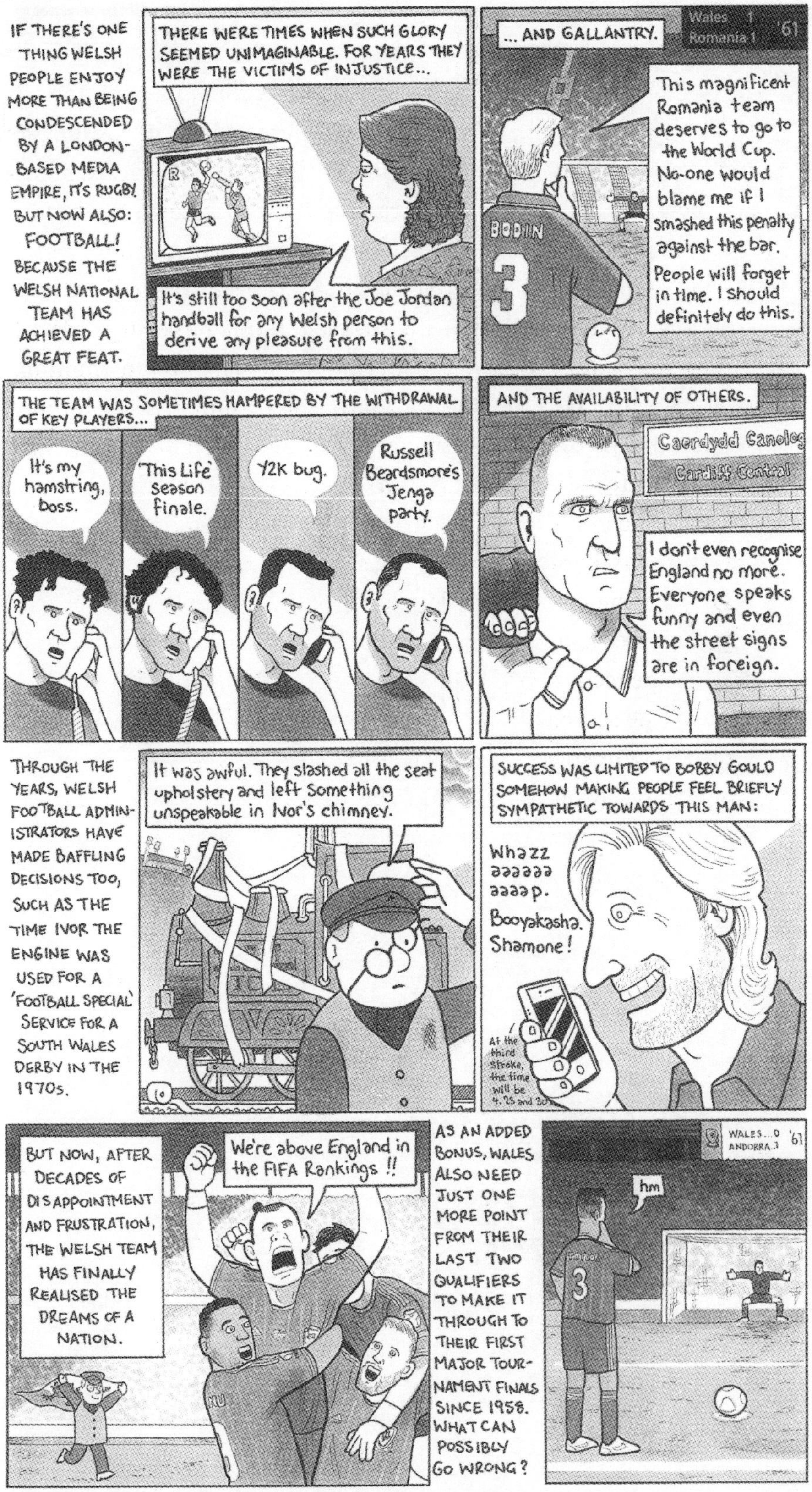
IF THERE'S ONE THING WELSH PEOPLE ENJOY MORE THAN BEING CONDESCENDED BY A LONDON-BASED MEDIA EMPIRE, IT'S RUGBY. BUT NOW ALSO: FOOTBALL! BECAUSE THE WELSH NATIONAL TEAM HAS ACHIEVED A GREAT FEAT.
THERE WERE TIMES WHEN SUCH GLORY SEEMED UNIMAGINABLE. FOR YEARS THEY WERE THE VICTIMS OF INJUSTICE...
It's still too soon after the Joe Jordan handball for any Welsh person to derive any pleasure from this.
... AND GALLANTRY.
Wales 1
Romania 1
'61
This magnificent Romania team deserves to go to the World Cup. No-one would blame me if I smashed this penalty against the bar. People will forget in time. I should definitely do this.
BODIN
3
THE TEAM WAS SOMETIMES HAMPERED BY THE WITHDRAWAL OF KEY PLAYERS...
It's my hamstring, boss.
'This Life' season finale.
Y2K bug.
Russell Beardsmore's Jenga party.
AND THE AVAILABILITY OF OTHERS.
Caerdydd Canolog
Cardiff Central
I don't even recognise England no more. Everyone speaks funny and even the street signs are in foreign.
THROUGH THE YEARS, WELSH FOOTBALL ADMINISTRATORS HAVE MADE BAFFLING DECISIONS TOO, SUCH AS THE TIME IVOR THE ENGINE WAS USED FOR A 'FOOTBALL SPECIAL' SERVICE FOR A SOUTH WALES DERBY IN THE 1970s.
It was awful. They slashed all the seat upholstery and left something unspeakable in Ivor's chimney.
SUCCESS WAS LIMITED TO BOBBY GOULD SOMEHOW MAKING PEOPLE FEEL BRIEFLY SYMPATHETIC TOWARDS THIS MAN:
Whazz aaaaaa aaaap.
Booyakasha.
Shamone!
At the third stroke, the time will be 4.23 and 30
BUT NOW, AFTER DECADES OF DISAPPOINTMENT AND FRUSTRATION, THE WELSH TEAM HAS FINALLY REALISED THE DREAMS OF A NATION.
We're above England in the FIFA Rankings !!
AS AN ADDED BONUS, WALES ALSO NEED JUST ONE MORE POINT FROM THEIR LAST TWO QUALIFIERS TO MAKE IT THROUGH TO THEIR FIRST MAJOR TOURNAMENT FINALS SINCE 1958. WHAT CAN POSSIBLY GO WRONG?
WALES...0
ANDORRA..1
'61
hm
3

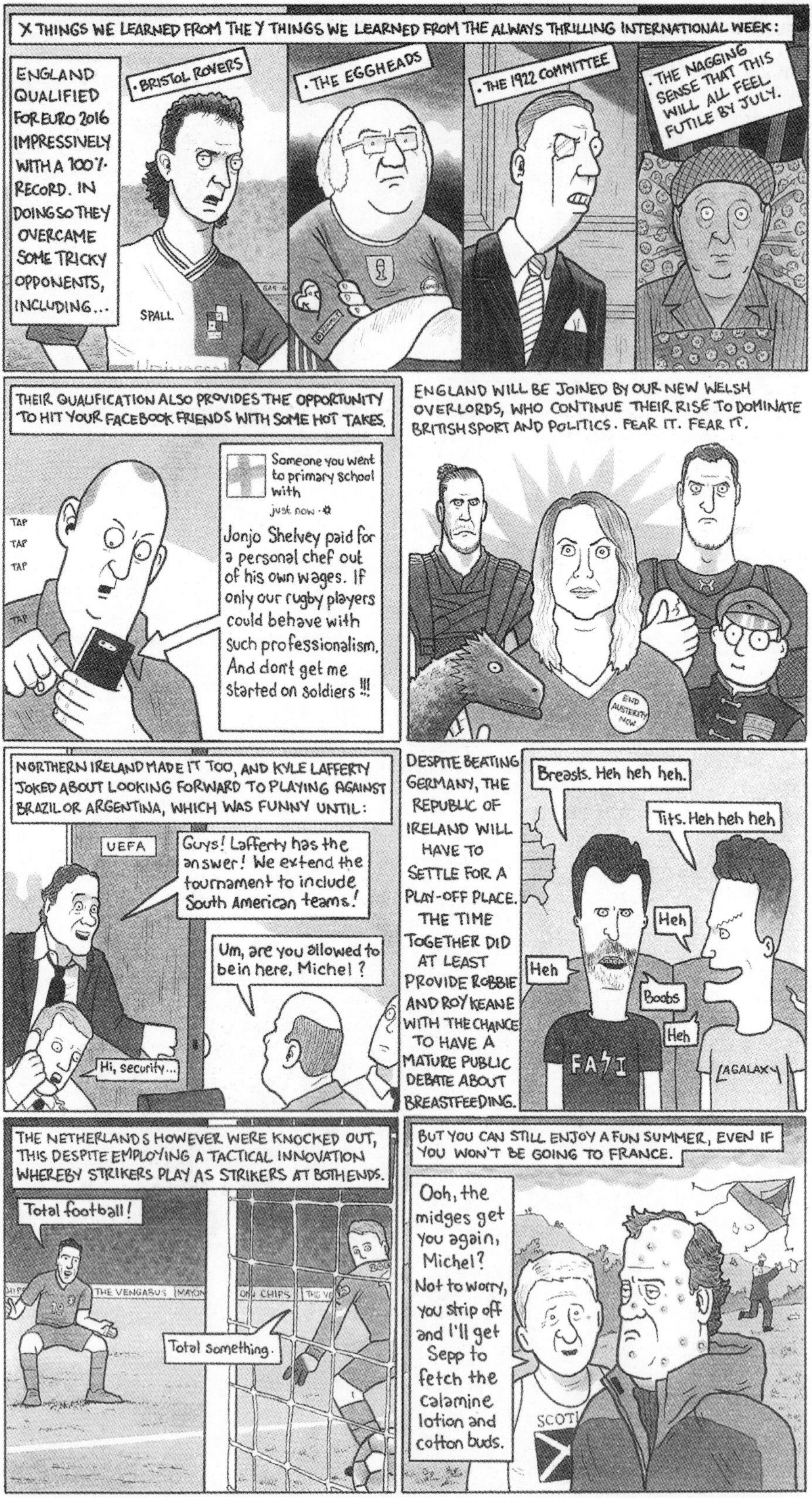
X THINGS WE LEARNED FROM THE Y THINGS WE LEARNED FROM THE ALWAYS THRILLING INTERNATIONAL WEEK:
ENGLAND QUALIFIED FOR EURO 2016 IMPRESSIVELY WITH A 100% RECORD. IN DOING SO THEY OVERCAME SOME TRICKY OPPONENTS, INCLUDING...
• BRISTOL ROVERS
SPALL
• THE EGGHEADS
• THE 1922 COMMITTEE
• THE NAGGING SENSE THAT THIS WILL ALL FEEL FUTILE BY JULY.
THEIR QUALIFICATION ALSO PROVIDES THE OPPORTUNITY TO HIT YOUR FACEBOOK FRIENDS WITH SOME HOT TAKES.
Someone you went to primary school with
just now
Jonjo Shelvey paid for a personal chef out of his own wages. If only our rugby players could behave with such professionalism. And don't get me started on soldiers !!!
TAP
TAP
TAP
TAP
ENGLAND WILL BE JOINED BY OUR NEW WELSH OVERLORDS, WHO CONTINUE THEIR RISE TO DOMINATE BRITISH SPORT AND POLITICS. FEAR IT. FEAR IT.
END AUSTERITY NOW
NORTHERN IRELAND MADE IT TOO, AND KYLE LAFFERTY JOKED ABOUT LOOKING FORWARD TO PLAYING AGAINST BRAZIL OR ARGENTINA, WHICH WAS FUNNY UNTIL:
UEFA
Guys! Lafferty has the answer! We extend the tournament to include South American teams!
Um, are you allowed to be in here, Michel ?
Hi, security...
DESPITE BEATING GERMANY, THE REPUBLIC OF IRELAND WILL HAVE TO SETTLE FOR A PLAY-OFF PLACE. THE TIME TOGETHER DID AT LEAST PROVIDE ROBBIE AND ROY KEANE WITH THE CHANCE TO HAVE A MATURE PUBLIC DEBATE ABOUT BREASTFEEDING.
Breasts. Heh heh heh.
Tits. Heh heh heh
Heh
Heh
Boobs
Heh
FAI
LAGALAXY
THE NETHERLANDS HOWEVER WERE KNOCKED OUT, THIS DESPITE EMPLOYING A TACTICAL INNOVATION WHEREBY STRIKERS PLAY AS STRIKERS AT BOTH ENDS.
Total football!
Total something.
THE VENGABUS
BUT YOU CAN STILL ENJOY A FUN SUMMER, EVEN IF YOU WON'T BE GOING TO FRANCE.
Ooh, the midges get you again, Michel? Not to worry, you strip off and I'll get Sepp to fetch the calamine lotion and cotton buds.
SCOTL

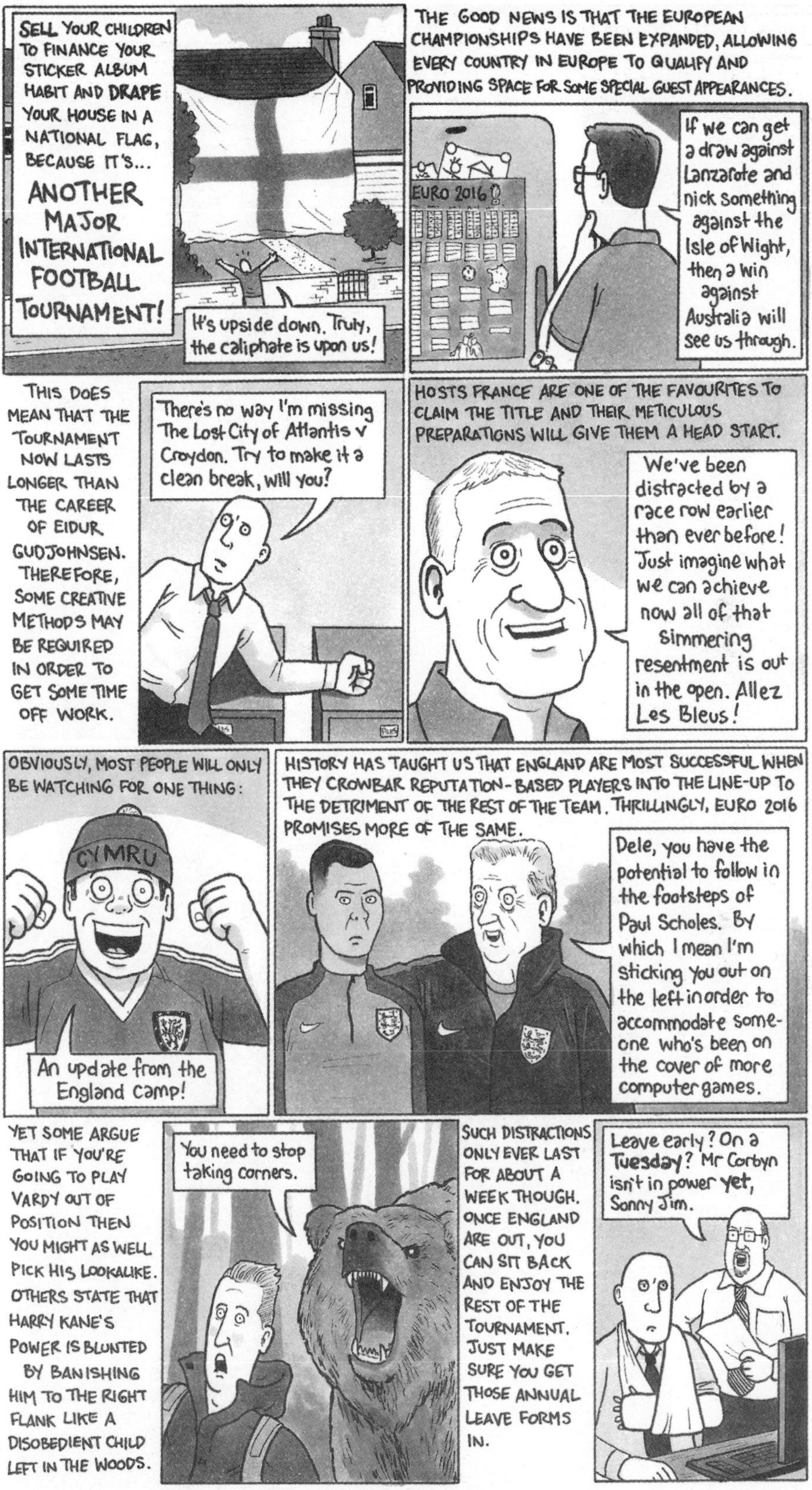
SELL YOUR CHILDREN TO FINANCE YOUR STICKER ALBUM HABIT AND DRAPE YOUR HOUSE IN A NATIONAL FLAG, BECAUSE IT'S... ANOTHER MAJOR INTERNATIONAL FOOTBALL TOURNAMENT!
It's upside down. Truly, the caliphate is upon us!
THE GOOD NEWS IS THAT THE EUROPEAN CHAMPIONSHIPS HAVE BEEN EXPANDED, ALLOWING EVERY COUNTRY IN EUROPE TO QUALIFY AND PROVIDING SPACE FOR SOME SPECIAL GUEST APPEARANCES.
EURO 2016
If we can get a draw against Lanzarote and nick something against the Isle of Wight, then a win against Australia will see us through.
THIS DOES MEAN THAT THE TOURNAMENT NOW LASTS LONGER THAN THE CAREER OF EIDUR GUDJOHNSEN. THEREFORE, SOME CREATIVE METHODS MAY BE REQUIRED IN ORDER TO GET SOME TIME OFF WORK.
There's no way I'm missing The Lost City of Atlantis v Croydon. Try to make it a clean break, will you?
HOSTS FRANCE ARE ONE OF THE FAVOURITES TO CLAIM THE TITLE AND THEIR METICULOUS PREPARATIONS WILL GIVE THEM A HEAD START.
We've been distracted by a race row earlier than ever before! Just imagine what we can achieve now all of that simmering resentment is out in the open. Allez Les Bleus!
OBVIOUSLY, MOST PEOPLE WILL ONLY BE WATCHING FOR ONE THING:
CYMRU
An update from the England camp!
HISTORY HAS TAUGHT US THAT ENGLAND ARE MOST SUCCESSFUL WHEN THEY CROWBAR REPUTATION-BASED PLAYERS INTO THE LINE-UP TO THE DETRIMENT OF THE REST OF THE TEAM. THRILLINGLY, EURO 2016 PROMISES MORE OF THE SAME.
Dele, you have the potential to follow in the footsteps of Paul Scholes. By which I mean I'm sticking you out on the left in order to accommodate someone who's been on the cover of more computer games.
YET SOME ARGUE THAT IF YOU'RE GOING TO PLAY VARDY OUT OF POSITION THEN YOU MIGHT AS WELL PICK HIS LOOKALIKE. OTHERS STATE THAT HARRY KANE'S POWER IS BLUNTED BY BANISHING HIM TO THE RIGHT FLANK LIKE A DISOBEDIENT CHILD LEFT IN THE WOODS.
You need to stop taking corners.
SUCH DISTRACTIONS ONLY EVER LAST FOR ABOUT A WEEK THOUGH. ONCE ENGLAND ARE OUT, YOU CAN SIT BACK AND ENJOY THE REST OF THE TOURNAMENT. JUST MAKE SURE YOU GET THOSE ANNUAL LEAVE FORMS IN.
Leave early? On a Tuesday? Mr Corbyn isn't in power yet, Sonny Jim.

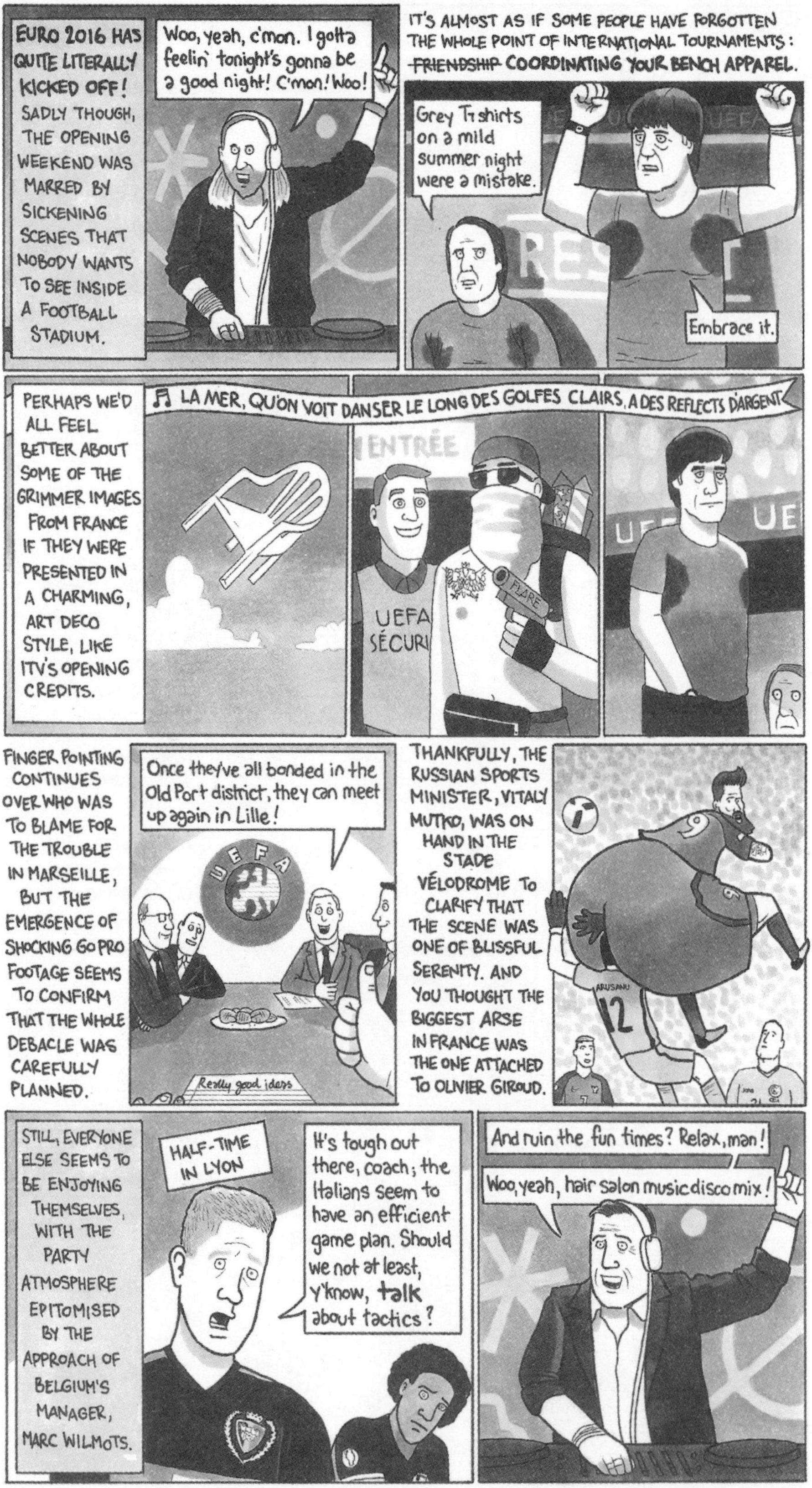
EURO 2016 HAS QUITE LITERALLY KICKED OFF! SADLY THOUGH, THE OPENING WEEKEND WAS MARRED BY SICKENING SCENES THAT NOBODY WANTS TO SEE INSIDE A FOOTBALL STADIUM.
Woo, yeah, c'mon. I gotta feelin' tonight's gonna be a good night! C'mon! Woo!
IT'S ALMOST AS IF SOME PEOPLE HAVE FORGOTTEN THE WHOLE POINT OF INTERNATIONAL TOURNAMENTS: ~~FRIENDSHIP~~ COORDINATING YOUR BENCH APPAREL.
Grey T-shirts on a mild summer night were a mistake.
Embrace it.
PERHAPS WE'D ALL FEEL BETTER ABOUT SOME OF THE GRIMMER IMAGES FROM FRANCE IF THEY WERE PRESENTED IN A CHARMING, ART DECO STYLE, LIKE ITV'S OPENING CREDITS.
♫ LA MER, QU'ON VOIT DANSER LE LONG DES GOLFES CLAIRS, A DES REFLECTS D'ARGENT
ENTRÉE
UEFA SÉCURI
FLARE
UEF
UE
FINGER POINTING CONTINUES OVER WHO WAS TO BLAME FOR THE TROUBLE IN MARSEILLE, BUT THE EMERGENCE OF SHOCKING GO PRO FOOTAGE SEEMS TO CONFIRM THAT THE WHOLE DEBACLE WAS CAREFULLY PLANNED.
Once they've all bonded in the Old Port district, they can meet up again in Lille!
UEFA
Really good ideas
THANKFULLY, THE RUSSIAN SPORTS MINISTER, VITALY MUTKO, WAS ON HAND IN THE STADE VÉLODROME TO CLARIFY THAT THE SCENE WAS ONE OF BLISSFUL SERENITY. AND YOU THOUGHT THE BIGGEST ARSE IN FRANCE WAS THE ONE ATTACHED TO OLIVIER GIROUD.
ARUSANU
12
STILL, EVERYONE ELSE SEEMS TO BE ENJOYING THEMSELVES, WITH THE PARTY ATMOSPHERE EPITOMISED BY THE APPROACH OF BELGIUM'S MANAGER, MARC WILMOTS.
HALF-TIME IN LYON
It's tough out there, coach; the Italians seem to have an efficient game plan. Should we not at least, y'know, talk about tactics?
And ruin the fun times? Relax, man!
Woo, yeah, hair salon music disco mix!

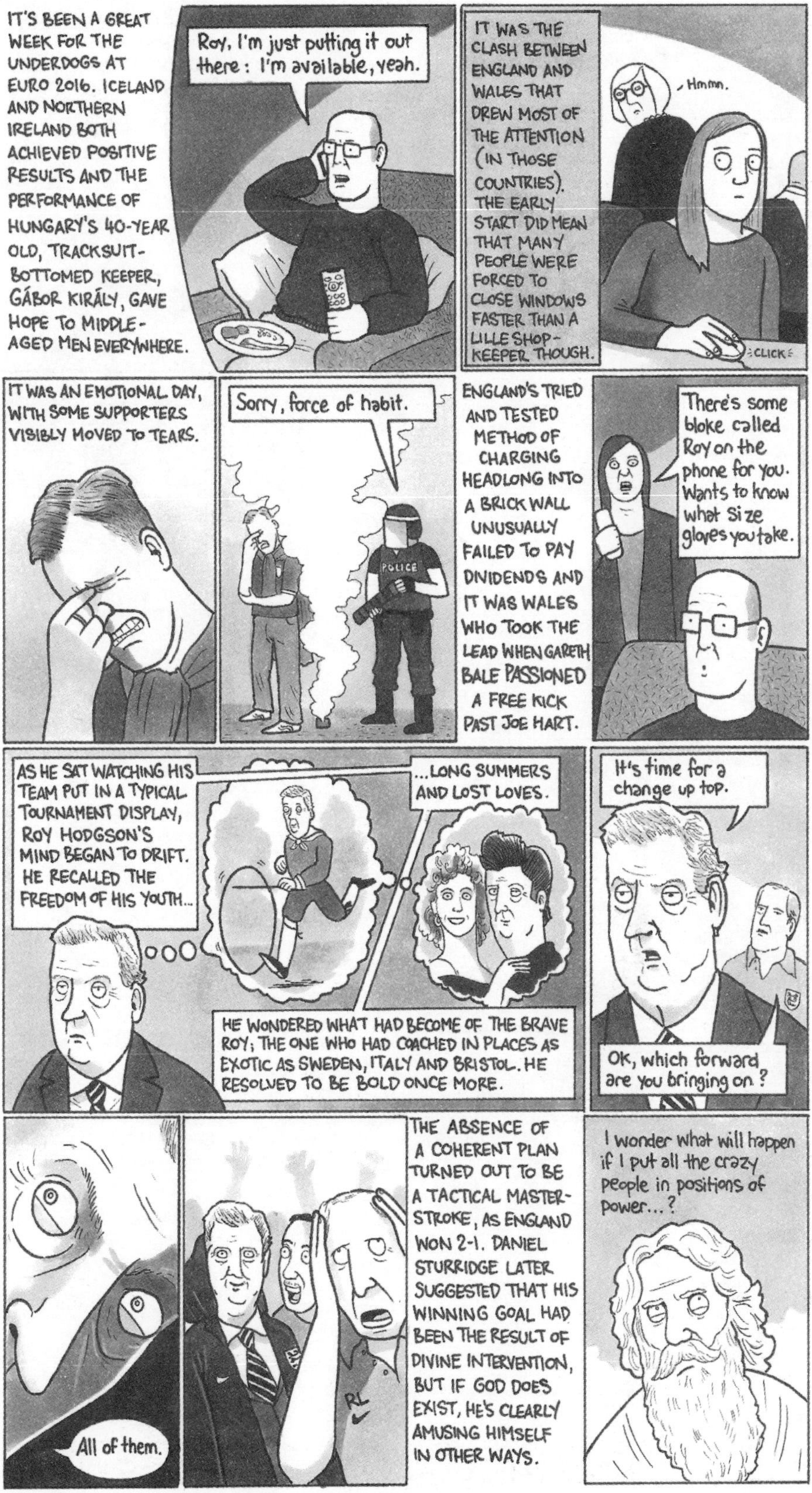
IT'S BEEN A GREAT WEEK FOR THE UNDERDOGS AT EURO 2016. ICELAND AND NORTHERN IRELAND BOTH ACHIEVED POSITIVE RESULTS AND THE PERFORMANCE OF HUNGARY'S 40-YEAR OLD, TRACKSUIT-BOTTOMED KEEPER, GÁBOR KIRÁLY, GAVE HOPE TO MIDDLE-AGED MEN EVERYWHERE.
Roy, I'm just putting it out there : I'm available, yeah.
IT WAS THE CLASH BETWEEN ENGLAND AND WALES THAT DREW MOST OF THE ATTENTION (IN THOSE COUNTRIES). THE EARLY START DID MEAN THAT MANY PEOPLE WERE FORCED TO CLOSE WINDOWS FASTER THAN A LILLE SHOP-KEEPER THOUGH.
Hmmn.
CLICK
IT WAS AN EMOTIONAL DAY, WITH SOME SUPPORTERS VISIBLY MOVED TO TEARS.
Sorry, force of habit.
POLICE
ENGLAND'S TRIED AND TESTED METHOD OF CHARGING HEADLONG INTO A BRICK WALL UNUSUALLY FAILED TO PAY DIVIDENDS AND IT WAS WALES WHO TOOK THE LEAD WHEN GARETH BALE PASSIONED A FREE KICK PAST JOE HART.
There's some bloke called Roy on the phone for you. Wants to know what size gloves you take.
AS HE SAT WATCHING HIS TEAM PUT IN A TYPICAL TOURNAMENT DISPLAY, ROY HODGSON'S MIND BEGAN TO DRIFT. HE RECALLED THE FREEDOM OF HIS YOUTH...
...LONG SUMMERS AND LOST LOVES.
HE WONDERED WHAT HAD BECOME OF THE BRAVE ROY; THE ONE WHO HAD COACHED IN PLACES AS EXOTIC AS SWEDEN, ITALY AND BRISTOL. HE RESOLVED TO BE BOLD ONCE MORE.
It's time for a change up top.
OK, which forward are you bringing on ?
All of them.
RL
THE ABSENCE OF A COHERENT PLAN TURNED OUT TO BE A TACTICAL MASTER-STROKE, AS ENGLAND WON 2-1. DANIEL STURRIDGE LATER SUGGESTED THAT HIS WINNING GOAL HAD BEEN THE RESULT OF DIVINE INTERVENTION, BUT IF GOD DOES EXIST, HE'S CLEARLY AMUSING HIMSELF IN OTHER WAYS.
I wonder what will happen if I put all the crazy people in positions of power...?

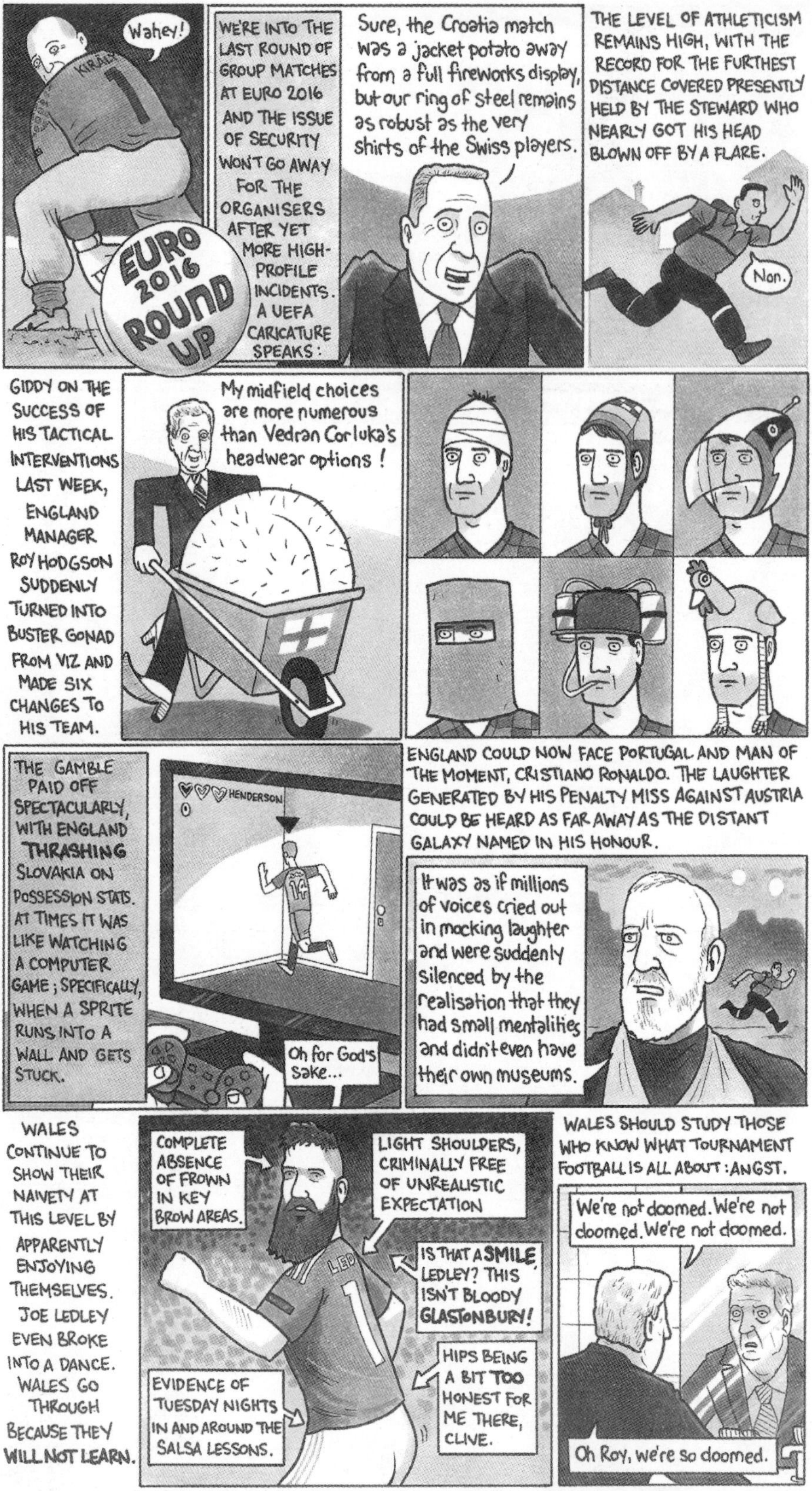
Wahey!
KIRALY
1
EURO 2016 ROUND UP
WE'RE INTO THE LAST ROUND OF GROUP MATCHES AT EURO 2016 AND THE ISSUE OF SECURITY WON'T GO AWAY FOR THE ORGANISERS AFTER YET MORE HIGH-PROFILE INCIDENTS. A UEFA CARICATURE SPEAKS:
Sure, the Croatia match was a jacket potato away from a full fireworks display, but our ring of steel remains as robust as the very shirts of the Swiss players.
THE LEVEL OF ATHLETICISM REMAINS HIGH, WITH THE RECORD FOR THE FURTHEST DISTANCE COVERED PRESENTLY HELD BY THE STEWARD WHO NEARLY GOT HIS HEAD BLOWN OFF BY A FLARE.
Non.
GIDDY ON THE SUCCESS OF HIS TACTICAL INTERVENTIONS LAST WEEK, ENGLAND MANAGER ROY HODGSON SUDDENLY TURNED INTO BUSTER GONAD FROM VIZ AND MADE SIX CHANGES TO HIS TEAM.
My midfield choices are more numerous than Vedran Corluka's headwear options!
THE GAMBLE PAID OFF SPECTACULARLY, WITH ENGLAND THRASHING SLOVAKIA ON POSSESSION STATS. AT TIMES IT WAS LIKE WATCHING A COMPUTER GAME; SPECIFICALLY, WHEN A SPRITE RUNS INTO A WALL AND GETS STUCK.
HENDERSON
0
14
Oh for God's sake...
ENGLAND COULD NOW FACE PORTUGAL AND MAN OF THE MOMENT, CRISTIANO RONALDO. THE LAUGHTER GENERATED BY HIS PENALTY MISS AGAINST AUSTRIA COULD BE HEARD AS FAR AWAY AS THE DISTANT GALAXY NAMED IN HIS HONOUR.
It was as if millions of voices cried out in mocking laughter and were suddenly silenced by the realisation that they had small mentalities and didn't even have their own museums.
WALES CONTINUE TO SHOW THEIR NAIVETY AT THIS LEVEL BY APPARENTLY ENJOYING THEMSELVES. JOE LEDLEY EVEN BROKE INTO A DANCE. WALES GO THROUGH BECAUSE THEY WILL NOT LEARN.
COMPLETE ABSENCE OF FROWN IN KEY BROW AREAS.
LIGHT SHOULDERS, CRIMINALLY FREE OF UNREALISTIC EXPECTATION
LED
1
IS THAT A SMILE, LEDLEY? THIS ISN'T BLOODY GLASTONBURY!
EVIDENCE OF TUESDAY NIGHTS IN AND AROUND THE SALSA LESSONS.
HIPS BEING A BIT TOO HONEST FOR ME THERE, CLIVE.
WALES SHOULD STUDY THOSE WHO KNOW WHAT TOURNAMENT FOOTBALL IS ALL ABOUT: ANGST.
We're not doomed. We're not doomed. We're not doomed.
Oh Roy, we're so doomed.

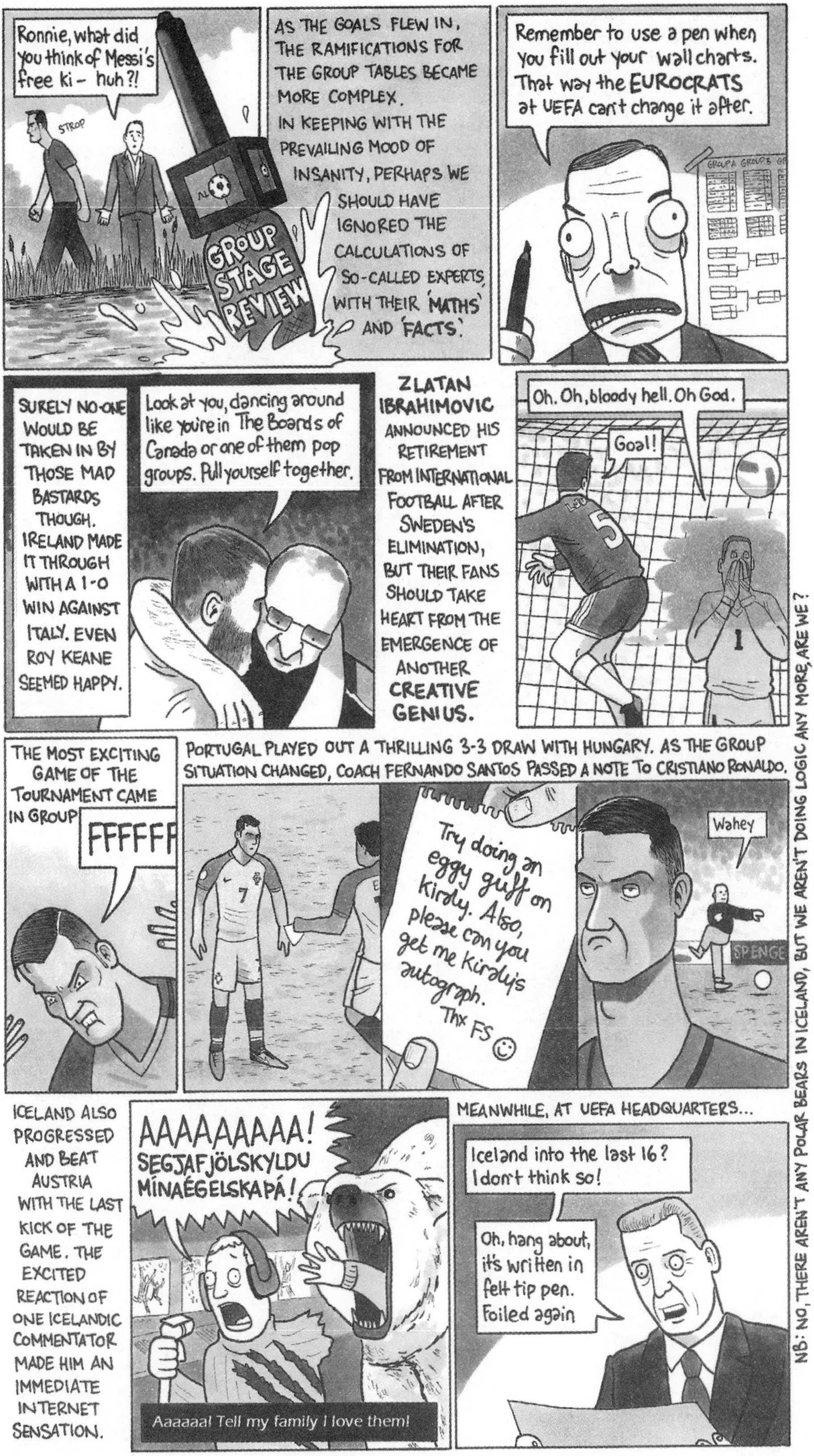
Ronnie, what did you think of Messi's free ki- huh?!
STROP
GROUP STAGE REVIEW
AS THE GOALS FLEW IN, THE RAMIFICATIONS FOR THE GROUP TABLES BECAME MORE COMPLEX.
IN KEEPING WITH THE PREVAILING MOOD OF INSANITY, PERHAPS WE SHOULD HAVE IGNORED THE CALCULATIONS OF SO-CALLED EXPERTS, WITH THEIR 'MATHS' AND 'FACTS'.
Remember to use a pen when you fill out your wall charts. That way the EUROCRATS at UEFA can't change it after.
SURELY NO-ONE WOULD BE TAKEN IN BY THOSE MAD BASTARDS THOUGH. IRELAND MADE IT THROUGH WITH A 1-0 WIN AGAINST ITALY. EVEN ROY KEANE SEEMED HAPPY.
Look at you, dancing around like you're in The Boards of Canada or one of them pop groups. Pull yourself together.
ZLATAN IBRAHIMOVIC ANNOUNCED HIS RETIREMENT FROM INTERNATIONAL FOOTBALL AFTER SWEDEN'S ELIMINATION, BUT THEIR FANS SHOULD TAKE HEART FROM THE EMERGENCE OF ANOTHER CREATIVE GENIUS.
Oh. Oh, bloody hell. Oh God.
Goal!
THE MOST EXCITING GAME OF THE TOURNAMENT CAME IN GROUP
FFFFFF
PORTUGAL PLAYED OUT A THRILLING 3-3 DRAW WITH HUNGARY. AS THE GROUP SITUATION CHANGED, COACH FERNANDO SANTOS PASSED A NOTE TO CRISTIANO RONALDO.
Try doing an eggy guff on Kiraly. Also, please can you get me Kiraly's autograph. Thx FS
Wahey
SPENGE
ICELAND ALSO PROGRESSED AND BEAT AUSTRIA WITH THE LAST KICK OF THE GAME. THE EXCITED REACTION OF ONE ICELANDIC COMMENTATOR MADE HIM AN IMMEDIATE INTERNET SENSATION.
AAAAAAAAA! SEGJAFJÖLSKYLDU MÍNAÉGELSKAPÁ!
Aaaaaa! Tell my family I love them!
MEANWHILE, AT UEFA HEADQUARTERS...
Iceland into the last 16? I don't think so!
Oh, hang about, it's written in felt tip pen. Foiled again
NB: NO, THERE AREN'T ANY POLAR BEARS IN ICELAND, BUT WE AREN'T DOING LOGIC ANY MORE, ARE WE?

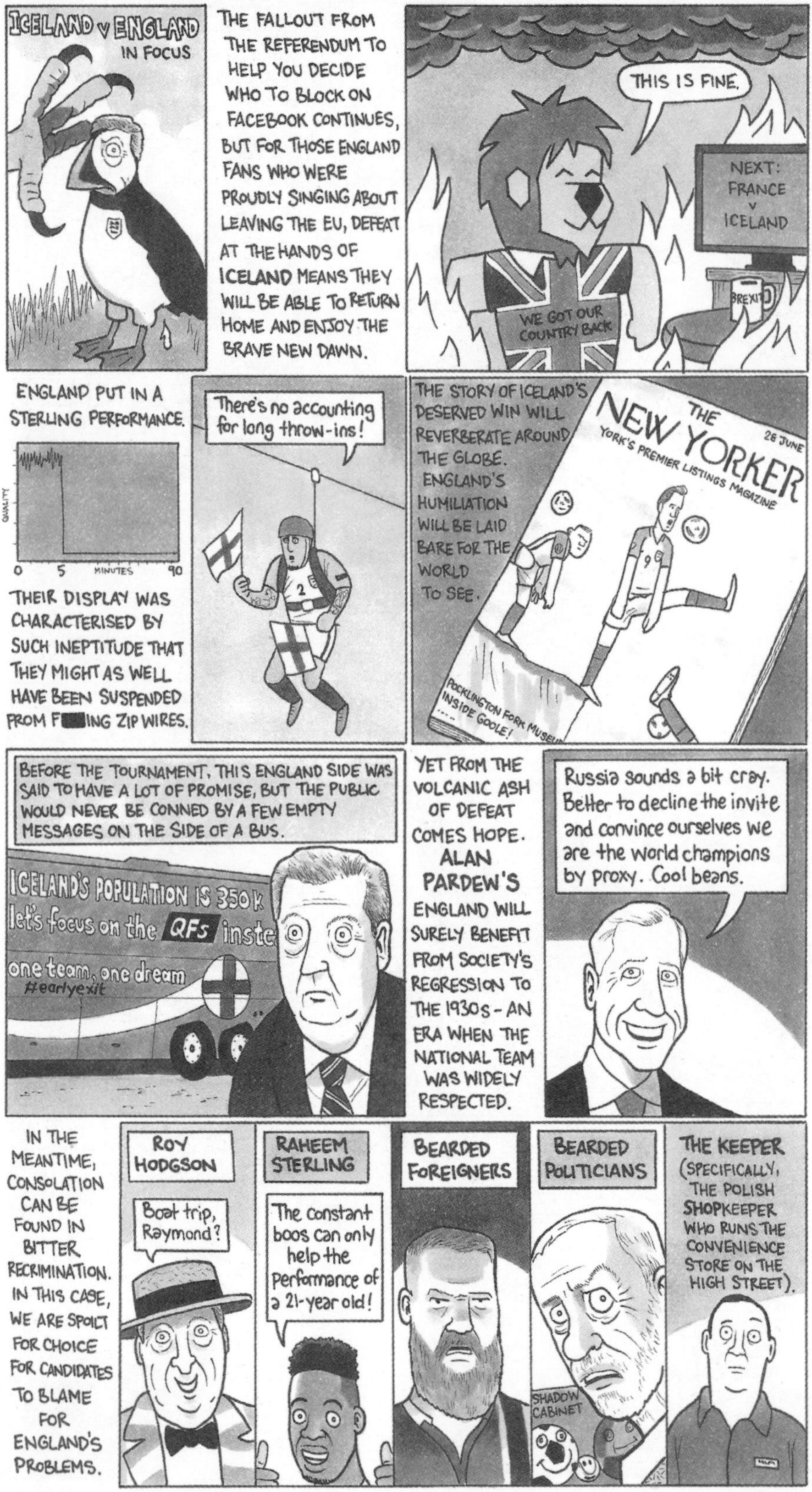
ICELAND v ENGLAND
IN FOCUS
THE FALLOUT FROM THE REFERENDUM TO HELP YOU DECIDE WHO TO BLOCK ON FACEBOOK CONTINUES, BUT FOR THOSE ENGLAND FANS WHO WERE PROUDLY SINGING ABOUT LEAVING THE EU, DEFEAT AT THE HANDS OF ICELAND MEANS THEY WILL BE ABLE TO RETURN HOME AND ENJOY THE BRAVE NEW DAWN.
THIS IS FINE.
NEXT: FRANCE v ICELAND
WE GOT OUR COUNTRY BACK
BREXIT
ENGLAND PUT IN A STERLING PERFORMANCE.
QUALITY
0 5 MINUTES 90
THEIR DISPLAY WAS CHARACTERISED BY SUCH INEPTITUDE THAT THEY MIGHT AS WELL HAVE BEEN SUSPENDED FROM F[redacted]ING ZIP WIRES.
There's no accounting for long throw-ins!
2
THE STORY OF ICELAND'S DESERVED WIN WILL REVERBERATE AROUND THE GLOBE. ENGLAND'S HUMILIATION WILL BE LAID BARE FOR THE WORLD TO SEE.
THE NEW YORKER
26 JUNE
YORK'S PREMIER LISTINGS MAGAZINE
9
POCKLINGTON FORK MUSEUM INSIDE GOOLE!
BEFORE THE TOURNAMENT, THIS ENGLAND SIDE WAS SAID TO HAVE A LOT OF PROMISE, BUT THE PUBLIC WOULD NEVER BE CONNED BY A FEW EMPTY MESSAGES ON THE SIDE OF A BUS.
ICELAND'S POPULATION IS 350k
let's focus on the QFs inste
one team, one dream
#earlyexit
YET FROM THE VOLCANIC ASH OF DEFEAT COMES HOPE. ALAN PARDEW'S ENGLAND WILL SURELY BENEFIT FROM SOCIETY'S REGRESSION TO THE 1930s - AN ERA WHEN THE NATIONAL TEAM WAS WIDELY RESPECTED.
Russia sounds a bit cray. Better to decline the invite and convince ourselves we are the world champions by proxy. Cool beans.
IN THE MEANTIME, CONSOLATION CAN BE FOUND IN BITTER RECRIMINATION. IN THIS CASE, WE ARE SPOILT FOR CHOICE FOR CANDIDATES TO BLAME FOR ENGLAND'S PROBLEMS.
ROY HODGSON
Boat trip, Raymond?
RAHEEM STERLING
The constant boos can only help the performance of a 21-year old!
BEARDED FOREIGNERS
BEARDED POLITICIANS
SHADOW CABINET
THE KEEPER (SPECIFICALLY, THE POLISH SHOPKEEPER WHO RUNS THE CONVENIENCE STORE ON THE HIGH STREET).

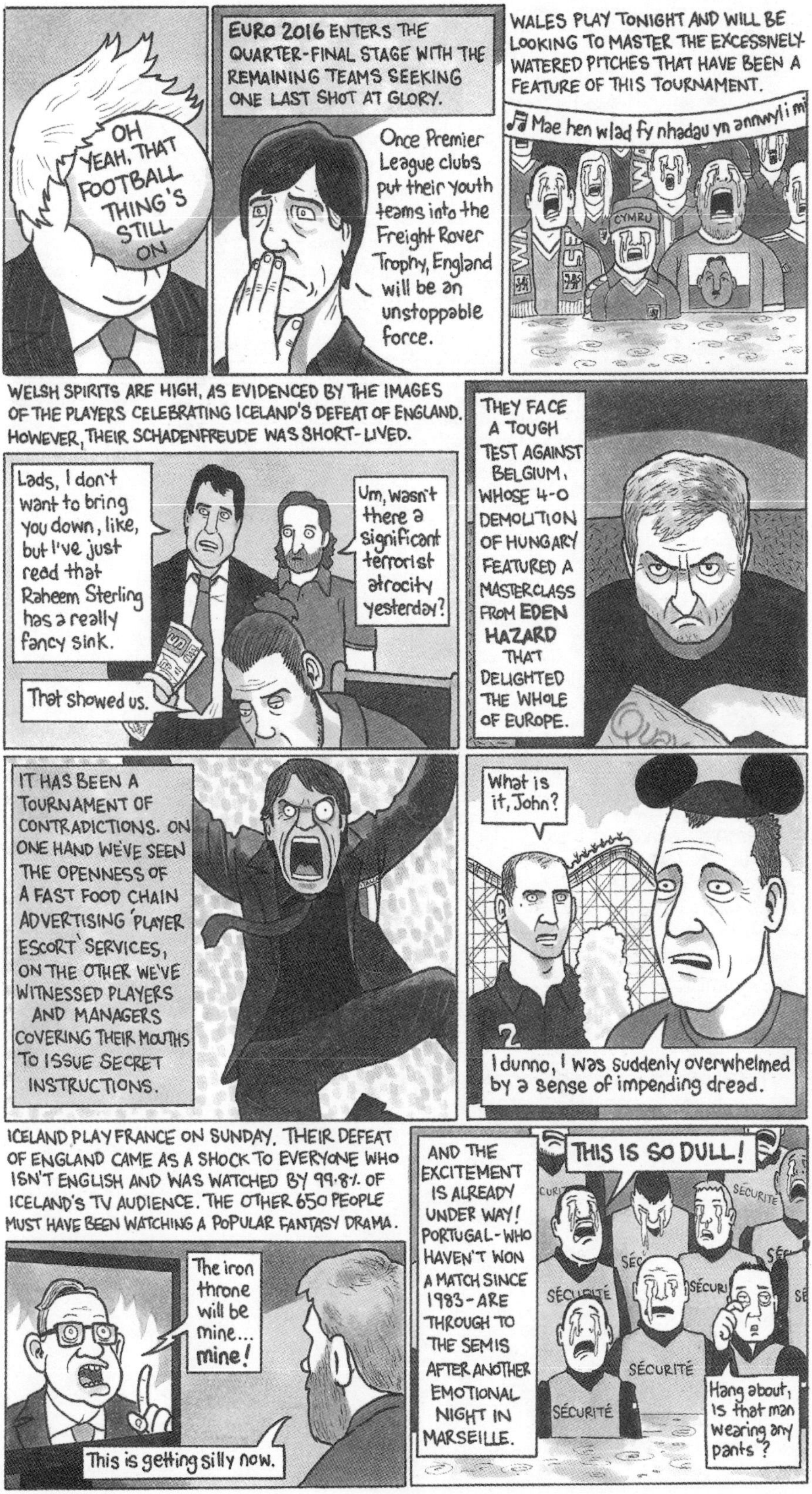
OH YEAH, THAT FOOTBALL THING'S STILL ON
EURO 2016 ENTERS THE QUARTER-FINAL STAGE WITH THE REMAINING TEAMS SEEKING ONE LAST SHOT AT GLORY.
Once Premier League clubs put their youth teams into the Freight Rover Trophy, England will be an unstoppable force.
WALES PLAY TONIGHT AND WILL BE LOOKING TO MASTER THE EXCESSIVELY-WATERED PITCHES THAT HAVE BEEN A FEATURE OF THIS TOURNAMENT.
♫ Mae hen wlad fy nhadau yn annwyl i mi
CYMRU
WELSH SPIRITS ARE HIGH, AS EVIDENCED BY THE IMAGES OF THE PLAYERS CELEBRATING ICELAND'S DEFEAT OF ENGLAND. HOWEVER, THEIR SCHADENFREUDE WAS SHORT-LIVED.
Lads, I don't want to bring you down, like, but I've just read that Raheem Sterling has a really fancy sink.
Um, wasn't there a significant terrorist atrocity yesterday?
That showed us.
THEY FACE A TOUGH TEST AGAINST BELGIUM, WHOSE 4-0 DEMOLITION OF HUNGARY FEATURED A MASTERCLASS FROM EDEN HAZARD THAT DELIGHTED THE WHOLE OF EUROPE.
IT HAS BEEN A TOURNAMENT OF CONTRADICTIONS. ON ONE HAND WE'VE SEEN THE OPENNESS OF A FAST FOOD CHAIN ADVERTISING 'PLAYER ESCORT' SERVICES, ON THE OTHER WE'VE WITNESSED PLAYERS AND MANAGERS COVERING THEIR MOUTHS TO ISSUE SECRET INSTRUCTIONS.
What is it, John?
I dunno, I was suddenly overwhelmed by a sense of impending dread.
ICELAND PLAY FRANCE ON SUNDAY. THEIR DEFEAT OF ENGLAND CAME AS A SHOCK TO EVERYONE WHO ISN'T ENGLISH AND WAS WATCHED BY 99.8% OF ICELAND'S TV AUDIENCE. THE OTHER 650 PEOPLE MUST HAVE BEEN WATCHING A POPULAR FANTASY DRAMA.
The iron throne will be mine... mine!
This is getting silly now.
AND THE EXCITEMENT IS ALREADY UNDER WAY! PORTUGAL - WHO HAVEN'T WON A MATCH SINCE 1983 - ARE THROUGH TO THE SEMIS AFTER ANOTHER EMOTIONAL NIGHT IN MARSEILLE.
THIS IS SO DULL!
SÉCURITÉ
Hang about, is that man wearing any pants?

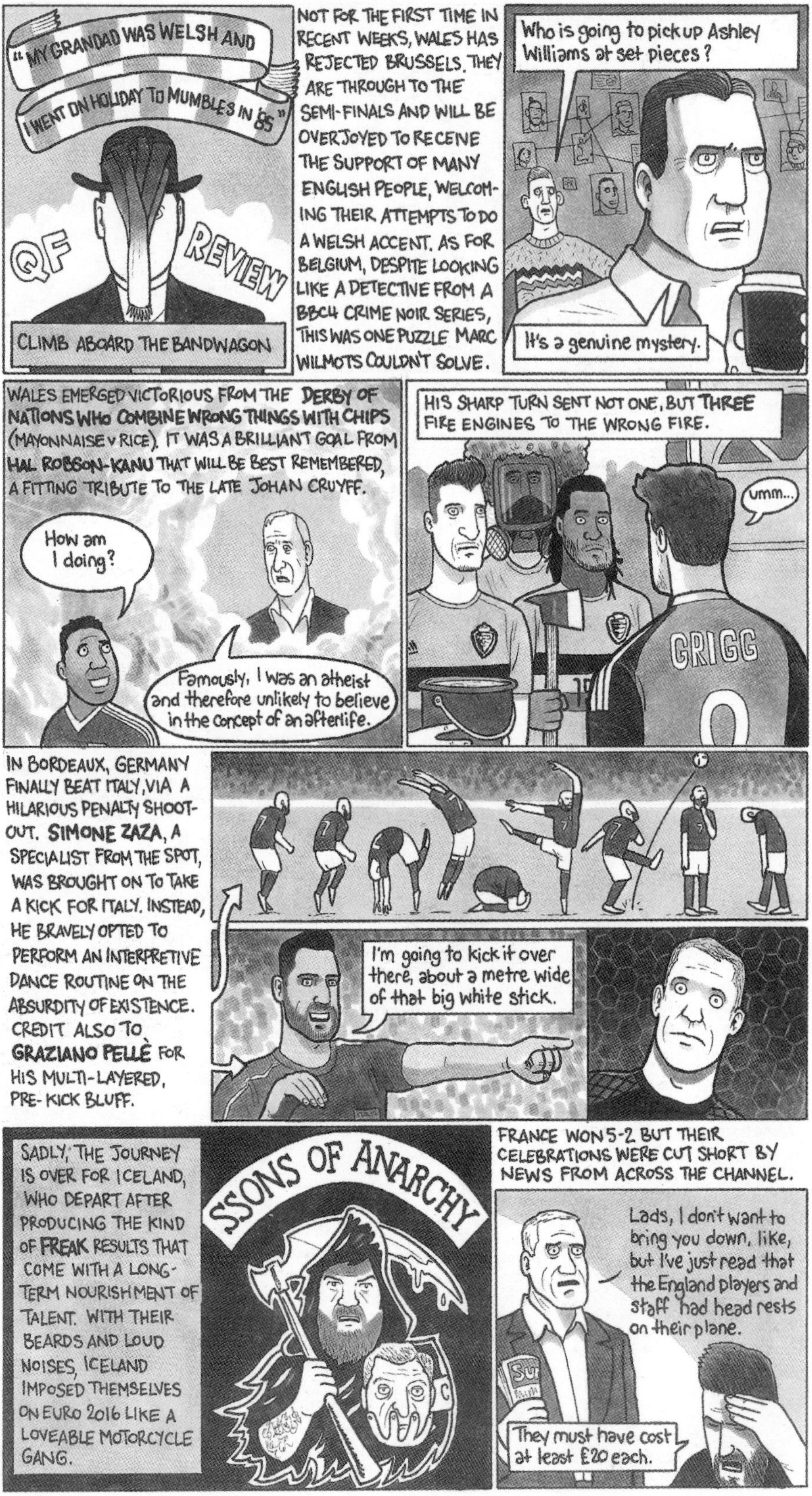

"MY GRANDAD WAS WELSH AND I WENT ON HOLIDAY TO MUMBLES IN '85"
QF REVIEW
CLIMB ABOARD THE BANDWAGON
NOT FOR THE FIRST TIME IN RECENT WEEKS, WALES HAS REJECTED BRUSSELS. THEY ARE THROUGH TO THE SEMI-FINALS AND WILL BE OVERJOYED TO RECEIVE THE SUPPORT OF MANY ENGLISH PEOPLE, WELCOMING THEIR ATTEMPTS TO DO A WELSH ACCENT. AS FOR BELGIUM, DESPITE LOOKING LIKE A DETECTIVE FROM A BBC4 CRIME NOIR SERIES, THIS WAS ONE PUZZLE MARC WILMOTS COULDN'T SOLVE.
Who is going to pick up Ashley Williams at set pieces?
It's a genuine mystery.
WALES EMERGED VICTORIOUS FROM THE DERBY OF NATIONS WHO COMBINE WRONG THINGS WITH CHIPS (MAYONNAISE V RICE). IT WAS A BRILLIANT GOAL FROM HAL ROBSON-KANU THAT WILL BE BEST REMEMBERED, A FITTING TRIBUTE TO THE LATE JOHAN CRUYFF.
How am I doing?
Famously, I was an atheist and therefore unlikely to believe in the concept of an afterlife.
HIS SHARP TURN SENT NOT ONE, BUT THREE FIRE ENGINES TO THE WRONG FIRE.
umm...
GRIGG
IN BORDEAUX, GERMANY FINALLY BEAT ITALY, VIA A HILARIOUS PENALTY SHOOT-OUT. SIMONE ZAZA, A SPECIALIST FROM THE SPOT, WAS BROUGHT ON TO TAKE A KICK FOR ITALY. INSTEAD, HE BRAVELY OPTED TO PERFORM AN INTERPRETIVE DANCE ROUTINE ON THE ABSURDITY OF EXISTENCE. CREDIT ALSO TO GRAZIANO PELLÈ FOR HIS MULTI-LAYERED, PRE-KICK BLUFF.
I'm going to kick it over there, about a metre wide of that big white stick.
SADLY, THE JOURNEY IS OVER FOR ICELAND, WHO DEPART AFTER PRODUCING THE KIND OF FREAK RESULTS THAT COME WITH A LONG-TERM NOURISHMENT OF TALENT. WITH THEIR BEARDS AND LOUD NOISES, ICELAND IMPOSED THEMSELVES ON EURO 2016 LIKE A LOVEABLE MOTORCYCLE GANG.
SSONS OF ANARCHY
FRANCE WON 5-2 BUT THEIR CELEBRATIONS WERE CUT SHORT BY NEWS FROM ACROSS THE CHANNEL.
Lads, I don't want to bring you down, like, but I've just read that the England players and staff had head rests on their plane.
They must have cost at least £20 each.

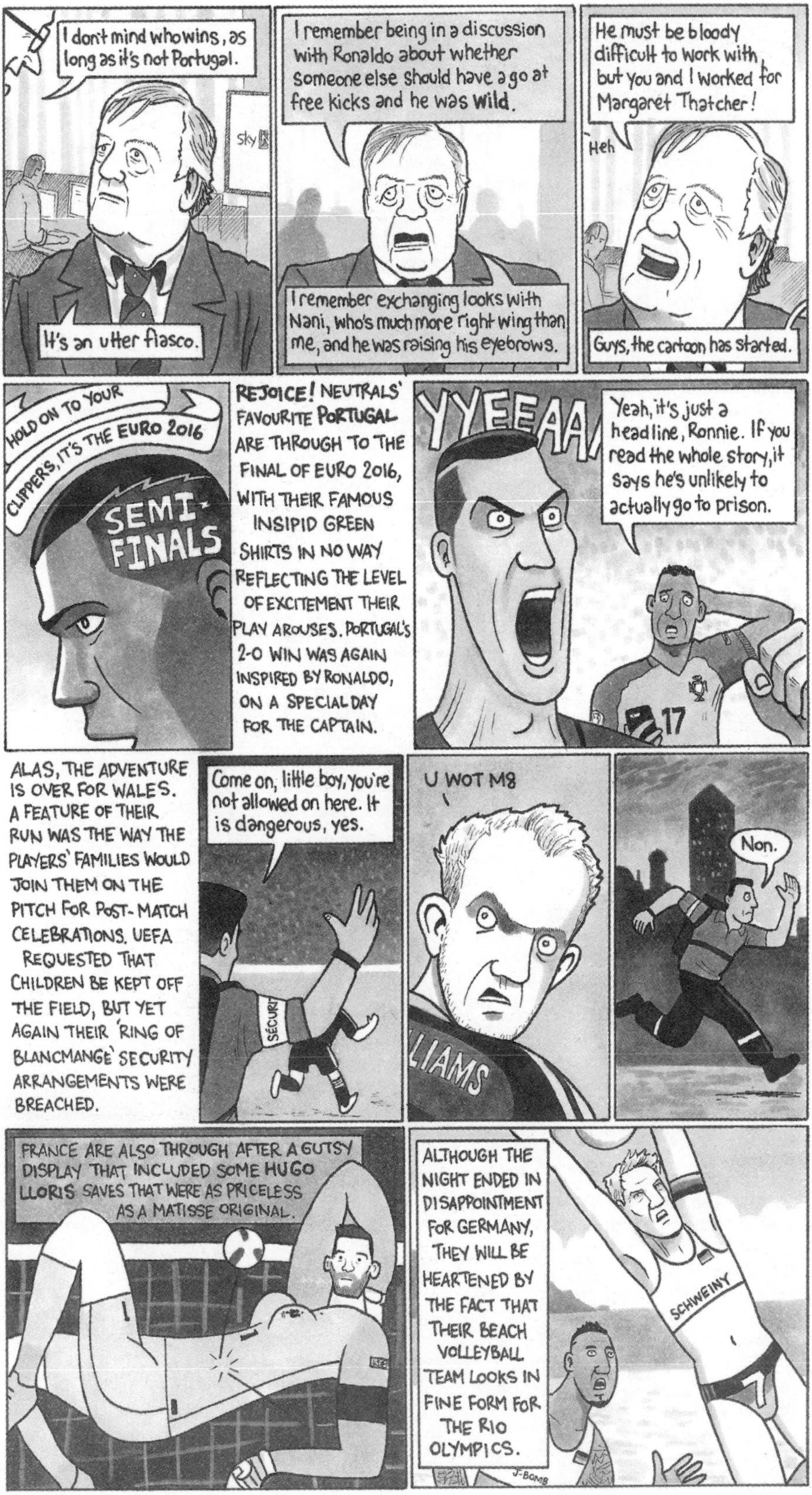
I don't mind who wins, as long as it's not Portugal.
It's an utter fiasco.
I remember being in a discussion with Ronaldo about whether someone else should have a go at free kicks and he was wild.
I remember exchanging looks with Nani, who's much more right wing than me, and he was raising his eyebrows.
He must be bloody difficult to work with but you and I worked for Margaret Thatcher!
Heh
Guys, the cartoon has started.
HOLD ON TO YOUR CLIPPERS, IT'S THE EURO 2016
SEMI-FINALS
REJOICE! NEUTRALS' FAVOURITE PORTUGAL ARE THROUGH TO THE FINAL OF EURO 2016, WITH THEIR FAMOUS INSIPID GREEN SHIRTS IN NO WAY REFLECTING THE LEVEL OF EXCITEMENT THEIR PLAY AROUSES. PORTUGAL'S 2-0 WIN WAS AGAIN INSPIRED BY RONALDO, ON A SPECIAL DAY FOR THE CAPTAIN.
YYEEAAA
Yeah, it's just a headline, Ronnie. If you read the whole story, it says he's unlikely to actually go to prison.
17
ALAS, THE ADVENTURE IS OVER FOR WALES. A FEATURE OF THEIR RUN WAS THE WAY THE PLAYERS' FAMILIES WOULD JOIN THEM ON THE PITCH FOR POST-MATCH CELEBRATIONS. UEFA REQUESTED THAT CHILDREN BE KEPT OFF THE FIELD, BUT YET AGAIN THEIR 'RING OF BLANCMANGE' SECURITY ARRANGEMENTS WERE BREACHED.
Come on, little boy, you're not allowed on here. It is dangerous, yes.
U WOT M8
LIAMS
Non.
FRANCE ARE ALSO THROUGH AFTER A GUTSY DISPLAY THAT INCLUDED SOME HUGO LLORIS SAVES THAT WERE AS PRICELESS AS A MATISSE ORIGINAL.
ALTHOUGH THE NIGHT ENDED IN DISAPPOINTMENT FOR GERMANY, THEY WILL BE HEARTENED BY THE FACT THAT THEIR BEACH VOLLEYBALL TEAM LOOKS IN FINE FORM FOR THE RIO OLYMPICS.
SCHWEINY
J-BOMB

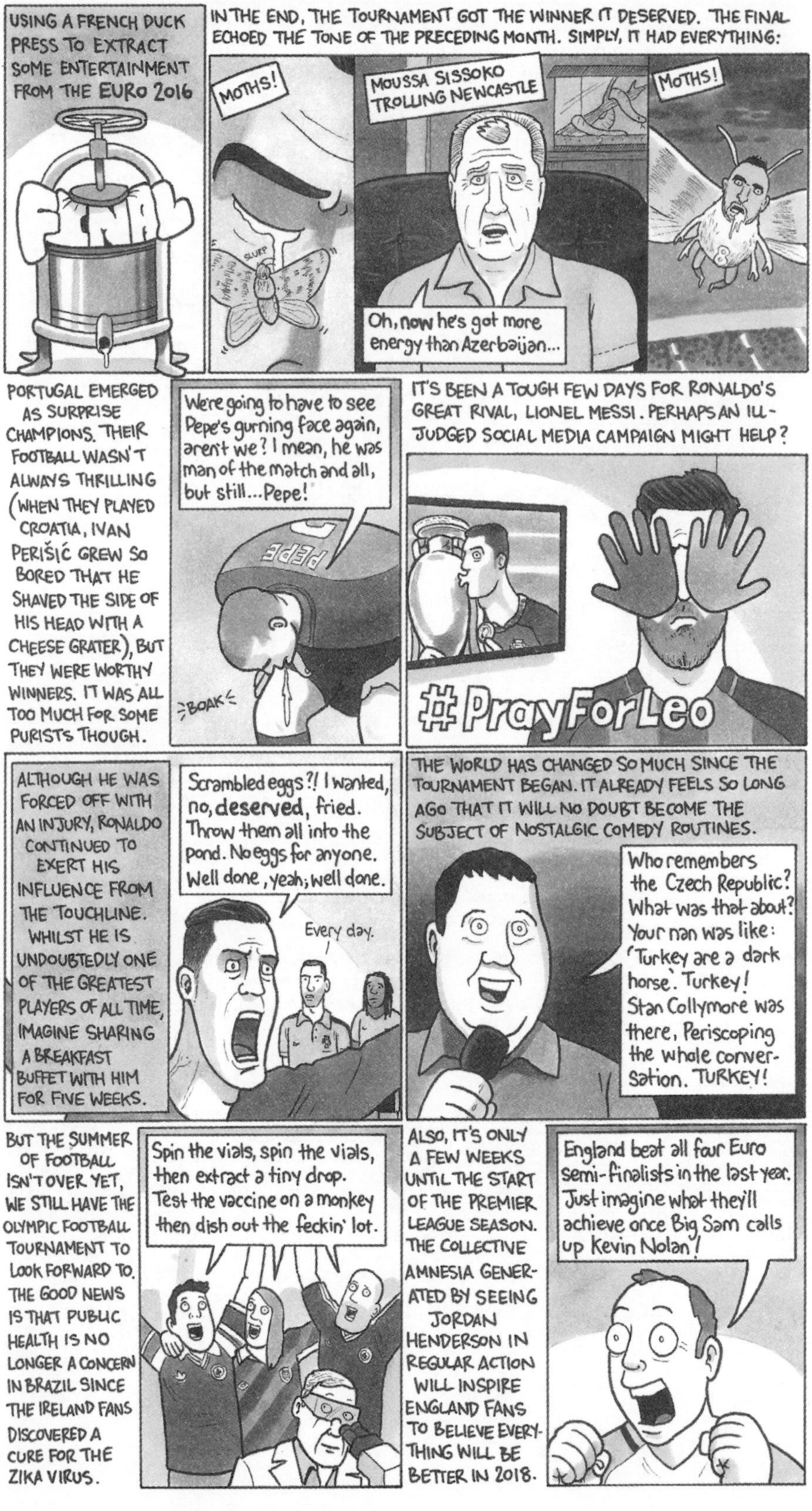
USING A FRENCH DUCK PRESS TO EXTRACT SOME ENTERTAINMENT FROM THE EURO 2016
FINAL
IN THE END, THE TOURNAMENT GOT THE WINNER IT DESERVED. THE FINAL ECHOED THE TONE OF THE PRECEDING MONTH. SIMPLY, IT HAD EVERYTHING:
MOTHS!
SLURP
MOUSSA SISSOKO TROLLING NEWCASTLE
Oh, now he's got more energy than Azerbaijan...
MOTHS!
PORTUGAL EMERGED AS SURPRISE CHAMPIONS. THEIR FOOTBALL WASN'T ALWAYS THRILLING (WHEN THEY PLAYED CROATIA, IVAN PERIŠIĆ GREW SO BORED THAT HE SHAVED THE SIDE OF HIS HEAD WITH A CHEESE GRATER), BUT THEY WERE WORTHY WINNERS. IT WAS ALL TOO MUCH FOR SOME PURISTS THOUGH.
We're going to have to see Pepe's gurning face again, aren't we? I mean, he was man of the match and all, but still... Pepe!
PEPE
BOAK
IT'S BEEN A TOUGH FEW DAYS FOR RONALDO'S GREAT RIVAL, LIONEL MESSI. PERHAPS AN ILL-JUDGED SOCIAL MEDIA CAMPAIGN MIGHT HELP?
#PrayForLeo
ALTHOUGH HE WAS FORCED OFF WITH AN INJURY, RONALDO CONTINUED TO EXERT HIS INFLUENCE FROM THE TOUCHLINE. WHILST HE IS UNDOUBTEDLY ONE OF THE GREATEST PLAYERS OF ALL TIME, IMAGINE SHARING A BREAKFAST BUFFET WITH HIM FOR FIVE WEEKS.
Scrambled eggs?! I wanted, no, deserved, fried. Throw them all into the pond. No eggs for anyone. Well done, yeah; well done.
Every day.
THE WORLD HAS CHANGED SO MUCH SINCE THE TOURNAMENT BEGAN. IT ALREADY FEELS SO LONG AGO THAT IT WILL NO DOUBT BECOME THE SUBJECT OF NOSTALGIC COMEDY ROUTINES.
Who remembers the Czech Republic? What was that about? Your nan was like: 'Turkey are a dark horse'. Turkey! Stan Collymore was there, Periscoping the whole conversation. TURKEY!
BUT THE SUMMER OF FOOTBALL ISN'T OVER YET, WE STILL HAVE THE OLYMPIC FOOTBALL TOURNAMENT TO LOOK FORWARD TO. THE GOOD NEWS IS THAT PUBLIC HEALTH IS NO LONGER A CONCERN IN BRAZIL SINCE THE IRELAND FANS DISCOVERED A CURE FOR THE ZIKA VIRUS.
Spin the vials, spin the vials, then extract a tiny drop. Test the vaccine on a monkey then dish out the feckin' lot.
ALSO, IT'S ONLY A FEW WEEKS UNTIL THE START OF THE PREMIER LEAGUE SEASON. THE COLLECTIVE AMNESIA GENERATED BY SEEING JORDAN HENDERSON IN REGULAR ACTION WILL INSPIRE ENGLAND FANS TO BELIEVE EVERYTHING WILL BE BETTER IN 2018.
England beat all four Euro semi-finalists in the last year. Just imagine what they'll achieve once Big Sam calls up Kevin Nolan!

JOSÉ MOURINHO

José Mourinho is the perfect manager for whatever awful age we're living through, a period so depressing that no one can even face giving this decade a nickname. The 'twenty-tens' doesn't quite scan, the 'tweenies' is inappropriately cute. The 'oh what nows' could be a goer, but people are too busy for three syllables.

Negative, cynical, disingenuous; by right, Mourinho's aptitude for doublespeak should have seen him elevated to a senior position in the UK government years ago. Clubs who can't afford his wage demands might as well appoint Michael Gove instead: that spongey little bastard will state the exact opposite of what you can see with your own eyes, and he'll do it for a fraction of the price. Just endured ninety minutes of Mourinho's team sitting deep and playing for a goalless draw at home? It was the opposition's fault. Knocked out of a tournament because of an aversion to attack? The fans were too quiet. Your expensive star player is played out of position and is unable to express himself? Luke Shaw's fat.

Some of José's outbursts are almost Trumpist in their duplicity. Perhaps the only surprising thing about Mourinho is that his regular assaults on the football media haven't yet included the term 'fake news'. He even worked as a summariser for Russia Today during the 2018 World Cup. If he starts organising mid-season rallies in aircraft hangars to help boost his ego, then we know it's time to hide his phone and put a parental lock on his television. At least he's not on Twitter, and although Manchester United sell a lot of replica shirts, they haven't yet developed intercontinental nuclear weapons.

Listening to his interviews provides an insight into how it must feel to play against (or, indeed, for) one of his teams. You feel yourself becoming gradually ground down, the repetition draining you. In recent years, it has seemed that his powers are on the wane; he appears less able to relate to and inspire younger players. Perhaps the *esprit de corps* he was able to so competently establish in the earlier years of his coaching career has been compromised by his constant public bullying of individual players.

It wasn't always this way. When he arrived at Chelsea in 2004, the charismatic young coach was all teeth and dimples, a tanned silver fox with an impressive track record to back up his arrogant demeanour. Instantly quotable, the media lapped up his every proclamation. You didn't get this with Nigel Worthington.[7]

Most British football fans became aware of Mourinho during his time at Porto: firstly, after they overcame Celtic in the 2003 UEFA Cup final (after which Celtic manager Martin O'Neill criticised the poor sportsmanship and play-acting of the Porto players – the early signs of a template forming); and then when he guided them to Champions League success in 2004. Porto had knocked out Manchester United in the round of sixteen, thanks to a last-minute Costinha goal that sent them through on aggregate. Mourinho famously celebrated by sprinting along the Old Trafford touchline and skidding on his knees. This probably explains why, when he later became the Manchester United manager, he was absolutely *fine* with rivals Manchester City celebrating a derby win in December 2017. He only got into a tiny scuffle with their

7 My partner, who has never shown the vaguest interest in football, looked up at *Match of the Day* once, eyes widening, and asked, 'Who is *that*?' It was Nigel Worthington, but she looked up again a few minutes later when José appeared on the screen, and noted that he was quite good-looking.

players, in the style of a middle-aged man seething with impotent rage and humiliating himself in front of a group of rowdy teenagers – which is pretty much exactly what he was doing.

Mourinho's first spell at Chelsea saw him become the most successful manager in their history, winning two Premier League titles in 2005 and 2006, and an FA Cup in 2007. He also won the League Cup in 2005 and 2007, and the Community Shield in 2005, which he would later count as a legitimate trophy as he became ever more desperate to boost his stats. However, Mourinho's time at Chelsea came to an end early in the 2007/8 season, when he clashed with Roman Abramovich and was jettisoned, possibly via the sewage outlet of a luxury yacht. He was fished out of the water by Inter, to whom he showed his gratitude by winning Serie A in 2009 and a treble of league, cup and Champions League a year later.

Mourinho's stock had never been higher, and it was at this point that Real Madrid came knocking. The loveable Spanish giants were a perfect fit for Mourinho's win-at-all-costs attitude. It also signalled a return to a country where José had enjoyed happy times at the outset of his career, working for Barcelona as a translator for Bobby Robson (the nicest man in football) and Louis van Gaal (also a man). However, in the intervening years, José had hardened, the young apprentice seduced by the dark side. His spell in Madrid was toxic. They won a league title in 2012, but he was consumed by a personal battle with Barcelona coach Pep Guardiola.

Such personal grudges became a more prominent feature of Mourinho's management style, as would his glowing tributes to the same men when they were no longer perceived to be a threat. He ridiculed Claudio Ranieri for his age, but when the Italian was fired by Leicester, Mourinho wore a top bearing his initials. His animosity towards Arsène Wenger saw the two of them come to blows on the touchline in 2014 in the weakest fight you'll see outside of a Waitrose car park. He famously described Wenger as a 'specialist in failure', a tag he later tried to convince us was meant respectfully. Mourinho was again treating the public like it didn't have the capacity to remember things that had happened quite recently nor had access to the information stored in a worldwide network of computers to jog our memories.

Mourinho's time at Madrid ended at the conclusion of the 2012/13 season, when the only trophy he'd collected was the eyeball he plucked from the head of Barcelona's assistant coach, Tito Vilanova. A return to Chelsea followed, a place where he said he felt loved, his memory perhaps damaged by banging his head as he was shot out of Abramovich's vacuum pipe.

Steady progress in the first season culminated in them denying Liverpool a league title with a classic Mourinho heist at Anfield, aided by the Reds' manager, Brendan Rodgers, leaving all the doors and windows open, and captain Steven Gerrard holding the burglars' ladder for them. Mourinho drank in the atmosphere of despair, intoxicated by the misery his team had caused – he was back. Chelsea won the league easily the following year, but everything crumbled in his third season, a campaign that started with him shouting insults at team doctor Eva Carneiro as she attended to an injured Eden Hazard. He was fired by Christmas, the team languishing amusingly close to the relegation zone.

Yet his reputation endured, and he was appointed by Manchester United in 2016. Like anyone who lands their dream job, he was happy for a while, keen to make a good impression on his new employers. But gradually his personality shone through, and before long the angry scowl and pouting bottom lip had returned. By his second season, following an embarrassing Champions League defeat to Sevilla, he was back to rambling, self-aggrandising press conferences designed to distract from the failure of the team he had picked and the tactics they had employed – a Mourinho move more classic than holding onto the ball when it goes out for a throw-in.

Yet despite all of this, there's a hard truth to face: I need him. The task of writing a weekly satirical football cartoon would be immeasurably more difficult if every team's manager spoke honestly and respectfully about refereeing decisions and transfer budgets. It seems unlikely that Paolo Di Canio will get another gig, Alan Pardew has salted the earth occupied by mid- to lower-ranking Premier League clubs, and after being fired by Everton, Sam Allardyce is rich enough to buy the Monster Munch factory and live out his days in a corn-snack paradise. My vision of hell: all Premier League teams being issued with an Eddie Howe clone, an amicable plague devouring my material like locusts.

Yes, I need Mourinho like Sherlock Holmes needs Moriarty, like the Daleks need Doctor Who. And much like in *Doctor Who*, in these cartoons José's appearance changes frequently.

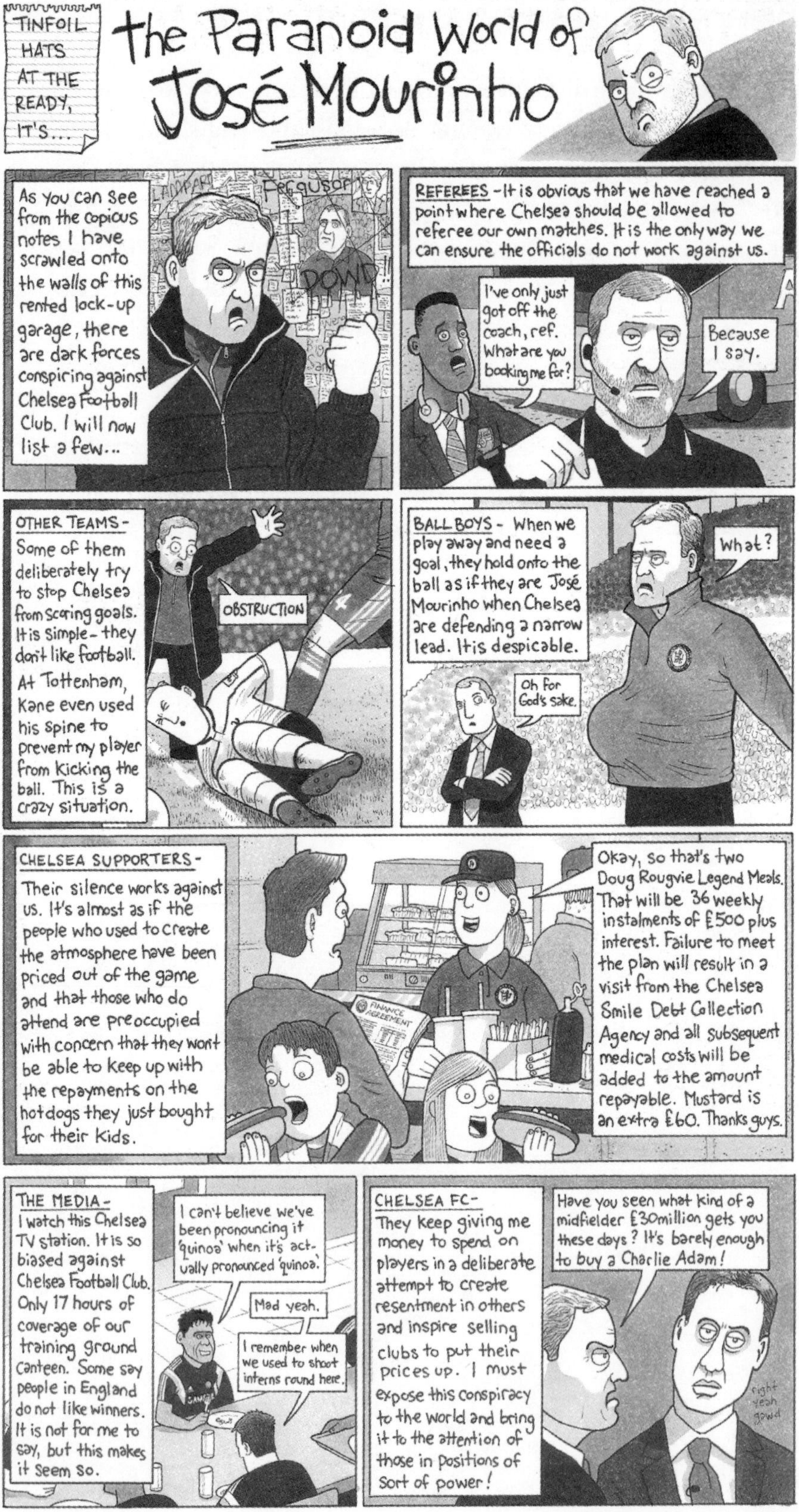
TINFOIL HATS AT THE READY, IT'S...
the Paranoid World of José Mourinho
As you can see from the copious notes I have scrawled onto the walls of this rented lock-up garage, there are dark forces conspiring against Chelsea Football Club. I will now list a few...
Ferguson
DOWD!!
REFEREES - It is obvious that we have reached a point where Chelsea should be allowed to referee our own matches. It is the only way we can ensure the officials do not work against us.
I've only just got off the coach, ref. What are you booking me for?
Because I say.
OTHER TEAMS - Some of them deliberately try to stop Chelsea from scoring goals. It is simple - they don't like football. At Tottenham, Kane even used his spine to prevent my player from kicking the ball. This is a crazy situation.
OBSTRUCTION
BALL BOYS - When we play away and need a goal, they hold onto the ball as if they are José Mourinho when Chelsea are defending a narrow lead. It is despicable.
What?
Oh for God's sake.
CHELSEA SUPPORTERS - Their silence works against us. It's almost as if the people who used to create the atmosphere have been priced out of the game and that those who do attend are preoccupied with concern that they won't be able to keep up with the repayments on the hotdogs they just bought for their kids.
Okay, so that's two Doug Rougvie Legend Meals. That will be 36 weekly instalments of £500 plus interest. Failure to meet the plan will result in a visit from the Chelsea Smile Debt Collection Agency and all subsequent medical costs will be added to the amount repayable. Mustard is an extra £60. Thanks guys.
FINANCE AGREEMENT
THE MEDIA - I watch this Chelsea TV station. It is so biased against Chelsea Football Club. Only 17 hours of coverage of our training ground canteen. Some say people in England do not like winners. It is not for me to say, but this makes it seem so.
I can't believe we've been pronouncing it 'quinoa' when it's actually pronounced 'quinoa'.
Mad yeah.
I remember when we used to shoot interns round here.
CHELSEA FC - They keep giving me money to spend on players in a deliberate attempt to create resentment in others and inspire selling clubs to put their prices up. I must expose this conspiracy to the world and bring it to the attention of those in positions of sort of power!
Have you seen what kind of a midfielder £30million gets you these days? It's barely enough to buy a Charlie Adam!
right yeah gawd

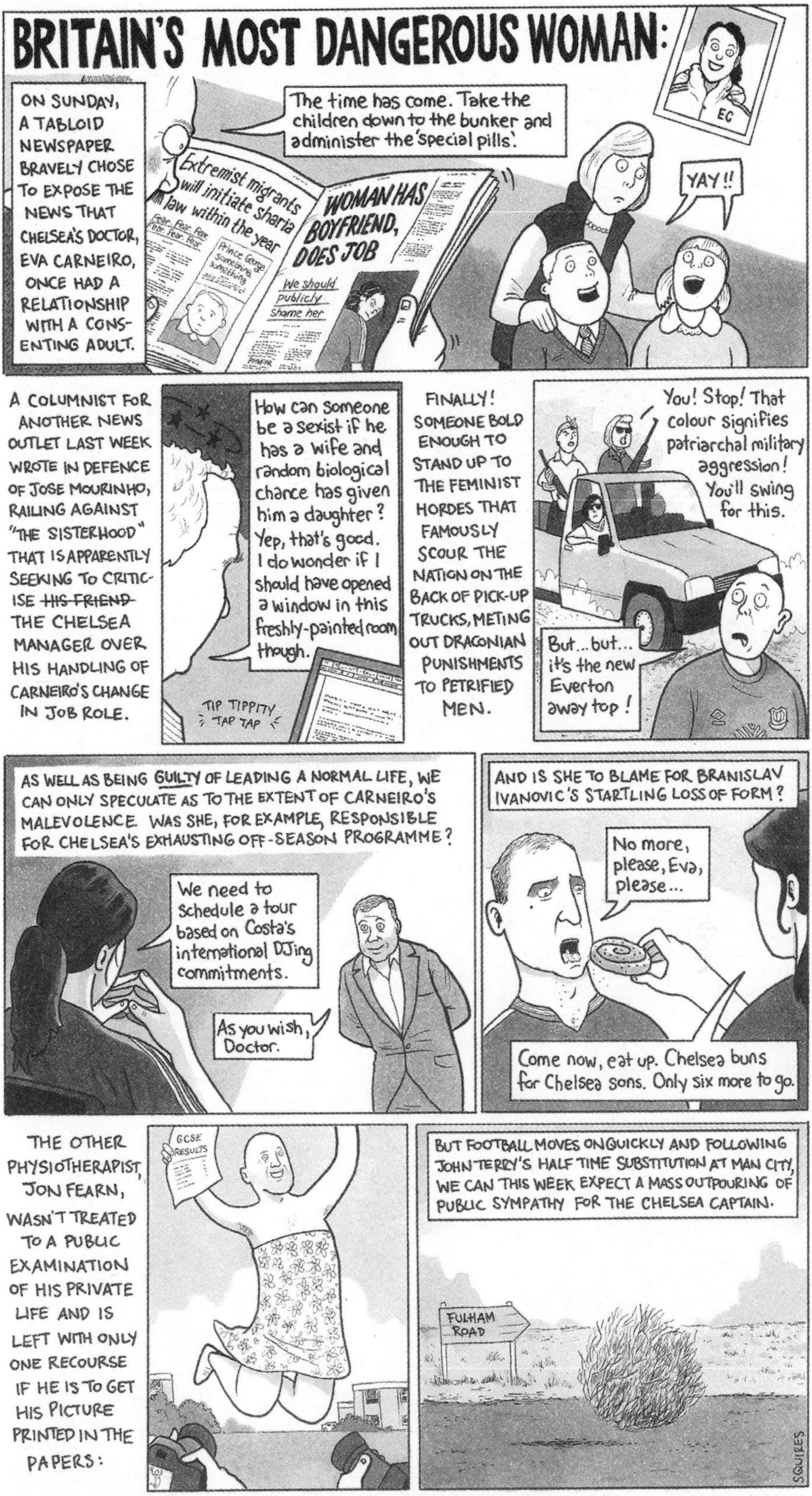
BRITAIN'S MOST DANGEROUS WOMAN:
EC
ON SUNDAY, A TABLOID NEWSPAPER BRAVELY CHOSE TO EXPOSE THE NEWS THAT CHELSEA'S DOCTOR, EVA CARNEIRO, ONCE HAD A RELATIONSHIP WITH A CONSENTING ADULT.
The time has come. Take the children down to the bunker and administer the 'special pills'.
Extremist migrants will initiate sharia law within the year
Fear. Fear. Fear. Fear. Fear. Fear.
WOMAN HAS BOYFRIEND, DOES JOB
We should publicly shame her
YAY!!
A COLUMNIST FOR ANOTHER NEWS OUTLET LAST WEEK WROTE IN DEFENCE OF JOSE MOURINHO, RAILING AGAINST "THE SISTERHOOD" THAT IS APPARENTLY SEEKING TO CRITICISE ~~HIS FRIEND~~ THE CHELSEA MANAGER OVER HIS HANDLING OF CARNEIRO'S CHANGE IN JOB ROLE.
How can someone be a sexist if he has a wife and random biological chance has given him a daughter? Yep, that's good. I do wonder if I should have opened a window in this freshly-painted room though.
TIP TIPPITY TAP TAP
FINALLY! SOMEONE BOLD ENOUGH TO STAND UP TO THE FEMINIST HORDES THAT FAMOUSLY SCOUR THE NATION ON THE BACK OF PICK-UP TRUCKS, METING OUT DRACONIAN PUNISHMENTS TO PETRIFIED MEN.
You! Stop! That colour signifies patriarchal military aggression! You'll swing for this.
But...but... it's the new Everton away top!
AS WELL AS BEING GUILTY OF LEADING A NORMAL LIFE, WE CAN ONLY SPECULATE AS TO THE EXTENT OF CARNEIRO'S MALEVOLENCE. WAS SHE, FOR EXAMPLE, RESPONSIBLE FOR CHELSEA'S EXHAUSTING OFF-SEASON PROGRAMME?
We need to schedule a tour based on Costa's international DJing commitments.
As you wish, Doctor.
AND IS SHE TO BLAME FOR BRANISLAV IVANOVIC'S STARTLING LOSS OF FORM?
No more, please, Eva, please...
Come now, eat up. Chelsea buns for Chelsea sons. Only six more to go.
THE OTHER PHYSIOTHERAPIST, JON FEARN, WASN'T TREATED TO A PUBLIC EXAMINATION OF HIS PRIVATE LIFE AND IS LEFT WITH ONLY ONE RECOURSE IF HE IS TO GET HIS PICTURE PRINTED IN THE PAPERS:
GCSE RESULTS
BUT FOOTBALL MOVES ON QUICKLY AND FOLLOWING JOHN TERRY'S HALF TIME SUBSTITUTION AT MAN CITY, WE CAN THIS WEEK EXPECT A MASS OUTPOURING OF PUBLIC SYMPATHY FOR THE CHELSEA CAPTAIN.
FULHAM ROAD
SQUIRES

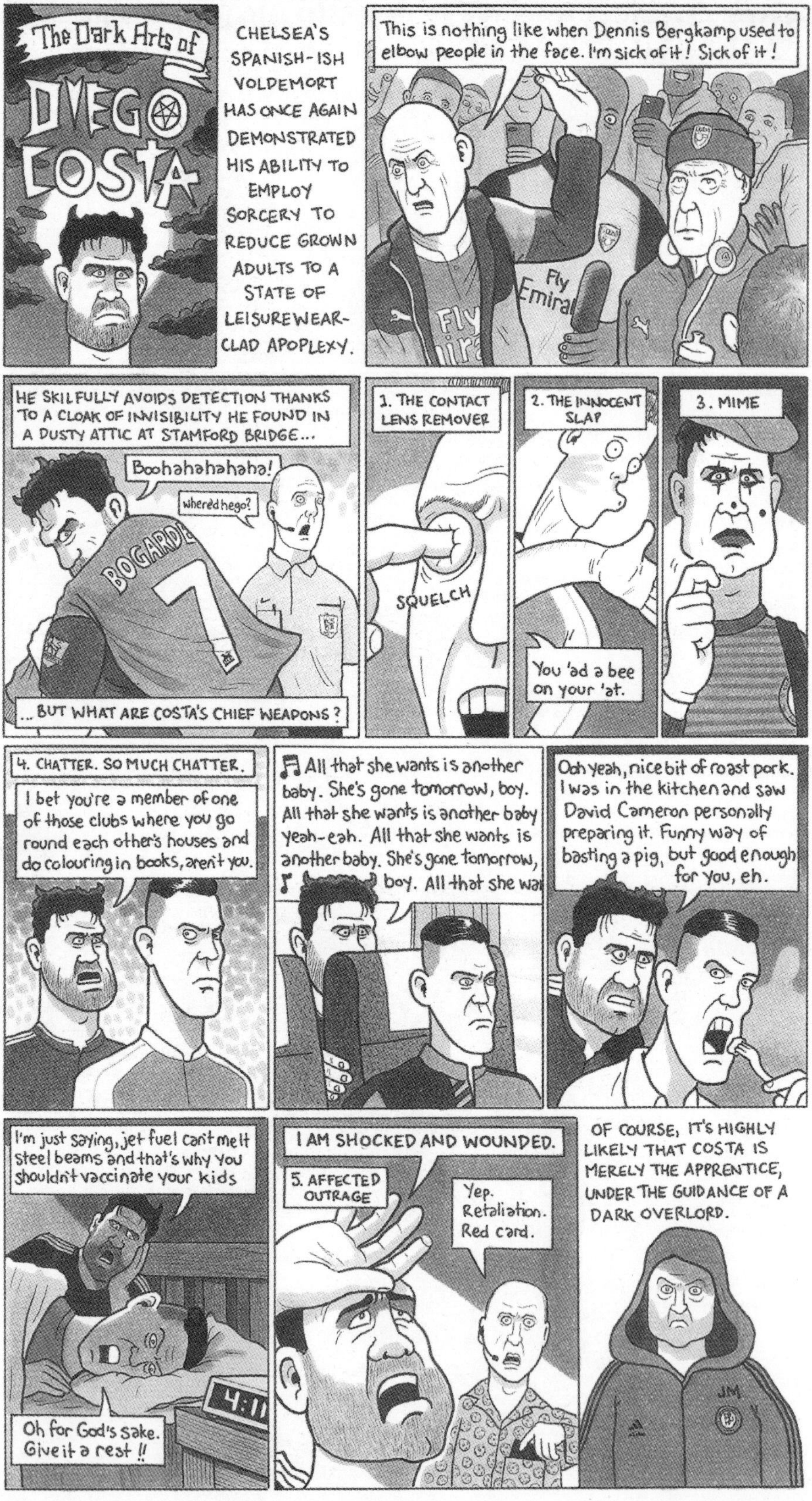
The Dark Arts of
DIEGO COSTA
CHELSEA'S SPANISH-ISH VOLDEMORT HAS ONCE AGAIN DEMONSTRATED HIS ABILITY TO EMPLOY SORCERY TO REDUCE GROWN ADULTS TO A STATE OF LEISUREWEAR-CLAD APOPLEXY.
This is nothing like when Dennis Bergkamp used to elbow people in the face. I'm sick of it! Sick of it!
Fly Emirat
HE SKILFULLY AVOIDS DETECTION THANKS TO A CLOAK OF INVISIBILITY HE FOUND IN A DUSTY ATTIC AT STAMFORD BRIDGE...
Boohahahahaha!
where'd he go?
BOGARDE 7
... BUT WHAT ARE COSTA'S CHIEF WEAPONS?
1. THE CONTACT LENS REMOVER
SQUELCH
2. THE INNOCENT SLAP
You 'ad a bee on your 'at.
3. MIME
4. CHATTER. SO MUCH CHATTER.
I bet you're a member of one of those clubs where you go round each other's houses and do colouring in books, aren't you.
All that she wants is another baby. She's gone tomorrow, boy. All that she wants is another baby yeah-eah. All that she wants is another baby. She's gone tomorrow, boy. All that she wa
Ooh yeah, nice bit of roast pork. I was in the kitchen and saw David Cameron personally preparing it. Funny way of basting a pig, but good enough for you, eh.
I'm just saying, jet fuel can't melt steel beams and that's why you shouldn't vaccinate your kids
Oh for God's sake. Give it a rest!!
I AM SHOCKED AND WOUNDED.
5. AFFECTED OUTRAGE
Yep. Retaliation. Red card.
OF COURSE, IT'S HIGHLY LIKELY THAT COSTA IS MERELY THE APPRENTICE, UNDER THE GUIDANCE OF A DARK OVERLORD.
JM

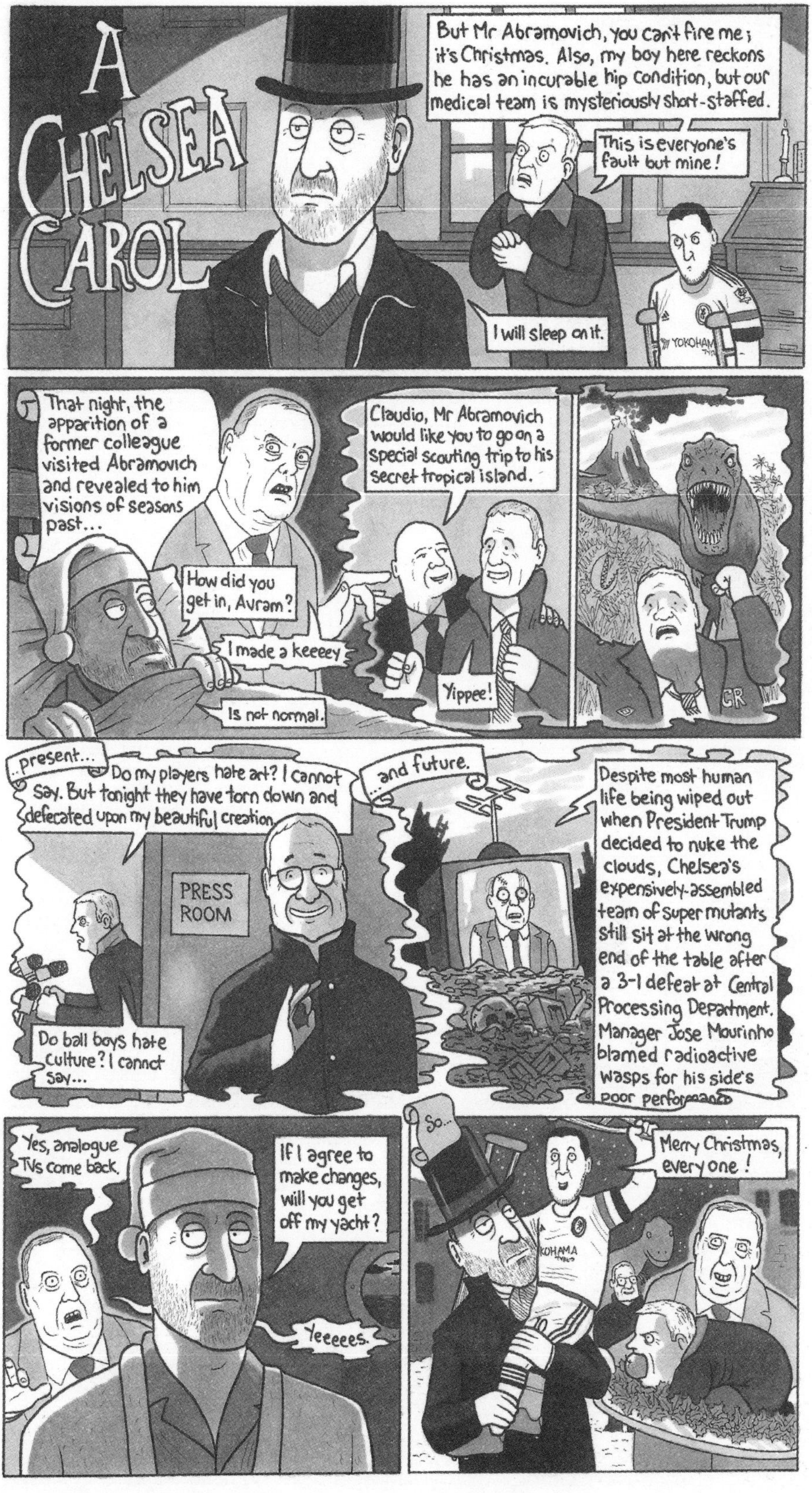
A CHELSEA CAROL
But Mr Abramovich, you can't fire me; it's Christmas. Also, my boy here reckons he has an incurable hip condition, but our medical team is mysteriously short-staffed.
This is everyone's fault but mine!
I will sleep on it.
YOKOHAMA
That night, the apparition of a former colleague visited Abramovich and revealed to him visions of seasons past...
How did you get in, Avram?
I made a keeeey
Is not normal.
Claudio, Mr Abramovich would like you to go on a special scouting trip to his secret tropical island.
Yippee!
CR
..present...
Do my players hate art? I cannot say. But tonight they have torn down and defecated upon my beautiful creation.
PRESS ROOM
Do ball boys hate culture? I cannot say...
...and future.
Despite most human life being wiped out when President Trump decided to nuke the clouds, Chelsea's expensively-assembled team of super mutants still sit at the wrong end of the table after a 3-1 defeat at Central Processing Department. Manager Jose Mourinho blamed radioactive wasps for his side's poor perfor
Yes, analogue TVs come back.
If I agree to make changes, will you get off my yacht?
Yeeeees.
So...
Merry Christmas, every one!
KOHAMA

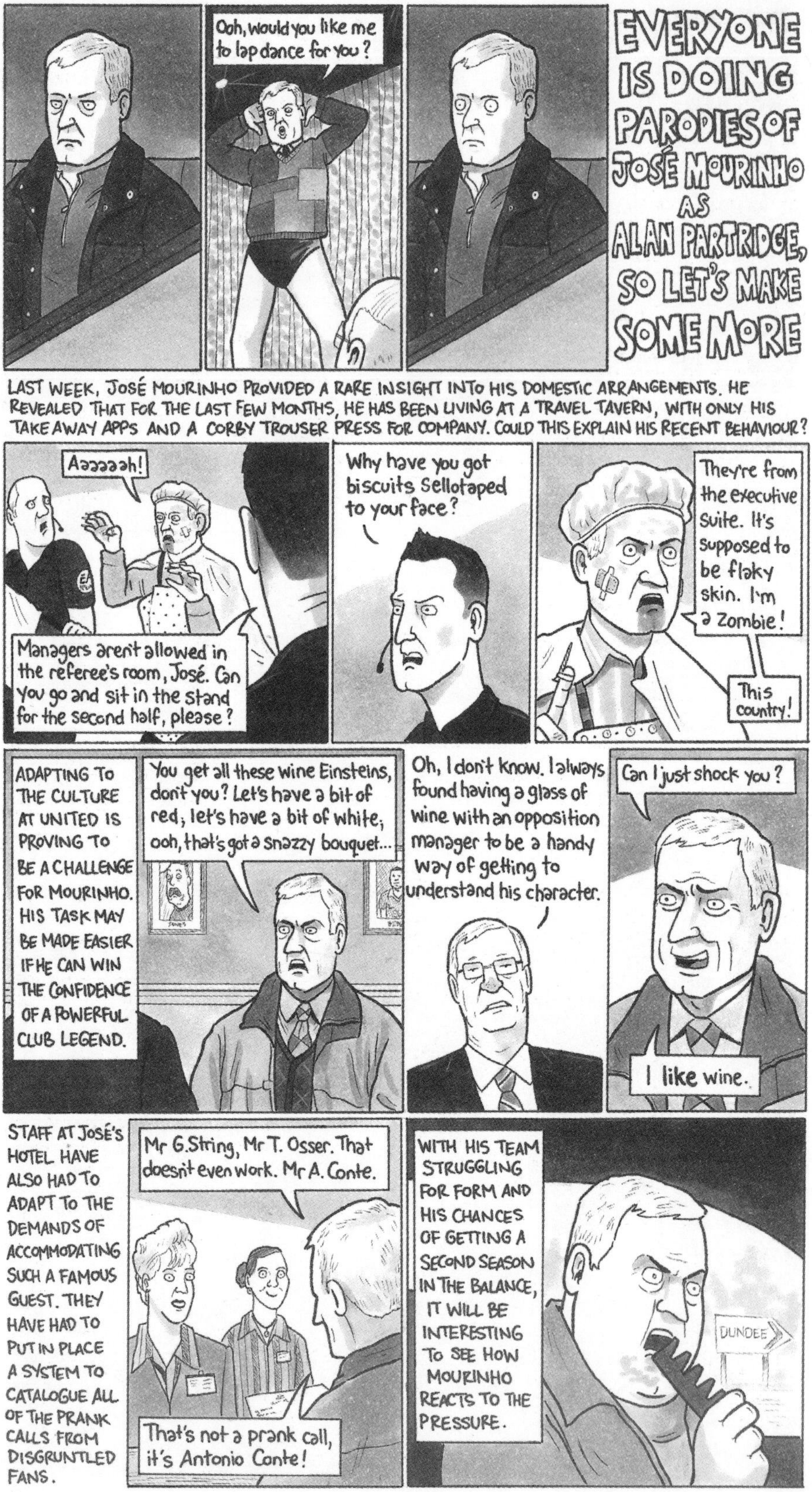
Ooh, would you like me to lap dance for you?
EVERYONE IS DOING PARODIES OF JOSÉ MOURINHO AS ALAN PARTRIDGE, SO LET'S MAKE SOME MORE
LAST WEEK, JOSÉ MOURINHO PROVIDED A RARE INSIGHT INTO HIS DOMESTIC ARRANGEMENTS. HE REVEALED THAT FOR THE LAST FEW MONTHS, HE HAS BEEN LIVING AT A TRAVEL TAVERN, WITH ONLY HIS TAKE AWAY APPS AND A CORBY TROUSER PRESS FOR COMPANY. COULD THIS EXPLAIN HIS RECENT BEHAVIOUR?
Aaaaaah!
Managers aren't allowed in the referee's room, José. Can you go and sit in the stand for the second half, please?
Why have you got biscuits Sellotaped to your face?
They're from the executive suite. It's supposed to be flaky skin. I'm a Zombie!
This country!
ADAPTING TO THE CULTURE AT UNITED IS PROVING TO BE A CHALLENGE FOR MOURINHO. HIS TASK MAY BE MADE EASIER IF HE CAN WIN THE CONFIDENCE OF A POWERFUL CLUB LEGEND.
You get all these wine Einsteins, don't you? Let's have a bit of red; let's have a bit of white; ooh, that's got a snazzy bouquet...
Oh, I don't know. I always found having a glass of wine with an opposition manager to be a handy way of getting to understand his character.
Can I just shock you?
I like wine.
STAFF AT JOSÉ'S HOTEL HAVE ALSO HAD TO ADAPT TO THE DEMANDS OF ACCOMMODATING SUCH A FAMOUS GUEST. THEY HAVE HAD TO PUT IN PLACE A SYSTEM TO CATALOGUE ALL OF THE PRANK CALLS FROM DISGRUNTLED FANS.
Mr G.String, Mr T. Osser. That doesn't even work. Mr A. Conte.
That's not a prank call, it's Antonio Conte!
WITH HIS TEAM STRUGGLING FOR FORM AND HIS CHANCES OF GETTING A SECOND SEASON IN THE BALANCE, IT WILL BE INTERESTING TO SEE HOW MOURINHO REACTS TO THE PRESSURE.
DUNDEE

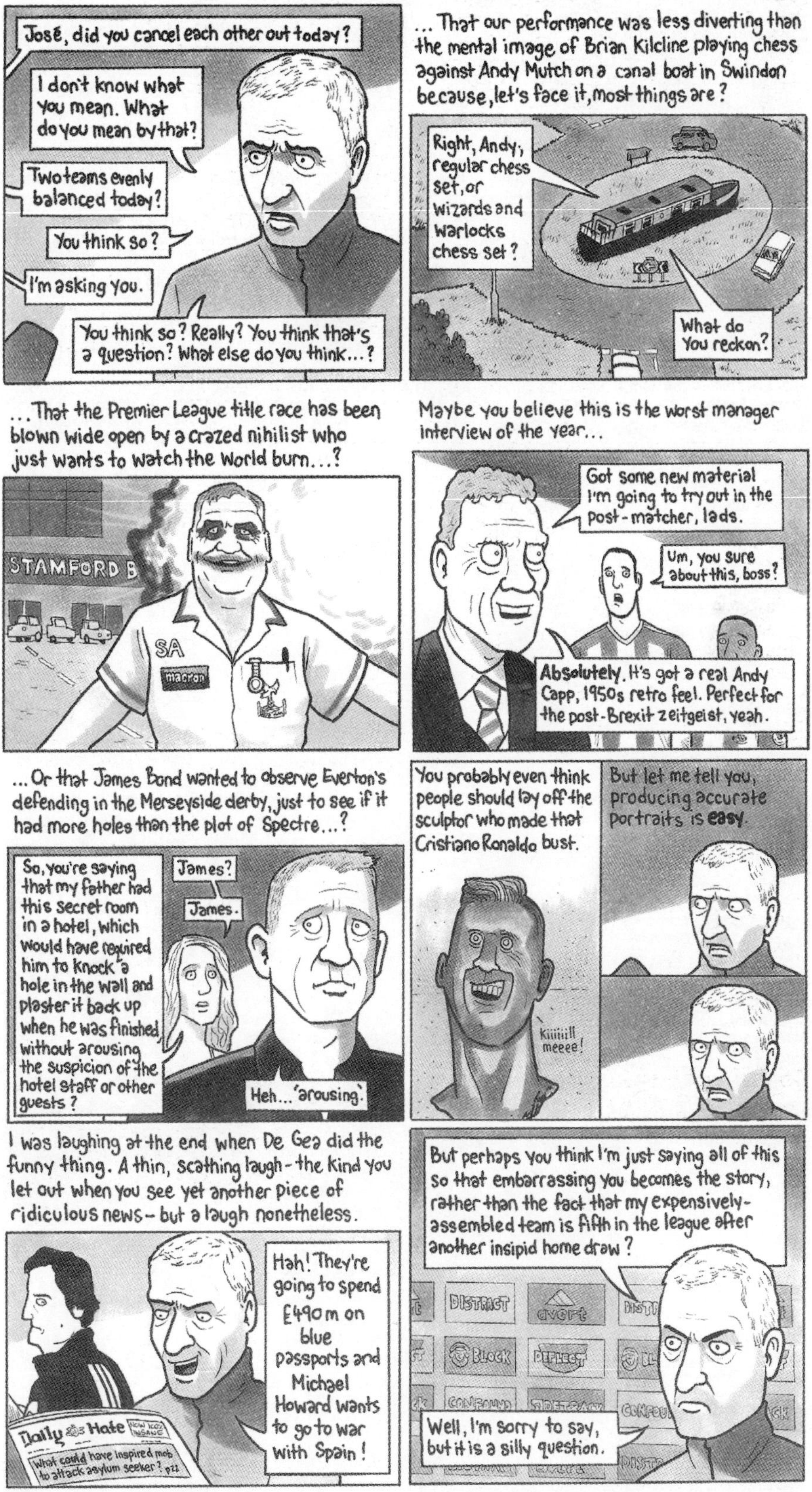
José, did you cancel each other out today?
I don't know what you mean. What do you mean by that?
Two teams evenly balanced today?
You think so?
I'm asking you.
You think so? Really? You think that's a question? What else do you think...?
... That our performance was less diverting than the mental image of Brian Kilcline playing chess against Andy Mutch on a canal boat in Swindon because, let's face it, most things are?
Right, Andy, regular chess set, or wizards and warlocks chess set?
What do you reckon?
... That the Premier League title race has been blown wide open by a crazed nihilist who just wants to watch the world burn...?
STAMFORD B
SA
macron
Maybe you believe this is the worst manager interview of the year...
Got some new material I'm going to try out in the post-matcher, lads.
Um, you sure about this, boss?
Absolutely. It's got a real Andy Capp, 1950s retro feel. Perfect for the post-Brexit zeitgeist, yeah.
... Or that James Bond wanted to observe Everton's defending in the Merseyside derby, just to see if it had more holes than the plot of Spectre...?
So, you're saying that my father had this secret room in a hotel, which would have required him to knock a hole in the wall and plaster it back up when he was finished without arousing the suspicion of the hotel staff or other guests?
James?
James.
Heh... 'arousing'.
You probably even think people should lay off the sculptor who made that Cristiano Ronaldo bust.
Kiiiiill meeee!
But let me tell you, producing accurate portraits is **easy**.
I was laughing at the end when De Gea did the funny thing. A thin, scathing laugh – the kind you let out when you see yet another piece of ridiculous news – but a laugh nonetheless.
Hah! They're going to spend £490m on blue passports and Michael Howard wants to go to war with Spain!
Daily Hate
What could have inspired mob to attack asylum seeker? p22
But perhaps you think I'm just saying all of this so that embarrassing you becomes the story, rather than the fact that my expensively-assembled team is fifth in the league after another insipid home draw?
DISTRACT
avert
BLOCK
DEFLECT
CONFOUND
SIDETRACK
Well, I'm sorry to say, but it is a silly question.

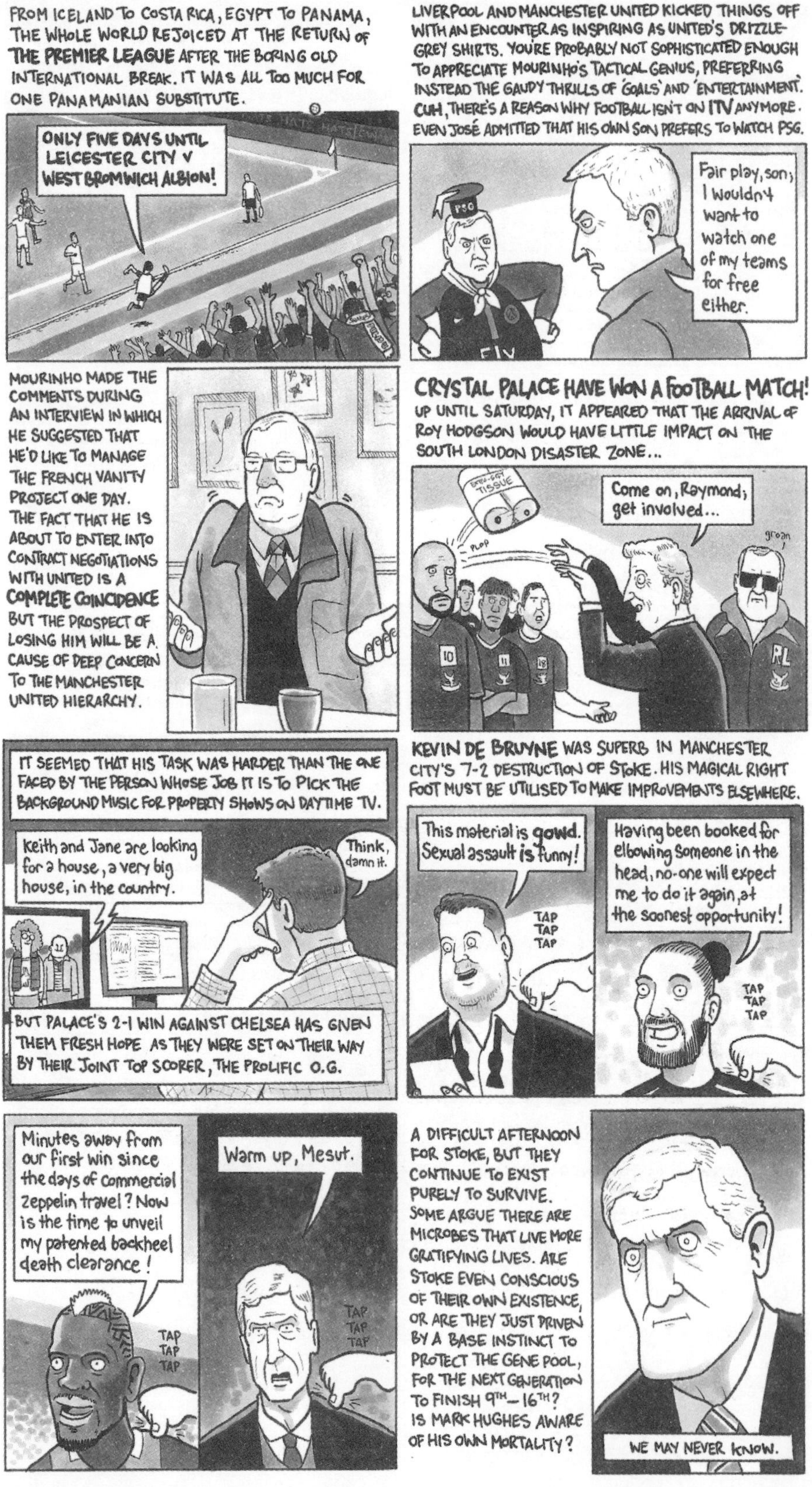
FROM ICELAND TO COSTA RICA, EGYPT TO PANAMA, THE WHOLE WORLD REJOICED AT THE RETURN OF THE PREMIER LEAGUE AFTER THE BORING OLD INTERNATIONAL BREAK. IT WAS ALL TOO MUCH FOR ONE PANAMANIAN SUBSTITUTE.
ONLY FIVE DAYS UNTIL LEICESTER CITY V WEST BROMWICH ALBION!
LIVERPOOL AND MANCHESTER UNITED KICKED THINGS OFF WITH AN ENCOUNTER AS INSPIRING AS UNITED'S DRIZZLE-GREY SHIRTS. YOU'RE PROBABLY NOT SOPHISTICATED ENOUGH TO APPRECIATE MOURINHO'S TACTICAL GENIUS, PREFERRING INSTEAD THE GAUDY THRILLS OF 'GOALS' AND 'ENTERTAINMENT'. CUH, THERE'S A REASON WHY FOOTBALL ISN'T ON ITV ANYMORE. EVEN JOSÉ ADMITTED THAT HIS OWN SON PREFERS TO WATCH PSG.
PSG
Fair play, son; I wouldn't want to watch one of my teams for free either.
MOURINHO MADE THE COMMENTS DURING AN INTERVIEW IN WHICH HE SUGGESTED THAT HE'D LIKE TO MANAGE THE FRENCH VANITY PROJECT ONE DAY. THE FACT THAT HE IS ABOUT TO ENTER INTO CONTRACT NEGOTIATIONS WITH UNITED IS A COMPLETE COINCIDENCE BUT THE PROSPECT OF LOSING HIM WILL BE A CAUSE OF DEEP CONCERN TO THE MANCHESTER UNITED HIERARCHY.
CRYSTAL PALACE HAVE WON A FOOTBALL MATCH!
UP UNTIL SATURDAY, IT APPEARED THAT THE ARRIVAL OF ROY HODGSON WOULD HAVE LITTLE IMPACT ON THE SOUTH LONDON DISASTER ZONE...
TISSUE
Come on, Raymond; get involved...
PLOP
groan
10
11
18
RL
IT SEEMED THAT HIS TASK WAS HARDER THAN THE ONE FACED BY THE PERSON WHOSE JOB IT IS TO PICK THE BACKGROUND MUSIC FOR PROPERTY SHOWS ON DAYTIME TV.
Keith and Jane are looking for a house, a very big house, in the country.
Think, damn it.
BUT PALACE'S 2-1 WIN AGAINST CHELSEA HAS GIVEN THEM FRESH HOPE AS THEY WERE SET ON THEIR WAY BY THEIR JOINT TOP SCORER, THE PROLIFIC O.G.
KEVIN DE BRUYNE WAS SUPERB IN MANCHESTER CITY'S 7-2 DESTRUCTION OF STOKE. HIS MAGICAL RIGHT FOOT MUST BE UTILISED TO MAKE IMPROVEMENTS ELSEWHERE.
This material is gowd. Sexual assault is funny!
TAP TAP TAP
Having been booked for elbowing someone in the head, no-one will expect me to do it again, at the soonest opportunity!
TAP TAP TAP
Minutes away from our first win since the days of commercial zeppelin travel? Now is the time to unveil my patented backheel death clearance!
TAP TAP TAP
Warm up, Mesut.
TAP TAP TAP
A DIFFICULT AFTERNOON FOR STOKE, BUT THEY CONTINUE TO EXIST PURELY TO SURVIVE. SOME ARGUE THERE ARE MICROBES THAT LIVE MORE GRATIFYING LIVES. ARE STOKE EVEN CONSCIOUS OF THEIR OWN EXISTENCE, OR ARE THEY JUST DRIVEN BY A BASE INSTINCT TO PROTECT THE GENE POOL, FOR THE NEXT GENERATION TO FINISH 9TH–16TH? IS MARK HUGHES AWARE OF HIS OWN MORTALITY?
WE MAY NEVER KNOW.

STICK TO FOOTBALL:
Politics and the World Outside

For anyone who saw Theresa May's attempt at a Mexican wave during a friendly between France and England in 2017, the argument that football and politics shouldn't mix was compelling. However, football doesn't exist in a vacuum and hasn't been immune to the social and political upheavals of recent years.

Brexit, Trump, global and domestic terrorism, the resumption of the cold war, the return of Nazis (who thought *those* guys would make a comeback?), the growing threat of nuclear obliteration: the last few years of turmoil have affected us all at some point. This is true whether we be football players, fans or simply people tasked with producing weekly cartoons about sport while being distracted by the thought that digging a nuclear bunker in the back garden might be a better use of a Tuesday afternoon (but would probably breach the tenancy agreement).

The British general election of 2015 already feels like it took place in a different century. The electorate looked back lovingly at the government's record of punishing the weakest people in society and resoundingly cried, 'More please!' They pulled up the ladder, safe in the knowledge that another term of David Cameron meant a bright and stable future for anyone who wasn't planning to be sick, poor, disabled, unemployed or foreign.

Even those who remained unconvinced by his bum-faced vanity must have been impressed by the sincerity with which he affected a fondness for footy. His team was, of course, Aston Villa (not West

95

Ham, as he said once, frantically trying to remember which claret and blue side the focus groups had said would play best with the proles), and his 2015/16 term would turn out to be every bit as impressive as that of the famous Midlands club.

On the other side of Parliament, an Arsenal fan called Jeremy Corbyn had become Labour leader. Much like the Gunners, the Labour Party is, of course, renowned for its ability not to humiliate itself with face-palming regularity, so with Corbyn's rise there was no doubt that the opposition benches would soon be the very picture of unity.

Cameron's decision to take Britain to the polls again to vote in a referendum on its continued membership of the European Union was a political masterstroke, as it allowed him to quit Parliament and spend more time in the Mediterranean with his collection of pink polo shirts. No skin off his Teflon-coated nose.

A resounding 52 per cent of voters chose to leave the EU, with a few of them even knowing what they were voting for! And so Article 50 was triggered, and the Brexit process began. And can you think of anything more British than a stubborn commitment to do something self-destructive because we said we would, and because changing our minds now would be more embarrassing than condemning future generations to unknown calamitous hardships? If you're reading this in the future (which you are, because I'm only writing it now), presumably it all worked out well. Even if it didn't, you can always blame its failure on the people who said it was a fucking shit idea for not being sufficiently enthusiastic about the fucking shit idea.

Somehow, 2016 had yet more joy to deliver: the election of a bigoted human Wotsit as the most powerful person in the world! Two years later, it's still difficult to comprehend quite how Donald Trump hasn't killed us all yet. There was, of course, a knock-on effect for the football world, too, as it would be hard for the fixture calendar to be completed if the world were covered in a glowing blanket of radioactive ash. Yet the sport struggled on gamely, with World Cup qualifiers taking place and Swindon providing Tim Sherwood with a route back into football management. Sherwood wasn't given an official job title, but his main responsibilities appeared to be to undermine the incumbent manager and not bother with any media obligations.

Guiding us through the mayhem was the steady hand of the British tabloid press, always to be relied upon for a measured response to any news story. In October 2016, it had Gary Lineker in its crosshairs for outrageously expressing some humanity towards the plight of refugee children, the socialist pig. Thankfully, the *Sun* was there to hold him to account, pointing out that some of the desperate people who had travelled great distances to escape persecution in war-torn lands looked slightly older than they claimed. How many refugees have you personally housed, eh, Gary? Oh, it's a glib solution to a complex problem, is it? Tell it to Leonid Brezhnev, crisp boy!

Come April 2017, it was time for the same newspaper's annual assault on the city of Liverpool by cuddly old Kelvin MacKenzie. This time, the columnist and former editor who famously oversaw the printing of egregious lies in the aftermath of the Hillsborough disaster likened Ross Barkley – Everton's young midfielder of Nigerian heritage – to a gorilla.

Yep.

However, in recent times the way in which people access the news has changed, which is great for people whose livelihood is reliant upon the continued rude health of the print media. News is now consumed in tasty, bite-sized chunks that are as gratifying and beneficial as living on a diet of Skittles alone. A sample of stories making the news in September 2017 included the tale of a young woman who had got trapped in a window while trying to retrieve a turd, a viral video of an Irish man trying to capture a bat in his kitchen (which admittedly was very funny) and the protracted transfer saga of Philippe Coutinho joining Barcelona. It was also the week that Alex Oxlade-Chamberlain joined Liverpool from Arsenal and Roy Hodgson returned to management with Crystal Palace. They both went on to enjoy successful seasons, and I was happy to have my inaccurate cartoon predictions shoved down my own throat.

A couple of weeks later and the issue of freedom of speech came to the fore, as a section of Manchester United fans were determined to sing a chant about Romelu Lukaku based on a racial stereotype, despite his respectful requests for them to pack it in (like it's got anything to do with *him*). Around the same time, those other bastions of giving the people the right to be racist without consequence – UKIP – launched a new logo that bore a startling resemblance to that of the Premier League, providing me with the excuse to draw a cartoon about them under the tenuous guise of it having something to do with football.

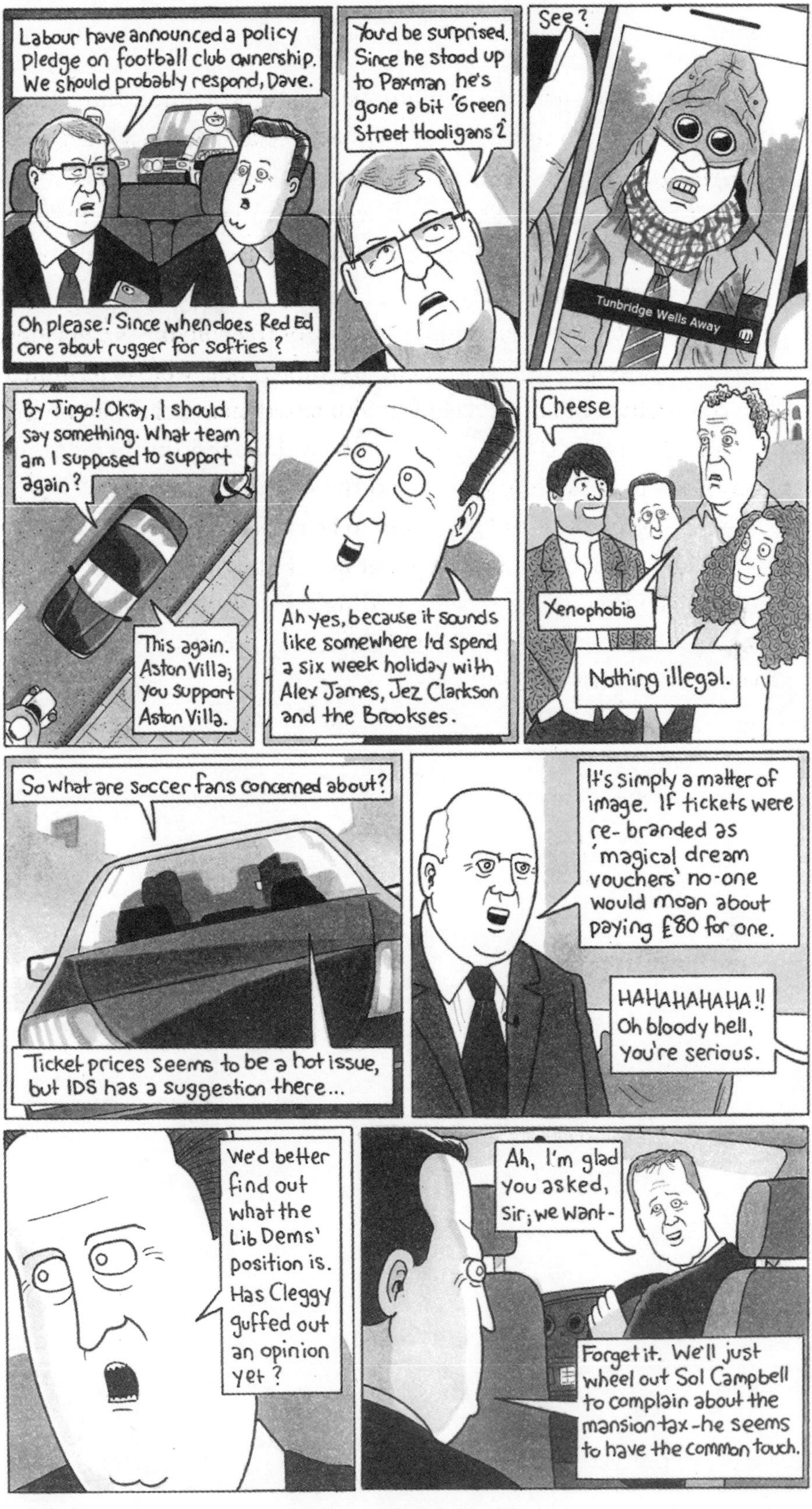
Labour have announced a policy pledge on football club ownership. We should probably respond, Dave.
Oh please! Since when does Red Ed care about rugger for softies?
You'd be surprised. Since he stood up to Paxman he's gone a bit 'Green Street Hooligans 2'
See?
Tunbridge Wells Away
By Jingo! Okay, I should say something. What team am I supposed to support again?
This again. Aston Villa; you support Aston Villa.
Ah yes, because it sounds like somewhere I'd spend a six week holiday with Alex James, Jez Clarkson and the Brookses.
Cheese
Xenophobia
Nothing illegal.
So what are soccer fans concerned about?
Ticket prices seems to be a hot issue, but IDS has a suggestion there...
It's simply a matter of image. If tickets were re-branded as 'magical dream vouchers' no-one would moan about paying £80 for one.
HAHAHAHAHA!! Oh bloody hell, you're serious.
We'd better find out what the Lib Dems' position is. Has Cleggy guffed out an opinion yet?
Ah, I'm glad you asked, sir; we want-
Forget it. We'll just wheel out Sol Campbell to complain about the mansion tax-he seems to have the common touch.

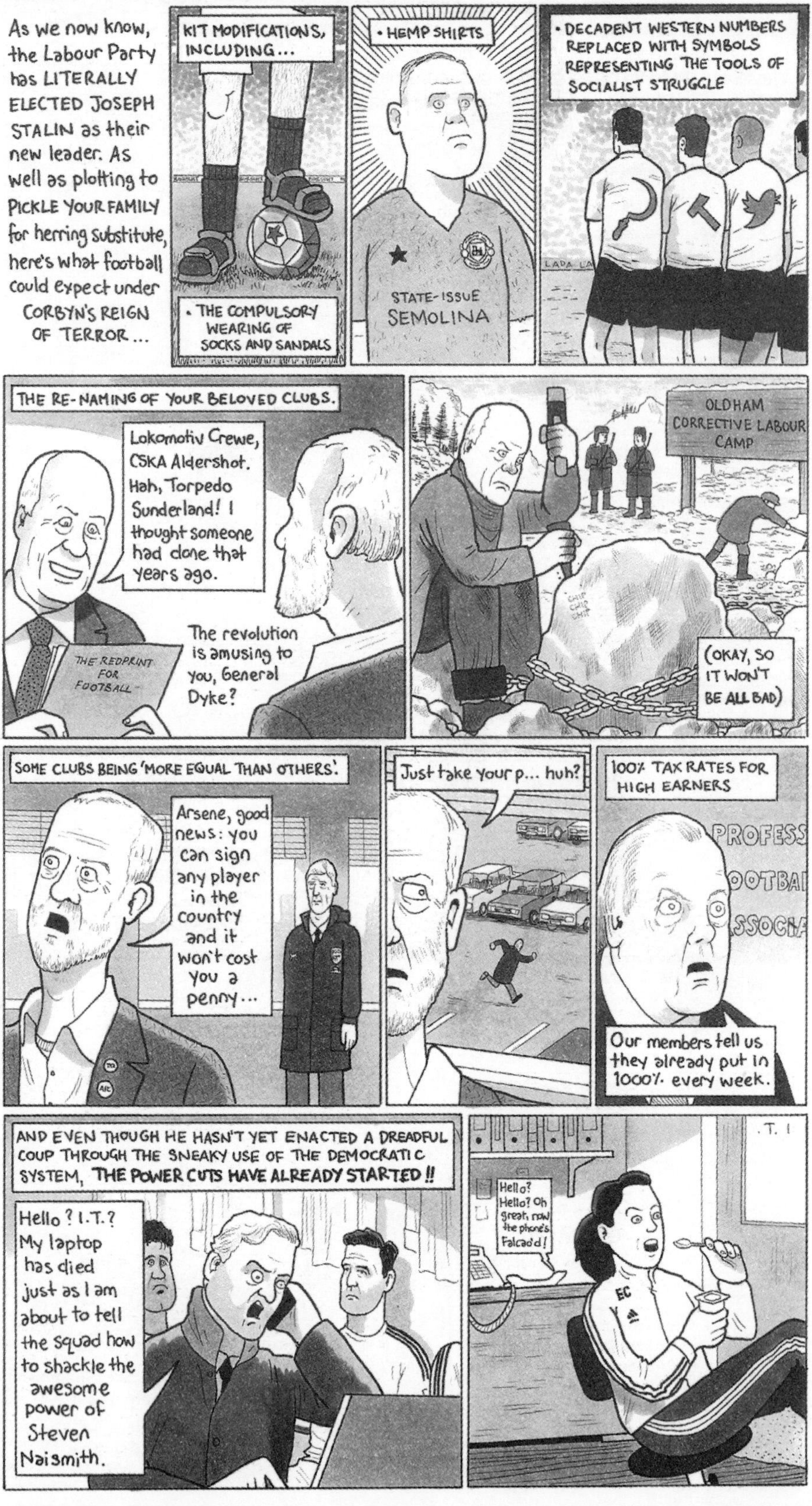
As we now know, the Labour Party has LITERALLY ELECTED JOSEPH STALIN as their new leader. As well as plotting to PICKLE YOUR FAMILY for herring substitute, here's what football could expect under CORBYN'S REIGN OF TERROR...
KIT MODIFICATIONS, INCLUDING...
• THE COMPULSORY WEARING OF SOCKS AND SANDALS
• HEMP SHIRTS
STATE-ISSUE SEMOLINA
• DECADENT WESTERN NUMBERS REPLACED WITH SYMBOLS REPRESENTING THE TOOLS OF SOCIALIST STRUGGLE
THE RE-NAMING OF YOUR BELOVED CLUBS.
Lokomotiv Crewe, CSKA Aldershot. Hah, Torpedo Sunderland! I thought someone had done that years ago.
THE REDPRINT FOR FOOTBALL
The revolution is amusing to you, General Dyke?
OLDHAM CORRECTIVE LABOUR CAMP
(OKAY, SO IT WON'T BE ALL BAD)
SOME CLUBS BEING 'MORE EQUAL THAN OTHERS'.
Arsene, good news: you can sign any player in the country and it won't cost you a penny...
Just take your p... huh?
100% TAX RATES FOR HIGH EARNERS
Our members tell us they already put in 1000% every week.
AND EVEN THOUGH HE HASN'T YET ENACTED A DREADFUL COUP THROUGH THE SNEAKY USE OF THE DEMOCRATIC SYSTEM, THE POWER CUTS HAVE ALREADY STARTED!!
Hello? I.T.? My laptop has died just as I am about to tell the squad how to shackle the awesome power of Steven Naismith.
Hello? Hello? Oh great, now the phone's Falcao'd!

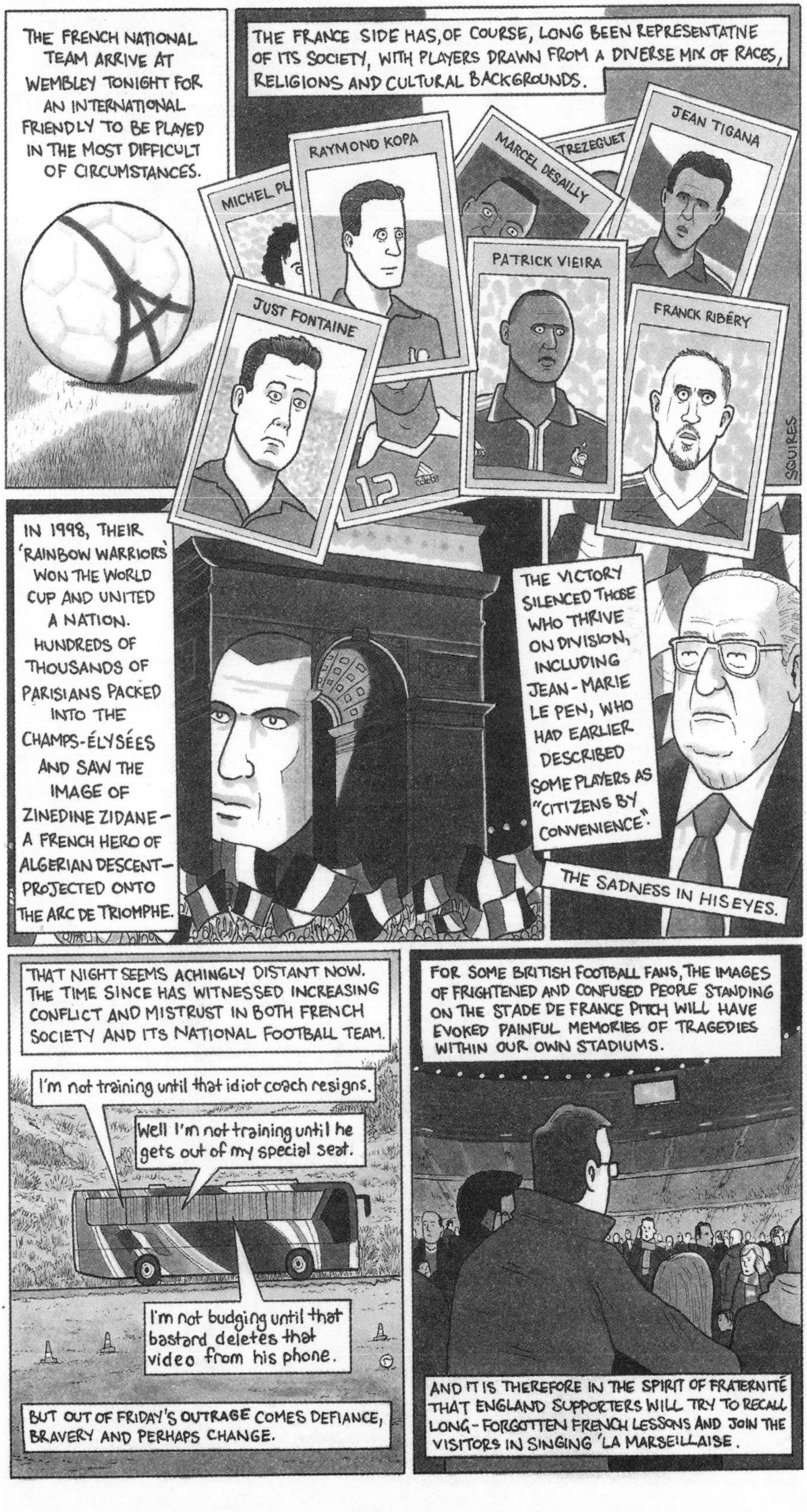
THE FRENCH NATIONAL TEAM ARRIVE AT WEMBLEY TONIGHT FOR AN INTERNATIONAL FRIENDLY TO BE PLAYED IN THE MOST DIFFICULT OF CIRCUMSTANCES.
THE FRANCE SIDE HAS, OF COURSE, LONG BEEN REPRESENTATIVE OF ITS SOCIETY, WITH PLAYERS DRAWN FROM A DIVERSE MIX OF RACES, RELIGIONS AND CULTURAL BACKGROUNDS.
RAYMOND KOPA
MARCEL DESAILLY
TREZEGUET
JEAN TIGANA
PATRICK VIEIRA
JUST FONTAINE
FRANCK RIBÉRY
SQUIRES
IN 1998, THEIR 'RAINBOW WARRIORS' WON THE WORLD CUP AND UNITED A NATION. HUNDREDS OF THOUSANDS OF PARISIANS PACKED INTO THE CHAMPS-ÉLYSÉES AND SAW THE IMAGE OF ZINEDINE ZIDANE – A FRENCH HERO OF ALGERIAN DESCENT – PROJECTED ONTO THE ARC DE TRIOMPHE.
THE VICTORY SILENCED THOSE WHO THRIVE ON DIVISION, INCLUDING JEAN-MARIE LE PEN, WHO HAD EARLIER DESCRIBED SOME PLAYERS AS "CITIZENS BY CONVENIENCE".
THE SADNESS IN HIS EYES.
THAT NIGHT SEEMS ACHINGLY DISTANT NOW. THE TIME SINCE HAS WITNESSED INCREASING CONFLICT AND MISTRUST IN BOTH FRENCH SOCIETY AND ITS NATIONAL FOOTBALL TEAM.
I'm not training until that idiot coach resigns.
Well I'm not training until he gets out of my special seat.
I'm not budging until that bastard deletes that video from his phone.
BUT OUT OF FRIDAY'S OUTRAGE COMES DEFIANCE, BRAVERY AND PERHAPS CHANGE.
FOR SOME BRITISH FOOTBALL FANS, THE IMAGES OF FRIGHTENED AND CONFUSED PEOPLE STANDING ON THE STADE DE FRANCE PITCH WILL HAVE EVOKED PAINFUL MEMORIES OF TRAGEDIES WITHIN OUR OWN STADIUMS.
AND IT IS THEREFORE IN THE SPIRIT OF FRATERNITÉ THAT ENGLAND SUPPORTERS WILL TRY TO RECALL LONG-FORGOTTEN FRENCH LESSONS AND JOIN THE VISITORS IN SINGING 'LA MARSEILLAISE'.

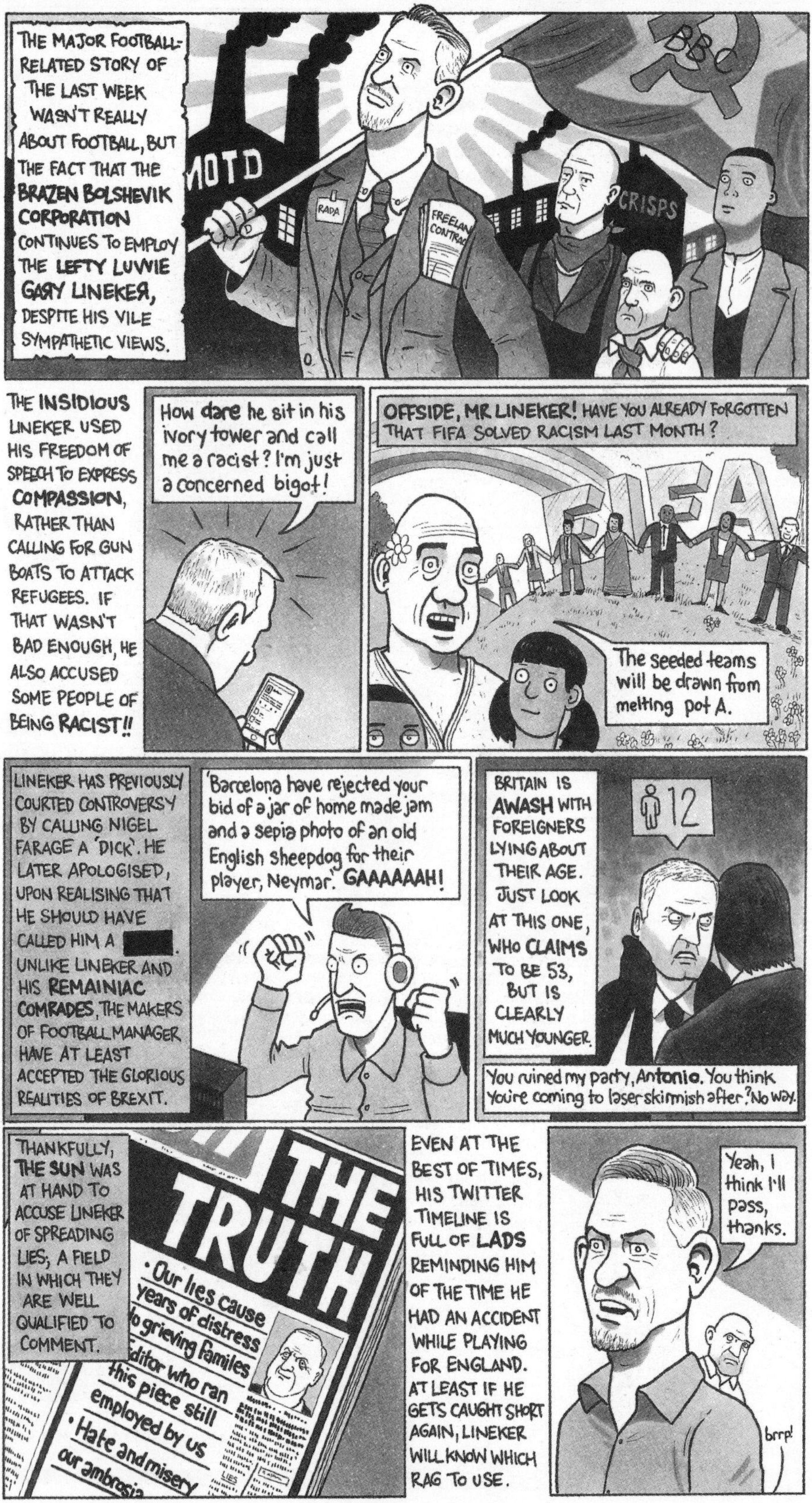

THE MAJOR FOOTBALL-RELATED STORY OF THE LAST WEEK WASN'T REALLY ABOUT FOOTBALL, BUT THE FACT THAT THE BRAZEN BOLSHEVIK CORPORATION CONTINUES TO EMPLOY THE LEFTY LUVVIE GARY LINEKER, DESPITE HIS VILE SYMPATHETIC VIEWS.
MOTD
RADA
BBC
CRISPS
THE INSIDIOUS LINEKER USED HIS FREEDOM OF SPEECH TO EXPRESS COMPASSION, RATHER THAN CALLING FOR GUN BOATS TO ATTACK REFUGEES. IF THAT WASN'T BAD ENOUGH, HE ALSO ACCUSED SOME PEOPLE OF BEING RACIST!!
How dare he sit in his ivory tower and call me a racist? I'm just a concerned bigot!
OFFSIDE, MR LINEKER! HAVE YOU ALREADY FORGOTTEN THAT FIFA SOLVED RACISM LAST MONTH?
FIFA
The seeded teams will be drawn from melting pot A.
LINEKER HAS PREVIOUSLY COURTED CONTROVERSY BY CALLING NIGEL FARAGE A 'DICK'. HE LATER APOLOGISED, UPON REALISING THAT HE SHOULD HAVE CALLED HIM A [redacted].
UNLIKE LINEKER AND HIS REMAINIAC COMRADES, THE MAKERS OF FOOTBALL MANAGER HAVE AT LEAST ACCEPTED THE GLORIOUS REALITIES OF BREXIT.
'Barcelona have rejected your bid of a jar of home made jam and a sepia photo of an old English sheepdog for their player, Neymar.' GAAAAAAH!
BRITAIN IS AWASH WITH FOREIGNERS LYING ABOUT THEIR AGE. JUST LOOK AT THIS ONE, WHO CLAIMS TO BE 53, BUT IS CLEARLY MUCH YOUNGER.
12
You ruined my party, Antonio. You think You're coming to laser skirmish after? No way.
THANKFULLY, THE SUN WAS AT HAND TO ACCUSE LINEKER OF SPREADING LIES; A FIELD IN WHICH THEY ARE WELL QUALIFIED TO COMMENT.
THE TRUTH
• Our lies cause years of distress to grieving familes
• Editor who ran this piece still employed by us
• Hate and misery our ambrosia
EVEN AT THE BEST OF TIMES, HIS TWITTER TIMELINE IS FULL OF LADS REMINDING HIM OF THE TIME HE HAD AN ACCIDENT WHILE PLAYING FOR ENGLAND. AT LEAST IF HE GETS CAUGHT SHORT AGAIN, LINEKER WILL KNOW WHICH RAG TO USE.
Yeah, I think I'll pass, thanks.
brrp!

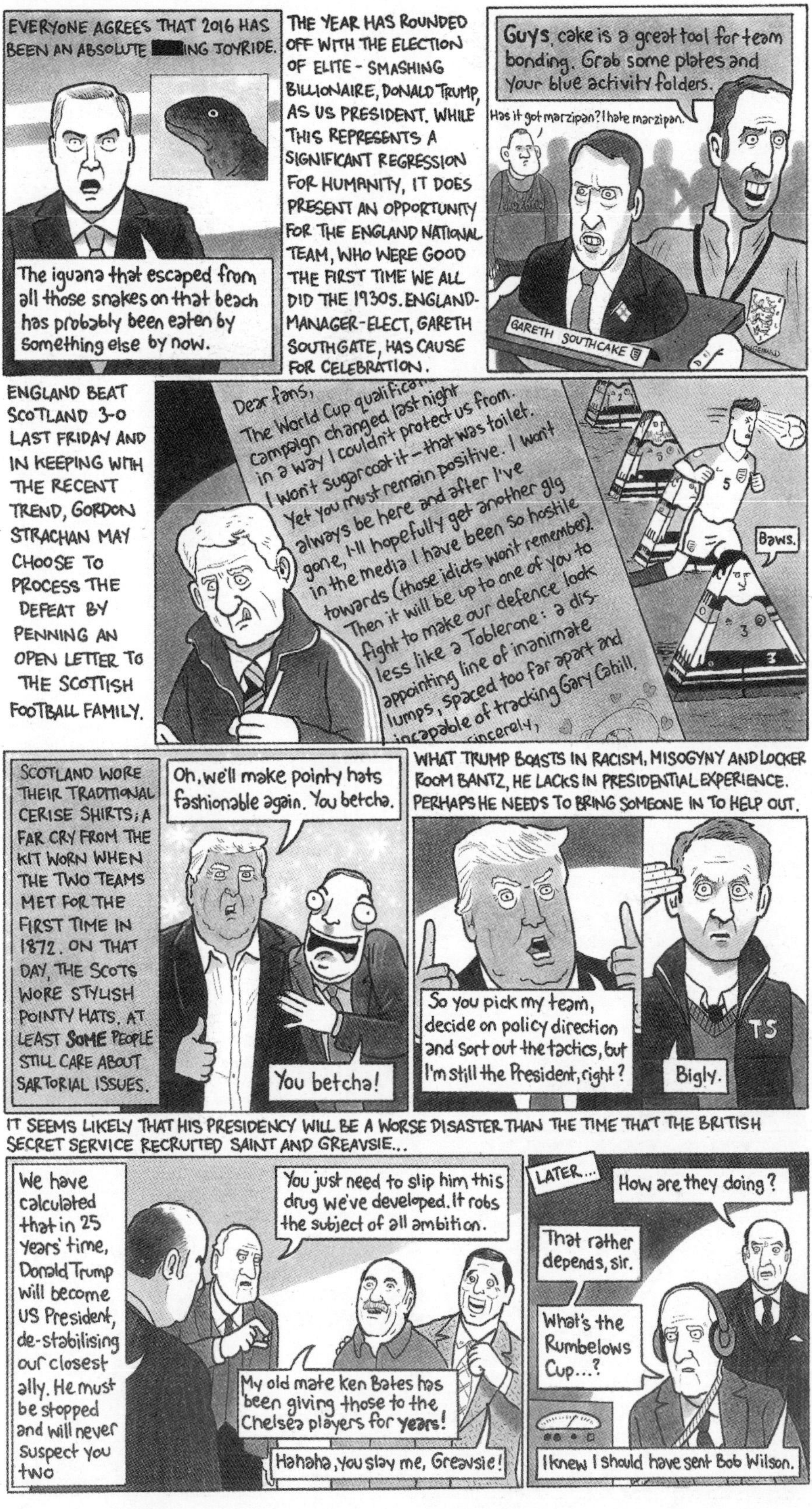
EVERYONE AGREES THAT 2016 HAS BEEN AN ABSOLUTE [redacted]ING JOYRIDE.
The iguana that escaped from all those snakes on that beach has probably been eaten by something else by now.
THE YEAR HAS ROUNDED OFF WITH THE ELECTION OF ELITE - SMASHING BILLIONAIRE, DONALD TRUMP, AS US PRESIDENT. WHILE THIS REPRESENTS A SIGNIFICANT REGRESSION FOR HUMANITY, IT DOES PRESENT AN OPPORTUNITY FOR THE ENGLAND NATIONAL TEAM, WHO WERE GOOD THE FIRST TIME WE ALL DID THE 1930s. ENGLAND-MANAGER-ELECT, GARETH SOUTHGATE, HAS CAUSE FOR CELEBRATION.
Guys, cake is a great tool for team bonding. Grab some plates and your blue activity folders.
Has it got marzipan? I hate marzipan.
GARETH SOUTHCAKE
ENGLAND BEAT SCOTLAND 3-0 LAST FRIDAY AND IN KEEPING WITH THE RECENT TREND, GORDON STRACHAN MAY CHOOSE TO PROCESS THE DEFEAT BY PENNING AN OPEN LETTER TO THE SCOTTISH FOOTBALL FAMILY.
Dear fans,
The World Cup qualifica
campaign changed last night
in a way I couldn't protect us from.
I won't sugarcoat it – that was toilet.
Yet you must remain positive. I won't
always be here and after I've
gone, I'll hopefully get another gig
in the media I have been so hostile
towards (those idiots won't remember).
Then it will be up to one of you to
fight to make our defence look
less like a Toblerone: a dis-
appointing line of inanimate
lumps, spaced too far apart and
incapable of tracking Gary Cahill.
sincerely,
Baws.
SCOTLAND WORE THEIR TRADITIONAL CERISE SHIRTS; A FAR CRY FROM THE KIT WORN WHEN THE TWO TEAMS MET FOR THE FIRST TIME IN 1872. ON THAT DAY, THE SCOTS WORE STYLISH POINTY HATS. AT LEAST SOME PEOPLE STILL CARE ABOUT SARTORIAL ISSUES.
Oh, we'll make pointy hats fashionable again. You betcha.
You betcha!
WHAT TRUMP BOASTS IN RACISM, MISOGYNY AND LOCKER ROOM BANTZ, HE LACKS IN PRESIDENTIAL EXPERIENCE. PERHAPS HE NEEDS TO BRING SOMEONE IN TO HELP OUT.
So you pick my team, decide on policy direction and sort out the tactics, but I'm still the President, right?
TS
Bigly.
IT SEEMS LIKELY THAT HIS PRESIDENCY WILL BE A WORSE DISASTER THAN THE TIME THAT THE BRITISH SECRET SERVICE RECRUITED SAINT AND GREAVSIE...
We have calculated that in 25 years' time, Donald Trump will become US President, de-stabilising our closest ally. He must be stopped and will never suspect you two
You just need to slip him this drug we've developed. It robs the subject of all ambition.
My old mate Ken Bates has been giving those to the Chelsea players for years!
Hahaha, you slay me, Greavsie!
LATER...
How are they doing?
That rather depends, sir.
What's the Rumbelows Cup...?
I knew I should have sent Bob Wilson.

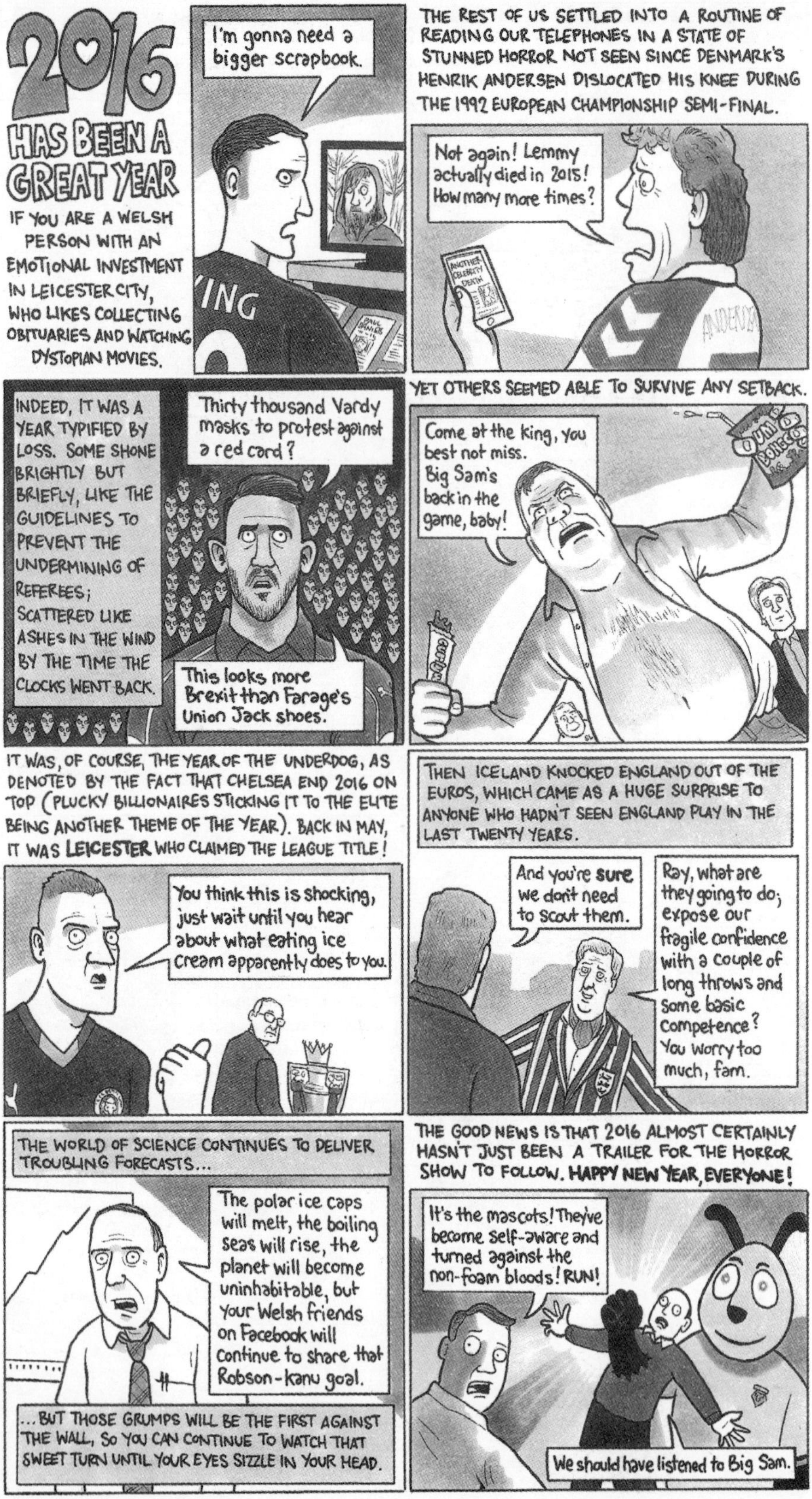

2016 HAS BEEN A GREAT YEAR
IF YOU ARE A WELSH PERSON WITH AN EMOTIONAL INVESTMENT IN LEICESTER CITY, WHO LIKES COLLECTING OBITUARIES AND WATCHING DYSTOPIAN MOVIES.
I'm gonna need a bigger scrapbook.
THE REST OF US SETTLED INTO A ROUTINE OF READING OUR TELEPHONES IN A STATE OF STUNNED HORROR NOT SEEN SINCE DENMARK'S HENRIK ANDERSEN DISLOCATED HIS KNEE DURING THE 1992 EUROPEAN CHAMPIONSHIP SEMI-FINAL.
Not again! Lemmy actually died in 2015! How many more times?
ANOTHER CELEBRITY DEATH
INDEED, IT WAS A YEAR TYPIFIED BY LOSS. SOME SHONE BRIGHTLY BUT BRIEFLY, LIKE THE GUIDELINES TO PREVENT THE UNDERMINING OF REFEREES; SCATTERED LIKE ASHES IN THE WIND BY THE TIME THE CLOCKS WENT BACK.
Thirty thousand Vardy masks to protest against a red card?
This looks more Brexit than Farage's Union Jack shoes.
YET OTHERS SEEMED ABLE TO SURVIVE ANY SETBACK.
Come at the king, you best not miss. Big Sam's back in the game, baby!
IT WAS, OF COURSE, THE YEAR OF THE UNDERDOG, AS DENOTED BY THE FACT THAT CHELSEA END 2016 ON TOP (PLUCKY BILLIONAIRES STICKING IT TO THE ELITE BEING ANOTHER THEME OF THE YEAR). BACK IN MAY, IT WAS LEICESTER WHO CLAIMED THE LEAGUE TITLE!
You think this is shocking, just wait until you hear about what eating ice cream apparently does to you.
THEN ICELAND KNOCKED ENGLAND OUT OF THE EUROS, WHICH CAME AS A HUGE SURPRISE TO ANYONE WHO HADN'T SEEN ENGLAND PLAY IN THE LAST TWENTY YEARS.
And you're sure we don't need to scout them.
Ray, what are they going to do; expose our fragile confidence with a couple of long throws and some basic competence? You worry too much, fam.
THE WORLD OF SCIENCE CONTINUES TO DELIVER TROUBLING FORECASTS...
The polar ice caps will melt, the boiling seas will rise, the planet will become uninhabitable, but your Welsh friends on Facebook will continue to share that Robson-Kanu goal.
...BUT THOSE GRUMPS WILL BE THE FIRST AGAINST THE WALL, SO YOU CAN CONTINUE TO WATCH THAT SWEET TURN UNTIL YOUR EYES SIZZLE IN YOUR HEAD.
THE GOOD NEWS IS THAT 2016 ALMOST CERTAINLY HASN'T JUST BEEN A TRAILER FOR THE HORROR SHOW TO FOLLOW. HAPPY NEW YEAR, EVERYONE!
It's the mascots! They've become self-aware and turned against the non-foam bloods! RUN!
We should have listened to Big Sam.

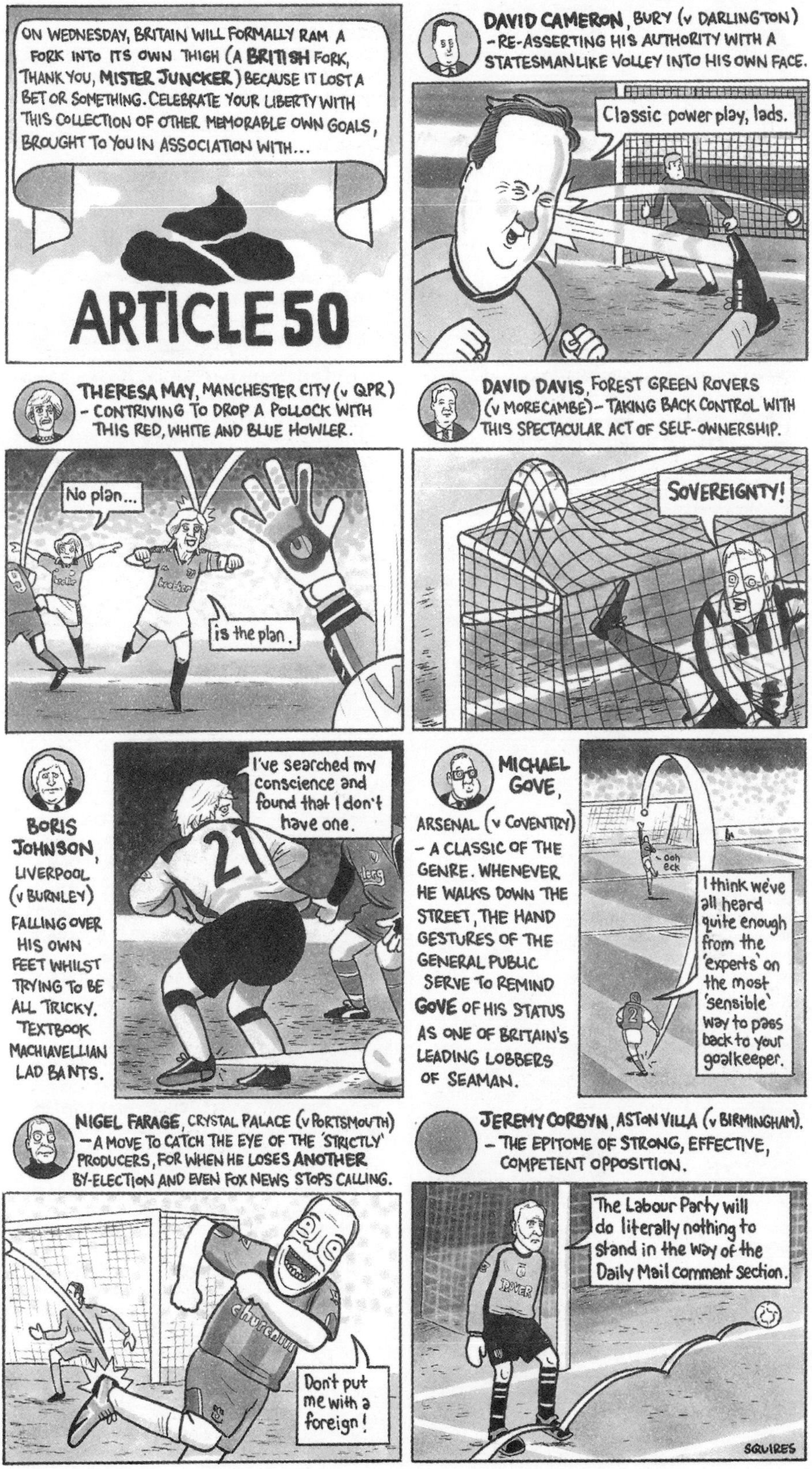
ON WEDNESDAY, BRITAIN WILL FORMALLY RAM A FORK INTO ITS OWN THIGH (A BRITISH FORK, THANK YOU, MISTER JUNCKER) BECAUSE IT LOST A BET OR SOMETHING. CELEBRATE YOUR LIBERTY WITH THIS COLLECTION OF OTHER MEMORABLE OWN GOALS, BROUGHT TO YOU IN ASSOCIATION WITH...
ARTICLE 50
DAVID CAMERON, BURY (v DARLINGTON) – RE-ASSERTING HIS AUTHORITY WITH A STATESMANLIKE VOLLEY INTO HIS OWN FACE.
Classic power play, lads.
THERESA MAY, MANCHESTER CITY (v QPR) – CONTRIVING TO DROP A POLLOCK WITH THIS RED, WHITE AND BLUE HOWLER.
No plan...
is the plan.
DAVID DAVIS, FOREST GREEN ROVERS (v MORECAMBE) – TAKING BACK CONTROL WITH THIS SPECTACULAR ACT OF SELF-OWNERSHIP.
SOVEREIGNTY!
BORIS JOHNSON, LIVERPOOL (v BURNLEY) FALLING OVER HIS OWN FEET WHILST TRYING TO BE ALL TRICKY. TEXTBOOK MACHIAVELLIAN LAD BANTS.
I've searched my conscience and found that I don't have one.
MICHAEL GOVE, ARSENAL (v COVENTRY) – A CLASSIC OF THE GENRE. WHENEVER HE WALKS DOWN THE STREET, THE HAND GESTURES OF THE GENERAL PUBLIC SERVE TO REMIND GOVE OF HIS STATUS AS ONE OF BRITAIN'S LEADING LOBBERS OF SEAMAN.
ooh eck
I think we've all heard quite enough from the 'experts' on the most 'sensible' way to pass back to your goalkeeper.
NIGEL FARAGE, CRYSTAL PALACE (v PORTSMOUTH) – A MOVE TO CATCH THE EYE OF THE 'STRICTLY' PRODUCERS, FOR WHEN HE LOSES ANOTHER BY-ELECTION AND EVEN FOX NEWS STOPS CALLING.
Don't put me with a foreign!
JEREMY CORBYN, ASTON VILLA (v BIRMINGHAM). – THE EPITOME OF STRONG, EFFECTIVE, COMPETENT OPPOSITION.
The Labour Party will do literally nothing to stand in the way of the Daily Mail comment section.
SQUIRES

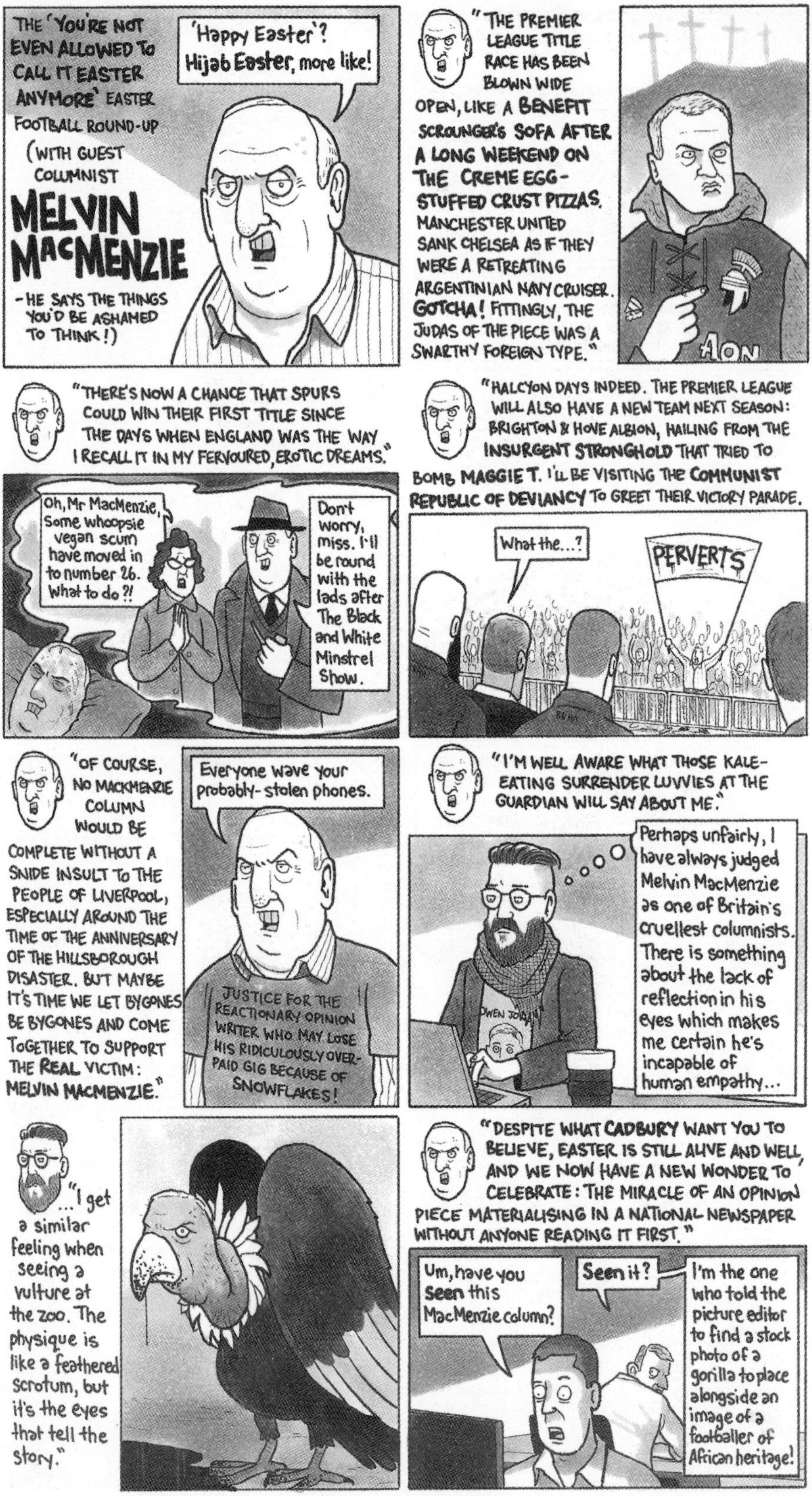
THE 'YOU'RE NOT EVEN ALLOWED TO CALL IT EASTER ANYMORE' EASTER FOOTBALL ROUND-UP
(WITH GUEST COLUMNIST
MELVIN MACMENZIE
- HE SAYS THE THINGS YOU'D BE ASHAMED TO THINK!)
'Happy Easter'? Hijab Easter, more like!
"THE PREMIER LEAGUE TITLE RACE HAS BEEN BLOWN WIDE OPEN, LIKE A BENEFIT SCROUNGER'S SOFA AFTER A LONG WEEKEND ON THE CREME EGG-STUFFED CRUST PIZZAS. MANCHESTER UNITED SANK CHELSEA AS IF THEY WERE A RETREATING ARGENTINIAN NAVY CRUISER. GOTCHA! FITTINGLY, THE JUDAS OF THE PIECE WAS A SWARTHY FOREIGN TYPE."
AON
"THERE'S NOW A CHANCE THAT SPURS COULD WIN THEIR FIRST TITLE SINCE THE DAYS WHEN ENGLAND WAS THE WAY I RECALL IT IN MY FERVOURED, EROTIC DREAMS."
Oh, Mr MacMenzie, Some whoopsie vegan scum have moved in to number 26. What to do?!
Don't worry, miss. I'll be round with the lads after The Black and White Minstrel Show.
"HALCYON DAYS INDEED. THE PREMIER LEAGUE WILL ALSO HAVE A NEW TEAM NEXT SEASON: BRIGHTON & HOVE ALBION, HAILING FROM THE INSURGENT STRONGHOLD THAT TRIED TO BOMB MAGGIE T. I'LL BE VISITING THE COMMUNIST REPUBLIC OF DEVIANCY TO GREET THEIR VICTORY PARADE."
What the...?
PERVERTS
"OF COURSE, NO MACMENZIE COLUMN WOULD BE COMPLETE WITHOUT A SNIDE INSULT TO THE PEOPLE OF LIVERPOOL, ESPECIALLY AROUND THE TIME OF THE ANNIVERSARY OF THE HILLSBOROUGH DISASTER. BUT MAYBE IT'S TIME WE LET BYGONES BE BYGONES AND COME TOGETHER TO SUPPORT THE REAL VICTIM: MELVIN MACMENZIE."
Everyone wave your probably-stolen phones.
JUSTICE FOR THE REACTIONARY OPINION WRITER WHO MAY LOSE HIS RIDICULOUSLY OVER-PAID GIG BECAUSE OF SNOWFLAKES!
"I'M WELL AWARE WHAT THOSE KALE-EATING SURRENDER LUVVIES AT THE GUARDIAN WILL SAY ABOUT ME."
Perhaps unfairly, I have always judged Melvin MacMenzie as one of Britain's cruellest columnists. There is something about the lack of reflection in his eyes which makes me certain he's incapable of human empathy...
...."I get a similar feeling when seeing a vulture at the zoo. The physique is like a feathered scrotum, but it's the eyes that tell the story."
"DESPITE WHAT CADBURY WANT YOU TO BELIEVE, EASTER IS STILL ALIVE AND WELL, AND WE NOW HAVE A NEW WONDER TO CELEBRATE: THE MIRACLE OF AN OPINION PIECE MATERIALISING IN A NATIONAL NEWSPAPER WITHOUT ANYONE READING IT FIRST."
Um, have you seen this MacMenzie column?
Seen it?
I'm the one who told the picture editor to find a stock photo of a gorilla to place alongside an image of a footballer of African heritage!

MANCHESTER UNITED FACED AJAX IN A EUROPA LEAGUE FINAL THAT MEANT BOTH EVERYTHING AND NOTHING.

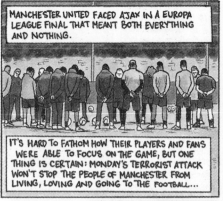

IT'S HARD TO FATHOM HOW THEIR PLAYERS AND FANS WERE ABLE TO FOCUS ON THE GAME, BUT ONE THING IS CERTAIN: MONDAY'S TERRORIST ATTACK WON'T STOP THE PEOPLE OF MANCHESTER FROM LIVING, LOVING AND GOING TO THE FOOTBALL...

WE ALL KNOW A MANCUNIAN. THEY'LL TELL YOU THEY HAVE THE BEST FOOTBALL, THE BEST TRAINERS AND THE BEST MUSIC. INFURIATINGLY, THEY'RE OFTEN RIGHT (NORTH-SIDE REMAIN CRITICALLY UNDERRATED). THE CHARACTERISTICS OF THE CITY CAN BE SEEN IN ITS FOOTBALL CLUBS AND THROUGH THE PEOPLE WHO HAVE REPRESENTED THEM.

SWAGGERING

FASHION CONSCIOUS

CREATIVE (CITY'S KENNY CLEMENTS USED TO PAINT WATER-COLOURS).

TOUGH

Um. Are you ok, Bert?

FUNNY

SQUAD!

Oh yes, it's just the one broken vertebra. Plenty more where that came from.

THE CULTURE AND MUSIC OF THE CITY ARE IMBUED IN BOTH CLUBS, THE GREAT BANDS OF THE PAST CONTINUING TO PROVIDE A LYRIC FOR EVERY OCCASION.

♫ There's a club if you'd like to go. You could meet someone who really loves you...

... So you go and you stand on your own...

Morning, Sir Alex!

Hmn.

AON

... and you leave on your own... and you go home, and you cry and you ring Depay. ♪

This country.

I know we didn't part on the best of terms, but what can you tell me about Ajax?

Yes, I know what time it is. Hello? Memphis?

THE REACTION TO MONDAY'S ATROCITY IS TYPICAL OF THE CITY: AN OUTPOURING OF LOVE AND SUPPORT; OFFERS OF FREE TAXI RIDES AND BEDS FOR THE NIGHT; AN OVERSUPPLY OF PEOPLE WANTING TO DONATE BLOOD, AND ENOUGH CUPS OF TEA TO FILL OLD TRAFFORD.

SUGAR

THIS IS THE STUFF THAT BAFFLES AND SCARES THOSE BIG BRAVE LADS WHO SEE CHILDREN CARRYING PINK BALLOONS AS A LEGITIMATE TARGET FOR THEIR FUCKED UP CAUSE. IT ALSO DEFIES THOSE WHO SEE THE ATTACK AS AN OPPORTUNITY TO DIVIDE SOCIETY VIA THE EFFLUENT PIPE OF THEIR TWITTER ACCOUNT. MANCHESTER KNOWS WHAT YOU CAN DO WITH YOUR NIHILISTIC ARSEHOLERY.

IN TODAY'S FAST-PACED WORLD, IT CAN BE HARD TO KEEP TRACK OF ALL THE DELICIOUS CLICK-BAIT STORIES IN YOUR SOCIAL MEDIA TIMELINE...

Heh. Luke Skywalker's a Wolves fan.

WHAT YOU NEED IS...

A HANDY ROUNDUP OF QUIRKY NEWS FROM AROUND THE INTERNET!

A 24-YEAR OLD MAN WAS EMBARRASSED IN A TRANSFER WINDOW-RELATED INCIDENT ON SATURDAY LUNCHTIME. ALEX OXLADE-CHAMBERLAIN IS BELIEVED TO HAVE BEEN ATTEMPTING TO POLISH A TURD WHEN HE BECAME TRAPPED IN A SLIGHTLY WORSE SITUATION THAN THE ONE HE HAD RECENTLY LEFT.

This is not my preferred position.

AT THE SAME EVENT, A BRAZILIAN GOALKEEPER SURVIVED HAVING HIS HEAD KICKED OFF. THE REAL VICTIM, SADIO MANÉ (25), WAS HELPED FROM THE SCENE AS AN AGITATED WITNESS WORKED HARD TO GET HIS PRIORITIES RIGHT.

I demand to know whether Ederson (who hasn't moved for five minutes and could be completely Trautmanned, for all I know) is OK. Only then will I rant on about the relative triviality of a footballer receiving a red card!!

PEOPLE ARE LOSING THEIR MINDS ABOUT THIS MAN, WHO SUFFERED A SERIOUS BACK INJURY BUT BRAVELY TRAVELLED TO SOUTH AMERICA AND SCORED A GOAL FOR BRAZIL. YOU WON'T BELIEVE WHAT HAPPENED WHEN HE RETURNED TO LIVERPOOL...!!

My bones are old, my back is weak, my eyes are dim, my ears are grey. ≈cough≈

A HEARTBROKEN MAN HAS VOWED TO PLAY THE PIANO UNTIL HE GETS WHAT HE WANTS. FRANK DE BOER (47) WAS DUMPED AFTER A RELATIONSHIP THAT LASTED JUST 10 WEEKS. DE BOER WILL PLAY A MEDLEY OF DUTCH LOVE SONGS, IN AN ACT OF PERFECTLY NORMAL BEHAVIOUR.

He's still out there, Mr Parish.

Come away from the window, you'll only encourage him.

Boom, boom, boom, boom, I want you in my room

IN OTHER SELF-RESPECT NEWS, TWO WHITE-HAIRED MEN HAVE REFUSED TO SHAKE HANDS. ONLOOKERS REPORTED THAT THEY COULDN'T HAVE LOOKED LESS DIGNIFIED IF THEY WERE TRYING TO CATCH A BAT IN THEIR KITCHEN.

Catch him! Catch him, Sparky.

AMERICANS HAVE BEEN WARNED ABOUT THE PERILS OF FIRING BULLETS INTO A HURRICANE, BECAUSE THAT'S WHERE WE'RE AT NOW, AS A SPECIES. HOWEVER, NOT EVEN THE FORCES OF NATURE OR STRATEGY COULD STOP THESE TRIGGER-HAPPY BUSINESSMEN...

LONG-TERM PLAN

CPFC

AND FINALLY...
A BRITISH MAN WILL BECOME THE OLDEST PERSON TO PARACHUTE DIRECTLY INTO A VOLCANO. ROY HODGSON (136) OF CROYDON IS EXPECTING TO LAND IN THE LAKE OF MOLTEN DISAPPOINTMENT LATER TODAY, AND EXPERTS ARE ALREADY PREDICTING THAT THIS WILL DEFINITELY END WELL.

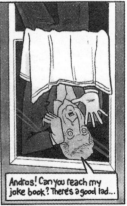

Andros! Can you reach my joke book? There's a good lad...

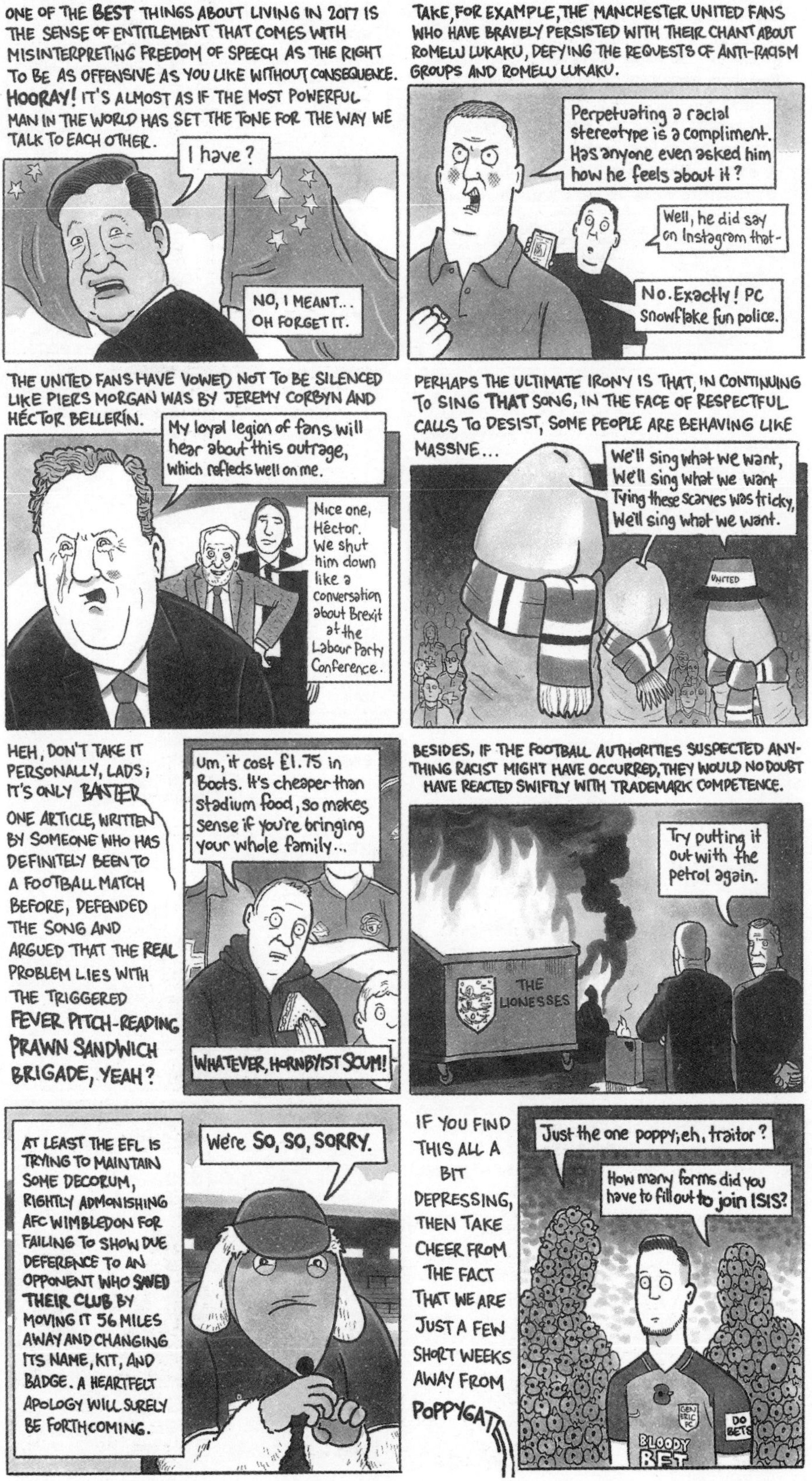
ONE OF THE BEST THINGS ABOUT LIVING IN 2017 IS THE SENSE OF ENTITLEMENT THAT COMES WITH MISINTERPRETING FREEDOM OF SPEECH AS THE RIGHT TO BE AS OFFENSIVE AS YOU LIKE WITHOUT CONSEQUENCE. HOORAY! IT'S ALMOST AS IF THE MOST POWERFUL MAN IN THE WORLD HAS SET THE TONE FOR THE WAY WE TALK TO EACH OTHER.
I have?
NO, I MEANT... OH FORGET IT.
TAKE, FOR EXAMPLE, THE MANCHESTER UNITED FANS WHO HAVE BRAVELY PERSISTED WITH THEIR CHANT ABOUT ROMELU LUKAKU, DEFYING THE REQUESTS OF ANTI-RACISM GROUPS AND ROMELU LUKAKU.
Perpetuating a racial stereotype is a compliment. Has anyone even asked him how he feels about it?
Well, he did say on Instagram that-
No. Exactly! PC snowflake fun police.
THE UNITED FANS HAVE VOWED NOT TO BE SILENCED LIKE PIERS MORGAN WAS BY JEREMY CORBYN AND HÉCTOR BELLERÍN.
My loyal legion of fans will hear about this outrage, which reflects well on me.
Nice one, Héctor. We shut him down like a conversation about Brexit at the Labour Party Conference.
PERHAPS THE ULTIMATE IRONY IS THAT, IN CONTINUING TO SING THAT SONG, IN THE FACE OF RESPECTFUL CALLS TO DESIST, SOME PEOPLE ARE BEHAVING LIKE MASSIVE...
We'll sing what we want, We'll sing what we want Tying these scarves was tricky, We'll sing what we want.
UNITED
HEH, DON'T TAKE IT PERSONALLY, LADS; IT'S ONLY BANTER
ONE ARTICLE, WRITTEN BY SOMEONE WHO HAS DEFINITELY BEEN TO A FOOTBALL MATCH BEFORE, DEFENDED THE SONG AND ARGUED THAT THE REAL PROBLEM LIES WITH THE TRIGGERED FEVER PITCH-READING PRAWN SANDWICH BRIGADE, YEAH?
Um, it cost £1.75 in Boots. It's cheaper than stadium food, so makes sense if you're bringing your whole family...
WHATEVER, HORNBYIST SCUM!
BESIDES, IF THE FOOTBALL AUTHORITIES SUSPECTED ANYTHING RACIST MIGHT HAVE OCCURRED, THEY WOULD NO DOUBT HAVE REACTED SWIFTLY WITH TRADEMARK COMPETENCE.
Try putting it out with the petrol again.
THE LIONESSES
AT LEAST THE EFL IS TRYING TO MAINTAIN SOME DECORUM, RIGHTLY ADMONISHING AFC WIMBLEDON FOR FAILING TO SHOW DUE DEFERENCE TO AN OPPONENT WHO SAVED THEIR CLUB BY MOVING IT 56 MILES AWAY AND CHANGING ITS NAME, KIT, AND BADGE. A HEARTFELT APOLOGY WILL SURELY BE FORTHCOMING.
We're SO, SO, SORRY.
IF YOU FIND THIS ALL A BIT DEPRESSING, THEN TAKE CHEER FROM THE FACT THAT WE ARE JUST A FEW SHORT WEEKS AWAY FROM POPPYGATE
Just the one poppy, eh, traitor?
How many forms did you have to fill out to join ISIS?
GEN ERIC FC
DO BETS
BLOODY BET

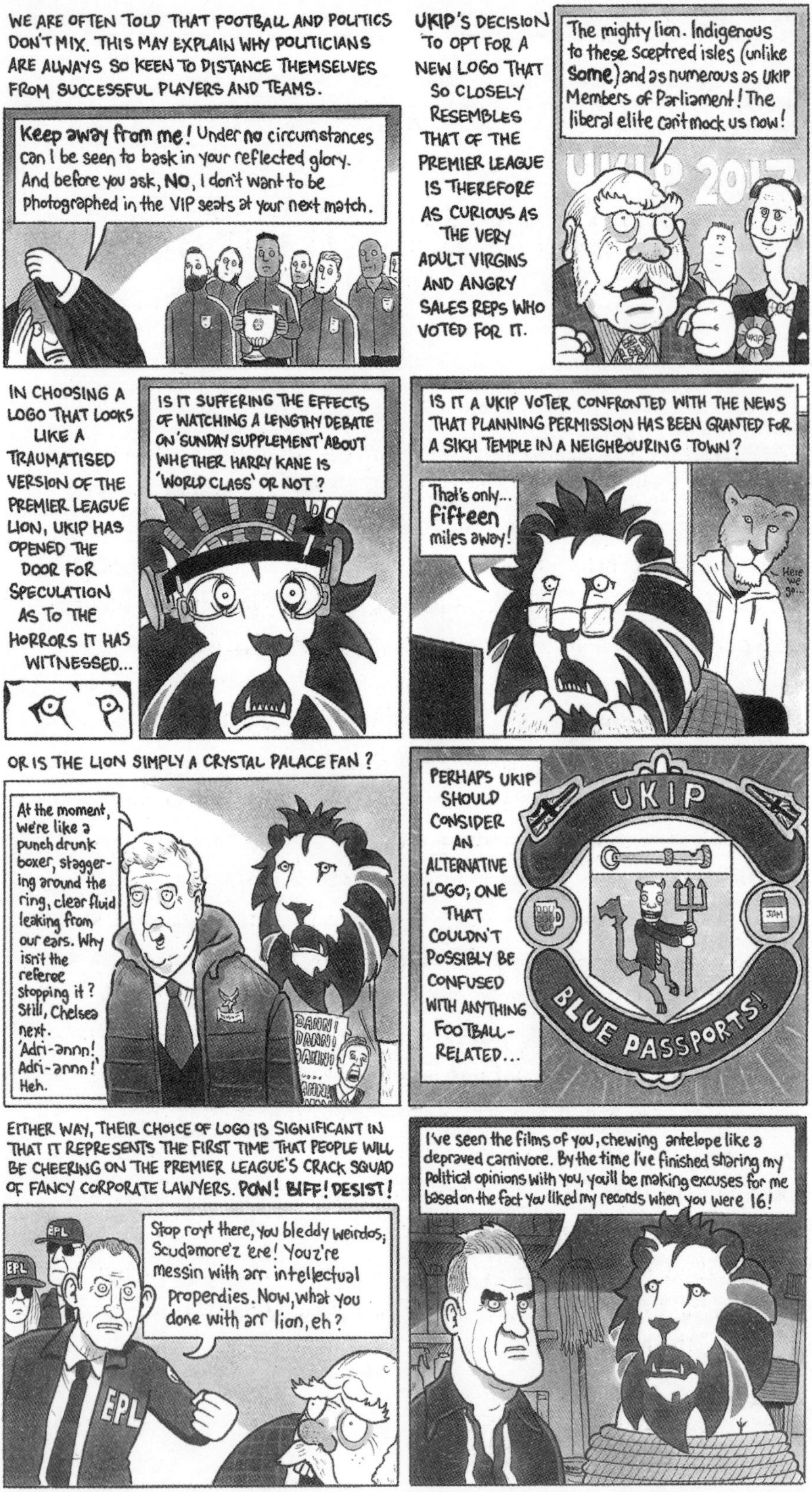
WE ARE OFTEN TOLD THAT FOOTBALL AND POLITICS DON'T MIX. THIS MAY EXPLAIN WHY POLITICIANS ARE ALWAYS SO KEEN TO DISTANCE THEMSELVES FROM SUCCESSFUL PLAYERS AND TEAMS.
Keep away from me! Under no circumstances can I be seen to bask in your reflected glory. And before you ask, NO, I don't want to be photographed in the VIP seats at your next match.
UKIP'S DECISION TO OPT FOR A NEW LOGO THAT SO CLOSELY RESEMBLES THAT OF THE PREMIER LEAGUE IS THEREFORE AS CURIOUS AS THE VERY ADULT VIRGINS AND ANGRY SALES REPS WHO VOTED FOR IT.
The mighty lion. Indigenous to these sceptred isles (unlike some) and as numerous as UKIP Members of Parliament! The liberal elite can't mock us now!
UKIP 2017
UKIP
IN CHOOSING A LOGO THAT LOOKS LIKE A TRAUMATISED VERSION OF THE PREMIER LEAGUE LION, UKIP HAS OPENED THE DOOR FOR SPECULATION AS TO THE HORRORS IT HAS WITNESSED...
IS IT SUFFERING THE EFFECTS OF WATCHING A LENGTHY DEBATE ON 'SUNDAY SUPPLEMENT' ABOUT WHETHER HARRY KANE IS 'WORLD CLASS' OR NOT?
IS IT A UKIP VOTER CONFRONTED WITH THE NEWS THAT PLANNING PERMISSION HAS BEEN GRANTED FOR A SIKH TEMPLE IN A NEIGHBOURING TOWN?
That's only... Fifteen miles away!
Here we go...
OR IS THE LION SIMPLY A CRYSTAL PALACE FAN?
At the moment, we're like a punch drunk boxer, staggering around the ring, clear fluid leaking from our ears. Why isn't the referee stopping it? Still, Chelsea next. 'Adri-annn! Adri-annn!' Heh.
DANNI! DANNI! DANNI!
PERHAPS UKIP SHOULD CONSIDER AN ALTERNATIVE LOGO; ONE THAT COULDN'T POSSIBLY BE CONFUSED WITH ANYTHING FOOTBALL-RELATED...
UKIP
JAM
BLUE PASSPORTS!
EITHER WAY, THEIR CHOICE OF LOGO IS SIGNIFICANT IN THAT IT REPRESENTS THE FIRST TIME THAT PEOPLE WILL BE CHEERING ON THE PREMIER LEAGUE'S CRACK SQUAD OF FANCY CORPORATE LAWYERS. POW! BIFF! DESIST!
EPL
EPL
Stop royt there, you bleddy weirdos; Scudamore'z 'ere! Youz're messin with arr intellectual properdies. Now, what you done with arr lion, eh?
EPL
I've seen the films of you, chewing antelope like a depraved carnivore. By the time I've finished sharing my political opinions with you, you'll be making excuses for me based on the fact you liked my records when you were 16!

WINNERS AND LOSERS

Arsène Wenger was widely ridiculed when, speaking at Arsenal's AGM in 2012, he equated qualifying for the Champions League with winning a trophy. His viewpoint has since been supported and repeated by other Premier League managers, most notably Louis van Gaal, during his time at Manchester United, and Mauricio Pochettino, when faced with the inconvenience of an FA Cup semi-final in 2018.

In a purely financial sense, finishing fourth in the league *is* more rewarding than winning a trophy, but we are yet to see a team conduct an open-top bus tour while lifting aloft a spreadsheet to a mass of fans waving replica spreadsheets (give it time). It stands to reason that Pochettino would prioritise the Champions League, and Spurs fans seemed largely supportive of this position, their hunger for silverware satisfied by the memory of last winning a meaningful trophy as recently as 1991.

Only a handful of teams can experience success each season, and for elite clubs scrapping it out at the top anything less than the Premier League title is considered a failure. Winning the FA Cup isn't enough to save a manager's job, and winning the Carabao Cup is almost more insulting than losing it. You might get away with it if you can do it in an arch, knowing fashion, but imagine the gossip among the other Big Clubs if you got caught in the moment, exhibiting non-ironic delight. ('Ohmygod, have you *seen* Pep? Dancing around with the trophy like he's drunk on Thai energy drink? #embarrassing.')

Given the ever-widening financial chasm that exists between a handful of clubs at the top of the Premier League and Everyone Else, it's likely that fans of only five or six teams will ever see their boys finish top of the pile. Certainly, going into the 2015/16 season there were no signs to suggest that the status quo would be broken.

Chelsea were reigning champions, having routinely swept aside all opponents the previous season. The only battle they had to endure was the feeling that the media weren't treating them with due deference, as if they were universally regarded as objectionable. How could anyone not like a team captained by John Terry and managed by José Mourinho? It was a weird one all right, but we soon discovered that 2016 would be an even stranger year.

Chelsea's title defence went off the rails almost from the first day, when Mourinho abused Eva Carneiro. Perhaps it was at that point that the Chelsea players began to wonder whether their loveable coach, with his sardonic laugh and fondness for blaming others, might be a bullying prick. Just to be on the safe side, for the next few months they did a passable impression of Sunderland, and he was fired by Christmas.

None of the other usual title contenders were able to take advantage of Chelsea's misfortune, so by November it was Leicester City who were top of the league, the kind of anomaly you usually only see on the opening weekend of the season, when not all the teams have played. When I drew a strip about 'Our New Leicester City Overlords', I didn't believe for one second that they would retain that position. I was as confident that they would slide down the table as I was in the belief that I'd always be able to make cartoon references to the films of Kevin Spacey. There was a natural order to things, and it didn't involve Leicester.

However, as is often the case, I was wrong. It's still incomprehensible that Leicester won the Premier League; it's like Trump in the White House, but with a bit less racism. They were now part of the football aristocracy, a situation that would be as permanent as the employment of Claudio Ranieri.

Europe awaited them, where Real Madrid were just about to win the 2016 Champions League final with a penalty shoot-out win against local rivals Atlético. The general consensus was that this Real side were limited and lucky. So rubbish and jammy were they that they won the competition for the next two years in a row, aided by the phenomenal hunger of Cristiano Ronaldo and the unerring commitment to bastardry of Sergio Ramos.

Speaking of which, Mourinho was back in the game at Manchester United, where they must have spent the previous nine months enjoying some kind of information detox, putting all their phones and tablets into a vault and avoiding all forms of news media. His former club Chelsea hired Antonio Conte and won the Premier League again in 2017. Hooray, normality restored, provincial clubs whose owners didn't make their fortune by pillaging a nation's mineral wealth put back in their place. However, there was still a shock element to the victory, as for the first time in living memory Chelsea seemed . . . if not quite *likeable*, then Not Contemptible (John Terry didn't play much).

Inter seemed intent on coaxing Conte back to Italy, and maybe he should have gone, as his relationship with Chelsea's hierarchy deteriorated over the course of the following season, his open acts of defiance extending to publicly complaining about transfer budgets, failing to qualify for the Champions League and, worst of all, winning the FA Cup. This was expert-level trolling.

2018 was Manchester City's year, though, as they won the league by a record number of points. At one stage it seemed that Pep Guardiola's team might go the whole season unbeaten, but then they began to wobble, in a manner most unusual for Manchester City. Having blown a two-goal lead to lose the Manchester derby at the Etihad Stadium, there existed a slim chance that United could catch them. However, the following Sunday Mourinho's team lost at home to West Brom – who were enjoying the turnaround in fortunes experienced by many clubs who no longer have Alan Pardew on their payroll – and the title was City's. The result sparked wild celebrations among their players and staff, apart from Pep, who spent the afternoon playing golf.

Almost as impressive as their football was the advert by an Abu Dhabi telecommunications company that accompanied it. Set to the tune of 'If You're Happy and You Know It', it managed to combine tired football tropes with lyrics more jarring than a Fernandinho reducer. Although it had all the realism of a football-themed birthday card from your nan, the advert did provide a crumb of familiar comfort: even when Manchester City were the best team in the country, they were still capable of screwing it up spectacularly.

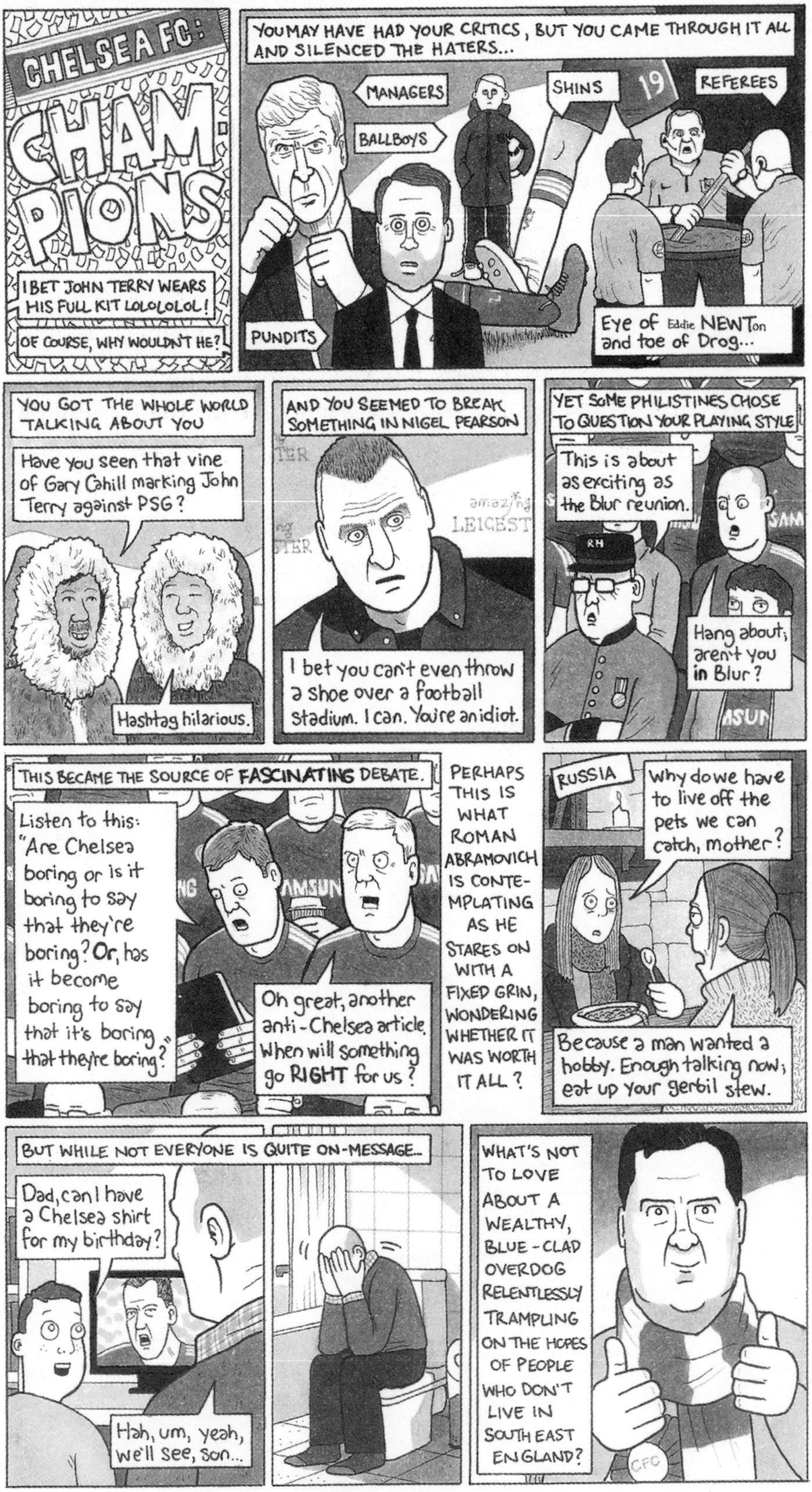
CHELSEA FC:
CHAMPIONS
I BET JOHN TERRY WEARS HIS FULL KIT LOLOLOLOL!
OF COURSE, WHY WOULDN'T HE?
YOU MAY HAVE HAD YOUR CRITICS, BUT YOU CAME THROUGH IT ALL AND SILENCED THE HATERS...
MANAGERS
BALLBOYS
SHINS
REFEREES
PUNDITS
Eye of Eddie NEWTon and toe of Drog...
YOU GOT THE WHOLE WORLD TALKING ABOUT YOU
Have you seen that vine of Gary Cahill marking John Terry against PSG?
Hashtag hilarious.
AND YOU SEEMED TO BREAK SOMETHING IN NIGEL PEARSON
I bet you can't even throw a shoe over a football stadium. I can. You're an idiot.
YET SOME PHILISTINES CHOSE TO QUESTION YOUR PLAYING STYLE
This is about as exciting as the Blur reunion.
Hang about, aren't you in Blur?
THIS BECAME THE SOURCE OF FASCINATING DEBATE.
Listen to this: "Are Chelsea boring or is it boring to say that they're boring? Or, has it become boring to say that it's boring that they're boring?"
Oh great, another anti-Chelsea article. When will something go RIGHT for us?
PERHAPS THIS IS WHAT ROMAN ABRAMOVICH IS CONTEMPLATING AS HE STARES ON WITH A FIXED GRIN, WONDERING WHETHER IT WAS WORTH IT ALL?
RUSSIA
Why do we have to live off the pets we can catch, mother?
Because a man wanted a hobby. Enough talking now; eat up your gerbil stew.
BUT WHILE NOT EVERYONE IS QUITE ON-MESSAGE...
Dad, can I have a Chelsea shirt for my birthday?
Hah, um, yeah, we'll see, son...
WHAT'S NOT TO LOVE ABOUT A WEALTHY, BLUE-CLAD OVERDOG RELENTLESSLY TRAMPLING ON THE HOPES OF PEOPLE WHO DON'T LIVE IN SOUTH EAST ENGLAND?
CFC

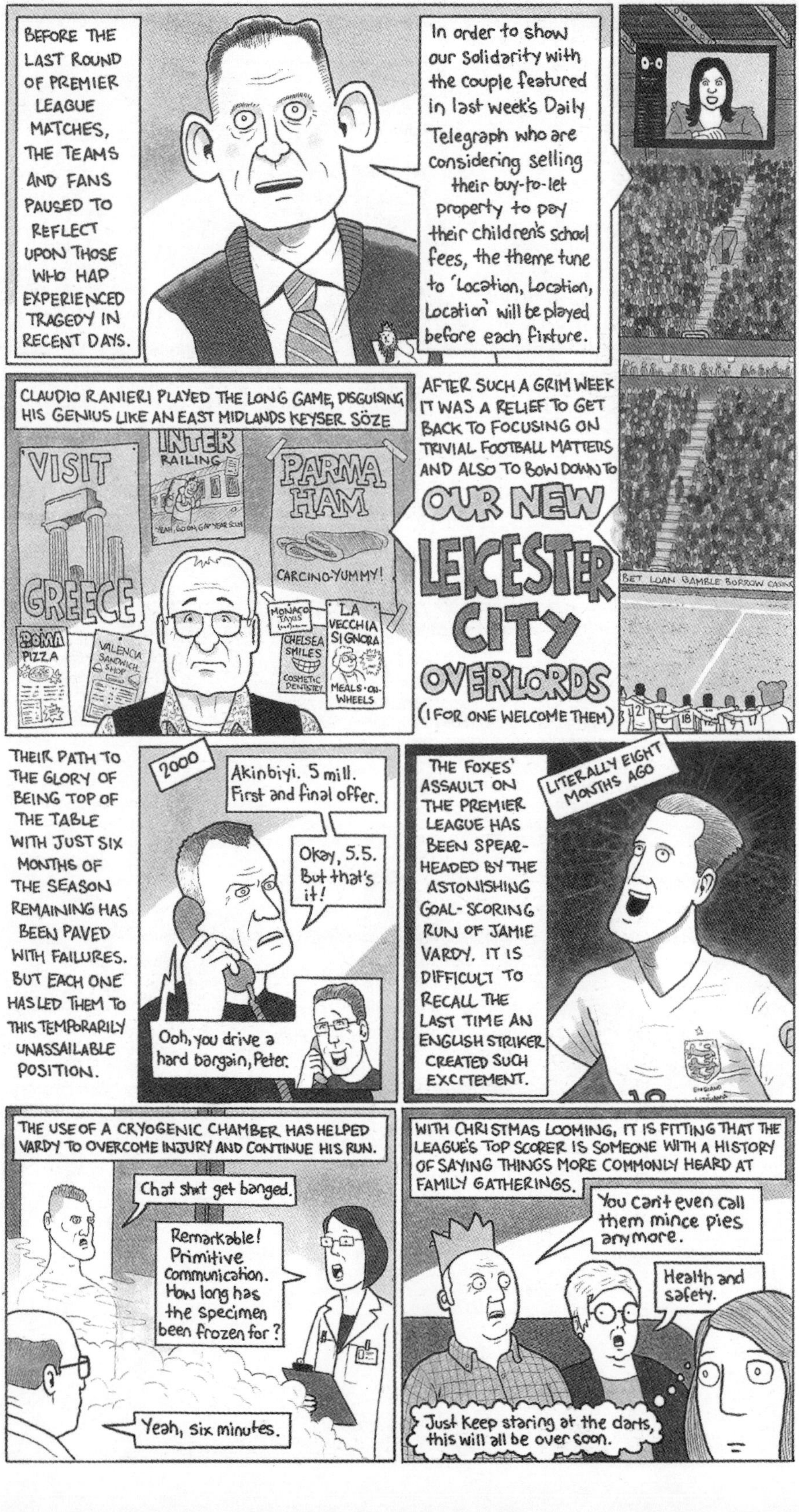
BEFORE THE LAST ROUND OF PREMIER LEAGUE MATCHES, THE TEAMS AND FANS PAUSED TO REFLECT UPON THOSE WHO HAD EXPERIENCED TRAGEDY IN RECENT DAYS.
In order to show our solidarity with the couple featured in last week's Daily Telegraph who are considering selling their buy-to-let property to pay their children's school fees, the theme tune to 'Location, Location, Location' will be played before each fixture.
CLAUDIO RANIERI PLAYED THE LONG GAME, DISGUISING HIS GENIUS LIKE AN EAST MIDLANDS KEYSER SÖZE
VISIT GREECE
INTER RAILING
YEAH, GO ON, GAP YEAR SCUM
PARMA HAM
CARCINO-YUMMY!
ROMA PIZZA
VALENCIA SANDWICH SHOP
MONACO TAXIS
CHELSEA SMILES
COSMETIC DENTISTRY
LA VECCHIA SIGNORA
MEALS-ON-WHEELS
AFTER SUCH A GRIM WEEK IT WAS A RELIEF TO GET BACK TO FOCUSING ON TRIVIAL FOOTBALL MATTERS AND ALSO TO BOW DOWN TO
OUR NEW LEICESTER CITY OVERLORDS
(I FOR ONE WELCOME THEM)
BET LOAN GAMBLE BORROW CASINO
THEIR PATH TO THE GLORY OF BEING TOP OF THE TABLE WITH JUST SIX MONTHS OF THE SEASON REMAINING HAS BEEN PAVED WITH FAILURES. BUT EACH ONE HAS LED THEM TO THIS TEMPORARILY UNASSAILABLE POSITION.
2000
Akinbiyi. 5 mill. First and final offer.
Okay, 5.5. But that's it!
Ooh, you drive a hard bargain, Peter.
THE FOXES' ASSAULT ON THE PREMIER LEAGUE HAS BEEN SPEAR-HEADED BY THE ASTONISHING GOAL-SCORING RUN OF JAMIE VARDY. IT IS DIFFICULT TO RECALL THE LAST TIME AN ENGLISH STRIKER CREATED SUCH EXCITEMENT.
LITERALLY EIGHT MONTHS AGO
THE USE OF A CRYOGENIC CHAMBER HAS HELPED VARDY TO OVERCOME INJURY AND CONTINUE HIS RUN.
Chat shit get banged.
Remarkable! Primitive communication. How long has the specimen been frozen for?
Yeah, six minutes.
WITH CHRISTMAS LOOMING, IT IS FITTING THAT THE LEAGUE'S TOP SCORER IS SOMEONE WITH A HISTORY OF SAYING THINGS MORE COMMONLY HEARD AT FAMILY GATHERINGS.
You can't even call them mince pies anymore.
Health and safety.
Just keep staring at the darts, this will all be over soon.

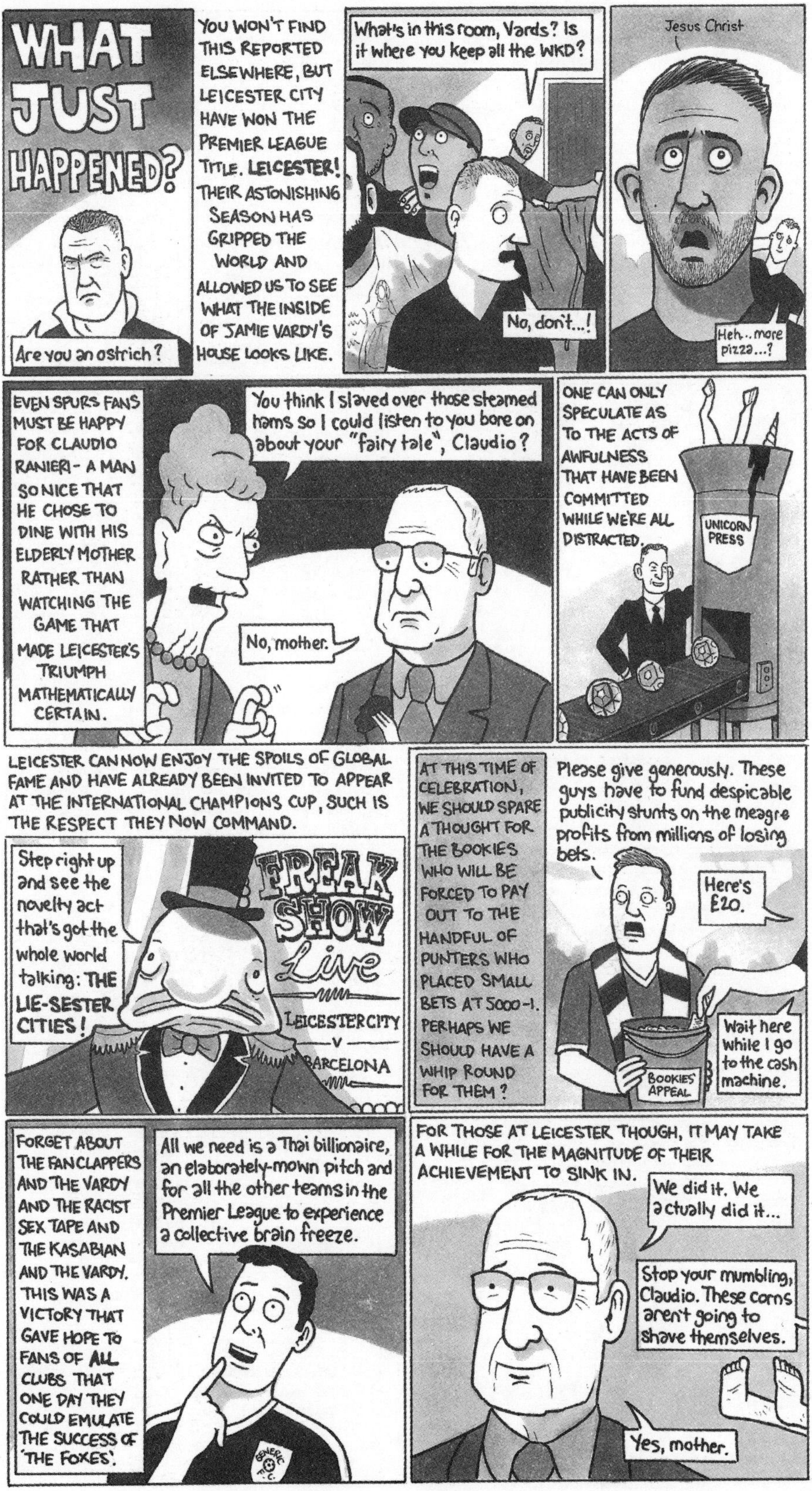

WHAT JUST HAPPENED?
Are you an ostrich?
YOU WON'T FIND THIS REPORTED ELSEWHERE, BUT LEICESTER CITY HAVE WON THE PREMIER LEAGUE TITLE. LEICESTER! THEIR ASTONISHING SEASON HAS GRIPPED THE WORLD AND ALLOWED US TO SEE WHAT THE INSIDE OF JAMIE VARDY'S HOUSE LOOKS LIKE.
What's in this room, Vards? Is it where you keep all the WKD?
No, don't...!
Jesus Christ
Heh... more pizza...?
EVEN SPURS FANS MUST BE HAPPY FOR CLAUDIO RANIERI - A MAN SO NICE THAT HE CHOSE TO DINE WITH HIS ELDERLY MOTHER RATHER THAN WATCHING THE GAME THAT MADE LEICESTER'S TRIUMPH MATHEMATICALLY CERTAIN.
You think I slaved over those steamed hams so I could listen to you bore on about your "fairy tale", Claudio?
No, mother.
ONE CAN ONLY SPECULATE AS TO THE ACTS OF AWFULNESS THAT HAVE BEEN COMMITTED WHILE WE'RE ALL DISTRACTED.
UNICORN PRESS
LEICESTER CAN NOW ENJOY THE SPOILS OF GLOBAL FAME AND HAVE ALREADY BEEN INVITED TO APPEAR AT THE INTERNATIONAL CHAMPIONS CUP, SUCH IS THE RESPECT THEY NOW COMMAND.
Step right up and see the novelty act that's got the whole world talking: THE LIE-SESTER CITIES!
FREAK SHOW Live
LEICESTER CITY v BARCELONA
AT THIS TIME OF CELEBRATION, WE SHOULD SPARE A THOUGHT FOR THE BOOKIES WHO WILL BE FORCED TO PAY OUT TO THE HANDFUL OF PUNTERS WHO PLACED SMALL BETS AT 5000-1. PERHAPS WE SHOULD HAVE A WHIP ROUND FOR THEM?
Please give generously. These guys have to fund despicable publicity stunts on the meagre profits from millions of losing bets.
Here's £20.
Wait here while I go to the cash machine.
BOOKIES' APPEAL
FORGET ABOUT THE FAN CLAPPERS AND THE VARDY AND THE RACIST SEX TAPE AND THE KASABIAN AND THE VARDY. THIS WAS A VICTORY THAT GAVE HOPE TO FANS OF ALL CLUBS THAT ONE DAY THEY COULD EMULATE THE SUCCESS OF 'THE FOXES'.
All we need is a Thai billionaire, an elaborately-mown pitch and for all the other teams in the Premier League to experience a collective brain freeze.
GENERIC F.C.
FOR THOSE AT LEICESTER THOUGH, IT MAY TAKE A WHILE FOR THE MAGNITUDE OF THEIR ACHIEVEMENT TO SINK IN.
We did it. We actually did it...
Stop your mumbling, Claudio. These corns aren't going to shave themselves.
Yes, mother.

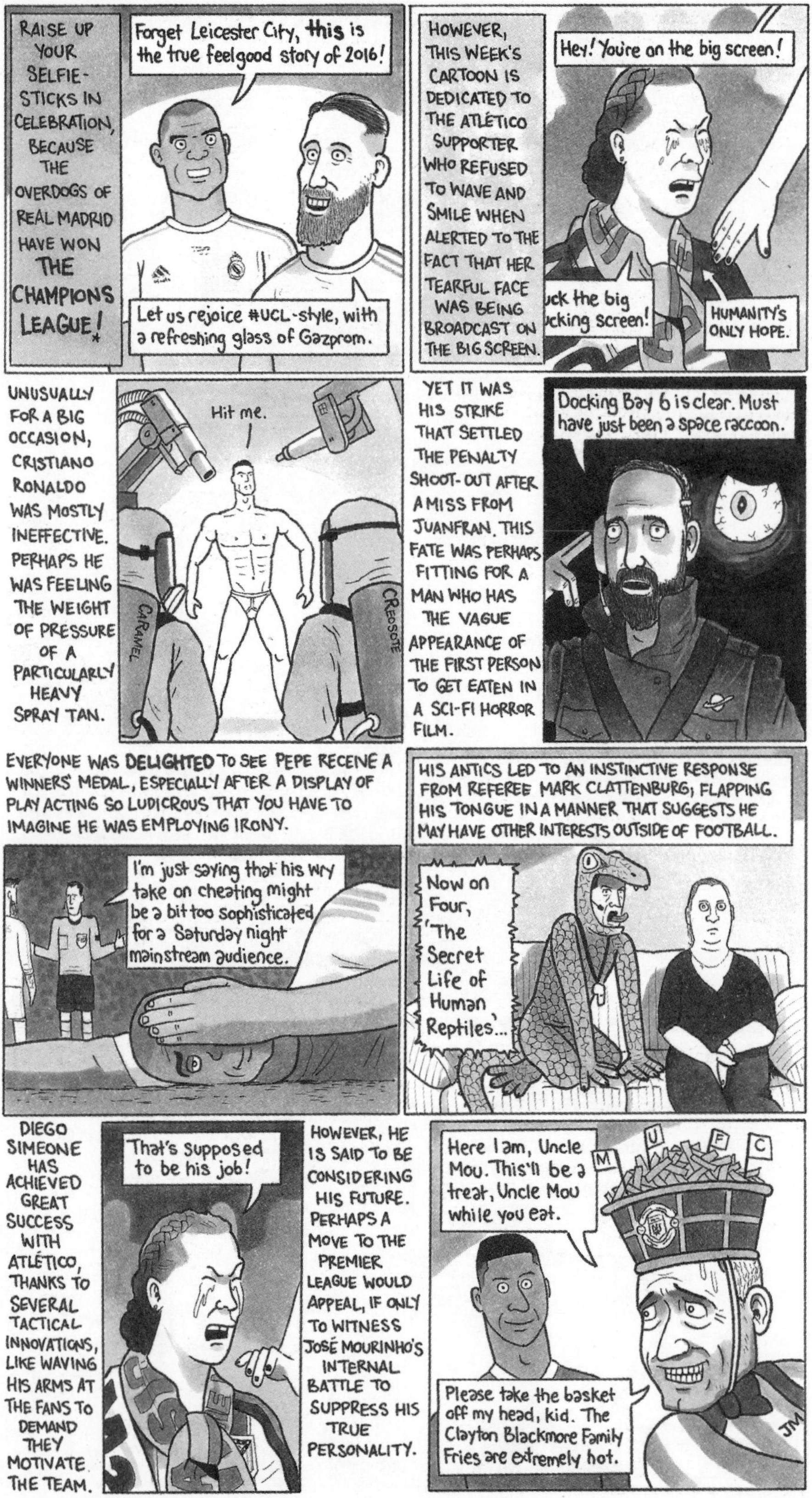

RAISE UP YOUR SELFIE-STICKS IN CELEBRATION, BECAUSE THE OVERDOGS OF REAL MADRID HAVE WON THE CHAMPIONS LEAGUE!*
Forget Leicester City, this is the true feelgood story of 2016!
Let us rejoice #UCL-style, with a refreshing glass of Gazprom.
HOWEVER, THIS WEEK'S CARTOON IS DEDICATED TO THE ATLÉTICO SUPPORTER WHO REFUSED TO WAVE AND SMILE WHEN ALERTED TO THE FACT THAT HER TEARFUL FACE WAS BEING BROADCAST ON THE BIG SCREEN.
Hey! You're on the big screen!
uck the big ucking screen!
HUMANITY'S ONLY HOPE.
UNUSUALLY FOR A BIG OCCASION, CRISTIANO RONALDO WAS MOSTLY INEFFECTIVE. PERHAPS HE WAS FEELING THE WEIGHT OF PRESSURE OF A PARTICULARLY HEAVY SPRAY TAN.
Hit me.
CARAMEL
CREOSOTE
YET IT WAS HIS STRIKE THAT SETTLED THE PENALTY SHOOT-OUT AFTER A MISS FROM JUANFRAN. THIS FATE WAS PERHAPS FITTING FOR A MAN WHO HAS THE VAGUE APPEARANCE OF THE FIRST PERSON TO GET EATEN IN A SCI-FI HORROR FILM.
Docking Bay 6 is clear. Must have just been a space raccoon.
EVERYONE WAS DELIGHTED TO SEE PEPE RECEIVE A WINNERS' MEDAL, ESPECIALLY AFTER A DISPLAY OF PLAY ACTING SO LUDICROUS THAT YOU HAVE TO IMAGINE HE WAS EMPLOYING IRONY.
I'm just saying that his wry take on cheating might be a bit too sophisticated for a Saturday night mainstream audience.
HIS ANTICS LED TO AN INSTINCTIVE RESPONSE FROM REFEREE MARK CLATTENBURG; FLAPPING HIS TONGUE IN A MANNER THAT SUGGESTS HE MAY HAVE OTHER INTERESTS OUTSIDE OF FOOTBALL.
Now on Four, 'The Secret Life of Human Reptiles'...
DIEGO SIMEONE HAS ACHIEVED GREAT SUCCESS WITH ATLÉTICO, THANKS TO SEVERAL TACTICAL INNOVATIONS, LIKE WAVING HIS ARMS AT THE FANS TO DEMAND THEY MOTIVATE THE TEAM.
That's supposed to be his job!
HOWEVER, HE IS SAID TO BE CONSIDERING HIS FUTURE. PERHAPS A MOVE TO THE PREMIER LEAGUE WOULD APPEAL, IF ONLY TO WITNESS JOSÉ MOURINHO'S INTERNAL BATTLE TO SUPPRESS HIS TRUE PERSONALITY.
Here I am, Uncle Mou. This'll be a treat, Uncle Mou while you eat.
M U F C
Please take the basket off my head, kid. The Clayton Blackmore Family Fries are extremely hot.
JM

CHELSEA ARE PREMIER LEAGUE CHAMPIONS! IN PREVIOUS YEARS, SUCH NEWS MAY HAVE BEEN MET AS ENTHUSIASTICALLY AS THE ARRIVAL OF A BLADDER INFECTION, BUT THIS YEAR CHELSEA SEEM LESS, WELL, CHELSEA. THEY'VE PLAYED THE BEST FOOTBALL, WON THE MOST GAMES, AND HAVE, AT TIMES VEERED DANGEROUSLY CLOSE TO BEING — OH GOD — LIKEABLE. PERHAPS IT'S JUST THAT WE'VE ALL BECOME DESENSITISED TO AWFUL EVENTS, OR MAYBE IT'S THE KNOWLEDGE THAT IT MUST REALLY ANNOY JOSÉ MOURINHO, BUT CHELSEA WINNING THE LEAGUE DOESN'T SEEM COMPLETELY TERRIBLE. CONGRATULATIONS!

SEVERAL PLAYERS CAME TO THE FORE AND MADE THE SUCCESS POSSIBLE. AMONG THEM WERE...

THE NEWLY-SERIOUS COMIC ACTOR DAVID LUIZ

Wow, keep this up and you'll get your own ITV detective series!

REFORMED SNAKE, EDEN HAZARD

It's odd, as soon as I started to play well, the fans forgot I was a José-murdering reptile man.

...AND, OF COURSE, THE OMNIPRESENT N'GOLO KANTÉ, WHO CONTINUES TO ASTOUND WITH HIS ABILITY TO SOLVE PROBLEMS ALL OVER THE PITCH AND BEYOND.

TACKLE!

RUN!

INTERCEPT!

BAH!

BLOCK!

If I've heard the critics correctly, they want another Alien prequel, with a more convoluted backstory...

RIDLEY SCOTT

INTERVENE!

Nuclear codes? Of course I know them. Sure, I can prove it—

STUFF

БАХ!

THE TURNING POINT OF THEIR SEASON CAME WITH A 3-0 DEFEAT TO ARSENAL IN SEPTEMBER (ARSÈNE WENGER WILL TAKE PRIDE IN THE ROLE HIS TEAM PLAYED IN DECIDING THE DIRECTION OF THE LEAGUE TITLE). ANTONIO CONTE'S SUBSEQUENT DECISION TO SWITCH TO THREE AT THE BACK WAS HIS 'DYLAN GOES ELECTRIC' MOMENT, BUT WAS INITIALLY MET WITH SOME HOSTILITY BY TRADITIONALISTS.

BOOOOOO!

COURTOIS
AZPILICUETA LUIZ CAHILL
MOSES KANTE MATIC ALONSO
PEDRO HAZARD
COSTA

The times they are a-changin, Bog brush 'ed.

TERRY

CONTE HAS SUCCESSFULLY TRANSFORMED CHELSEA, BUT THE CLUB NOW FACES A BATTLE TO KEEP HIM. IT SEEMS INTER ARE TRYING TO LURE HIM BACK TO ITALY. HAVING HIRED ALL OF HIS FRIENDS IN KEY ROLES, THEY MAY NOW MOVE ON TO APPOINTING MEMBERS OF HIS IMMEDIATE FAMILY.

I made one simple request: sign me Batman. What do you bring me? Ben Sodding Affleck! I'm Director of Football, not a restorer of exploded sofas!

Hey!

HOWEVER, CHELSEA ARE APPARENTLY PLANNING TO THROW A ROMELU LUKAKU-SIZED PILE OF CASH HIS WAY, SO THERE IS PROBABLY NO CAUSE FOR THEIR FANS TO BE TOO CONCERNED.

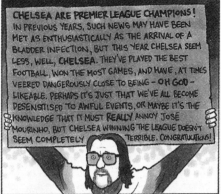

YOU...

∨ THE GUY THEY TOLD YOU NOT TO WORRY ABOUT.

Blue is a colour, football is a thing. Dum-dum-de-dum dum...

PERIŠIĆ

HAVING SECURED THE LEAGUE TITLE, MONDAY NIGHT'S EXHIBITION GAME WITH WATFORD WAS PLAYED IN A PARTY ATMOSPHERE, BUT AS THE ASSORTED RESERVES AND COMPETITION WINNERS TOOK THEIR PLACE IN THE CHELSEA LINE UP, THE THOUGHTS OF THE MORE SERIOUS PLAYERS TURNED TO THE NEXT BIG PROJECT.

itv2

LIKESCHURCH

DORSET'S CRIME-FIGHTING EVANGELICAL DETECTIVE

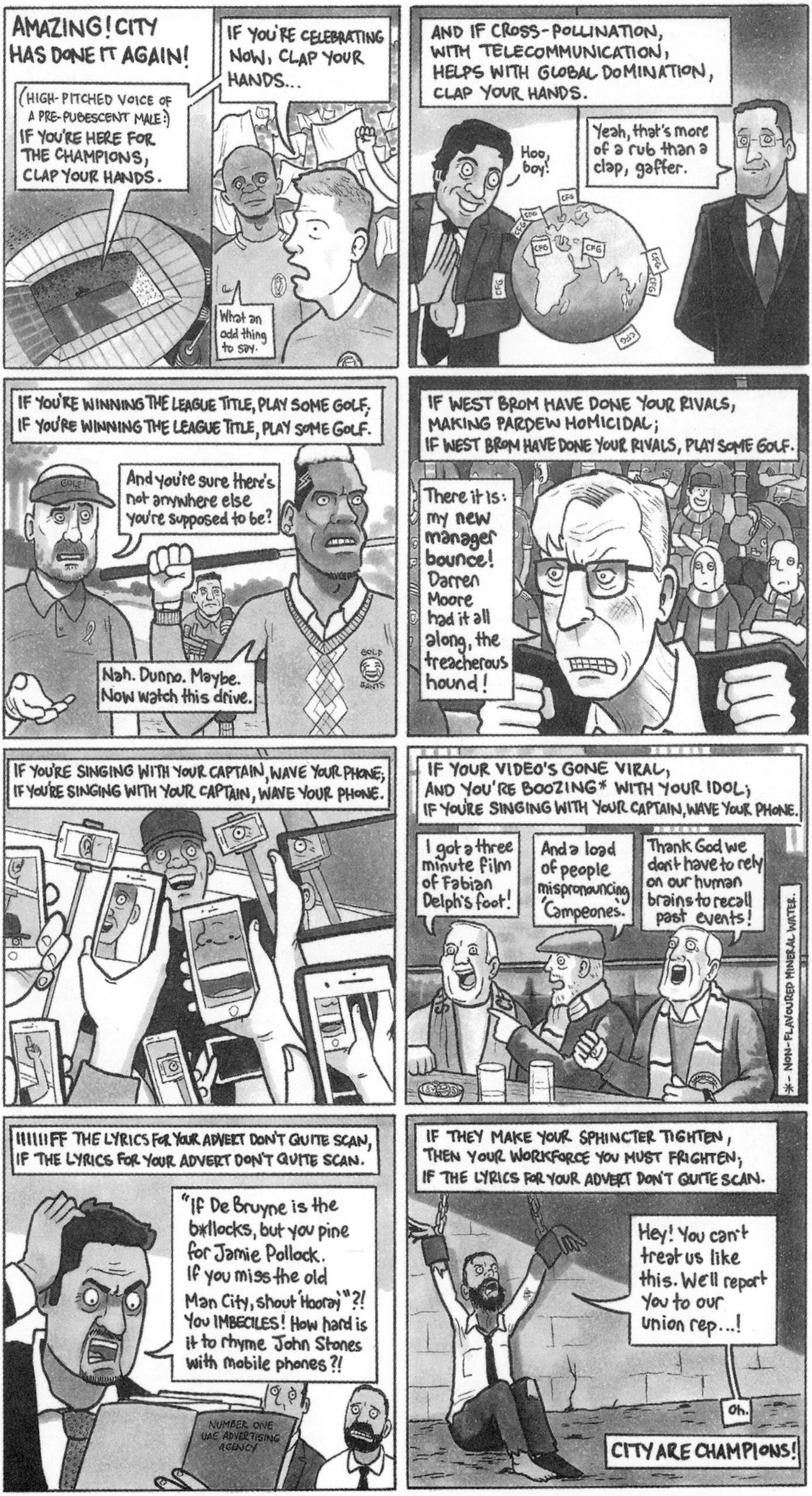
AMAZING! CITY HAS DONE IT AGAIN!
(HIGH-PITCHED VOICE OF A PRE-PUBESCENT MALE:) IF YOU'RE HERE FOR THE CHAMPIONS, CLAP YOUR HANDS.
IF YOU'RE CELEBRATING NOW, CLAP YOUR HANDS...
What an odd thing to say.
AND IF CROSS-POLLINATION, WITH TELECOMMUNICATION, HELPS WITH GLOBAL DOMINATION, CLAP YOUR HANDS.
Hoo, boy!
Yeah, that's more of a rub than a clap, gaffer.
CFG
IF YOU'RE WINNING THE LEAGUE TITLE, PLAY SOME GOLF, IF YOU'RE WINNING THE LEAGUE TITLE, PLAY SOME GOLF.
And you're sure there's not anywhere else you're supposed to be?
Nah. Dunno. Maybe. Now watch this drive.
GOLF BANTS
IF WEST BROM HAVE DONE YOUR RIVALS, MAKING PARDEW HOMICIDAL; IF WEST BROM HAVE DONE YOUR RIVALS, PLAY SOME GOLF.
There it is: my new manager bounce! Darren Moore had it all along, the treacherous hound!
IF YOU'RE SINGING WITH YOUR CAPTAIN, WAVE YOUR PHONE; IF YOU'RE SINGING WITH YOUR CAPTAIN, WAVE YOUR PHONE.
IF YOUR VIDEO'S GONE VIRAL, AND YOU'RE BOOZING* WITH YOUR IDOL; IF YOU'RE SINGING WITH YOUR CAPTAIN, WAVE YOUR PHONE.
I got a three minute film of Fabian Delph's foot!
And a load of people mispronouncing 'Campeones'.
Thank God we don't have to rely on our human brains to recall past events!
* - NON-FLAVOURED MINERAL WATER.
IIIIIIFF THE LYRICS FOR YOUR ADVERT DON'T QUITE SCAN, IF THE LYRICS FOR YOUR ADVERT DON'T QUITE SCAN.
"If De Bruyne is the b*llocks, but you pine for Jamie Pollock. If you miss the old Man City, shout 'Hooray'"?! You IMBECILES! How hard is it to rhyme 'John Stones' with 'mobile phones'?!
NUMBER ONE UAE ADVERTISING AGENCY
IF THEY MAKE YOUR SPHINCTER TIGHTEN, THEN YOUR WORKFORCE YOU MUST FRIGHTEN; IF THE LYRICS FOR YOUR ADVERT DON'T QUITE SCAN.
Hey! You can't treat us like this. We'll report you to our union rep...!
Oh.
CITY ARE CHAMPIONS!

ENGLAND EXPECTS

(at Best to Go Out to the
First Good Team They Play)

England has a weird relationship with its national football team. It's tied up in history and an often misplaced sense of its status in the world. As a political and footballing force, England hasn't been a major power for some time, the glory days a distant memory. Just as the Industrial Revolution gave Britain the upper hand on the world stage, England's national team had the advantage of being one of football's early adopters, a superpower before others caught up and overtook.

Up until the 2018 World Cup, England's record at major tournaments was poor. It was over fifty years since they'd reached a major final (Le Tournoi was a group-based competition, so didn't have a final), and they hadn't seriously bothered the latter stages of a tournament since 1996. Yet throughout much of this barren period, a false sense of entitlement endured, an attitude based in myth and propagated by a chauvinistic tabloid media. This outlook was famously summed up by a headline in the *Sun*, when the draw was made for the 2010 World Cup group stage: 'England, Algeria, Slovenia, Yanks – EASY'. Naturally, England finished second and got thrashed by Germany in the second round.

Yet it is the same outlets that strive to destabilise the efforts of the national team, digging deep before every tournament to unearth some dirt on the players or manager. After all, it's in the public interest to make life as relentlessly grim as possible, so if you can make a scapegoat out of a young man for getting a tattoo or buying a sausage roll in Greggs, then it helps to cultivate the blame culture that props up your noxious empire of misery.

At major tournaments, England's deficiencies are often painfully exposed, their dour football in tune with grim renditions of the *Dambusters* theme from that bloody band, and with costumed reminders of the Crusades and world war bombing campaigns contributing to the carnival atmosphere. Even if you want them to win, you want them to lose.

The public attitude towards England seemed to hit a nadir in the early 2000s, with the arrival of a talented group of players who were tagged 'The Golden Generation' by the FA's Adam Crozier. With expectation levels helpfully heightened, the team's inability to deliver success was met with frustration and anger. There was a feeling of resentment towards some of the squad's superstars, especially as this period coincided with lucrative TV deals that inflated the top players' wages. Footballers had always been well paid, but the riches of the Premier League era forced them deeper into their gated communities. There was no longer a chance you'd kick your ball into a garden and be surprised to see Ashley Cole answer the door when you went to knock for it.

Each elimination from a major tournament is followed by a period of soul searching. Why aren't our players comfortable on the ball? Is coaching to blame? How come they can perform well against the likes of Bournemouth and Watford in the best league in the world, but can't do it against the finest eleven players from Germany? Unlike most other countries, lots of people like football in England, so why aren't we the best at it? Is it possible to trace hate mail, because I have a special package I want to send to that lad who was photographed buying a pastry-based snack just three weeks after we lost a football match?

Up until Russia, my own theory was that English people just don't like being away from home for longer than two weeks. We're not good travellers. Yeah, you say you'd tour the world if you won the lottery, but after a couple of weeks you'd be wanting to get home to have a proper cuppa and visit Mum.

At least the current England crop aren't weighed down with the burden of national hope. They have a squad of young players, relatively free of star names (apologies, Fabian Delph), and in Gareth Southgate have a likeable, articulate manager whose measured approach and humble character makes him annoyingly difficult to take the piss out of. Somehow, I have soldiered on, so I'll leave it up to you to decide who the *real* good guy is in this scenario (it's me).

This group of cartoons mostly focuses on the period following England's disastrous performance at Euro 2016, through to qualification for the 2018 World Cup (which is covered in full in the final chapter of the book). After the departure of Roy Hodgson, there was hope for a new era. Sam Allardyce took charge and immediately became the most potent manager in England's history, boasting a 100 per cent win record, thanks to a solitary 1–0 win against Slovakia in Trnava. Alas, he was also the manager most likely to show off to a group of undercover reporters, and he was 100 per cent fired after just sixty-seven days in the job.

Southgate was hired as caretaker manager, eventually getting the job on a permanent basis. At the time, anyone could have been handed the job, as the rest of the world was distracted by the increasing likelihood of a seventy-year old baby becoming the US president, which also presented me with the chance to draw Ken Bone. (Remember Ken Bone? From the televised presidential debates? He wore red knitwear and had a moustache! He was a human man for a while and then became a meme! What? You've got a job? OK, forget it.)

However, the first cartoon in this section goes back further and is titled 'Images from a Match Against Norway in September 2014, Set to the Lyrics of "The Dead Flag Blues" by Canadian Post-Rock Outfit Godspeed You! Black Emperor'. I hope it encapsulates the enthusiasm for England friendlies in the months following a poor showing at a big tournament.

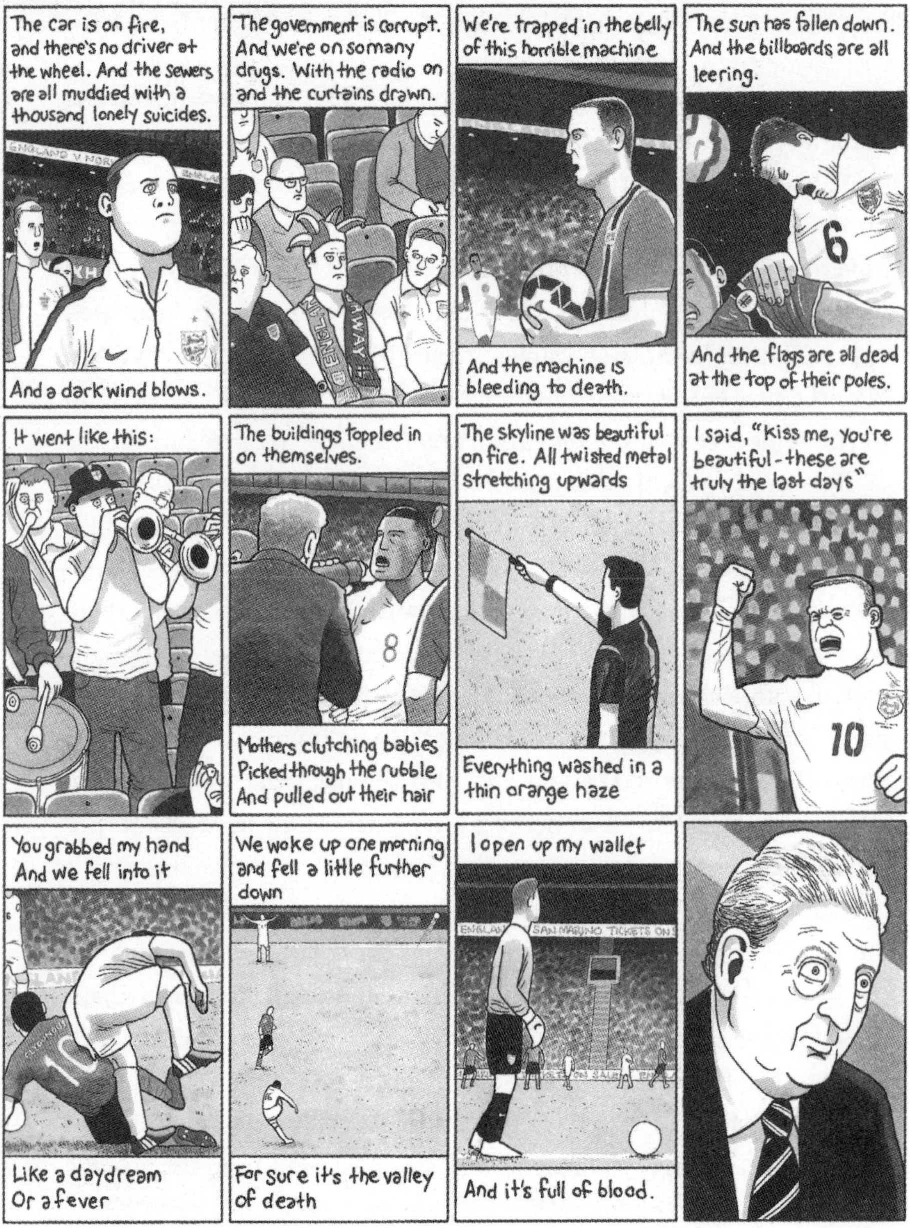

The car is on fire, and there's no driver at the wheel. And the sewers are all muddied with a thousand lonely suicides.
And a dark wind blows.
The government is corrupt. And we're on so many drugs. With the radio on and the curtains drawn.
We're trapped in the belly of this horrible machine
And the machine is bleeding to death.
The sun has fallen down. And the billboards are all leering.
And the flags are all dead at the top of their poles.
It went like this:
The buildings toppled in on themselves.
Mothers clutching babies
Picked through the rubble
And pulled out their hair
The skyline was beautiful on fire. All twisted metal stretching upwards
Everything washed in a thin orange haze
I said, "Kiss me, you're beautiful - these are truly the last days"
You grabbed my hand
And we fell into it
Like a daydream
Or a fever
We woke up one morning and fell a little further down
For sure it's the valley of death
I open up my wallet
And it's full of blood.

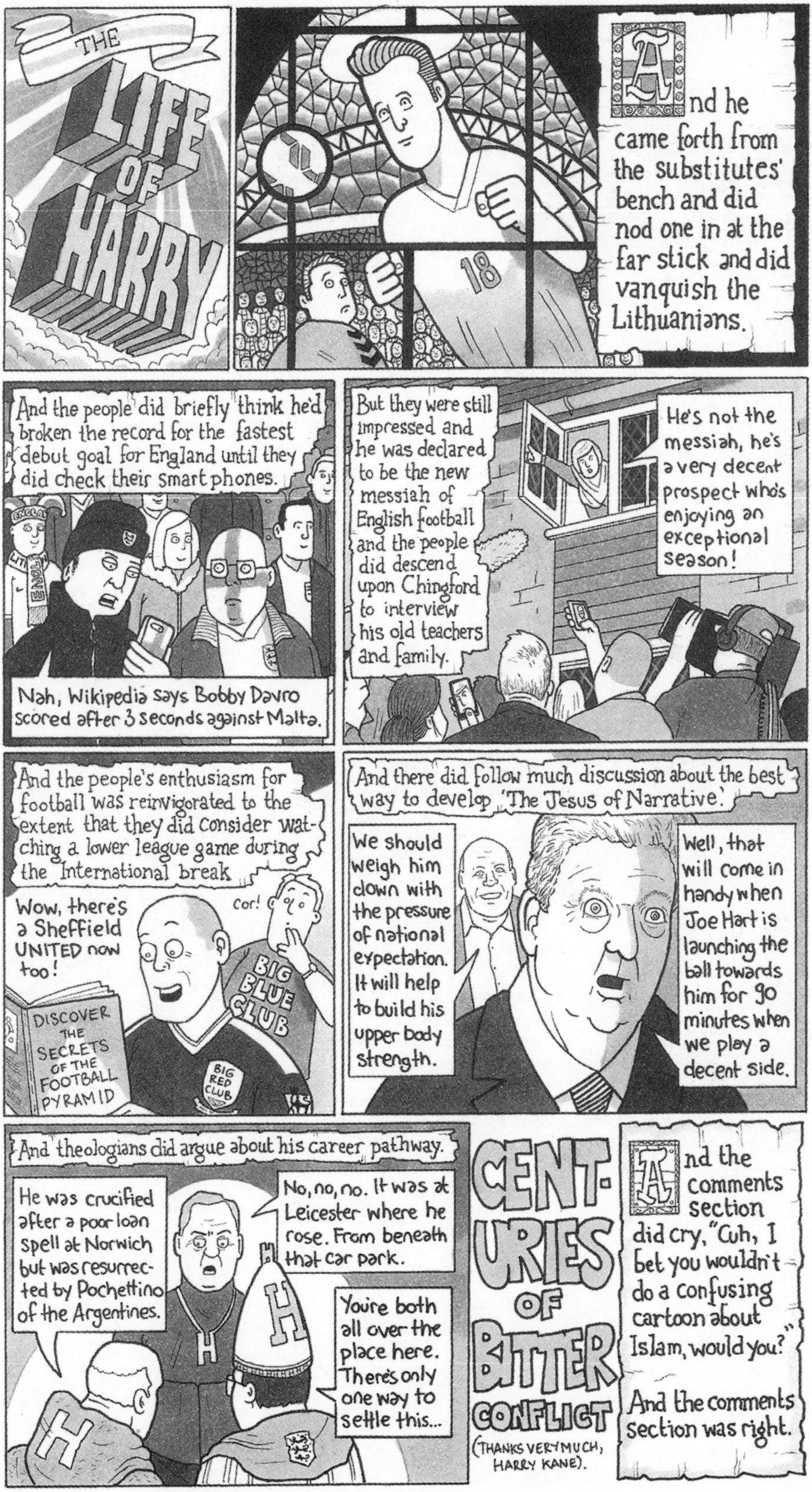
THE
LIFE OF HARRY
And he came forth from the substitutes' bench and did nod one in at the far stick and did vanquish the Lithuanians.
18
And the people did briefly think he'd broken the record for the fastest debut goal for England until they did check their smart phones.
Nah, Wikipedia says Bobby Davro scored after 3 seconds against Malta.
But they were still impressed and he was declared to be the new messiah of English football and the people did descend upon Chingford to interview his old teachers and family.
He's not the messiah, he's a very decent prospect who's enjoying an exceptional season!
And the people's enthusiasm for football was reinvigorated to the extent that they did consider watching a lower league game during the International break
Wow, there's a Sheffield UNITED now too!
Cor!
BIG BLUE CLUB
DISCOVER THE SECRETS OF THE FOOTBALL PYRAMID
BIG RED CLUB
And there did follow much discussion about the best way to develop 'The Jesus of Narrative'.
We should weigh him down with the pressure of national expectation. It will help to build his upper body strength.
Well, that will come in handy when Joe Hart is launching the ball towards him for 90 minutes when we play a decent side.
And theologians did argue about his career pathway.
He was crucified after a poor loan spell at Norwich but was resurrected by Pochettino of the Argentines.
No, no, no. It was at Leicester where he rose. From beneath that car park.
You're both all over the place here. There's only one way to settle this...
CENTURIES OF BITTER CONFLICT
(THANKS VERY MUCH, HARRY KANE).
And the comments section did cry, "Cuh, I bet you wouldn't do a confusing cartoon about Islam, would you?"
And the comments section was right.

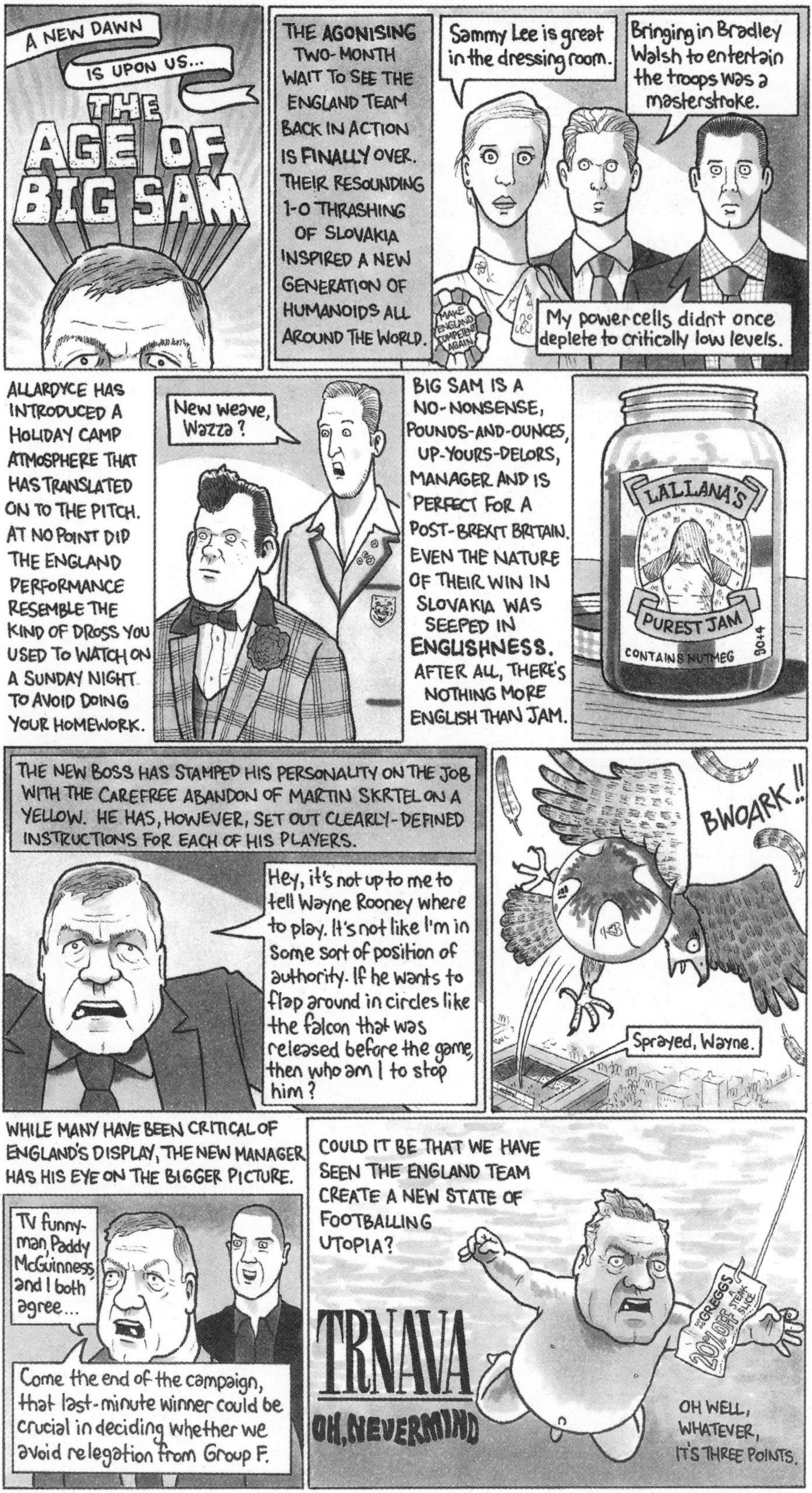

A NEW DAWN IS UPON US...
THE AGE OF BIG SAM
THE AGONISING TWO-MONTH WAIT TO SEE THE ENGLAND TEAM BACK IN ACTION IS FINALLY OVER. THEIR RESOUNDING 1-0 THRASHING OF SLOVAKIA INSPIRED A NEW GENERATION OF HUMANOIDS ALL AROUND THE WORLD.
Sammy Lee is great in the dressing room.
Bringing in Bradley Walsh to entertain the troops was a masterstroke.
MAKE ENGLAND COMPETENT AGAIN
My power cells didn't once deplete to critically low levels.
ALLARDYCE HAS INTRODUCED A HOLIDAY CAMP ATMOSPHERE THAT HAS TRANSLATED ON TO THE PITCH. AT NO POINT DID THE ENGLAND PERFORMANCE RESEMBLE THE KIND OF DROSS YOU USED TO WATCH ON A SUNDAY NIGHT TO AVOID DOING YOUR HOMEWORK.
New weave, Wazza?
BIG SAM IS A NO-NONSENSE, POUNDS-AND-OUNCES, UP-YOURS-DELORS, MANAGER AND IS PERFECT FOR A POST-BREXIT BRITAIN. EVEN THE NATURE OF THEIR WIN IN SLOVAKIA WAS SEEPED IN ENGLISHNESS. AFTER ALL, THERE'S NOTHING MORE ENGLISH THAN JAM.
LALLANA'S
PUREST JAM
CONTAINS NUTMEG
THE NEW BOSS HAS STAMPED HIS PERSONALITY ON THE JOB WITH THE CAREFREE ABANDON OF MARTIN SKRTEL ON A YELLOW. HE HAS, HOWEVER, SET OUT CLEARLY-DEFINED INSTRUCTIONS FOR EACH OF HIS PLAYERS.
Hey, it's not up to me to tell Wayne Rooney where to play. It's not like I'm in some sort of position of authority. If he wants to flap around in circles like the falcon that was released before the game, then who am I to stop him?
BWOARK!!
Sprayed, Wayne.
WHILE MANY HAVE BEEN CRITICAL OF ENGLAND'S DISPLAY, THE NEW MANAGER HAS HIS EYE ON THE BIGGER PICTURE.
TV funny-man, Paddy McGuinness, and I both agree...
Come the end of the campaign, that last-minute winner could be crucial in deciding whether we avoid relegation from Group F.
COULD IT BE THAT WE HAVE SEEN THE ENGLAND TEAM CREATE A NEW STATE OF FOOTBALLING UTOPIA?
TRNAVA
OH, NEVERMIND
GREGGS
20% OFF A STEAK SLICE
OH WELL, WHATEVER, IT'S THREE POINTS.

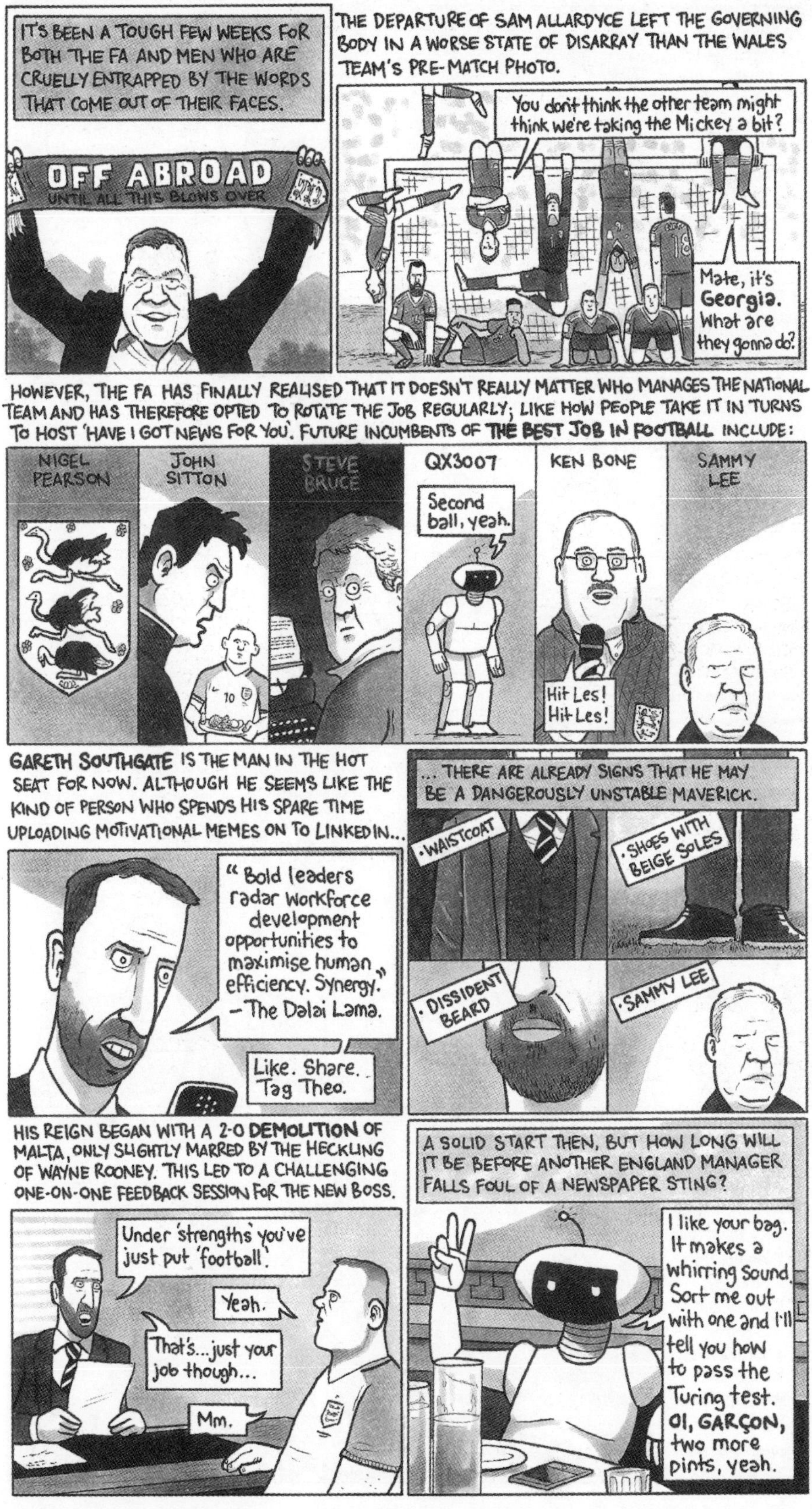
IT'S BEEN A TOUGH FEW WEEKS FOR BOTH THE FA AND MEN WHO ARE CRUELLY ENTRAPPED BY THE WORDS THAT COME OUT OF THEIR FACES.
OFF ABROAD
UNTIL ALL THIS BLOWS OVER
THE DEPARTURE OF SAM ALLARDYCE LEFT THE GOVERNING BODY IN A WORSE STATE OF DISARRAY THAN THE WALES TEAM'S PRE-MATCH PHOTO.
You don't think the other team might think we're taking the Mickey a bit?
Mate, it's Georgia. What are they gonna do?
HOWEVER, THE FA HAS FINALLY REALISED THAT IT DOESN'T REALLY MATTER WHO MANAGES THE NATIONAL TEAM AND HAS THEREFORE OPTED TO ROTATE THE JOB REGULARLY; LIKE HOW PEOPLE TAKE IT IN TURNS TO HOST 'HAVE I GOT NEWS FOR YOU'. FUTURE INCUMBENTS OF THE BEST JOB IN FOOTBALL INCLUDE:
NIGEL PEARSON
JOHN SITTON
STEVE BRUCE
QX3007
Second ball, yeah.
KEN BONE
Hit Les! Hit Les!
SAMMY LEE
GARETH SOUTHGATE IS THE MAN IN THE HOT SEAT FOR NOW. ALTHOUGH HE SEEMS LIKE THE KIND OF PERSON WHO SPENDS HIS SPARE TIME UPLOADING MOTIVATIONAL MEMES ON TO LINKEDIN...
"Bold leaders radar workforce development opportunities to maximise human efficiency. Synergy." – The Dalai Lama.
Like. Share. Tag Theo.
... THERE ARE ALREADY SIGNS THAT HE MAY BE A DANGEROUSLY UNSTABLE MAVERICK.
• WAISTCOAT
• SHOES WITH BEIGE SOLES
• DISSIDENT BEARD
• SAMMY LEE
HIS REIGN BEGAN WITH A 2-0 DEMOLITION OF MALTA, ONLY SLIGHTLY MARRED BY THE HECKLING OF WAYNE ROONEY. THIS LED TO A CHALLENGING ONE-ON-ONE FEEDBACK SESSION FOR THE NEW BOSS.
Under 'strengths' you've just put 'football'.
Yeah.
That's... just your job though...
Mm.
A SOLID START THEN, BUT HOW LONG WILL IT BE BEFORE ANOTHER ENGLAND MANAGER FALLS FOUL OF A NEWSPAPER STING?
I like your bag. It makes a whirring sound. Sort me out with one and I'll tell you how to pass the Turing test. OI, GARÇON, two more pints, yeah.

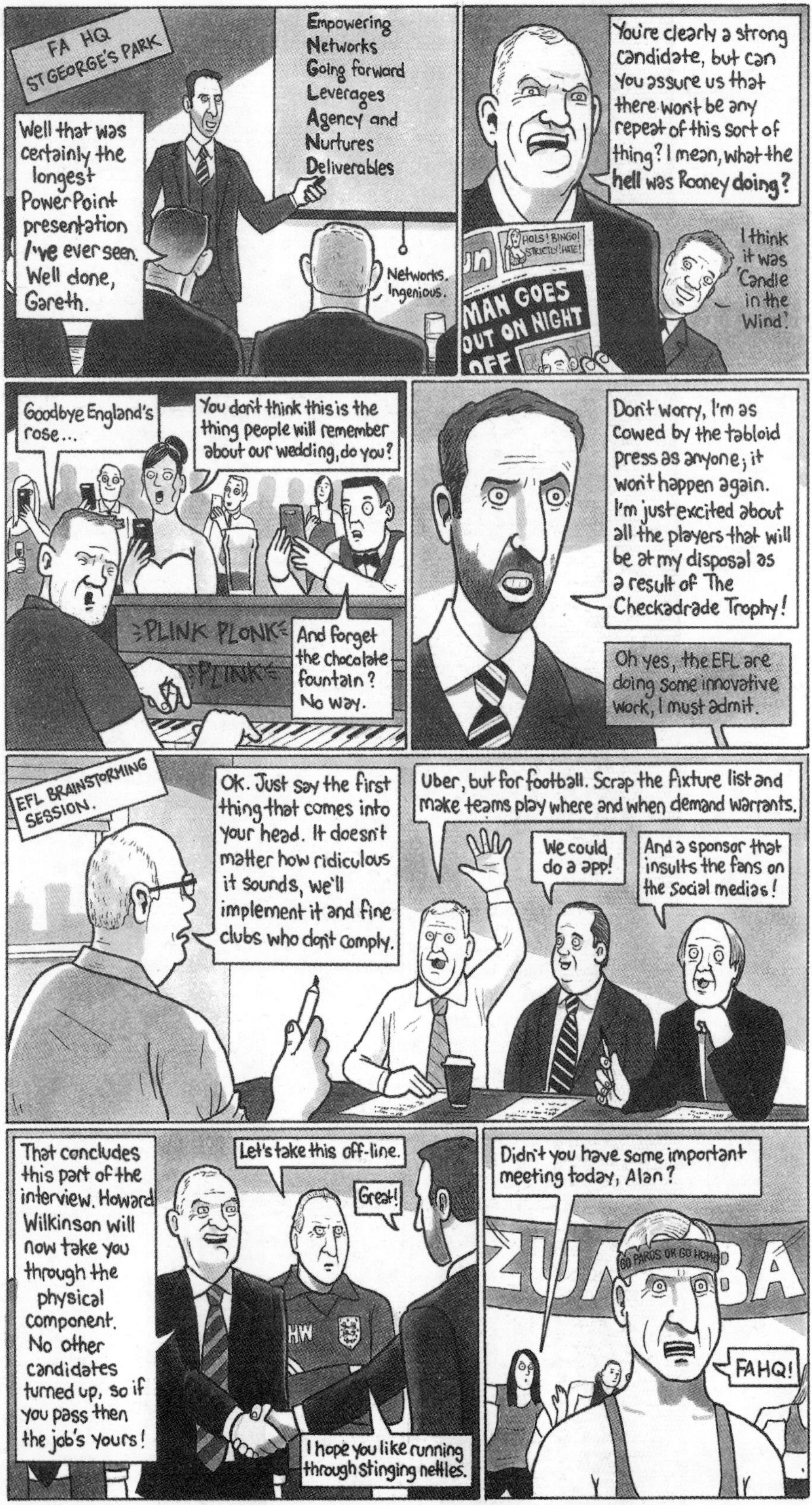

FA HQ
ST GEORGE'S PARK
Empowering
Networks
Going forward
Leverages
Agency and
Nurtures
Deliverables
Well that was certainly the longest PowerPoint presentation I've ever seen. Well done, Gareth.
Networks. Ingenious.
You're clearly a strong candidate, but can you assure us that there won't be any repeat of this sort of thing? I mean, what the **hell** was Rooney **doing**?
HOLS! BINGO! STRICTLY! HATE!
MAN GOES OUT ON NIGHT OFF
I think it was 'Candle in the Wind'.
Goodbye England's rose...
You don't think this is the thing people will remember about our wedding, do you?
PLINK PLONK
PLINK
And forget the chocolate fountain? No way.
Don't worry, I'm as cowed by the tabloid press as anyone; it won't happen again. I'm just excited about all the players that will be at my disposal as a result of The Checkadrade Trophy!
Oh yes, the EFL are doing some innovative work, I must admit.
EFL BRAINSTORMING SESSION.
OK. Just say the first thing that comes into your head. It doesn't matter how ridiculous it sounds, we'll implement it and fine clubs who don't comply.
Uber, but for football. Scrap the fixture list and make teams play where and when demand warrants.
We could do a app!
And a sponsor that insults the fans on the social medias!
That concludes this part of the interview. Howard Wilkinson will now take you through the physical component. No other candidates turned up, so if you pass then the job's yours!
Let's take this off-line.
Great!
HW
I hope you like running through stinging nettles.
Didn't you have some important meeting today, Alan?
ZUMBA
FAHQ!

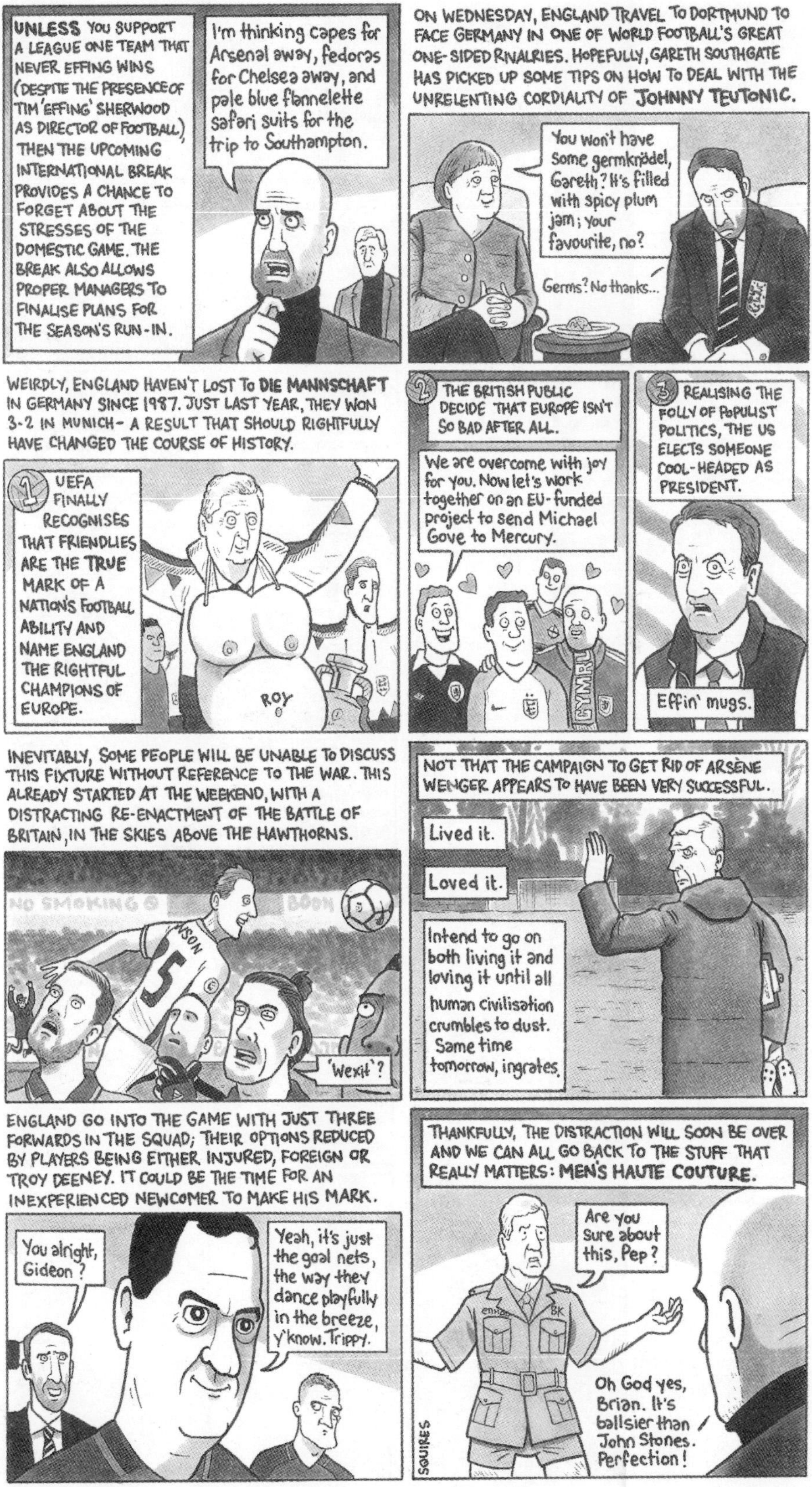

UNLESS YOU SUPPORT A LEAGUE ONE TEAM THAT NEVER EFFING WINS (DESPITE THE PRESENCE OF TIM 'EFFING' SHERWOOD AS DIRECTOR OF FOOTBALL) THEN THE UPCOMING INTERNATIONAL BREAK PROVIDES A CHANCE TO FORGET ABOUT THE STRESSES OF THE DOMESTIC GAME. THE BREAK ALSO ALLOWS PROPER MANAGERS TO FINALISE PLANS FOR THE SEASON'S RUN-IN.
I'm thinking capes for Arsenal away, fedoras for Chelsea away, and pale blue flannelette safari suits for the trip to Southampton.
ON WEDNESDAY, ENGLAND TRAVEL TO DORTMUND TO FACE GERMANY IN ONE OF WORLD FOOTBALL'S GREAT ONE-SIDED RIVALRIES. HOPEFULLY, GARETH SOUTHGATE HAS PICKED UP SOME TIPS ON HOW TO DEAL WITH THE UNRELENTING CORDIALITY OF JOHNNY TEUTONIC.
You won't have some germknödel, Gareth? It's filled with spicy plum jam; your favourite, no?
Germs? No thanks...
WEIRDLY, ENGLAND HAVEN'T LOST TO DIE MANNSCHAFT IN GERMANY SINCE 1987. JUST LAST YEAR, THEY WON 3-2 IN MUNICH - A RESULT THAT SHOULD RIGHTFULLY HAVE CHANGED THE COURSE OF HISTORY.
1
UEFA FINALLY RECOGNISES THAT FRIENDLIES ARE THE TRUE MARK OF A NATION'S FOOTBALL ABILITY AND NAME ENGLAND THE RIGHTFUL CHAMPIONS OF EUROPE.
ROY
2
THE BRITISH PUBLIC DECIDE THAT EUROPE ISN'T SO BAD AFTER ALL.
We are overcome with joy for you. Now let's work together on an EU-funded project to send Michael Gove to Mercury.
CYMRU
3
REALISING THE FOLLY OF POPULIST POLITICS, THE US ELECTS SOMEONE COOL-HEADED AS PRESIDENT.
Effin' mugs.
INEVITABLY, SOME PEOPLE WILL BE UNABLE TO DISCUSS THIS FIXTURE WITHOUT REFERENCE TO THE WAR. THIS ALREADY STARTED AT THE WEEKEND, WITH A DISTRACTING RE-ENACTMENT OF THE BATTLE OF BRITAIN, IN THE SKIES ABOVE THE HAWTHORNS.
NO SMOKING
5
'Wexit'?
NOT THAT THE CAMPAIGN TO GET RID OF ARSÈNE WENGER APPEARS TO HAVE BEEN VERY SUCCESSFUL.
Lived it.
Loved it.
Intend to go on both living it and loving it until all human civilisation crumbles to dust. Same time tomorrow, ingrates.
ENGLAND GO INTO THE GAME WITH JUST THREE FORWARDS IN THE SQUAD; THEIR OPTIONS REDUCED BY PLAYERS BEING EITHER INJURED, FOREIGN OR TROY DEENEY. IT COULD BE THE TIME FOR AN INEXPERIENCED NEWCOMER TO MAKE HIS MARK.
You alright, Gideon?
Yeah, it's just the goal nets, the way they dance playfully in the breeze, y'know. Trippy.
THANKFULLY, THE DISTRACTION WILL SOON BE OVER AND WE CAN ALL GO BACK TO THE STUFF THAT REALLY MATTERS: MEN'S HAUTE COUTURE.
Are you sure about this, Pep?
BK
Oh God yes, Brian. It's ballsier than John Stones. Perfection!
SQUIRES

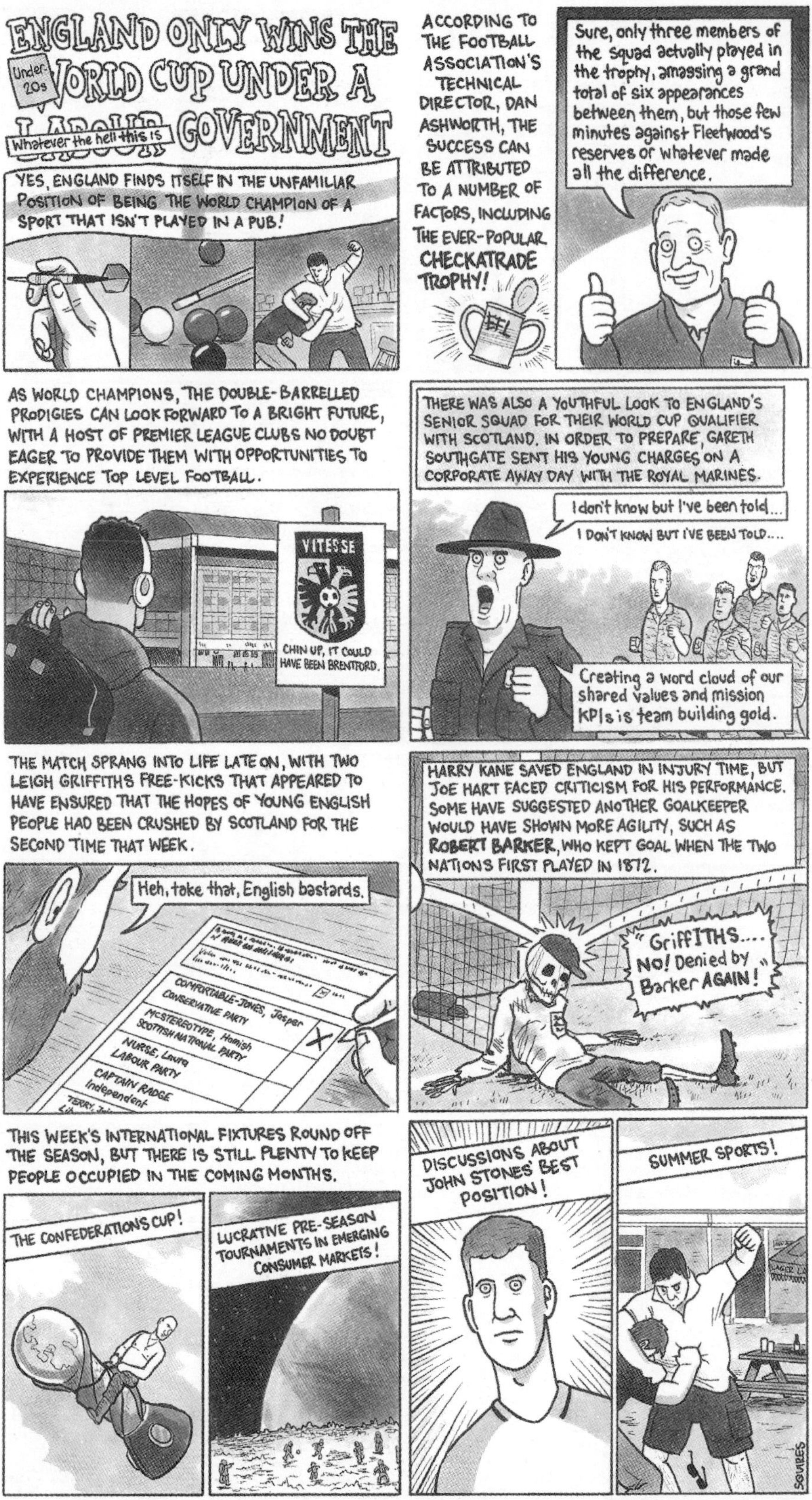

ENGLAND ONLY WINS THE
Under-20s
WORLD CUP UNDER A
LABOUR
Whatever the hell this is
GOVERNMENT
YES, ENGLAND FINDS ITSELF IN THE UNFAMILIAR POSITION OF BEING THE WORLD CHAMPION OF A SPORT THAT ISN'T PLAYED IN A PUB!
ACCORDING TO THE FOOTBALL ASSOCIATION'S TECHNICAL DIRECTOR, DAN ASHWORTH, THE SUCCESS CAN BE ATTRIBUTED TO A NUMBER OF FACTORS, INCLUDING THE EVER-POPULAR CHECKATRADE TROPHY!
EFL
Sure, only three members of the squad actually played in the trophy, amassing a grand total of six appearances between them, but those few minutes against Fleetwood's reserves or whatever made all the difference.
AS WORLD CHAMPIONS, THE DOUBLE-BARRELLED PRODIGIES CAN LOOK FORWARD TO A BRIGHT FUTURE, WITH A HOST OF PREMIER LEAGUE CLUBS NO DOUBT EAGER TO PROVIDE THEM WITH OPPORTUNITIES TO EXPERIENCE TOP LEVEL FOOTBALL.
VITESSE
CHIN UP, IT COULD HAVE BEEN BRENTFORD.
THERE WAS ALSO A YOUTHFUL LOOK TO ENGLAND'S SENIOR SQUAD FOR THEIR WORLD CUP QUALIFIER WITH SCOTLAND. IN ORDER TO PREPARE, GARETH SOUTHGATE SENT HIS YOUNG CHARGES ON A CORPORATE AWAY DAY WITH THE ROYAL MARINES.
I don't know but I've been told...
I DON'T KNOW BUT I'VE BEEN TOLD....
Creating a word cloud of our shared values and mission KPIs is team building gold.
THE MATCH SPRANG INTO LIFE LATE ON, WITH TWO LEIGH GRIFFITHS FREE-KICKS THAT APPEARED TO HAVE ENSURED THAT THE HOPES OF YOUNG ENGLISH PEOPLE HAD BEEN CRUSHED BY SCOTLAND FOR THE SECOND TIME THAT WEEK.
Heh, take that, English bastards.
COMFORTABLE-JONES, Jasper
CONSERVATIVE PARTY
McSTEREOTYPE, Hamish
SCOTTISH NATIONAL PARTY
NURSE, Laura
LABOUR PARTY
CAPTAIN RADGE
Independent
HARRY KANE SAVED ENGLAND IN INJURY TIME, BUT JOE HART FACED CRITICISM FOR HIS PERFORMANCE. SOME HAVE SUGGESTED ANOTHER GOALKEEPER WOULD HAVE SHOWN MORE AGILITY, SUCH AS ROBERT BARKER, WHO KEPT GOAL WHEN THE TWO NATIONS FIRST PLAYED IN 1872.
"GriffITHS.... No! Denied by Barker AGAIN!"
THIS WEEK'S INTERNATIONAL FIXTURES ROUND OFF THE SEASON, BUT THERE IS STILL PLENTY TO KEEP PEOPLE OCCUPIED IN THE COMING MONTHS.
THE CONFEDERATIONS CUP!
LUCRATIVE PRE-SEASON TOURNAMENTS IN EMERGING CONSUMER MARKETS!
DISCUSSIONS ABOUT JOHN STONES' BEST POSITION!
SUMMER SPORTS!
SQUIRES

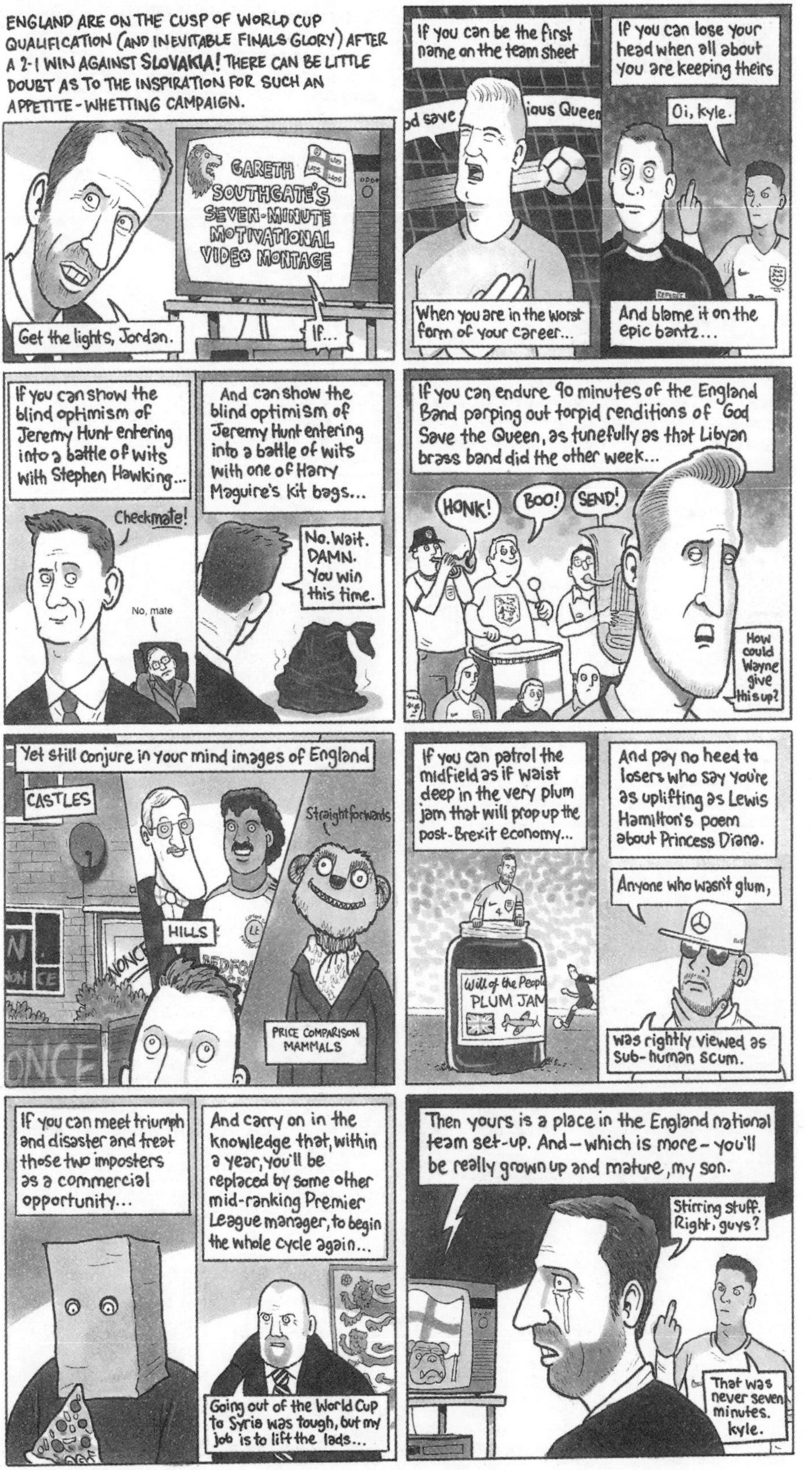

ENGLAND ARE ON THE CUSP OF WORLD CUP QUALIFICATION (AND INEVITABLE FINALS GLORY) AFTER A 2-1 WIN AGAINST SLOVAKIA! THERE CAN BE LITTLE DOUBT AS TO THE INSPIRATION FOR SUCH AN APPETITE-WHETTING CAMPAIGN.
GARETH SOUTHGATE'S SEVEN-MINUTE MOTIVATIONAL VIDEO MONTAGE
Get the lights, Jordan.
If...
If you can be the first name on the team sheet
When you are in the worst form of your career...
If you can lose your head when all about you are keeping theirs
Oi, kyle.
And blame it on the epic bantz...
If you can show the blind optimism of Jeremy Hunt entering into a battle of wits with Stephen Hawking...
Checkmate!
No, mate
And can show the blind optimism of Jeremy Hunt entering into a battle of wits with one of Harry Maguire's kit bags...
No. Wait. DAMN. You win this time.
If you can endure 90 minutes of the England Band parping out torpid renditions of God Save the Queen, as tunefully as that Libyan brass band did the other week...
HONK!
BOO!
SEND!
How could Wayne give this up?
Yet still conjure in your mind images of England
CASTLES
HILLS
NONCE
Straight forwards
PRICE COMPARISON MAMMALS
If you can patrol the midfield as if waist deep in the very plum jam that will prop up the post-Brexit economy...
Will of the People PLUM JAM
And pay no heed to losers who say you're as uplifting as Lewis Hamilton's poem about Princess Diana.
Anyone who wasn't glum,
was rightly viewed as sub-human scum.
If you can meet triumph and disaster and treat those two imposters as a commercial opportunity...
And carry on in the knowledge that, within a year, you'll be replaced by some other mid-ranking Premier League manager, to begin the whole cycle again...
Going out of the World Cup to Syria was tough, but my job is to lift the lads...
Then yours is a place in the England national team set-up. And – which is more – you'll be really grown up and mature, my son.
Stirring stuff. Right, guys?
That was never seven minutes, kyle.

QUALIFICATION FOR THE 2050 OFF-WORLD CUP HAS BEEN CONFIRMED, WITH A NARROW HOME WIN AGAINST A RADIOACTIVE DUST CLOUD. THE CROWD DRIFTS AWAY, A SEXY INTERACTIVE HOLOGRAM OFFERS BETTING ODDS FOR THE UPCOMING FRIENDLY AGAINST A NEW FORM OF SYNTHETIC MOSS.

First goal scorer: whoever we're completely reliant upon now. 3 to 1. Get on it, mush.

AFTER THE LIFE SAPPING DISASTERS OF SUCCESSIVE MAJOR TOURNAMENTS, FA TECHNICAL DIRECTOR **DAN ASHWORTH** MANUFACTURED A BREED OF DRONE-LIKE ACADEMY PLAYERS; INCAPABLE OF INDEPENDENT THOUGHT, BEREFT OF IMAGINATION.

MOST OF THE SURVIVING MEMBERS OF THE LAST ENGLAND TEAM TO GET FURTHER THAN THE QUARTER-FINALS HAVE BEEN SOLD INTO PUNDITRY, BUT ONE IS RETAINED AND GIVEN THE THANKLESS TASK OF SEARCHING FOR A CREATIVE MIDFIELDER.

(HE STILL LOOKS LIKE HE DID IN 2017 BECAUSE OF MOISTURISING)

WHEN NOT SCOURING THE LAND IN ONE OF THE FLYING CARS WE'LL DEFINITELY HAVE IN UNDER 30 YEARS' TIME, HE TRAWLS THROUGH THE DATA ON ENGLISH PLAYERS.

Enhance 352. Pull back. Scroll. Stop. Enhance 3421.

BLEEP
BLEEP
CLICK
BLEEP

Move right. Scroll. Scroll. Enhance 433.

Stop.

≥sigh≤

x8610	33918333821	336812
22286	ggp88931451	352251
33364	36811sf18899	399631
33385	sf74sf48g1s7b	335512
zz963	1s7447644411	2862s6
f9f888	51398183323	3sf5f2h
tt9853	52df2f55f233r	215g8b
m2777	12gdd2c7h2bh	bdgwsc
4458g	Mark Noble	v83823
88143	3383388zczv5	2b8b62
13386	55sgj7488581	33f82v
96191	ssf82gdh8882	185gb8
55hh5	15856841275	b3b2b8
6561s	889548s585h	y1h4h2
1484d	599sg5h8511	hh4g2s
sfg588	1sfg59996559	333f8gv

Give me a hard copy.

ENGLAND 0
SOME MOSS 0
89:18

THE SEARCH CONTINUES.

BUT OUT IN THE WILDERNESS OF THE INTERNATIONAL SCRAPHEAP, THERE ARE MANY WHO WOULD GLADLY SWAP PLACES WITH HIM.

Jammy bastards. It's all about genetics, Dickie son.

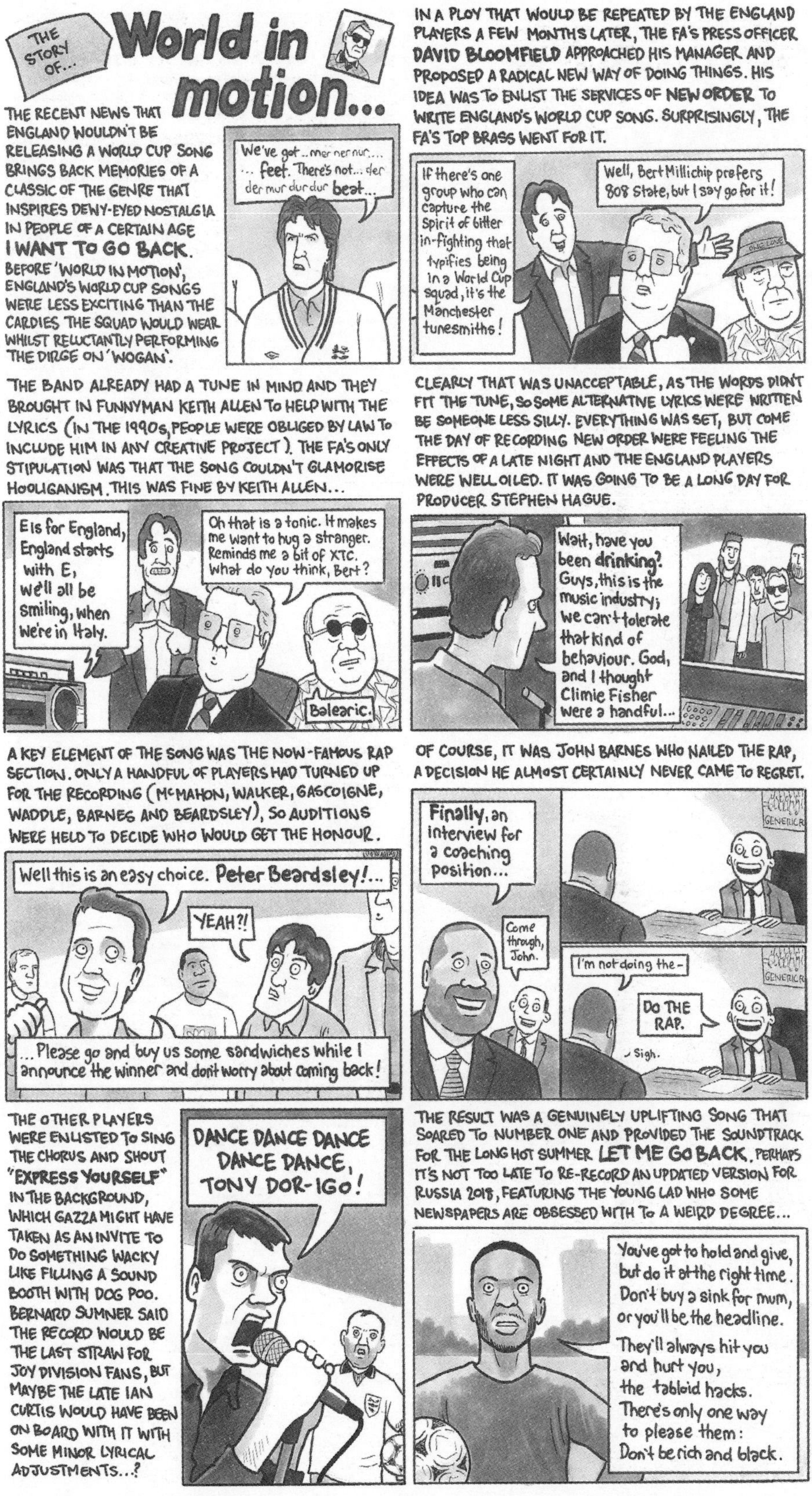
THE STORY OF...
World in motion...
THE RECENT NEWS THAT ENGLAND WOULDN'T BE RELEASING A WORLD CUP SONG BRINGS BACK MEMORIES OF A CLASSIC OF THE GENRE THAT INSPIRES DEWY-EYED NOSTALGIA IN PEOPLE OF A CERTAIN AGE I WANT TO GO BACK. BEFORE 'WORLD IN MOTION', ENGLAND'S WORLD CUP SONGS WERE LESS EXCITING THAN THE CARDIES THE SQUAD WOULD WEAR WHILST RELUCTANTLY PERFORMING THE DIRGE ON 'WOGAN'.
We've got... mer ner nur.... ... feet. There's not... der der mur dur dur beat...
IN A PLOY THAT WOULD BE REPEATED BY THE ENGLAND PLAYERS A FEW MONTHS LATER, THE FA'S PRESS OFFICER DAVID BLOOMFIELD APPROACHED HIS MANAGER AND PROPOSED A RADICAL NEW WAY OF DOING THINGS. HIS IDEA WAS TO ENLIST THE SERVICES OF NEW ORDER TO WRITE ENGLAND'S WORLD CUP SONG. SURPRISINGLY, THE FA'S TOP BRASS WENT FOR IT.
If there's one group who can capture the spirit of bitter in-fighting that typifies being in a World Cup squad, it's the Manchester tunesmiths!
Well, Bert Millichip prefers 808 State, but I say go for it!
THE BAND ALREADY HAD A TUNE IN MIND AND THEY BROUGHT IN FUNNYMAN KEITH ALLEN TO HELP WITH THE LYRICS (IN THE 1990s, PEOPLE WERE OBLIGED BY LAW TO INCLUDE HIM IN ANY CREATIVE PROJECT). THE FA'S ONLY STIPULATION WAS THAT THE SONG COULDN'T GLAMORISE HOOLIGANISM. THIS WAS FINE BY KEITH ALLEN...
E is for England, England starts with E, We'll all be smiling, when we're in Italy.
Oh that is a tonic. It makes me want to hug a stranger. Reminds me a bit of XTC. What do you think, Bert?
Balearic.
CLEARLY THAT WAS UNACCEPTABLE, AS THE WORDS DIDN'T FIT THE TUNE, SO SOME ALTERNATIVE LYRICS WERE WRITTEN BE SOMEONE LESS SILLY. EVERYTHING WAS SET, BUT COME THE DAY OF RECORDING NEW ORDER WERE FEELING THE EFFECTS OF A LATE NIGHT AND THE ENGLAND PLAYERS WERE WELL OILED. IT WAS GOING TO BE A LONG DAY FOR PRODUCER STEPHEN HAGUE.
Wait, have you been drinking? Guys, this is the music industry; we can't tolerate that kind of behaviour. God, and I thought Climie Fisher were a handful...
A KEY ELEMENT OF THE SONG WAS THE NOW-FAMOUS RAP SECTION. ONLY A HANDFUL OF PLAYERS HAD TURNED UP FOR THE RECORDING (McMAHON, WALKER, GASCOIGNE, WADDLE, BARNES AND BEARDSLEY), SO AUDITIONS WERE HELD TO DECIDE WHO WOULD GET THE HONOUR.
Well this is an easy choice. Peter Beardsley!...
YEAH?!
...Please go and buy us some sandwiches while I announce the winner and don't worry about coming back!
OF COURSE, IT WAS JOHN BARNES WHO NAILED THE RAP, A DECISION HE ALMOST CERTAINLY NEVER CAME TO REGRET.
Finally, an interview for a coaching position...
Come through, John.
I'm not doing the-
Do THE RAP.
Sigh.
THE OTHER PLAYERS WERE ENLISTED TO SING THE CHORUS AND SHOUT "EXPRESS YOURSELF" IN THE BACKGROUND, WHICH GAZZA MIGHT HAVE TAKEN AS AN INVITE TO DO SOMETHING WACKY LIKE FILLING A SOUND BOOTH WITH DOG POO. BERNARD SUMNER SAID THE RECORD WOULD BE THE LAST STRAW FOR JOY DIVISION FANS, BUT MAYBE THE LATE IAN CURTIS WOULD HAVE BEEN ON BOARD WITH IT WITH SOME MINOR LYRICAL ADJUSTMENTS...?
DANCE DANCE DANCE DANCE DANCE, TONY DOR-IGO!
THE RESULT WAS A GENUINELY UPLIFTING SONG THAT SOARED TO NUMBER ONE AND PROVIDED THE SOUNDTRACK FOR THE LONG HOT SUMMER LET ME GO BACK. PERHAPS IT'S NOT TOO LATE TO RE-RECORD AN UPDATED VERSION FOR RUSSIA 2018, FEATURING THE YOUNG LAD WHO SOME NEWSPAPERS ARE OBSESSED WITH TO A WEIRD DEGREE...
You've got to hold and give, but do it at the right time. Don't buy a sink for mum, or you'll be the headline.
They'll always hit you and hurt you, the tabloid hacks. There's only one way to please them: Don't be rich and black.

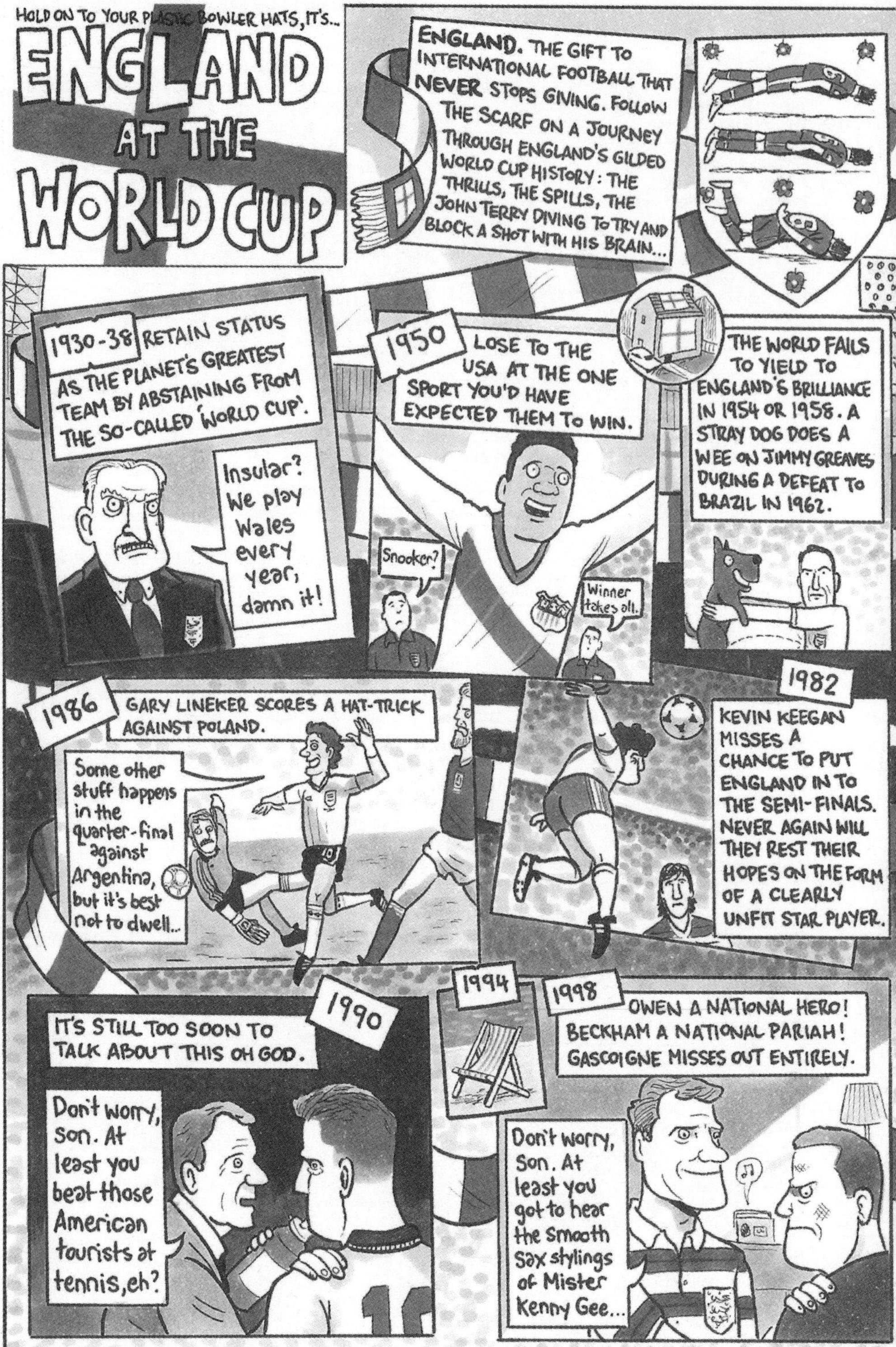
HOLD ON TO YOUR PLASTIC BOWLER HATS, IT'S...
ENGLAND AT THE WORLD CUP
ENGLAND. THE GIFT TO INTERNATIONAL FOOTBALL THAT NEVER STOPS GIVING. FOLLOW THE SCARF ON A JOURNEY THROUGH ENGLAND'S GILDED WORLD CUP HISTORY: THE THRILLS, THE SPILLS, THE JOHN TERRY DIVING TO TRY AND BLOCK A SHOT WITH HIS BRAIN...
1930-38
RETAIN STATUS AS THE PLANET'S GREATEST TEAM BY ABSTAINING FROM THE SO-CALLED 'WORLD CUP'.
Insular? We play Wales every year, damn it!
1950
LOSE TO THE USA AT THE ONE SPORT YOU'D HAVE EXPECTED THEM TO WIN.
Snooker?
Winner takes all.
THE WORLD FAILS TO YIELD TO ENGLAND'S BRILLIANCE IN 1954 OR 1958. A STRAY DOG DOES A WEE ON JIMMY GREAVES DURING A DEFEAT TO BRAZIL IN 1962.
1986
GARY LINEKER SCORES A HAT-TRICK AGAINST POLAND.
Some other stuff happens in the quarter-final against Argentina, but it's best not to dwell...
1982
KEVIN KEEGAN MISSES A CHANCE TO PUT ENGLAND IN TO THE SEMI-FINALS. NEVER AGAIN WILL THEY REST THEIR HOPES ON THE FORM OF A CLEARLY UNFIT STAR PLAYER.
1990
IT'S STILL TOO SOON TO TALK ABOUT THIS OH GOD.
Don't worry, son. At least you beat those American tourists at tennis, eh?
1994
1998
OWEN A NATIONAL HERO! BECKHAM A NATIONAL PARIAH! GASCOIGNE MISSES OUT ENTIRELY.
Don't worry, son. At least you got to hear the smooth sax stylings of Mister Kenny Gee...

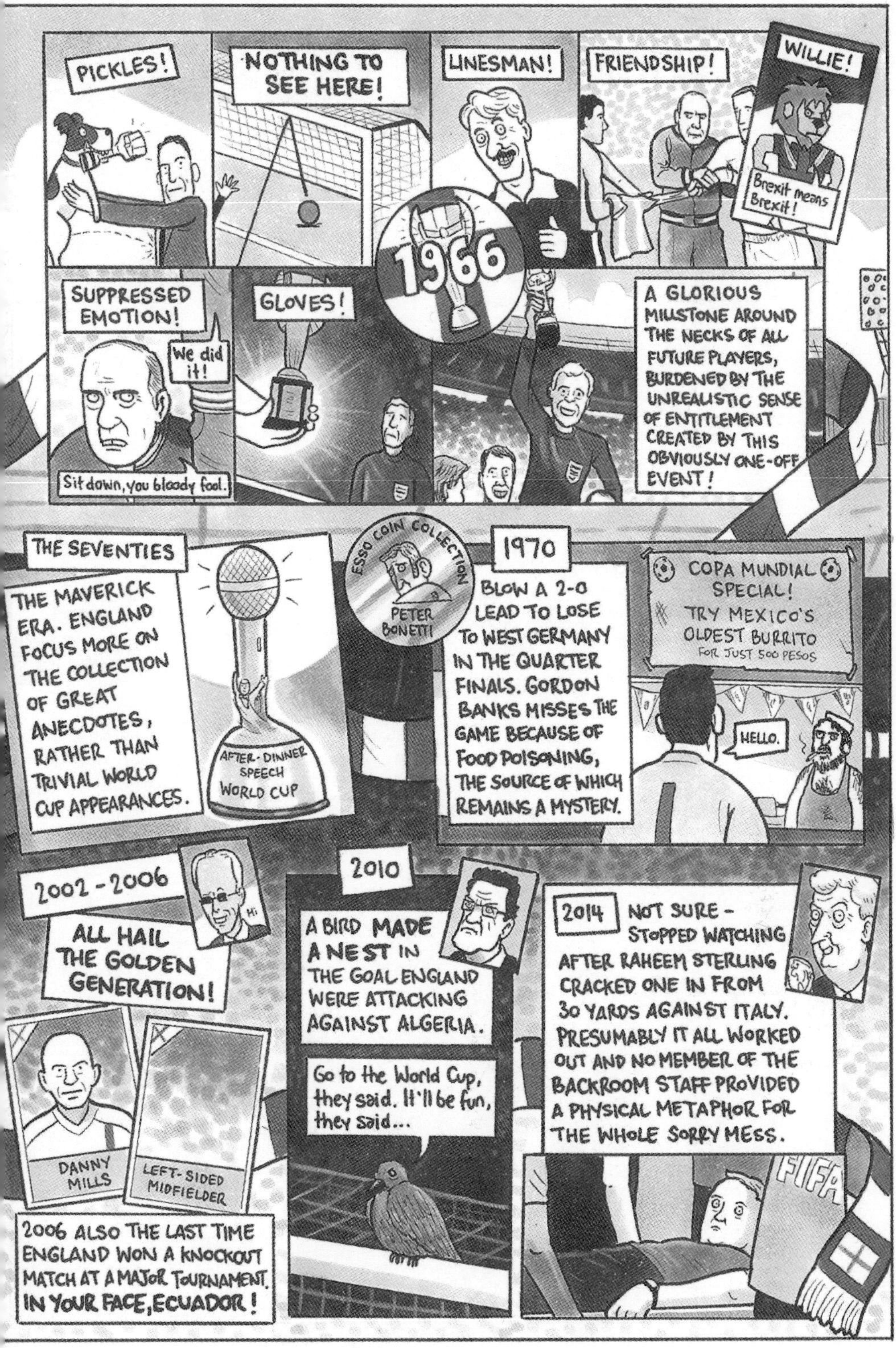
PICKLES!
NOTHING TO SEE HERE!
LINESMAN!
FRIENDSHIP!
WILLIE!
Brexit means Brexit!
1966
SUPPRESSED EMOTION!
We did it!
Sit down, you bloody fool.
GLOVES!
A GLORIOUS MILLSTONE AROUND THE NECKS OF ALL FUTURE PLAYERS, BURDENED BY THE UNREALISTIC SENSE OF ENTITLEMENT CREATED BY THIS OBVIOUSLY ONE-OFF EVENT!
THE SEVENTIES
THE MAVERICK ERA. ENGLAND FOCUS MORE ON THE COLLECTION OF GREAT ANECDOTES, RATHER THAN TRIVIAL WORLD CUP APPEARANCES.
AFTER-DINNER SPEECH WORLD CUP
ESSO COIN COLLECTION
PETER BONETTI
1970
BLOW A 2-0 LEAD TO LOSE TO WEST GERMANY IN THE QUARTER FINALS. GORDON BANKS MISSES THE GAME BECAUSE OF FOOD POISONING, THE SOURCE OF WHICH REMAINS A MYSTERY.
COPA MUNDIAL SPECIAL!
TRY MEXICO'S OLDEST BURRITO
FOR JUST 500 PESOS
HELLO.
2002 - 2006
Hi
ALL HAIL THE GOLDEN GENERATION!
DANNY MILLS
LEFT-SIDED MIDFIELDER
2006 ALSO THE LAST TIME ENGLAND WON A KNOCKOUT MATCH AT A MAJOR TOURNAMENT. IN YOUR FACE, ECUADOR!
2010
A BIRD MADE A NEST IN THE GOAL ENGLAND WERE ATTACKING AGAINST ALGERIA.
Go to the World Cup, they said. It'll be fun, they said...
2014
NOT SURE - STOPPED WATCHING AFTER RAHEEM STERLING CRACKED ONE IN FROM 30 YARDS AGAINST ITALY. PRESUMABLY IT ALL WORKED OUT AND NO MEMBER OF THE BACKROOM STAFF PROVIDED A PHYSICAL METAPHOR FOR THE WHOLE SORRY MESS.
FIFA

TRIBUTES

Every club has its legends, the names that fans are able to have printed on their shirts or tattooed on their chests without fear of disappointment. Bobby Moore isn't going to leave West Ham for Tottenham; Sir Matt Busby isn't going to say something abhorrent on talk radio; Sammy Lee isn't going to turn down a cushy corporate ambassador's job at Liverpool to become assistant manager at Everton.

Some of these individuals make such a deep and lasting impact that their popularity transcends petty rivalry. Who among us can honestly say they did not feel a lump in their throats when John Terry organised a spontaneous standing ovation for his pre-arranged substitution in his last Chelsea appearance?

Despite the impression you might have got from reading the rest of this book, I quite like football. Therefore, it has been my great pleasure to be able to pay cartoon tributes to some of the icons of the game, as included in this section. These have sometimes been players or managers who formed an important part of my childhood, the giants of football when my mind was a healthy young sponge rather than the cynical dried-up walnut of today.

I was a relative latecomer to the game, not becoming a full addict until I was nine years old. At the time, Everton were emerging as the team to beat (look, it was the 1980s, it was a strange decade), with a great attacking line-up and a bright young manager, Howard Kendall. His death in 2015 led to a flood of anecdotes attesting to his generosity of spirit, and for once the comments sections of online obituaries were a pleasant place to be. Even in death, Kendall was still performing minor miracles.

The same could be said of one of Kendall's contemporaries: the man who sat in the opposite dugout for the 1984 FA Cup final, Graham Taylor. Both men acknowledged the importance and dedication of the fans who followed their clubs, and they had a humanist approach to all they encountered. Taylor's meteoric career rise was, of course, stymied by the England job and the accompanying documentary, but he recovered from that setback, his obvious enthusiasm for the game and his warmly intelligent observations making him something of a national treasure by the time of his death in 2017.

Another star of the era was Cyrille Regis, who tragically passed away in 2018 at the age of fifty-nine. I was too young to appreciate him in his pioneering West Brom days, but knew him as an explosive threat in the Coventry forward line. By then, it wasn't unusual to see black footballers playing for English teams, thanks to the bravery and talent of Regis and other people of colour who fought to overcome discrimination. They still endured foul abuse from the terraces, and institutional racism was still rife at many clubs, but attitudes were slowly starting to change. As a player, Regis had a deserved reputation as a powerful, intelligent player. So much so that Johan Cruyff tried to sign him for Ajax as a replacement for the Milan-bound Marco van Basten. The board's failure to land his target led to Cruyff quitting.

Cruyff himself passed away in 2016 – a year when it felt like every person who'd brought joy to the planet was ascending to a better place (the infinite void of death being preferable to seeing another news interview with Nigel Farage). The Dutchman was one of the most important figures in football history, a colossus whose innovative skill as a player was matched by his vision as a coach. He was the great creator whose influence is still felt to this day. As well as teaching some of the world's greatest players and building phenomenal sides, such as Barcelona's 'Dream Team' of the early 1990s, he also put in place the training academy that helped to produce talents like Guardiola, Xavi, Iniesta and Messi.

Perhaps less aesthetic were the unique talents of Trifon Ivanov, the Bulgarian full-back who also departed that year, aged just fifty. Beauty does indeed die young. Ivanov brought a different kind of pleasure to football fans; it was always a great feeling to switch on a game and see his mad, grizzled face in the line-up. He looked and played like he'd emerged from the woods and no one had the confidence to stop him from marching onto the field.

Of course, you don't need to have died to earn a permanent place in the hearts of football fans. It is rare in the modern era for players to stay at one club throughout their careers, so those who show loyalty are treated as heroes. Two such examples are Steven Gerrard and John Terry, neither of whom are one-club men.

When Gerrard announced his intention to leave Liverpool in January 2015, there followed a period of public mourning, the rest of the Merseyside club's season being reminiscent of Princess Diana's funeral procession. A year later, Terry was threatening to leave Chelsea, but ended up signing a contract extension before eventually shuffling off to the next realm, joining Aston Villa in the Championship.

More complex was the case of Arsène Wenger, who ended his twenty-two-year relationship with Arsenal in 2018. It would be strange to think of Arsenal without Wenger; he had almost become part of the furniture at the Emirates Stadium – specifically, the coat stand. Memories of his exceptional early successes and the cultural shift he had brought about at the club were dimmed by time, and Arsenal fans had grown frustrated after a period of stagnation that only saw them win a handful of major trophies. Although they were grateful for what he had done – a gratitude they expressed via the medium of airborne 'WENGER OUT' banners – they saw that it was time for a change, and eventually so did he.

One individual who defies categorisation but is worthy of tribute is Zlatan Ibrahimović. His arrival at LA Galaxy in 2018 was typically Hollywood, coming off the bench to win a local derby with two goals, one of which was a spectacular dipping effort from distance. However, much like many of Tinseltown's products, this debut feature was followed by a number of underwhelming sequels.

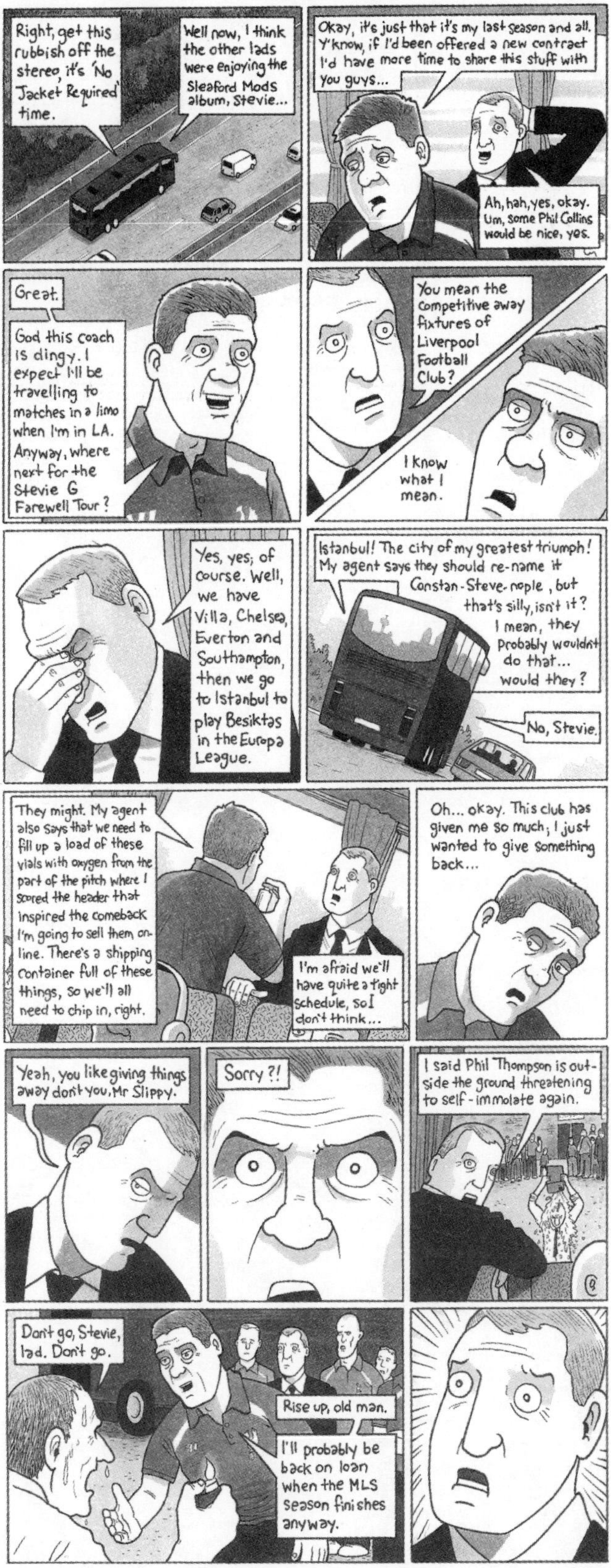
Right, get this rubbish off the stereo, it's 'No Jacket Required' time.
Well now, I think the other lads were enjoying the Sleaford Mods album, Stevie...
Okay, it's just that it's my last season and all. Y'know, if I'd been offered a new contract I'd have more time to share this stuff with you guys...
Ah, hah, yes, okay. Um, some Phil Collins would be nice, yes.
Great.
God this coach is dingy. I expect I'll be travelling to matches in a limo when I'm in LA. Anyway, where next for the Stevie G Farewell Tour?
You mean the competitive away fixtures of Liverpool Football Club?
I know what I mean.
Yes, yes; of course. Well, we have Villa, Chelsea, Everton and Southampton, then we go to Istanbul to play Besiktas in the Europa League.
Istanbul! The city of my greatest triumph! My agent says they should re-name it Constan-Steve-nople, but that's silly, isn't it? I mean, they probably wouldn't do that... would they?
No, Stevie.
They might. My agent also says that we need to fill up a load of these vials with oxygen from the part of the pitch where I scored the header that inspired the comeback I'm going to sell them on-line. There's a shipping container full of these things, so we'll all need to chip in, right.
I'm afraid we'll have quite a tight schedule, so I don't think...
Oh... okay. This club has given me so much; I just wanted to give something back...
Yeah, you like giving things away don't you, Mr Slippy.
Sorry?!
I said Phil Thompson is out-side the ground threatening to self-immolate again.
Don't go, Stevie, lad. Don't go.
Rise up, old man.
I'll probably be back on loan when the MLS season finishes anyway.

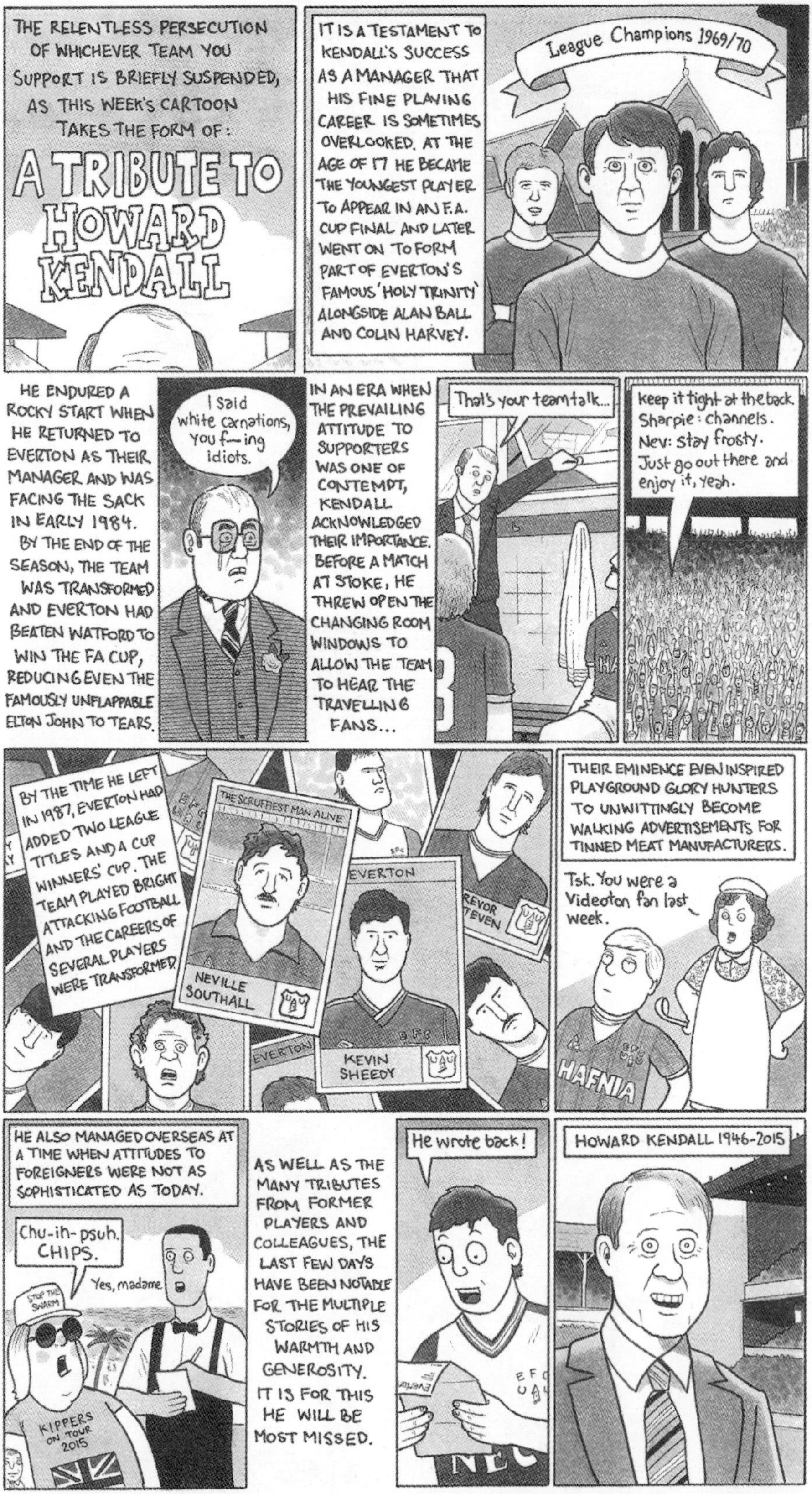
THE RELENTLESS PERSECUTION OF WHICHEVER TEAM YOU SUPPORT IS BRIEFLY SUSPENDED, AS THIS WEEK'S CARTOON TAKES THE FORM OF:
A TRIBUTE TO HOWARD KENDALL
IT IS A TESTAMENT TO KENDALL'S SUCCESS AS A MANAGER THAT HIS FINE PLAYING CAREER IS SOMETIMES OVERLOOKED. AT THE AGE OF 17 HE BECAME THE YOUNGEST PLAYER TO APPEAR IN AN F.A. CUP FINAL AND LATER WENT ON TO FORM PART OF EVERTON'S FAMOUS 'HOLY TRINITY' ALONGSIDE ALAN BALL AND COLIN HARVEY.
League Champions 1969/70
HE ENDURED A ROCKY START WHEN HE RETURNED TO EVERTON AS THEIR MANAGER AND WAS FACING THE SACK IN EARLY 1984. BY THE END OF THE SEASON, THE TEAM WAS TRANSFORMED AND EVERTON HAD BEATEN WATFORD TO WIN THE FA CUP, REDUCING EVEN THE FAMOUSLY UNFLAPPABLE ELTON JOHN TO TEARS.
I said white carnations, you f—ing idiots.
IN AN ERA WHEN THE PREVAILING ATTITUDE TO SUPPORTERS WAS ONE OF CONTEMPT, KENDALL ACKNOWLEDGED THEIR IMPORTANCE. BEFORE A MATCH AT STOKE, HE THREW OPEN THE CHANGING ROOM WINDOWS TO ALLOW THE TEAM TO HEAR THE TRAVELLING FANS...
That's your team talk...
keep it tight at the back. Sharpie: channels. Nev: stay frosty. Just go out there and enjoy it, yeah.
BY THE TIME HE LEFT IN 1987, EVERTON HAD ADDED TWO LEAGUE TITLES AND A CUP WINNERS' CUP. THE TEAM PLAYED BRIGHT ATTACKING FOOTBALL AND THE CAREERS OF SEVERAL PLAYERS WERE TRANSFORMED.
THE SCRUFFIEST MAN ALIVE
NEVILLE SOUTHALL
EVERTON
KEVIN SHEEDY
EVERTON
THEIR EMINENCE EVEN INSPIRED PLAYGROUND GLORY HUNTERS TO UNWITTINGLY BECOME WALKING ADVERTISEMENTS FOR TINNED MEAT MANUFACTURERS.
Tsk. You were a Videoton fan last week.
HAFNIA
HE ALSO MANAGED OVERSEAS AT A TIME WHEN ATTITUDES TO FOREIGNERS WERE NOT AS SOPHISTICATED AS TODAY.
Chu-ih-psuh. CHIPS.
Yes, madame
STOP THE SWARM
KIPPERS ON TOUR 2015
AS WELL AS THE MANY TRIBUTES FROM FORMER PLAYERS AND COLLEAGUES, THE LAST FEW DAYS HAVE BEEN NOTABLE FOR THE MULTIPLE STORIES OF HIS WARMTH AND GENEROSITY. IT IS FOR THIS HE WILL BE MOST MISSED.
He wrote back!
HOWARD KENDALL 1946-2015

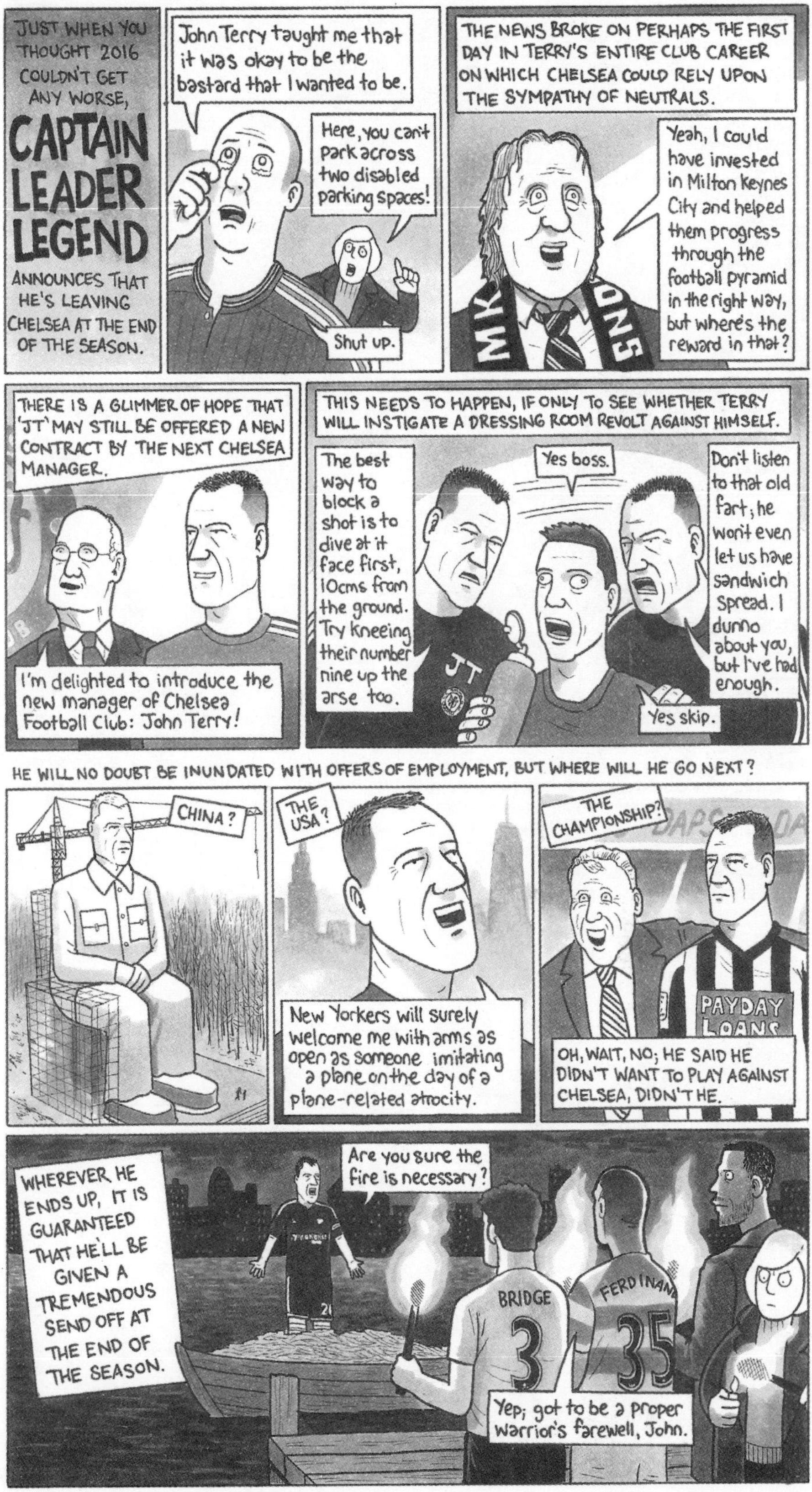
JUST WHEN YOU THOUGHT 2016 COULDN'T GET ANY WORSE,
CAPTAIN LEADER LEGEND
ANNOUNCES THAT HE'S LEAVING CHELSEA AT THE END OF THE SEASON.
John Terry taught me that it was okay to be the bastard that I wanted to be.
Here, you can't park across two disabled parking spaces!
Shut up.
THE NEWS BROKE ON PERHAPS THE FIRST DAY IN TERRY'S ENTIRE CLUB CAREER ON WHICH CHELSEA COULD RELY UPON THE SYMPATHY OF NEUTRALS.
Yeah, I could have invested in Milton Keynes City and helped them progress through the football pyramid in the right way, but where's the reward in that?
THERE IS A GLIMMER OF HOPE THAT 'JT' MAY STILL BE OFFERED A NEW CONTRACT BY THE NEXT CHELSEA MANAGER.
I'm delighted to introduce the new manager of Chelsea Football Club: John Terry!
THIS NEEDS TO HAPPEN, IF ONLY TO SEE WHETHER TERRY WILL INSTIGATE A DRESSING ROOM REVOLT AGAINST HIMSELF.
The best way to block a shot is to dive at it face first, 10cms from the ground. Try kneeing their number nine up the arse too.
Yes boss.
Don't listen to that old fart; he won't even let us have sandwich spread. I dunno about you, but I've had enough.
Yes skip.
HE WILL NO DOUBT BE INUNDATED WITH OFFERS OF EMPLOYMENT, BUT WHERE WILL HE GO NEXT?
CHINA?
THE USA?
New Yorkers will surely welcome me with arms as open as someone imitating a plane on the day of a plane-related atrocity.
THE CHAMPIONSHIP?
PAYDAY LOANS
OH, WAIT, NO; HE SAID HE DIDN'T WANT TO PLAY AGAINST CHELSEA, DIDN'T HE.
WHEREVER HE ENDS UP, IT IS GUARANTEED THAT HE'LL BE GIVEN A TREMENDOUS SEND OFF AT THE END OF THE SEASON.
Are you sure the fire is necessary?
BRIDGE 3
FERDINAN 35
Yep; got to be a proper warrior's farewell, John.

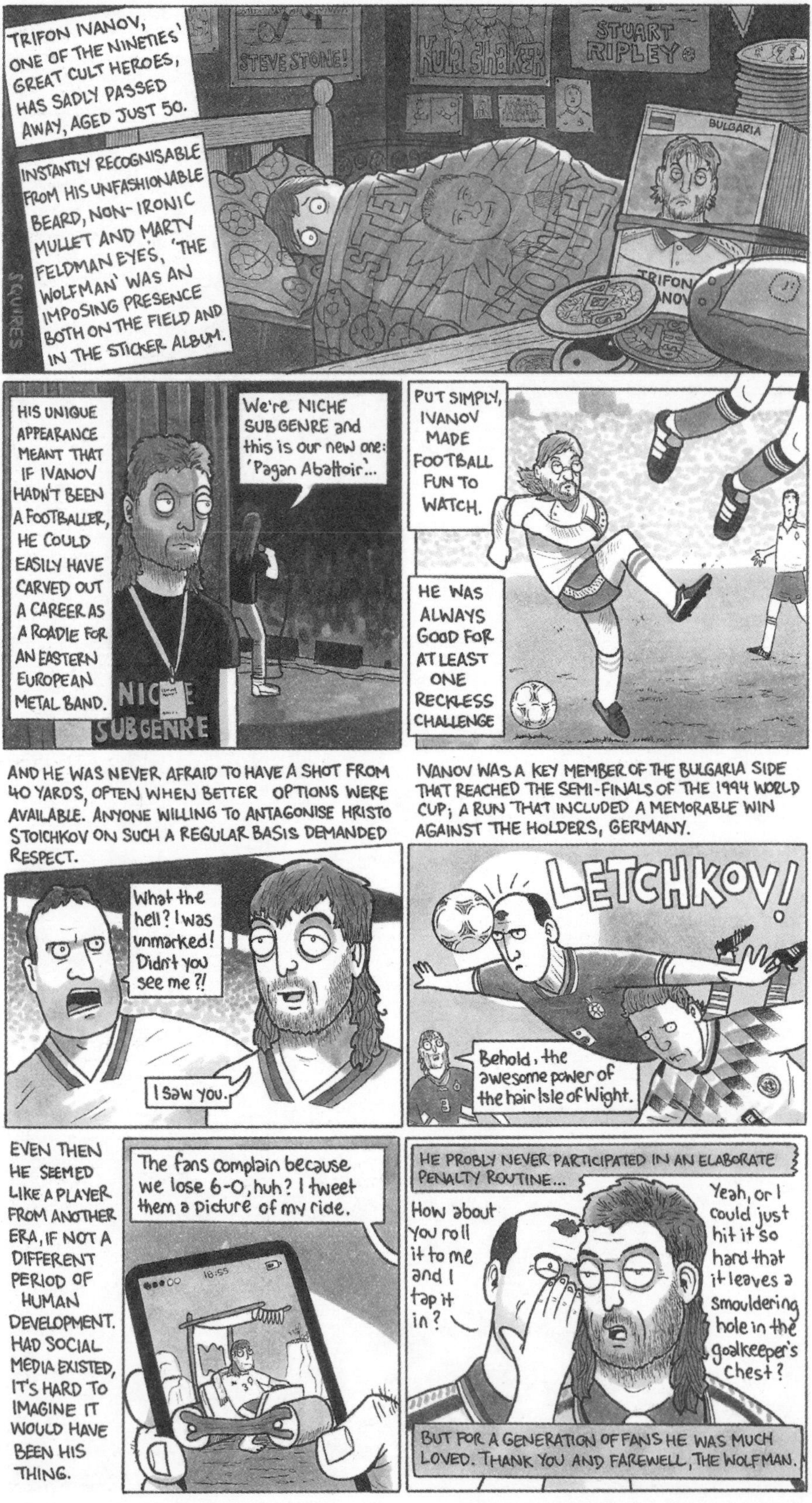
STEVE STONE!
Kula Shaker
STUART RIPLEY
TRIFON IVANOV, ONE OF THE NINETIES' GREAT CULT HEROES, HAS SADLY PASSED AWAY, AGED JUST 50.
BULGARIA
INSTANTLY RECOGNISABLE FROM HIS UNFASHIONABLE BEARD, NON-IRONIC MULLET AND MARTY FELDMAN EYES, 'THE WOLFMAN' WAS AN IMPOSING PRESENCE BOTH ON THE FIELD AND IN THE STICKER ALBUM.
SQUIRES
HIS UNIQUE APPEARANCE MEANT THAT IF IVANOV HADN'T BEEN A FOOTBALLER, HE COULD EASILY HAVE CARVED OUT A CAREER AS A ROADIE FOR AN EASTERN EUROPEAN METAL BAND.
We're NICHE SUBGENRE and this is our new one: 'Pagan Abattoir'...
NICHE SUBGENRE
PUT SIMPLY, IVANOV MADE FOOTBALL FUN TO WATCH.
HE WAS ALWAYS GOOD FOR AT LEAST ONE RECKLESS CHALLENGE
AND HE WAS NEVER AFRAID TO HAVE A SHOT FROM 40 YARDS, OFTEN WHEN BETTER OPTIONS WERE AVAILABLE. ANYONE WILLING TO ANTAGONISE HRISTO STOICHKOV ON SUCH A REGULAR BASIS DEMANDED RESPECT.
What the hell? I was unmarked! Didn't you see me?!
I saw you.
IVANOV WAS A KEY MEMBER OF THE BULGARIA SIDE THAT REACHED THE SEMI-FINALS OF THE 1994 WORLD CUP; A RUN THAT INCLUDED A MEMORABLE WIN AGAINST THE HOLDERS, GERMANY.
LETCHKOV!
Behold, the awesome power of the hair Isle of Wight.
EVEN THEN HE SEEMED LIKE A PLAYER FROM ANOTHER ERA, IF NOT A DIFFERENT PERIOD OF HUMAN DEVELOPMENT. HAD SOCIAL MEDIA EXISTED, IT'S HARD TO IMAGINE IT WOULD HAVE BEEN HIS THING.
The fans complain because we lose 6-0, huh? I tweet them a picture of my ride.
18:55
HE PROBLY NEVER PARTICIPATED IN AN ELABORATE PENALTY ROUTINE...
How about you roll it to me and I tap it in?
Yeah, or I could just hit it so hard that it leaves a smouldering hole in the goalkeeper's chest?
BUT FOR A GENERATION OF FANS HE WAS MUCH LOVED. THANK YOU AND FAREWELL, THE WOLFMAN.

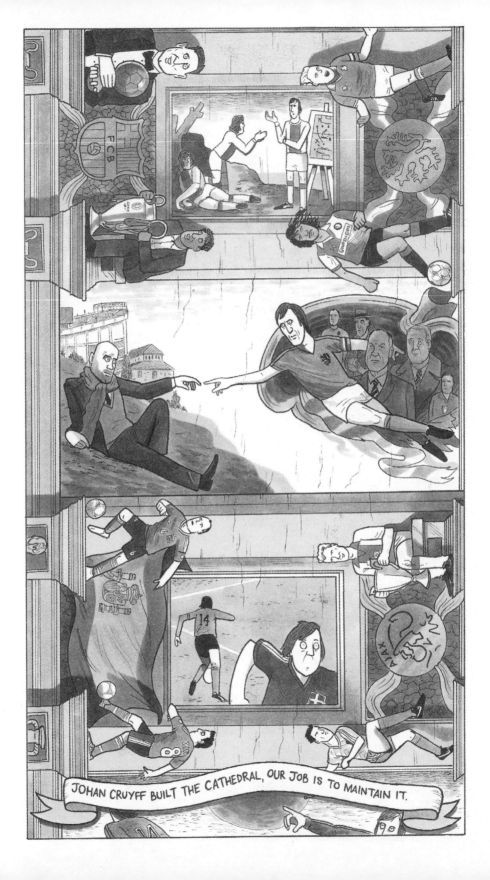

JOHAN CRUYFF BUILT THE CATHEDRAL, OUR JOB IS TO MAINTAIN IT.

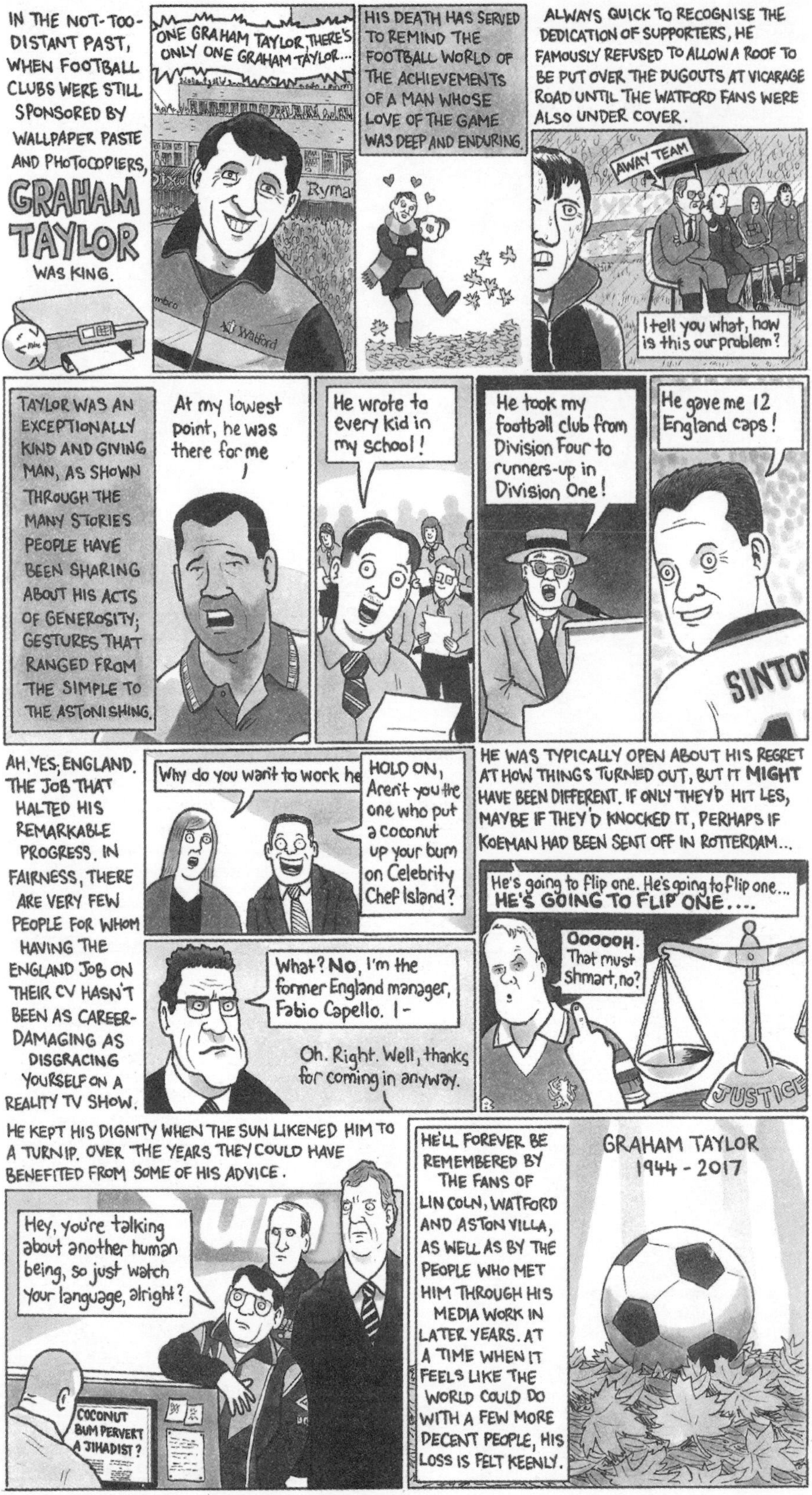

IN THE NOT-TOO-DISTANT PAST, WHEN FOOTBALL CLUBS WERE STILL SPONSORED BY WALLPAPER PASTE AND PHOTOCOPIERS,
GRAHAM TAYLOR
WAS KING.
ONE GRAHAM TAYLOR, THERE'S ONLY ONE GRAHAM TAYLOR...
Ryman
Watford
HIS DEATH HAS SERVED TO REMIND THE FOOTBALL WORLD OF THE ACHIEVEMENTS OF A MAN WHOSE LOVE OF THE GAME WAS DEEP AND ENDURING.
ALWAYS QUICK TO RECOGNISE THE DEDICATION OF SUPPORTERS, HE FAMOUSLY REFUSED TO ALLOW A ROOF TO BE PUT OVER THE DUGOUTS AT VICARAGE ROAD UNTIL THE WATFORD FANS WERE ALSO UNDER COVER.
AWAY TEAM
I tell you what, how is this our problem?
TAYLOR WAS AN EXCEPTIONALLY KIND AND GIVING MAN, AS SHOWN THROUGH THE MANY STORIES PEOPLE HAVE BEEN SHARING ABOUT HIS ACTS OF GENEROSITY; GESTURES THAT RANGED FROM THE SIMPLE TO THE ASTONISHING.
At my lowest point, he was there for me
He wrote to every kid in my school!
He took my football club from Division Four to runners-up in Division One!
He gave me 12 England caps!
SINTON
AH, YES, ENGLAND. THE JOB THAT HALTED HIS REMARKABLE PROGRESS. IN FAIRNESS, THERE ARE VERY FEW PEOPLE FOR WHOM HAVING THE ENGLAND JOB ON THEIR CV HASN'T BEEN AS CAREER-DAMAGING AS DISGRACING YOURSELF ON A REALITY TV SHOW.
Why do you want to work he
HOLD ON, Aren't you the one who put a coconut up your bum on Celebrity Chef Island?
What? NO, I'm the former England manager, Fabio Capello. I-
Oh. Right. Well, thanks for coming in anyway.
HE WAS TYPICALLY OPEN ABOUT HIS REGRET AT HOW THINGS TURNED OUT, BUT IT MIGHT HAVE BEEN DIFFERENT. IF ONLY THEY'D HIT LES, MAYBE IF THEY'D KNOCKED IT, PERHAPS IF KOEMAN HAD BEEN SENT OFF IN ROTTERDAM...
He's going to flip one. He's going to flip one... HE'S GOING TO FLIP ONE....
Oooooh. That must shmart, no?
JUSTICE
HE KEPT HIS DIGNITY WHEN THE SUN LIKENED HIM TO A TURNIP. OVER THE YEARS THEY COULD HAVE BENEFITED FROM SOME OF HIS ADVICE.
Hey, you're talking about another human being, so just watch your language, alright?
COCONUT BUM PERVERT A JIHADIST?
HE'LL FOREVER BE REMEMBERED BY THE FANS OF LINCOLN, WATFORD AND ASTON VILLA, AS WELL AS BY THE PEOPLE WHO MET HIM THROUGH HIS MEDIA WORK IN LATER YEARS. AT A TIME WHEN IT FEELS LIKE THE WORLD COULD DO WITH A FEW MORE DECENT PEOPLE, HIS LOSS IS FELT KEENLY.
GRAHAM TAYLOR
1944 - 2017

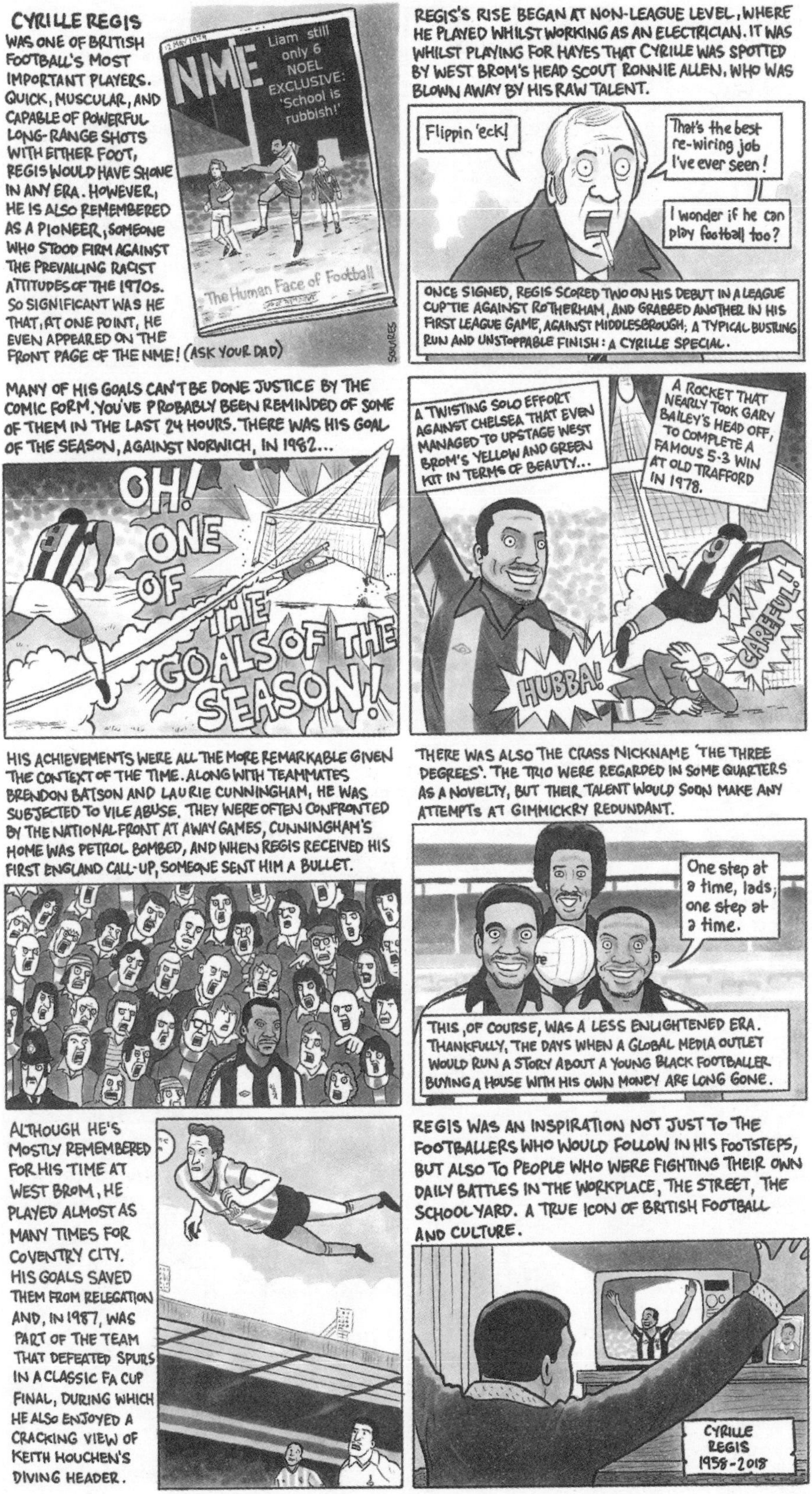
CYRILLE REGIS
WAS ONE OF BRITISH FOOTBALL'S MOST IMPORTANT PLAYERS. QUICK, MUSCULAR, AND CAPABLE OF POWERFUL LONG-RANGE SHOTS WITH EITHER FOOT, REGIS WOULD HAVE SHONE IN ANY ERA. HOWEVER, HE IS ALSO REMEMBERED AS A PIONEER, SOMEONE WHO STOOD FIRM AGAINST THE PREVAILING RACIST ATTITUDES OF THE 1970s. SO SIGNIFICANT WAS HE THAT, AT ONE POINT, HE EVEN APPEARED ON THE FRONT PAGE OF THE NME! (ASK YOUR DAD)
NME
Liam still only 6
NOEL EXCLUSIVE: 'School is rubbish!'
The Human Face of Football
SQUIRES
REGIS'S RISE BEGAN AT NON-LEAGUE LEVEL, WHERE HE PLAYED WHILST WORKING AS AN ELECTRICIAN. IT WAS WHILST PLAYING FOR HAYES THAT CYRILLE WAS SPOTTED BY WEST BROM'S HEAD SCOUT RONNIE ALLEN, WHO WAS BLOWN AWAY BY HIS RAW TALENT.
Flippin 'eck!
That's the best re-wiring job I've ever seen!
I wonder if he can play football too?
ONCE SIGNED, REGIS SCORED TWO ON HIS DEBUT IN A LEAGUE CUP TIE AGAINST ROTHERHAM, AND GRABBED ANOTHER IN HIS FIRST LEAGUE GAME, AGAINST MIDDLESBROUGH; A TYPICAL BUSTLING RUN AND UNSTOPPABLE FINISH: A CYRILLE SPECIAL.
MANY OF HIS GOALS CAN'T BE DONE JUSTICE BY THE COMIC FORM. YOU'VE PROBABLY BEEN REMINDED OF SOME OF THEM IN THE LAST 24 HOURS. THERE WAS HIS GOAL OF THE SEASON, AGAINST NORWICH, IN 1982...
OH! ONE OF THE GOALS OF THE SEASON!
A TWISTING SOLO EFFORT AGAINST CHELSEA THAT EVEN MANAGED TO UPSTAGE WEST BROM'S YELLOW AND GREEN KIT IN TERMS OF BEAUTY...
A ROCKET THAT NEARLY TOOK GARY BAILEY'S HEAD OFF, TO COMPLETE A FAMOUS 5-3 WIN AT OLD TRAFFORD IN 1978.
HUBBA!
CAREFUL!
HIS ACHIEVEMENTS WERE ALL THE MORE REMARKABLE GIVEN THE CONTEXT OF THE TIME. ALONG WITH TEAMMATES BRENDON BATSON AND LAURIE CUNNINGHAM, HE WAS SUBJECTED TO VILE ABUSE. THEY WERE OFTEN CONFRONTED BY THE NATIONAL FRONT AT AWAY GAMES, CUNNINGHAM'S HOME WAS PETROL BOMBED, AND WHEN REGIS RECEIVED HIS FIRST ENGLAND CALL-UP, SOMEONE SENT HIM A BULLET.
THERE WAS ALSO THE CRASS NICKNAME 'THE THREE DEGREES'. THE TRIO WERE REGARDED IN SOME QUARTERS AS A NOVELTY, BUT THEIR TALENT WOULD SOON MAKE ANY ATTEMPTS AT GIMMICKRY REDUNDANT.
One step at a time, lads; one step at a time.
THIS, OF COURSE, WAS A LESS ENLIGHTENED ERA. THANKFULLY, THE DAYS WHEN A GLOBAL MEDIA OUTLET WOULD RUN A STORY ABOUT A YOUNG BLACK FOOTBALLER BUYING A HOUSE WITH HIS OWN MONEY ARE LONG GONE.
ALTHOUGH HE'S MOSTLY REMEMBERED FOR HIS TIME AT WEST BROM, HE PLAYED ALMOST AS MANY TIMES FOR COVENTRY CITY. HIS GOALS SAVED THEM FROM RELEGATION AND, IN 1987, WAS PART OF THE TEAM THAT DEFEATED SPURS IN A CLASSIC FA CUP FINAL, DURING WHICH HE ALSO ENJOYED A CRACKING VIEW OF KEITH HOUCHEN'S DIVING HEADER.
REGIS WAS AN INSPIRATION NOT JUST TO THE FOOTBALLERS WHO WOULD FOLLOW IN HIS FOOTSTEPS, BUT ALSO TO PEOPLE WHO WERE FIGHTING THEIR OWN DAILY BATTLES IN THE WORKPLACE, THE STREET, THE SCHOOLYARD. A TRUE ICON OF BRITISH FOOTBALL AND CULTURE.
CYRILLE REGIS 1958–2018

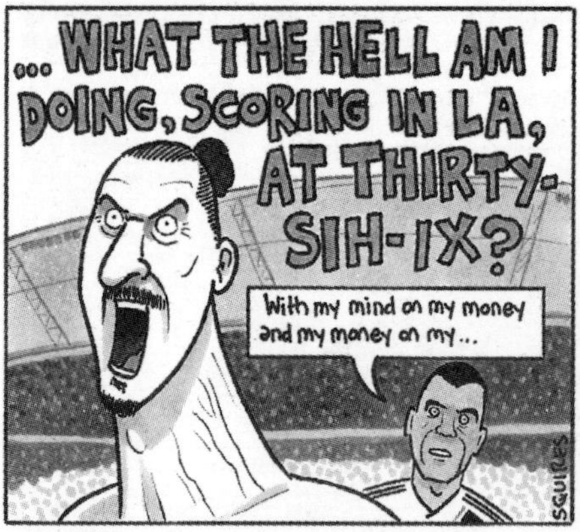
...WHAT THE HELL AM I DOING, SCORING IN LA, AT THIRTY-SIH-IX?
With my mind on my money and my money on my...
SQUIRES

ZLATAN IS RISEN! IBRAHIMOVIĆ ANNOUNCED HIS ARRIVAL AT LA GALAXY WITH A PIECE OF ART SECOND ONLY TO THE RENAISSANCE CROWD SCENE THAT MET ONE OF DELE ALLI'S GOALS FOR TOTTENHAM AT CHELSEA.

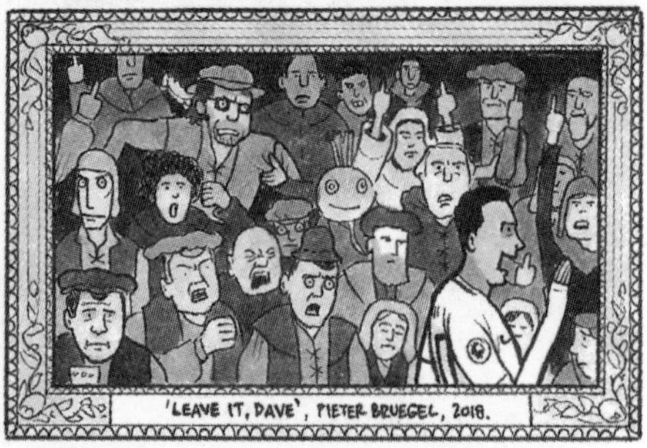
'LEAVE IT, DAVE', PIETER BRUEGEL, 2018.

THIS TIME LAST YEAR IT WAS FEARED THAT ZLATAN'S CAREER MIGHT BE OVER, BUT JUST AS HE PREDICTED, HE RECOVERED FROM A CRUCIATE LIGAMENT INJURY AS QUICKLY AS A **LION** WHO'D HAD ACCESS TO THE BEST HEALTHCARE PROVISION AND FANCY HARLEY STREET VETS. HE MIGHT EVEN HAVE MADE HIS GALAXY DEBUT EARLIER IF IT WEREN'T FOR THE PUNISHING SCHEDULE OF FILMING HUBRISTIC PROMOTIONAL VIDEOS TO ACCOMPANY HIS ARRIVAL.

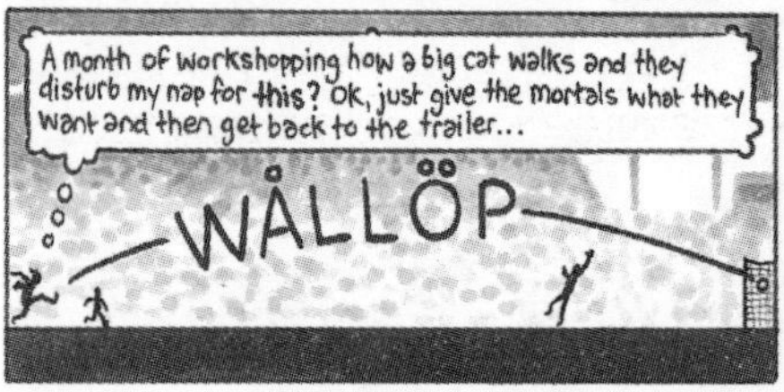
A month of workshopping how a big cat walks and they disturb my nap for this? Ok, just give the mortals what they want and then get back to the trailer...
WALLÖP

IBRAHIMOVIĆ'S LONG-RANGE GOAL AGAINST **LAFC** CIRCULATED THE INTERNET LIKE ONE OF HIS TRADEMARK ROUNDHOUSE KICKS TO A TEAMMATE'S EAR. THE SHEER WONDER OF THE GOAL WAS CAPTURED PERFECTLY BY THE AMERICAN COMMENTATORS...

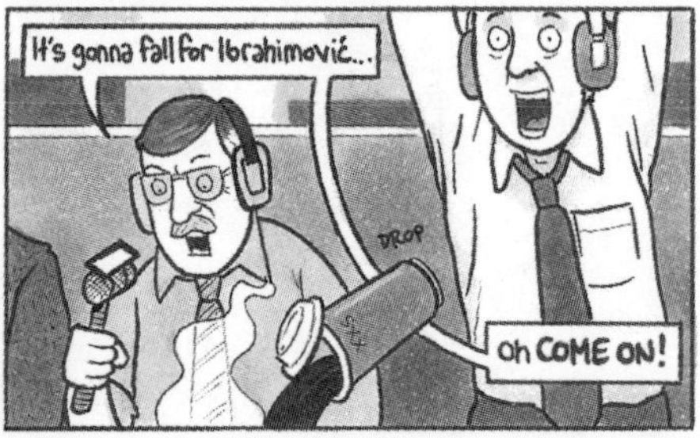
It's gonna fall for Ibrahimović...
DROP
Oh COME ON!

ZLATAN HAD ARRIVED IN LA ONLY A COUPLE OF NIGHTS BEFORE; HIS NEW COLLEAGUES NO DOUBT IN AWE OF HIS SHEER **ALPHA** PRESENCE, AS IF THE CLUB HAD BROKEN ITS WAGE STRUCTURE TO SIGN **JOHNSON FROM PEEP SHOW.**

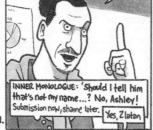

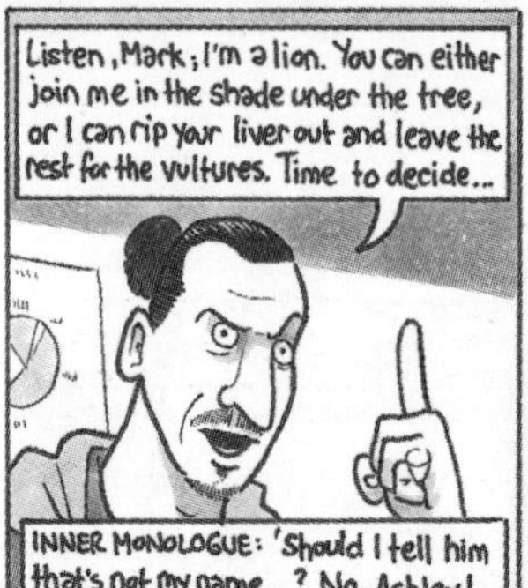
Listen, Mark; I'm a lion. You can either join me in the shade under the tree, or I can rip your liver out and leave the rest for the vultures. Time to decide...
INNER MONOLOGUE: 'Should I tell him that's not my name...? No, Ashley! Submission now, shame later.
Yes, Zlatan

THE STRIKE ENTERED THE SCRAPBOOK OF ZLATAN'S CAREER HIGHLIGHTS. PERHAPS THE GOAL EVEN MATCHES THE ACHIEVEMENT OF PROVING TO ENGLISH PEOPLE THAT HE WASN'T JUST AN IAN ORMONDROYD WITH PRISON-STYLE TATTOOS BY SCORING AGAINST **JOE HART!**

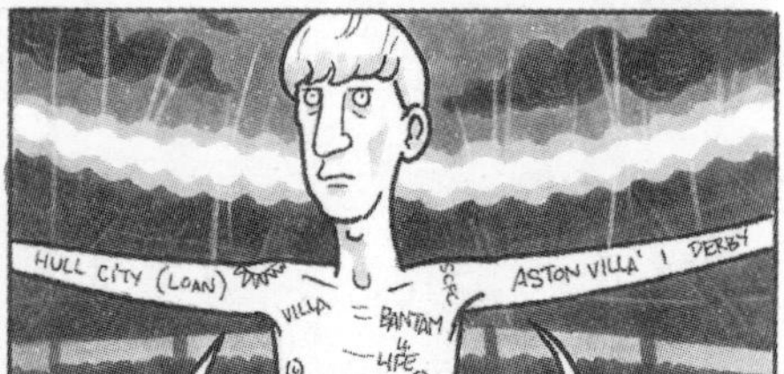
HULL CITY (LOAN)
ASTON VILLA
DERBY
VILLA
BANTAM 4 LIFE
LEICESTER
I am IAN.
You're welcome, yeah.

THE BEST PART OF ZLATAN'S MOVE TO LA IS THAT IT PUTS HIM IN CLOSE PROXIMITY TO HOLLYWOOD, MAKING IT INEVITABLE THAT HE WILL BECOME A STAR OF THE SILVER SCREEN. POTENTIAL FILM PROJECTS INCLUDE:

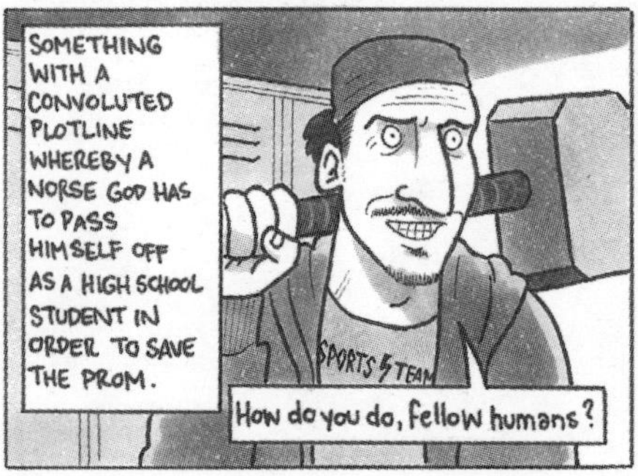
SOMETHING WITH A CONVOLUTED PLOTLINE WHEREBY A NORSE GOD HAS TO PASS HIMSELF OFF AS A HIGH SCHOOL STUDENT IN ORDER TO SAVE THE PROM.
SPORTS TEAM
How do you do, fellow humans?

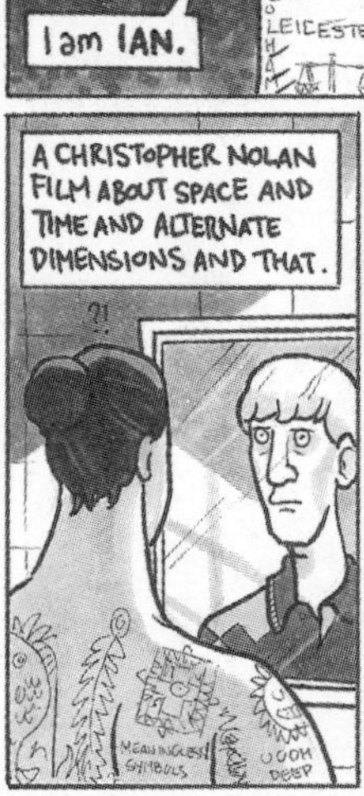
A CHRISTOPHER NOLAN FILM ABOUT SPACE AND TIME AND ALTERNATE DIMENSIONS AND THAT.
?!
MEANINGFUL SYMBOLS
OOOH DEEP

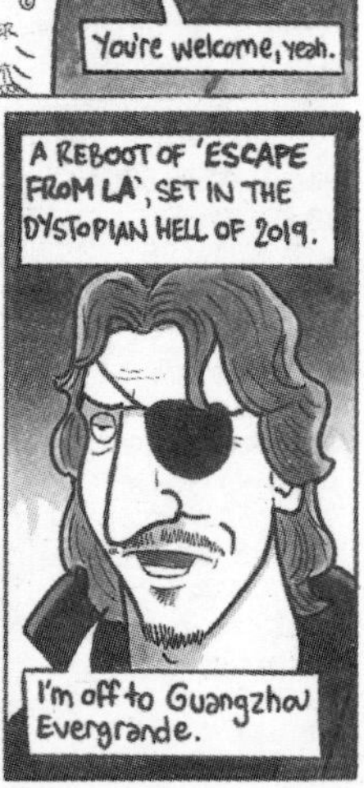
A REBOOT OF 'ESCAPE FROM LA', SET IN THE DYSTOPIAN HELL OF 2019.
I'm off to Guangzhou Evergrande.

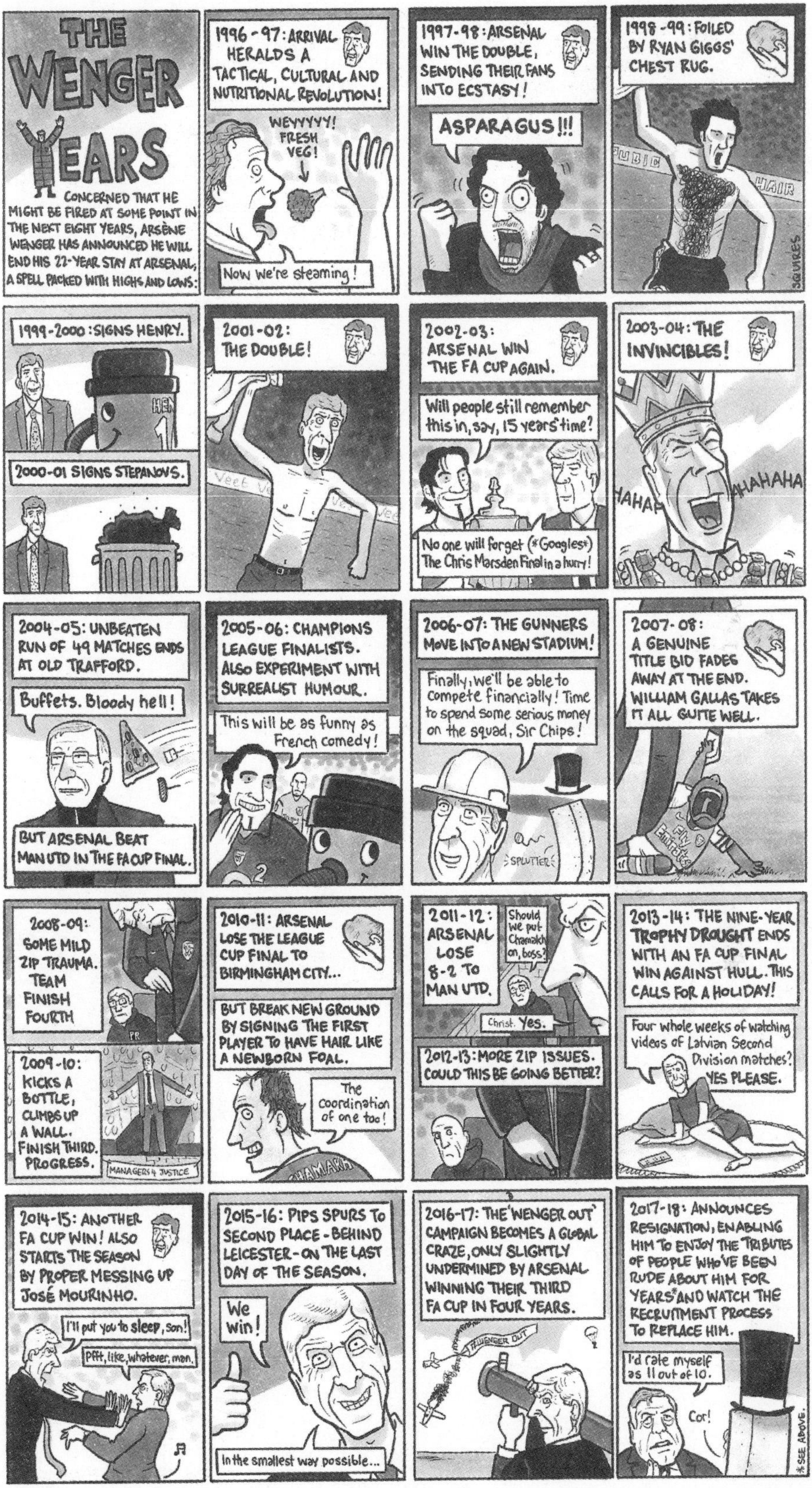
THE WENGER YEARS
CONCERNED THAT HE MIGHT BE FIRED AT SOME POINT IN THE NEXT EIGHT YEARS, ARSÈNE WENGER HAS ANNOUNCED HE WILL END HIS 22-YEAR STAY AT ARSENAL, A SPELL PACKED WITH HIGHS AND LOWS:
1996-97: ARRIVAL HERALDS A TACTICAL, CULTURAL AND NUTRITIONAL REVOLUTION!
WEYYYYY! FRESH VEG!
Now we're steaming!
1997-98: ARSENAL WIN THE DOUBLE, SENDING THEIR FANS INTO ECSTASY!
ASPARAGUS!!!
1998-99: FOILED BY RYAN GIGGS' CHEST RUG.
PUBIC
HAIR
SQUIRES
1999-2000: SIGNS HENRY.
HEN 1
2000-01 SIGNS STEPANOVS.
2001-02: THE DOUBLE!
2002-03: ARSENAL WIN THE FA CUP AGAIN.
Will people still remember this in, say, 15 years' time?
No one will forget (*Googles*) The Chris Marsden Final in a hurry!
2003-04: THE INVINCIBLES!
HAHA
HAHAHA
2004-05: UNBEATEN RUN OF 49 MATCHES ENDS AT OLD TRAFFORD.
Buffets. Bloody hell!
BUT ARSENAL BEAT MAN UTD IN THE FA CUP FINAL.
2005-06: CHAMPIONS LEAGUE FINALISTS. ALSO EXPERIMENT WITH SURREALIST HUMOUR.
This will be as funny as French comedy!
2006-07: THE GUNNERS MOVE INTO A NEW STADIUM!
Finally, we'll be able to compete financially! Time to spend some serious money on the squad, Sir Chips!
SPLUTTER
2007-08: A GENUINE TITLE BID FADES AWAY AT THE END. WILLIAM GALLAS TAKES IT ALL QUITE WELL.
Fly Emirates
2008-09: SOME MILD ZIP TRAUMA. TEAM FINISH FOURTH
PR
2009-10: KICKS A BOTTLE, CLIMBS UP A WALL. FINISH THIRD. PROGRESS.
MANAGERS 4 JUSTICE
2010-11: ARSENAL LOSE THE LEAGUE CUP FINAL TO BIRMINGHAM CITY...
BUT BREAK NEW GROUND BY SIGNING THE FIRST PLAYER TO HAVE HAIR LIKE A NEWBORN FOAL.
The coordination of one too!
CHAMAKH
2011-12: ARSENAL LOSE 8-2 TO MAN UTD.
Should we put Chamakh on, boss?
Christ. Yes.
2012-13: MORE ZIP ISSUES. COULD THIS BE GOING BETTER?
2013-14: THE NINE-YEAR TROPHY DROUGHT ENDS WITH AN FA CUP FINAL WIN AGAINST HULL. THIS CALLS FOR A HOLIDAY!
Four whole weeks of watching videos of Latvian Second Division matches? YES PLEASE.
2014-15: ANOTHER FA CUP WIN! ALSO STARTS THE SEASON BY PROPER MESSING UP JOSÉ MOURINHO.
I'll put you to sleep, son!
Pfft, like, whatever, man.
2015-16: PIPS SPURS TO SECOND PLACE - BEHIND LEICESTER - ON THE LAST DAY OF THE SEASON.
We win!
In the smallest way possible...
2016-17: THE 'WENGER OUT' CAMPAIGN BECOMES A GLOBAL CRAZE, ONLY SLIGHTLY UNDERMINED BY ARSENAL WINNING THEIR THIRD FA CUP IN FOUR YEARS.
WENGER OUT
2017-18: ANNOUNCES RESIGNATION, ENABLING HIM TO ENJOY THE TRIBUTES OF PEOPLE WHO'VE BEEN RUDE ABOUT HIM FOR YEARS* AND WATCH THE RECRUITMENT PROCESS TO REPLACE HIM.
I'd rate myself as 11 out of 10.
Cor!
*SEE ABOVE.

SHUT THE FA CUP

(and Read These Cartoons)

We all know that winning the oldest cup competition in the world and providing a club's supporters with a day they will never forget is not as good as finishing fourth. Indeed, many Premier League clubs now regard the competition as an unwelcome distraction, preferring the spare weekends that elimination affords – time that can be better spent taking the squad overseas for warm-weather training in the bars and nightclubs of southern European cities.

The competition's status has not even been revived by the intrusive sponsorship of a state-owned airline from the Arabian peninsula nor by moving the kick-off time to maximise the inconvenience for any travelling fan who lives outside Greater London – a section of the population that I'm led to believe numbers literally hundreds.

In spite of all this, the FA Cup is still warmly regarded by many football fans (the old ones, and those who support Wigan). For decades, the FA Cup final was the biggest match in the football calendar, and one of just a handful of games that were shown live on British television, with two-thirds of all the TV stations available in England screening the match. If you could be bothered to get up and manually change channels, you could switch between the washed-out, beige-jacket vibe of BBC1 and the kaleidoscope of wrongness that was ITV's coverage.

The match would be preceded by a three-hour build-up, which seemed like an age but was essential viewing. It was only on these occasions that the cameras would grant us access to the players, allowing us to discover the wacky nicknames they had for one another (Reidy, Sharpy, Sheedy-y, etc.). Helicopters would film the team buses as they snaked their way through the crowds to Wembley Stadium, the whole event having the air of a royal wedding (except it wasn't an Establishment propaganda tool designed to normalise the tyranny of inherited power and wealth – APART FROM THE YEARS MAN UNITED WERE IN IT, EH? EH?).

Ah yes, comedy (that's what that was). The cup final coverage would always include a segment featuring a star of light entertainment who had some connection to the finalists. If a Merseyside club was involved, you'd better have a spare pair of pants at the ready because after five minutes of Jimmy Tarbuck bantering with Stan Boardman they would be filled to the brim with hot piss.

The humorous segments didn't always hit the mark, though. Famously, in 1984, teatime funnyman Michael Barrymore did an impersonation of Watford's John Barnes that involved an 'Afro wig' and comedy West Indian voice. A video of the performance was up on YouTube for a while, but has since been taken down, presumably because of the threat to public health caused by a mass outbreak of people curling up into a ball and saying, 'No, no, no, no, no, no, no, no, no, no, no, no, no' until they die.

The journey to the final starts many months earlier, at amateur level. As the competition stretches into the winter months, professional teams enter the fray, but some retain the spirit of amateurism by failing to progress beyond the second round for bloody years, Swindon, you utterly useless . . .

At least the FA Cup draw still provides a sensual treat: the clack of the balls as they fall from the velvet bag into a goldfish bowl. These are glitzy affairs now, as you would expect from any event that occasionally involves Martin Keown. Back in the day, there was no live audience to provide reaction to two people reading out the names of football teams. Instead, the draw would be conducted from an oak-panelled room within the FA's headquarters at Lancaster Gate, two poker-faced men in blazers reading out the team numbers, displaying no hint of emotion no matter how exciting the tie. Manchester United v. Liverpool? Nothing. Tottenham v. Arsenal? Not so much as an eyebrow-raise. Eleven genetically modified cockroach men v. Space Nazis XI? Next.

The FA Cup still means a lot to me (old) and I enjoy the opportunity to draw cartoons about it. This section includes a few strips from events in recent seasons, starting with the 2016 final, which most people remember as the one where Alan Pardew did a little dance after his Crystal Palace side took the lead. His career never really recovered from that. Manchester United came back to win the final, Palace had a poor start to the following season and Pardew was sacked before Christmas. He made such a mess of his next job at West Bromwich Albion that they had to leave all the windows open at the Hawthorns for months after he was fired. Louis van Gaal didn't even last that long, and was mutually consented before the engraver had even finished putting United's name on the trophy.

There was a time when the crowd was trusted to sing the national anthem before the final, but at some point it was decided that it would be better to hire an opera singer to belt it out over the booming PA system. In 2016, singer Karen Harding decided to hark back to the good old days by missing her cue and only raising her microphone for the last few bars. Or maybe, as the brass band struck up, it dawned upon her that national anthems are inherently rubbish, especially Britain's celebration of subservience, which doesn't even mention mountains or fire.

The 2016/17 competition provided plenty of stories and a surprisingly entertaining final. At the quarter-final stage Manchester City strolled past Middlesbrough, in a week when the world was distracted by a viral video of the BBC's expert on Korean diplomatic relations having a live interview interrupted by his strutting children and panicked wife. Meanwhile, Spurs were faced with the

153

daunting prospect of a trip to Wembley, which at the time was considered to be a cursed venue for them. They'd used the stadium as their home ground for European fixtures, which saw them knocked out of the Champions League in the group stage and then eliminated by Gent in the Europa League. Chelsea would beat them in the semi-final, so maybe there was something in it.

Chelsea would play Arsenal in the final, who had shocked Manchester City's magnificently coiffured fans in the other semi-final. Also doing the rounds that week was a photo of some serious-looking West Ham fans who'd photographed themselves with various items of ancient weaponry. What is the FA Cup about if not spotty-arsed teenagers making spectacles of themselves on social media platforms while brandishing one of their dad's putters in a vaguely menacing fashion?

Arsenal went on to win the final 2–1, which ruined John Terry's last day as a Chelsea player but provided entertainment for the rest of the country, not least Wayne Bridge and Anton Ferdinand.

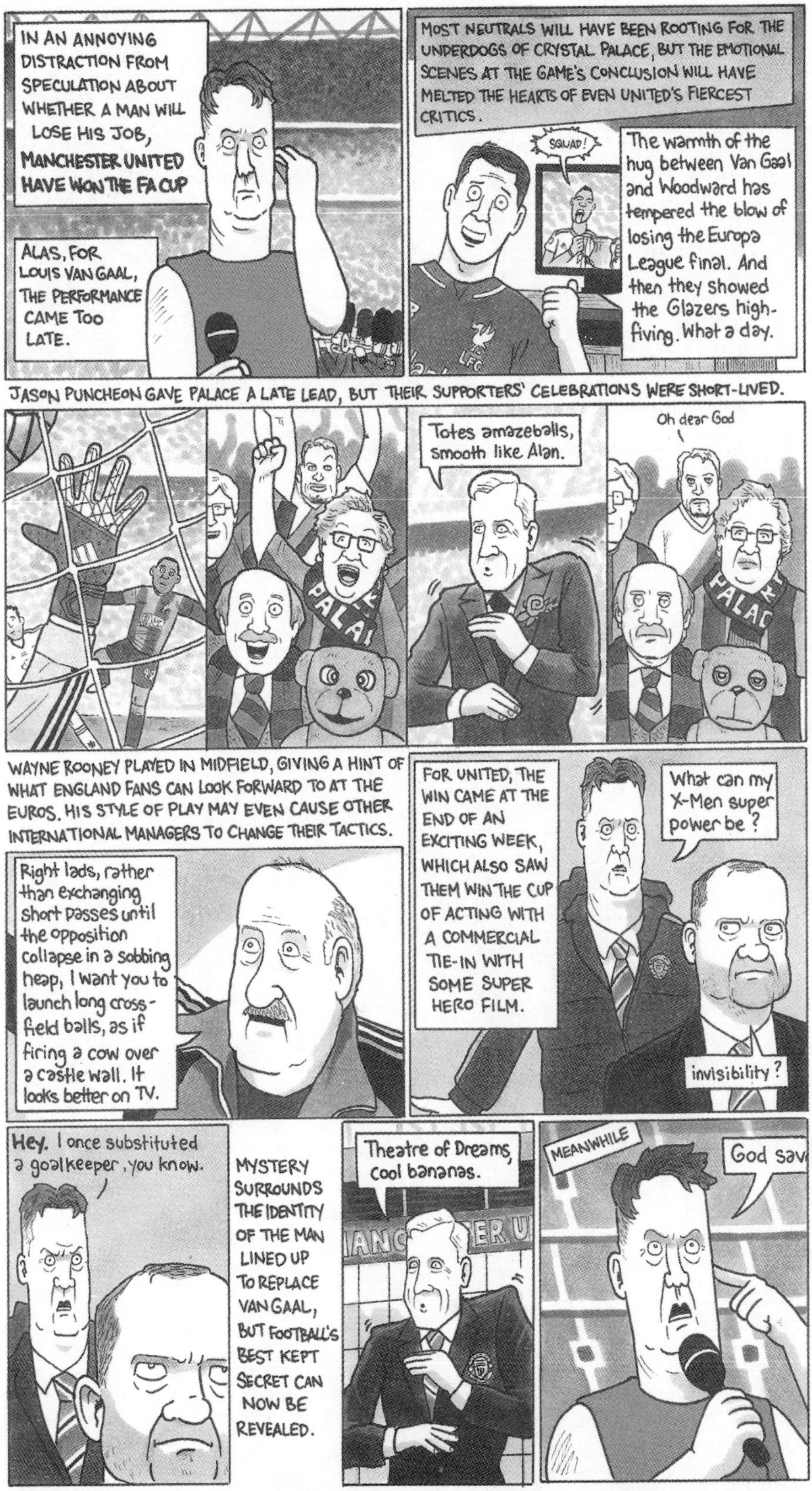
IN AN ANNOYING DISTRACTION FROM SPECULATION ABOUT WHETHER A MAN WILL LOSE HIS JOB, MANCHESTER UNITED HAVE WON THE FA CUP
ALAS, FOR LOUIS VAN GAAL, THE PERFORMANCE CAME TOO LATE.
MOST NEUTRALS WILL HAVE BEEN ROOTING FOR THE UNDERDOGS OF CRYSTAL PALACE, BUT THE EMOTIONAL SCENES AT THE GAME'S CONCLUSION WILL HAVE MELTED THE HEARTS OF EVEN UNITED'S FIERCEST CRITICS.
SQUAD!
The warmth of the hug between Van Gaal and Woodward has tempered the blow of losing the Europa League final. And then they showed the Glazers high-fiving. What a day.
JASON PUNCHEON GAVE PALACE A LATE LEAD, BUT THEIR SUPPORTERS' CELEBRATIONS WERE SHORT-LIVED.
Totes amazeballs, smooth like Alan.
Oh dear God
WAYNE ROONEY PLAYED IN MIDFIELD, GIVING A HINT OF WHAT ENGLAND FANS CAN LOOK FORWARD TO AT THE EUROS. HIS STYLE OF PLAY MAY EVEN CAUSE OTHER INTERNATIONAL MANAGERS TO CHANGE THEIR TACTICS.
Right lads, rather than exchanging short passes until the opposition collapse in a sobbing heap, I want you to launch long cross-field balls, as if firing a cow over a castle wall. It looks better on TV.
FOR UNITED, THE WIN CAME AT THE END OF AN EXCITING WEEK, WHICH ALSO SAW THEM WIN THE CUP OF ACTING WITH A COMMERCIAL TIE-IN WITH SOME SUPER HERO FILM.
What can my X-Men super power be?
invisibility?
Hey. I once substituted a goalkeeper, you know.
MYSTERY SURROUNDS THE IDENTITY OF THE MAN LINED UP TO REPLACE VAN GAAL, BUT FOOTBALL'S BEST KEPT SECRET CAN NOW BE REVEALED.
Theatre of Dreams, cool bananas.
MEANWHILE
God sav

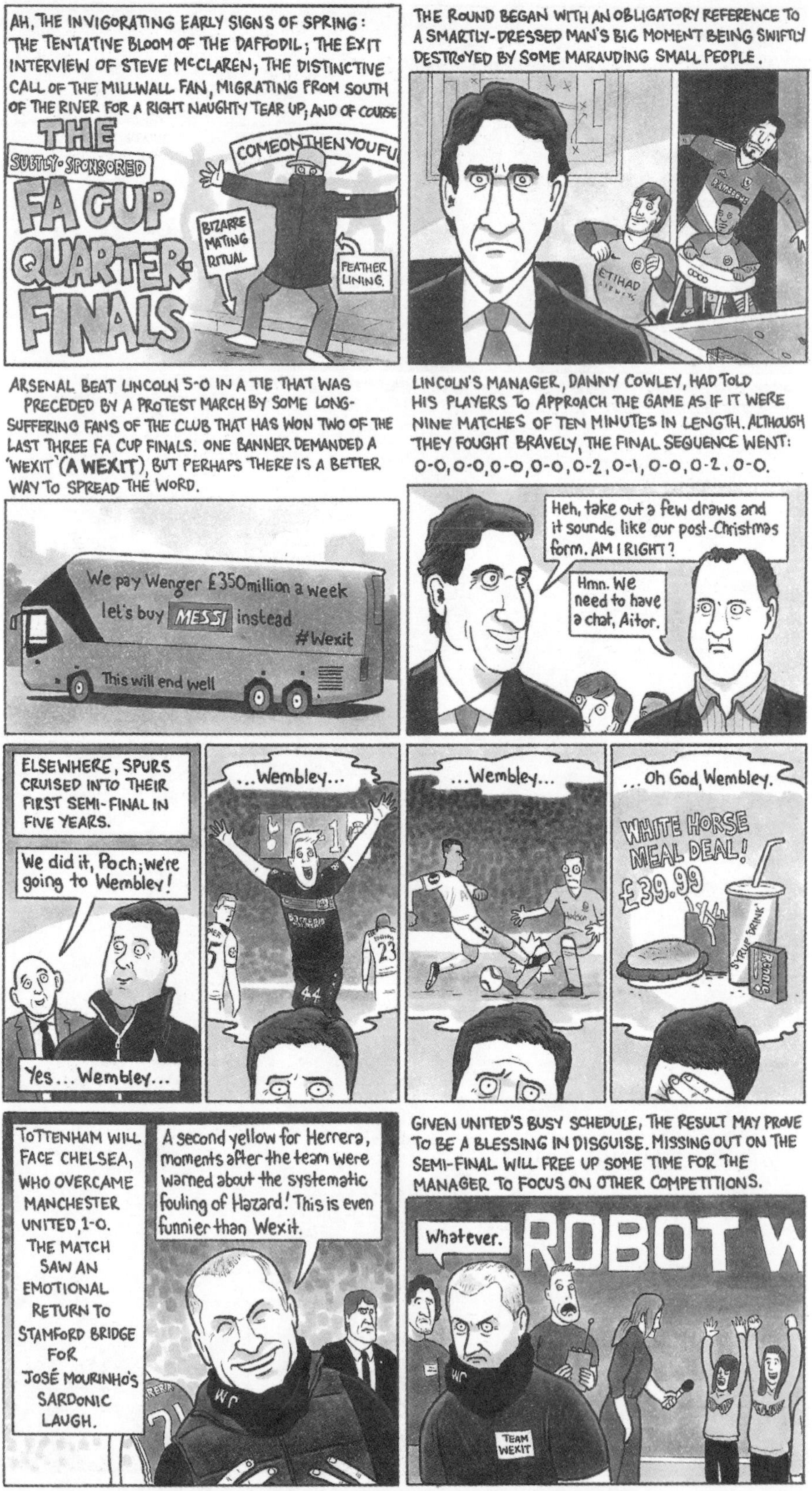
AH, THE INVIGORATING EARLY SIGNS OF SPRING: THE TENTATIVE BLOOM OF THE DAFFODIL; THE EXIT INTERVIEW OF STEVE McCLAREN; THE DISTINCTIVE CALL OF THE MILLWALL FAN, MIGRATING FROM SOUTH OF THE RIVER FOR A RIGHT NAUGHTY TEAR UP; AND OF COURSE
THE SUBTLY-SPONSORED FA CUP QUARTER-FINALS
COMEONTHENYOUFU
BIZARRE MATING RITUAL
FEATHER LINING.
THE ROUND BEGAN WITH AN OBLIGATORY REFERENCE TO A SMARTLY-DRESSED MAN'S BIG MOMENT BEING SWIFTLY DESTROYED BY SOME MARAUDING SMALL PEOPLE.
ETIHAD
ARSENAL BEAT LINCOLN 5-0 IN A TIE THAT WAS PRECEDED BY A PROTEST MARCH BY SOME LONG-SUFFERING FANS OF THE CLUB THAT HAS WON TWO OF THE LAST THREE FA CUP FINALS. ONE BANNER DEMANDED A 'WEXIT' (A WEXIT), BUT PERHAPS THERE IS A BETTER WAY TO SPREAD THE WORD.
We pay Wenger £350million a week
let's buy MESSI instead
#Wexit
This will end well
LINCOLN'S MANAGER, DANNY COWLEY, HAD TOLD HIS PLAYERS TO APPROACH THE GAME AS IF IT WERE NINE MATCHES OF TEN MINUTES IN LENGTH. ALTHOUGH THEY FOUGHT BRAVELY, THE FINAL SEQUENCE WENT: 0-0, 0-0, 0-0, 0-0, 0-2, 0-1, 0-0, 0-2, 0-0.
Heh, take out a few draws and it sounds like our post-Christmas form. AM I RIGHT?
Hmn. We need to have a chat, Aitor.
ELSEWHERE, SPURS CRUISED INTO THEIR FIRST SEMI-FINAL IN FIVE YEARS.
We did it, Poch; we're going to Wembley!
Yes... Wembley...
...Wembley...
...Wembley...
...Oh God, Wembley.
WHITE HORSE MEAL DEAL!
£39.99
SYRUP DRINK
TOTTENHAM WILL FACE CHELSEA, WHO OVERCAME MANCHESTER UNITED, 1-0. THE MATCH SAW AN EMOTIONAL RETURN TO STAMFORD BRIDGE FOR JOSÉ MOURINHO'S SARDONIC LAUGH.
A second yellow for Herrera, moments after the team were warned about the systematic fouling of Hazard! This is even funnier than Wexit.
GIVEN UNITED'S BUSY SCHEDULE, THE RESULT MAY PROVE TO BE A BLESSING IN DISGUISE. MISSING OUT ON THE SEMI-FINAL WILL FREE UP SOME TIME FOR THE MANAGER TO FOCUS ON OTHER COMPETITIONS.
Whatever.
ROBOT W
TEAM WEXIT

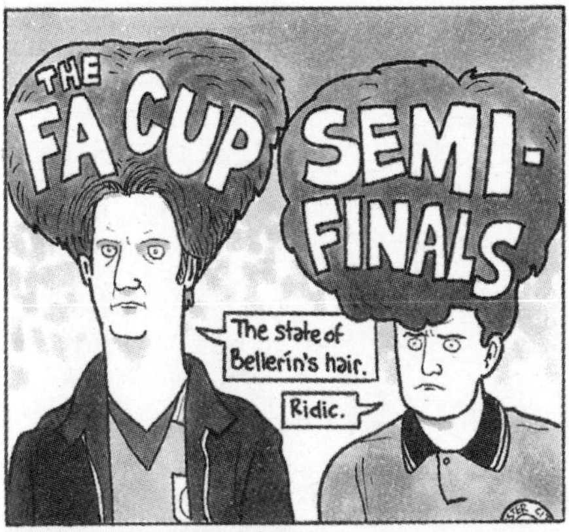
THE
FA CUP
SEMI-FINALS
The state of Bellerín's hair.
Ridic.

CHELSEA OVERCAME SPURS IN THE FIRST SEMI, THANKS IN PART TO SOME INDIVIDUAL BRILLIANCE AND A PENALTY CONCEDED BY SON HEUNG-MIN, WITH A FOUL THAT WAS SIGNALLED WELL IN ADVANCE.

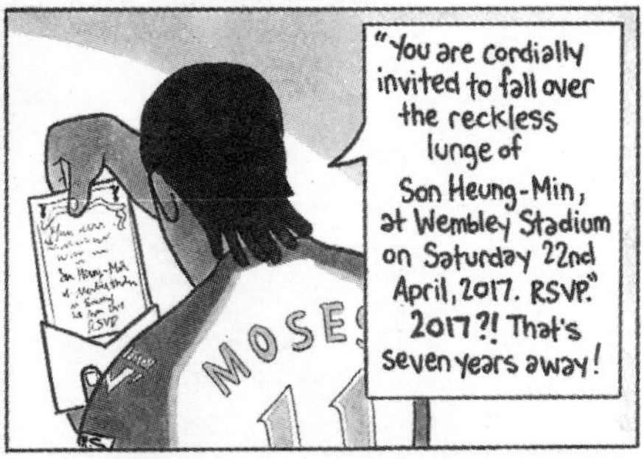
"You are cordially invited to fall over the reckless lunge of Son Heung-Min, at Wembley Stadium on Saturday 22nd April, 2017. RSVP." 2017?! That's seven years away!
MOSES

CONTE'S BOLD SELECTION CHOICES PAID DIVIDENDS, AND ALSO REVEALED THE LIST OF PEOPLE APPARENTLY NOW AHEAD OF JOHN TERRY IN THE PECKING ORDER.

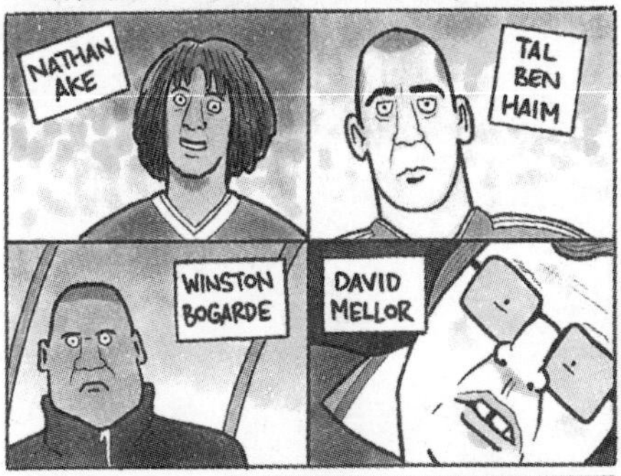
NATHAN AKE
TAL BEN HAIM
WINSTON BOGARDE
DAVID MELLOR

DESPITE THIS OUTRAGEOUS SNUB (ON THE EVE OF ST GEORGE'S DAY, NO LESS!), TERRY SEEMED CONTENT ENOUGH ON THE BENCH AND WAS SEEN CELEBRATING WITH A STUNNED KURT ZOUMA AFTER NEMANJA MATIC HAD TRACTION-ENGINED THE TIE BEYOND SPURS' REACH.

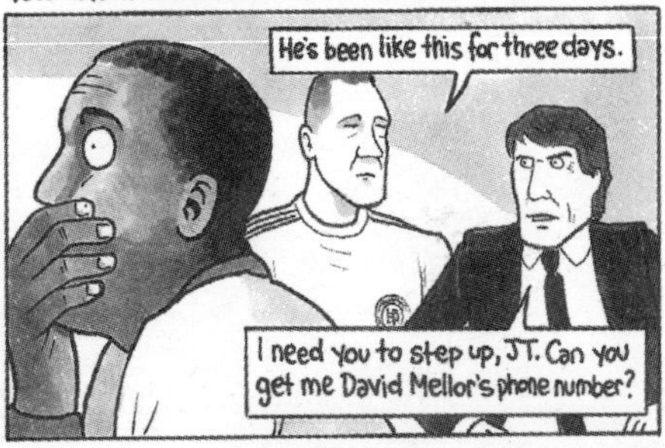
He's been like this for three days.
I need you to step up, JT. Can you get me David Mellor's phone number?

ARSENAL WON THEIR SEMI-FINAL WITH MAN CITY – A TIMELY BOOST AFTER THEIR RECENT TROUBLES. JUST LAST WEEK THEY HAD TO SUFFER THE INDIGNITY OF SEEING THEIR FAMOUS KIT BEING WORN BY ONE OF DONALD TRUMP'S CHINLESS, PATRICK-BATEMAN-LOOKING, FRAT BOY SONS (I FORGET WHICH ONE).

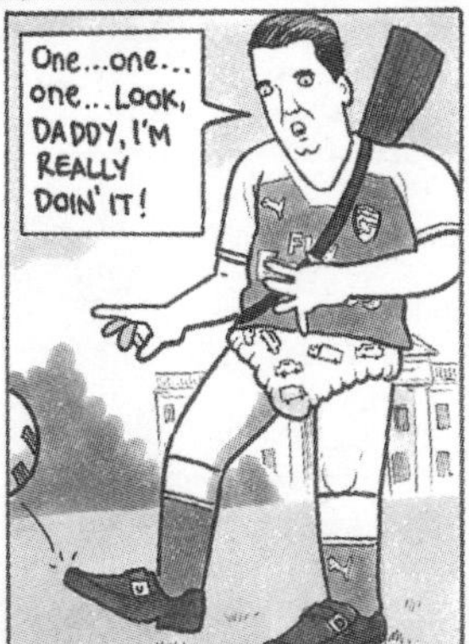
One...one... one...LOOK, DADDY, I'M REALLY DOIN' IT!

ARSENAL NOW HAVE A CHANCE TO WIN THEIR THIRD FA CUP IN FOUR YEARS (AND YOU THOUGHT LEYTON ORIENT HAD IT TOUGH). AFTER THE ABUSE HE HAS TAKEN OF LATE, ARSÈNE WENGER MUST HAVE BEEN TEMPTED TO CELEBRATE IN A MORE THEATRICAL MANNER.

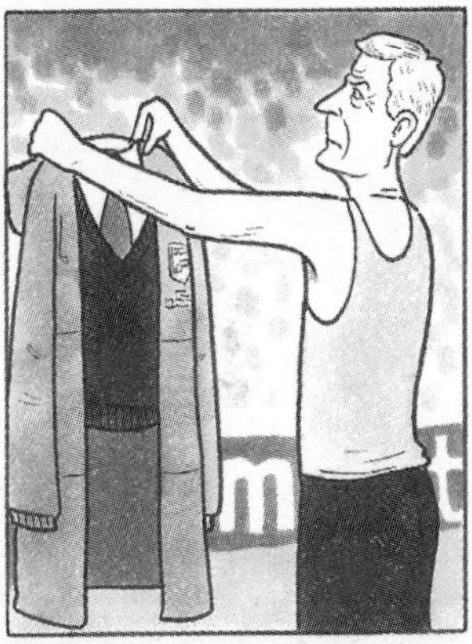

IT WAS A TOUGH DAY FOR MANCHESTER CITY, WHO CAN AT LEAST TAKE SOLACE FROM THE FACT THEY WERE ABLE TO ESCAPE FROM LONDON AFTER A CONFRONTATION WITH THE CAPITAL'S SECOND TOUGHEST HOOLIE FIRM.

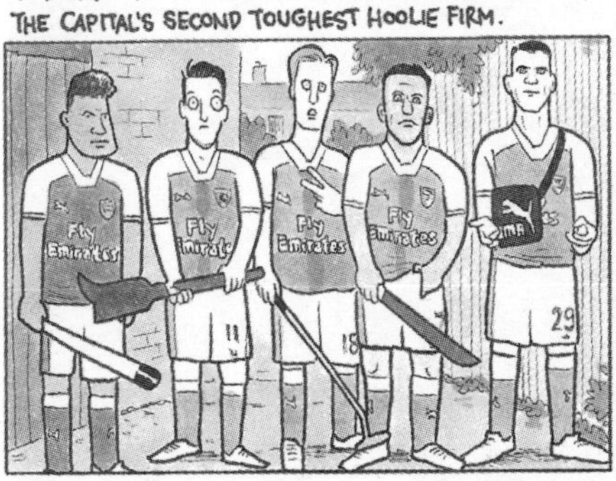
Fly Emirates
Fly Emirates
Fly Emirates
Fly Emirates
29

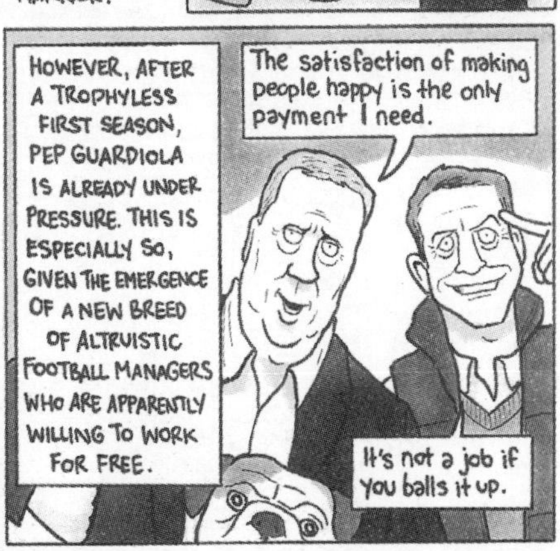
HOWEVER, AFTER A TROPHYLESS FIRST SEASON, PEP GUARDIOLA IS ALREADY UNDER PRESSURE. THIS IS ESPECIALLY SO, GIVEN THE EMERGENCE OF A NEW BREED OF ALTRUISTIC FOOTBALL MANAGERS WHO ARE APPARENTLY WILLING TO WORK FOR FREE.
The satisfaction of making people happy is the only payment I need.
It's not a job if you balls it up.

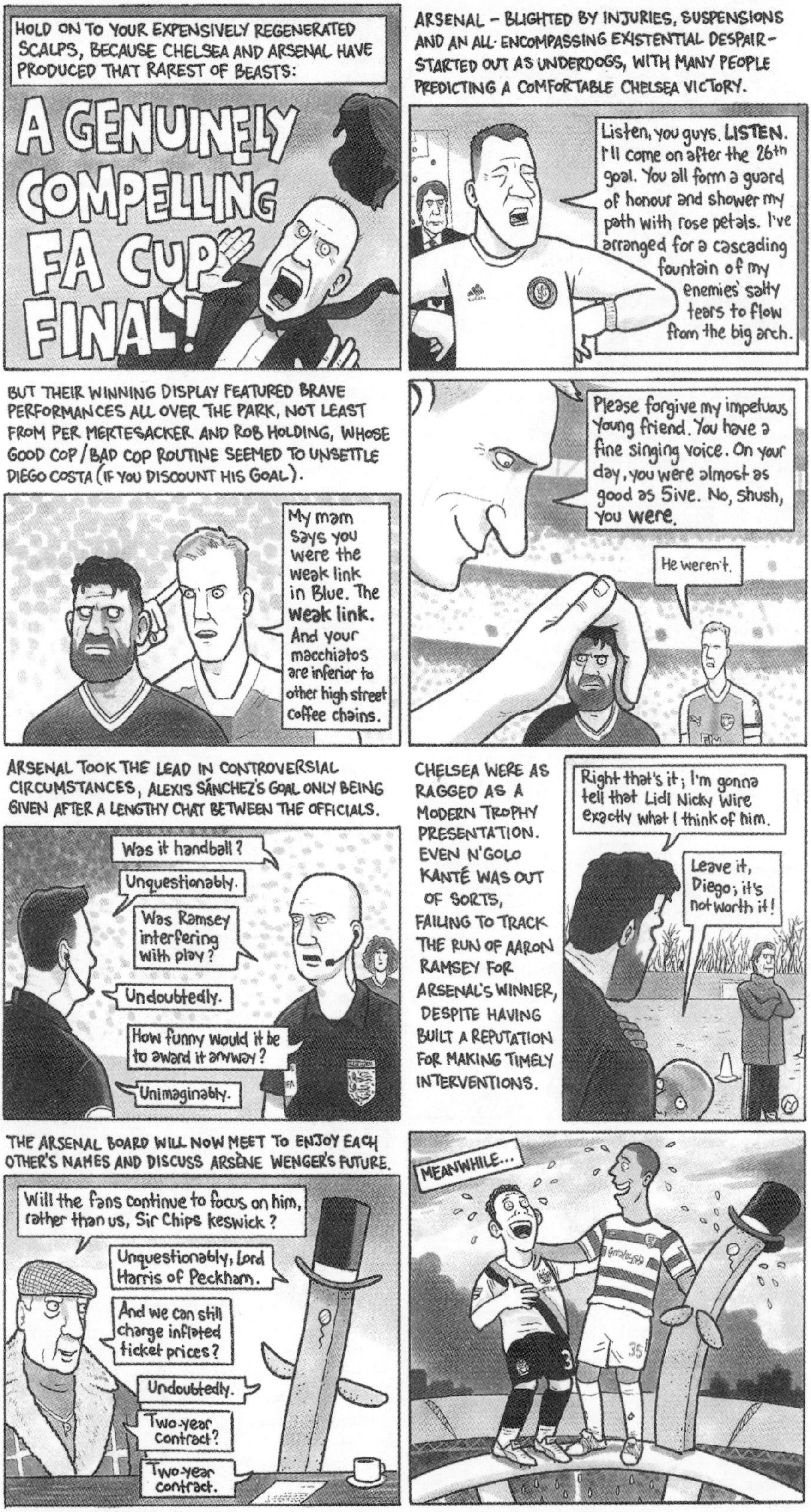
HOLD ON TO YOUR EXPENSIVELY REGENERATED SCALPS, BECAUSE CHELSEA AND ARSENAL HAVE PRODUCED THAT RAREST OF BEASTS:
A GENUINELY COMPELLING FA CUP FINAL!
ARSENAL – BLIGHTED BY INJURIES, SUSPENSIONS AND AN ALL-ENCOMPASSING EXISTENTIAL DESPAIR – STARTED OUT AS UNDERDOGS, WITH MANY PEOPLE PREDICTING A COMFORTABLE CHELSEA VICTORY.
Listen, you guys. LISTEN. I'll come on after the 26th goal. You all form a guard of honour and shower my path with rose petals. I've arranged for a cascading fountain of my enemies' salty tears to flow from the big arch.
BUT THEIR WINNING DISPLAY FEATURED BRAVE PERFORMANCES ALL OVER THE PARK, NOT LEAST FROM PER MERTESACKER AND ROB HOLDING, WHOSE GOOD COP/BAD COP ROUTINE SEEMED TO UNSETTLE DIEGO COSTA (IF YOU DISCOUNT HIS GOAL).
My mam says you were the weak link in Blue. The weak link. And your macchiatos are inferior to other high street coffee chains.
Please forgive my impetuous young friend. You have a fine singing voice. On your day, you were almost as good as 5ive. No, shush, you were.
He weren't.
ARSENAL TOOK THE LEAD IN CONTROVERSIAL CIRCUMSTANCES, ALEXIS SÁNCHEZ'S GOAL ONLY BEING GIVEN AFTER A LENGTHY CHAT BETWEEN THE OFFICIALS.
Was it handball?
Unquestionably.
Was Ramsey interfering with play?
Undoubtedly.
How funny would it be to award it anyway?
Unimaginably.
CHELSEA WERE AS RAGGED AS A MODERN TROPHY PRESENTATION. EVEN N'GOLO KANTÉ WAS OUT OF SORTS, FAILING TO TRACK THE RUN OF AARON RAMSEY FOR ARSENAL'S WINNER, DESPITE HAVING BUILT A REPUTATION FOR MAKING TIMELY INTERVENTIONS.
Right that's it; I'm gonna tell that Lidl Nicky Wire exactly what I think of him.
Leave it, Diego; it's not worth it!
THE ARSENAL BOARD WILL NOW MEET TO ENJOY EACH OTHER'S NAMES AND DISCUSS ARSÈNE WENGER'S FUTURE.
Will the fans continue to focus on him, rather than us, Sir Chips Keswick?
Unquestionably, Lord Harris of Peckham.
And we can still charge inflated ticket prices?
Undoubtedly.
Two-year contract?
Two-year contract.
MEANWHILE...

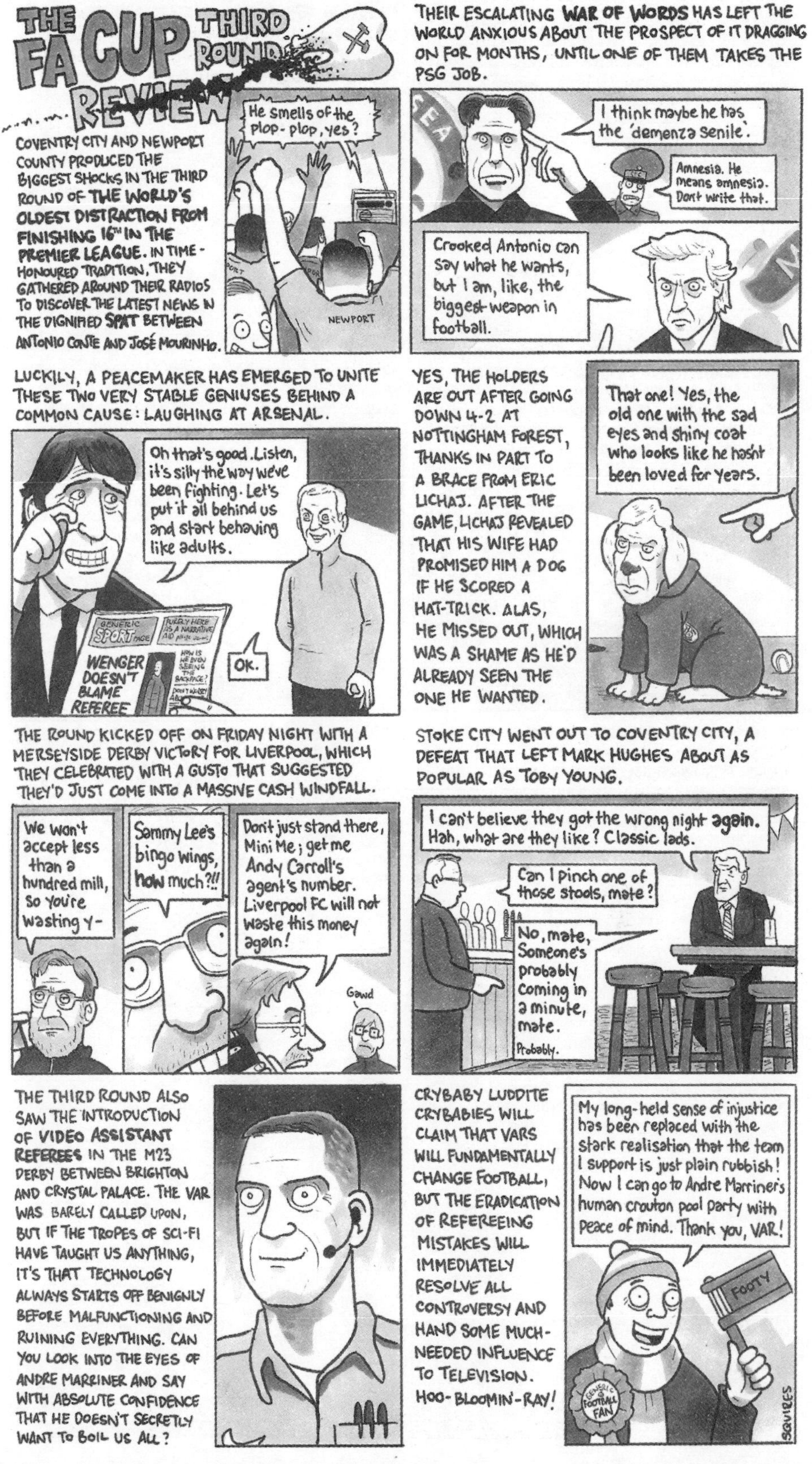

THE FA CUP THIRD ROUND REVIEW
COVENTRY CITY AND NEWPORT COUNTY PRODUCED THE BIGGEST SHOCKS IN THE THIRD ROUND OF THE WORLD'S OLDEST DISTRACTION FROM FINISHING 16TH IN THE PREMIER LEAGUE. IN TIME-HONOURED TRADITION, THEY GATHERED AROUND THEIR RADIOS TO DISCOVER THE LATEST NEWS IN THE DIGNIFIED SPAT BETWEEN ANTONIO CONTE AND JOSÉ MOURINHO.
He smells of the plop-plop, yes?
NEWPORT
THEIR ESCALATING WAR OF WORDS HAS LEFT THE WORLD ANXIOUS ABOUT THE PROSPECT OF IT DRAGGING ON FOR MONTHS, UNTIL ONE OF THEM TAKES THE PSG JOB.
I think maybe he has the 'demenza senile'.
Amnesia. He means amnesia. Don't write that.
Crooked Antonio can say what he wants, but I am, like, the biggest weapon in football.
LUCKILY, A PEACEMAKER HAS EMERGED TO UNITE THESE TWO VERY STABLE GENIUSES BEHIND A COMMON CAUSE: LAUGHING AT ARSENAL.
Oh that's good. Listen, it's silly the way we've been fighting. Let's put it all behind us and start behaving like adults.
OK.
GENERIC SPORT PAGE
WENGER DOESN'T BLAME REFEREE
YES, THE HOLDERS ARE OUT AFTER GOING DOWN 4-2 AT NOTTINGHAM FOREST, THANKS IN PART TO A BRACE FROM ERIC LICHAJ. AFTER THE GAME, LICHAJ REVEALED THAT HIS WIFE HAD PROMISED HIM A DOG IF HE SCORED A HAT-TRICK. ALAS, HE MISSED OUT, WHICH WAS A SHAME AS HE'D ALREADY SEEN THE ONE HE WANTED.
That one! Yes, the old one with the sad eyes and shiny coat who looks like he hasn't been loved for years.
THE ROUND KICKED OFF ON FRIDAY NIGHT WITH A MERSEYSIDE DERBY VICTORY FOR LIVERPOOL, WHICH THEY CELEBRATED WITH A GUSTO THAT SUGGESTED THEY'D JUST COME INTO A MASSIVE CASH WINDFALL.
We won't accept less than a hundred mill, so you're wasting y-
Sammy Lee's bingo wings, how much?!!
Don't just stand there, Mini Me; get me Andy Carroll's agent's number. Liverpool FC will not waste this money again!
Gawd
STOKE CITY WENT OUT TO COVENTRY CITY, A DEFEAT THAT LEFT MARK HUGHES ABOUT AS POPULAR AS TOBY YOUNG.
I can't believe they got the wrong night again. Hah, what are they like? Classic lads.
Can I pinch one of those stools, mate?
No, mate, Someone's probably coming in a minute, mate.
Probably.
THE THIRD ROUND ALSO SAW THE INTRODUCTION OF VIDEO ASSISTANT REFEREES IN THE M23 DERBY BETWEEN BRIGHTON AND CRYSTAL PALACE. THE VAR WAS BARELY CALLED UPON, BUT IF THE TROPES OF SCI-FI HAVE TAUGHT US ANYTHING, IT'S THAT TECHNOLOGY ALWAYS STARTS OFF BENIGNLY BEFORE MALFUNCTIONING AND RUINING EVERYTHING. CAN YOU LOOK INTO THE EYES OF ANDRE MARRINER AND SAY WITH ABSOLUTE CONFIDENCE THAT HE DOESN'T SECRETLY WANT TO BOIL US ALL?
CRYBABY LUDDITE CRYBABIES WILL CLAIM THAT VARS WILL FUNDAMENTALLY CHANGE FOOTBALL, BUT THE ERADICATION OF REFEREEING MISTAKES WILL IMMEDIATELY RESOLVE ALL CONTROVERSY AND HAND SOME MUCH-NEEDED INFLUENCE TO TELEVISION. HOO-BLOOMIN'-RAY!
My long-held sense of injustice has been replaced with the stark realisation that the team I support is just plain rubbish! Now I can go to Andre Marriner's human crouton pool party with peace of mind. Thank you, VAR!
FOOTY
GENERIC FOOTBALL FAN
SQUIRES

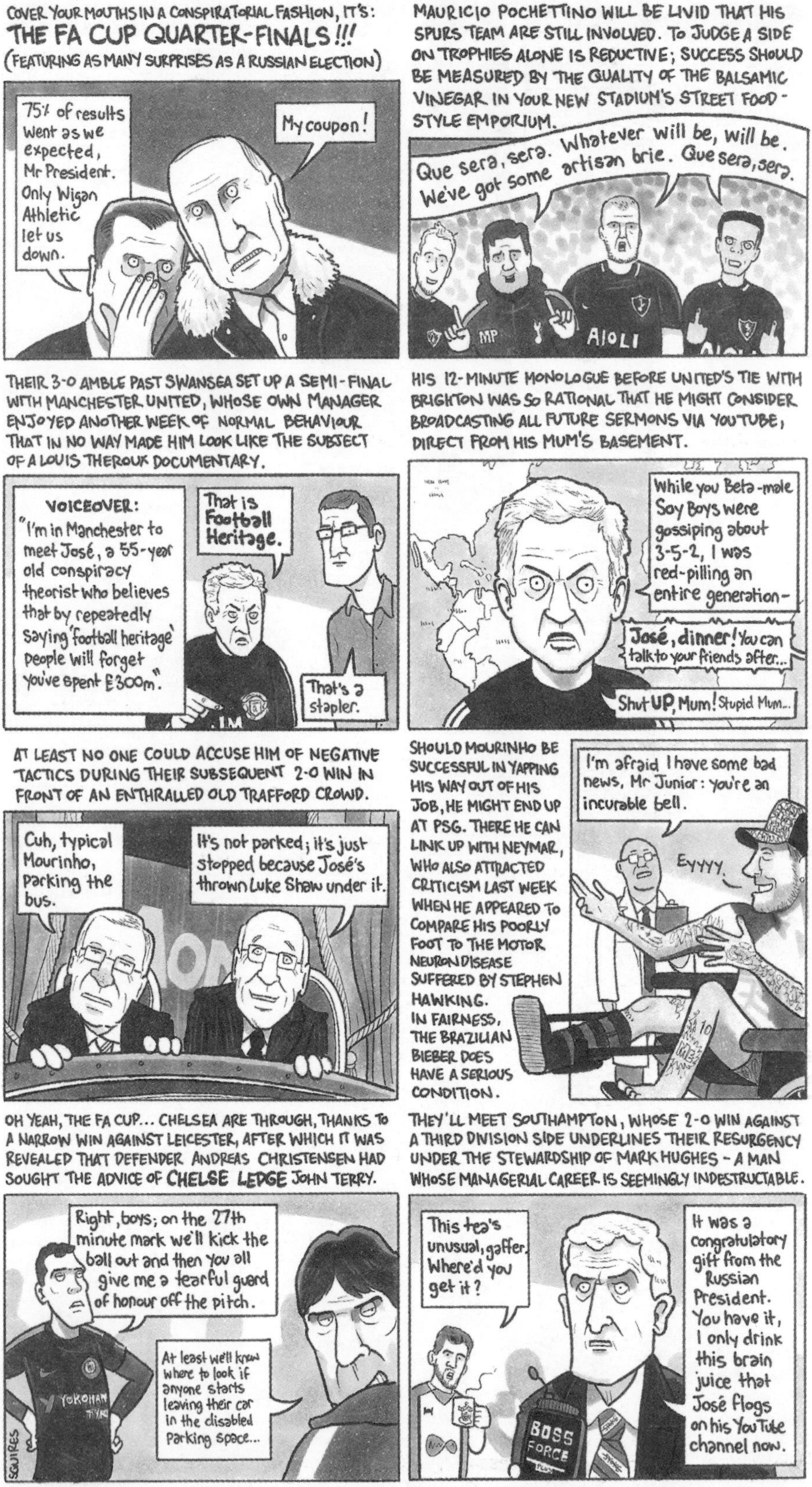

COVER YOUR MOUTHS IN A CONSPIRATORIAL FASHION, IT'S:
THE FA CUP QUARTER-FINALS!!!
(FEATURING AS MANY SURPRISES AS A RUSSIAN ELECTION)
75% of results went as we expected, Mr President. Only Wigan Athletic let us down.
My coupon!
MAURICIO POCHETTINO WILL BE LIVID THAT HIS SPURS TEAM ARE STILL INVOLVED. TO JUDGE A SIDE ON TROPHIES ALONE IS REDUCTIVE; SUCCESS SHOULD BE MEASURED BY THE QUALITY OF THE BALSAMIC VINEGAR IN YOUR NEW STADIUM'S STREET FOOD-STYLE EMPORIUM.
Que sera, sera. Whatever will be, will be. We've got some artisan brie. Que sera, sera.
MP
AIOLI
THEIR 3-0 AMBLE PAST SWANSEA SET UP A SEMI-FINAL WITH MANCHESTER UNITED, WHOSE OWN MANAGER ENJOYED ANOTHER WEEK OF NORMAL BEHAVIOUR THAT IN NO WAY MADE HIM LOOK LIKE THE SUBJECT OF A LOUIS THEROUX DOCUMENTARY.
VOICEOVER: "I'm in Manchester to meet José, a 55-year old conspiracy theorist who believes that by repeatedly saying 'football heritage' people will forget you've spent £300m."
That is Football Heritage.
That's a stapler.
HIS 12-MINUTE MONOLOGUE BEFORE UNITED'S TIE WITH BRIGHTON WAS SO RATIONAL THAT HE MIGHT CONSIDER BROADCASTING ALL FUTURE SERMONS VIA YOUTUBE, DIRECT FROM HIS MUM'S BASEMENT.
While you Beta-male Soy Boys were gossiping about 3-5-2, I was red-pilling an entire generation-
José, dinner! You can talk to your friends after...
Shut UP, Mum! Stupid Mum...
AT LEAST NO ONE COULD ACCUSE HIM OF NEGATIVE TACTICS DURING THEIR SUBSEQUENT 2-0 WIN IN FRONT OF AN ENTHRALLED OLD TRAFFORD CROWD.
Cuh, typical Mourinho, parking the bus.
It's not parked; it's just stopped because José's thrown Luke Shaw under it.
SHOULD MOURINHO BE SUCCESSFUL IN YAPPING HIS WAY OUT OF HIS JOB, HE MIGHT END UP AT PSG. THERE HE CAN LINK UP WITH NEYMAR, WHO ALSO ATTRACTED CRITICISM LAST WEEK WHEN HE APPEARED TO COMPARE HIS POORLY FOOT TO THE MOTOR NEURON DISEASE SUFFERED BY STEPHEN HAWKING.
IN FAIRNESS, THE BRAZILIAN BIEBER DOES HAVE A SERIOUS CONDITION.
I'm afraid I have some bad news, Mr Junior: you're an incurable bell.
Eyyyy.
OH YEAH, THE FA CUP... CHELSEA ARE THROUGH, THANKS TO A NARROW WIN AGAINST LEICESTER, AFTER WHICH IT WAS REVEALED THAT DEFENDER ANDREAS CHRISTENSEN HAD SOUGHT THE ADVICE OF CHELSE LEDGE JOHN TERRY.
Right, boys; on the 27th minute mark we'll kick the ball out and then you all give me a tearful guard of honour off the pitch.
At least we'll know where to look if anyone starts leaving their car in the disabled parking space...
SQUIRES
THEY'LL MEET SOUTHAMPTON, WHOSE 2-0 WIN AGAINST A THIRD DIVISION SIDE UNDERLINES THEIR RESURGENCY UNDER THE STEWARDSHIP OF MARK HUGHES - A MAN WHOSE MANAGERIAL CAREER IS SEEMINGLY INDESTRUCTABLE.
This tea's unusual, gaffer. Where'd you get it?
It was a congratulatory gift from the Russian President. You have it, I only drink this brain juice that José flogs on his YouTube channel now.
BOSS FORCE

JANET

A recurring character in many of these cartoons is Gunnersaurus Rex, but also, occasionally, Janet.

Janet started off as a sympathetic character, another innocent bystander in the glorious caustic pantomime that is Diego Costa. She soon morphed into something more insidious: an amalgamation of line managers, supervisors and superiors I have worked for, each of whom neglected to bend to my huffy, entitled attitude and entrenched sense of victimhood. It was, and remains, unfair.

Mostly, though, Janet is based on one particular ex-boss, who had the charm of a ferry disaster and whose only kind words were, I suspect, spared for her correspondence with the Moors murderers. True, we're all just trying to make our way through life, but she picked her path over a trail of corpses and passive-aggressive Post-it notes. Luckily, being a cartoonist is the most stable and sustainable career choice a person can make, so the chances that I'll have to go crawling to her for a reference are as unlikely as the print media industry crumbling to dust.

Janet's hobbies include being rude to call-centre workers who have Indian accents, and she was at the vanguard of the Zumba craze of the early 2010s. Holidays are taken once a year: two weeks on the same Mediterranean cruise, where you can connect with nice people from Dudley who also believe that Brexit means Brexit and that *we're* the real refugees in our own bloody country. If she was being interviewed in the Q&A style of a 1970s football magazine, her answers would be as follows:

Full name: Janet Jane Anette King.
Birthplace/date: The Enoch Powell Memorial Hospital, Wolverhampton. I'll not tell you the year of my birth, but I'll give you a hint: I'm a Pisces.
Married: Twice, to Ed. Fool me once, shame on you; fool me twice, fuck you, Ed.
Car: Audi A5, the only choice when you're cruising in the middle lane to get to the annual conference in Stevenage, and it's the car issued to you by your company.
Nickname: My team have too much respect for me to give me a nickname to my face.
Worst-ever injury: Rolled ankle during intense Jazzercise session back in '14. I told Karen those yoga mats were a deathtrap, but did she listen? Did she tits.
Most difficult opponent: Stephen Robertson in Human Resources absolutely boils my piss.
Favourite band/musician: Ed Sheeran.
Miscellaneous likes: Discipline, performance reviews, denying holiday requests, Ed Sheeran.
Miscellaneous dislikes: Political correctness, Human Resources, anything halal, Lily Allen.
Best country visited: England!
Favourite TV show: Anything that includes James Corden being wacky in an enclosed space.
Favourite food: Curry, pizza, Chinese, carbonara – good British fayre.
Favourite drink: Espresso Martinis. We were drinking them after an ideas symposium in Didcot last year. I was with a younger crowd of cool millennial influencers – BTEC business graduates and the like. They didn't need to say anything, but I could tell they

were blown away when they discovered I was older than them, especially when I interrupted their conversation about Stormzy to profess a fondness for 'The Mumfords', as I call them.

Biggest influence on my career: My first manager, Robert Watson. He somehow held down a job while acting as the primary carer for his mother, who was suffering from dementia. Inevitably, the pressure affected his performance, but his bravery and humility taught me a valuable lesson: as soon as Mum hesitated in remembering the name of my python (Nigel), I put her in a home. She protested that she was only sixty-two, but you can't let personal detritus litter your journey.

Superstitions: I don't trust Greek people.

Greatest achievement: Nine words: South-East Sales Team of the Year nominee, 2011.

Biggest disappointment: When Harry married Meghan Markle. A betrayal.

Personal ambition: Nine words: South-East Sales Team of the Year nominee, 2019. As we say at the ideas symposium: dream big.

Who would you most like to meet: Jeff Weiner (the CEO of LinkedIn).

Advice to youngsters: You come at the King, you best not miss.

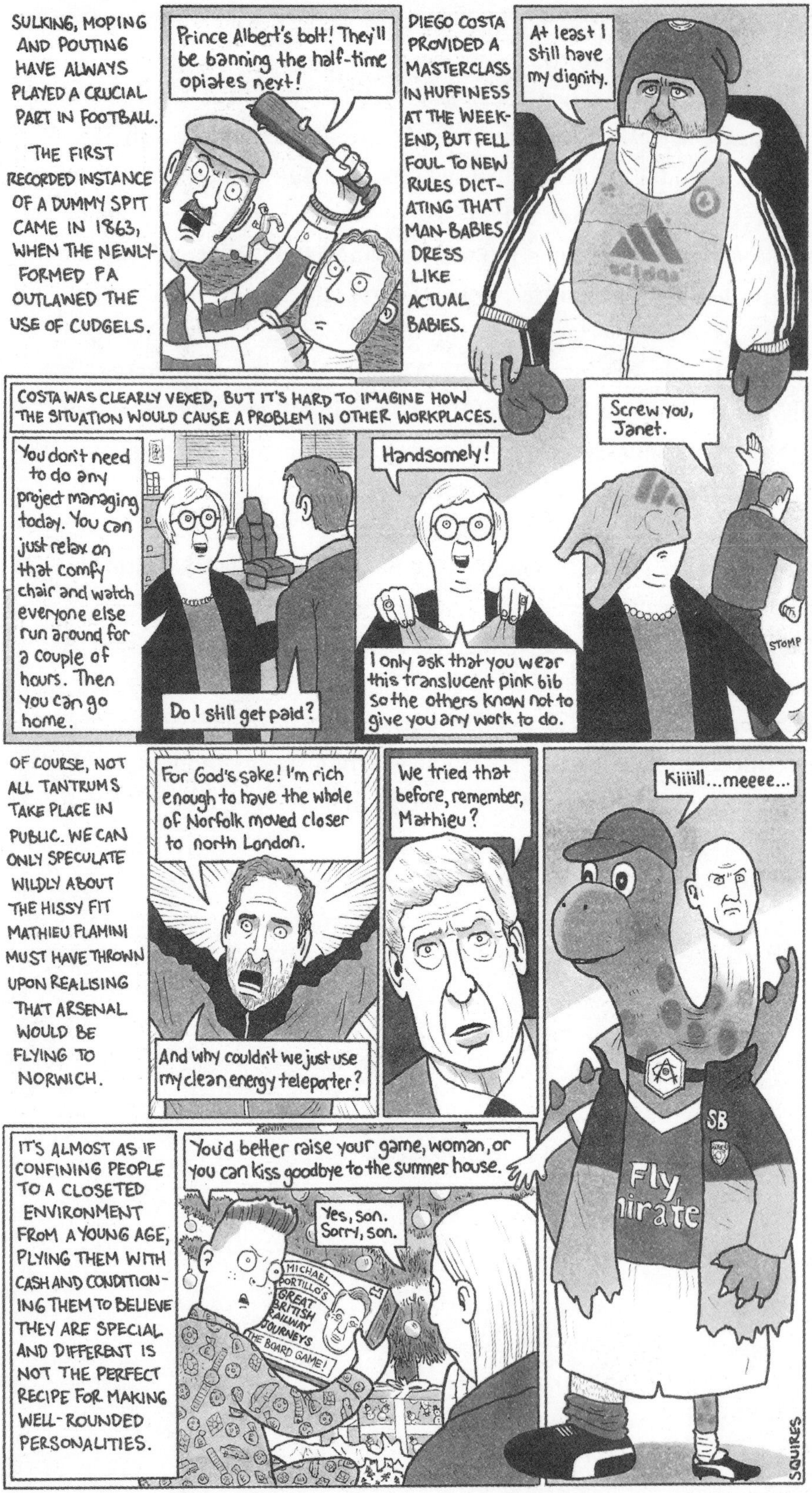
SULKING, MOPING AND POUTING HAVE ALWAYS PLAYED A CRUCIAL PART IN FOOTBALL.
THE FIRST RECORDED INSTANCE OF A DUMMY SPIT CAME IN 1863, WHEN THE NEWLY-FORMED FA OUTLAWED THE USE OF CUDGELS.
Prince Albert's bolt! They'll be banning the half-time opiates next!
DIEGO COSTA PROVIDED A MASTERCLASS IN HUFFINESS AT THE WEEK-END, BUT FELL FOUL TO NEW RULES DICTATING THAT MAN-BABIES DRESS LIKE ACTUAL BABIES.
At least I still have my dignity.
COSTA WAS CLEARLY VEXED, BUT IT'S HARD TO IMAGINE HOW THE SITUATION WOULD CAUSE A PROBLEM IN OTHER WORKPLACES.
You don't need to do any project managing today. You can just relax on that comfy chair and watch everyone else run around for a couple of hours. Then you can go home.
Do I still get paid?
Handsomely!
I only ask that you wear this translucent pink bib so the others know not to give you any work to do.
Screw you, Janet.
STOMP
OF COURSE, NOT ALL TANTRUMS TAKE PLACE IN PUBLIC. WE CAN ONLY SPECULATE WILDLY ABOUT THE HISSY FIT MATHIEU FLAMINI MUST HAVE THROWN UPON REALISING THAT ARSENAL WOULD BE FLYING TO NORWICH.
For God's sake! I'm rich enough to have the whole of Norfolk moved closer to north London.
And why couldn't we just use my clean energy teleporter?
We tried that before, remember, Mathieu?
Kiiiill...meeee...
SB
Fly
irate
IT'S ALMOST AS IF CONFINING PEOPLE TO A CLOSETED ENVIRONMENT FROM A YOUNG AGE, PLYING THEM WITH CASH AND CONDITIONING THEM TO BELIEVE THEY ARE SPECIAL AND DIFFERENT IS NOT THE PERFECT RECIPE FOR MAKING WELL-ROUNDED PERSONALITIES.
You'd better raise your game, woman, or you can kiss goodbye to the summer house.
Yes, son. Sorry, son.
MICHAEL PORTILLO'S GREAT BRITISH RAILWAY JOURNEYS THE BOARD GAME!
SQUIRES

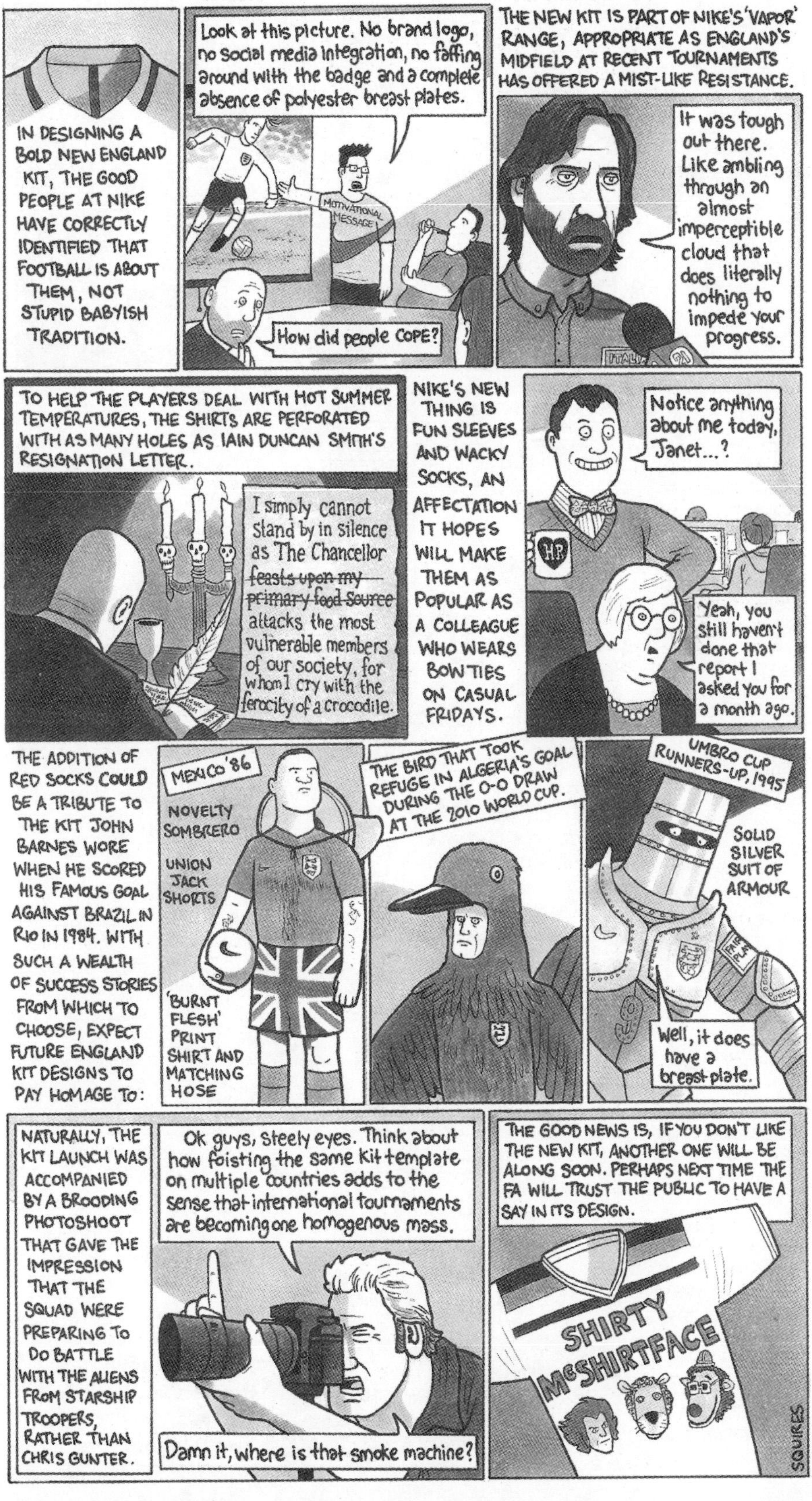

IN DESIGNING A BOLD NEW ENGLAND KIT, THE GOOD PEOPLE AT NIKE HAVE CORRECTLY IDENTIFIED THAT FOOTBALL IS ABOUT THEM, NOT STUPID BABYISH TRADITION.
Look at this picture. No brand logo, no social media integration, no faffing around with the badge and a complete absence of polyester breast plates.
MOTIVATIONAL MESSAGE
How did people cope?
THE NEW KIT IS PART OF NIKE'S 'VAPOR' RANGE, APPROPRIATE AS ENGLAND'S MIDFIELD AT RECENT TOURNAMENTS HAS OFFERED A MIST-LIKE RESISTANCE.
It was tough out there. Like ambling through an almost imperceptible cloud that does literally nothing to impede your progress.
TO HELP THE PLAYERS DEAL WITH HOT SUMMER TEMPERATURES, THE SHIRTS ARE PERFORATED WITH AS MANY HOLES AS IAIN DUNCAN SMITH'S RESIGNATION LETTER.
I simply cannot stand by in silence as The Chancellor ~~feasts upon my primary food source~~ attacks the most vulnerable members of our society, for whom I cry with the ferocity of a crocodile.
NIKE'S NEW THING IS FUN SLEEVES AND WACKY SOCKS, AN AFFECTATION IT HOPES WILL MAKE THEM AS POPULAR AS A COLLEAGUE WHO WEARS BOW TIES ON CASUAL FRIDAYS.
Notice anything about me today, Janet...?
H.R
Yeah, you still haven't done that report I asked you for a month ago.
THE ADDITION OF RED SOCKS COULD BE A TRIBUTE TO THE KIT JOHN BARNES WORE WHEN HE SCORED HIS FAMOUS GOAL AGAINST BRAZIL IN RIO IN 1984. WITH SUCH A WEALTH OF SUCCESS STORIES FROM WHICH TO CHOOSE, EXPECT FUTURE ENGLAND KIT DESIGNS TO PAY HOMAGE TO:
MEXICO '86
NOVELTY SOMBRERO
UNION JACK SHORTS
'BURNT FLESH' PRINT SHIRT AND MATCHING HOSE
THE BIRD THAT TOOK REFUGE IN ALGERIA'S GOAL DURING THE 0-0 DRAW AT THE 2010 WORLD CUP.
UMBRO CUP RUNNERS-UP, 1995
SOLID SILVER SUIT OF ARMOUR
Well, it does have a breast plate.
NATURALLY, THE KIT LAUNCH WAS ACCOMPANIED BY A BROODING PHOTOSHOOT THAT GAVE THE IMPRESSION THAT THE SQUAD WERE PREPARING TO DO BATTLE WITH THE ALIENS FROM STARSHIP TROOPERS, RATHER THAN CHRIS GUNTER.
Ok guys, steely eyes. Think about how foisting the same kit template on multiple countries adds to the sense that international tournaments are becoming one homogenous mass.
Damn it, where is that smoke machine?
THE GOOD NEWS IS, IF YOU DON'T LIKE THE NEW KIT, ANOTHER ONE WILL BE ALONG SOON. PERHAPS NEXT TIME THE FA WILL TRUST THE PUBLIC TO HAVE A SAY IN ITS DESIGN.
SHIRTY McSHIRTFACE
SQUIRES

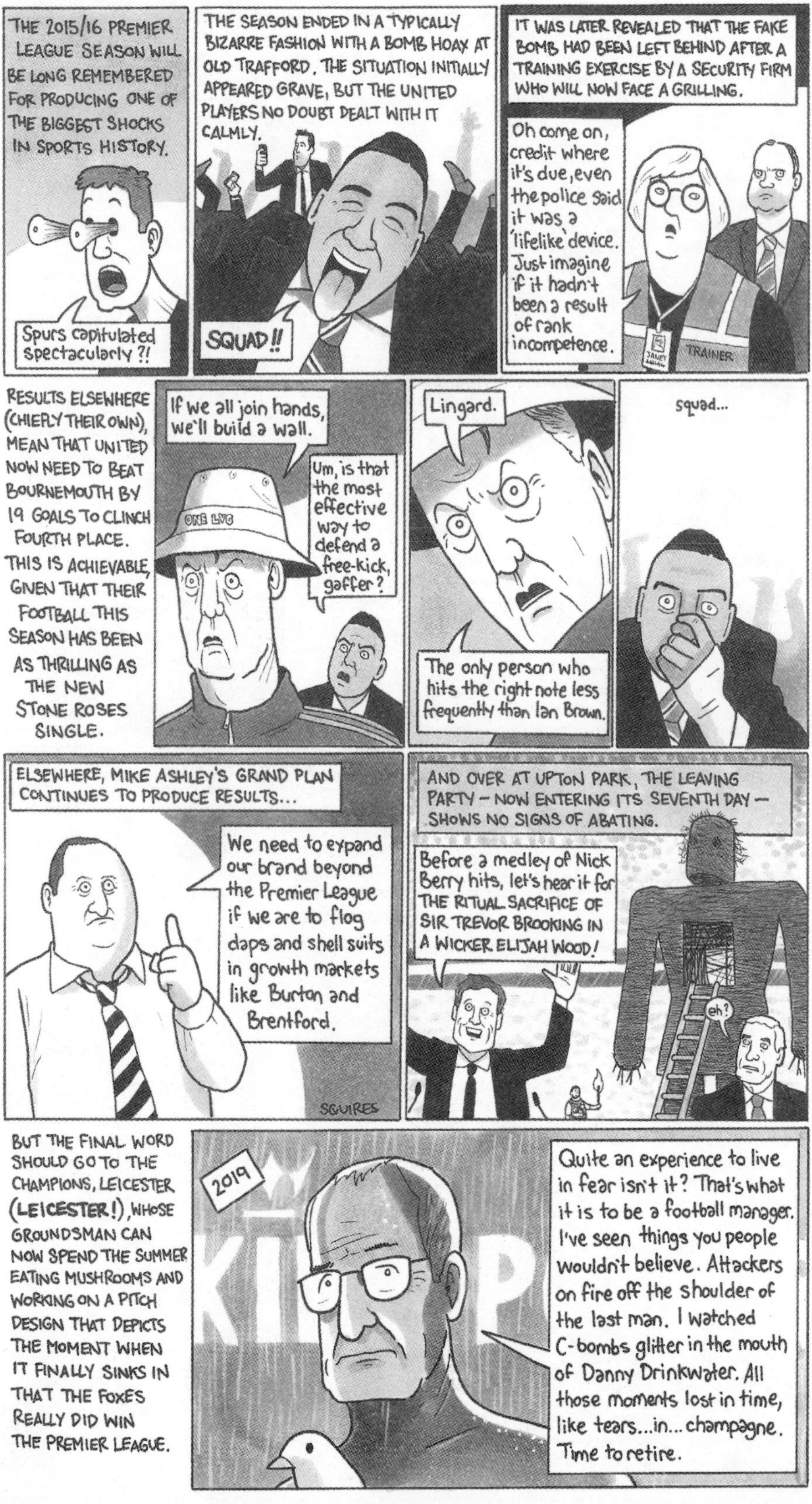

THE 2015/16 PREMIER LEAGUE SEASON WILL BE LONG REMEMBERED FOR PRODUCING ONE OF THE BIGGEST SHOCKS IN SPORTS HISTORY.
Spurs capitulated spectacularly ?!
THE SEASON ENDED IN A TYPICALLY BIZARRE FASHION WITH A BOMB HOAX AT OLD TRAFFORD. THE SITUATION INITIALLY APPEARED GRAVE, BUT THE UNITED PLAYERS NO DOUBT DEALT WITH IT CALMLY.
SQUAD!!
IT WAS LATER REVEALED THAT THE FAKE BOMB HAD BEEN LEFT BEHIND AFTER A TRAINING EXERCISE BY A SECURITY FIRM WHO WILL NOW FACE A GRILLING.
Oh come on, credit where it's due, even the police said it was a 'lifelike' device. Just imagine if it hadn't been a result of rank incompetence.
TRAINER
RESULTS ELSEWHERE (CHIEFLY THEIR OWN), MEAN THAT UNITED NOW NEED TO BEAT BOURNEMOUTH BY 19 GOALS TO CLINCH FOURTH PLACE. THIS IS ACHIEVABLE, GIVEN THAT THEIR FOOTBALL THIS SEASON HAS BEEN AS THRILLING AS THE NEW STONE ROSES SINGLE.
If we all join hands, we'll build a wall.
ONE LVG
Um, is that the most effective way to defend a free-kick, gaffer?
Lingard.
The only person who hits the right note less frequently than Ian Brown.
squad...
ELSEWHERE, MIKE ASHLEY'S GRAND PLAN CONTINUES TO PRODUCE RESULTS...
We need to expand our brand beyond the Premier League if we are to flog daps and shell suits in growth markets like Burton and Brentford.
SQUIRES
AND OVER AT UPTON PARK, THE LEAVING PARTY – NOW ENTERING ITS SEVENTH DAY – SHOWS NO SIGNS OF ABATING.
Before a medley of Nick Berry hits, let's hear it for THE RITUAL SACRIFICE OF SIR TREVOR BROOKING IN A WICKER ELIJAH WOOD!
eh?
BUT THE FINAL WORD SHOULD GO TO THE CHAMPIONS, LEICESTER (LEICESTER!), WHOSE GROUNDSMAN CAN NOW SPEND THE SUMMER EATING MUSHROOMS AND WORKING ON A PITCH DESIGN THAT DEPICTS THE MOMENT WHEN IT FINALLY SINKS IN THAT THE FOXES REALLY DID WIN THE PREMIER LEAGUE.
2019
Quite an experience to live in fear isn't it? That's what it is to be a football manager. I've seen things you people wouldn't believe. Attackers on fire off the shoulder of the last man. I watched C-bombs glitter in the mouth of Danny Drinkwater. All those moments lost in time, like tears...in... champagne. Time to retire.

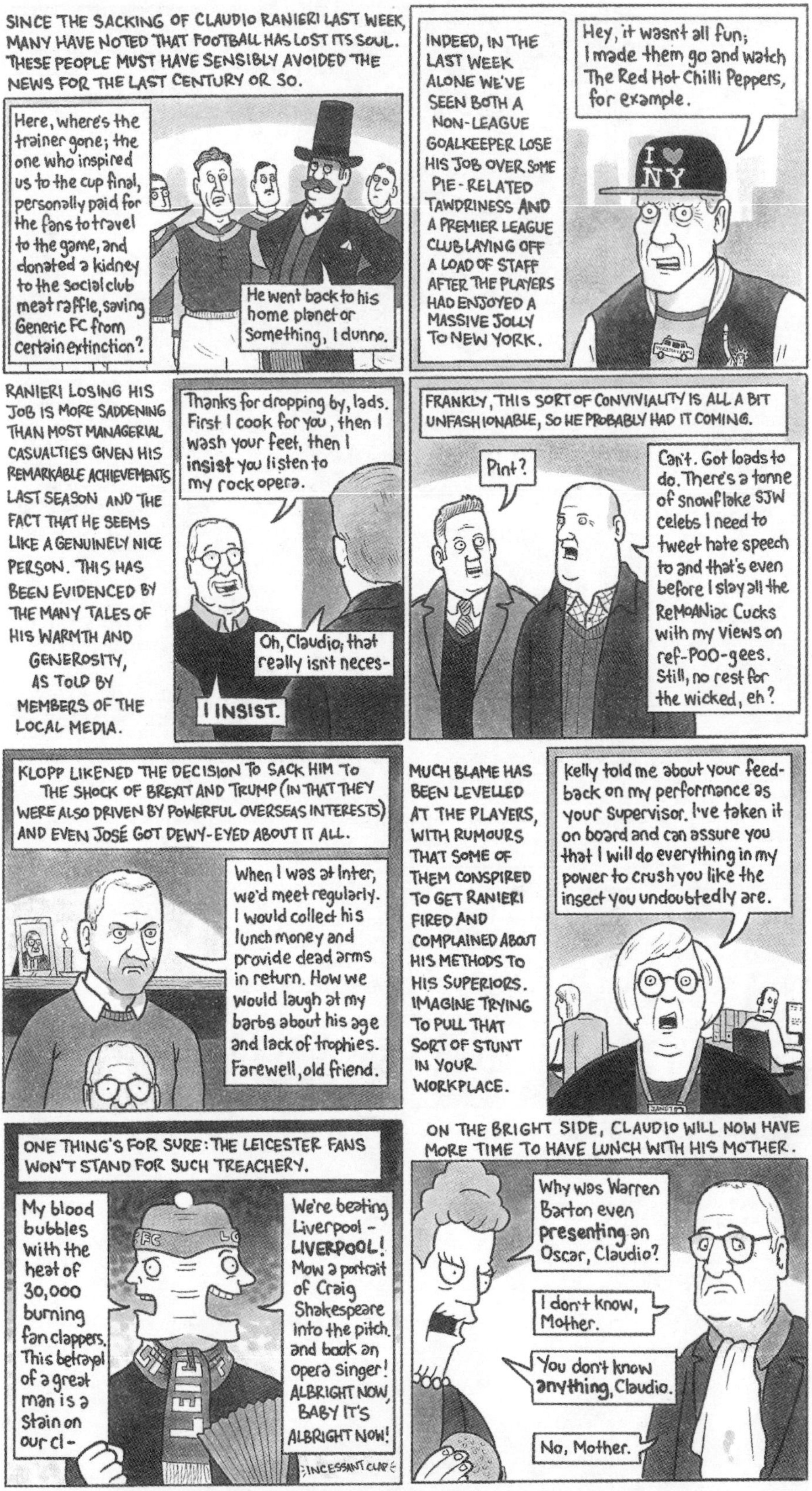

SINCE THE SACKING OF CLAUDIO RANIERI LAST WEEK, MANY HAVE NOTED THAT FOOTBALL HAS LOST ITS SOUL. THESE PEOPLE MUST HAVE SENSIBLY AVOIDED THE NEWS FOR THE LAST CENTURY OR SO.
Here, where's the trainer gone; the one who inspired us to the cup final, personally paid for the fans to travel to the game, and donated a kidney to the social club meat raffle, saving Generic FC from certain extinction?
He went back to his home planet or something, I dunno.
INDEED, IN THE LAST WEEK ALONE WE'VE SEEN BOTH A NON-LEAGUE GOALKEEPER LOSE HIS JOB OVER SOME PIE-RELATED TAWDRINESS AND A PREMIER LEAGUE CLUB LAYING OFF A LOAD OF STAFF AFTER THE PLAYERS HAD ENJOYED A MASSIVE JOLLY TO NEW YORK.
Hey, it wasn't all fun; I made them go and watch The Red Hot Chilli Peppers, for example.
I ♥ NY
RANIERI LOSING HIS JOB IS MORE SADDENING THAN MOST MANAGERIAL CASUALTIES GIVEN HIS REMARKABLE ACHIEVEMENTS LAST SEASON AND THE FACT THAT HE SEEMS LIKE A GENUINELY NICE PERSON. THIS HAS BEEN EVIDENCED BY THE MANY TALES OF HIS WARMTH AND GENEROSITY, AS TOLD BY MEMBERS OF THE LOCAL MEDIA.
Thanks for dropping by, lads. First I cook for you, then I wash your feet, then I insist you listen to my rock opera.
Oh, Claudio; that really isn't neces-
I INSIST.
FRANKLY, THIS SORT OF CONVIVIALITY IS ALL A BIT UNFASHIONABLE, SO HE PROBABLY HAD IT COMING.
Pint?
Can't. Got loads to do. There's a tonne of snowflake SJW celebs I need to tweet hate speech to and that's even before I slay all the ReMoaNiac Cucks with my views on ref-POO-gees. Still, no rest for the wicked, eh?
KLOPP LIKENED THE DECISION TO SACK HIM TO THE SHOCK OF BREXIT AND TRUMP (IN THAT THEY WERE ALSO DRIVEN BY POWERFUL OVERSEAS INTERESTS) AND EVEN JOSÉ GOT DEWY-EYED ABOUT IT ALL.
When I was at Inter, we'd meet regularly. I would collect his lunch money and provide dead arms in return. How we would laugh at my barbs about his age and lack of trophies. Farewell, old friend.
MUCH BLAME HAS BEEN LEVELLED AT THE PLAYERS, WITH RUMOURS THAT SOME OF THEM CONSPIRED TO GET RANIERI FIRED AND COMPLAINED ABOUT HIS METHODS TO HIS SUPERIORS. IMAGINE TRYING TO PULL THAT SORT OF STUNT IN YOUR WORKPLACE.
Kelly told me about your feedback on my performance as your supervisor. I've taken it on board and can assure you that I will do everything in my power to crush you like the insect you undoubtedly are.
ONE THING'S FOR SURE: THE LEICESTER FANS WON'T STAND FOR SUCH TREACHERY.
My blood bubbles with the heat of 30,000 burning fan clappers. This betrayal of a great man is a stain on our cl-
We're beating Liverpool - LIVERPOOL! Mow a portrait of Craig Shakespeare into the pitch, and book an opera singer! ALBRIGHT NOW, BABY IT'S ALBRIGHT NOW!
INCESSANT CLAP
ON THE BRIGHT SIDE, CLAUDIO WILL NOW HAVE MORE TIME TO HAVE LUNCH WITH HIS MOTHER.
Why was Warren Barton even presenting an Oscar, Claudio?
I don't know, Mother.
You don't know anything, Claudio.
No, Mother.

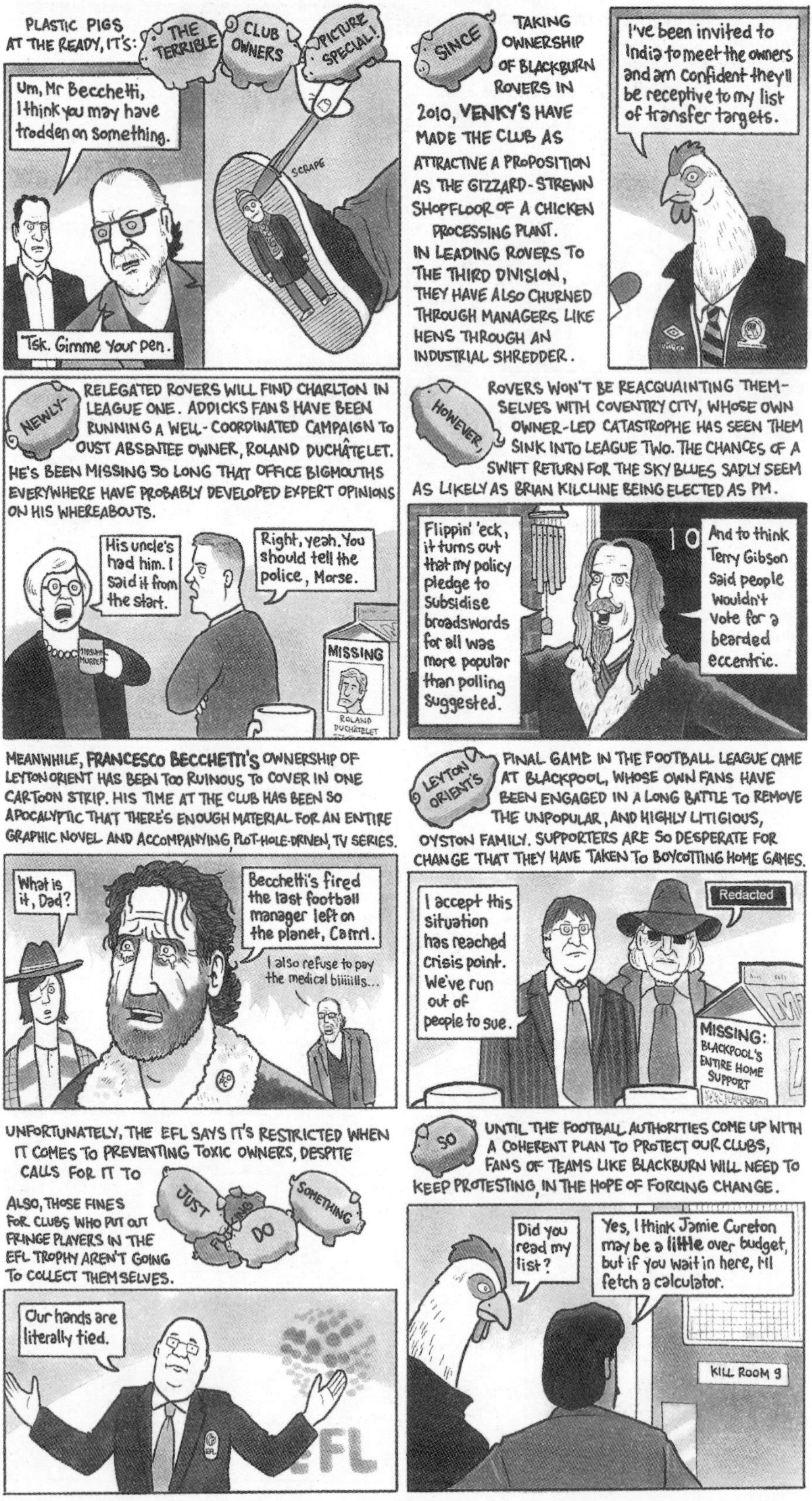

PLASTIC PIGS AT THE READY, IT'S:
THE TERRIBLE
CLUB OWNERS
PICTURE SPECIAL!
Um, Mr Becchetti, I think you may have trodden on something.
Tsk. Gimme your pen.
SCRAPE
SINCE
TAKING OWNERSHIP OF BLACKBURN ROVERS IN 2010, VENKY'S HAVE MADE THE CLUB AS ATTRACTIVE A PROPOSITION AS THE GIZZARD-STREWN SHOPFLOOR OF A CHICKEN PROCESSING PLANT.
IN LEADING ROVERS TO THE THIRD DIVISION, THEY HAVE ALSO CHURNED THROUGH MANAGERS LIKE HENS THROUGH AN INDUSTRIAL SHREDDER.
I've been invited to India to meet the owners and am confident they'll be receptive to my list of transfer targets.
NEWLY-
RELEGATED ROVERS WILL FIND CHARLTON IN LEAGUE ONE. ADDICKS FANS HAVE BEEN RUNNING A WELL-COORDINATED CAMPAIGN TO OUST ABSENTEE OWNER, ROLAND DUCHÂTELET.
HE'S BEEN MISSING SO LONG THAT OFFICE BIGMOUTHS EVERYWHERE HAVE PROBABLY DEVELOPED EXPERT OPINIONS ON HIS WHEREABOUTS.
His uncle's had him. I said it from the start.
Right, yeah. You should tell the police, Morse.
MISSING
ROLAND DUCHÂTELET
HOWEVER,
ROVERS WON'T BE REACQUAINTING THEMSELVES WITH COVENTRY CITY, WHOSE OWN OWNER-LED CATASTROPHE HAS SEEN THEM SINK INTO LEAGUE TWO. THE CHANCES OF A SWIFT RETURN FOR THE SKY BLUES SADLY SEEM AS LIKELY AS BRIAN KILCLINE BEING ELECTED AS PM.
10
Flippin' 'eck, it turns out that my policy pledge to subsidise broadswords for all was more popular than polling suggested.
And to think Terry Gibson said people wouldn't vote for a bearded eccentric.
MEANWHILE, FRANCESCO BECCHETTI'S OWNERSHIP OF LEYTON ORIENT HAS BEEN TOO RUINOUS TO COVER IN ONE CARTOON STRIP. HIS TIME AT THE CLUB HAS BEEN SO APOCALYPTIC THAT THERE'S ENOUGH MATERIAL FOR AN ENTIRE GRAPHIC NOVEL AND ACCOMPANYING, PLOT-HOLE-DRIVEN, TV SERIES.
What is it, Dad?
Becchetti's fired the last football manager left on the planet, Carrl.
I also refuse to pay the medical biiiiills...
LEYTON ORIENT'S
FINAL GAME IN THE FOOTBALL LEAGUE CAME AT BLACKPOOL, WHOSE OWN FANS HAVE BEEN ENGAGED IN A LONG BATTLE TO REMOVE THE UNPOPULAR, AND HIGHLY LITIGIOUS, OYSTON FAMILY. SUPPORTERS ARE SO DESPERATE FOR CHANGE THAT THEY HAVE TAKEN TO BOYCOTTING HOME GAMES.
I accept this situation has reached crisis point. We've run out of people to sue.
Redacted
MISSING: BLACKPOOL'S ENTIRE HOME SUPPORT
UNFORTUNATELY, THE EFL SAYS IT'S RESTRICTED WHEN IT COMES TO PREVENTING TOXIC OWNERS, DESPITE CALLS FOR IT TO
JUST
F*CKING
DO
SOMETHING
ALSO, THOSE FINES FOR CLUBS WHO PUT OUT FRINGE PLAYERS IN THE EFL TROPHY AREN'T GOING TO COLLECT THEMSELVES.
Our hands are literally tied.
EFL
SO
UNTIL THE FOOTBALL AUTHORITIES COME UP WITH A COHERENT PLAN TO PROTECT OUR CLUBS, FANS OF TEAMS LIKE BLACKBURN WILL NEED TO KEEP PROTESTING, IN THE HOPE OF FORCING CHANGE.
Did you read my list?
Yes, I think Jamie Cureton may be a little over budget, but if you wait in here, I'll fetch a calculator.
KILL ROOM 9

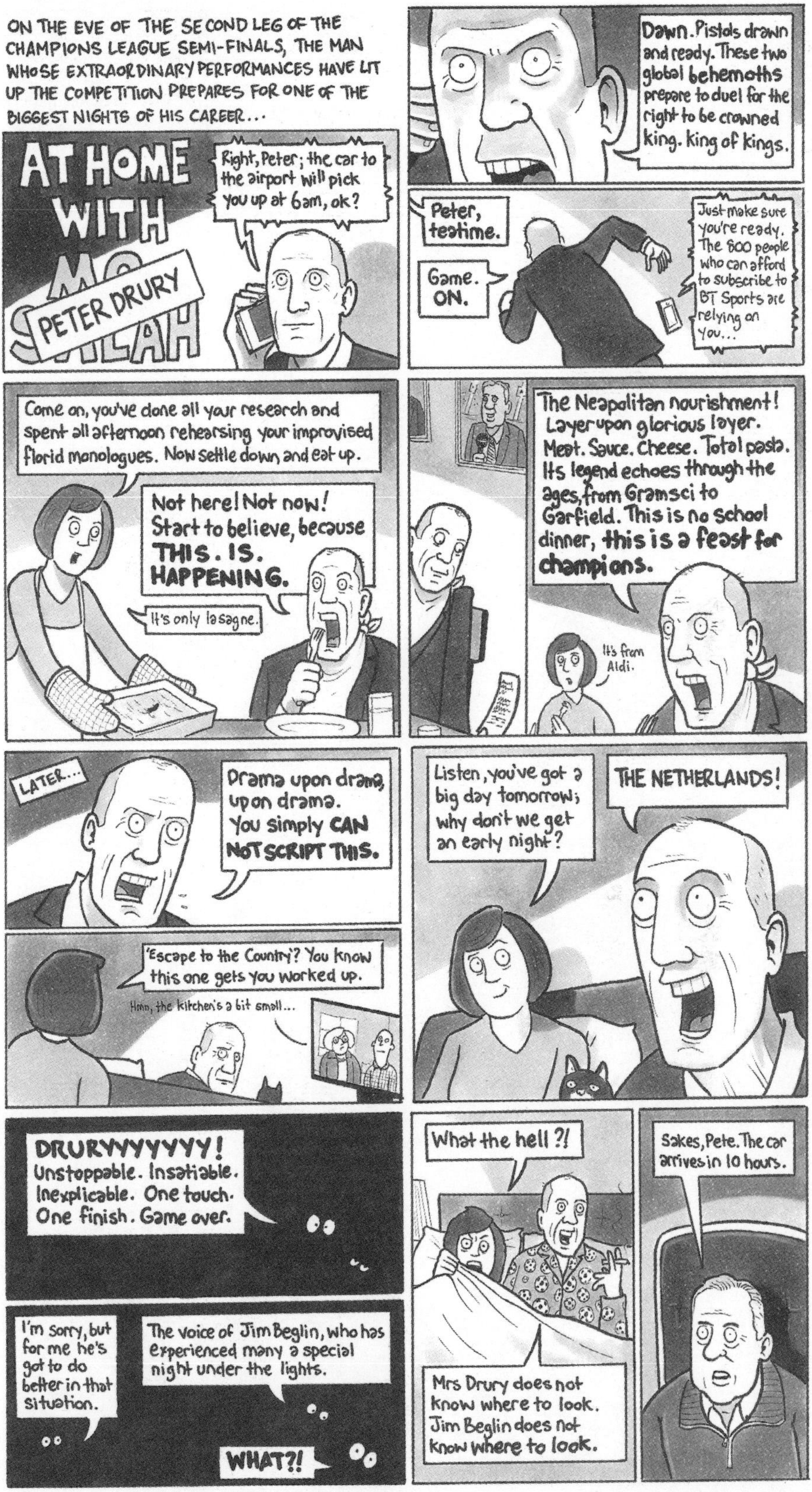
ON THE EVE OF THE SECOND LEG OF THE CHAMPIONS LEAGUE SEMI-FINALS, THE MAN WHOSE EXTRAORDINARY PERFORMANCES HAVE LIT UP THE COMPETITION PREPARES FOR ONE OF THE BIGGEST NIGHTS OF HIS CAREER...
AT HOME WITH MO SALAH
PETER DRURY
Right, Peter; the car to the airport will pick you up at 6am, ok?
Dawn. Pistols drawn and ready. These two global behemoths prepare to duel for the right to be crowned king. King of kings.
Peter, teatime.
Game. ON.
Just make sure you're ready. The 800 people who can afford to subscribe to BT Sports are relying on you...
Come on, you've done all your research and spent all afternoon rehearsing your improvised florid monologues. Now settle down and eat up.
Not here! Not now! Start to believe, because THIS. IS. HAPPENING.
It's only lasagne.
The Neapolitan nourishment! Layer upon glorious layer. Meat. Sauce. Cheese. Total pasta. Its legend echoes through the ages, from Gramsci to Garfield. This is no school dinner, this is a feast for champions.
It's from Aldi.
LATER...
Drama upon drama, upon drama. You simply CAN NOT SCRIPT THIS.
'Escape to the Country'? You know this one gets you worked up.
Hmn, the kitchen's a bit small...
Listen, you've got a big day tomorrow; why don't we get an early night?
THE NETHERLANDS!
DRURYYYYYYY! Unstoppable. Insatiable. Inexplicable. One touch. One finish. Game over.
I'm sorry, but for me he's got to do better in that situation.
The voice of Jim Beglin, who has experienced many a special night under the lights.
WHAT?!
What the hell?!
Mrs Drury does not know where to look. Jim Beglin does not know where to look.
Sakes, Pete. The car arrives in 10 hours.

FOOTBALL HERITAGE

In an ideal world, it would be 1998. It's no generalisation to say that we'd all still be twenty-three years old, be able to drink more than five beers without feeling like someone had replaced your soul with a public toilet filled with spiders, and have the confidence to strut into the club in your brown moleskin jeans, turning heads as you mouthed the words to All Saints' version of 'Lady Marmalade'. Sizzle.

The Internet would be slow but nice. If you wanted to abuse someone, you'd have to do it the old-fashioned way, by going round to their house and pushing dog muck through their door; tricky if they had one of those brush things across the letterbox, but it was the 1990s, guys – we *coped*! Generally, the world was a simpler, more peaceful place, unless you lived in Kosovo, Sierra Leone, Burundi, Afghanistan or any of the other nations or regions torn apart by the infinite horrors of war. Altogether now: 'Vindaloo, vindaloo, la la.'

Nostalgia is big business, especially in football. The retro shirt industry is thriving as people try to revive memories of past glories. Even the clubs themselves have got wise to it, tapping into the yearning for bygone eras. The fact that they change their shirts each season means these tribute designs sometimes hark back to periods that weren't even particularly successful. 'Here's this season's third kit, with a collar that makes reference to the famous 1991/2 Rumbelows Cup run that ended in a heavy aggregate defeat

171

to Oldham Athletic in the second round.' Lads, you had me at collar.

Studying history allows us to observe the mistakes made by previous generations and then repeat them. This chapter contains a group of cartoons that delve into the past of some of English football's most cherished institutions, starting with everyone's second-favourite club, Leeds United.

The cartoon was published in November 2015, at a time when Leeds were in a state of turmoil under the leadership of owner Massimo Cellino, the kind of reasonable, level-headed businessman anyone would want involved with their club. Yes, he had a criminal record, was prone to wildly eccentric behaviour and went through managers like a bandsaw through a choc-ice (he fired thirty-six managers in twenty-two years at Cagliari), but he wasn't Ken Bates, which is all you can really ask of a person.

During his three years at Leeds, he fired seven managers (upping his average to 2.3 managers a year). Darko Milanič was sacked after thirty-two days, an even shorter stay than those of Brian Clough and Jock Stein, who lasted forty-four days each – Clough being fired after winning only one of his six games in charge and Stein leaving of his own accord to manage the Scottish national team. However, Cellino had inherited a mess from the previous owners and famously admitted that the strain of owning Leeds was affecting his physical well-being ('I'm losing my balls. Ten years ago, I had more balls but since I came here it's been a nightmare. Now I have a low quality of life. I feel shame when I walk to the shop to buy cigarettes if we lose a game'). Eventually, he sold his shares in the club to businessman Andrea Radrizzani and returned to Italy, purchasing Serie B side Brescia in June 2017 (his manager turnover rate as of June 2018: an impressive 5.0 per year).

The next cartoon looks at Manchester United under Louis van Gaal. At the time the cartoon was published, the Dutchman had been their head coach for a season and a half, and people were beginning to notice that they weren't exactly playing the free-flowing Total Football that none of van Gaal's teams had played for at least the previous fifteen years. Still, at the end of the season he would be replaced by José Mourinho, and that's when the feast of free-spirited attacking football would *really* begin.

That is followed by a cartoon about Arsène Wenger's first twenty years at Arsenal. At the time, it felt like he would be there for another twenty years, something I'd have been absolutely fine with if it (a) provided me with more cartoon material, and (b) caused Piers Morgan to have an aneurism.

Millwall were in the headlines in January 2017, and not for the *usual* reasons (their great work in the community and campaigning efforts to save local health services), and so became the subject of my cartoon that week. Their ground was under threat from the one group of people with a worse reputation than Millwall fans: offshore property developers.

It was also a week when Paul Merson and the Sky *Soccer Saturday* lads had displayed a surprisingly in-depth knowledge of Greek football by dismissing the coaching credentials of Hull City's new manager, Marco Silva (although he won only a few games, got them relegated and then stank out Watford, so maybe they were on to something, accidentally).

The chapter also includes a short series of cartoons celebrating the twenty-fifth anniversary of the formation of the Premier League, looking back at some of its most iconic moments: Newcastle imploding in 1996, Arsenal's 'Invincible' team, and the takeovers of Chelsea and Manchester City by mega-rich oil tycoons.

Finally, there are a couple of cartoons relating to stories from the 2017/18 season. Firstly, two members of Manchester United's Class of '92 landed themselves managerial jobs (a cartoon that required me to study a photograph of Paul Scholes's genitals falling out of his shorts during the 1996 FA Cup final – *never* underestimate the lengths to which I am prepared to suffer for my art); and secondly, the frustration of West Ham fans that boiled over and led to pitch invasions amid chaotic scenes during a 3–0 home defeat to Burnley. It was a weekend for bad behaviour. In Greece, the owner of PAOK marched onto the pitch with a handgun tucked into his belt, and there was even a pitch invasion at Crufts dog show. Elsewhere, Jamie Carragher managed to entangle himself in a high-speed gobbing incident, leaning out of his car to flob at a fellow motorist who'd been goading him about a football result. The gentleman correctly ignored the desperate pleas of his teenage daughter to stop it, as he filmed the Sky Sports pundit on his phone while travelling along a motorway.

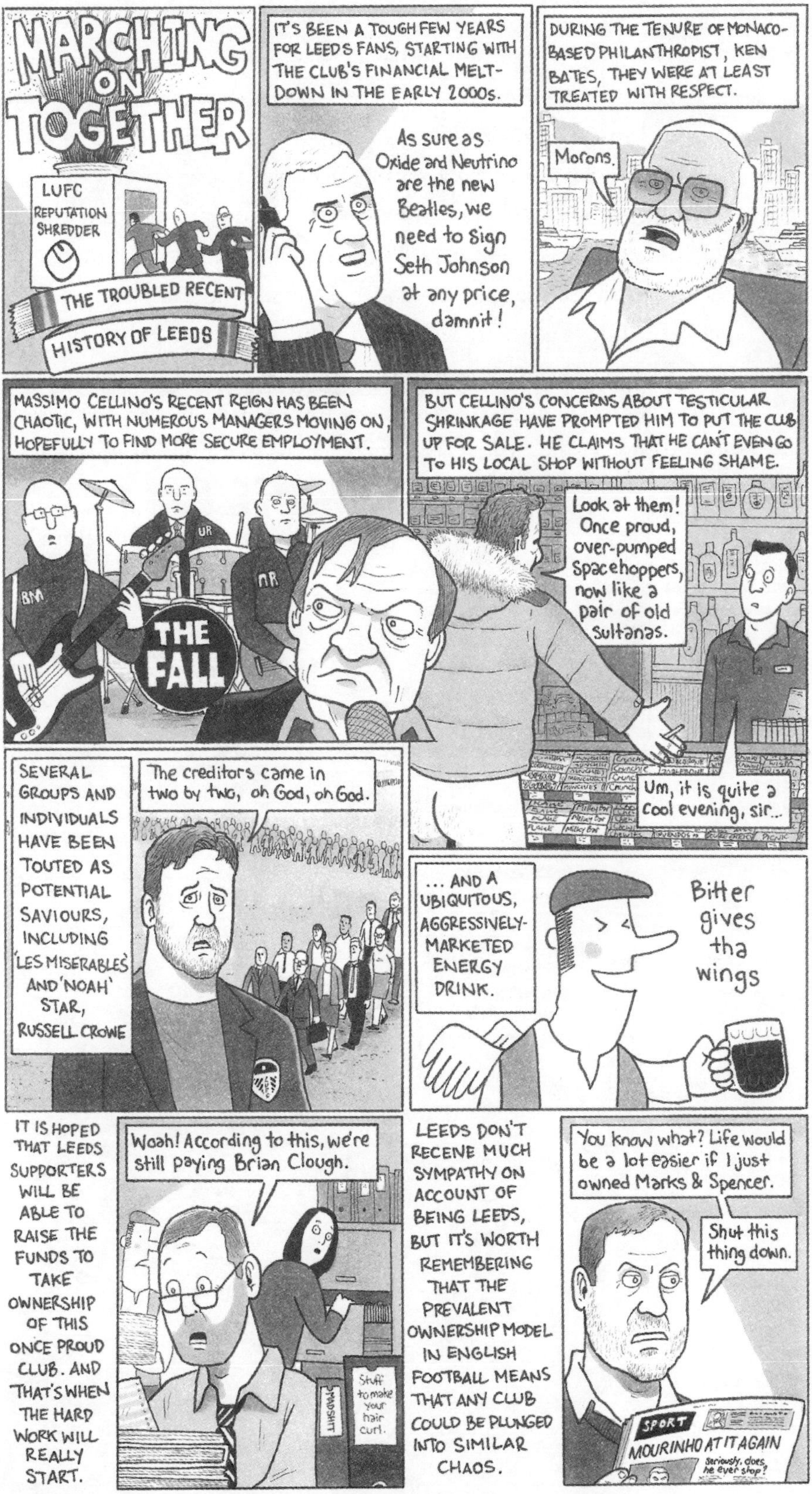

MARCHING ON TOGETHER
LUFC REPUTATION SHREDDER
THE TROUBLED RECENT HISTORY OF LEEDS
IT'S BEEN A TOUGH FEW YEARS FOR LEEDS FANS, STARTING WITH THE CLUB'S FINANCIAL MELT-DOWN IN THE EARLY 2000s.
As sure as Oxide and Neutrino are the new Beatles, we need to sign Seth Johnson at any price, damnit!
DURING THE TENURE OF MONACO-BASED PHILANTHROPIST, KEN BATES, THEY WERE AT LEAST TREATED WITH RESPECT.
Morons.
MASSIMO CELLINO'S RECENT REIGN HAS BEEN CHAOTIC, WITH NUMEROUS MANAGERS MOVING ON, HOPEFULLY TO FIND MORE SECURE EMPLOYMENT.
UR
BM
NR
THE FALL
BUT CELLINO'S CONCERNS ABOUT TESTICULAR SHRINKAGE HAVE PROMPTED HIM TO PUT THE CLUB UP FOR SALE. HE CLAIMS THAT HE CAN'T EVEN GO TO HIS LOCAL SHOP WITHOUT FEELING SHAME.
Look at them! Once proud, over-pumped Spacehoppers, now like a pair of old sultanas.
Um, it is quite a cool evening, sir...
SEVERAL GROUPS AND INDIVIDUALS HAVE BEEN TOUTED AS POTENTIAL SAVIOURS, INCLUDING 'LES MISERABLES' AND 'NOAH' STAR, RUSSELL CROWE
The creditors came in two by two, oh God, oh God.
... AND A UBIQUITOUS, AGGRESSIVELY-MARKETED ENERGY DRINK.
Bitter gives tha wings
IT IS HOPED THAT LEEDS SUPPORTERS WILL BE ABLE TO RAISE THE FUNDS TO TAKE OWNERSHIP OF THIS ONCE PROUD CLUB. AND THAT'S WHEN THE HARD WORK WILL REALLY START.
Woah! According to this, we're still paying Brian Clough.
Stuff to make your hair curl.
LEEDS DON'T RECEIVE MUCH SYMPATHY ON ACCOUNT OF BEING LEEDS, BUT IT'S WORTH REMEMBERING THAT THE PREVALENT OWNERSHIP MODEL IN ENGLISH FOOTBALL MEANS THAT ANY CLUB COULD BE PLUNGED INTO SIMILAR CHAOS.
You know what? Life would be a lot easier if I just owned Marks & Spencer.
Shut this thing down.
SPORT
MOURINHO AT IT AGAIN
Seriously, does he ever stop?

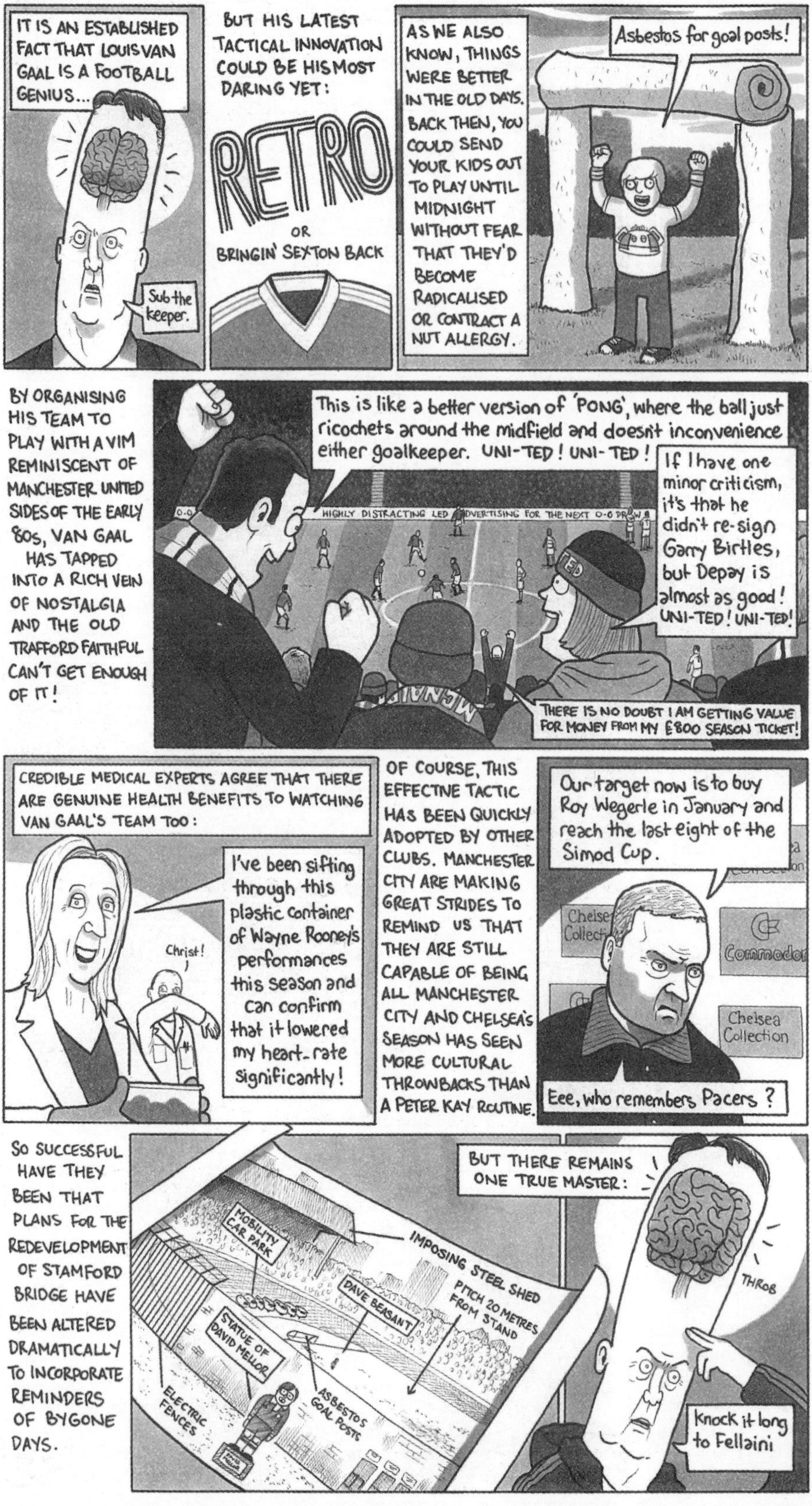
IT IS AN ESTABLISHED FACT THAT LOUIS VAN GAAL IS A FOOTBALL GENIUS...
Sub the keeper.
BUT HIS LATEST TACTICAL INNOVATION COULD BE HIS MOST DARING YET:
RETRO
OR
BRINGIN' SEXTON BACK
AS WE ALSO KNOW, THINGS WERE BETTER IN THE OLD DAYS. BACK THEN, YOU COULD SEND YOUR KIDS OUT TO PLAY UNTIL MIDNIGHT WITHOUT FEAR THAT THEY'D BECOME RADICALISED OR CONTRACT A NUT ALLERGY.
Asbestos for goal posts!
BY ORGANISING HIS TEAM TO PLAY WITH A VIM REMINISCENT OF MANCHESTER UNITED SIDES OF THE EARLY '80s, VAN GAAL HAS TAPPED INTO A RICH VEIN OF NOSTALGIA AND THE OLD TRAFFORD FAITHFUL CAN'T GET ENOUGH OF IT!
This is like a better version of 'PONG', where the ball just ricochets around the midfield and doesn't inconvenience either goalkeeper. UNI-TED! UNI-TED!
0-0
HIGHLY DISTRACTING LED ADVERTISING FOR THE NEXT 0-0 DRAW
If I have one minor criticism, it's that he didn't re-sign Garry Birtles, but Depay is almost as good! UNI-TED! UNI-TED!
THERE IS NO DOUBT I AM GETTING VALUE FOR MONEY FROM MY £800 SEASON TICKET!
CREDIBLE MEDICAL EXPERTS AGREE THAT THERE ARE GENUINE HEALTH BENEFITS TO WATCHING VAN GAAL'S TEAM TOO:
I've been sifting through this plastic container of Wayne Rooney's performances this season and can confirm that it lowered my heart-rate significantly!
Christ!
OF COURSE, THIS EFFECTIVE TACTIC HAS BEEN QUICKLY ADOPTED BY OTHER CLUBS. MANCHESTER CITY ARE MAKING GREAT STRIDES TO REMIND US THAT THEY ARE STILL CAPABLE OF BEING ALL MANCHESTER CITY AND CHELSEA'S SEASON HAS SEEN MORE CULTURAL THROWBACKS THAN A PETER KAY ROUTINE.
Our target now is to buy Roy Wegerle in January and reach the last eight of the Simod Cup.
Chelsea Collection
Commodore
Chelsea Collection
Eee, who remembers Pacers?
SO SUCCESSFUL HAVE THEY BEEN THAT PLANS FOR THE REDEVELOPMENT OF STAMFORD BRIDGE HAVE BEEN ALTERED DRAMATICALLY TO INCORPORATE REMINDERS OF BYGONE DAYS.
MOBILITY CAR PARK
IMPOSING STEEL SHED
DAVE BEASANT
PITCH 20 METRES FROM STAND
STATUE OF DAVID MELLOR
ASBESTOS GOAL POSTS
ELECTRIC FENCES
BUT THERE REMAINS ONE TRUE MASTER:
THROB
Knock it long to Fellaini

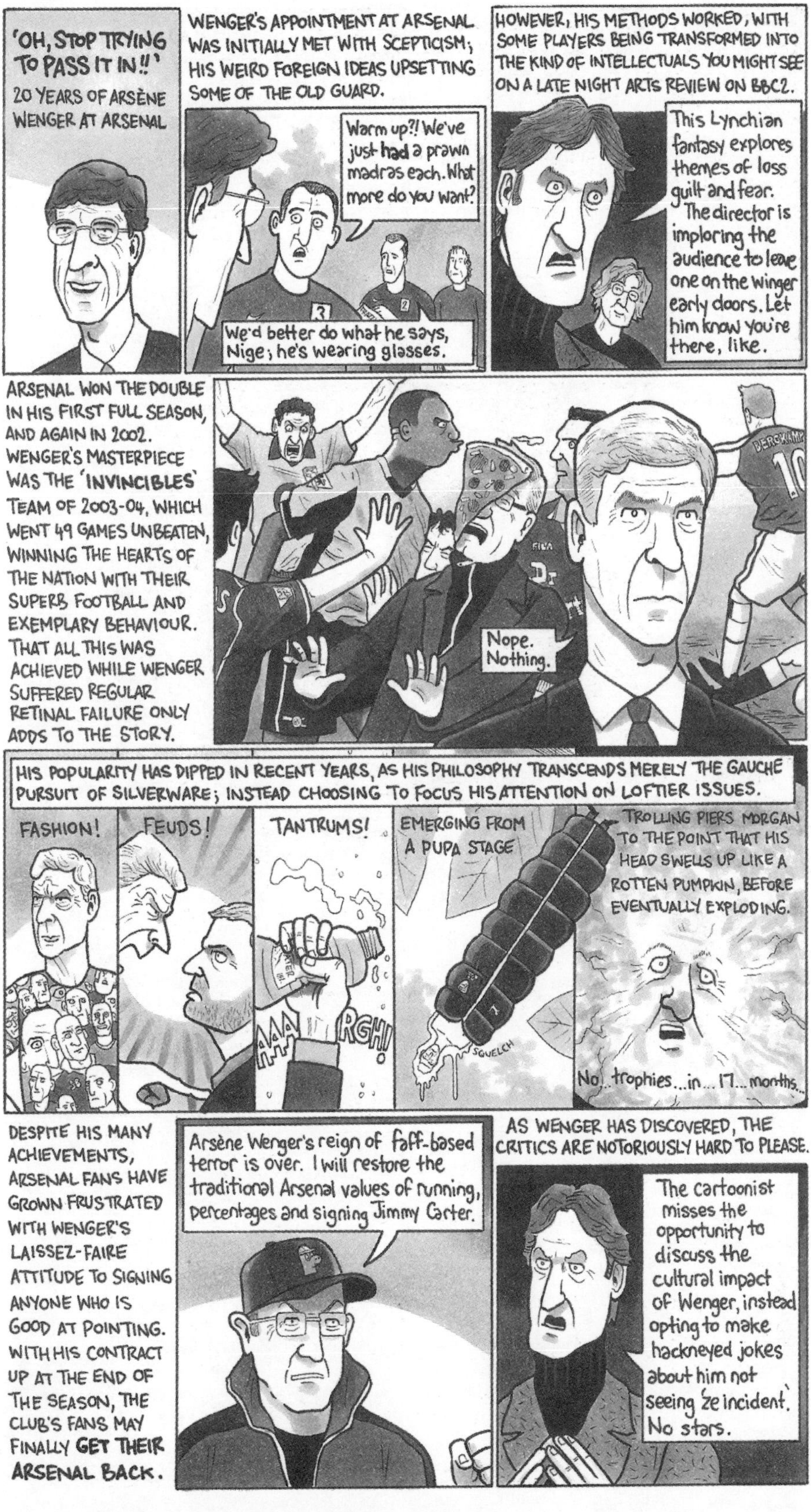

'OH, STOP TRYING TO PASS IT IN!!'
20 YEARS OF ARSÈNE WENGER AT ARSENAL
WENGER'S APPOINTMENT AT ARSENAL WAS INITIALLY MET WITH SCEPTICISM; HIS WEIRD FOREIGN IDEAS UPSETTING SOME OF THE OLD GUARD.
Warm up?! We've just had a prawn madras each. What more do you want?
We'd better do what he says, Nige; he's wearing glasses.
HOWEVER, HIS METHODS WORKED, WITH SOME PLAYERS BEING TRANSFORMED INTO THE KIND OF INTELLECTUALS YOU MIGHT SEE ON A LATE NIGHT ARTS REVIEW ON BBC2.
This Lynchian fantasy explores themes of loss guilt and fear. The director is imploring the audience to leave one on the winger early doors. Let him know you're there, like.
ARSENAL WON THE DOUBLE IN HIS FIRST FULL SEASON, AND AGAIN IN 2002. WENGER'S MASTERPIECE WAS THE 'INVINCIBLES' TEAM OF 2003-04, WHICH WENT 49 GAMES UNBEATEN, WINNING THE HEARTS OF THE NATION WITH THEIR SUPERB FOOTBALL AND EXEMPLARY BEHAVIOUR. THAT ALL THIS WAS ACHIEVED WHILE WENGER SUFFERED REGULAR RETINAL FAILURE ONLY ADDS TO THE STORY.
BERGKAMP 10
Nope. Nothing.
HIS POPULARITY HAS DIPPED IN RECENT YEARS, AS HIS PHILOSOPHY TRANSCENDS MERELY THE GAUCHE PURSUIT OF SILVERWARE; INSTEAD CHOOSING TO FOCUS HIS ATTENTION ON LOFTIER ISSUES.
FASHION!
FEUDS!
TANTRUMS!
AAAARGH!
EMERGING FROM A PUPA STAGE
SQUELCH
TROLLING PIERS MORGAN TO THE POINT THAT HIS HEAD SWELLS UP LIKE A ROTTEN PUMPKIN, BEFORE EVENTUALLY EXPLODING.
No... trophies... in... 17... months...
DESPITE HIS MANY ACHIEVEMENTS, ARSENAL FANS HAVE GROWN FRUSTRATED WITH WENGER'S LAISSEZ-FAIRE ATTITUDE TO SIGNING ANYONE WHO IS GOOD AT POINTING. WITH HIS CONTRACT UP AT THE END OF THE SEASON, THE CLUB'S FANS MAY FINALLY GET THEIR ARSENAL BACK.
Arsène Wenger's reign of faff-based terror is over. I will restore the traditional Arsenal values of running, percentages and signing Jimmy Carter.
AS WENGER HAS DISCOVERED, THE CRITICS ARE NOTORIOUSLY HARD TO PLEASE.
The cartoonist misses the opportunity to discuss the cultural impact of Wenger, instead opting to make hackneyed jokes about him not seeing 'ze incident'. No stars.

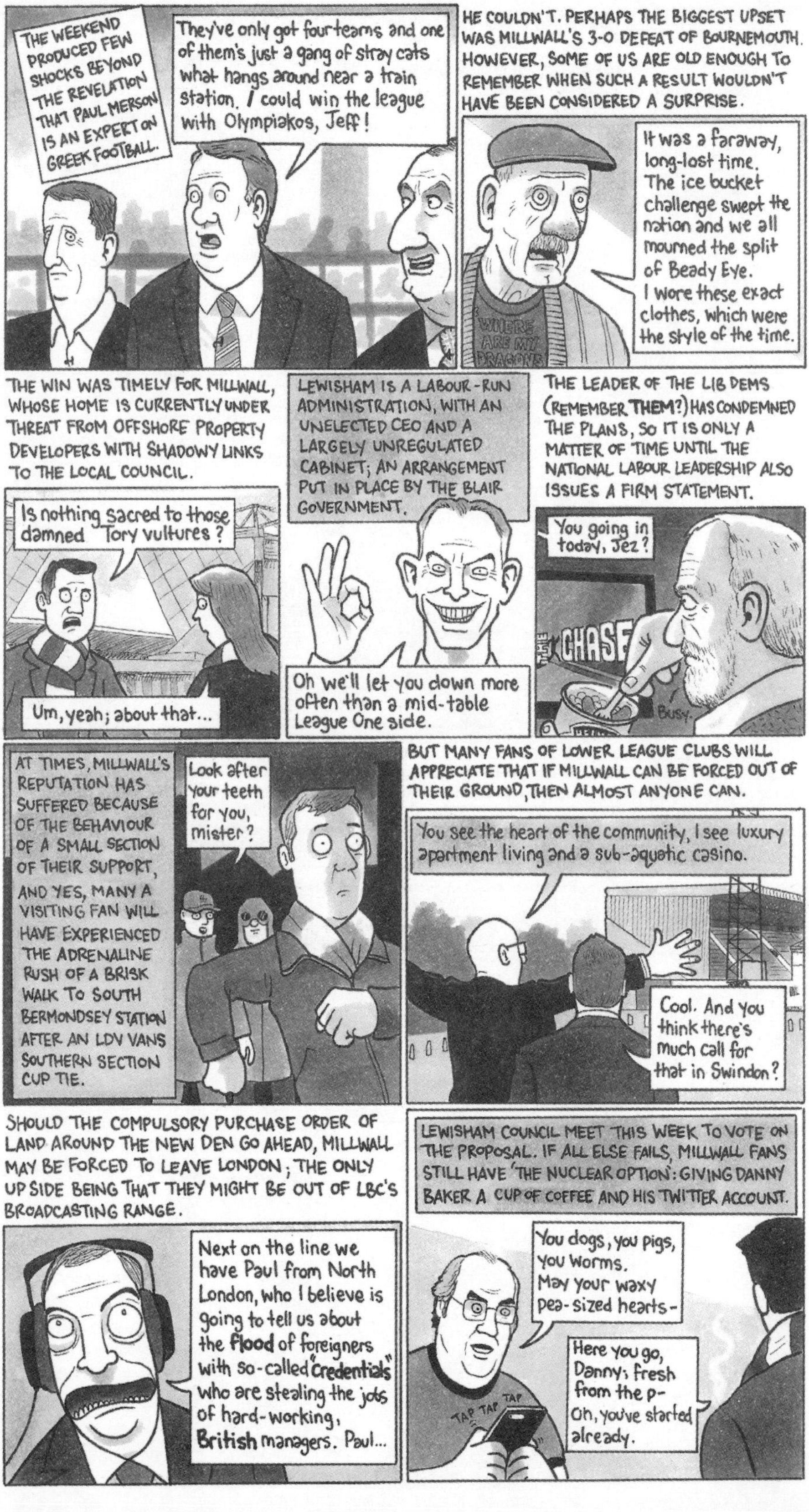
THE WEEKEND PRODUCED FEW SHOCKS BEYOND THE REVELATION THAT PAUL MERSON IS AN EXPERT ON GREEK FOOTBALL.
They've only got four teams and one of them's just a gang of stray cats what hangs around near a train station. I could win the league with Olympiakos, Jeff!
HE COULDN'T. PERHAPS THE BIGGEST UPSET WAS MILLWALL'S 3-0 DEFEAT OF BOURNEMOUTH. HOWEVER, SOME OF US ARE OLD ENOUGH TO REMEMBER WHEN SUCH A RESULT WOULDN'T HAVE BEEN CONSIDERED A SURPRISE.
It was a faraway, long-lost time. The ice bucket challenge swept the nation and we all mourned the split of Beady Eye. I wore these exact clothes, which were the style of the time.
WHERE ARE MY DRAGONS
THE WIN WAS TIMELY FOR MILLWALL, WHOSE HOME IS CURRENTLY UNDER THREAT FROM OFFSHORE PROPERTY DEVELOPERS WITH SHADOWY LINKS TO THE LOCAL COUNCIL.
Is nothing sacred to those damned Tory vultures?
Um, yeah; about that...
LEWISHAM IS A LABOUR-RUN ADMINISTRATION, WITH AN UNELECTED CEO AND A LARGELY UNREGULATED CABINET; AN ARRANGEMENT PUT IN PLACE BY THE BLAIR GOVERNMENT.
Oh we'll let you down more often than a mid-table League One side.
THE LEADER OF THE LIB DEMS (REMEMBER THEM?) HAS CONDEMNED THE PLANS, SO IT IS ONLY A MATTER OF TIME UNTIL THE NATIONAL LABOUR LEADERSHIP ALSO ISSUES A FIRM STATEMENT.
You going in today, Jez?
THE CHASE
BUSY
AT TIMES, MILLWALL'S REPUTATION HAS SUFFERED BECAUSE OF THE BEHAVIOUR OF A SMALL SECTION OF THEIR SUPPORT, AND YES, MANY A VISITING FAN WILL HAVE EXPERIENCED THE ADRENALINE RUSH OF A BRISK WALK TO SOUTH BERMONDSEY STATION AFTER AN LDV VANS SOUTHERN SECTION CUP TIE.
Look after your teeth for you, mister?
BUT MANY FANS OF LOWER LEAGUE CLUBS WILL APPRECIATE THAT IF MILLWALL CAN BE FORCED OUT OF THEIR GROUND, THEN ALMOST ANYONE CAN.
You see the heart of the community, I see luxury apartment living and a sub-aquatic casino.
Cool. And you think there's much call for that in Swindon?
SHOULD THE COMPULSORY PURCHASE ORDER OF LAND AROUND THE NEW DEN GO AHEAD, MILLWALL MAY BE FORCED TO LEAVE LONDON; THE ONLY UP SIDE BEING THAT THEY MIGHT BE OUT OF LBC'S BROADCASTING RANGE.
Next on the line we have Paul from North London, who I believe is going to tell us about the **flood** of foreigners with so-called "credentials" who are stealing the jobs of hard-working, **British** managers. Paul...
LEWISHAM COUNCIL MEET THIS WEEK TO VOTE ON THE PROPOSAL. IF ALL ELSE FAILS, MILLWALL FANS STILL HAVE 'THE NUCLEAR OPTION': GIVING DANNY BAKER A CUP OF COFFEE AND HIS TWITTER ACCOUNT.
You dogs, you pigs, you worms. May your waxy pea-sized hearts-
TAP TAP TAP
Here you go, Danny; fresh from the p- Oh, you've started already.

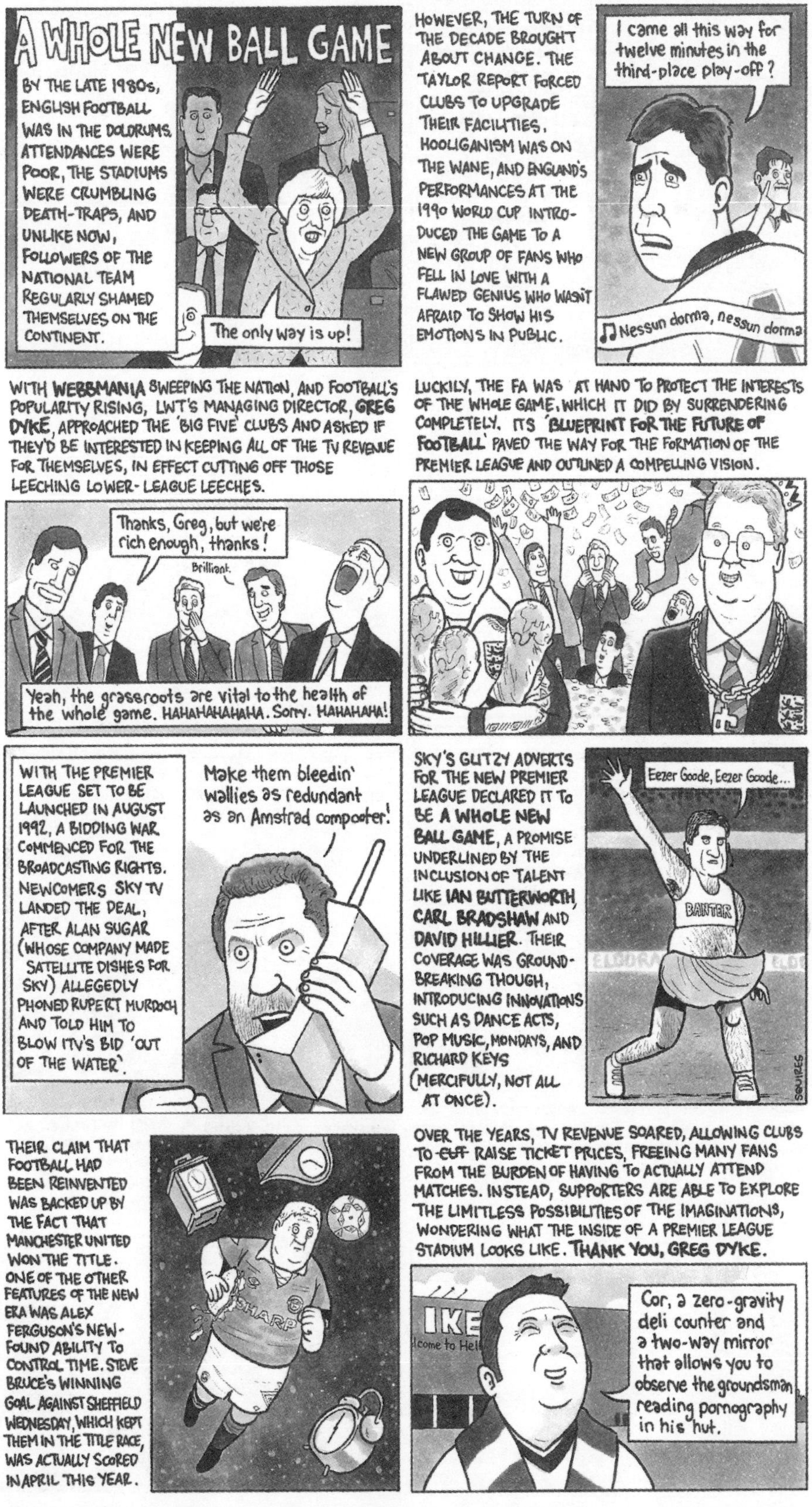

A WHOLE NEW BALL GAME
BY THE LATE 1980s, ENGLISH FOOTBALL WAS IN THE DOLDRUMS. ATTENDANCES WERE POOR, THE STADIUMS WERE CRUMBLING DEATH-TRAPS, AND UNLIKE NOW, FOLLOWERS OF THE NATIONAL TEAM REGULARLY SHAMED THEMSELVES ON THE CONTINENT.
The only way is up!
HOWEVER, THE TURN OF THE DECADE BROUGHT ABOUT CHANGE. THE TAYLOR REPORT FORCED CLUBS TO UPGRADE THEIR FACILITIES. HOOLIGANISM WAS ON THE WANE, AND ENGLAND'S PERFORMANCES AT THE 1990 WORLD CUP INTRODUCED THE GAME TO A NEW GROUP OF FANS WHO FELL IN LOVE WITH A FLAWED GENIUS WHO WASN'T AFRAID TO SHOW HIS EMOTIONS IN PUBLIC.
I came all this way for twelve minutes in the third-place play-off?
♫ Nessun dorma, nessun dorma
WITH WEBBMANIA SWEEPING THE NATION, AND FOOTBALL'S POPULARITY RISING, LWT'S MANAGING DIRECTOR, GREG DYKE, APPROACHED THE 'BIG FIVE' CLUBS AND ASKED IF THEY'D BE INTERESTED IN KEEPING ALL OF THE TV REVENUE FOR THEMSELVES, IN EFFECT CUTTING OFF THOSE LEECHING LOWER-LEAGUE LEECHES.
Thanks, Greg, but we're rich enough, thanks!
Brilliant.
Yeah, the grassroots are vital to the health of the whole game. HAHAHAHAHAHA. Sorry. HAHAHAHA!
LUCKILY, THE FA WAS AT HAND TO PROTECT THE INTERESTS OF THE WHOLE GAME, WHICH IT DID BY SURRENDERING COMPLETELY. ITS 'BLUEPRINT FOR THE FUTURE OF FOOTBALL' PAVED THE WAY FOR THE FORMATION OF THE PREMIER LEAGUE AND OUTLINED A COMPELLING VISION.
WITH THE PREMIER LEAGUE SET TO BE LAUNCHED IN AUGUST 1992, A BIDDING WAR COMMENCED FOR THE BROADCASTING RIGHTS. NEWCOMERS SKY TV LANDED THE DEAL, AFTER ALAN SUGAR (WHOSE COMPANY MADE SATELLITE DISHES FOR SKY) ALLEGEDLY PHONED RUPERT MURDOCH AND TOLD HIM TO BLOW ITV'S BID 'OUT OF THE WATER'.
Make them bleedin' wallies as redundant as an Amstrad compooter!
SKY'S GLITZY ADVERTS FOR THE NEW PREMIER LEAGUE DECLARED IT TO BE A WHOLE NEW BALL GAME, A PROMISE UNDERLINED BY THE INCLUSION OF TALENT LIKE IAN BUTTERWORTH, CARL BRADSHAW AND DAVID HILLIER. THEIR COVERAGE WAS GROUND-BREAKING THOUGH, INTRODUCING INNOVATIONS SUCH AS DANCE ACTS, POP MUSIC, MONDAYS, AND RICHARD KEYS (MERCIFULLY, NOT ALL AT ONCE).
Eezer Goode, Eezer Goode...
BANTER
SQUIRES
THEIR CLAIM THAT FOOTBALL HAD BEEN REINVENTED WAS BACKED UP BY THE FACT THAT MANCHESTER UNITED WON THE TITLE. ONE OF THE OTHER FEATURES OF THE NEW ERA WAS ALEX FERGUSON'S NEW-FOUND ABILITY TO CONTROL TIME. STEVE BRUCE'S WINNING GOAL AGAINST SHEFFIELD WEDNESDAY, WHICH KEPT THEM IN THE TITLE RACE, WAS ACTUALLY SCORED IN APRIL THIS YEAR.
SHARP
OVER THE YEARS, TV REVENUE SOARED, ALLOWING CLUBS TO ~~CUT~~ RAISE TICKET PRICES, FREEING MANY FANS FROM THE BURDEN OF HAVING TO ACTUALLY ATTEND MATCHES. INSTEAD, SUPPORTERS ARE ABLE TO EXPLORE THE LIMITLESS POSSIBILITIES OF THE IMAGINATIONS, WONDERING WHAT THE INSIDE OF A PREMIER LEAGUE STADIUM LOOKS LIKE. THANK YOU, GREG DYKE.
IKE
lcome to Hel
Cor, a zero-gravity deli counter and a two-way mirror that allows you to observe the groundsman reading pornography in his hut.

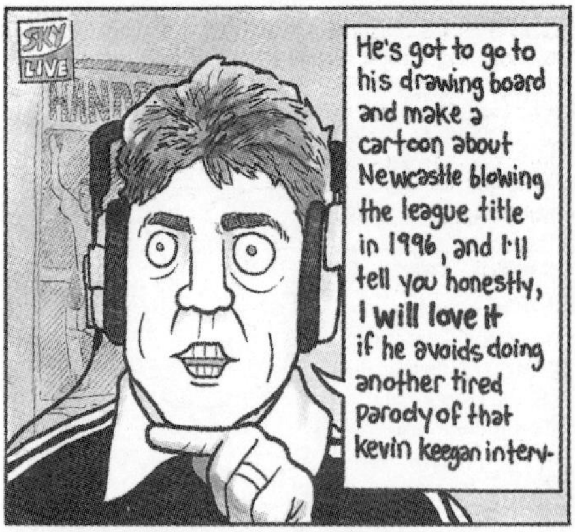
SKY LIVE
He's got to go to his drawing board and make a cartoon about Newcastle blowing the league title in 1996, and I'll tell you honestly, I **will love it** if he avoids doing another tired parody of that kevin keegan interv-

IN JANUARY 1996, NEWCASTLE UNITED HAD A 12-POINT LEAD AT THE TOP OF THE PREMIER LEAGUE. THAT THEY WOULD BE CROWNED CHAMPIONS SEEMED AS CERTAIN AS THE FACT THAT NUMBER ONE ARTISTS BABYLON ZOO WOULD DOMINATE THE BRITISH MUSIC SCENE FOR GENERATIONS TO COME. THE MAGPIES' SUCCESS WAS THE RESULT OF KEVIN KEEGAN'S FOOTBALL PHILOSOPHY OF:

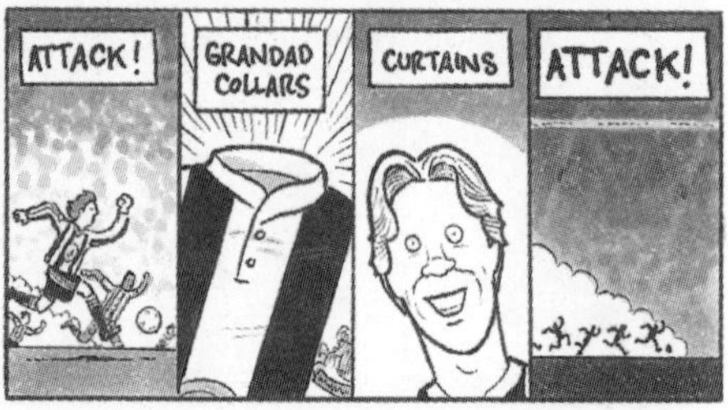
ATTACK!
GRANDAD COLLARS
CURTAINS
ATTACK!

THEIR GUNG-HO APPROACH, THOUGH THRILLING, DID MEAN THEY LET IN A LOT OF GOALS. THE SOLUTION WAS OBVIOUS: **SIGN ANOTHER STRIKER!**

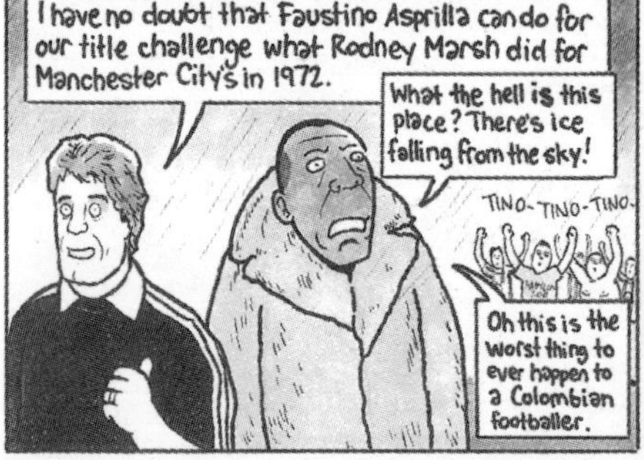
I have no doubt that Faustino Asprilla can do for our title challenge what Rodney Marsh did for Manchester City's in 1972.
What the hell **is** this place? There's ice falling from the sky!
TINO-TINO-TINO
Oh this is the worst thing to ever happen to a Colombian footballer.

HE MADE A STRONG START, COMING OFF THE BENCH TO SET UP A GOAL IN A 2-1 WIN AT MIDDLESBROUGH; AN IMPRESSIVE CONTRIBUTION CONSIDERING HE HADN'T EXPECTED TO PLAY AND ENJOYED A LARGE GLASS OF WINE WITH LUNCH.

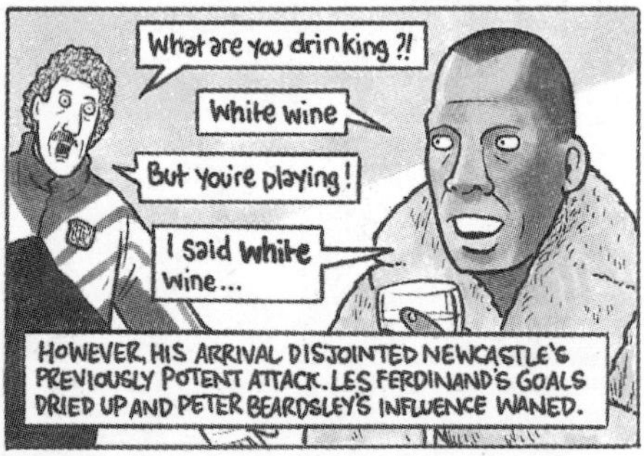
What are you drinking?!
White wine
But you're playing!
I said **white** wine...
HOWEVER, HIS ARRIVAL DISJOINTED NEWCASTLE'S PREVIOUSLY POTENT ATTACK. LES FERDINAND'S GOALS DRIED UP AND PETER BEARDSLEY'S INFLUENCE WANED.

THEY HAD A BIGGER PROBLEM THOUGH: MANCHESTER UNITED. WITH CANTONA BACK FROM A NINE MONTH BAN, UNITED WENT ON A RELENTLESS WINNING RUN, SLOWLY REELING NEWCASTLE IN. A SOLITARY CANTONA GOAL SETTLED THE MATCH WHEN THE TWO SIDES MET IN EARLY MARCH. NEWCASTLE SIMPLY COULDN'T FIND A WAY PAST **SCHMEICHEL** - THE GIANT STARFISH UNITED'S SCOUTS HAD DISCOVERED IN THE DEPTHS OF THE NORTH SEA.

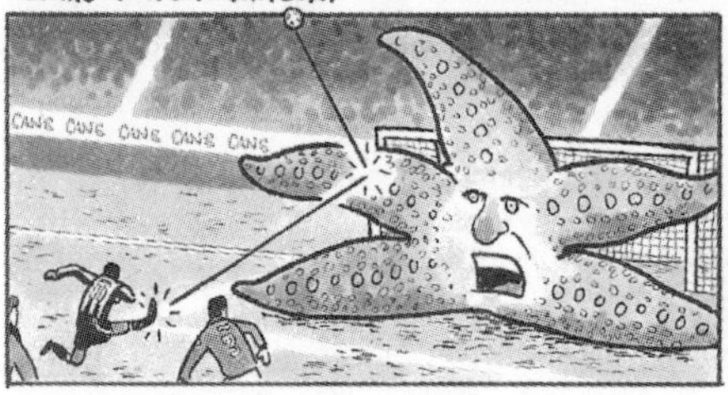

THEY EVENTUALLY OVERHAULED NEWCASTLE LATER THAT MONTH AND WHEN KEEGAN'S SIDE LOST A 4-3 **THRILLER** TO LIVERPOOL THERE WAS A SENSE OF INEVITABILITY THAT THE TITLE WOULD BE HEADING TO OLD TRAFFORD.

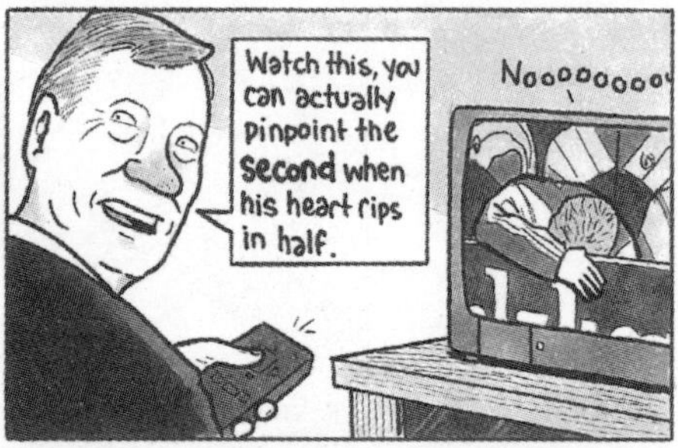
Watch this, you can actually pinpoint the **second** when his heart rips in half.
Noooooooo

WHEN KEEGAN LAUNCHED INTO HIS FAMOUS TELEVISED RANT, ALEX FERGUSON WAS HAILED AS A PSYCHOLOGICAL GENIUS; A DARK MASTER WHO COULD MANIPULATE THE MINDS OF OPPOSITION MANAGERS AT WILL. WHILE HIS POWERS WERE EXAGGERATED, THEY CERTAINLY WORKED ON KEEGAN.

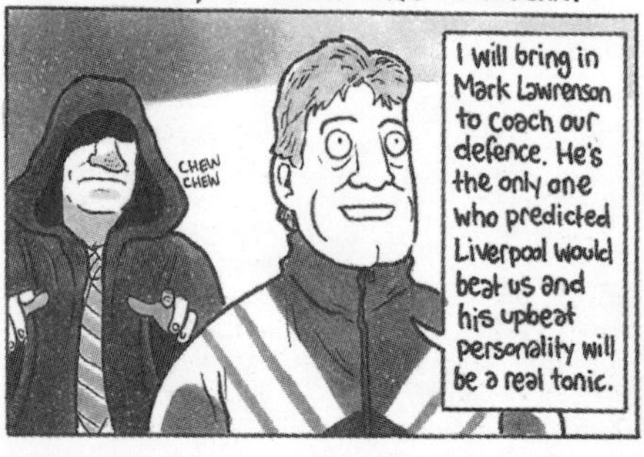
CHEW CHEW
I will bring in Mark Lawrenson to coach our defence. He's the only one who predicted Liverpool would beat us and his upbeat personality will be a real tonic.

MANCHESTER UNITED SECURED THE TITLE ON THE LAST DAY OF THE SEASON, BUT NEWCASTLE'S BRAND OF OPEN, BREEZY FOOTBALL HAD DELIGHTED AND AMUSED. PLUS, WITH THE SUMMER SIGNING OF ALAN SHEARER, AND SOME SHREWD ADDITIONS TO THE COACHING STAFF, 1997 WAS SURE TO BRING MORE JOY.

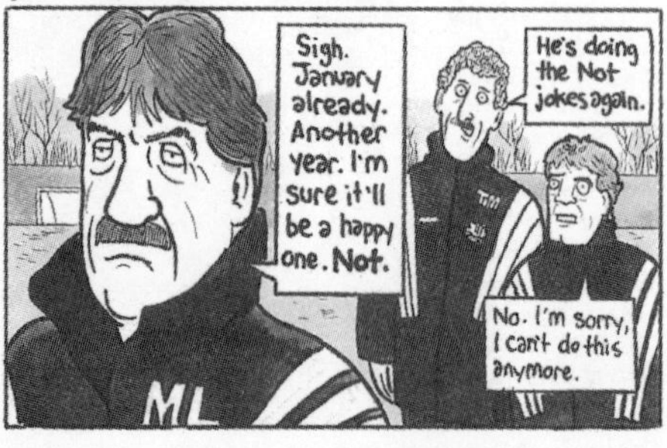
Sigh. January already. Another year. I'm sure it'll be a happy one. **Not.**
He's doing the Not jokes again.
No. I'm sorry, I can't do this anymore.
ML

AT THE START OF THE 2003-04 SEASON, ARSÈNE WENGER THOUGHT HIS ARSENAL TEAM WAS CAPABLE OF GOING THE WHOLE LEAGUE CAMPAIGN UNBEATEN; A FEAT LAST ACHIEVED BY PRESTON NORTH END IN 1889, AND THEY HAD THE BENEFIT OF PLAYING FEWER MATCHES AND ADVANCES IN SPORT SCIENCE.

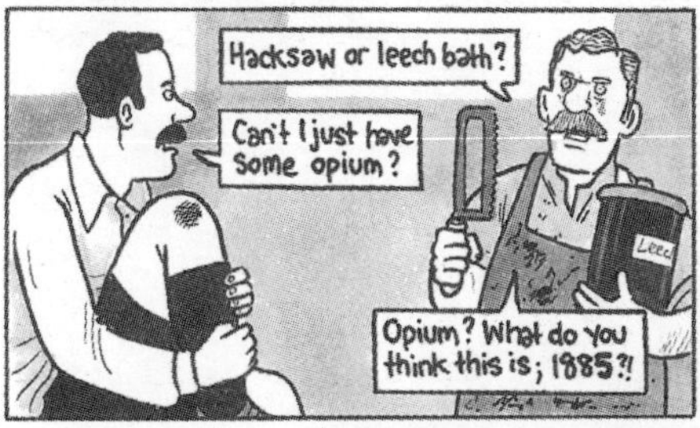

Hacksaw or leech bath?
Can't I just have some opium?
Opium? What do you think this is; 1885?!

WENGER WAS WORKING TO A TIGHT BUDGET AS ARSENAL WERE BUILDING A NEW STADIUM THAT WOULD GUARANTEE THEIR SUCCESS FOR YEARS TO COME. THEIR MOST SIGNIFICANT SIGNING WAS THE £1.5M CAPTURE OF JENS LEHMANN FROM BORUSSIA DORTMUND. THE 33-YEAR OLD GOALKEEPER WOULD PREPARE FOR GAMES BY BLASTING GERMAN TECHNO.

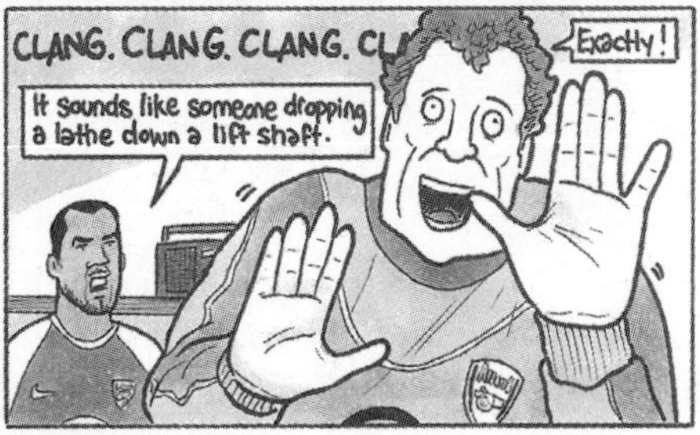

CLANG. CLANG. CLANG. CL
Exactly!
It sounds like someone dropping a lathe down a lift shaft.

ARSENAL STARTED THE SEASON STRONGLY, BUT NEARLY CAME UNSTUCK AFTER JUST SIX GAMES, WHEN THEY WERE LUCKY TO ESCAPE WITH A POINT FROM A TRIP TO OLD TRAFFORD; RUUD VAN NISTELROOY CRACKING AN INJURY-TIME PENALTY AGAINST THE BAR. THIS WOULD TURN OUT TO BE THE FOOTBALL EQUIVALENT OF A BATSMAN BEING DROPPED ON FOUR RUNS AND THEN GOING ON TO SCORE A DOUBLE CENTURY.

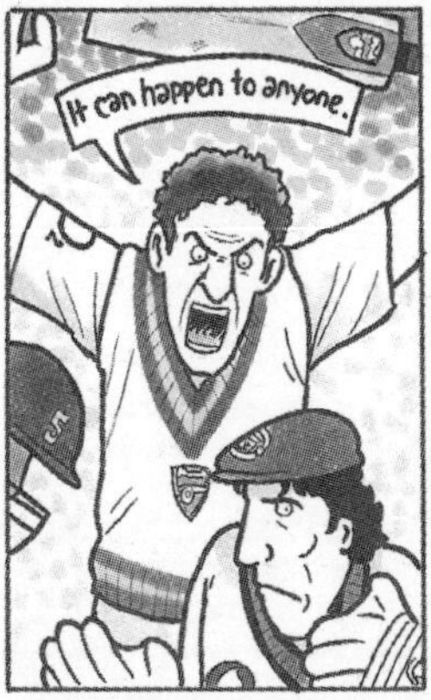

It can happen to anyone.

BY APRIL THEY WERE STILL IN THE HUNT FOR THREE TROPHIES, BUT WITHIN THE SPACE OF A WEEK IT SEEMED THEIR SEASON WAS COLLAPSING. IT MUST HAVE BEEN AN EXHAUSTING TIME FOR THE SHRIEKING ARSENAL FAN WHO ALWAYS SAT NEAR A TOUCHLINE MICROPHONE.

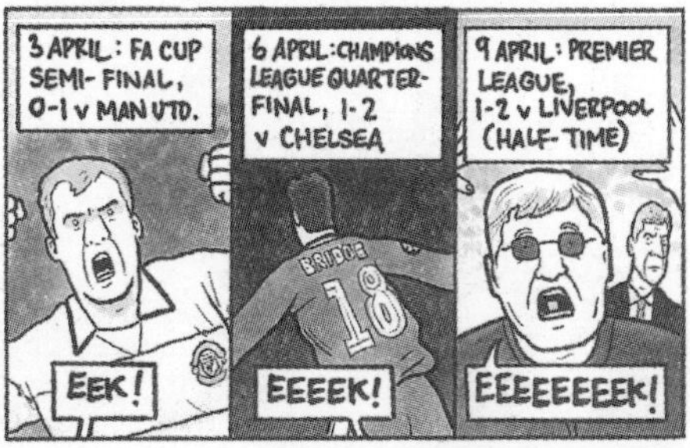

3 APRIL: FA CUP SEMI-FINAL, 0-1 v MAN UTD.
EEK!
6 APRIL: CHAMPIONS LEAGUE QUARTER-FINAL, 1-2 v CHELSEA
BRIDGE
18
EEEEK!
9 APRIL: PREMIER LEAGUE, 1-2 v LIVERPOOL (HALF-TIME)
EEEEEEEEK!

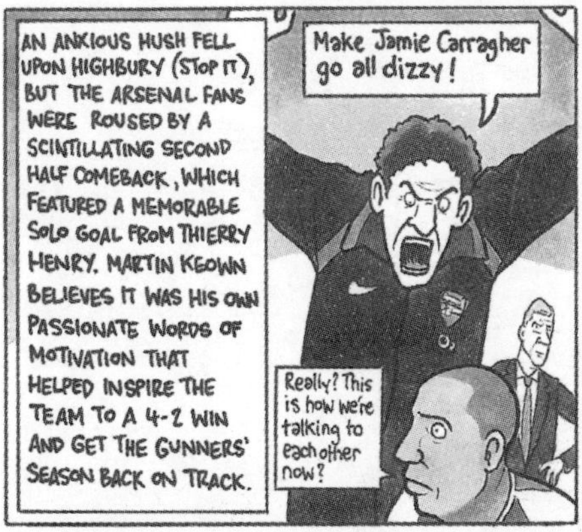

AN ANXIOUS HUSH FELL UPON HIGHBURY (STOP IT), BUT THE ARSENAL FANS WERE ROUSED BY A SCINTILLATING SECOND HALF COMEBACK, WHICH FEATURED A MEMORABLE SOLO GOAL FROM THIERRY HENRY. MARTIN KEOWN BELIEVES IT WAS HIS OWN PASSIONATE WORDS OF MOTIVATION THAT HELPED INSPIRE THE TEAM TO A 4-2 WIN AND GET THE GUNNERS' SEASON BACK ON TRACK.
Make Jamie Carragher go all dizzy!
Really? This is how we're talking to each other now?

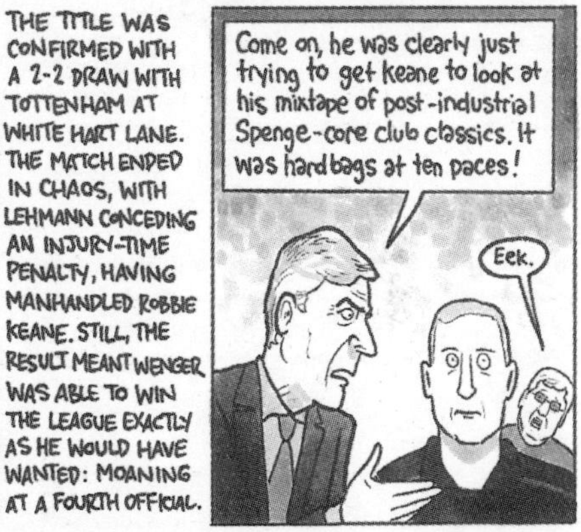

THE TITLE WAS CONFIRMED WITH A 2-2 DRAW WITH TOTTENHAM AT WHITE HART LANE. THE MATCH ENDED IN CHAOS, WITH LEHMANN CONCEDING AN INJURY-TIME PENALTY, HAVING MANHANDLED ROBBIE KEANE. STILL, THE RESULT MEANT WENGER WAS ABLE TO WIN THE LEAGUE EXACTLY AS HE WOULD HAVE WANTED: MOANING AT A FOURTH OFFICIAL.
Come on, he was clearly just trying to get keane to look at his mixtape of post-industrial Spenge-core club classics. It was hard bags at ten paces!
Eek.

THEIR STATUS AS **INVINCIBLES** WAS SECURED WITH A 2-1 WIN AGAINST LEICESTER ON THE LAST DAY OF THE SEASON. THIS INCREDIBLE ACHIEVEMENT GAVE THEM THE CONFIDENCE TO LATER CREATE THEIR GREATEST TRIUMPH: A DADAIST INSTALLATION TITLED 'PENALTY-A STUDY IN HUBRIS', DESIGNED TO PROVOKE AN EMOTIONAL RESPONSE FROM DANNY MILLS.

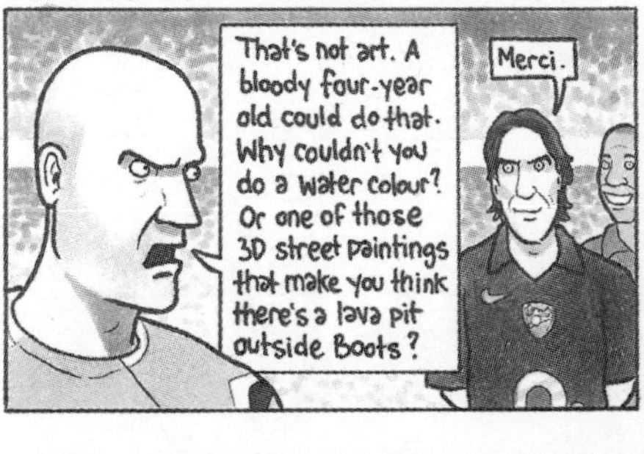

That's not art. A bloody four-year old could do that. Why couldn't you do a water colour? Or one of those 3D street paintings that make you think there's a lava pit outside Boots?
Merci.

ARSENAL'S UNDEFEATED RUN CONTINUED INTO THE NEXT SEASON, STRETCHING TO A RECORD 49 MATCHES BEFORE THEY LOST 2-0 AT MANCHESTER UNITED IN CONTROVERSIAL CIRCUMSTANCES. A HUGE SCRAP IN THE PLAYERS' TUNNEL SAW THE CONTENTS OF A BUFFET BECOMING AIRBORNE AND SOME GUNNERS FANS STILL BELIEVE A CONSPIRACY TOOK PLACE.

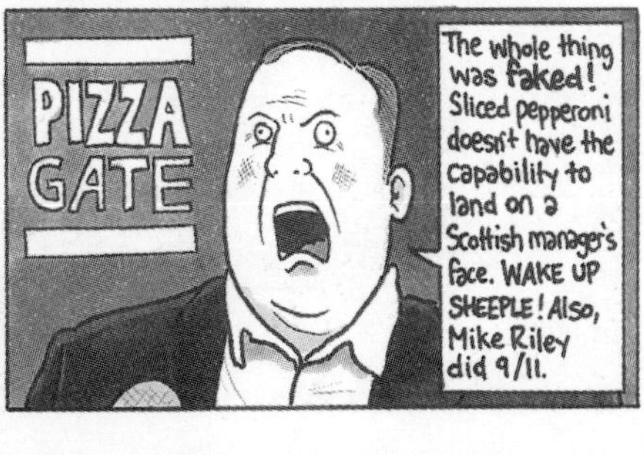

PIZZA GATE
The whole thing was faked! Sliced pepperoni doesn't have the capability to land on a Scottish manager's face. WAKE UP SHEEPLE! Also, Mike Riley did 9/11.

FOR FOOTBALL FANS OF A CERTAIN AGE, IT WAS ODD TO HEAR CHELSEA'S NEW SIGNING TIEMOUÉ BAKAYOKO TALK ABOUT SUPPORTING THE CLUB SINCE HE WAS A BOY. IN THE MINDS OF SOME, CHELSEA WILL ALWAYS BE THE CLUB THEY WERE BEFORE ROMAN ABRAMOVICH BOUGHT THEM.

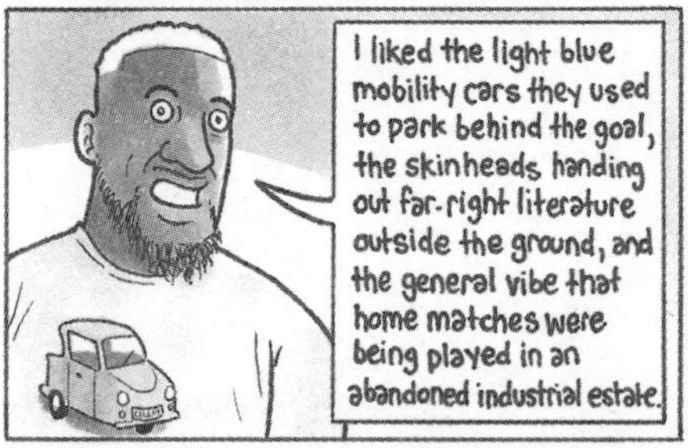
I liked the light blue mobility cars they used to park behind the goal, the skinheads handing out far-right literature outside the ground, and the general vibe that home matches were being played in an abandoned industrial estate.

IN 2003, CHELSEA WERE MILLIONS IN DEBT, BUT WERE STILL AN ATTRACTIVE PROSPECT, HAVING QUALIFIED FOR THE CHAMPIONS LEAGUE WITH A GOOD SQUAD. HOWEVER, BEFORE ABRAMOVICH COULD BUY THEM, HE HAD TO DEAL WITH THE ANGRY GOBLIN WHO HAD CAST A SPELL OVER THE CLUB.

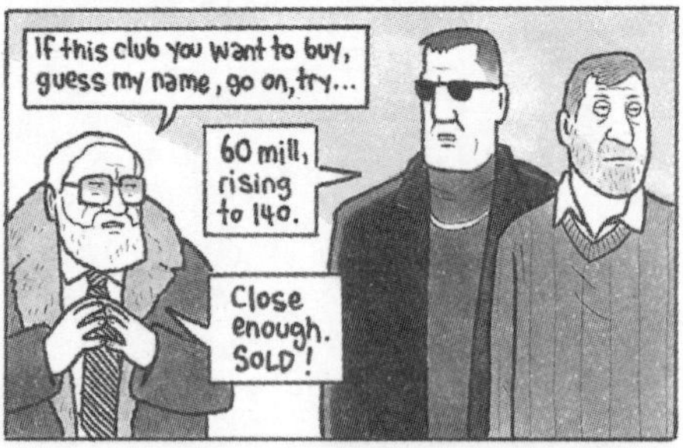
If this club you want to buy, guess my name, go on, try...
60 mill, rising to 140.
Close enough. SOLD!

CHELSEA'S CEO AT THE TIME, TREVOR BIRCH, SAID THAT THE DEAL WAS COMPLETED IN TEN MINUTES, AND THAT HE SUGGESTED TO ABRAMOVICH THAT HE LOWER TICKET PRICES AS A GESTURE OF GOODWILL TO SUPPORTERS.

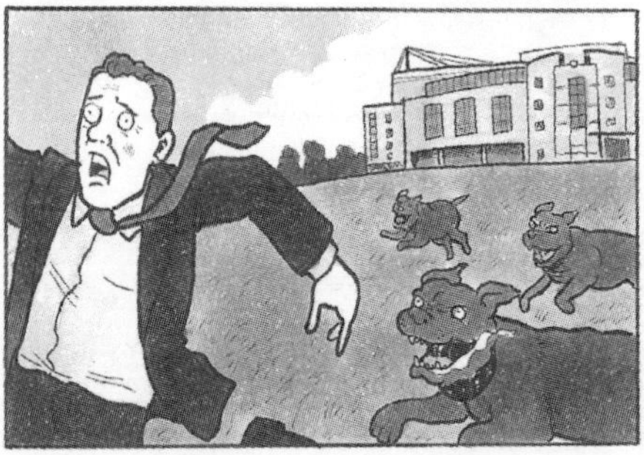

AT THE TIME, ABRAMOVICH WAS THE SECOND RICHEST PERSON IN RUSSIA. HE AND THE OTHER OLIGARCHS HAD DONE A DEAL WITH BORIS YELTSIN TO PURCHASE RUSSIAN OIL AT A HUGELY REDUCED PRICE. THE CONSEQUENT SALE OF THIS OIL MADE THEM ALL RICHER THAN KYLE WALKER, WHILE THE PEOPLE OF RUSSIA MISSED OUT. THIS PRESENTED CHELSEA FANS WITH A DIFFICULT ETHICAL CONUNDRUM.

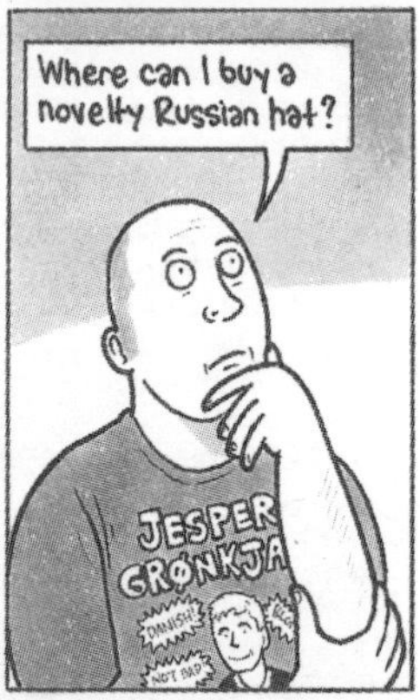
Where can I buy a novelty Russian hat?
JESPER GRØNKJA
DANISH!
NOT BAD

HIS ARRIVAL HERALDED A PERIOD OF UNPRECEDENTED SPENDING. MANAGER CLAUDIO RANIERI DIVED INTO THE TRANSFER MARKET WITH THE CAREFREE ABANDON OF AN OLIGARCH'S SPOUSE ON A BOND STREET SHOPPING SPREE.

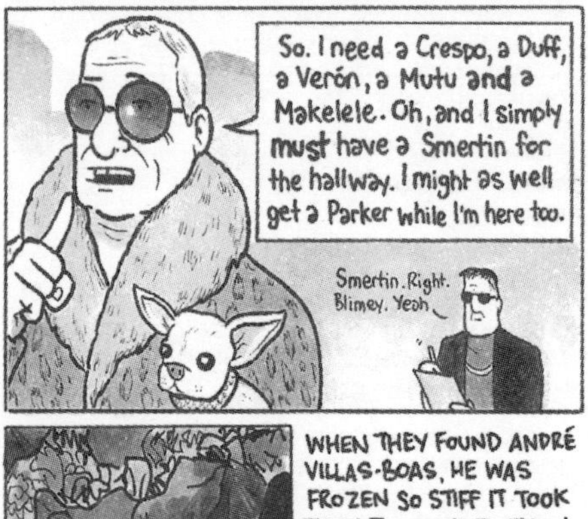
So. I need a Crespo, a Duff, a Verón, a Mutu and a Makelele. Oh, and I simply **must** have a Smertin for the hallway. I might as well get a Parker while I'm here too.
Smertin. Right. Blimey. Yeah.

RANIERI GUIDED CHELSEA TO SECOND PLACE IN THE LEAGUE AND TO THE SEMI-FINALS OF THE CHAMPIONS LEAGUE, BUT STILL GOT THE CHOP. OVER THE YEARS, ABRAMOVICH'S MANAGERIAL CASUALTIES WOULD STACK UP.

♫ LAYLA (PIANO EXIT) ♫

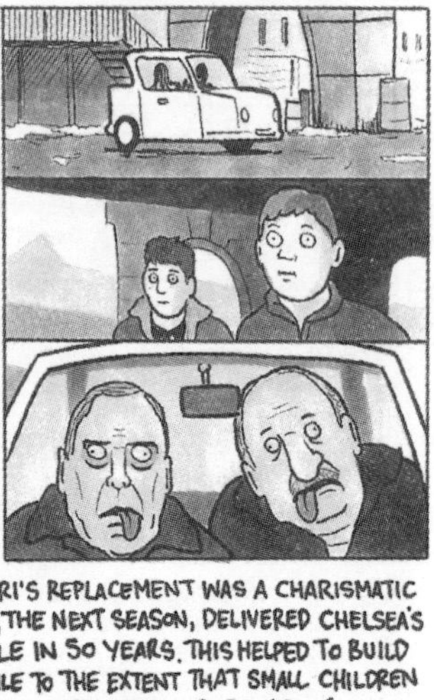

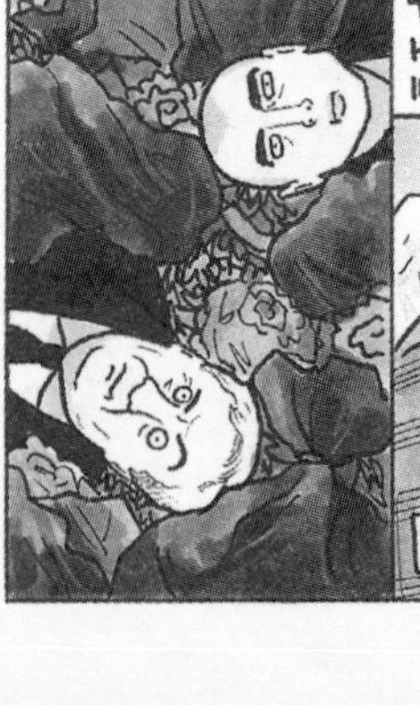

WHEN THEY FOUND ANDRÉ VILLAS-BOAS, HE WAS FROZEN SO STIFF IT TOOK THEM TWO DAYS TO THAW HIM OUT FOR HIS JOB INTERVIEW AT SPURS.

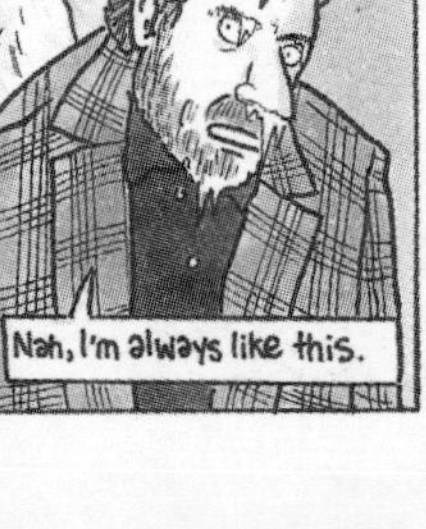
Nah, I'm always like this.

HOWEVER, RANIERI'S REPLACEMENT WAS A CHARISMATIC PRAGMATIST WHO, THE NEXT SEASON, DELIVERED CHELSEA'S FIRST LEAGUE TITLE IN 50 YEARS. THIS HELPED TO BUILD THE CLUB'S PROFILE TO THE EXTENT THAT SMALL CHILDREN IN PARIS BECAME AWARE OF THEM. SURELY JOSÉ MOURINHO WOULD BE SAFE FROM THE BULLET.

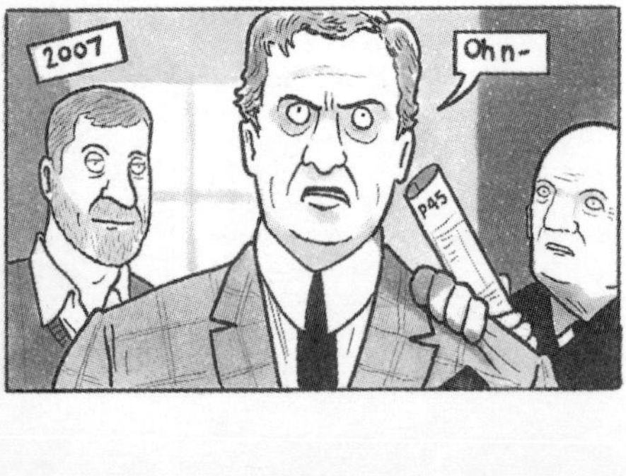
2007
Oh n-
P45

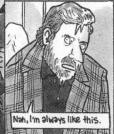

AFTER YEARS OF DISAPPOINTMENT, OVERSEEN BY A SUCCESSION OF HAPLESS CHAIRMEN, MANCHESTER CITY FANS WERE DELIGHTED TO DISCOVER THAT THEIR CLUB WAS BEING BOUGHT BY SOMEONE WITH THE FINANCIAL CLOUT AND BUSINESS ACUMEN TO PUT CITY BACK IN THE BIG TIME: DEPOSED THAI PRIME MINISTER, THAKSIN SHINAWATRA!!

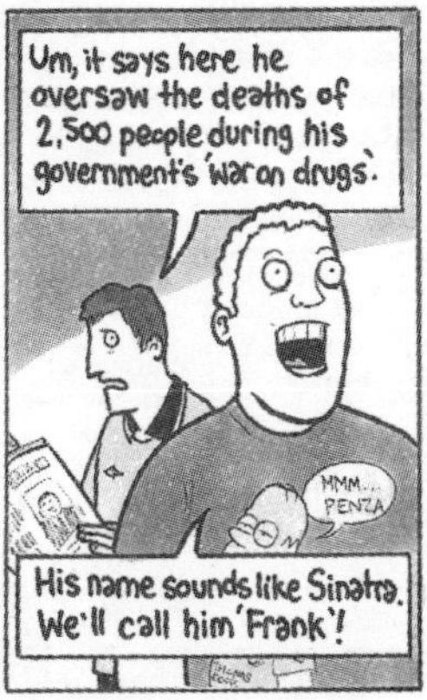
Um, it says here he oversaw the deaths of 2,500 people during his government's 'war on drugs'.
MMM... PENZA
His name sounds like Sinatra. We'll call him 'Frank'!

HOWEVER, AS THE 2007-08 SEASON RUMBLED ON, THINGS WENT 'A BIT CITY'. SHINAWATRA HAD HIS FINANCES FROZEN, THE FANS LAUNCHED A PROTEST TO SAVE POPULAR MANAGER SVEN-GÖRAN ERIKSSON FROM THE SACK, AND DESPITE A STRONG START THE TEAM SLUMPED TO NINTH PLACE, LOSING THEIR LAST GAME 8-1 TO MIDDLESBROUGH.

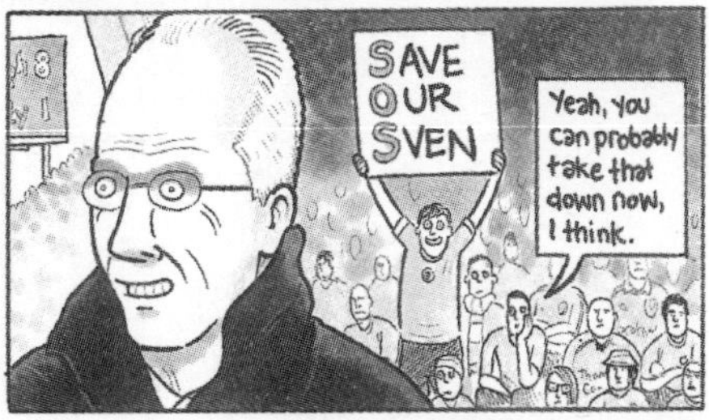
SAVE OUR SVEN
Yeah, you can probably take that down now, I think.

THEIR LUCK WAS ABOUT TO CHANGE THOUGH, BECAUSE ON 1 SEPTEMBER 2008, A TAKEOVER OF THE CLUB BY THE OIL-RICH ABU DHABI UNITED GROUP WAS COMPLETED, JUST IN TIME FOR THEM TO SIGN ROBINHO FOR A BRITISH RECORD OF £32.5M ON TRANSFER DEADLINE DAY.

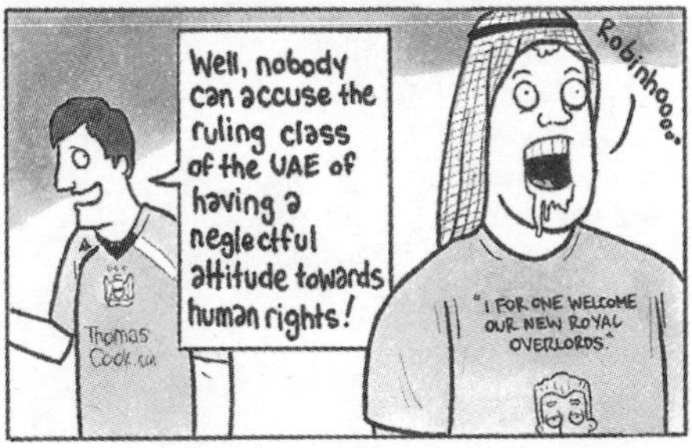
Well, nobody can accuse the ruling class of the UAE of having a neglectful attitude towards human rights!
Robinhooo...
"I FOR ONE WELCOME OUR NEW ROYAL OVERLORDS."

IN THE FIRST FEW YEARS UNDER THE NEW OWNERSHIP, CITY ADOPTED AN AGGRESSIVE MARKETING STRATEGY, LED BY CEO GARRY COOK, TO RAISE THE CLUB'S PROFILE AND ANTAGONISE NEIGHBOURS MANCHESTER UNITED.

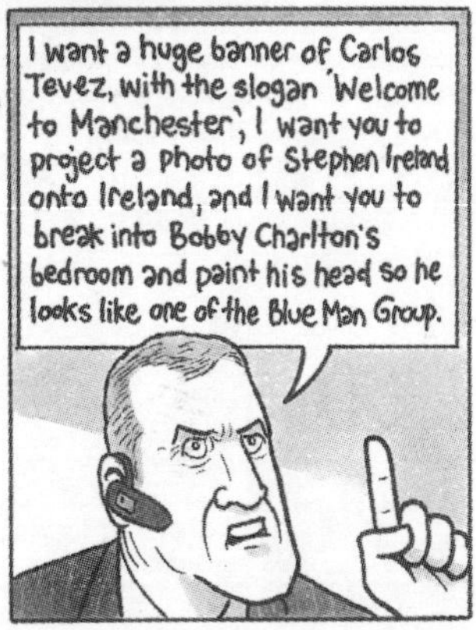
I want a huge banner of Carlos Tevez, with the slogan 'Welcome to Manchester', I want you to project a photo of Stephen Ireland onto Ireland, and I want you to break into Bobby Charlton's bedroom and paint his head so he looks like one of the Blue Man Group.

A STEADY IMPROVEMENT OVER THE NEXT FEW YEARS MEANT CITY WENT INTO THE LAST GAME OF THE 2011-12 SEASON KNOWING THAT VICTORY AGAINST LOWLY QPR WOULD SECURE THE LEAGUE TITLE. AFTER AN HOUR, WITH THE SCORES LEVEL AT 1-1, A SIGNAL WAS GIVEN TO ACTIVATE FORMER CITY PLAYER AND 'MANCUNIAN CANDIDATE' JOEY BARTON INTO DOING SOMETHING DAFT.

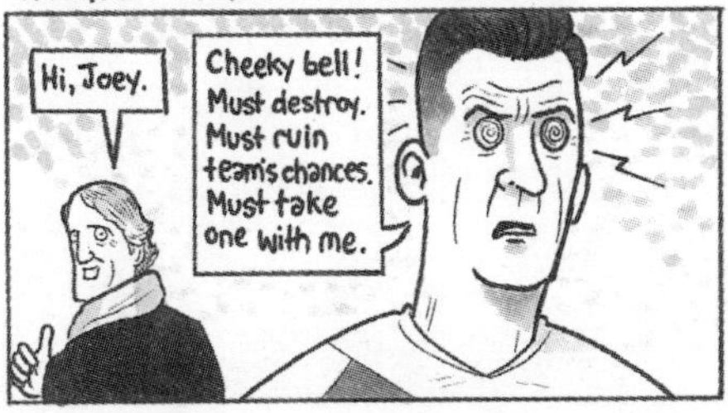
Hi, Joey.
Cheeky bell! Must destroy. Must ruin team's chances. Must take one with me.

DESPITE (OR BECAUSE OF) BARTON'S SUBSEQUENT RED CARD, QPR THEN TOOK A SHOCK LEAD. IT APPEARED THAT CITY WERE ABOUT TO PRODUCE THE MOST CITY RESULT POSSIBLE – ALMOST KNOWINGLY SO.

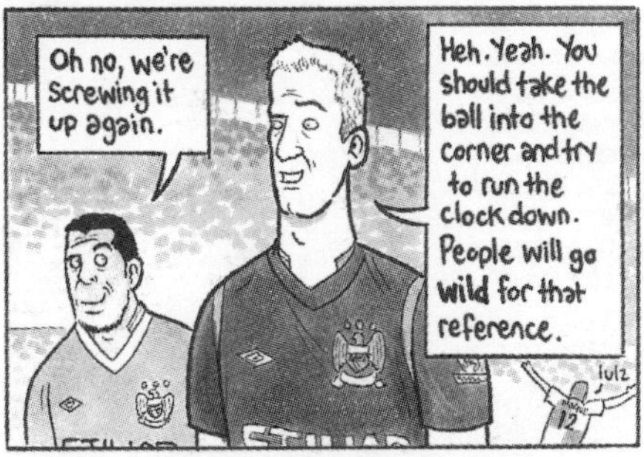
Oh no, we're screwing it up again.
Heh. Yeah. You should take the ball into the corner and try to run the clock down. People will go wild for that reference.
lulz

BUT TWO INJURY-TIME GOALS FROM DŽEKO AND AGÜERO SAVED THE DAY; THE ADDED BONUS BEING THAT THE WIN SNATCHED THE PREMIER LEAGUE TITLE FROM THE GRASP OF MANCHESTER UNITED, WHOSE FANS COULD ONLY LOOK ON IN DISMAY.

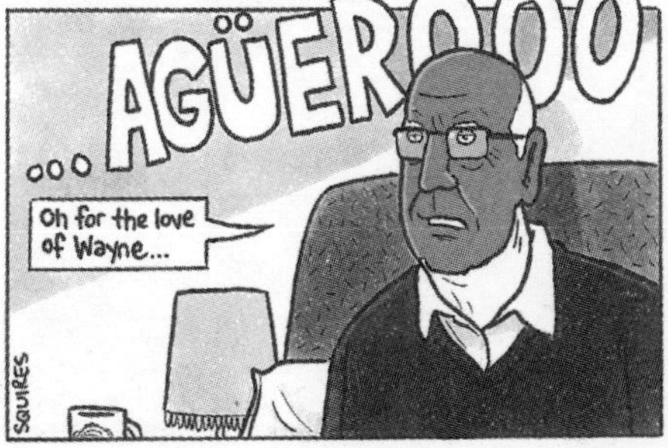
...AGÜEROOOO
Oh for the love of Wayne...
SQUIRES

ANOTHER TITLE FOLLOWED IN 2014, LAYING THE FOUNDATIONS FOR THE NEXT STAGE OF THE CITY FOOTBALL GROUP'S PLAN FOR GLOBAL DOMINATION, WHICH APPARENTLY INVOLVES THE FORCEFUL ACQUISITION OF ALL THE FULL-BACKS.

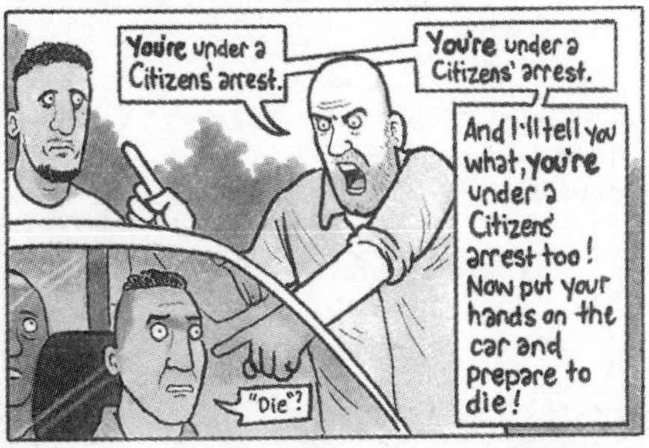
You're under a Citizens' arrest.
You're under a Citizens' arrest.
And I'll tell you what, you're under a Citizens' arrest too! Now put your hands on the car and prepare to die!
"Die"?

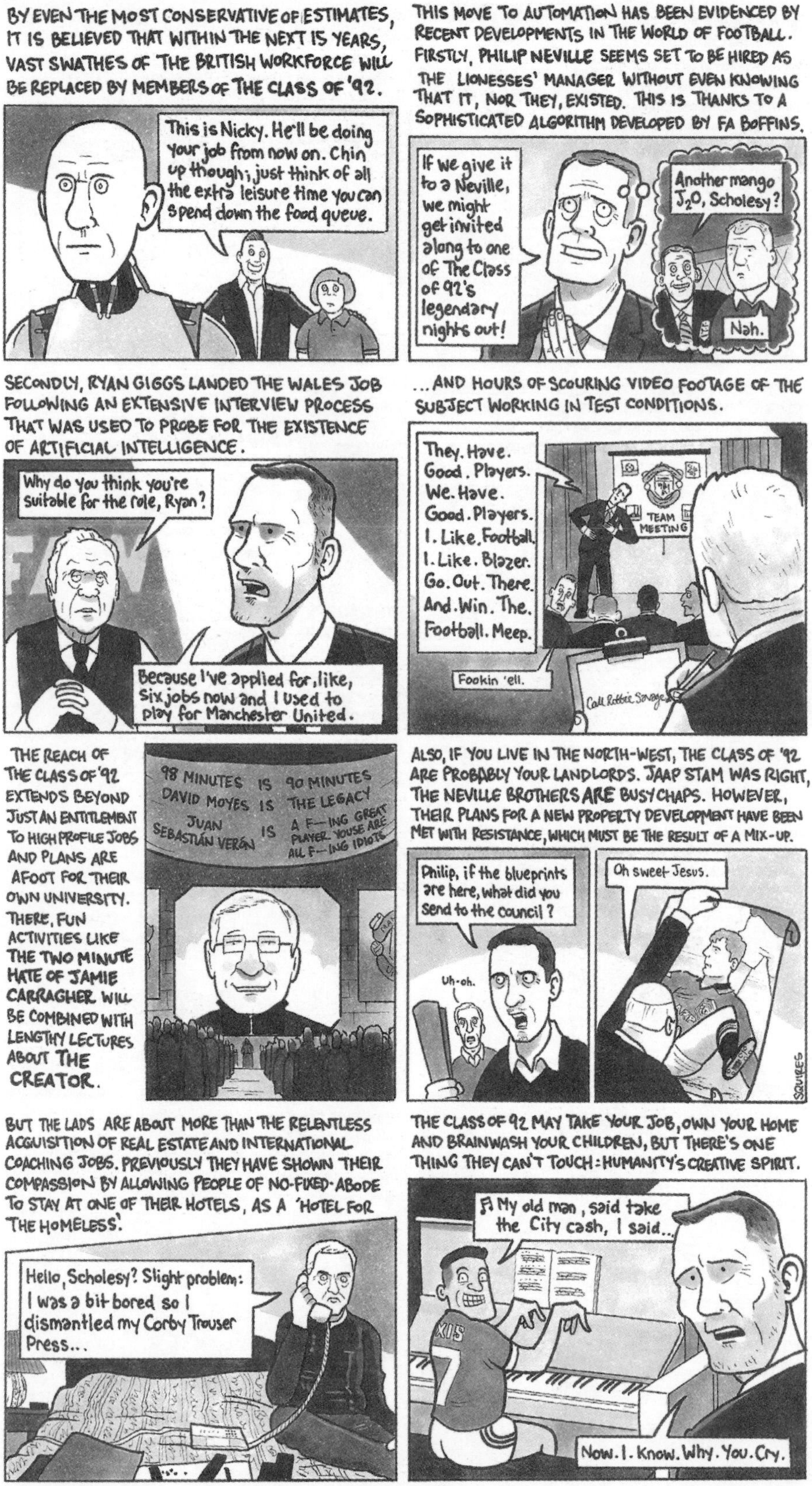

BY EVEN THE MOST CONSERVATIVE OF ESTIMATES, IT IS BELIEVED THAT WITHIN THE NEXT 15 YEARS, VAST SWATHES OF THE BRITISH WORKFORCE WILL BE REPLACED BY MEMBERS OF THE CLASS OF '92.
This is Nicky. He'll be doing your job from now on. Chin up though; just think of all the extra leisure time you can spend down the food queue.
THIS MOVE TO AUTOMATION HAS BEEN EVIDENCED BY RECENT DEVELOPMENTS IN THE WORLD OF FOOTBALL. FIRSTLY, PHILIP NEVILLE SEEMS SET TO BE HIRED AS THE LIONESSES' MANAGER WITHOUT EVEN KNOWING THAT IT, NOR THEY, EXISTED. THIS IS THANKS TO A SOPHISTICATED ALGORITHM DEVELOPED BY FA BOFFINS.
If we give it to a Neville, we might get invited along to one of The Class of 92's legendary nights out!
Another mango J2O, Scholesy?
Nah.
SECONDLY, RYAN GIGGS LANDED THE WALES JOB FOLLOWING AN EXTENSIVE INTERVIEW PROCESS THAT WAS USED TO PROBE FOR THE EXISTENCE OF ARTIFICIAL INTELLIGENCE.
Why do you think you're suitable for the role, Ryan?
Because I've applied for, like, six jobs now and I used to play for Manchester United.
...AND HOURS OF SCOURING VIDEO FOOTAGE OF THE SUBJECT WORKING IN TEST CONDITIONS.
They. Have. Good. Players. We. Have. Good. Players. I. Like. Football. I. Like. Blazer. Go. Out. There. And. Win. The. Football. Meep.
TEAM MEETING
Fookin 'ell.
Call Robbie Savage
THE REACH OF THE CLASS OF '92 EXTENDS BEYOND JUST AN ENTITLEMENT TO HIGH PROFILE JOBS AND PLANS ARE AFOOT FOR THEIR OWN UNIVERSITY. THERE, FUN ACTIVITIES LIKE THE TWO MINUTE HATE OF JAMIE CARRAGHER WILL BE COMBINED WITH LENGTHY LECTURES ABOUT THE CREATOR.
98 MINUTES IS 90 MINUTES
DAVID MOYES IS THE LEGACY
JUAN SEBASTIÁN VERÓN IS A F— ING GREAT PLAYER. YOUSE ARE ALL F— ING IDIOTS
ALSO, IF YOU LIVE IN THE NORTH-WEST, THE CLASS OF '92 ARE PROBABLY YOUR LANDLORDS. JAAP STAM WAS RIGHT, THE NEVILLE BROTHERS ARE BUSY CHAPS. HOWEVER, THEIR PLANS FOR A NEW PROPERTY DEVELOPMENT HAVE BEEN MET WITH RESISTANCE, WHICH MUST BE THE RESULT OF A MIX-UP.
Philip, if the blueprints are here, what did you send to the council?
Uh-oh.
Oh sweet Jesus.
SQUIRES
BUT THE LADS ARE ABOUT MORE THAN THE RELENTLESS ACQUISITION OF REAL ESTATE AND INTERNATIONAL COACHING JOBS. PREVIOUSLY THEY HAVE SHOWN THEIR COMPASSION BY ALLOWING PEOPLE OF NO-FIXED-ABODE TO STAY AT ONE OF THEIR HOTELS, AS A 'HOTEL FOR THE HOMELESS'.
Hello, Scholesy? Slight problem: I was a bit bored so I dismantled my Corby Trouser Press...
THE CLASS OF 92 MAY TAKE YOUR JOB, OWN YOUR HOME AND BRAINWASH YOUR CHILDREN, BUT THERE'S ONE THING THEY CAN'T TOUCH: HUMANITY'S CREATIVE SPIRIT.
♫ My old man, said take the City cash, I said...
Now. I. Know. Why. You. Cry.

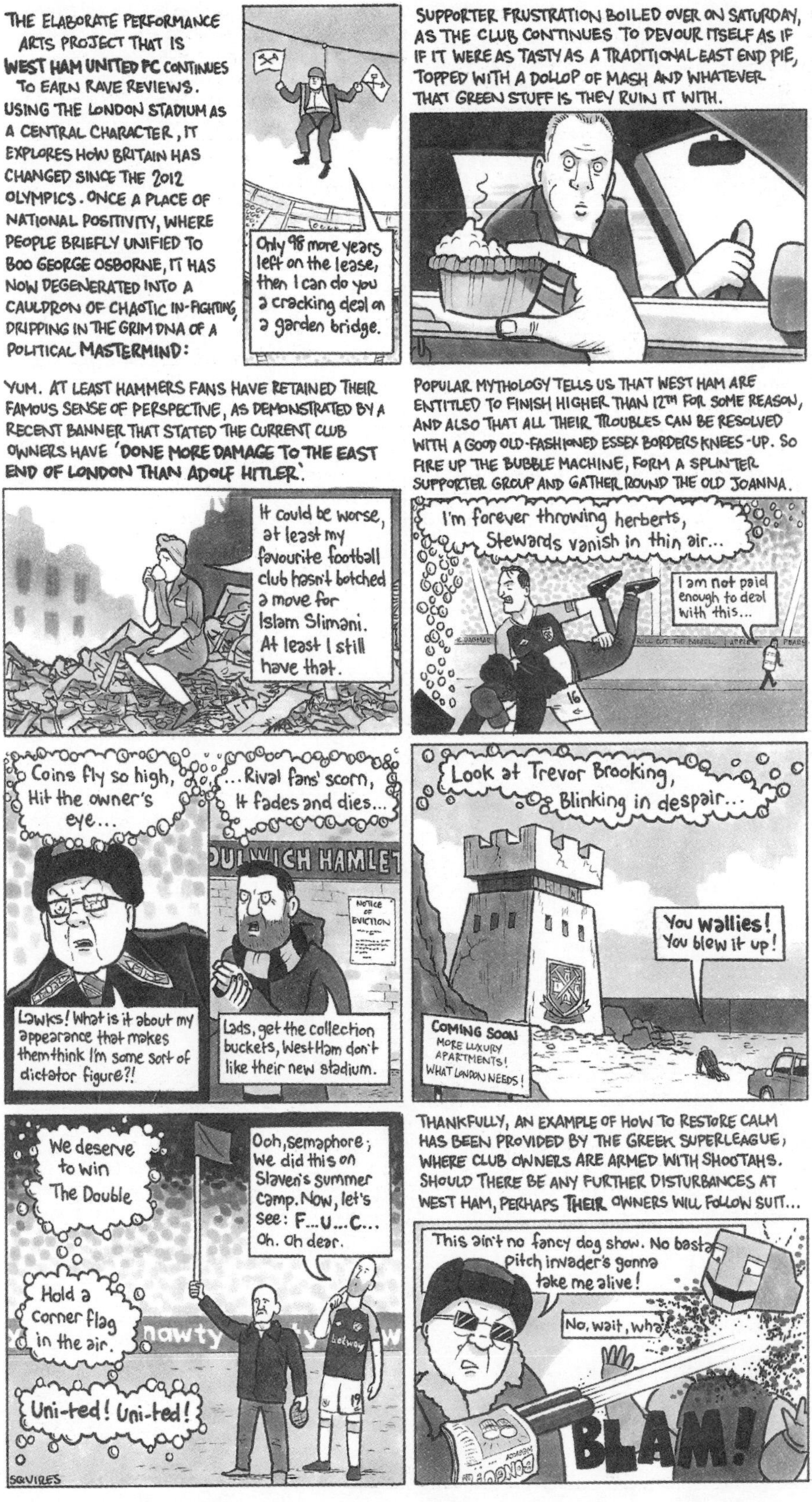
THE ELABORATE PERFORMANCE ARTS PROJECT THAT IS WEST HAM UNITED FC CONTINUES TO EARN RAVE REVIEWS. USING THE LONDON STADIUM AS A CENTRAL CHARACTER, IT EXPLORES HOW BRITAIN HAS CHANGED SINCE THE 2012 OLYMPICS. ONCE A PLACE OF NATIONAL POSITIVITY, WHERE PEOPLE BRIEFLY UNIFIED TO BOO GEORGE OSBORNE, IT HAS NOW DEGENERATED INTO A CAULDRON OF CHAOTIC IN-FIGHTING, DRIPPING IN THE GRIM DNA OF A POLITICAL MASTERMIND:
Only 98 more years left on the lease, then I can do you a cracking deal on a garden bridge.
SUPPORTER FRUSTRATION BOILED OVER ON SATURDAY, AS THE CLUB CONTINUES TO DEVOUR ITSELF AS IF IF IT WERE AS TASTY AS A TRADITIONAL EAST END PIE, TOPPED WITH A DOLLOP OF MASH AND WHATEVER THAT GREEN STUFF IS THEY RUIN IT WITH.
YUM. AT LEAST HAMMERS FANS HAVE RETAINED THEIR FAMOUS SENSE OF PERSPECTIVE, AS DEMONSTRATED BY A RECENT BANNER THAT STATED THE CURRENT CLUB OWNERS HAVE 'DONE MORE DAMAGE TO THE EAST END OF LONDON THAN ADOLF HITLER'.
It could be worse, at least my favourite football club hasn't botched a move for Islam Slimani. At least I still have that.
POPULAR MYTHOLOGY TELLS US THAT WEST HAM ARE ENTITLED TO FINISH HIGHER THAN 12TH FOR SOME REASON, AND ALSO THAT ALL THEIR TROUBLES CAN BE RESOLVED WITH A GOOD OLD-FASHIONED ESSEX BORDERS KNEES-UP. SO FIRE UP THE BUBBLE MACHINE, FORM A SPLINTER SUPPORTER GROUP AND GATHER ROUND THE OLD JOANNA.
I'm forever throwing herberts, Stewards vanish in thin air...
I am not paid enough to deal with this...
ROLL OUT THE BARREL
16
Coins fly so high, Hit the owner's eye...
...Rival fans' scorn, It fades and dies...
DULWICH HAMLET
NOTICE OF EVICTION
Lawks! What is it about my appearance that makes them think I'm some sort of dictator figure?!
Lads, get the collection buckets, West Ham don't like their new stadium.
Look at Trevor Brooking, Blinking in despair...
You wallies! You blew it up!
COMING SOON MORE LUXURY APARTMENTS! WHAT LONDON NEEDS!
We deserve to win The Double
Hold a corner flag in the air.
Uni-ted! Uni-ted!
Ooh, semaphore; We did this on Slaven's summer camp. Now, let's see: F...U...C... Oh. Oh dear.
betway
19
THANKFULLY, AN EXAMPLE OF HOW TO RESTORE CALM HAS BEEN PROVIDED BY THE GREEK SUPERLEAGUE, WHERE CLUB OWNERS ARE ARMED WITH SHOOTAHS. SHOULD THERE BE ANY FURTHER DISTURBANCES AT WEST HAM, PERHAPS THEIR OWNERS WILL FOLLOW SUIT...
This ain't no fancy dog show. No basta pitch invader's gonna take me alive!
No, wait, wha
BLAM!
SQUIRES

COMPLETISTS' CORNER

When you work from home, it is important to maintain a routine: breakfast at seven, lunch at twelve, wash at least twice a week, try to leave the house on a monthly basis, remembering to put some trousers on first, which is easier in winter, when you are already wearing all of your clothes to save on energy bills.

Since 2015, I have added to my Thursday-morning routine the duty of reading the baffled, hurt and angry posts of people who have clicked on a link to one of my cartoons, only to discover it is about Australia's Hyundai A-League – for some readers, a niche reference too far.

When I moved to Australia in 2009, one of the first things I did was to seek out the local football scene. While other migrants will have headed for the iconic Sydney Harbour Bridge, booked a trip to Uluru or headed north to swim with the deadly jellyfish on the north Queensland coast, it was the Moore Park stadium for me, and an uninspiring 1–0 victory for Sydney FC against Adelaide United, in a contest of questionable quality. I was home.

Despite its impressive participation rates, Australia isn't a football country. It is an isolated and relatively young nation, and as such often seeks the validation and attention of the outside world. José Mourinho predicting Australia would get out of their World Cup group made the national news here in 2018. International sporting defeats are quickly brushed over and receive little media attention. The most popular sports are the ones that hardly anyone else plays (Aussie rules and rugby league), meaning the nation's self-confidence cannot be dented.

A sneering attitude to football persists, a bias founded in barely veiled xenophobia. For many, football is still a game played by the descendants of post-war immigrants from southern and central Europe. Many mainstream news outlets report minor crowd disturbances as if they were mass riots, while laughing off crowd trouble in other sports as rowdy horseplay. You quickly grow tired of conversations with football sceptics who tell you how boring the sport is on account of its lack of goals, and how all the players are wimps who dive and cry and cheat (the Australian cricket team ball-tampering scandal of 2018 was a moment of divine smugness for football fans). I've only been here a decade and rarely go outside (have you *been* out there?), and even I get ground down by it.

However, this is mostly offset by the fact that being a football supporter in Australia is otherwise an overwhelmingly positive experience. The community is large, passionate and diverse, has progressive attitudes for the most part, and the women's game is respected and valued. People take pride in the achievements of the Matildas and Socceroos on the international stage, aware that they are often punching above their weight.

The A-League is a relatively new competition, only coming into being after a restructuring of the sport in 2005. It owes a debt to the clubs across the country who were vital to the development of the game in Australia, providing a focal point for communities and a place of belonging for European migrants whose foreign names and accents made them a target for racist bullies. Football in Australia is welcoming, even to sarcastic Brits making jokes about the thing they hold most dear on a weekly basis.

The big matches, especially the derbies between Sydney FC and Western Sydney Wanderers, attract large, enthusiastic crowds that can create an atmosphere as intense as anything I ever experienced in England. I've yet to see any serious crowd trouble, and away from the areas where the ultras bounce and sing, fans of opposing teams are able to sit together in relative harmony. This was something of a culture shock to me at first. I remember seeing a Melbourne Victory fan stand up within a section of Sydney fans to openly celebrate a goal, mocking those sat around him. I sank in my seat, fully expecting him to be murdered before my eyes, but everyone just ignored him and he eventually sat down sheepishly.

However, the fear of the football fan endures. Fans in Melbourne are often bewildered to be confronted by a battalion of riot police as they arrive for matches, and Sydney supporters are routinely scanned with metal detectors.[8] Attitudes towards football supporters were encapsulated by the Police Association NSW president Scott Weber in 2015, when he likened Western Sydney Wanderers fans to 'grubs'. This is the basis for the first cartoon in the following collection.

The 'Code Wars' cartoon probably needs a little more explanation for context. It was drawn on the week *The Force Awakens* was released and in the wake of an article in Sydney's Murdoch tabloid, the *Daily Telegraph*, which publicly outed a number of football supporters who, it claimed, had been ignoring stadium bans. The story was accompanied by an opinion piece that pointed the finger of blame at the Football Federation Australia for being soft on 'football louts'. There followed a predictable deluge of knee-jerk comments from the usual football sceptics.

As for the characters in the cartoon, Darth Vader is Alan Jones, a right-wing shock-jock whose broadcasting career somehow wasn't impeded by being found guilty by a tribunal of inciting racial hatred in the lead-up to the Cronulla race riot of 2005. Unlike Darth, it's unlikely that before Jones dies he'll reveal himself as not being a shit.

The Emperor is Murdoch and the Imperial Officer, Rebecca

8 I once saw a fan take a yoga mat into a ground, which is possibly the most Sydney thing in recorded history.

Wilson – the person who wrote the inflammatory article about football fans. Obi-Wan is Craig Foster, the former player turned pundit; Yoda is Frank Lowy, whose cash injection funded the restructuring of Australian football. The musicians from the Mos Eisley Cantina are Central Coast Mariners fans (they have a brass band that plays to welcome the team onto the pitch). Han Solo and Admiral Ackbar are commentator Simon Hill and Mark Bosnich respectively, who both spoke out in defence of fans. Chewbacca is Nutmeg, the mascot from the 2015 Asian Cup, hosted and won by Australia. Jar Jar Binks is Damien De Bohun, the much maligned former head of the A-League, and C-3PO and R2-D2 are played by David Gallop and Steven Lowy, Football Federation Australia's head honchos. The guy in the middle is a generic football fan, holding aloft a flare – the worst crime a person can commit in Australia.

The next cartoon celebrates that most glorious of football sights: the disallowed goal. On this occasion, Western Sydney Wanderers' striker Kerem Bulut raced off to leap into the joyous arms of supporters for a prolonged celebration, before realising with perfect comedy timing that his goal against Melbourne City had been chalked off for offside.

Sydney FC won the league by a mile in 2017, but were still forced to take part in a series of play-offs at the end of the season to decide who the *real* champions were. It's a curiosity of Australian sport, and one that outsiders find baffling. The third cartoon imagines the scene where Sydney's manager Graham Arnold explains the situation to his Brazilian striker, Bobô. Arnold makes another appearance in the next cartoon, which was basically an excuse to draw Arsène Wenger's ankle-length jeans. The section concludes with a look at the press conference when veteran grump Bert van Marwijk was appointed as the coach of Australia's national team, a replacement for the popular Ange Postecoglou, who'd resigned to focus on sniping from the sidelines, his reputation intact.

Look, if you decide to skip this bit, I'll never know.

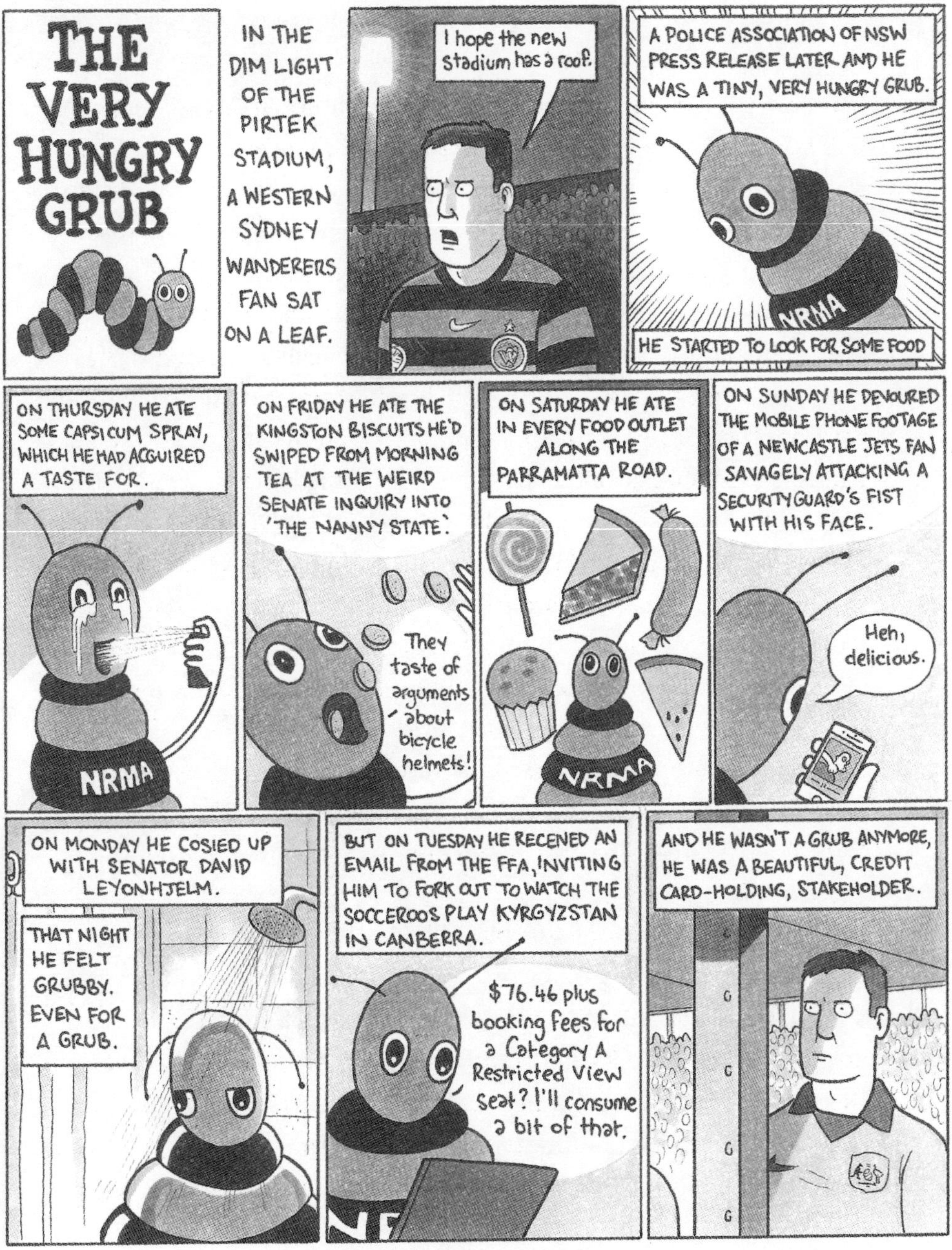
THE VERY HUNGRY GRUB
IN THE DIM LIGHT OF THE PIRTEK STADIUM, A WESTERN SYDNEY WANDERERS FAN SAT ON A LEAF.
I hope the new stadium has a roof.
A POLICE ASSOCIATION OF NSW PRESS RELEASE LATER AND HE WAS A TINY, VERY HUNGRY GRUB.
NRMA
HE STARTED TO LOOK FOR SOME FOOD
ON THURSDAY HE ATE SOME CAPSICUM SPRAY, WHICH HE HAD ACQUIRED A TASTE FOR.
NRMA
ON FRIDAY HE ATE THE KINGSTON BISCUITS HE'D SWIPED FROM MORNING TEA AT THE WEIRD SENATE INQUIRY INTO 'THE NANNY STATE'.
They taste of arguments about bicycle helmets!
ON SATURDAY HE ATE IN EVERY FOOD OUTLET ALONG THE PARRAMATTA ROAD.
NRMA
ON SUNDAY HE DEVOURED THE MOBILE PHONE FOOTAGE OF A NEWCASTLE JETS FAN SAVAGELY ATTACKING A SECURITY GUARD'S FIST WITH HIS FACE.
Heh, delicious.
ON MONDAY HE COSIED UP WITH SENATOR DAVID LEYONHJELM.
THAT NIGHT HE FELT GRUBBY. EVEN FOR A GRUB.
BUT ON TUESDAY HE RECEIVED AN EMAIL FROM THE FFA, INVITING HIM TO FORK OUT TO WATCH THE SOCCEROOS PLAY KYRGYZSTAN IN CANBERRA.
$76.46 plus booking fees for a Category A Restricted View seat? I'll consume a bit of that.
AND HE WASN'T A GRUB ANYMORE, HE WAS A BEAUTIFUL, CREDIT CARD-HOLDING, STAKEHOLDER.

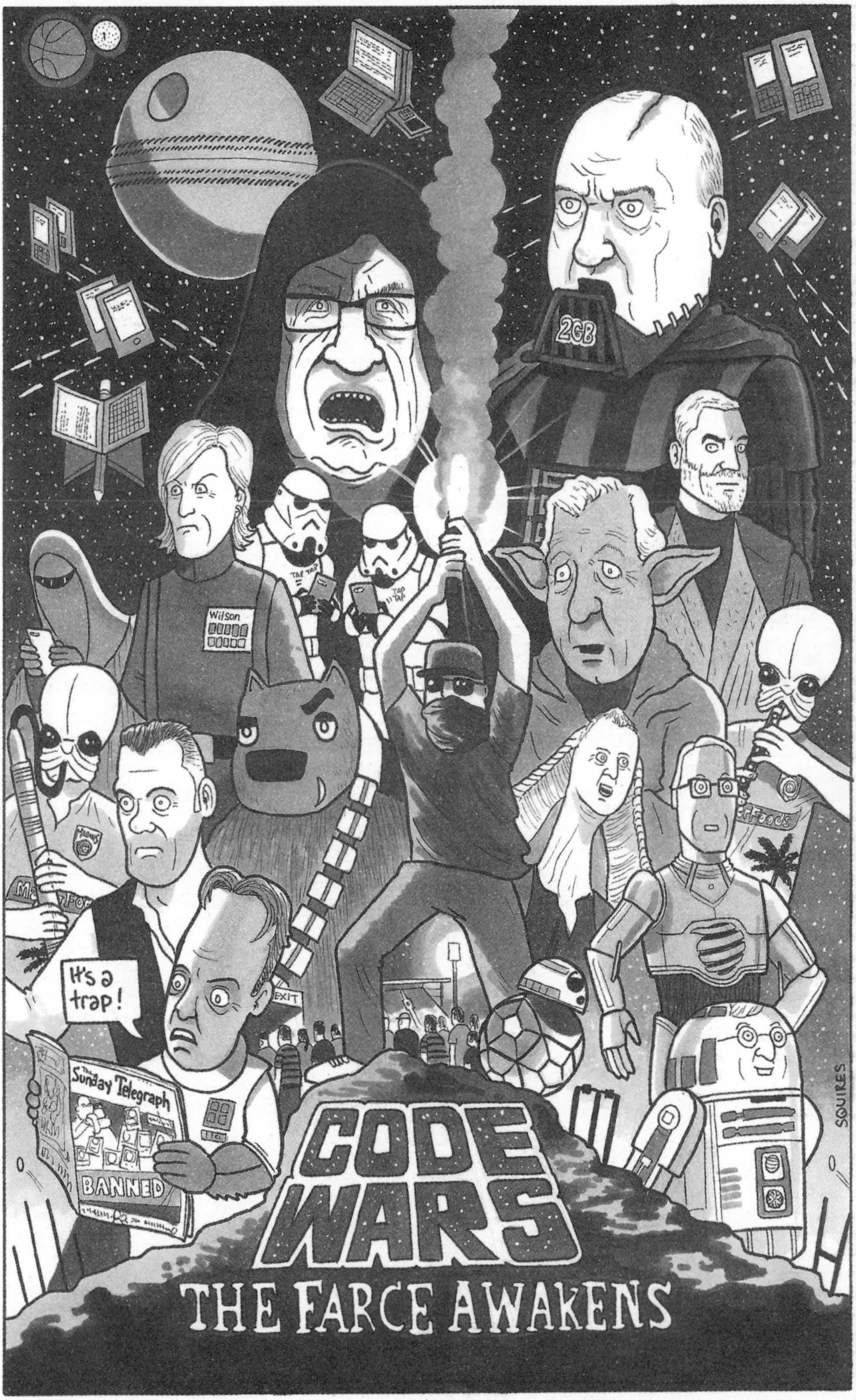
2GB
Wilson
TAP TAP
It's a trap!
EXIT
Sunday Telegraph
BANNED
CODE WARS
THE FARCE AWAKENS
SQUIRES

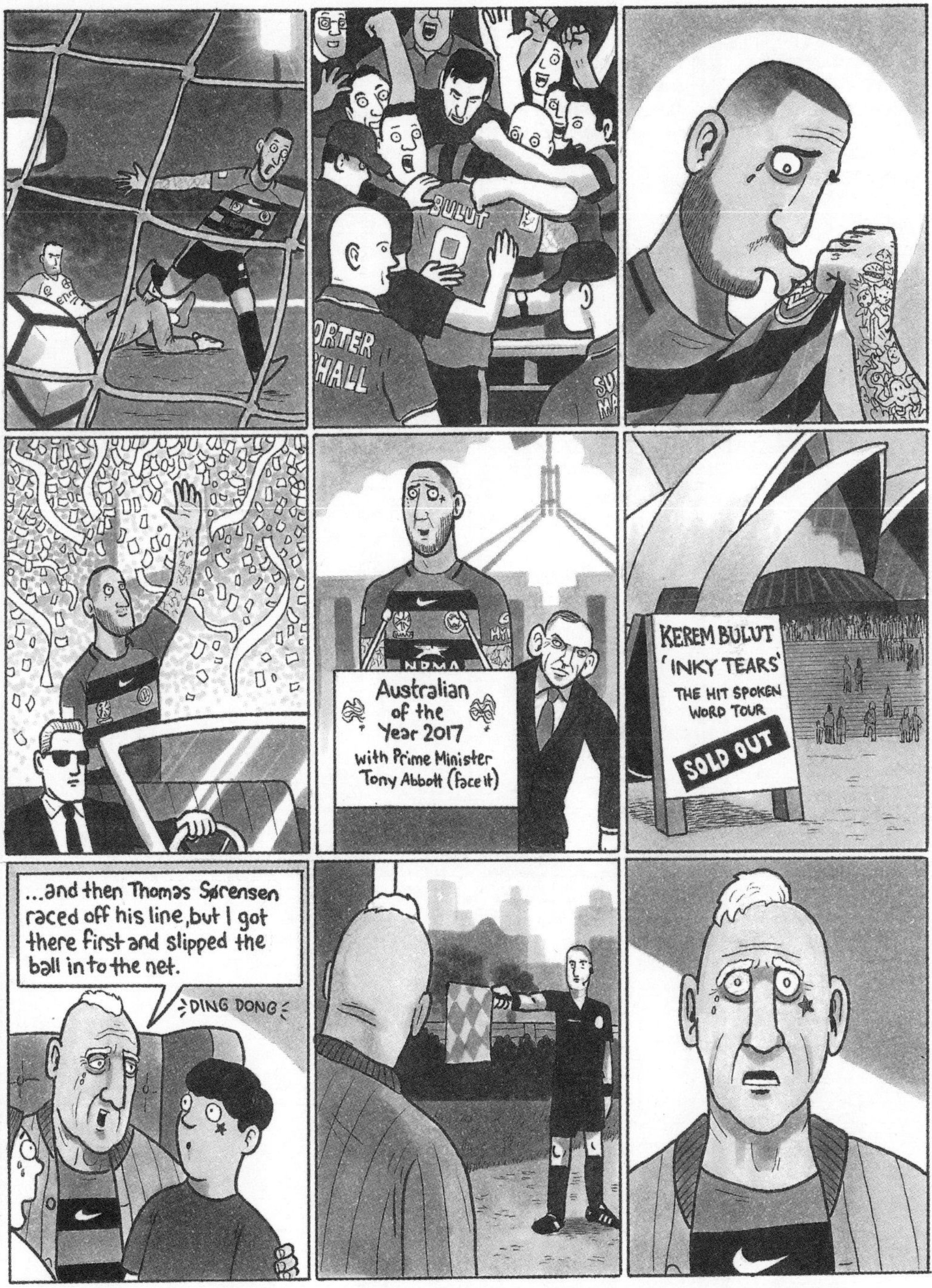
BULUT
Australian of the Year 2017
with Prime Minister Tony Abbott (face it)
KEREM BULUT
'INKY TEARS'
THE HIT SPOKEN WORD TOUR
SOLD OUT
...and then Thomas Sørensen raced off his line, but I got there first and slipped the ball in to the net.
DING DONG

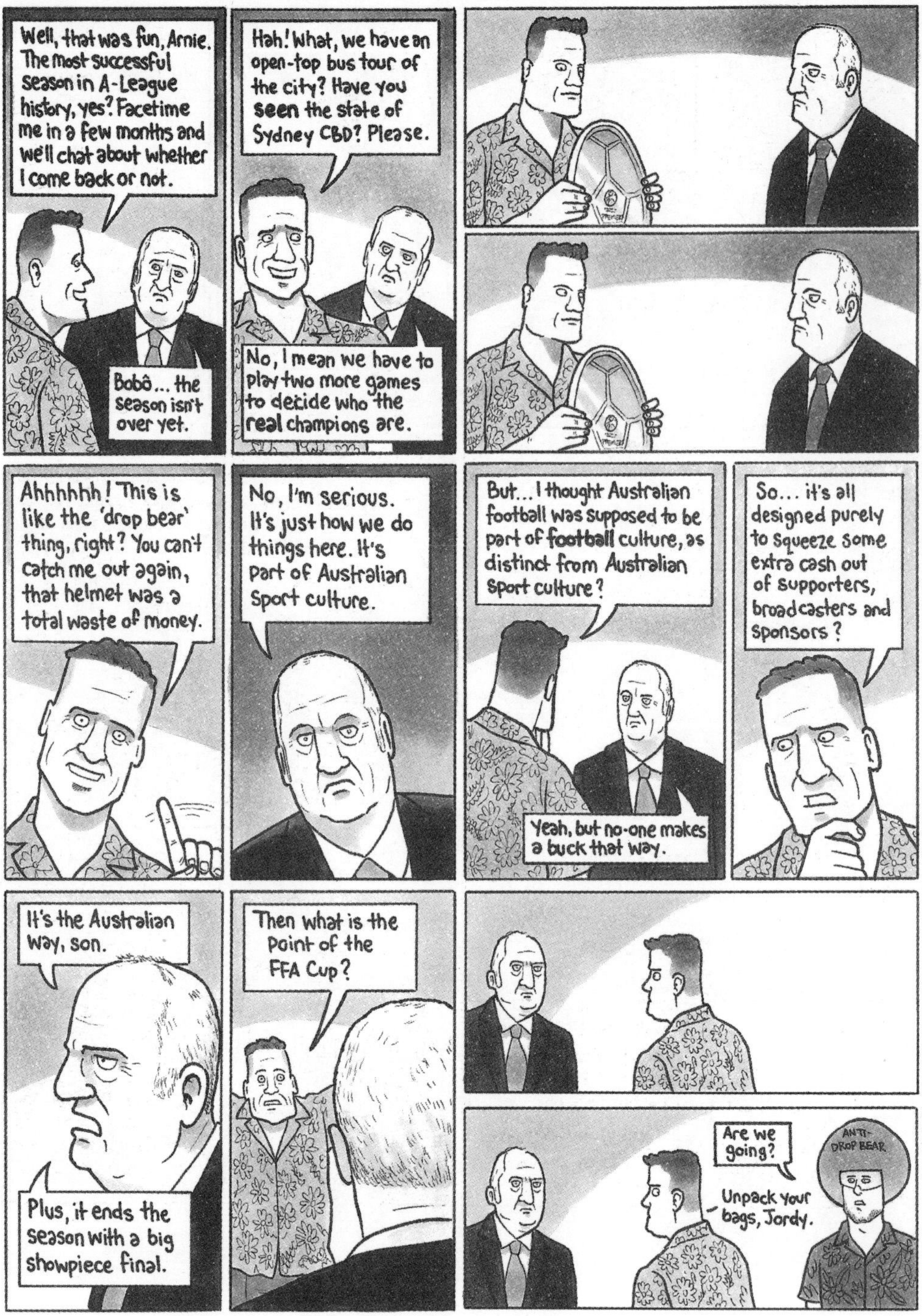
Well, that was fun, Arnie. The most successful season in A-League history, yes? Facetime me in a few months and we'll chat about whether I come back or not.
Bobô... the season isn't over yet.
Hah! What, we have an open-top bus tour of the city? Have you **seen** the state of Sydney CBD? Please.
No, I mean we have to play two more games to decide who the **real** champions are.
Ahhhhhh! This is like the 'drop bear' thing, right? You can't catch me out again, that helmet was a total waste of money.
No, I'm serious. It's just how we do things here. It's part of Australian Sport culture.
But... I thought Australian football was supposed to be part of **football** culture, as distinct from Australian sport culture?
Yeah, but no-one makes a buck that way.
So... it's all designed purely to squeeze some extra cash out of supporters, broadcasters and sponsors?
It's the Australian way, son.
Plus, it ends the season with a big showpiece final.
Then what is the point of the FFA Cup?
Are we going?
ANTI-DROP BEAR
Unpack your bags, Jordy.

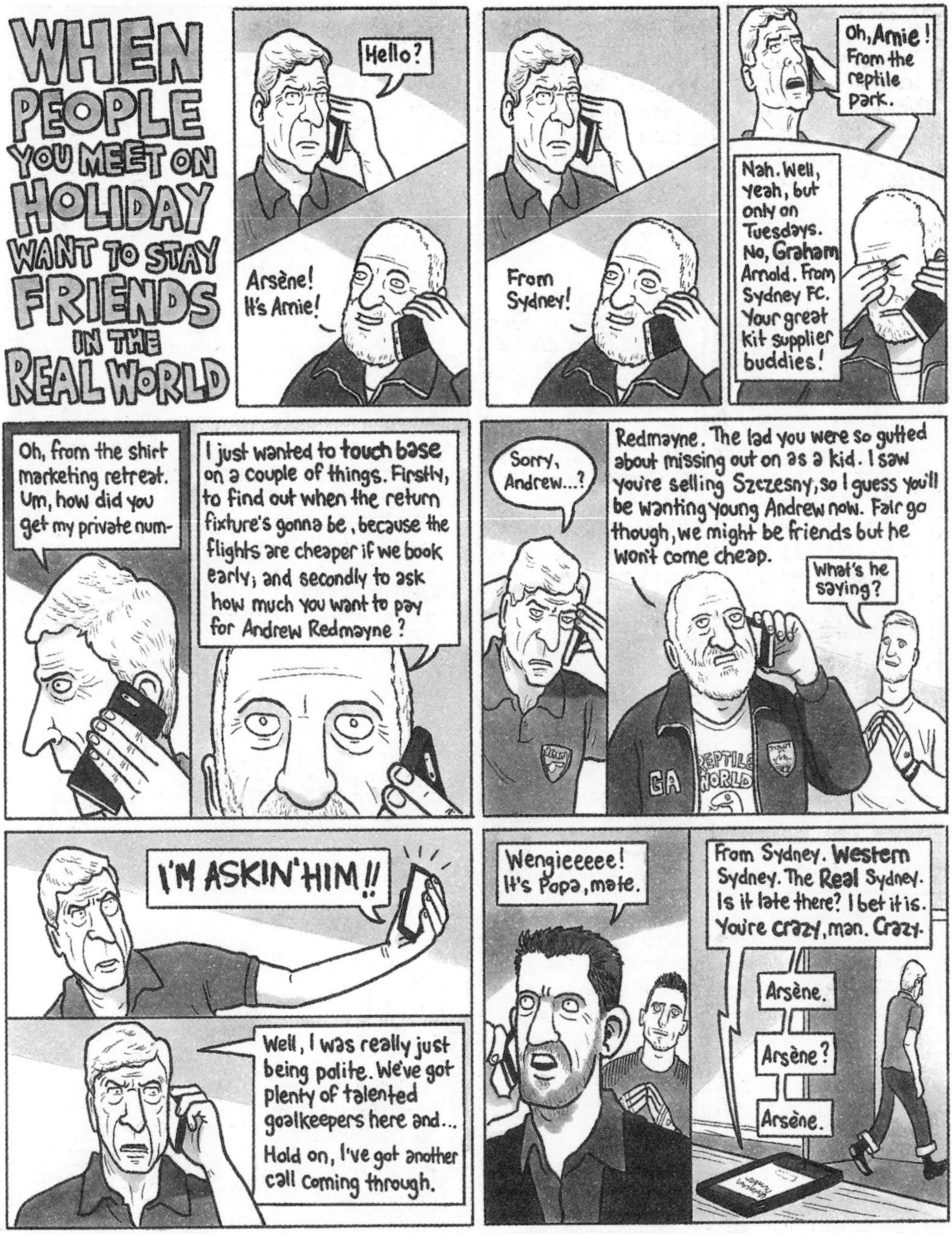
WHEN PEOPLE YOU MEET ON HOLIDAY WANT TO STAY FRIENDS IN THE REAL WORLD
Hello?
Arsène! It's Arnie!
From Sydney!
Oh, Arnie! From the reptile park.
Nah. Well, yeah, but only on Tuesdays. No, Graham Arnold. From Sydney FC. Your great kit supplier buddies!
Oh, from the shirt marketing retreat. Um, how did you get my private num-
I just wanted to touch base on a couple of things. Firstly, to find out when the return fixture's gonna be, because the flights are cheaper if we book early; and secondly to ask how much you want to pay for Andrew Redmayne?
Sorry, Andrew...?
Redmayne. The lad you were so gutted about missing out on as a kid. I saw you're selling Szczesny, so I guess you'll be wanting young Andrew now. Fair go though, we might be friends but he won't come cheap.
What's he saying?
GA
REPTILE WORLD
I'M ASKIN' HIM!!
Well, I was really just being polite. We've got plenty of talented goalkeepers here and...
Hold on, I've got another call coming through.
Wengieeeee! It's Popa, mate.
From Sydney. Western Sydney. The Real Sydney. Is it late there? I bet it is. You're crazy, man. Crazy.
Arsène.
Arsène?
Arsène.

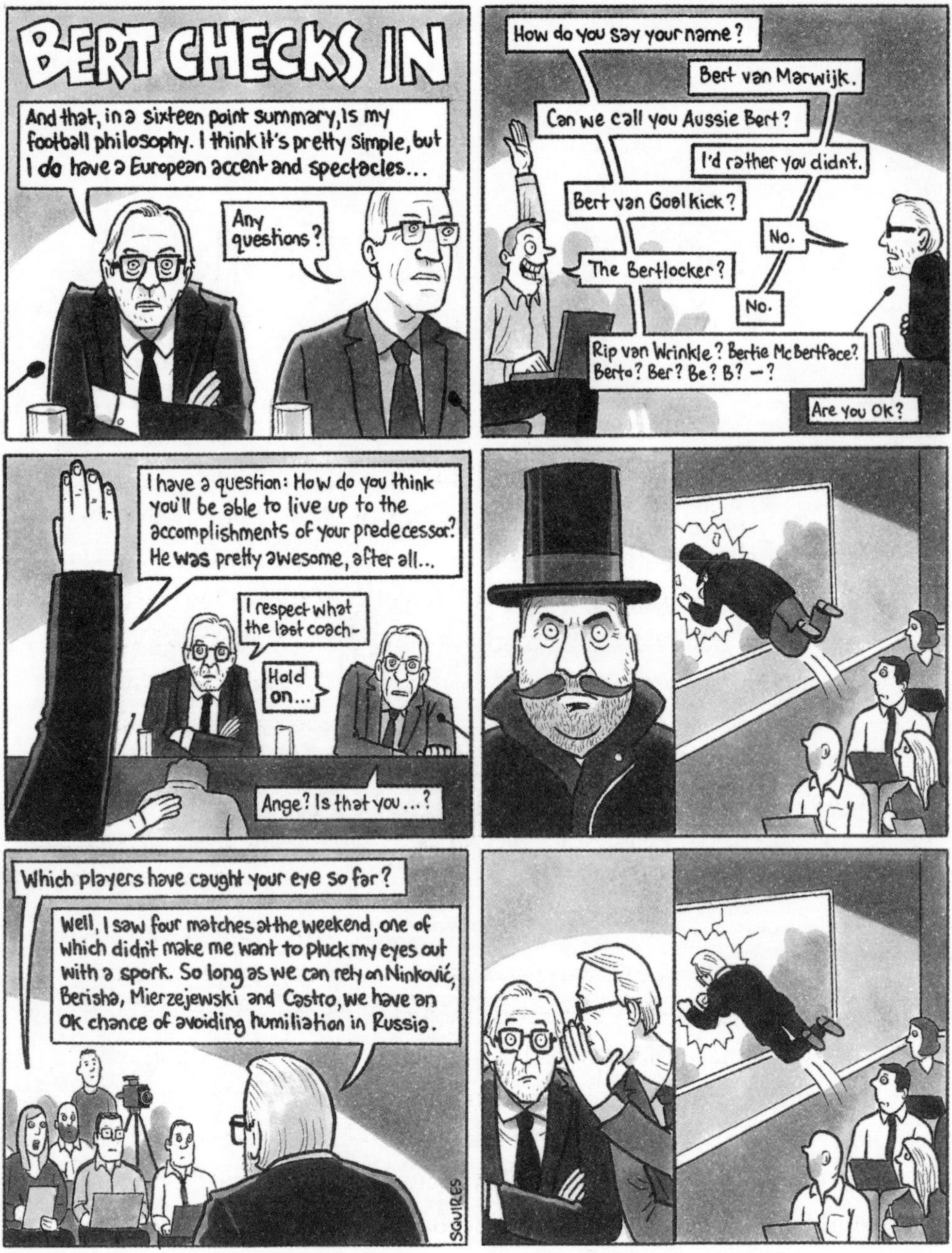

BERT CHECKS IN
And that, in a sixteen point summary, is my football philosophy. I think it's pretty simple, but I *do* have a European accent and spectacles...
Any questions?
How do you say your name?
Bert van Marwijk.
Can we call you Aussie Bert?
I'd rather you didn't.
Bert van Goal Kick?
No.
The Bertlocker?
No.
Rip van Wrinkle? Bertie McBertface? Berto? Ber? Be? B? – ?
Are you OK?
I have a question: How do you think you'll be able to live up to the accomplishments of your predecessor? He was pretty awesome, after all...
I respect what the last coach-
Hold on...
Ange? Is that you...?
Which players have caught your eye so far?
Well, I saw four matches at the weekend, one of which didn't make me want to pluck my eyes out with a spork. So long as we can rely on Ninković, Berisha, Mierzejewski and Castro, we have an OK chance of avoiding humiliation in Russia.
SQUIRES

NO FIGHTING IN THE VAR ROOM!

Russia 2018

When the curiously puffy face of Vladimir Putin delivered a sermon to a rapturous home crowd before the first game of Russia 2018, it's fair to say that enthusiasm was muted for the twenty-first edition of the World Cup. After all, a global audience had just sat through an opening ceremony that comprised a Robbie Williams megamix, and now here was one of the world's other most notorious bastards. Russia then strolled to a 5–0 victory against Saudi Arabia, each goal met with a camera cutaway to Putin affecting affability with Crown Prince Mohammad bin Salman, with FIFA president Gianni Infantino a flaccid rose sandwiched between two thorny despots.

However, despite concerns that the tournament would be marred by the violence witnessed at the European Championships two years earlier and the racist incidents frequently reported in Russian domestic football, visitors soon realised that Russia was a beautiful country full of warm and friendly people. Even the notoriously draconian security forces seemed as chilled out as bobbies dancing at the Notting Hill Carnival, a tolerant attitude that would no doubt continue once the gaze of the world's media had switched elsewhere.

On the pitch, it was the maddest tournament of recent years, not least because England exceeded all expectations by reaching the semi-finals. They might even have made it further had Croatia run out of steam, as we were all promised they would. Instead, Luka

Modrić took control of the midfield and exposed England's age-old deficiencies.

However, there was something bigger at play: the cultural change that manager Gareth Southgate had engineered helped to create a positive atmosphere around the squad and improved relationships with the public and press. No longer was it acceptable to say, for example, that Jordan Henderson was less capable of hitting his intended target than a short-circuiting tennis-ball machine. No, for this was the New England, a beacon of positivity for a divided nation. Obviously, this blame amnesty did not apply to Raheem Sterling, who continued to act as the world's tiniest lightning rod for newspaper columnists and talk-radio callers.

Back home, a heatwave burned the lawns and shoulders of many England fans. They flocked to pubs and fan parks, cooling themselves by queuing at the bar for half an hour and then throwing thirty quid's worth of cooking lager in the air. Some climbed up bus shelters, others invaded furniture shops; many just watched it at home and dared to dream that they really might see England win the World Cup at a tournament without age restrictions. Yeah, the national team were completely reliant on set-pieces and didn't play anyone decent until Croatia, but for a couple of weeks they provided a welcome distraction from Life. They even had the good grace to go out before too many politicians could climb upon the bandwagon (just imagine the state of Farage if they'd won it).

England winning a match on penalties illustrated just how unusual this World Cup was. Even before it had started there was chaos, with Spain rolling back the years by descending into calamity two days before their first match. Coach Julen Lopetegui was fired after it was announced that he would be leaving post-tournament to manage Real Madrid, who never cease to amaze in their ability to not give one solitary eff.

The inexperienced Fernando Hierro stepped into the breach, and under his stewardship Spain didn't stick around for long, but they did play their part in arguably the best match of the tournament, a 3–3 draw with Portugal. It was a game that had everything: a Ronaldo hat-trick, sealed with a last-breath free-kick; a Nacho goal that flew like an arrow into the bottom corner; a terrible goalkeeping error from David de Gea; and a Diego Costa goal that involved him scrapping the entire Portugal defence like the corridor fight scene in *Oldboy*.

The biggest casualty of the group stage were the holders, Germany, who added to the global 1930s revival vibe by going out in the first round for the first time in eighty years. It looked like they had saved themselves with a beautifully worked Toni Kroos free-kick against Sweden, but they somehow conspired to lose their final group game to South Korea and were eliminated. With five minutes left, and the game scoreless, they could yet have salvaged the situation, but Mats Hummels Keeganed a header from close range and Korea hit them with two late, hilarious goals. South Korea's second involved Manuel Neuer being dispossessed in the left-wing position and then having to race back with the blind optimism of a man hoping a bus would stop for him. Never gonna happen, mate, they've got a schedule to stick to.

Notwithstanding Spain and Germany's ignominious exits, it was a tournament dominated by European nations, with the fancied teams from South America failing to progress past the quarter-finals. Lionel Messi was unable to drag Argentina beyond the second round, where they fell to France in an entertaining 4–3 defeat, amid rumours of a dressing-room coup against manager Jorge Sampaoli. The anarchy of their campaign was mirrored by the antics of Diego Maradona in the VIP seats. This was especially the case during Argentina's decisive group win against Nigeria, when Maradona was pictured roaring at the sky, enjoying a nap, wildly flicking the bird to crestfallen opposition fans, and then being attended to by worried-looking medics. He never has been one for holding back his emotions, nor for keeping his powder dry . . .

Not even the excellent Year 10 drama skills of Neymar Jr could prevent Brazil from being knocked out by Belgium. Perhaps they could have gone further in the tournament if they weren't required to accommodate an egomaniac doing The Worm for ninety minutes. Belgium's team of Premier League stars – including the surprisingly effective Nacer Chadli and Marouane Fellaini – went out to eventual champions France, who went through the tournament doing just what they needed to do. Grimly efficient in the group stage, scintillating in flashes against Argentina, defensively disciplined against Uruguay and Belgium, they then did enough in a twenty-minute spell to put Croatia out of reach in the final.

France were also the first team to benefit from VAR, when Antoine Griezmann was awarded a penalty in their opening game against Australia. The sight of referees touching their ear and then trotting over to watch a replay on the pitch-side screen became commonplace in the group stage. For a while, nobody seemed entirely sure what constituted a penalty any more, and many were left questioning whether they understood the laws of the game at all in this anarchic new era.

VAR interventions became less frequent during the knockout stages, as better, more confident referees were less likely to be bullied into reviewing their decisions by mobs of complaining players. It did, however, make a roaring comeback in the final, when referee Néstor Pitana – a former actor with a fine sense of occasion – used video technology to award a penalty to France, deciding that Croatia's Ivan Perišić had deliberately handled the ball, when his arm was behind his back.

The penalty, converted by Griezmann, gave France a 2–1 lead going into half-time, and exhaustion finally caught up with the Croatians, who over the course of the competition had played the equivalent of 846 matches. France added two more after the break, from Pogba and Mbappé, and that was that.

All that was left to do was for Vladimir Putin to hand out the medals. The Moscow skies opened in a torrential downpour, but the French players didn't care a jot, and nor did Vlad, who was the only one with an umbrella.

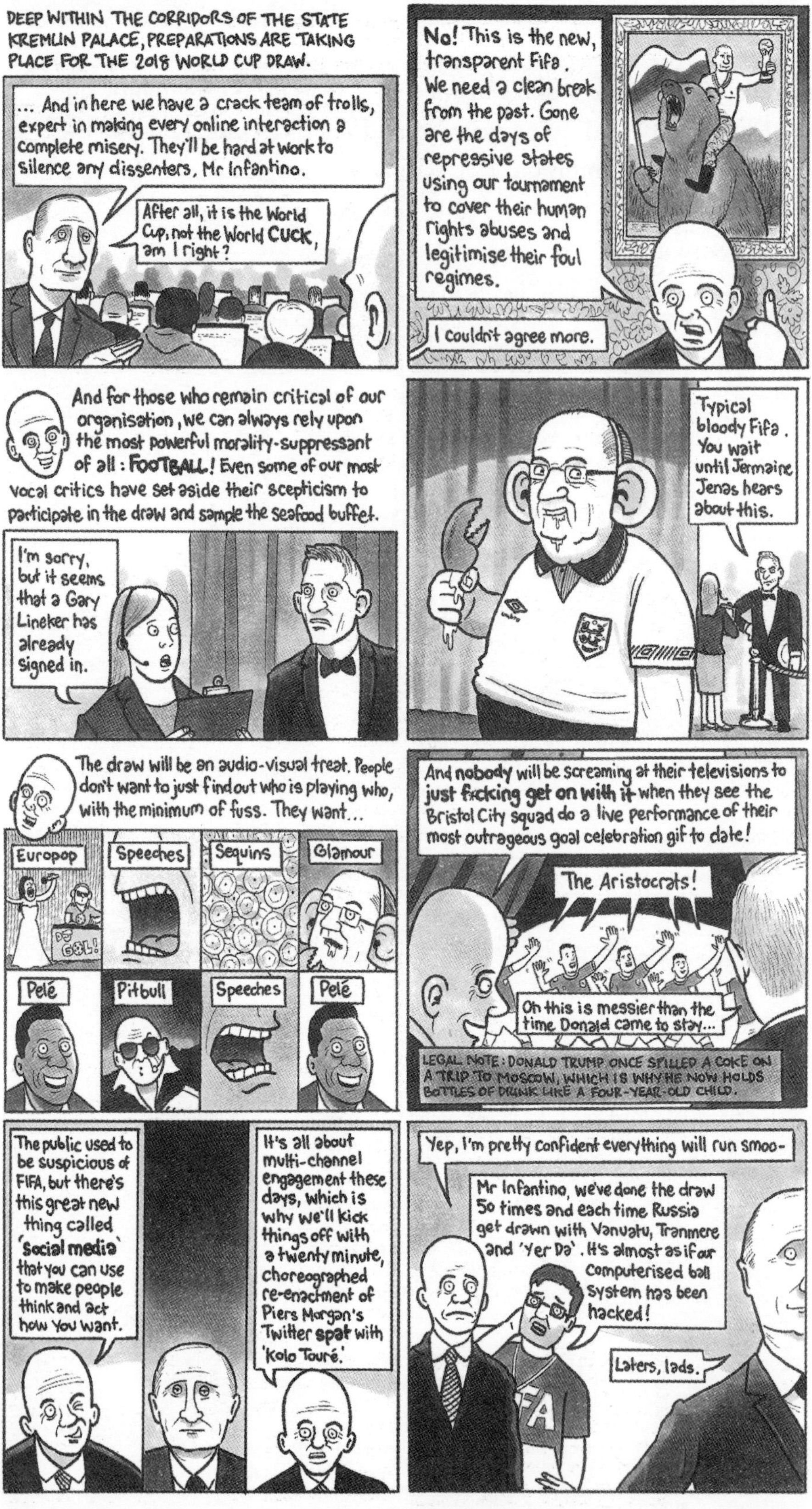
DEEP WITHIN THE CORRIDORS OF THE STATE KREMLIN PALACE, PREPARATIONS ARE TAKING PLACE FOR THE 2018 WORLD CUP DRAW.
... And in here we have a crack team of trolls, expert in making every online interaction a complete misery. They'll be hard at work to silence any dissenters, Mr Infantino.
After all, it is the World Cup, not the World CUCK, am I right?
No! This is the new, transparent Fifa. We need a clean break from the past. Gone are the days of repressive states using our tournament to cover their human rights abuses and legitimise their foul regimes.
I couldn't agree more.
And for those who remain critical of our organisation, we can always rely upon the most powerful morality-suppressant of all: FOOTBALL! Even some of our most vocal critics have set aside their scepticism to participate in the draw and sample the seafood buffet.
I'm sorry, but it seems that a Gary Lineker has already signed in.
Typical bloody Fifa. You wait until Jermaine Jenas hears about this.
The draw will be an audio-visual treat. People don't want to just find out who is playing who, with the minimum of fuss. They want...
Europop
DJ GOL!
Speeches
Sequins
Glamour
Pelé
Pitbull
Speeches
Pelé
And nobody will be screaming at their televisions to just f*cking get on with it when they see the Bristol City squad do a live performance of their most outrageous goal celebration gif to date!
The Aristocrats!
Oh this is messier than the time Donald came to stay...
LEGAL NOTE: DONALD TRUMP ONCE SPILLED A COKE ON A TRIP TO MOSCOW, WHICH IS WHY HE NOW HOLDS BOTTLES OF DRINK LIKE A FOUR-YEAR-OLD CHILD.
The public used to be suspicious of FIFA, but there's this great new thing called 'social media' that you can use to make people think and act how you want.
It's all about multi-channel engagement these days, which is why we'll kick things off with a twenty minute, choreographed re-enactment of Piers Morgan's Twitter spat with 'Kolo Touré.'
Yep, I'm pretty confident everything will run smoo-
Mr Infantino, we've done the draw 50 times and each time Russia get drawn with Vanuatu, Tranmere and 'Yer Da'. It's almost as if our computerised ball system has been hacked!
Laters, lads.

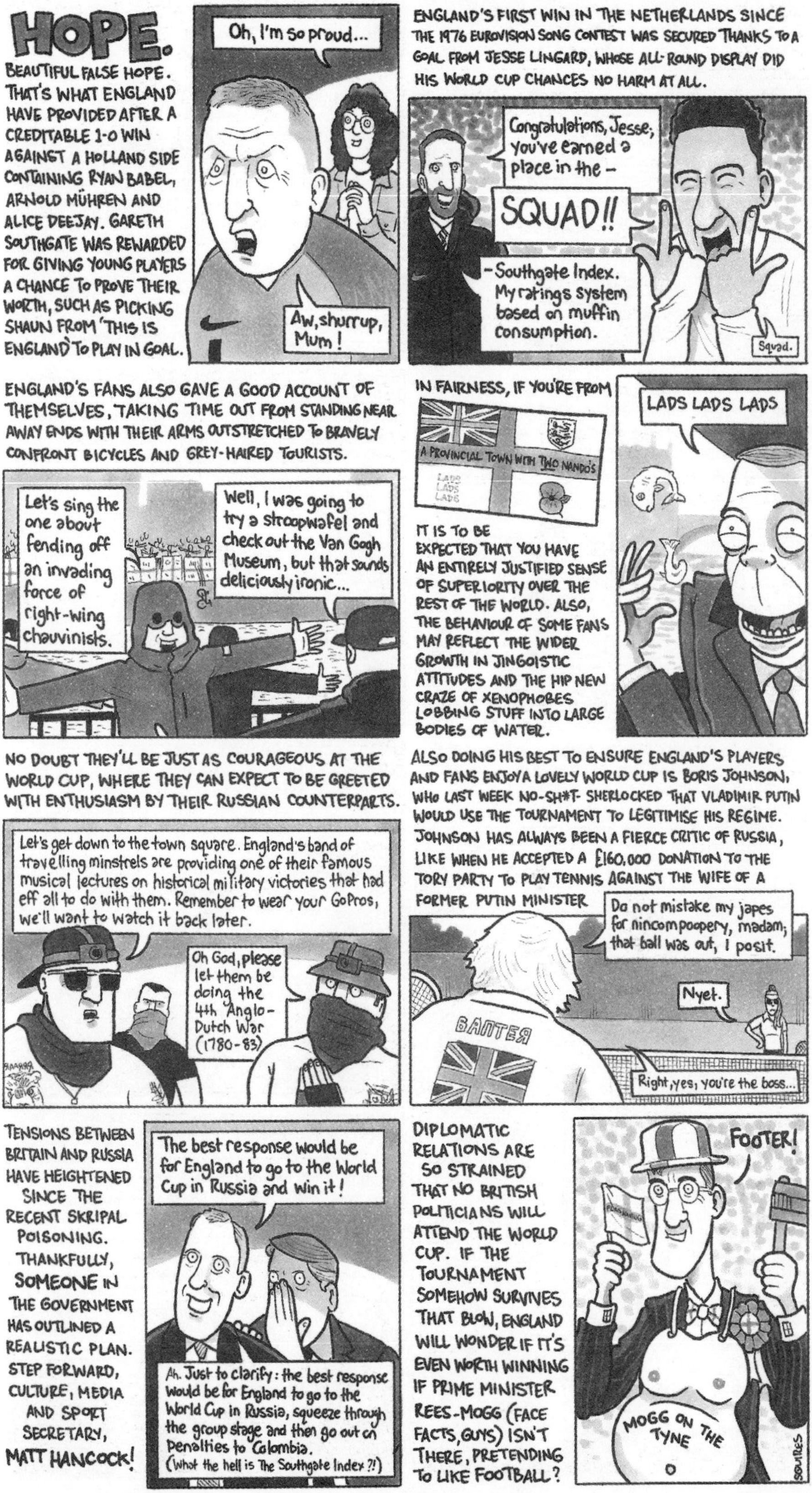
HOPE.
BEAUTIFUL FALSE HOPE. THAT'S WHAT ENGLAND HAVE PROVIDED AFTER A CREDITABLE 1-0 WIN AGAINST A HOLLAND SIDE CONTAINING RYAN BABEL, ARNOLD MÜHREN AND ALICE DEEJAY. GARETH SOUTHGATE WAS REWARDED FOR GIVING YOUNG PLAYERS A CHANCE TO PROVE THEIR WORTH, SUCH AS PICKING SHAUN FROM 'THIS IS ENGLAND' TO PLAY IN GOAL.
Oh, I'm so proud...
Aw, shurrup, Mum!
ENGLAND'S FIRST WIN IN THE NETHERLANDS SINCE THE 1976 EUROVISION SONG CONTEST WAS SECURED THANKS TO A GOAL FROM JESSE LINGARD, WHOSE ALL-ROUND DISPLAY DID HIS WORLD CUP CHANCES NO HARM AT ALL.
Congratulations, Jesse; you've earned a place in the –
SQUAD!!
– Southgate Index. My ratings system based on muffin consumption.
Squad.
ENGLAND'S FANS ALSO GAVE A GOOD ACCOUNT OF THEMSELVES, TAKING TIME OUT FROM STANDING NEAR AWAY ENDS WITH THEIR ARMS OUTSTRETCHED TO BRAVELY CONFRONT BICYCLES AND GREY-HAIRED TOURISTS.
Let's sing the one about fending off an invading force of right-wing chauvinists.
Well, I was going to try a stroopwafel and check out the Van Gogh Museum, but that sounds deliciously ironic...
IN FAIRNESS, IF YOU'RE FROM
A PROVINCIAL TOWN WITH TWO NANDO'S
LADS LADS LADS
IT IS TO BE EXPECTED THAT YOU HAVE AN ENTIRELY JUSTIFIED SENSE OF SUPERIORITY OVER THE REST OF THE WORLD. ALSO, THE BEHAVIOUR OF SOME FANS MAY REFLECT THE WIDER GROWTH IN JINGOISTIC ATTITUDES AND THE HIP NEW CRAZE OF XENOPHOBES LOBBING STUFF INTO LARGE BODIES OF WATER.
LADS LADS LADS
NO DOUBT THEY'LL BE JUST AS COURAGEOUS AT THE WORLD CUP, WHERE THEY CAN EXPECT TO BE GREETED WITH ENTHUSIASM BY THEIR RUSSIAN COUNTERPARTS.
Let's get down to the town square. England's band of travelling minstrels are providing one of their famous musical lectures on historical military victories that had eff all to do with them. Remember to wear your GoPros, we'll want to watch it back later.
Oh God, please let them be doing the 4th Anglo-Dutch War (1780–83)
ALSO DOING HIS BEST TO ENSURE ENGLAND'S PLAYERS AND FANS ENJOY A LOVELY WORLD CUP IS BORIS JOHNSON, WHO LAST WEEK NO-SH*T-SHERLOCKED THAT VLADIMIR PUTIN WOULD USE THE TOURNAMENT TO LEGITIMISE HIS REGIME. JOHNSON HAS ALWAYS BEEN A FIERCE CRITIC OF RUSSIA, LIKE WHEN HE ACCEPTED A £160,000 DONATION TO THE TORY PARTY TO PLAY TENNIS AGAINST THE WIFE OF A FORMER PUTIN MINISTER
Do not mistake my japes for nincompoopery, madam; that ball was out, I posit.
Nyet.
БAПTEЯ
Right, yes, you're the boss...
TENSIONS BETWEEN BRITAIN AND RUSSIA HAVE HEIGHTENED SINCE THE RECENT SKRIPAL POISONING. THANKFULLY, SOMEONE IN THE GOVERNMENT HAS OUTLINED A REALISTIC PLAN. STEP FORWARD, CULTURE, MEDIA AND SPORT SECRETARY, MATT HANCOCK!
The best response would be for England to go to the World Cup in Russia and win it!
Ah. Just to clarify: the best response would be for England to go to the World Cup in Russia, squeeze through the group stage and then go out on penalties to Colombia.
(What the hell is The Southgate Index?!)
DIPLOMATIC RELATIONS ARE SO STRAINED THAT NO BRITISH POLITICIANS WILL ATTEND THE WORLD CUP. IF THE TOURNAMENT SOMEHOW SURVIVES THAT BLOW, ENGLAND WILL WONDER IF IT'S EVEN WORTH WINNING IF PRIME MINISTER REES-MOGG (FACE FACTS, GUYS) ISN'T THERE, PRETENDING TO LIKE FOOTBALL?
FOOTER!
MOGG ON THE TYNE
SQUIRES

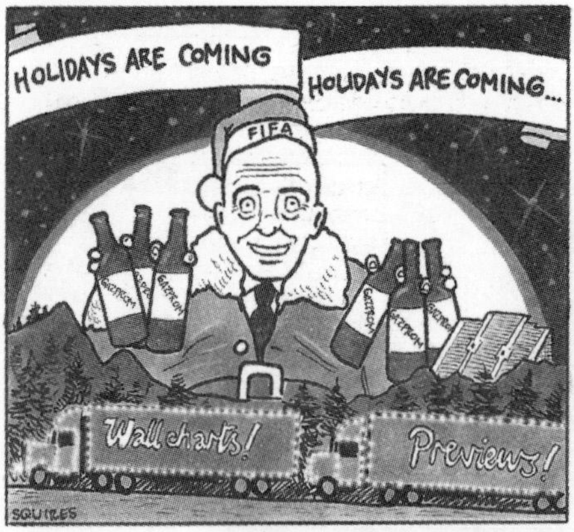
HOLIDAYS ARE COMING
HOLIDAYS ARE COMING...
FIFA
Wall charts!
Previews!
SQUIRES

FOOTBALL CHRISTMAS IS HERE. A TIME FOR HOPE. A TIME FOR TOGETHERNESS. A TIME FOR FAMILY TO MANAGE THEIR EXPECTATIONS ABOUT HOW MUCH THEY'LL SEE YOU OVER THE NEXT MONTH. SOME PEOPLE HAVE EVEN TAKEN EXTREME PRECAUTIONS TO ENSURE THEIR CALENDAR REMAINS FREE OF SOCIAL COMMITMENTS.

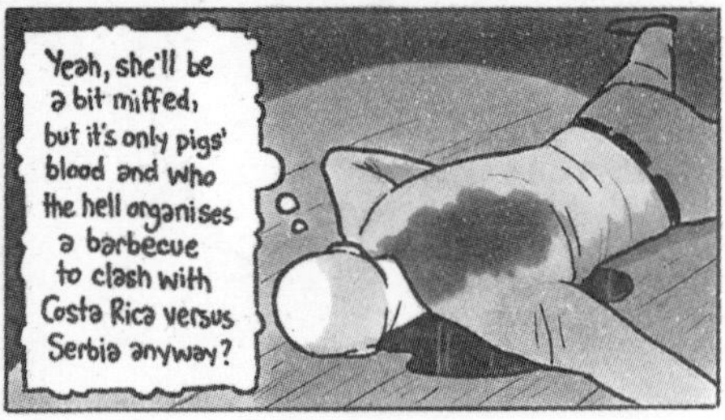
Yeah, she'll be a bit miffed, but it's only pigs' blood and who the hell organises a barbecue to clash with Costa Rica versus Serbia anyway?

PREPARATIONS ARE ALSO TAKING PLACE IN RUSSIA; THE TOURNAMENT OFFERING A CHANCE FOR VLADIMIR PUTIN TO SHOWCASE HIS FRIENDLY AUTOCRACY. ANY CROWD TROUBLE OR POLITICAL DISSENT WILL BE SWIFTLY DEALT WITH BY HIS SMILING SECURITY FORCES, SO AFFABLE THEY COULD STAR IN THEIR OWN CARTOON!

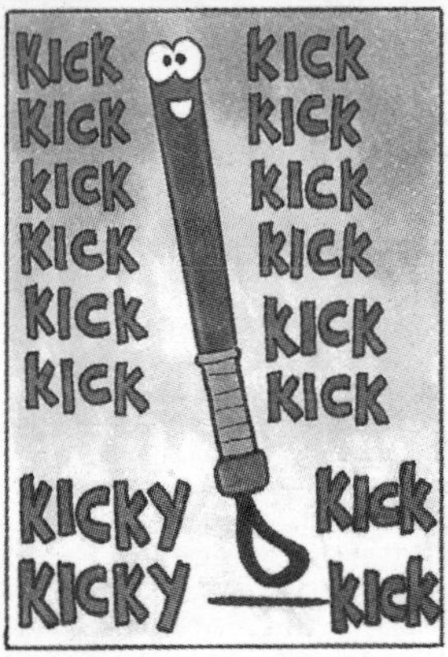
KICK KICK KICK KICK KICK KICK
KICK KICK KICK KICK KICK KICK
KICKY KICKY
KICK KICK

FUNNY TO THINK THAT THE WORLD CUP COULD HAVE BEEN HELD IN ENGLAND HAD THE FIFA EXECUTIVE COMMITTEE NOT BEEN INEXPLICABLY UNIMPRESSED BY EMPTY HANDBAGS AND THE INTERVENTION OF DAVID CAMERON.

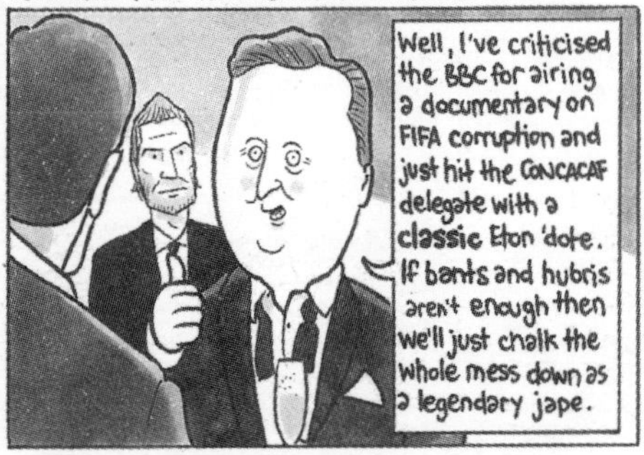
Well, I've criticised the BBC for airing a documentary on FIFA corruption and just hit the CONCACAF delegate with a classic Eton 'dote. If bants and hubris aren't enough then we'll just chalk the whole mess down as a legendary jape.

AS FOOTBALL'S GREATEST PLAYERS ARRIVE IN RUSSIA, SOME ARE WONDERING WHETHER THIS COULD FINALLY BE LIONEL MESSI'S YEAR. AS WELL AS CARRYING THE HOPES OF A NATION, THIS YEAR MESSI WILL ALSO BE REQUIRED TO CARRY A GOAT WITH HIM AT ALL TIMES, FOR THE PURPOSES OF VISUAL METAPHOR.

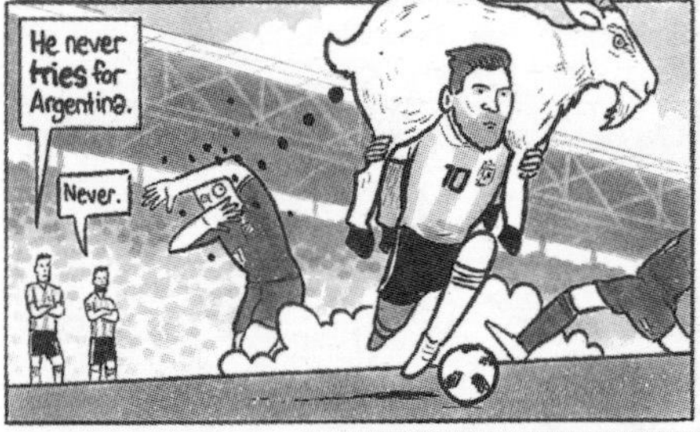
He never tries for Argentina.
Never.
10

IN THESE LAST FEW DAYS BEFORE THE BIG KICK-OFF, TEAMS WILL BE HOPING THEIR STAR TALENT CAN STAY INJURY-FREE, UNLIKE ITV'S CLIVE TYLDESLEY, WHO SEEMED TO EXPERIENCE SOME KIND OF CATASTROPHIC MALFUNCTION WHILST COMMENTATING ON A CHARITY MATCH ON SUNDAY.

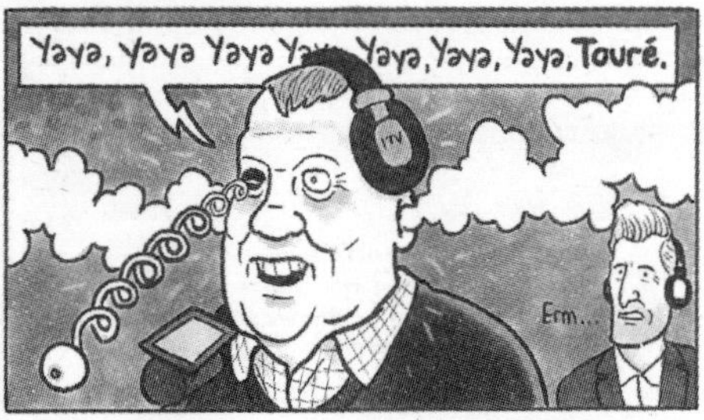
Yaya, Yaya Yaya Ya... Yaya, Yaya, Yaya, Touré.
ITV
Erm...

FOR ONCE THERE ARE REALISTIC EXPECTATIONS OF HOW WELL ENGLAND WILL DO. PERHAPS THIS IS BECAUSE THEY ARE GUARANTEED TO WIN THE NEXT WORLD CUP AFTER THE INTRODUCTION OF A WINTER BREAK THAT WILL EXCLUSIVELY BENEFIT THE HANDFUL OF PREMIER LEAGUE PLAYERS ELIGIBLE TO PLAY FOR ENGLAND. AS WE KNOW, EVEN THE WORST IDEAS CAN BE JUSTIFIED BY CLAIMING TO ASSIST ENGLAND.

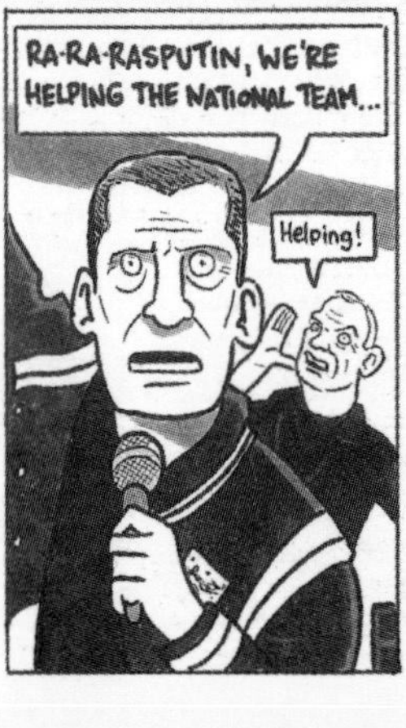
RA-RA-RASPUTIN, WE'RE HELPING THE NATIONAL TEAM...
Helping!

BUT IF NONE OF THIS IS FOR YOU, THERE ARE ALWAYS THE VOYEURISTIC DELIGHTS OF A REALITY SHOW WHERE A GROUP OF FIT YOUNG PEOPLE ARE LOCKED AWAY FOR AN EXTENDED PERIOD OF TIME, ENJOYING INANE CONVERSATIONS ABOUT POLITICAL AFFAIRS, ON HOTEL SUN LOUNGERS.

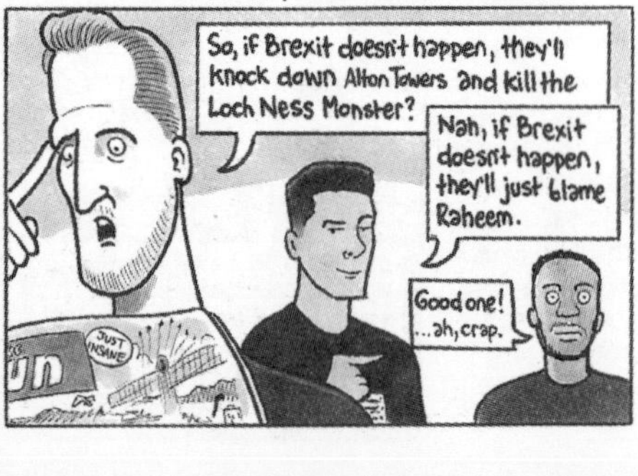
So, if Brexit doesn't happen, they'll knock down Alton Towers and kill the Loch Ness Monster?
Nah, if Brexit doesn't happen, they'll just blame Raheem.
Good one! ...ah, crap.
JUST INSANE

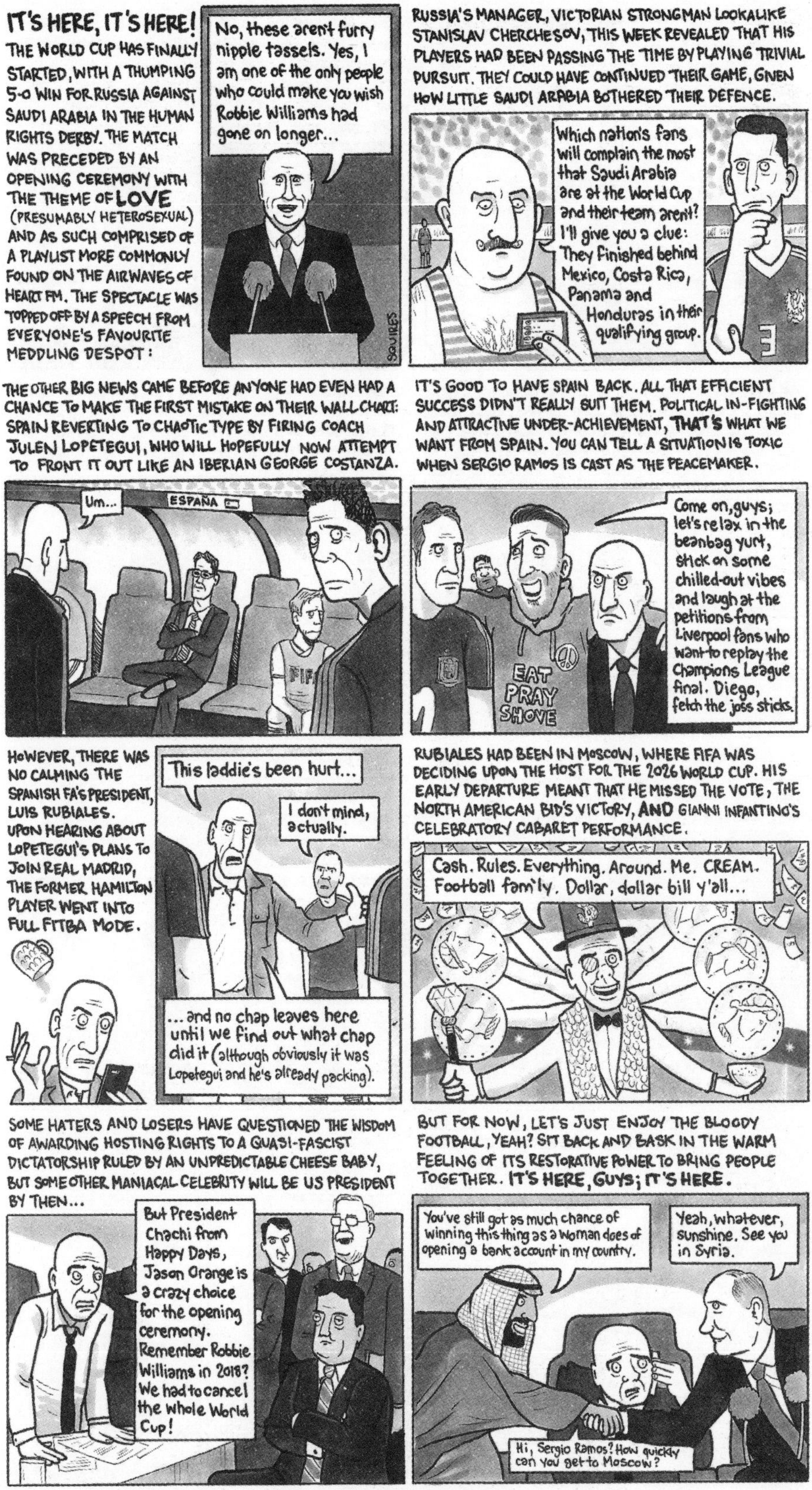
IT'S HERE, IT'S HERE!
THE WORLD CUP HAS FINALLY STARTED, WITH A THUMPING 5-0 WIN FOR RUSSIA AGAINST SAUDI ARABIA IN THE HUMAN RIGHTS DERBY. THE MATCH WAS PRECEDED BY AN OPENING CEREMONY WITH THE THEME OF LOVE (PRESUMABLY HETEROSEXUAL) AND AS SUCH COMPRISED OF A PLAYLIST MORE COMMONLY FOUND ON THE AIRWAVES OF HEART FM. THE SPECTACLE WAS TOPPED OFF BY A SPEECH FROM EVERYONE'S FAVOURITE MEDDLING DESPOT:
No, these aren't furry nipple tassels. Yes, I am one of the only people who could make you wish Robbie Williams had gone on longer...
SQUIRES
RUSSIA'S MANAGER, VICTORIAN STRONGMAN LOOKALIKE STANISLAV CHERCHESOV, THIS WEEK REVEALED THAT HIS PLAYERS HAD BEEN PASSING THE TIME BY PLAYING TRIVIAL PURSUIT. THEY COULD HAVE CONTINUED THEIR GAME, GIVEN HOW LITTLE SAUDI ARABIA BOTHERED THEIR DEFENCE.
Which nation's fans will complain the most that Saudi Arabia are at the World Cup and their team aren't? I'll give you a clue: They finished behind Mexico, Costa Rica, Panama and Honduras in their qualifying group.
THE OTHER BIG NEWS CAME BEFORE ANYONE HAD EVEN HAD A CHANCE TO MAKE THE FIRST MISTAKE ON THEIR WALL CHART: SPAIN REVERTING TO CHAOTIC TYPE BY FIRING COACH JULEN LOPETEGUI, WHO WILL HOPEFULLY NOW ATTEMPT TO FRONT IT OUT LIKE AN IBERIAN GEORGE COSTANZA.
Um...
ESPAÑA
FIFA
IT'S GOOD TO HAVE SPAIN BACK. ALL THAT EFFICIENT SUCCESS DIDN'T REALLY SUIT THEM. POLITICAL IN-FIGHTING AND ATTRACTIVE UNDER-ACHIEVEMENT, THAT'S WHAT WE WANT FROM SPAIN. YOU CAN TELL A SITUATION IS TOXIC WHEN SERGIO RAMOS IS CAST AS THE PEACEMAKER.
Come on, guys; let's relax in the beanbag yurt, stick on some chilled-out vibes and laugh at the petitions from Liverpool fans who want to replay the Champions League final. Diego, fetch the joss sticks.
EAT PRAY SHOVE
HOWEVER, THERE WAS NO CALMING THE SPANISH FA'S PRESIDENT, LUIS RUBIALES. UPON HEARING ABOUT LOPETEGUI'S PLANS TO JOIN REAL MADRID, THE FORMER HAMILTON PLAYER WENT INTO FULL FITBA MODE.
This laddie's been hurt...
I don't mind, actually.
...and no chap leaves here until we find out what chap did it (although obviously it was Lopetegui and he's already packing).
RUBIALES HAD BEEN IN MOSCOW, WHERE FIFA WAS DECIDING UPON THE HOST FOR THE 2026 WORLD CUP. HIS EARLY DEPARTURE MEANT THAT HE MISSED THE VOTE, THE NORTH AMERICAN BID'S VICTORY, AND GIANNI INFANTINO'S CELEBRATORY CABARET PERFORMANCE.
Cash. Rules. Everything. Around. Me. CREAM. Football fam'ly. Dollar, dollar bill y'all...
SOME HATERS AND LOSERS HAVE QUESTIONED THE WISDOM OF AWARDING HOSTING RIGHTS TO A QUASI-FASCIST DICTATORSHIP RULED BY AN UNPREDICTABLE CHEESE BABY, BUT SOME OTHER MANIACAL CELEBRITY WILL BE US PRESIDENT BY THEN...
But President Chachi from Happy Days, Jason Orange is a crazy choice for the opening ceremony. Remember Robbie Williams in 2018? We had to cancel the whole World Cup!
BUT FOR NOW, LET'S JUST ENJOY THE BLOODY FOOTBALL, YEAH? SIT BACK AND BASK IN THE WARM FEELING OF ITS RESTORATIVE POWER TO BRING PEOPLE TOGETHER. IT'S HERE, GUYS; IT'S HERE.
You've still got as much chance of winning this thing as a woman does of opening a bank account in my country.
Yeah, whatever, sunshine. See you in Syria.
Hi, Sergio Ramos? How quickly can you get to Moscow?

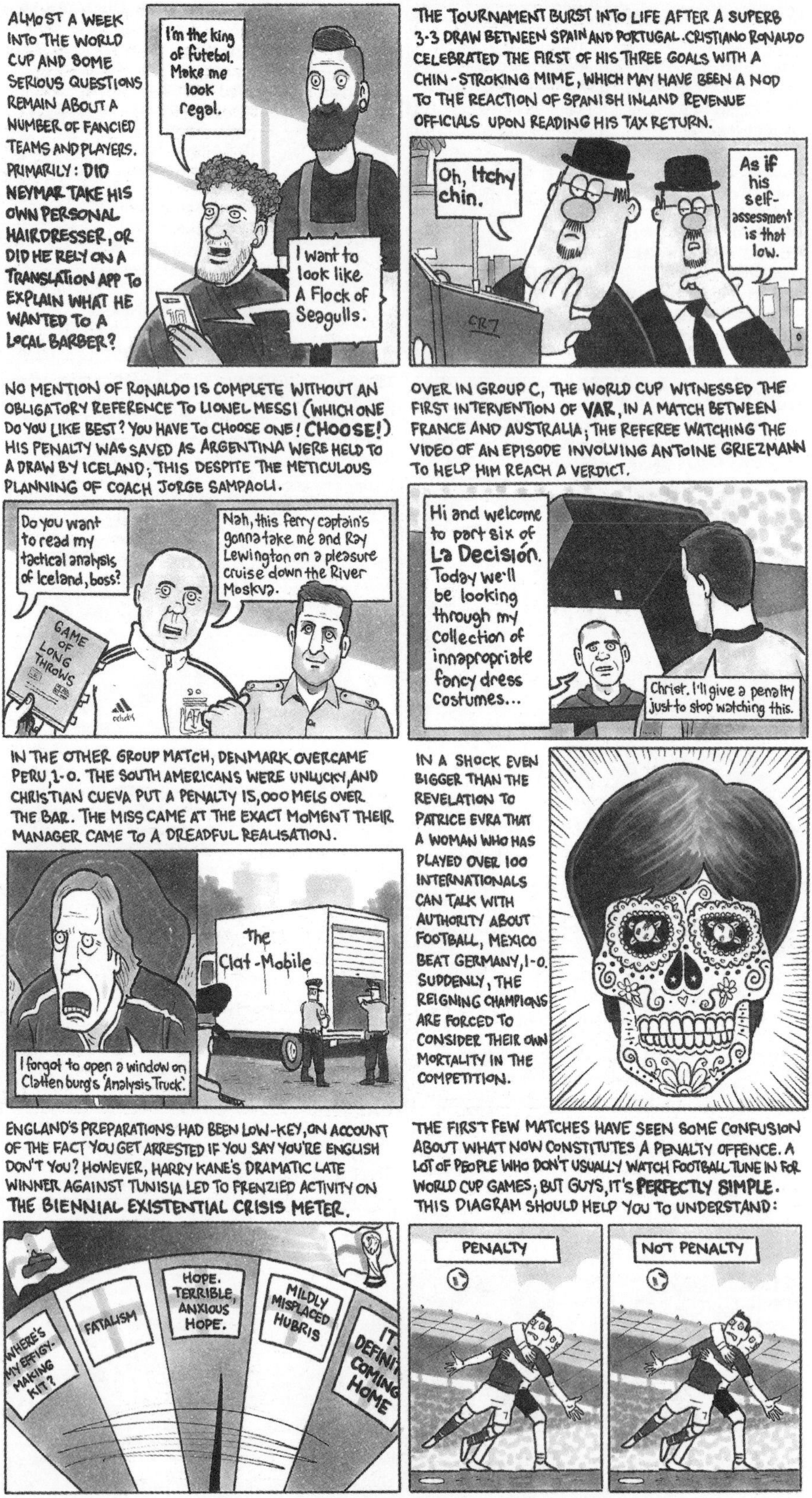
ALMOST A WEEK INTO THE WORLD CUP AND SOME SERIOUS QUESTIONS REMAIN ABOUT A NUMBER OF FANCIED TEAMS AND PLAYERS. PRIMARILY: DID NEYMAR TAKE HIS OWN PERSONAL HAIRDRESSER, OR DID HE RELY ON A TRANSLATION APP TO EXPLAIN WHAT HE WANTED TO A LOCAL BARBER?
I'm the king of futebol. Make me look regal.
I want to look like A Flock of Seagulls.
THE TOURNAMENT BURST INTO LIFE AFTER A SUPERB 3-3 DRAW BETWEEN SPAIN AND PORTUGAL. CRISTIANO RONALDO CELEBRATED THE FIRST OF HIS THREE GOALS WITH A CHIN-STROKING MIME, WHICH MAY HAVE BEEN A NOD TO THE REACTION OF SPANISH INLAND REVENUE OFFICIALS UPON READING HIS TAX RETURN.
Oh, Itchy chin.
As if his self-assessment is that low.
CR7
NO MENTION OF RONALDO IS COMPLETE WITHOUT AN OBLIGATORY REFERENCE TO LIONEL MESSI (WHICH ONE DO YOU LIKE BEST? YOU HAVE TO CHOOSE ONE! CHOOSE!) HIS PENALTY WAS SAVED AS ARGENTINA WERE HELD TO A DRAW BY ICELAND; THIS DESPITE THE METICULOUS PLANNING OF COACH JORGE SAMPAOLI.
Do you want to read my tactical analysis of Iceland, boss?
Nah, this ferry captain's gonna take me and Ray Lewington on a pleasure cruise down the River Moskva.
GAME OF LONG THROWS
OVER IN GROUP C, THE WORLD CUP WITNESSED THE FIRST INTERVENTION OF VAR, IN A MATCH BETWEEN FRANCE AND AUSTRALIA; THE REFEREE WATCHING THE VIDEO OF AN EPISODE INVOLVING ANTOINE GRIEZMANN TO HELP HIM REACH A VERDICT.
Hi and welcome to part six of La Decisión. Today we'll be looking through my collection of innapropriate fancy dress costumes...
Christ. I'll give a penalty just to stop watching this.
IN THE OTHER GROUP MATCH, DENMARK OVERCAME PERU, 1-0. THE SOUTH AMERICANS WERE UNLUCKY, AND CHRISTIAN CUEVA PUT A PENALTY 15,000 MELS OVER THE BAR. THE MISS CAME AT THE EXACT MOMENT THEIR MANAGER CAME TO A DREADFUL REALISATION.
I forgot to open a window on Clattenburg's 'Analysis Truck'.
The Clat-Mobile
IN A SHOCK EVEN BIGGER THAN THE REVELATION TO PATRICE EVRA THAT A WOMAN WHO HAS PLAYED OVER 100 INTERNATIONALS CAN TALK WITH AUTHORITY ABOUT FOOTBALL, MEXICO BEAT GERMANY, 1-0. SUDDENLY, THE REIGNING CHAMPIONS ARE FORCED TO CONSIDER THEIR OWN MORTALITY IN THE COMPETITION.
ENGLAND'S PREPARATIONS HAD BEEN LOW-KEY, ON ACCOUNT OF THE FACT YOU GET ARRESTED IF YOU SAY YOU'RE ENGLISH DON'T YOU? HOWEVER, HARRY KANE'S DRAMATIC LATE WINNER AGAINST TUNISIA LED TO FRENZIED ACTIVITY ON THE BIENNIAL EXISTENTIAL CRISIS METER.
WHERE'S MY EFFIGY-MAKING KIT?
FATALISM
HOPE. TERRIBLE, ANXIOUS HOPE.
MILDLY MISPLACED HUBRIS
COMING HOME
THE FIRST FEW MATCHES HAVE SEEN SOME CONFUSION ABOUT WHAT NOW CONSTITUTES A PENALTY OFFENCE. A LOT OF PEOPLE WHO DON'T USUALLY WATCH FOOTBALL TUNE IN FOR WORLD CUP GAMES; BUT GUYS, IT'S PERFECTLY SIMPLE. THIS DIAGRAM SHOULD HELP YOU TO UNDERSTAND:
PENALTY
NOT PENALTY

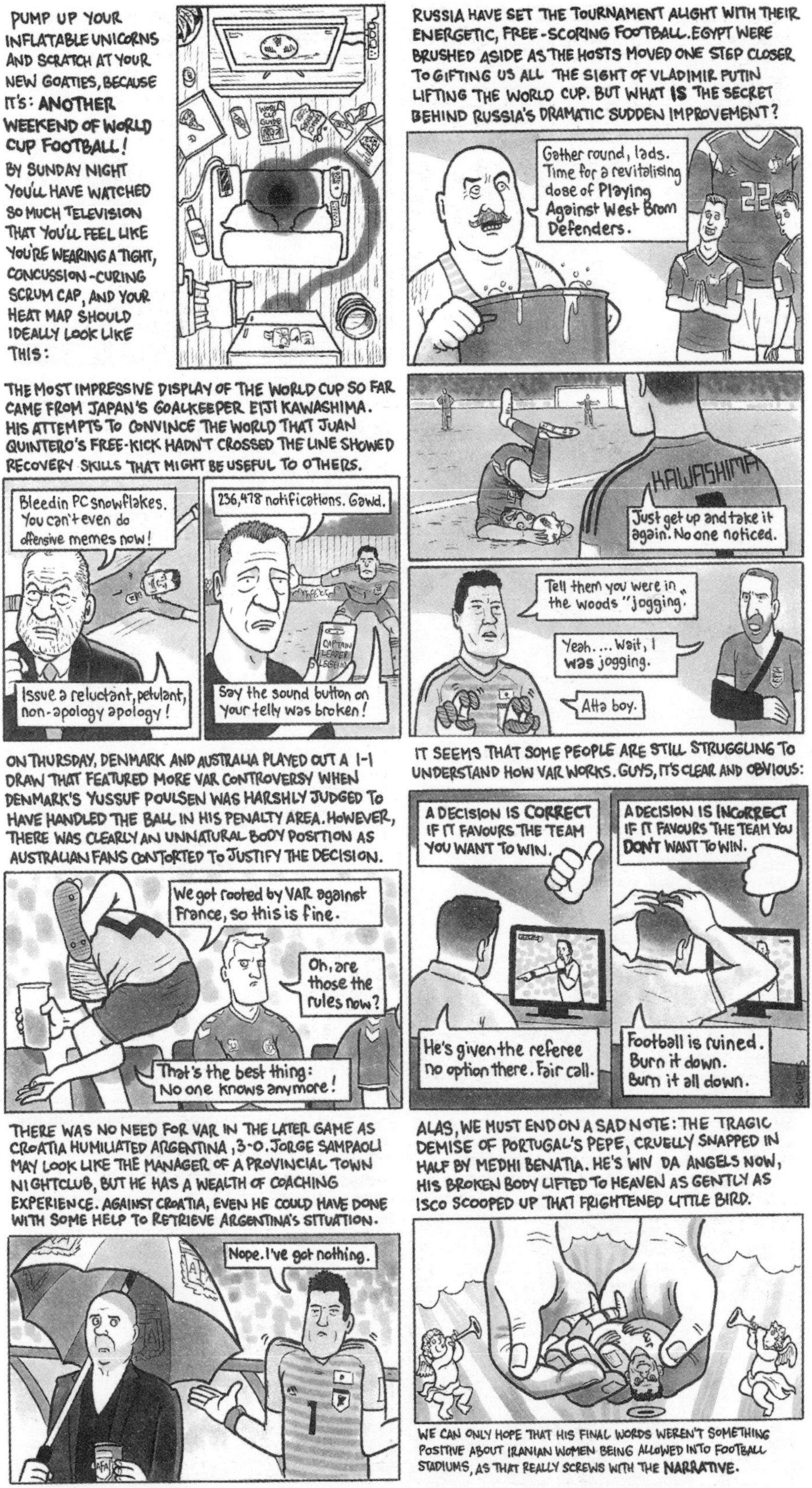
PUMP UP YOUR INFLATABLE UNICORNS AND SCRATCH AT YOUR NEW GOATIES, BECAUSE IT'S: ANOTHER WEEKEND OF WORLD CUP FOOTBALL!
BY SUNDAY NIGHT YOU'LL HAVE WATCHED SO MUCH TELEVISION THAT YOU'LL FEEL LIKE YOU'RE WEARING A TIGHT, CONCUSSION-CURING SCRUM CAP, AND YOUR HEAT MAP SHOULD IDEALLY LOOK LIKE THIS:
WORLD CUP GUIDE
RUSSIA HAVE SET THE TOURNAMENT ALIGHT WITH THEIR ENERGETIC, FREE-SCORING FOOTBALL. EGYPT WERE BRUSHED ASIDE AS THE HOSTS MOVED ONE STEP CLOSER TO GIFTING US ALL THE SIGHT OF VLADIMIR PUTIN LIFTING THE WORLD CUP. BUT WHAT IS THE SECRET BEHIND RUSSIA'S DRAMATIC SUDDEN IMPROVEMENT?
Gather round, lads. Time for a revitalising dose of Playing Against West Brom Defenders.
THE MOST IMPRESSIVE DISPLAY OF THE WORLD CUP SO FAR CAME FROM JAPAN'S GOALKEEPER EIJI KAWASHIMA. HIS ATTEMPTS TO CONVINCE THE WORLD THAT JUAN QUINTERO'S FREE-KICK HADN'T CROSSED THE LINE SHOWED RECOVERY SKILLS THAT MIGHT BE USEFUL TO OTHERS.
KAWASHIMA
Just get up and take it again. No one noticed.
Bleedin PC snowflakes. You can't even do offensive memes now!
Issue a reluctant, petulant, non-apology apology!
236,478 notifications. Gawd.
CAPTAIN LEADER LEGEND
Say the sound button on your telly was broken!
Tell them you were in the woods "jogging."
Yeah.... Wait, I was jogging.
Atta boy.
ON THURSDAY, DENMARK AND AUSTRALIA PLAYED OUT A 1-1 DRAW THAT FEATURED MORE VAR CONTROVERSY WHEN DENMARK'S YUSSUF POULSEN WAS HARSHLY JUDGED TO HAVE HANDLED THE BALL IN HIS PENALTY AREA. HOWEVER, THERE WAS CLEARLY AN UNNATURAL BODY POSITION AS AUSTRALIAN FANS CONTORTED TO JUSTIFY THE DECISION.
We got rooted by VAR against France, so this is fine.
Oh, are those the rules now?
That's the best thing: No one knows anymore!
IT SEEMS THAT SOME PEOPLE ARE STILL STRUGGLING TO UNDERSTAND HOW VAR WORKS. GUYS, IT'S CLEAR AND OBVIOUS:
A DECISION IS CORRECT IF IT FAVOURS THE TEAM YOU WANT TO WIN.
He's given the referee no option there. Fair call.
A DECISION IS INCORRECT IF IT FAVOURS THE TEAM YOU DON'T WANT TO WIN.
Football is ruined. Burn it down. Burn it all down.
THERE WAS NO NEED FOR VAR IN THE LATER GAME AS CROATIA HUMILIATED ARGENTINA, 3-0. JORGE SAMPAOLI MAY LOOK LIKE THE MANAGER OF A PROVINCIAL TOWN NIGHTCLUB, BUT HE HAS A WEALTH OF COACHING EXPERIENCE. AGAINST CROATIA, EVEN HE COULD HAVE DONE WITH SOME HELP TO RETRIEVE ARGENTINA'S SITUATION.
Nope. I've got nothing.
ALAS, WE MUST END ON A SAD NOTE: THE TRAGIC DEMISE OF PORTUGAL'S PEPE, CRUELLY SNAPPED IN HALF BY MEDHI BENATIA. HE'S WIV DA ANGELS NOW, HIS BROKEN BODY LIFTED TO HEAVEN AS GENTLY AS ISCO SCOOPED UP THAT FRIGHTENED LITTLE BIRD.
WE CAN ONLY HOPE THAT HIS FINAL WORDS WEREN'T SOMETHING POSITIVE ABOUT IRANIAN WOMEN BEING ALLOWED INTO FOOTBALL STADIUMS, AS THAT REALLY SCREWS WITH THE NARRATIVE.

ONE OF THE GREAT THINGS ABOUT THE WORLD CUP IS THAT IT PROVIDES OPPORTUNITIES TO LEARN ABOUT CULTURES THAT AREN'T BASED ON CRISPS AND SALAD CREAM. FOOTBALL BRINGS US TOGETHER, INCREASING OUR UNDERSTANDING OF LANGUAGE, GEOGRAPHY AND POLITICAL HOSTILITIES.

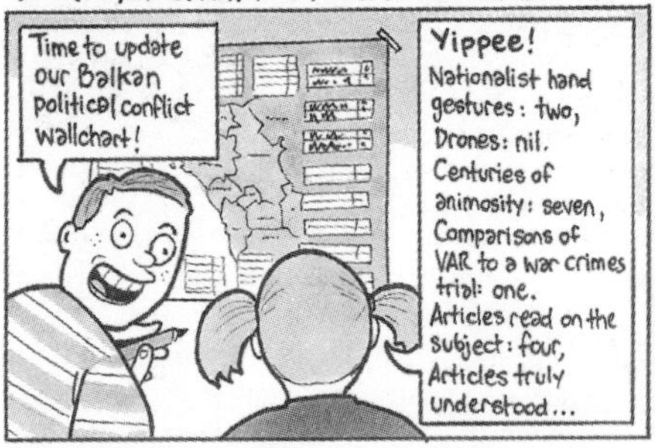

Time to update our Balkan political conflict wallchart!
Yippee! Nationalist hand gestures: two, Drones: nil. Centuries of animosity: seven, Comparisons of VAR to a war crimes trial: one. Articles read on the subject: four, Articles truly understood...

IN THE ACTUAL FOOTBALL, EVERYONE WAS **DELIGHTED** FOR BRAZIL, WHO SCORED TWO INJURY-TIME GOALS TO BEAT COSTA RICA. IT WAS ALL TOO MUCH FOR NEYMAR, WHO WAS OVERCOME WITH EMOTION AS HE CAME TO A SUDDEN, DREADFUL, REALISATION.

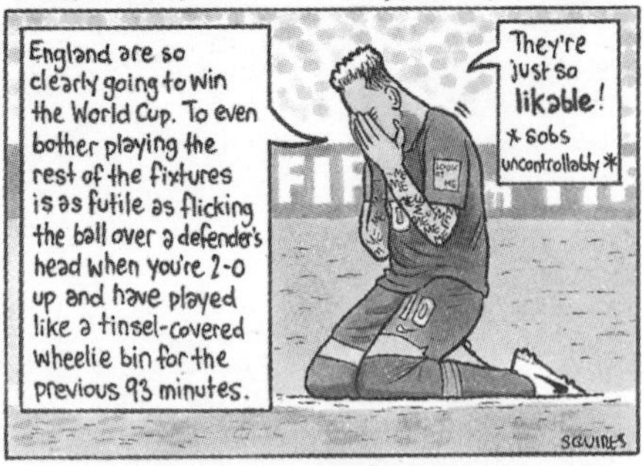

England are so clearly going to win the World Cup. To even bother playing the rest of the fixtures is as futile as flicking the ball over a defender's head when you're 2-0 up and have played like a tinsel-covered wheelie bin for the previous 93 minutes.
They're just so likable! *sobs uncontrollably*
FIFA
SQUIRES

YES, IN CASE YOU HAVEN'T HEARD, **FOOTBALL'S COMING HOME** (SO LONG AS FOOTBALL ONLY PLAYS VIOLENT UNDERDOGS WHO'D STRUGGLE AGAINST NOTTS COUNTY AND DON'T PRESS THE BACK THREE). TALK NOW TURNS TO WHICH RESULT AGAINST BELGIUM WILL GUARANTEE THE EASIEST QUARTER-FINAL; ENGLAND APPARENTLY BEING GRANTED A BYE FOR THE SECOND ROUND. SHOULD THE MATCH END IN A DRAW, THE GROUP SHOULD BE DECIDED BY WHOEVER CAN KICK PIERS MORGAN UP THE ARSE THE HARDEST. FIFA, MAKE THIS HAPPEN AND ALL IS FORGIVEN.

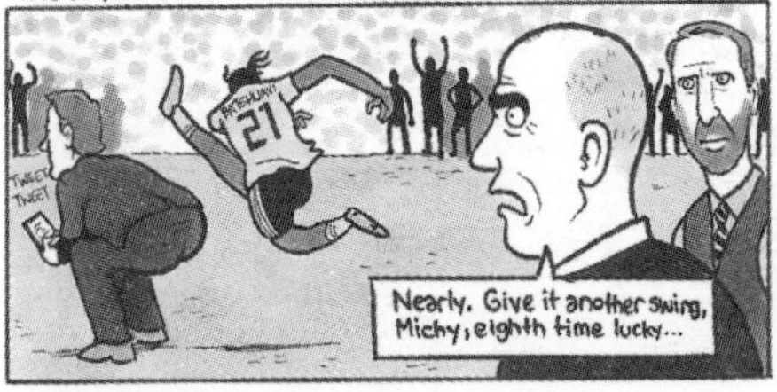

TWEET TWEET
21
Nearly. Give it another swing, Michy, eighth time lucky...

ALMOST AS GRATIFYING WAS GERMANY'S LATE WIN AGAINST SWEDEN. JUST WHEN IT SEEMED THAT THE HOLDERS WOULD BE LEFT FRUSTRATED BY AN IMPOSSIBLE SWEDISH PUZZLE, TONI KROOS FOUND THE ALLEN KEY TO UNLOCK THEIR DEFENCE.

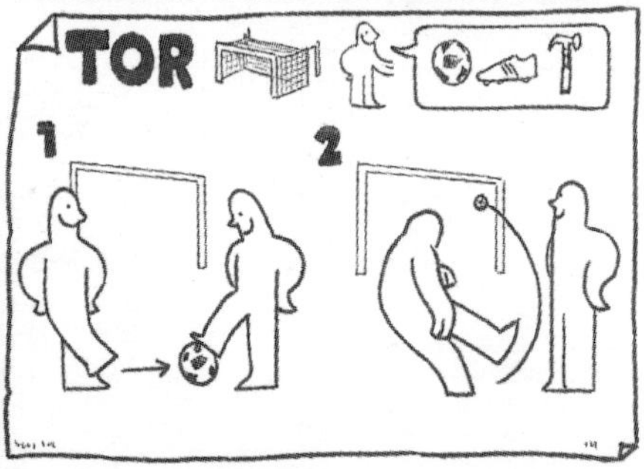

TOR
1
2

SO BRUTAL WAS THE INJURY-TIME WINNER THAT IT MAY BECOME THE SUBJECT OF YOUR NEXT FAVOURITE NORDIC NOIR CRIME SERIES.

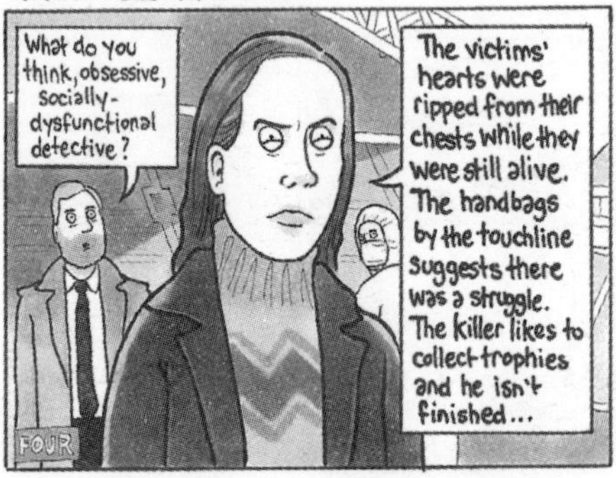

What do you think, obsessive, socially-dysfunctional detective?
The victims' hearts were ripped from their chests while they were still alive. The handbags by the touchline suggests there was a struggle. The killer likes to collect trophies and he isn't finished...
FOUR

SPAIN WON GROUP B THANKS TO A LAST-GASP EQUALISER AGAINST MOROCCO, WHO COULD HAVE DONE WITH THE OFFSIDE TRAP THAT JAPAN USED TO LEAVE THE ENTIRE SENEGAL TEAM STRANDED IN THE RYN DESERT OF WESTERN KAZAKHSTAN.

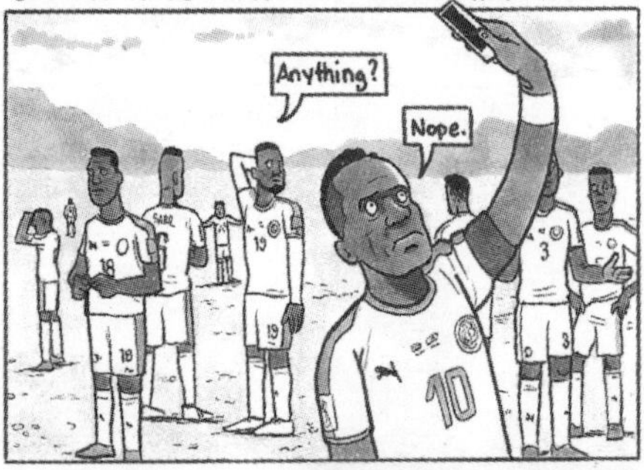

Anything?
Nope.

THE REFEREE IN THE OTHER GROUP MATCH – BETWEEN PORTUGAL AND IRAN – SPENT MORE TIME WATCHING THE TELLY THAN YOU HAVE OVER THE PAST FORTNIGHT. HIS DECISION TO AWARD PORTUGAL A PENALTY SAW CARLOS QUEIROZ...

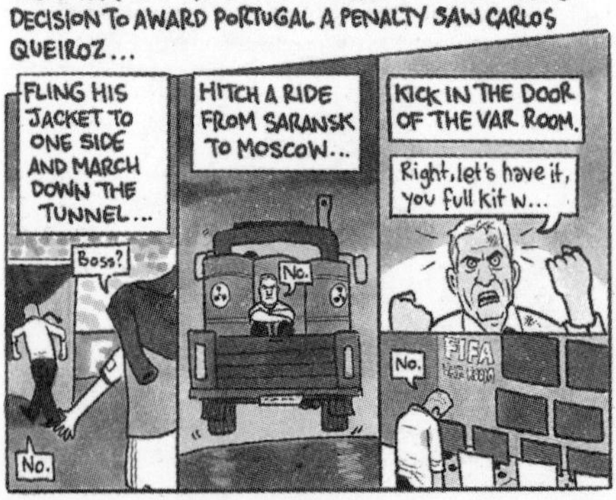

FLING HIS JACKET TO ONE SIDE AND MARCH DOWN THE TUNNEL...
Boss?
No.
HITCH A RIDE FROM SARANSK TO MOSCOW...
No.
KICK IN THE DOOR OF THE VAR ROOM.
Right, let's have it, you full kit w...
FIFA
No.

RONALDO MISSED IT, THEN IRAN LEVEL THROUGH A PENALTY OF THEIR OWN, AWARDED BY VAR FOR HUMOUR. THEN, IN THE DYING MOMENTS, MEHDI TAREMI SMASHES THE BALL INTO THE NET! **PORTUGAL ARE OUT! LOOK AT PEPE'S FACE! LOOK AT RONNIE! OH GOD IT'S HIT THE SIDE-NETTING, DAMN YOU FOOTBALL, YOU GLORIOUS, TERRIBLE B*STARD!** FINAL SCORE: 1-1, IRAN INCONSOLABLE.

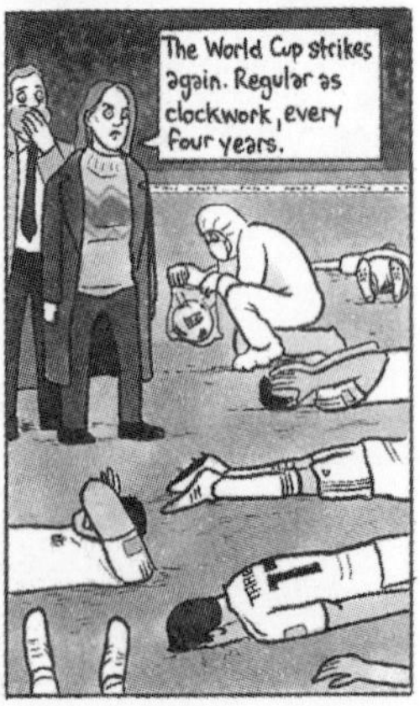

The World Cup strikes again. Regular as clockwork, every four years.

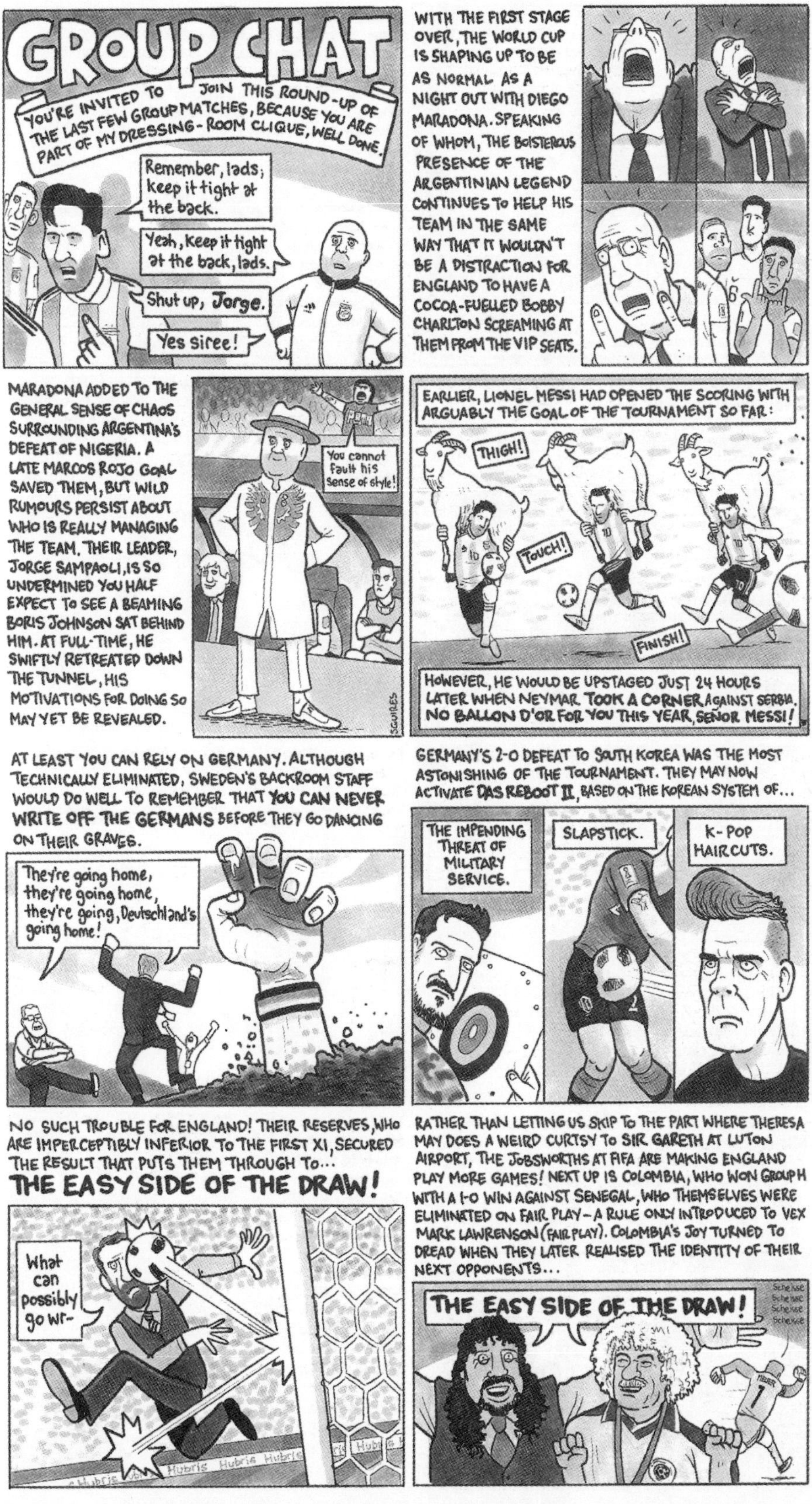
GROUP CHAT
YOU'RE INVITED TO JOIN THIS ROUND-UP OF THE LAST FEW GROUP MATCHES, BECAUSE YOU ARE PART OF MY DRESSING-ROOM CLIQUE, WELL DONE.
Remember, lads; keep it tight at the back.
Yeah, keep it tight at the back, lads.
Shut up, Jorge.
Yes siree!
WITH THE FIRST STAGE OVER, THE WORLD CUP IS SHAPING UP TO BE AS NORMAL AS A NIGHT OUT WITH DIEGO MARADONA. SPEAKING OF WHOM, THE BOISTEROUS PRESENCE OF THE ARGENTINIAN LEGEND CONTINUES TO HELP HIS TEAM IN THE SAME WAY THAT IT WOULDN'T BE A DISTRACTION FOR ENGLAND TO HAVE A COCOA-FUELLED BOBBY CHARLTON SCREAMING AT THEM FROM THE VIP SEATS.
MARADONA ADDED TO THE GENERAL SENSE OF CHAOS SURROUNDING ARGENTINA'S DEFEAT OF NIGERIA. A LATE MARCOS ROJO GOAL SAVED THEM, BUT WILD RUMOURS PERSIST ABOUT WHO IS REALLY MANAGING THE TEAM. THEIR LEADER, JORGE SAMPAOLI, IS SO UNDERMINED YOU HALF EXPECT TO SEE A BEAMING BORIS JOHNSON SAT BEHIND HIM. AT FULL-TIME, HE SWIFTLY RETREATED DOWN THE TUNNEL, HIS MOTIVATIONS FOR DOING SO MAY YET BE REVEALED.
You cannot fault his sense of style!
SQUIRES
EARLIER, LIONEL MESSI HAD OPENED THE SCORING WITH ARGUABLY THE GOAL OF THE TOURNAMENT SO FAR:
THIGH!
TOUCH!
FINISH!
HOWEVER, HE WOULD BE UPSTAGED JUST 24 HOURS LATER WHEN NEYMAR TOOK A CORNER AGAINST SERBIA. NO BALLON D'OR FOR YOU THIS YEAR, SEÑOR MESSI!
AT LEAST YOU CAN RELY ON GERMANY. ALTHOUGH TECHNICALLY ELIMINATED, SWEDEN'S BACKROOM STAFF WOULD DO WELL TO REMEMBER THAT YOU CAN NEVER WRITE OFF THE GERMANS BEFORE THEY GO DANCING ON THEIR GRAVES.
They're going home, they're going home, they're going, Deutschland's going home!
GERMANY'S 2-0 DEFEAT TO SOUTH KOREA WAS THE MOST ASTONISHING OF THE TOURNAMENT. THEY MAY NOW ACTIVATE DAS REBOOT II, BASED ON THE KOREAN SYSTEM OF...
THE IMPENDING THREAT OF MILITARY SERVICE.
SLAPSTICK.
K-POP HAIRCUTS.
NO SUCH TROUBLE FOR ENGLAND! THEIR RESERVES, WHO ARE IMPERCEPTIBLY INFERIOR TO THE FIRST XI, SECURED THE RESULT THAT PUTS THEM THROUGH TO...
THE EASY SIDE OF THE DRAW!
What can possibly go wr-
Hubris Hubris Hubris
RATHER THAN LETTING US SKIP TO THE PART WHERE THERESA MAY DOES A WEIRD CURTSY TO SIR GARETH AT LUTON AIRPORT, THE JOBSWORTHS AT FIFA ARE MAKING ENGLAND PLAY MORE GAMES! NEXT UP IS COLOMBIA, WHO WON GROUP H WITH A 1-0 WIN AGAINST SENEGAL, WHO THEMSELVES WERE ELIMINATED ON FAIR PLAY – A RULE ONLY INTRODUCED TO VEX MARK LAWRENSON (FAIR PLAY). COLOMBIA'S JOY TURNED TO DREAD WHEN THEY LATER REALISED THE IDENTITY OF THEIR NEXT OPPONENTS...
THE EASY SIDE OF THE DRAW!
Scheisse Scheisse Scheisse Scheisse

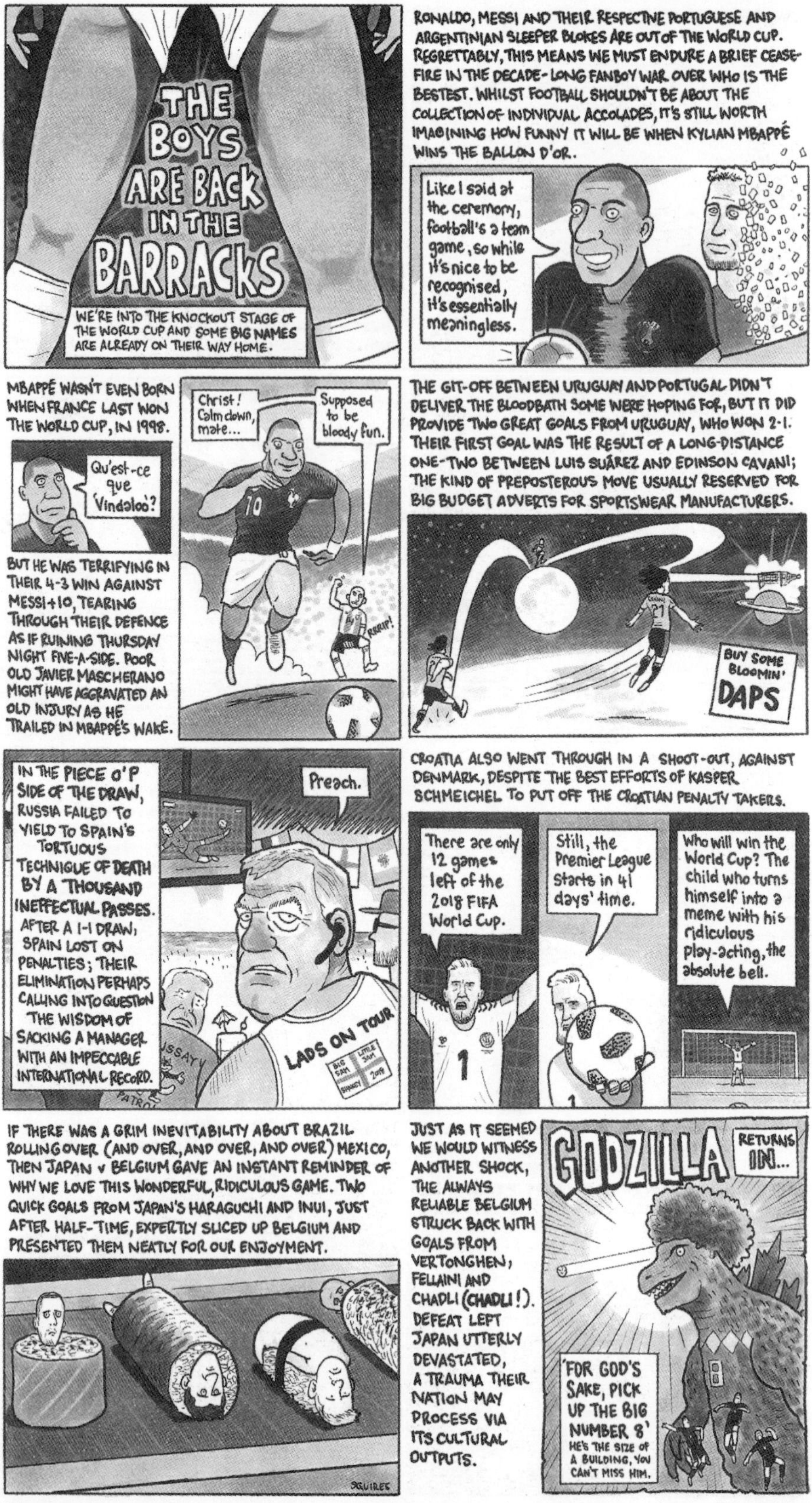
THE BOYS ARE BACK IN THE BARRACKS
WE'RE INTO THE KNOCKOUT STAGE OF THE WORLD CUP AND SOME BIG NAMES ARE ALREADY ON THEIR WAY HOME.
RONALDO, MESSI AND THEIR RESPECTIVE PORTUGUESE AND ARGENTINIAN SLEEPER BLOKES ARE OUT OF THE WORLD CUP. REGRETTABLY, THIS MEANS WE MUST ENDURE A BRIEF CEASE-FIRE IN THE DECADE-LONG FANBOY WAR OVER WHO IS THE BESTEST. WHILST FOOTBALL SHOULDN'T BE ABOUT THE COLLECTION OF INDIVIDUAL ACCOLADES, IT'S STILL WORTH IMAGINING HOW FUNNY IT WILL BE WHEN KYLIAN MBAPPÉ WINS THE BALLON D'OR.
Like I said at the ceremony, football's a team game, so while it's nice to be recognised, it's essentially meaningless.
MBAPPÉ WASN'T EVEN BORN WHEN FRANCE LAST WON THE WORLD CUP, IN 1998.
Qu'est-ce que 'Vindaloo'?
BUT HE WAS TERRIFYING IN THEIR 4-3 WIN AGAINST MESSI+10, TEARING THROUGH THEIR DEFENCE AS IF RUINING THURSDAY NIGHT FIVE-A-SIDE. POOR OLD JAVIER MASCHERANO MIGHT HAVE AGGRAVATED AN OLD INJURY AS HE TRAILED IN MBAPPÉ'S WAKE.
Christ! Calm down, mate...
Supposed to be bloody fun.
RRRIP!
THE GIT-OFF BETWEEN URUGUAY AND PORTUGAL DIDN'T DELIVER THE BLOODBATH SOME WERE HOPING FOR, BUT IT DID PROVIDE TWO GREAT GOALS FROM URUGUAY, WHO WON 2-1. THEIR FIRST GOAL WAS THE RESULT OF A LONG-DISTANCE ONE-TWO BETWEEN LUIS SUÁREZ AND EDINSON CAVANI; THE KIND OF PREPOSTEROUS MOVE USUALLY RESERVED FOR BIG BUDGET ADVERTS FOR SPORTSWEAR MANUFACTURERS.
BUY SOME BLOOMIN' DAPS
IN THE PIECE O'P SIDE OF THE DRAW, RUSSIA FAILED TO YIELD TO SPAIN'S TORTUOUS TECHNIQUE OF DEATH BY A THOUSAND INEFFECTUAL PASSES. AFTER A 1-1 DRAW, SPAIN LOST ON PENALTIES; THEIR ELIMINATION PERHAPS CALLING INTO QUESTION THE WISDOM OF SACKING A MANAGER WITH AN IMPECCABLE INTERNATIONAL RECORD.
Preach.
LADS ON TOUR
CROATIA ALSO WENT THROUGH IN A SHOOT-OUT, AGAINST DENMARK, DESPITE THE BEST EFFORTS OF KASPER SCHMEICHEL TO PUT OFF THE CROATIAN PENALTY TAKERS.
There are only 12 games left of the 2018 FIFA World Cup.
Still, the Premier League starts in 41 days' time.
Who will win the World Cup? The child who turns himself into a meme with his ridiculous play-acting, the absolute bell.
IF THERE WAS A GRIM INEVITABILITY ABOUT BRAZIL ROLLING OVER (AND OVER, AND OVER, AND OVER) MEXICO, THEN JAPAN V BELGIUM GAVE AN INSTANT REMINDER OF WHY WE LOVE THIS WONDERFUL, RIDICULOUS GAME. TWO QUICK GOALS FROM JAPAN'S HARAGUCHI AND INUI, JUST AFTER HALF-TIME, EXPERTLY SLICED UP BELGIUM AND PRESENTED THEM NEATLY FOR OUR ENJOYMENT.
SQUIRES
JUST AS IT SEEMED WE WOULD WITNESS ANOTHER SHOCK, THE ALWAYS RELIABLE BELGIUM STRUCK BACK WITH GOALS FROM VERTONGHEN, FELLAINI AND CHADLI (CHADLI!). DEFEAT LEFT JAPAN UTTERLY DEVASTATED, A TRAUMA THEIR NATION MAY PROCESS VIA ITS CULTURAL OUTPUTS.
GODZILLA
RETURNS IN...
'FOR GOD'S SAKE, PICK UP THE BIG NUMBER 8'
HE'S THE SIZE OF A BUILDING, YOU CAN'T MISS HIM.

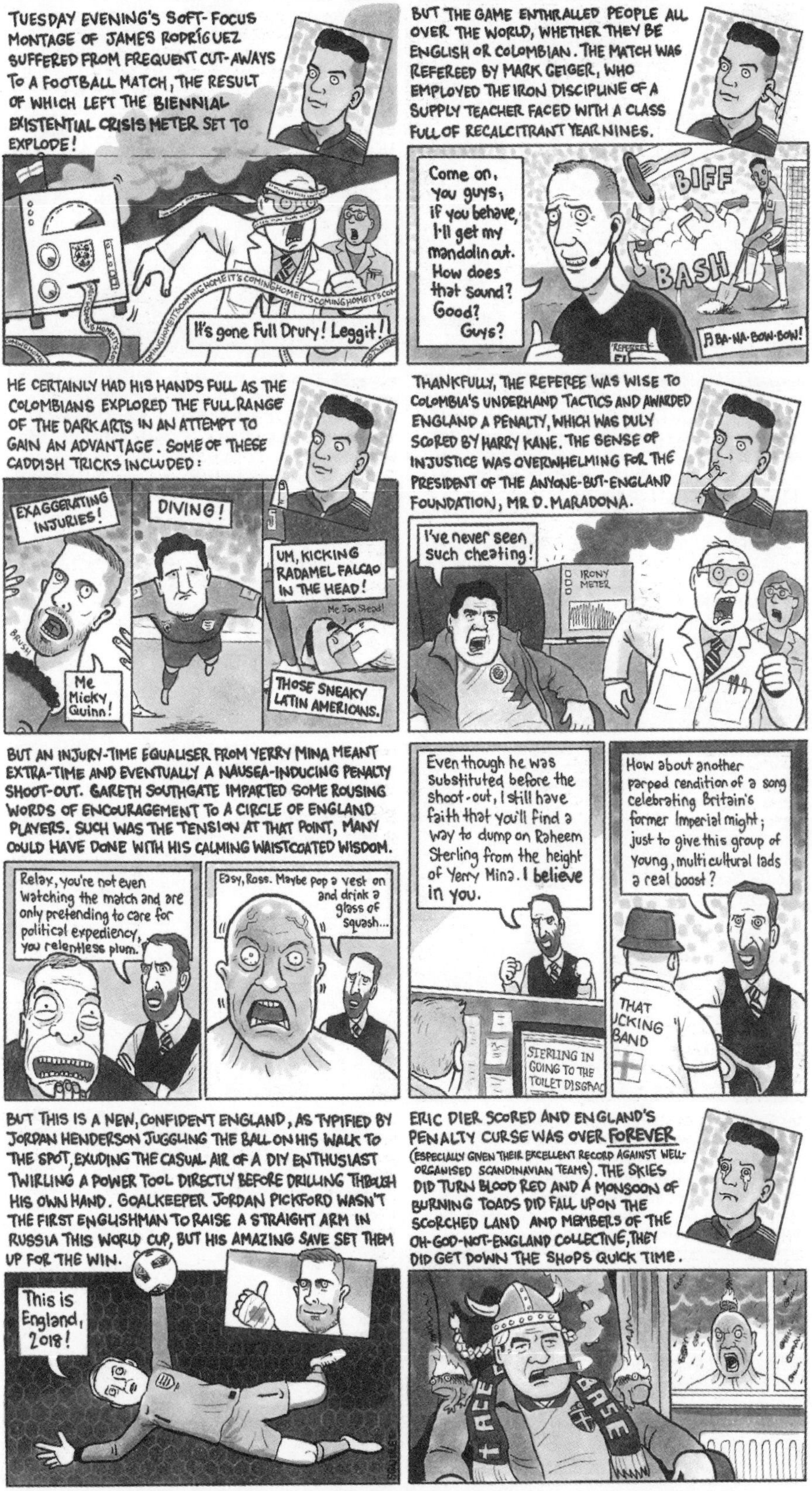

TUESDAY EVENING'S SOFT-FOCUS MONTAGE OF JAMES RODRÍGUEZ SUFFERED FROM FREQUENT CUT-AWAYS TO A FOOTBALL MATCH, THE RESULT OF WHICH LEFT THE BIENNIAL EXISTENTIAL CRISIS METER SET TO EXPLODE!
It's gone Full Drury! Leggit!
BUT THE GAME ENTHRALLED PEOPLE ALL OVER THE WORLD, WHETHER THEY BE ENGLISH OR COLOMBIAN. THE MATCH WAS REFEREED BY MARK GEIGER, WHO EMPLOYED THE IRON DISCIPLINE OF A SUPPLY TEACHER FACED WITH A CLASS FULL OF RECALCITRANT YEAR NINES.
Come on, you guys, if you behave, I'll get my mandolin out. How does that sound? Good? Guys?
BIFF
BASH
BA-NA-BOW-BOW!
HE CERTAINLY HAD HIS HANDS FULL AS THE COLOMBIANS EXPLORED THE FULL RANGE OF THE DARK ARTS IN AN ATTEMPT TO GAIN AN ADVANTAGE. SOME OF THESE CADDISH TRICKS INCLUDED:
EXAGGERATING INJURIES!
BRUSH
Me Micky Quinn!
DIVING!
UM, KICKING RADAMEL FALCAO IN THE HEAD!
Me Jon Stead!
THOSE SNEAKY LATIN AMERICANS.
THANKFULLY, THE REFEREE WAS WISE TO COLOMBIA'S UNDERHAND TACTICS AND AWARDED ENGLAND A PENALTY, WHICH WAS DULY SCORED BY HARRY KANE. THE SENSE OF INJUSTICE WAS OVERWHELMING FOR THE PRESIDENT OF THE ANYONE-BUT-ENGLAND FOUNDATION, MR D. MARADONA.
I've never seen such cheating!
IRONY METER
BUT AN INJURY-TIME EQUALISER FROM YERRY MINA MEANT EXTRA-TIME AND EVENTUALLY A NAUSEA-INDUCING PENALTY SHOOT-OUT. GARETH SOUTHGATE IMPARTED SOME ROUSING WORDS OF ENCOURAGEMENT TO A CIRCLE OF ENGLAND PLAYERS. SUCH WAS THE TENSION AT THAT POINT, MANY COULD HAVE DONE WITH HIS CALMING WAISTCOATED WISDOM.
Relax, you're not even watching the match and are only pretending to care for political expediency, you relentless plum.
Easy, Ross. Maybe pop a vest on and drink a glass of squash...
Even though he was substituted before the shoot-out, I still have faith that you'll find a way to dump on Raheem Sterling from the height of Yerry Mina. I believe in you.
STERLING IN GOING TO THE TOILET DISGRAC
How about another parped rendition of a song celebrating Britain's former Imperial might; just to give this group of young, multicultural lads a real boost?
THAT UCKING BAND
BUT THIS IS A NEW, CONFIDENT ENGLAND, AS TYPIFIED BY JORDAN HENDERSON JUGGLING THE BALL ON HIS WALK TO THE SPOT, EXUDING THE CASUAL AIR OF A DIY ENTHUSIAST TWIRLING A POWER TOOL DIRECTLY BEFORE DRILLING THROUGH HIS OWN HAND. GOALKEEPER JORDAN PICKFORD WASN'T THE FIRST ENGLISHMAN TO RAISE A STRAIGHT ARM IN RUSSIA THIS WORLD CUP, BUT HIS AMAZING SAVE SET THEM UP FOR THE WIN.
This is England, 2018!
ERIC DIER SCORED AND ENGLAND'S PENALTY CURSE WAS OVER FOREVER (ESPECIALLY GIVEN THEIR EXCELLENT RECORD AGAINST WELL-ORGANISED SCANDINAVIAN TEAMS). THE SKIES DID TURN BLOOD RED AND A MONSOON OF BURNING TOADS DID FALL UPON THE SCORCHED LAND AND MEMBERS OF THE OH-GOD-NOT-ENGLAND COLLECTIVE, THEY DID GET DOWN THE SHOPS QUICK TIME.

BULLDOZE A LIBRARY WITH MARTIN KEOWN! SCALE SOME TRANSPORT INFRASTRUCTURE! INVADE A RETAIL OUTLET LOOSELY ASSOCIATED WITH YOUR OPPONENTS! BECAUSE: ENGLAND ARE IN THE SEMI-FINALS OF THE FLIPPIN' WORLD CUP!

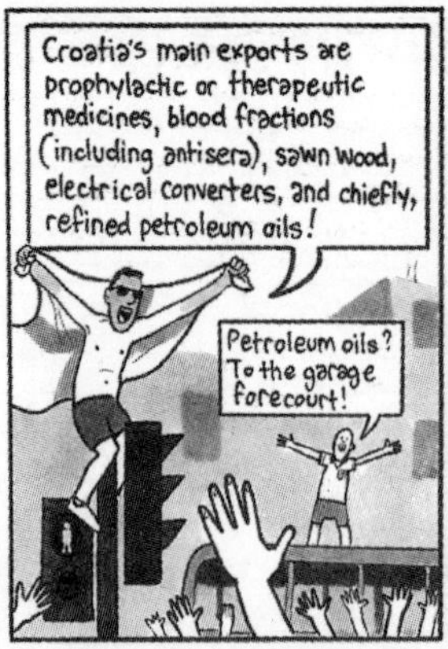
Croatia's main exports are prophylactic or therapeutic medicines, blood fractions (including antisera), sawn wood, electrical converters, and chiefly, refined petroleum oils!
Petroleum oils? To the garage forecourt!

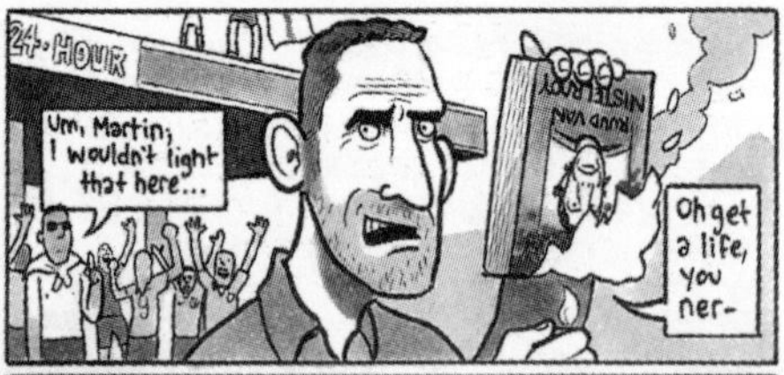
24-HOUR
Um, Martin, I wouldn't light that here...
Oh get a life, you ner-

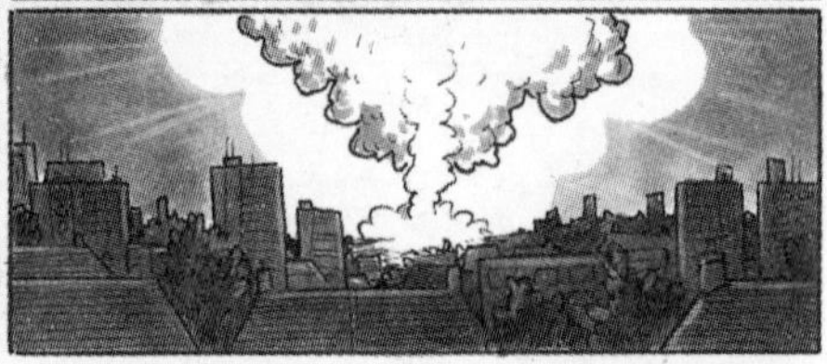

ENGLAND BREEZED THROUGH THEIR QUARTER-FINAL WITH SWEDEN, WITH JORDAN PICKFORD ONLY REQUIRED TO MAKE THREE WORLD CLASS SAVES (EAS-EH! EAS-EH!). THE PLAYERS' JUBILANT FAMILIES WATCHED ON WITH PRIDE, NOT LEAST FABIAN DELPH'S WIFE, WHO ACCORDING TO HIM IS 'AN ABSOLUTE MACHINE'; AN ODD CHOICE OF PHRASE, UNLESS HE WAS TALKING LITERALLY.

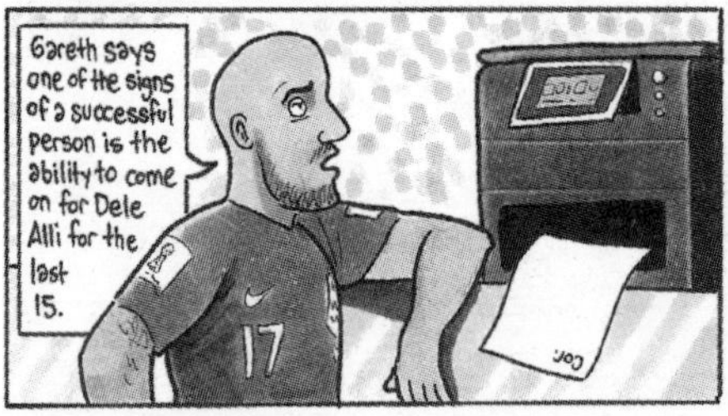
Gareth says one of the signs of a successful person is the ability to come on for Dele Alli for the last 15.
17

HOWEVER, THEIR NEXT OPPONENT - CROATIA - WILL PRESENT ENGLAND WITH SOMETHING THEY HAVEN'T FACED AT THIS WORLD CUP: A PLAYER WITH A SWEET UNDERCUT THAT MAKES HIM LOOK LIKE HE COLLECTS MARTIAL ARTS WEAPONRY.

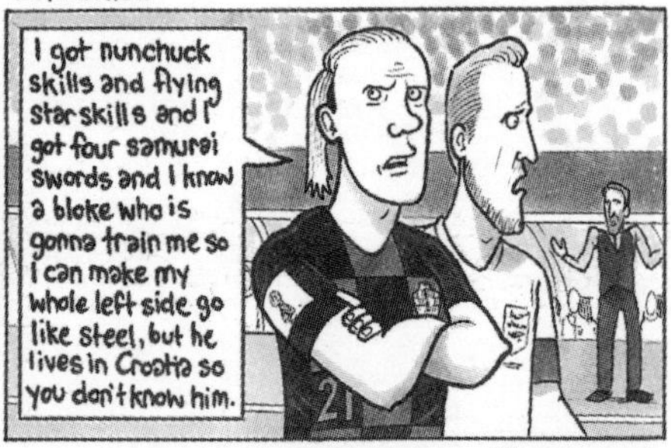
I got nunchuck skills and flying star skills and I got four samurai swords and I know a bloke who is gonna train me so I can make my whole left side go like steel, but he lives in Croatia so you don't know him.

CROATIA ARE ALSO RESILIENT, AS DEMONSTRATED DURING THEIR WIN AGAINST RUSSIA, WHEN INJURED GOALKEEPER DANIJEL SUBAŠIĆ PLAYED ON AND DID A 'WEEKEND AT BERNIE'S' FOR THE PENALTY SHOOT-OUT

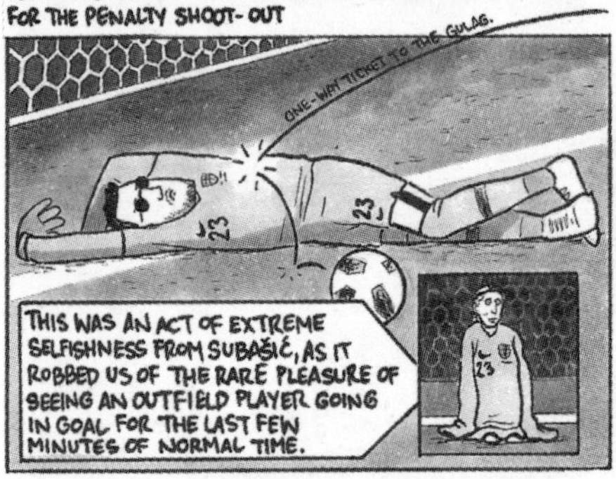
ONE-WAY TICKET TO THE GULAG
23
THIS WAS AN ACT OF EXTREME SELFISHNESS FROM SUBAŠIĆ, AS IT ROBBED US OF THE RARE PLEASURE OF SEEING AN OUTFIELD PLAYER GOING IN GOAL FOR THE LAST FEW MINUTES OF NORMAL TIME.

ALAS, THE FAVOURITES OF QUATRO-SIPPING NEUTRALS WHO STILL LIVE IN 1986 ARE OUT, BRAZIL LOSING 2-1 TO BELGIUM DESPITE EDEN HAZARD'S COMPLETE FAILURE TO GRASP THE CORE PRINCIPLES OF THE No 10 ROLE, AS DEMONSTRATED BY HIS OPPOSITE NUMBER:

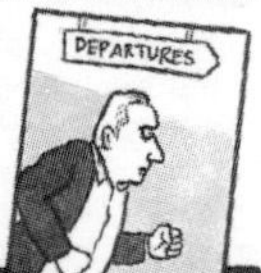
DEPARTURES

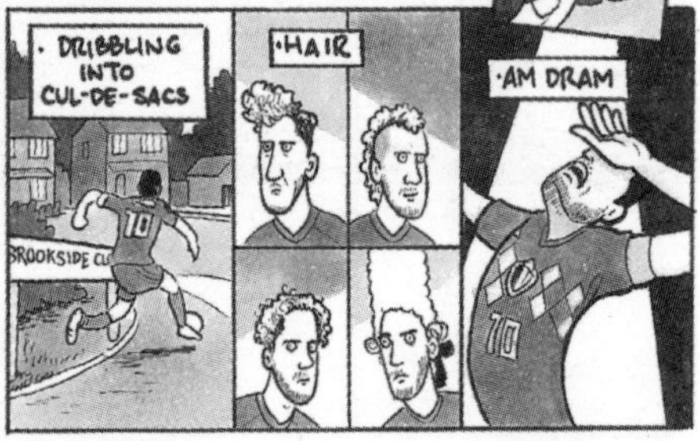
• DRIBBLING INTO CUL-DE-SACS
BROOKSIDE CL
10
• HAIR
• AM DRAM
10

THE QUARTER-FINALS PRESENTED A CHANCE FOR FIFA TO PROMOTE ITS 'SAY NO TO RACISM' CAMPAIGN; A MESSAGE THAT WAS ALMOST AS CONGRUOUS AS A TORY MP WEARING A BADGE CELEBRATING THE 70TH BIRTHDAY OF THE NHS. IT WAS FITTING THAT, IN THIS TONE OF RESPECT, URUGUAY'S MASCOT FOR THE DAY - ANTOINE GRIEZMANN - REFUSED TO CELEBRATE HIS GOAL IN FRANCE'S 2-0 WIN.

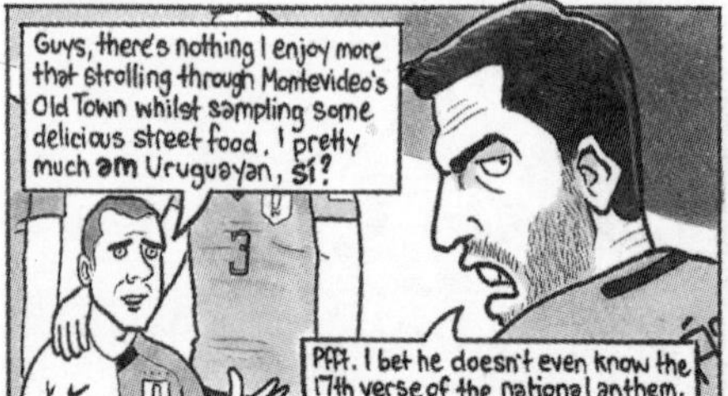
Guys, there's nothing I enjoy more that strolling through Montevideo's Old Town whilst sampling some delicious street food. I pretty much am Uruguayan, sí?
Pfft. I bet he doesn't even know the 17th verse of the national anthem.

THE RESULTS MEAN THAT THE SEMI-FINALS WILL BE CONTESTED BY THREE EUROPEAN TEAMS AND WHATEVER THE CLOTTED CREAM FUDGE ENGLAND IS NOW. SUDDENLY, ASTONISHINGLY, IT'S NOT COMPLETELY MAD TO BELIEVE THAT FOOTBALL REALLY MIGHT BE... YOU KNOW...

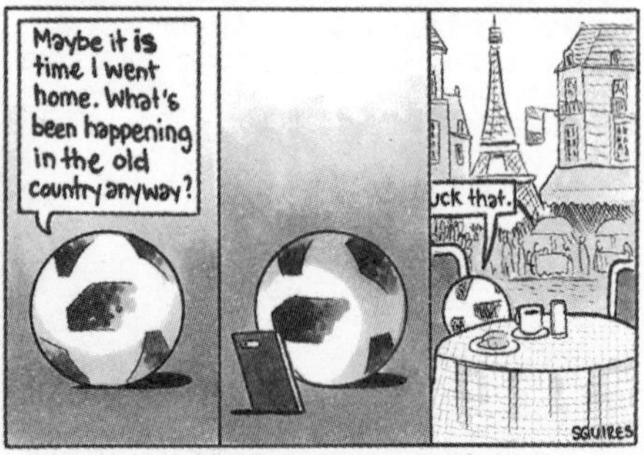
Maybe it is time I went home. What's been happening in the old country anyway?
uck that.
SQUIRES

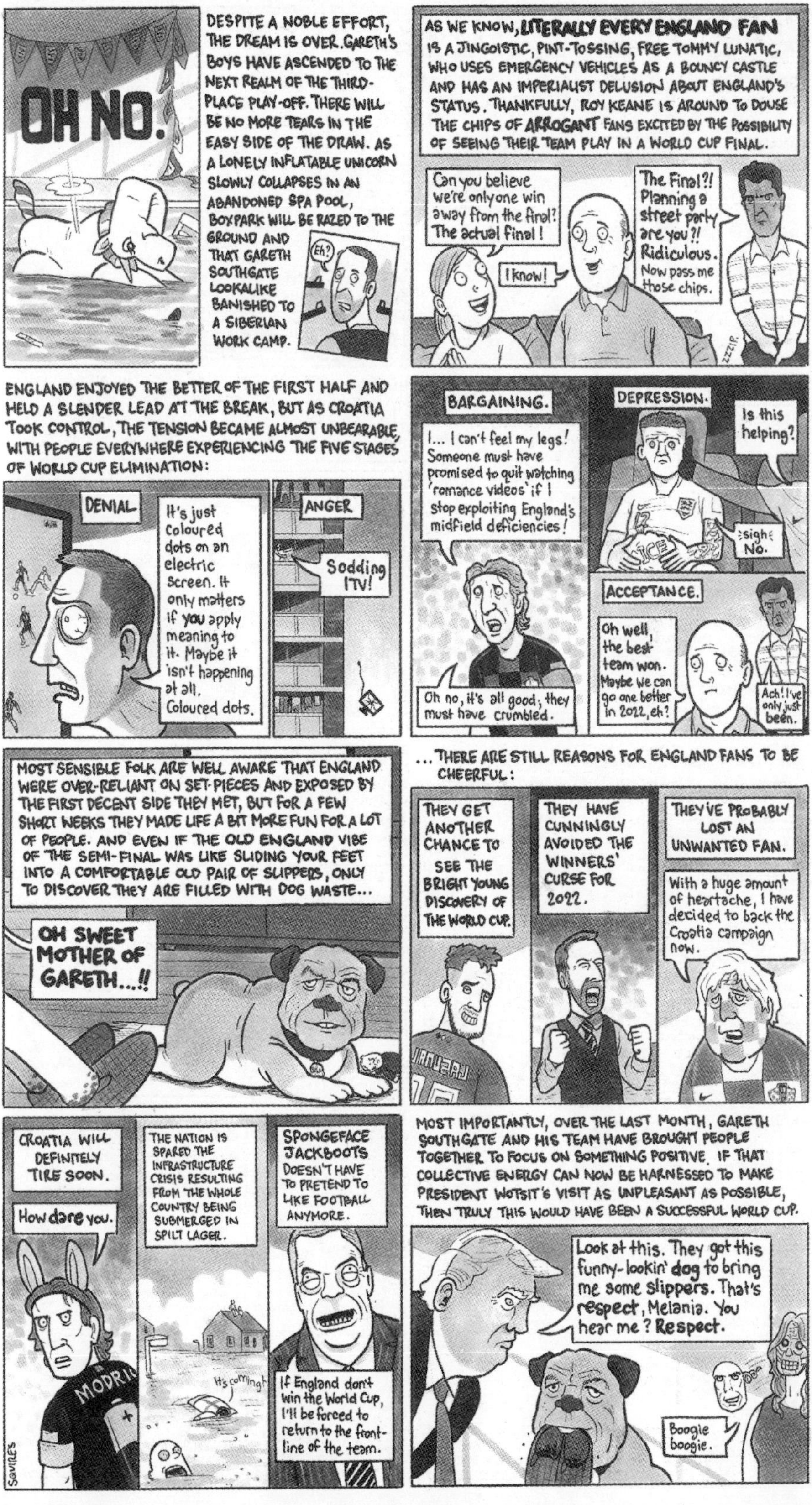

OH NO.
DESPITE A NOBLE EFFORT, THE DREAM IS OVER. GARETH'S BOYS HAVE ASCENDED TO THE NEXT REALM OF THE THIRD-PLACE PLAY-OFF. THERE WILL BE NO MORE TEARS IN THE EASY SIDE OF THE DRAW. AS A LONELY INFLATABLE UNICORN SLOWLY COLLAPSES IN AN ABANDONED SPA POOL, BOXPARK WILL BE RAZED TO THE GROUND AND THAT GARETH SOUTHGATE LOOKALIKE BANISHED TO A SIBERIAN WORK CAMP.
Eh?
AS WE KNOW, LITERALLY EVERY ENGLAND FAN IS A JINGOISTIC, PINT-TOSSING, FREE TOMMY LUNATIC, WHO USES EMERGENCY VEHICLES AS A BOUNCY CASTLE AND HAS AN IMPERIALIST DELUSION ABOUT ENGLAND'S STATUS. THANKFULLY, ROY KEANE IS AROUND TO DOUSE THE CHIPS OF ARROGANT FANS EXCITED BY THE POSSIBILITY OF SEEING THEIR TEAM PLAY IN A WORLD CUP FINAL.
Can you believe we're only one win away from the final? The actual final!
I know!
The Final?! Planning a street party are you?! Ridiculous. Now pass me those chips.
ZZZIP.
ENGLAND ENJOYED THE BETTER OF THE FIRST HALF AND HELD A SLENDER LEAD AT THE BREAK, BUT AS CROATIA TOOK CONTROL, THE TENSION BECAME ALMOST UNBEARABLE, WITH PEOPLE EVERYWHERE EXPERIENCING THE FIVE STAGES OF WORLD CUP ELIMINATION:
DENIAL
It's just coloured dots on an electric screen. It only matters if you apply meaning to it. Maybe it isn't happening at all. Coloured dots.
ANGER
Sodding ITV!
BARGAINING.
I... I can't feel my legs! Someone must have promised to quit watching 'romance videos' if I stop exploiting England's midfield deficiencies!
Oh no, it's all good; they must have crumbled.
DEPRESSION.
Is this helping?
sigh
No.
ACCEPTANCE.
Oh well, the best team won. Maybe we can go one better in 2022, eh?
Ach! I've only just been.
MOST SENSIBLE FOLK ARE WELL AWARE THAT ENGLAND WERE OVER-RELIANT ON SET-PIECES AND EXPOSED BY THE FIRST DECENT SIDE THEY MET, BUT FOR A FEW SHORT WEEKS THEY MADE LIFE A BIT MORE FUN FOR A LOT OF PEOPLE. AND EVEN IF THE OLD ENGLAND VIBE OF THE SEMI-FINAL WAS LIKE SLIDING YOUR FEET INTO A COMFORTABLE OLD PAIR OF SLIPPERS, ONLY TO DISCOVER THEY ARE FILLED WITH DOG WASTE...
OH SWEET MOTHER OF GARETH...!!
... THERE ARE STILL REASONS FOR ENGLAND FANS TO BE CHEERFUL:
THEY GET ANOTHER CHANCE TO SEE THE BRIGHT YOUNG DISCOVERY OF THE WORLD CUP.
THEY HAVE CUNNINGLY AVOIDED THE WINNERS' CURSE FOR 2022.
THEY'VE PROBABLY LOST AN UNWANTED FAN.
With a huge amount of heartache, I have decided to back the Croatia campaign now.
CROATIA WILL DEFINITELY TIRE SOON.
How dare you.
MODRIC
THE NATION IS SPARED THE INFRASTRUCTURE CRISIS RESULTING FROM THE WHOLE COUNTRY BEING SUBMERGED IN SPILT LAGER.
It's coming h
SPONGEFACE JACKBOOTS DOESN'T HAVE TO PRETEND TO LIKE FOOTBALL ANYMORE.
If England don't win the World Cup, I'll be forced to return to the front-line of the team.
MOST IMPORTANTLY, OVER THE LAST MONTH, GARETH SOUTHGATE AND HIS TEAM HAVE BROUGHT PEOPLE TOGETHER TO FOCUS ON SOMETHING POSITIVE. IF THAT COLLECTIVE ENERGY CAN NOW BE HARNESSED TO MAKE PRESIDENT WOTSIT'S VISIT AS UNPLEASANT AS POSSIBLE, THEN TRULY THIS WOULD HAVE BEEN A SUCCESSFUL WORLD CUP.
Look at this. They got this funny-lookin' dog to bring me some slippers. That's respect, Melania. You hear me? Respect.
Boogie boogie.
SQUIRES

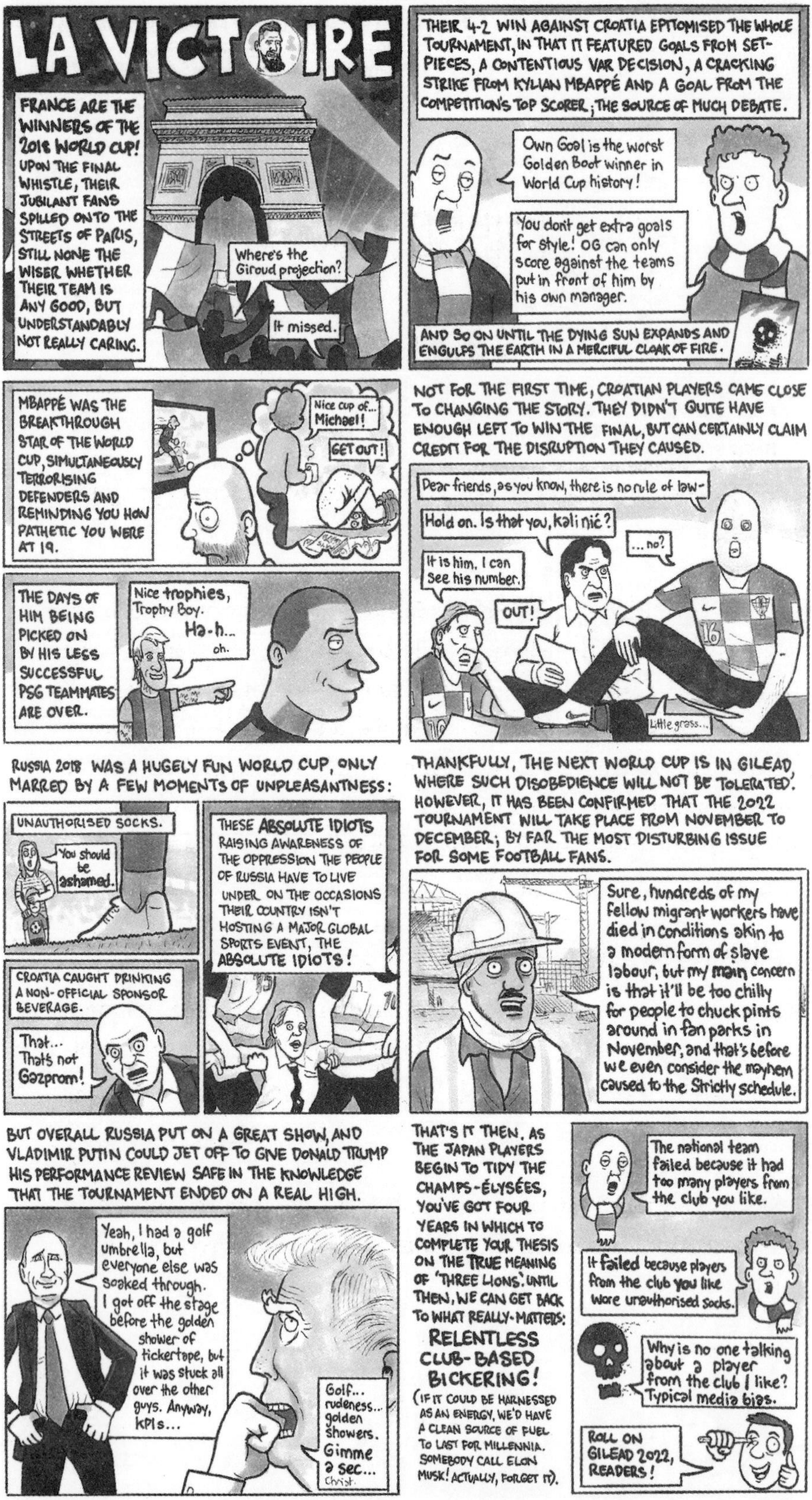
LA VICTOIRE
FRANCE ARE THE WINNERS OF THE 2018 WORLD CUP! UPON THE FINAL WHISTLE, THEIR JUBILANT FANS SPILLED ONTO THE STREETS OF PARIS, STILL NONE THE WISER WHETHER THEIR TEAM IS ANY GOOD, BUT UNDERSTANDABLY NOT REALLY CARING.
Where's the Giroud projection?
It missed.
THEIR 4-2 WIN AGAINST CROATIA EPITOMISED THE WHOLE TOURNAMENT, IN THAT IT FEATURED GOALS FROM SET-PIECES, A CONTENTIOUS VAR DECISION, A CRACKING STRIKE FROM KYLIAN MBAPPÉ AND A GOAL FROM THE COMPETITION'S TOP SCORER, THE SOURCE OF MUCH DEBATE.
Own Goal is the worst Golden Boot winner in World Cup history!
You don't get extra goals for style! OG can only score against the teams put in front of him by his own manager.
AND SO ON UNTIL THE DYING SUN EXPANDS AND ENGULFS THE EARTH IN A MERCIFUL CLOAK OF FIRE.
MBAPPÉ WAS THE BREAKTHROUGH STAR OF THE WORLD CUP, SIMULTANEOUSLY TERRORISING DEFENDERS AND REMINDING YOU HOW PATHETIC YOU WERE AT 19.
Nice cup of... Michael!
GET OUT!
THE DAYS OF HIM BEING PICKED ON BY HIS LESS SUCCESSFUL PSG TEAMMATES ARE OVER.
Nice trophies, Trophy Boy.
Ha-h... oh.
NOT FOR THE FIRST TIME, CROATIAN PLAYERS CAME CLOSE TO CHANGING THE STORY. THEY DIDN'T QUITE HAVE ENOUGH LEFT TO WIN THE FINAL, BUT CAN CERTAINLY CLAIM CREDIT FOR THE DISRUPTION THEY CAUSED.
Dear friends, as you know, there is no rule of law-
Hold on. Is that you, Kalinić?
...no?
It is him. I can see his number.
OUT!
Little grass...
RUSSIA 2018 WAS A HUGELY FUN WORLD CUP, ONLY MARRED BY A FEW MOMENTS OF UNPLEASANTNESS:
UNAUTHORISED SOCKS.
You should be ashamed.
THESE ABSOLUTE IDIOTS RAISING AWARENESS OF THE OPPRESSION THE PEOPLE OF RUSSIA HAVE TO LIVE UNDER ON THE OCCASIONS THEIR COUNTRY ISN'T HOSTING A MAJOR GLOBAL SPORTS EVENT, THE ABSOLUTE IDIOTS!
CROATIA CAUGHT DRINKING A NON-OFFICIAL SPONSOR BEVERAGE.
That... That's not Gazprom!
THANKFULLY, THE NEXT WORLD CUP IS IN GILEAD, WHERE SUCH DISOBEDIENCE WILL NOT BE TOLERATED. HOWEVER, IT HAS BEEN CONFIRMED THAT THE 2022 TOURNAMENT WILL TAKE PLACE FROM NOVEMBER TO DECEMBER; BY FAR THE MOST DISTURBING ISSUE FOR SOME FOOTBALL FANS.
Sure, hundreds of my fellow migrant workers have died in conditions akin to a modern form of slave labour, but my main concern is that it'll be too chilly for people to chuck pints around in fan parks in November, and that's before we even consider the mayhem caused to the Strictly schedule.
BUT OVERALL RUSSIA PUT ON A GREAT SHOW, AND VLADIMIR PUTIN COULD JET OFF TO GIVE DONALD TRUMP HIS PERFORMANCE REVIEW SAFE IN THE KNOWLEDGE THAT THE TOURNAMENT ENDED ON A REAL HIGH.
Yeah, I had a golf umbrella, but everyone else was soaked through. I got off the stage before the golden shower of tickertape, but it was stuck all over the other guys. Anyway, KPIs...
Golf... rudeness... golden showers. Gimme a sec...
Christ.
THAT'S IT THEN. AS THE JAPAN PLAYERS BEGIN TO TIDY THE CHAMPS-ÉLYSÉES, YOU'VE GOT FOUR YEARS IN WHICH TO COMPLETE YOUR THESIS ON THE TRUE MEANING OF 'THREE LIONS'. UNTIL THEN, WE CAN GET BACK TO WHAT REALLY MATTERS:
RELENTLESS CLUB-BASED BICKERING!
(IF IT COULD BE HARNESSED AS AN ENERGY, WE'D HAVE A CLEAN SOURCE OF FUEL TO LAST FOR MILLENNIA. SOMEBODY CALL ELON MUSK! ACTUALLY, FORGET IT).
The national team failed because it had too many players from the club you like.
It failed because players from the club you like wore unauthorised socks.
Why is no one talking about a player from the club I like? Typical media bias.
ROLL ON GILEAD 2022, READERS!

ENDNOTES

Rivalries

Page 48: Newcastle had just sacked Steve McClaren and appointed Rafa Benítez.

Page 49: The cable-car joke is a reference to a story in the news at the time, in which dozens of people had be rescued from a cable car that was suspended over Mont Blanc overnight. Elsewhere, one of Pep Guardiola's first acts as Manchester City manager was to send Joe Hart out on loan to Torino, which went about as well as expected. Also, former Manchester United manager David Moyes had given an interview in which he talked up his managerial credentials.

Just About Managing

Page 59: The second panel of this cartoon refers to an incident in which a man strapped with a fake bomb hijacked an Egypt-Air flight in 2016 and posed for photographs with a British passenger.

Page 62: The final frame of this one is a reference to Australian comedian Jim Jefferies insulting Piers Morgan on live television, which was pretty damn sweet.

Marc Wilmots's Disco Mix: Euro 2016

Page 73: The Harry Kane joke with Tactics Bear refers to a quirky news story that was doing the rounds at the time about a Japanese couple who left their seven-year-old son in bear-infested woods.

José Mourinho

Page 88: The last panel references an interview in the run-up to the 2015 general election, when Labour leader Ed Miliband had to shuffle from buttock to buttock while Myleene Klass complained about the injustice of his proposal to tax her mansion.

Shut the FA Cup (and Read These Cartoons)

Page 156: The final panel of the quarter-final cartoon refers to a contestant flouncing from the set of *Robot Wars*, having been defeated by some children. What is the FA Cup about if not niche references to Sunday-lunchtime children's television programmes watched by a tiny section of the public?

Janet

Page 169: Janet appears as a tiny cameo in the Peter Drury cartoon. After its publication, someone contacted me to tell me they had shown it to Drury's wife (WHY WOULD YOU?). Apparently, she found it 'funny', but denied shopping in Aldi, which means that football's most verbose commentator may never have tasted the sweet ambrosia of off-brand lager. Another person tweeted Jim Beglin to ask if he'd seen the cartoon. His reply: 'Yes.' Gulp.

Football Heritage

Page 183: The final panel of this cartoon refers to a viral video that was doing the rounds in the week of publication, featuring a red-faced man trying to conduct a citizen's arrest after an apparent road-rage incident, his moral high ground crumbling beneath him as he delivers furious individual insults to each member of a quivering family and tells them they are going to die. It's been a while since I moved overseas, but this is exactly how I remember England, my England (*wipes tear*).

ACKNOWLEDGEMENTS

This book has been nearly four years in the making, during which time life has changed a lot. I'd like to thank all of my family and friends, who have stuck by me even though working from home has deprived me of the few social skills I had in the first place. Primarily, I would like to thank my partner Sarah, without whose support and encouragement none of the cartoons or words in this book would have been possible.

Obviously, I'm also deeply grateful to all the team on the sports desk at the *Guardian*. In particular, I'm indebted to James Dart, whose editorial skills and eagle eye spares me from typo-based embarrassment each week. I'd also like to thank Mike Hytner at *Guardian Australia*, not only for giving me the opportunity to draw weekly cartoons on the A-League, the maniac, but for his friendship and encouragement over the years.

Big thanks also to my agent, David Luxton, and Fred Baty and the team at Faber for helping make this book happen.

Oh, and if you've liked, shared or commented on any of these cartoons over the years, then I thank you, too. It's a weird job, and you spend long periods of time inside your own head. Anyone who has ever sent me an email or tweet or shared kind words has helped me more than you could imagine. The Comments section: I know you are there and appreciate your presence, but much like the sun, looking at you directly will be detrimental to my health.

Finally, thanks to my dog Sally, who nudges my knee each day as the sun sets, encouraging me to venture into the outside world (the dog park) and free me from the regular bouts of writer's block. Speaking of which: *walkies!*